Solicitors' Negligence

Solicitors' Negligence

William Flenley

MA (Oxon), LLM (Cornell), BCL, Barrister

Tom Leech

MA (Oxon), BCL, Barrister

Butterworths
London, Dublin, Edinburgh
1999

United Kingdom	Butterworths, a Division of Reed Elsevier (UK) Ltd, Halsbury House, 35 Chancery Lane, LONDON WC2A 1EL and 4 Hill Street, EDINBURGH EH2 3JZ
Australia	Butterworths, a Division of Reed International Books Australia Pty Ltd, CHATSWOOD, New South Wales
Canada	Butterworths Canada Ltd, MARKHAM, Ontario
Hong Kong	Butterworths Asia (Hong Kong), HONG KONG
India	Butterworths India, NEW DELHI
Ireland	Butterworth (Ireland) Ltd, DUBLIN
Malaysia	Malayan Law Journal Sdn Bhd, KUALA LUMPUR
New Zealand	Butterworths of New Zealand Ltd, WELLINGTON
Singapore	Butterworths Asia, SINGAPORE
South Africa	Butterworths Publishers (Pty) Ltd, DURBAN
USA	Lexis Law Publishing, CHARLOTTESVILLE, Virginia

A CIP Catalogue record for this book is available from the British Library.

ISBN 0 406 052 255

Printed by Butler & Tanner Ltd, Frome and London

Visit us at our website: http://www.butterworths.co.uk

Foreword

Practitioners will agree that a textbook on solicitors' negligence is timely, if not overdue. This is not because solicitors are more prone to be negligent than other professionals. It is rather *because,* when they are, they tend to give rise to a wider range of problems than usual.

Professional negligence, other than medical negligence, is a discrete branch of the law of negligence. It occasions economic loss rather than personal injury, usually (though not always) arises in the course of a contractual relationship, and rarely gives rise to problems of proximity.

The difficulty in finding a sufficient relationship between the parties which has beset the development of the modern law of negligence is generally absent. But there are three problems which, though not peculiar to solicitors, are particularly acute in cases of solicitors' negligence.

The starting point in any case of professional negligence is to ascertain the scope of the defendant's duty. It is easy enough to say that the scope of a solicitor's duty depends on his retainer, but this is rarely in express and precise terms. There is no single or simple answer to the question whether a solicitor is under a general duty to give advice. Even if negligent breach of duty is established, it may give rise to particularly difficult questions of causation. Recent cases have explored the allied issues of causation and measure of damages in the case of valuers' negligence, but much more difficult questions remain to be decided in relation to solicitors. The distinction between the loss of a chance and other cases is better understood than it was, but the last word has certainly not been spoken on this subject.

Other problems arise from the fact that the relationship between a solicitor and his client is a fiduciary one. The solicitor is consequently subject to fiduciary obligations as well as duties in contract and tort. While the common law duties in contract and tort are similar and overlap, the equitable obligations imposed by the fiduciary nature of the solicitor's relationship with his client are distinct and yield different remedies in the event of breach. Moreover, the solicitor is a trustee of the money in his clients' account, so that misapplication of the money, even if merely the result of negligence, may render him liable to an action for breach of trust. Some of the problems to which these interacting relationships give rise have been considered in a spate of cases resulting from the mortgage frauds of the late 1980s. Those which relate to limitation are particularly difficult. Their authoritative resolution may have to await legislation when the Law Commission presents its report. In the meantime, practitioners will welcome all the help they can get.

This is a carefully researched and thoughtful book, which draws on the experience gained in some of the most difficult cases to have come before the courts. I unreservedly recommend it to practitioners, common law and equity alike.

The Rt Hon The Lord Millett

Preface

Over the last ten years claims against solicitors have multiplied. One of us started his professional career in a set of chambers specialising in property litigation and chancery work; the other in a common law set. Neither of us anticipated that, after ten years, a core part of our work would involve solicitors' negligence and liability. The volume of litigation together with the body of case law which has followed it justifies, we hope, a book dedicated to the subject.

The content of this book reflects the questions which we have faced in practice. As Lord Millett demonstrates in his foreword, difficult principles of law of widespread application often arise for determination in solicitors' cases. But the volume of litigation has also proved that claims against solicitors arise out of all aspects of their practice—from non-contentious business, such as conveyancing and wills, to all forms of litigation, both commercial and criminal. A practitioner needs not only to be familiar with the principles of the law of professional negligence, but also to have a working knowledge of the law and practice which form the backdrop to the claim. In this book we have attempted to meet both needs. Part 1 explores general principles. In Part 2 we have devoted equal space to analysing claims by reference to the fields of practice in which they arise. We hope that in many cases it will prove quicker and easier to identify the issue or problem in question, if not to find an answer, by using an analysis of this kind. In Part 3, we have added two procedural chapters: one to deal with the relatively new, but unfortunately fertile, area of wasted costs; the other to reflect the issues which often arise, particularly in relation to privilege, when considering disclosure in a solicitors' action. We have attempted to state the law as at 1 June 1999, but have in some cases been able to incorporate developments after that date.

As reference to the text which follows will show, in recent years many of the most important judgments in this area of the law have been given by Lord Millett. We are particularly grateful to him for writing a foreword for our book. We would also like to thank Dr Dominic Berry, Spike Charlwood, Nicholas Davidson QC, Ian Gatt, Tim Harry, Ted Johnson, Harvey McGregor QC, Tony Oakley, Nicholas Patten QC and Simon Shooter for their help and comments. Finally, we would like to thank everyone at Butterworths who has been involved in the project. This book is dedicated to the memory of William's father Professor David Flenley and to Tom's wife Jane.

William Flenley   Tom Leech
4 Paper Buildings,   Lincoln's Inn and Bermuda
Temple

July 1999

Contents

Foreword   v
Preface   vii
Table of statutes   xi
Table of statutory instruments   xiii
Table of cases   xv

Part 1   General principles

1   The solicitor's duties in contract and tort   3
2   Breach of duty   19
3   Damages at common law   37
4   Claims in equity   71
5   Limitation   110
6   Contributory negligence and contribution   141

Part 2   Specific claims

7   Lenders' claims   155
8   Conveyancing   203
9   Wills, estates and trusts   249
10 Litigation   262

Part 3   Procedure

11 Orders that solicitors pay the costs of litigation personally   299
12 Disclosure and privilege   325

Index   341

Table of statutes

PARA

Administration of Justice Act 1965
s 6(1) 4.61
Administration of Justice Act 1982 .... 9.10
s 20 .... **9.19**
(1)(b) 9.21
Agricultural Holdings Act 1986 .... 8.80
Arbitration Act 1950 .... 1.5

Civil Evidence Act 1972 .... 2.22; 5.76
s 3 .... 2.24
Civil Liability (Contribution) Act 1978: 6.22
s 1(4) 6.19
1(5) 6.21
2(3) 6.23
6(1) 6.16
Companies Act 1985
s 311 .... 5.54, 5.55
320 .... 3.26; 6.13
County Courts Act 1984
s 84 .... 3.62
Court and Legal Services Act 1990
s 58 .... 11.52
62 .... 10.36, 10.39

Data Protection Act 1984 .... 12.23

Human Rights Act 1998 .... 10.44

Income and Corporation Taxes Act 1988: 2.6
Inheritance Act 1984 .... 9.13
Inheritance (Provision for Family and
Dependants) Act 1975 .... 9.18
Insolvency Act 1986
s 306 .... 11.64
423 .... 12.20

Land Registration Act 1925 .... 8.09
s 70(1)(g) 8.61
123(1) 8.70
Landlord and Tenant Act 1954
s 25 .... 8.94
Pt II (ss 23-46) 3.31, 3.47; 8.93
Landlord and Tenant (Covenants) Act
1995 .... 2.35
Law of Property Act 1925
s 30 .... 7.112
199(1)(ii) 8.62
Law of Property (Miscellaneous Provisions)
Act 1989 .... 8.56

PARA

Law Reform (Contributory Negligence) Act
1945
s 1(1) **6.2**
s 1(1)(i) 6.8
Leasehold Reform Act 1967 ..... 3.33; 8.50
Legal Aid Act 1988
s 31(1) 11.43
Limitation Act 1980 ... 5.2, 5.22, 5.26, 5.75
s 2 .... 5.60
10 .... 6.20
11 .... 5.6
(1) **5.7**
11A(3) 5.60
12(1) 5.60
14 .... 5.6
(1)(b) 5.46
(10) 5.56
14A 5.1, 5.3, 5.5, 5.10, 5.38,
5.39, 5.40, 5.41, 5.50, 5.52,
5.53, 5.55, 5.59; 12.30, 12.31
(6) 5.44
(8) 5.44, 5.46, 5.48, 5.49
(9) 5.45, 5.51
(10)(a) 5.57
14B 5.40
19 .... 5.71
21 .... **5.70, 5.73**
(1)(a) 5.71
32 .... 5.1, 5.4, 5.5, 5.38,
5.60, 5.68; 12.30, 12.31
(1)(b) 5.41, 5.66
(c) 5.67
(2) 5.63
33 .... 10.7
35 .... 5.77
(1), (2) 5.82
(4), (5) 5.84
38 .... 5.70

Matrimonial Homes Act 1967 .... 8.59
Misrepresentation Act 1967
s 2(1) 6.5
3 .... 8.38

Nuclear Installations Act 1965
s 7 .... 3.67

Partnership Act 1890
s 10 .... 4.19; 6.19
Prosecution of Offences Act 1985
s 19A 11.57

PARA

Solicitors Act 1974
  s 14 .... 2.3
    20-25 .... 2.3
    59 .... 1.5
    60(5) 1.5
    68 .... 12.3
    87 .... 1.5
Supply of Goods and Services Act 1982
  s 13 .... 1.4; 7.38
Supreme Court Act 1981 .... 3.62
  s 35A 3.62, 3.65, 3.66, 3.67;
                         5.26; 7.67, 7.74
    51 .... **11.4**
    (1), (3) 11.68, 11.69, 11.70
    (6) 11.1, 11.11, 11.66, 11.69
    (7) 11.19
    56 .... 11.57
    (7) **11.55**
    128 .... 1.5

PARA

Trustee Act 1925
  s 68(17) 5.70
Trustees Act 1996
  s 14 .... 8.23
Trusts of Land and Appointment Trustees
  Act 1996
  s 14 .... 8.31
Unfair Contract Terms Act 1977:   1.06, 1.27;
                                       8.40
  s 1(1) 1.25
    2(2) 1.25
    11(3) 1.25
    13(1) 1.25
Victorian Wills Act 1958
  s 9(d) 9.9
Wills Act 1837 .... 9.9
  s 18 .... 9.10
    (4)(b) 9.10

Table of statutory instruments

PARA

Bar and Library Transcript 1990,
SI 1990/272 .... 8.7
Civil Procedure Rules 1998, SI 1998/
3132 .... 5.77
Pt 17.4 .... 5.84
Costs in Criminal Cases (General) Regulations
1986, SI 1986/1335
Reg 3A–3D 11.57

PARA

Rules of The Supreme Court 1965,
SI 1965/1776 .... 5.77
Ord 106 .... 12.04
Unfair Terms in Consumer
Contracts Regulations 1994,
SI 1994/3159 .... 1.06, 1.25

Table of cases

A

PARA

Abrams v Abrams [1996] PNLR 129 .... 1.22
ADT Ltd v BDO Binder Hamlyn [1996] BCC 808 .... 1.22, 1.24
Abbey National Building Society v Cann [1991] 1 AC 56, [1990] 1 All ER 1085, [1990]
    2 WLR 832, 60 P & CR 278, [1990] 2 FLR 122, [1990] Fam Law 397, 22 HLR
    360, [1990] 17 LS Gaz R 32, [1990] NLJR 477, HL 8.61
Abbey National plc v Forsyths (11 June 1997, unreported) 5.58
Abbey National plc v Solicitors' Indemnity Fund Ltd [1997] PNLR 306 .... 7.99
Acton v Graham Pearce (a firm) [1997] 3 All ER 909 .... 10.8, 10.9, 10.20, 10.62
Aiden Shipping Co Ltd v Interbulk Ltd, The Vimeira [1986] AC 965, [1986] 2 All ER
    409, [1986] 2 WLR 1051, [1986] 2 Lloyd's Rep 117, 130 Sol Jo 429, [1986] LS
    Gaz R 1895, [1986] NLJ Rep 514, HL 11.68
Al-Kandari v JR Brown & Co [1988] QB 665, [1988] 1 All ER 833, [1988] 2 WLR 671,
    [1988] Fam Law 382, 132 Sol Jo 462, [1988] 14 LS Gaz R 50, [1988] NLJR 62,
    CA 1.22,10.8
Al-Sabah v Ali [1999] EGCS 11 .... 8.7, 8.9
Alexander v Cambridge Credit Corpn Ltd (1987) 9 NSWLR 310, CA 3.25
Ali (Saif) v Sydney Mitchell & Co (a firm) [1980] AC 198, [1978] 3 All ER 1033, [1978]
    3 WLR 849, 122 Sol Jo 761, HL 1.3, 2.2, 2.25, 10.7, 10.15,
                                 10.29, 10.40, 10.41, 10.42,
                                     10.43, 10.45, 11.34
Allen v Sir Alfred McAlpine & Sons Ltd [1968] 2 QB 229, [1968] 1 All ER 543, [1968]
    2 WLR 366, 112 Sol Jo 49, CA 10.7
Allen v Unigate Dairies Ltd [1994] Ch 205, [1994] 3 WLR 462, CA 11.36
Alliance & Leicester Building Society v Edgestop Ltd (18 January 1991, unreported) . 4.12
Alliance and Leicester Building Society v Edgestop Ltd [1994] 2 All ER 38, [1993]
    1 WLR 1462, [1993] NPC 79, [1994] 2 EGLR 229; affd on other grounds [1995]
    CLY 2828, CA 6.5, 7.100
Alliance & Leicester v Wheelers (23 January 1997, unreported) 6.4, 7.31, 7.79
Allied Finance and Investments Ltd v Haddow & Co [1983] NZLR 22, NZCA . 1.23, 8.39,
                                                8.44
Allied Maples Group Ltd v Simmons & Simmons (a firm) [1995] 4 All ER 907, [1995] 1
    WLR 1602, [1995] NLJR 1646, CA 3.11, 3.12, 3.15, 3.16,
                                      3.17, 3.54, 8.85, 10.50
Alltrans Express Ltd v CVA Holdings Ltd [1984] 1 All ER 685, [1984] 1 WLR 394, 128
    Sol Jo 47, [1984] LS Gaz R 430, CA 7.59
Amerena v Barling (1993) 69 P & CR 252, CA 8.105, 8.106
Amonoo v Grant [1999] 01 LS Gaz R 25 .... 10.8, 10.52
Anns v Merton London Borough Council [1978] AC 728, [1977] 2 All ER 492, [1977] 2
    WLR 1024, 75 LGR 555, 141 JP 526, 121 Sol Jo 377, 5 BLR 1, 243 Estates Gazette
    523, 591, [1977] JPL 514, HL 8.39
Arbuthnot Latham Bank Ltd v Trafalgar Holding Ltd [1998] 2 All ER 181, [1998] 1 WLR
    1426, CA 10.5
Argyll (Duchess) v Beuselinck [1972] 2 Lloyd's Rep 172 .... 2.7, 2.8, 2.26
Armitage v Nurse [1998] Ch 241, [1997] 2 All ER 705, [1997] 3 WLR 1046, 74 P &
    CR D13, CA 4.3, 4.11, 4.14
Aslan v Clintons (1984) 134 NLJ 584 .... 8.47
Ata v American Express Bank Ltd (1998) Times, 26 June, CA 4.44, 4.47, 4.58
Atkins v Atkins [1993] EGCS 54 .... 8.25

PARA

Attard v Samson (1966) 110 Sol Jo 249, 198 Estates Gazette 121 .... 8.4, 8.51
A-G v Alford (1854) 18 Jur 592, 2 Sm & G 488, 2 WR 580, 23 LTOS 226; on appeal
    (1855) 4 De GM & G 843, 3 Eq Rep 952, 1 Jur NS 361, 102 RR 406, 3 WR 200,
    24 LTOS 265 .... 4.60
Atwell v Michael Perry & Co (a firm) [1998] 4 All ER 65 .... 10.47
Aylwin v Aylwin [1902] P 203, 71 LJP 130, 87 LT 142 .... 9.11

B

BRDC v Hextall Esrkine & Co (a firm). See British Racing Drivers' Club Ltd v Hextall
    Erskine & Co (a firm)
Bacon v Howard Kennedy [1999] PNLR 1 .... 5.37
Bailey v Bullock [1950] 2 All ER 1167, 94 Sol Jo 689, 66 (pt 2) TLR 791 ..... 8.72, 8.81
Baker v Ollard and Bentley (a firm) (1982) 126 Sol Jo 593, CA 5.19, 5.20
Baker (GL) Ltd v Medway Building and Supplies Ltd [1958] 3 All ER 540, [1958] 1
    WLR 1216, 102 Sol Jo 877, CA 5.62
Balabel v Air-India [1988] Ch 317, [1988] 2 All ER 246, [1988] 2 WLR 1036, 132 Sol
    Jo 699, [1988] NLJR 85, CA 12.16
Balamoan v Holden & Co (28 May 1999, unreported), CA 10.11
Banco de Portugal v Waterlow & Sons Ltd [1932] AC 452, 101 LJKB 417, [1932] All
    ER Rep 181, 76 Sol Jo 327, 147 LT 101, 48 TLR 404, HL 3.41
Banco Exterior Internacional v Mann [1995] 1 All ER 936, [1995] 2 FCR 282, [1995]
    1 FLR 602, [1995] Fam Law 297, 27 HLR 329, [1995] NLJR 179, CA .. 8.18, 8.21
Bank of Baroda v Shah [1988] 3 All ER 24, [1988] NLJR 98, CA 8.26
Bank of Credit and Commerce International (Overseas) v Price Waterhouse (No 3)
    (1998) Times, 2 April 3.25, 7.77
Bannister v SGB plc [1997] 4 All ER 129, [1998] 1 WLR 1123, [1997] 31 LS Gaz R 36,
    [1997] NLJR 685, [1997] PIQR P 165, CA 10.4, 10.12
Banque Bruxelles Lambert SA v Eagle Star Insurance Co Ltd [1995] 2 All ER 769,
    [1994] 2 EGLR 108, 68 BLR 39, [1994] 31 EG 68, 32 EG 89; revsd [1995]
    QB 375, [1995] 2 All ER 769, [1995] 2 WLR 607, [1995] 1 EGLR 129,
    [1995] 12 LS Gaz R 34, [1995] NLJR 343, [1995] 12 EG 144, CA; upheld [1997]
    AC 191, HL 3.1, 3.7, 3.8, 3.9, 3.10, 3.13,
    3.29, 3.32, 3.50, 3.63, 5.26, 6.7,
    6.14, 6.23, 7.2, 7.59, 7.62, 7.66,
    7.70, 7.77, 7.95, 7.100, 7.111, 8.89
Banque Bruxelles Lambert SA v Simmons & Simmons (24 November 1995,
    unreported) 12.27, 12.28
Banque Keyser Ullmann SA v Skandia (UK) Insurance Co Ltd [1990] 1 QB 665,
    [1987] 2 All ER 923, [1987] 2 WLR 1300, [1987] 1 Lloyd's Rep 69, 131 Sol
    Jo 775, [1987] LS Gaz R 1965; revsd [1990] 1 QB 665, [1989] 3 WLR 25, 133
    Sol Jo 817, [1989] 26 LS Gaz R 33, [1988] NLJR 287, sub nom Banque Financière
    de la Cité SA v Westgate Insurance Co Ltd [1989] 2 All ER 952, [1988] 2 Lloyd's
    Rep 513, CA; affd sub nom Banque Financière de la Cité SA (formerly Banque
    Keyser Ullmann SA) v Westgate Insurance Co Ltd (formerly Hodge General and
    Mercantile Co Ltd) [1991] 2 AC 249, [1990] 2 All ER 947, [1990] 3 WLR 364,
    [1990] 2 Lloyd's Rep 377, 134 Sol Jo 1265, [1990] NLJR 1074, HL 3.29, 3.39
Barclay-White v Guillaume & Sons [1996] EGCS 123 .... 8.53, 8.79
Barclays Bank v Schwartz [1995] CLY 2492, CA 8.13
Barclays Bank plc v Boulter [1997] 2 All ER 1002, [1998] 1 WLR 1, [1997] 3 FCR 252,
    [1997] 2 FLR 157, [1997] Fam Law 545, 30 HLR 134, CA 8.62
Barclays Bank plc v Eustice [1995] 4 All ER 511, [1995] 1 WLR 1238, [1995] 2 BCLC
    630, [1995] BCC 978, [1995] NLJR 1503, CA 12.20, 12.21, 12.22
Barclays Bank plc v Fairclough Building Ltd [1995] QB 214, [1995] 1 All ER 289,
    [1994] 3 WLR 1057, 39 Con LR 86, [1995] PIQR P 152, 68 BLR 1, [1994] BLM
    (June) 1, CA 6.3
Barclays Bank plc v Thomson [1997] 4 All ER 816, 75 P & CR 5, [1997] 1 FCR 541,
    [1997] 1 FLR 156, [1996] NLJR 1778, CA 1.8, 8.18
Barclays Bank plc v Weeks Legg & Dean (a firm) [1999] QB 309, [1998] 3 All ER 213,
    [1998] 3 WLR 656, 77 P & CR 320, [1998] 25 LS Gaz R 33, [1998] 21 LS Gaz
    R 38, [1998] 40 EG 182, 142 Sol Jo LB 180, 76 P & CR D27, CA 1.2, 7.32,
    7.33, 7.36, 8.27

PARA

Barnes v Hay (1988) 12 NSWLR 337, CA 3.23, 3.24, 3.39
Barrett v Enfield London Borough Council [1999] 3 WLR 79, HL 10.9
Barrister, a (No 1 of 1991), Re [1993] QB 293, [1992] 3 All ER 429, [1992] 3 WLR 662,
    95 Cr App Rep 288, [1992] 24 LS Gaz R 31, [1992] NLJR 636, 136 Sol Jo LB 147,
    CA 11.59
Bartlett v Barclays Bank Trust Co Ltd (No 2) [1980] Ch 515, [1980] 2 All ER 92, [1980]
    2 WLR 430, 124 Sol Jo 221 .... 4.61
Baxter v F W Gapp & Co Ltd and Gapp [1938] 4 All ER 457; affd [1939] 2 KB 271,
    [1939] 2 All ER 752, 108 LJKB 522, 83 Sol Jo 436, 160 LT 533, 55 TLR 739,
    CA 2.4
Baxter v Smith, 19 May 1999, NLD 10.10
Bayer v Balkin (1995) 31 ATR 295 .... 9.24
Beaman v ARTS Ltd [1949] 1 KB 550, [1949] 1 All ER 465, 93 Sol Jo 236, 65 TLR 389,
    CA 5.62
Bell v Peter Browne & Co [1990] 2 QB 495, [1990] 3 All ER 124, [1990] 3 WLR 510,
    [1990] NLJR 701, CA 1.9, 5.12, 5.13, 5.23, 8.59
Bell's Indenture, Re, Bell v Hickley [1980] 3 All ER 425, [1980] 1 WLR 1217, 123 Sol Jo
    322 .... 4.19, 6.19
Bennett v Greenland Houchen & Co [1998] PNLR 458, CA 5.7
Biggin & Co Ltd v Permanite Ltd [1951] 2 KB 314, [1951] 2 All ER 191, 95 Sol Jo 414,
    [1951] 2 TLR 159, CA 12.33
Birmingham Midshires Building Society v Infields (20 May 1999, unreported) 5.58
Birmingham Midshires Building Society v J D Wretham [1999] 07 EG 138, [1998] EGCS
    176, [1999] Lloyd's Rep PN 133 .... 5.59, 5.80
Birmingham Midshires Mortgage Services Ltd v Ansell (6 November 1997,
    unreported) 12.21
Birmingham Midshires Mortgage Services Ltd v David Parry & Co [1997] NPC 153,
    [1997] EGCS 150, CA 6.14, 7.27, 7.28, 7.47, 7.50
Birmingham Midshires Mortgage Services Ltd v Phillips [1998] PNLR 468 .... 3.60, 3.63,
    3.64, 7.69
Birse Construction Ltd v Haiste Ltd [1996] 2 All ER 1, [1996] 1 WLR 675, 47 Con LR 162,
    [1996] 02 LS Gaz R 29, 76 BLR 26, 140 Sol Jo LB 25, CA 6.17
Bishopsgate Investment Management Ltd (in liquidation) v Maxwell (No 2) [1994] 1 All
    ER 261, [1993] BCLC 1282, [1993] BCC 120, CA 4.53
Bittlestone v Keegan Williams [1997] EGCS 8 .... 8.53
Blue Circle Industries plc v Ministry of Defence [1998] 3 All ER 385, [1999] 2 WLR
    295, [1998] EGCS 93, CA 3.19, 3.45, 3.55, 3.60, 3.65
Bolam v Friern Hospital Management Committee [1957] 2 All ER 118, [1957] 1 WLR
    582, 101 Sol Jo 357, 1 BMLR 1 .... 2.2, 2.13
Bolitho v City and Hackney Health Authority [1998] AC 232, [1997] 4 All ER 771,
    [1997] 3 WLR 1151, 39 BMLR 1, [1997] 47 LS Gaz R 30, 141 Sol Jo LB 238,
    HL 2.13
Bolkiah v KPMG (a firm) [1999] 1 All ER 517, [1999] 2 WLR 215, [1999] 1 BCLC 1,
    [1999] NLJR 16, 143 Sol Jo LB 35, HL 4.20, 10.65, 10.66,
    10.68, 10.70, 10.72
Boscawen v Bajwa [1995] 4 All ER 769, [1996] 1 WLR 328, 70 P & CR 391, [1995] 21 LS
    Gaz R 37, CA 8.23, 8.68
Boston (Martin) & Co v Roberts [1995] NPC 28, [1996] PNLR 45, CA 2.2, 2.7, 2.8,
    2.25, 2.27, 10.10
Bowdage v Harold Michelmore & Co (1962) 106 Sol Jo 512, 183 Estates Gazette
    233 .... 2.36, 8.83
Bowers v Bowers (3 February 1987, unreported) 8.23
Bown v Gould & Swayne [1996] PNLR 130, CA 2.14, 2.15, 2.21, 2.23, 2.24, 10.48
Bradford & Bingley Building Society v Boyce Evans Shepherd [1998] PNLR 250; (6 July
    1998, unreported), CA 12.12
Bradstock Trustee Services Ltd v Nabarro Nathanson (a firm) [1995] 4 All ER 888,
    [1995] 1 WLR 1405 .... 5.52
Brenner v Gregory [1972] 30 DLR (3d) 672, [1973] 1 OR 252 .... 2.16, 8.49
Brickenden v London Loan & Savings Co [1934] 3 DLR 465, PC 4.42, 4.43
Bridgegrove Ltd v Smith [1997] 2 EGLR 40, [1997] 33 EG 96, CA 8.76
Bristol & West Building Society v A Kramer & Co [1995] NPC 14, Independent,
    26 January, Times, 6 February 6.4

PARA

Bristol and West Building Society v Baden Barnes Groves & Co (26 November 1996,
  unreported) 7.56
Bristol and West Building Society v Christie [1996] EGCS 53 .... 7.92
Bristol and West Building Society v Fancy and Jackson (a firm) [1997] 4 All ER 582:   4.34,
                                                  6.4, 7.2, 7.16, 7.17, 7.20, 7.21,
                                                  7.23, 7.24, 7.61, 7.64, 7.75, 7.76, 7.78,
                                               7.80, 7.85, 7.87, 7.89, 7.107, 7.110, 7.111, 7.112
Bristol and West Building Society v May May & Merrimans (a firm) [1996] 2 All ER 801,
  [1996] 19 LS Gaz R 30, [1996] NLJR 625, 140 Sol Jo LB 110 .... 4.35, 4.43,
                                                           7.2, 7.17, 7.30
Bristol and West Building Society v May May & Merrimans (a firm) (No 2) [1997] 3 All
  ER 206, [1998] 1 WLR 336 .... 7.87
Bristol and West Building Society v Mothew (t/a Stapley & Co) [1998] Ch 1, [1996] 4 All
  ER 698, [1997] 2 WLR 436, [1996] NLJR 1273, 140 Sol Jo LB 206, sub nom
  Mothew v Bristol & West Building Society 75 P & CR 241, CA 3.3, 3.5,
                                            3.6, 3.9, 4.1, 4.6, 4.9, 4.10, 4.13, 4.20,
                                               4.27, 4.28, 4.30, 4.32, 4.33, 4.51, 7.2,
                                                   7.54, 7.60, 7.61, 7.75, 7.77,
                                                   7.111, 7.114, 8.4, 12.7, 12.8
Bristol and West plc v Bhadresa (No 2) [1999] 01 LS Gaz R 23, [1999] Lloyd's Rep IR
  138 .... 11.71
Bristol and West plc v Mascarenhas (No 2) [1999] 01 LS Gaz R 23, [1999] Lloyd's Rep
  IR 138 .... 11.71
British & Commonwealth Holdings plc v Barclays Bank plc [1996] 1 WLR 1, CA 5.8
British & Commonwealth Holdings plc v Quadrex Holdings Inc (10 April 1995,
  unreported), CA 3.27, 3.29, 3.30
British Fame (Owners) v Macgregor (Owners), The Macgregor [1943] AC 197, [1943]
  1 All ER 33, 112 LJP 6, 86 Sol Jo 367, 168 LT 193, 59 TLR 61, 74 Ll L Rep 82,
  HL 6.21
British Racing Drivers' Club Ltd v Hextall Erskine & Co (a firm) [1996] 3 All ER 667,
  [1997] 1 BCLC 182 .... 3.38, 6.13
British Westinghouse Electric and Manufacturing Co Ltd v Underground Electric Rlys
  Co of London Ltd [1912] AC 673, 81 LJKB 1132, [1911-13] All ER Rep 63, 56
  Sol Jo 734, 107 LT 325, HL 3.1, 3.40
Broadley v Guy Clapham & Co [1994] 4 All ER 439, [1993] 4 Med LR 328, 17 BMLR
  56, CA 5.46
Brocklesby v Armitage & Guest, 9 July 1999, NLD, CA 5.63
Brown v IRC [1965] AC 244, [1964] 3 All ER 119, [1964] 3 WLR 511, 42 TC 42, 43
  ATC 244, [1964] TR 269, 108 Sol Jo 636, 192 Estates Gazette 457, 1964 SC (HL)
  180, 1964 SLT 302, HL 4.5
Brown v KMR Services Ltd [1995] 4 All ER 598, [1995] 2 Lloyd's Rep 513, [1995] 32
  LS Gaz R 29, CA 3.11, 3.28, 3.29
Buckland v Mackesy (1968) 112 Sol Jo 841, 208 Estates Gazette 969, CA 8.46, 8.47,
                                                           8.48, 8.49
Buckley v Lane Herdman & Co [1977] CLY 3143 .... 8.56
Buckley v National Union of General and Municipal Workers [1967] 3 All ER 767,
  112 Sol Jo 292 .... 10.56
Burdge & Burdge v John Hodge & Co (11 March 1996, unreported) 12.27, 12.32
Burdick v Garrick (1870) 5 Ch App 233, 39 LJ Ch 369, 18 WR 387 .... 4.5, 4.60, 4.64
Burrells Wharf Freeholds Ltd v Galliard Homes Ltd (1 July 1999, unreported) 12.2
Byrne v Hall Pain & Foster (a firm) [1999] 2 All ER 400, [1999] 12 EG 165, [1998]
  EGCS 182, 143 Sol Jo LB 36, [1999] Lloyd's Rep PN 147, CA 5.24

C

Cabassi v Vila (1940) 64 CLR 130, HC of A 10.42
Caffrey v Darby (1801) 6 Ves 488 .... 4.48, 4.49
Campbell v Meacocks [1995] NPC 141, CA 5.43
Cancer Research Campaign v Ernest Brown & Co (a firm) [1997] STC 1425, [1998]
  PNLR 592 .... 9.4, 9.6, 9.12
Canson Enterprises Ltd v Broughton & Co [1991] SCR 534, 131 NR 321, [1992] 1 WWR
  245, 9 CCLT (2d) 1, 85 DLR (4th) 129, 39 CPR (3d) 449 .... 4.39, 4.48, 4.49,
                                                   4.50, 4.51, 4.52, 6.6

PARA

Caparo Industries plc v Dickman [1990] 2 AC 605, [1990] 1 All ER 568, [1990] 2 WLR 358, [1990] BCLC 273, [1990] BCC 164, 134 Sol Jo 494, [1990] 12 LS Gaz R 42, [1990] NLJR 248, HL 1.12, 1.13, 1.14, 3.8

Carlton v Fulchers [1997] PNLR 337, CA 10.7

Carr-Glynn v Frearsons (a firm) [1998] 4 All ER 225, [1999] 2 WLR 1046, [1998] 3 FCR 487, [1999] 1 FLR 8, [1998] Fam Law 739, [1998] NLJR 1487, [1998] EGCS 128, CA 1.28, 9.2, 9.3, 9.4, 9.8

Carradine Properties Ltd v D J Freeman & Co (1982) 1 PN 41, 126 Sol Jo 157, CA ... 1.10

Carradine Properties Ltd v DJ Freeman & Co (a firm) (1989) 5 Const LJ 267, CA 2.32

Carter (t/a New Chapel Developments) v TG Baynes & Sons [1998] EGCS 109: 3.10, 8.53, 8.77, 8.78

Carvin v Dunham Brindley & Linn [1997] EGCS 90, CA 8.53

Casey v Hugh James Jones & Jenkins [1999] Lloyd's Rep PN 115 .... 10.8, 10.56

Cavendish Funding Ltd v Henry Spencer & Sons Ltd [1998] 06 EG 146, [1998] PNLR 122, CA 3.14

Cemp Properties (UK) Ltd v Dentsply Research and Development Corpn (Denton Hall & Burgin, third party) [1989] 2 EGLR 205, [1989] 37 EG 133 .... 8.35, 8.37, 8.84, 8.92

Central Trust Co v Rafuse (1986) 34 BLR 187, [1986] 2 SCR 147, 37 CCLT 117, 42 RPR 161, 31 DLR (4th) 481 .... 2.9

Chaplin v Hicks [1911] 2 KB 786, 80 LJKB 1292, [1911-13] All ER Rep 224, 55 Sol Jo 580, 105 LT 285, 27 TLR 458, CA 9.17

Chelsea Building Society v Goddard & Smith [1996] EGCS 157 .... 7.92

Christensen v Scott [1996] 1 NZLR 273, NZCA 1.8

Christie v Wilson [1999] 1 All ER 545, [1998] 1 WLR 1694, [1998] 30 LS Gaz R 25, 142 Sol Jo LB 205, CA 10.73

Citro (a bankrupt), Re [1991] Ch 142, [1990] 3 All ER 952, [1990] 3 WLR 880, [1991] 1 FLR 71, [1990] Fam Law 428, 134 Sol Jo 806, [1990] 28 LS Gaz R 43, [1990] NLJR 1073, CA 8.31

Clark v Kirby-Smith [1964] Ch 506, [1964] 2 All ER 835, [1964] 3 WLR 239, 108 Sol Jo 462, 190 Estates Gazette 865 .... 8.95

Clark Boyce v Mouat [1994] 1 AC 428, [1993] 4 All ER 268, [1993] 3 WLR 1021, [1993] 40 LS Gaz R 42, [1993] 3 NZLR 641, 137 Sol Jo LB 231, PC: . 2.36, 4.28, 8.3

Clarke v Bruce Lance & Co (a firm) [1988] 1 All ER 364, [1988] 1 WLR 881, 131 Sol Jo 1698, [1988] 2 LS Gaz R 37, [1987] NLJ Rep 1064, CA 9.3, 9.4

Clarke v Milford (1987) 38 DLR (4th) 139 .... 8.56, 8.71

Clough v Bond (1838) 3 My & Cr 490, 8 LJ Ch 51, 2 Jur 958, 45 RR 314, 40 ER 1159 .... 4.48

Cobeldick, ex p (1883) 12 QBD 149, 32 WR 239, 49 LT 741, CA 12.3

Collard v Saunders (1972) 222 Estates Gazette 795 .... 8.49, 8.73

Collie, Re, ex p Adamson (1878) 8 Ch D 807, 47 LJ Bcy 103, 26 WR 890, 38 LT 917, CA 4.39

Company, a (No 006798 of 1995), Re [1996] 2 All ER 417, [1996] 1 WLR 491, [1996] 2 BCLC 48 .... 11.29

Comphania de Seguros Imperio v Heath (REBX) Ltd (30 March 1999, unreported) 5.69, 5.72

Computastaff Ltd v Ingledew Brown Bennison and Garrett (1983) 268 Estates Gazette 906, [1983] EGD 983, 133 NLJ 598 .... 8.35, 8.52, 8.53, 8.80

Connell v Odlum [1993] 2 NZLR 257, NZCA 8.29

Connor & Labrum v Regoczi-Ritzman (1995) 70 P & CR D41-3 ... 3.39, 3.40, 3.55, 8.73, 8.77, 8.78

Cook v S [1967] 1 All ER 299, 110 Sol Jo 964, sub nom Cook v Swinfen [1967] 1 WLR 457, CA 10.53

Corfield v D S Bosher & Co [1992] 1 EGLR 163, [1992] 04 EG 127 .... 10.59

Costa v Georghiou (1983) 1 PN 201, [1984] NLJR 82, CA 8.56

Coulthard v Disco Mix Club Ltd [1999] 2 All ER 457 .... 5.75

County Personnel (Employment Agency) Ltd v Alan R Pulver & Co [1987] 1 All ER 289, [1987] 1 WLR 916, 131 Sol Jo 474, [1986] 2 EGLR 246, [1987] LS Gaz R 1409, [1986] NLJ Rep 1138, CA 2.32, 2.37, 3.10, 3.52, 8.55, 8.74, 10.55

Coxwold, The. See Yorkshire Dale Steamship Co Ltd v Minister of War Transport, The Coxwold

PARA

Crédit Lyonnais Bank Nederland NV v Burch [1997] 1 All ER 144, 74 P & CR 384,
    [1997] 2 FCR 1, [1997] 1 FLR 11, [1997] Fam Law 168, 29 HLR 513, [1996]
    32 LS Gaz R 33, [1996] NLJR 1421, 140 Sol Jo LB 158, CA . 8.14, 8.20, 8.22, 8.24
Creech v Mayorcas (1966) 198 Estates Gazette 1091 .... 2.28, 8.60, 8.79
Crocker, Re, Re Taxation of Costs [1936] Ch 696, [1936] 2 All ER 899, [1936] WN 192,
    105 LJ Ch 276, 80 Sol Jo 486, 155 LT 344, 52 TLR 565 .... 12.5
Cygnet Health Care plc v Elleston & Co (10 May 1999, unreported) 8.73

D

DSL Group Ltd v Unisys International Services Ltd (1994) 67 BLR 117 .... 12.33
Dace v Redland Aggregates Ltd [1997] EGCS 123 .... 11.48
Daniels (formerly practising as Deloittes Haskins & Sells) v Anderson (1995) 118 FLR
    248, 13 ACLC 614, 37 NSWLR 438, 16 ASCR 607 .... 6.13
Darlington Building Society v O'Rourke James Scourfield & McCarthy [1999] Lloyd's
    Rep PN 33, CA 5.78, 5.79, 7.56
Davey v Woolley (1982) 35 OR (2d) 599, CA 4.31
Davies v Davies (4 March 1999, unreported), CA 10.72
Davies v Swan Motor Co (Swansea) Ltd [1949] 2 KB 291, [1949] 1 All ER 620, 65 TLR
    278, CA 6.15, 6.21
Davis v Ministry of Defence [1985] CLY 2017, [1985] LS Gaz R 3265, [1985] CA
    Transcript 413 .... 5.44
Davy-Chiesman v Davy-Chiesman [1984] Fam 48, [1984] 1 All ER 321, [1984] 2
    WLR 291, 127 Sol Jo 805, [1984] LS Gaz R 44, CA 2.11, 11.47
Dawson, Re, Union Fidelity Trust Co Ltd v Perpetual Trustees Co Ltd (1966) 84 WN
    399, [1966] 2 NSWR 211 .... 4.55, 4.56, 4.64
Day v Mead [1987] 2 NZLR 443, NZCA 4.20, 4.51, 6.6
Deeny v Gooda Walker [1994] CLC 1224 .... 2.18
Deeny v Gooda Walker Ltd (in liquidation) [1995] 4 All ER 289, [1995] 1 WLR 1206,
    [1996] LRLR 176 .... 3.59
Dent (JJ) v National Farmers' Union, 17 June 1999, NLD 10.7
Derry v Peek (1889) 14 App Cas 337, 54 JP 148, 58 LJ Ch 864, 1 Meg 292, 38 WR 33,
    [1886-90] All ER Rep 1, 61 LT 265, 5 TLR 625, HL 7.99
Diamond v Campbell-Jones [1961] Ch 22, [1960] 1 All ER 583, [1960] 2 WLR 568, 39
    ATC 103, 53 R & IT 502, [1960] TR 131, 104 Sol Jo 249 .... 3.36
Dickinson v Jones Alexander & Co [1993] 2 FLR 521, [1990] Fam Law 137, 6 PN 205,
    [1989] NLJR 1525 .... 10.8, 10.53, 10.57
Dixon v Rigby, Golding & Co (13 March 1995, unreported), CA 3.39
Dobbie v Medway Health Authority [1994] 4 All ER 450, [1994] 1 WLR 1234, [1994]
    5 Med LR 160, 20 BMLR 61, [1994] NLJR 828, CA 5.46
Dogma Properties Ltd v Gale (1984) 136 NLJ 453 .... 8.64, 8.69
Donmez v Barnes [1996] EGCS 129 .... 2.32, 8.102
Downs v Chappell [1996] 3 All ER 344, [1997] 1 WLR 426, CA 3.4, 3.5, 3.6,
                                                                6.15, 6.21, 6.22, 7.60
Dubai Aluminium Co Ltd v Al Alawi [1999] 1 All ER 703, [1999] 1 Lloyd's Rep 478: 12.23
Dubai Aluminium Co Ltd v Salaam and Livingston [1999] 1 Lloyd's Rep 415, Times,
    4 September 4.19, 6.19, 6.22
Duncan v Cuelenaere, Beaubier, Walters, Kendall & Fisher [1987] 2 WWR 379 ...... 2.30
Dunkirk Colliery Co v Lever (1878) 9 Ch D 20, 26 WR 841, 39 LT 239, CA 3.1
Dunn v Fairs, Blissard, Barnes and Stowe (1961) 105 Sol Jo 932 .... 9.15
Dunn v Hallen (1861) 2 F & F 642 .... 10.7

E

Eckersley v Binnie (1988) 18 Con LR 1, CA 2.2, 2.9, 2.25
El Ajou v Dollar Land Holdings plc (No 2) [1995] 2 All ER 213 .... 4.65
Elcano Acceptance Ltd v Richmond, Richmond, Stambler & Mills [1989] 68 OR (2d) 165;
    affd [1991] 3 OR (3d) 123, (1991) 79 DLR (4th) 154 .... 2.7, 2.18
Elguzouli-Daf v Metropolitan Police Comr [1995] QB 335, [1995] 1 All ER 833, [1995]
    2 WLR 173, [1995] NLJR 151, CA 10.9
Elland Developments Ltd v Smith [1995] EGCS 141 .... 8.63

PARA

Embassy Art Products Ltd, Re [1988] BCLC 1, 3 BCC 292 .... 11.41
Empresa Exportadora de Azucar v Industria Azucarera Nacional SA, The Playa Larga
    and The Marble Islands [1983] 2 Lloyd's Rep 171, CA 4.58
Endhill Pty Ltd v Grasso, Searles & Romano [1993] 2 Qd R 136 .... 3.34, 8.72
Enterprises of Panama Inc, SS, Liverpool (Owners) v Ousel (Owners), The Liverpool (No 2)
    [1963] P 64, [1960] 3 All ER 307, [1960] 3 WLR 597, [1960] 2 Lloyd's Rep 66,
    104 Sol Jo 824, CA 3.41
Esso Petroleum Co Ltd v Mardon [1976] QB 801, [1976] 2 All ER 5, [1976] 2 WLR 583,
    [1976] 2 Lloyd's Rep 305, 120 Sol Jo 131, 2 BLR 85, CA 108
Esterhuizen v Allied Dunbar Assurance plc [1998] 2 FLR 668, [1998] Fam Law
    527 .... 2.15, 9.9
Europe Mortgage Co Ltd v GA Property Services Ltd (26 April 1999, unreported) 3.8

F

Faragher v Gerber [1994] EGCS 122 .... 8.52, 8.53, 8.73
Farrer v Copley Singleton (1997) 76 P & CR 169, [1998] PNLR 22, CA 8.7, 8.8
Fell v Brown (1791) 1 Peake 131 .... 10.38
Filmlab Systems International Ltd v Pennington [1994] 4 All ER 673, [1995] 1 WLR 673,
    [1993] NLJR 1405 .... 11.17
Finance For Mortgages Ltd v Farley & Co [1996] NPC 19, [1996] EGCS 35, [1998]
    PNLR 145 .... 5.58
Finers (a firm) v Miro [1991] 1 All ER 182, [1991] 1 WLR 35, 134 Sol Jo 1039, [1990]
    NLJR 1387, CA 4.4
Finlay (James) & Co Ltd v NV Kwik Hoo Tong Handel Maatschappij [1929] 1 KB 400,
    98 LJKB 251, 17 Asp MLC 566, 34 Com Cas 143, [1928] All ER Rep 110, 140
    LT 389, 45 TLR 149, CA 3.41
First Interstate Bank of California v Cohen Arnold & Co [1996] 5 Bank LR 150,
    140 Sol Jo LB 12, [1996] PNLR 17, CA 3.21
First National Commercial Bank plc v Humberts (a firm) [1995] 2 All ER 673,
    [1995] NPC 1, [1995] 1 EGLR 142, 73 BLR 90, [1995] 14 EG 140, [1995]
    NLJR 345n, CA 5.26
First National Commercial Bank plc v Loxleys (a firm) [1996] 43 LS Gaz R 26, 141
    Sol Jo LB 6, [1997] PNLR 211, CA 1.21, 1.25, 8.35, 8.37
Fletamentos Maritimos SA v Effijohn International BV (10 December 1997, unreported),
    CA 11.6, 11.28, 11.31, 11.42, 11.49
Fletamentos Maritimos SA v Effijohn International BV (No 2) [1997] 2 Lloyd's Rep
    302, CA 11.6, 11.28, 11.31
Fletcher & Son v Jubb, Booth and Helliwell [1920] 1 KB 275, 89 LJKB 236, 122 LT
    258, 36 TLR 19, CA 2.28
Forbes v Wandsworth Health Authority [1997] QB 402, [1996] 4 All ER 881, [1996]
    3 WLR 1108, [1996] 7 Med LR 175, 36 BMLR 1, [1996] 15 LS Gaz R 32, [1996]
    NLJR 477, 140 Sol Jo LB 85, CA 5.48, 5.49, 5.56
Forbouys v Gadhavi [1993] NPC 122 .... 2.37, 8.55
Ford v White & Co [1964] 2 All ER 755, [1964] 1 WLR 885, 108 Sol Jo 542 . 3.57, 8.53,
    8.73, 8.80
Forsikringsaktieselskapet Vesta v Butcher [1986] 2 All ER 488, [1986] 2 Lloyd's Rep
    179; on appeal sub nom Forsikringsaktieselskapet Vesta v Butcher, Bain Dawles
    Ltd and Aquacultural Insurance Services Ltd [1989] AC 852, [1988] 2 All ER 43,
    [1988] 3 WLR 565, [1988] 1 Lloyd's Rep 19, 132 Sol Jo 1181, CA; affd [1989]
    AC 852, [1989] 1 All ER 402, [1989] 2 WLR 290, [1989] 1 Lloyd's Rep 331,
    133 Sol Jo 184, [1989] 11 LS Gaz R 42, HL 6.3
Forster v Outred & Co (a firm) [1982] 2 All ER 753, [1982] 1 WLR 86, 125 Sol Jo
    309, CA 5.16, 5.17, 5.18, 5.37
Foster (a bankrupt), Re, Trustee of Property of Foster (bankrupts) v Crust (a firm) [1986]
    BCLC 307, 129 Sol Jo 333 .... 1.8, 8.42
Fozal v Gofur (1993) Times, 9 July, CA 11.1
Freeman v Marshall & Co (1966) 200 Estates Gazette 777 .... 2.4
Freudiana Holdings, Re (1995) Times, 4 December, CA 11.8
Friends' Provident Life Office v Hillier Parker May & Rowden (a firm) (Estates and
    General plc, third parties)) [1997] QB 85, [1995] 4 All ER 260, [1996] 2 WLR
    123, 71 P & CR 286, CA 6.16

G

GP & P Ltd v Bulcraig and Davis [1986] 2 EGLR 148, 280 Estates Gazette 356;
    on appeal [1988] 1 EGLR 138, [1988] 12 EG 103, CA 8.52, 8.53, 8.75
Galoo Ltd (in liquidation) v Bright Grahame Murray (a firm) [1995] 1 All ER 16,
    [1994] 1 WLR 1360, [1994] 2 BCLC 492, [1994] BCC 319, CA 3.22, 3.25
Gardner v Marsh and Parsons [1997] 3 All ER 871, [1997] 1 WLR 489, 75
    P & CR 319, [1996] 46 LS Gaz R 28, [1997] 15 EG 137, 140 Sol Jo LB 262,
    CA 3.44, 3.45, 3.47
Gartside v Sheffield, Young and Ellis [1983] NZLR 37, NZCA 9.9, 9.17
Gascoine v Ian Sheridan & Co and Latham [1994] 5 Med LR 437 .... 10.58
Gaud v Leeds Health Authority (1999) Times, 14 May 5.8
Giles v Thompson [1994] 1 AC 142, [1993] 3 All ER 321, [1993] 2 WLR 908, [1993] RTR
    289, [1993] 27 LS Gaz R 34, [1993] NLJR 884, 137 Sol Jo LB 151, HL 11.68
Glaverbel SA v British Coal Corpn [1995] RPC 255, CA 2.22
Globe Equities Ltd v Globe Legal Services Ltd [1999] BLR 232, CA 11.69
Goddard (Theodore) v Fletcher King Services Ltd [1997] 32 EG 90 .... 8.55, 8.85
Godefroy v Jay (1831) 7 Bing 413, 9 LJOS 122, 5 Moo & P 284, 131 ER 159 ...... 10.7
Goodwill v British Pregnancy Advisory Service [1996] 2 All ER 161, [1996] 1 WLR
    1397, [1996] 2 FCR 680, [1996] 2 FLR 55, [1996] Fam Law 471, 31 BMLR 83,
    [1996] 05 LS Gaz R 31, [1996] NLJR 173, 140 Sol Jo LB 37, CA 1.13
Goody v Baring [1956] 2 All ER 11, [1956] 1 WLR 448, 100 Sol Jo 320 .... 8.4, 8.52,
                                                                          8.53, 8.58
Gran Gelato Ltd v Richcliff (Group) Ltd [1992] Ch 560, [1992] 1 All ER 865,
    [1992] 2 WLR 867, [1992] 1 EGLR 297, [1992] 18 LS Gaz R 36, [1992]
    NLJR 51 .... 1.19, 1.20, 1.21, 1.22, 1.23,
                                                                   6.5, 6.6, 8.35, 8.39
Greaves & Co (Contractors) Ltd v Baynham, Meikle & Partners [1975] 3 All ER 99,
    [1975] 1 WLR 1095, [1975] 2 Lloyd's Rep 325, 119 Sol Jo 372, 4 BLR 56,
    CA 1.2, 2.2
Greaves & Co (Contractors) Ltd v Baynham Meikle & Partners (1978) 11 BLR 29, HL: 1.2
Green v Cunningham John & Co (1995) 46 Con LR 62, CA 10.56
Greenhoff v J Lyons & Co (30 June 1998, unreported), CA 11.27
Gregory v Tarlo (1964) 108 Sol Jo 219 .... 10.58
Griffin v Kingsmill [1998] PIQR P 24, [1998] PNLR 157 .... 10.47
Griffin v Kingsmill (No 2) (20 February 1998, unreported) 10.47
Griffin v Mersey Regional Ambulance [1998] PIQR P 34, CA 6.15
Griffiths v Fleming [1909] 1 KB 805, 78 LJKB 567, [1908-10] All ER Rep 760,
    53 Sol Jo 340, 100 LT 765, 25 TLR 377, CA 9.15
Groom v Crocker [1939] 1 KB 194, [1938] 2 All ER 394, 108 LJKB 296, 82 Sol Jo
    374, 158 LT 477, 54 TLR 861, 60 Ll L Rep 393, CA 1.8
Guardian Ocean Cargoes Ltd, Transorient Ship Cargoes Ltd, Middle East Agents SAL and
    Med Lines SA v Banco do Brasil SA (No 3) [1992] 2 Lloyd's Rep 193; affd sub
    nom Guardian Ocean Cargoes Ltd, Transorient Ship Cargoes Ltd, Middle East
    Agents SAL and Med Line SA v Banco do Brasil SA (Nos 1 and 3) [1994]
    2 Lloyd's Rep 152, CA 4.64, 4.65
Guerin v R [1984] 2 SCR 335, 13 DLR (4th) 321, 55 NR 161 (Can SC) ... 4.47, 4.50, 4.57
Gupta v Comer [1991] 1 QB 629, [1991] 1 All ER 289, [1991] 2 WLR 494, [1990]
    NLJR 1606, CA 11.66

H

HF Pension Trustees Ltd v Ellison (1999) Times, 5 March 5.52, 5.55
Hadley v Baxendale (1854) 23 LJ Ex 179, 9 Exch 341, 18 Jur 358, 2 WR 302, 156
    ER 145, [1843-60] All ER Rep 461, 2 CLR 517, 23 LTOS 69:   3.28, 3.64, 7.67, 7.68
Haigh v Wright Hassall & Co [1994] EGCS 54, CA 2.36, 8.47
Halford v Brookes [1991] 3 All ER 559, [1991] 1 WLR 428, CA 5.44
Halifax Building Society v Grosse [1997] EGCS 111 .... 8.55
Halifax Mortgage Services Ltd v Stepsky [1996] Ch 1, [1995] 4 All ER 656, [1995]
    3 WLR 701, [1996] 1 FCR 107, [1995] 27 LS Gaz R 31; affd [1996] Ch 207,
    [1996] 2 All ER 277, [1996] 2 WLR 230, [1996] 2 FCR 97, [1996] 1 FLR 620,
    [1996] Fam Law 279, 28 HLR 522, [1996] 01 LS Gaz R 21, 140 Sol Jo LB 9,
    CA 8.17, 8.18, 8.28, 8.33, 8.62

PARA

Halifax plc v Gould and Swayne [1998] EGCS 127, [1999] PNLR 184, CA 7.31
Hall v Meyrick [1957] 2 QB 455, [1957] 2 All ER 722, [1957] 3 WLR 273, 101 Sol Jo
    574, CA 9.10
        Hall (Arthur J S) & Co v Simons [1999] 2 FCR 193, [1999] 1 FLR 536, [1999] Fam
        Law 215, [1999] Lloyd's Rep PN 47, [1999] PNLR 374, CA   10.13, 10.14,
                                                               10.15, 10.17, 10.20, 10.28, 10.30,
                                                               10.31, 10.32, 10.33, 10.34, 10.35,
                                                  10.36,10.37, 10.42, 10.43, 10.46, 10.47
Hallam-Eames v Merrett Syndicates Ltd [1996] 7 Med LR 122, CA .. 5.43, 5.46, 5.47, 5.49
Hallewell Bunyard, Re (5 June 1996, unreported), CA 11.9
Hallmark Finance Insurance Brokers Ltd v Fraser & Beatty [1990] 1 OR (3d) 641: 2.33, 2.37
Hambros Bank Ltd v British Historic Buildings Trust and Din [1995] NPC 179, CA ... 8.13
Harris v Nantes and Wilde [1997] NPC 7, CA 1.8, 8.8, 8.23
Harrison v Battye [1974] 3 All ER 830, [1975] 1 WLR 58, 119 Sol Jo 31, CA 8.56
Hartle v Laceys [1997] CLY 3839, [1999] Lloyd's Rep PN 315, CA 3.18, 3.19, 3.20,
                                                         3.60, 3.64, 7.67, 7.69, 8.70
Hawkins v Clayton (1988) 164 CLR 539, 78 ALR 69, HC of A 9.12
Hawkins v Harwood (1849) 7 Dow & L 181, 19 LJ Ex 33, 4 Exch 503, 14 LTOS 273: 10.7
Hayes v Dowding [1996] PNLR 578 .... 12.27, 12.28
Hayes v James & Charles Dodd (a firm) [1990] 2 All ER 815, [1988] BTLC 380, [1988]
    NLJR 259, CA 3.10, 8.53, 8.76, 8.81, 10.64
Hedley Byrne & Co Ltd v Heller & Partners Ltd [1964] AC 465, [1963] 2 All
    ER 575, [1963] 3 WLR 101, [1963] 1 Lloyd's Rep 485, 107 Sol Jo 454,
    HL 1.12, 1.14, 1.16, 2.28, 4.20, 4.25, 10.39
Hellenic Mutual War Risks Association (Bermuda) Ltd and General Contractors
    Importing and Services Enterprises v Harrison (The Sagheera) [1997] 1 Lloyd's
    Rep 160 .... 12.18, 12.19
Hemmens v Wilson Browne (a firm) [1995] Ch 223, [1993] 4 All ER 826, [1994]
    2 WLR 323, [1994] 2 FLR 101, [1993] 45 LS Gaz R 45 .... 9.25, 9.26
Henderson v Merrett Syndicates [1995] 2 AC 145, [1994] 3 All ER 506, [1994] 3 WLR
    761, [1994] NLJR 1204, HL 1.10, 1.12, 1.14, 1.16, 1.18, 1.25, 1.29, 4.20, 5.2
Henderson v Merrett Syndicates Ltd and Ernst & Whinney (No 2) [1996] PNLR 32,
    [1997] LRLR 247 .... 2.7, 2.9, 6.13
Henderson v Temple Pier Co Ltd [1998] 3 All ER 324, [1998] 1 WLR 1540, [1998]
    20 LS Gaz R 35, 142 Sol Jo LB 156, CA 5.57
Heron II, The. See Koufos v C Czarnikow Ltd, The Heron II
Heywood v Wellers [1976] QB 446, [1976] 1 All ER 300, [1976] 2 WLR 101, [1976]
    2 Lloyd's Rep 88, 120 Sol Jo 9, CA 3.14, 10.8, 10.64
Hill v Harris [1965] 2 QB 601, [1965] 2 All ER 358, [1965] 2 WLR 1331, 109 Sol Jo 333,
    CA 8.55
Hillsdown Holdings plc v Pensions Ombudsman [1997] 1 All ER 862 .... 5.52
Hitchens v Higgens & Bacchus [1997] NPC 115, CA 3.43, 8.86
Hodge v Clifford Cowling & Co [1990] 2 EGLR 89, [1990] 46 EG 120, CA 8.94, 8.96
Hodgson v Imperial Tobacco Ltd [1998] 2 All ER 673, [1998] 1 WLR 1056,
    [1998] 15 LS Gaz R 31, [1998] NLJR 241, 142 Sol Jo LB 93, CA 11.2, 11.52,
                                                               11.60, 11.68, 11.70
Holden v Holden and Pearson (1910) 54 Sol Jo 328, 102 LT 398, 26 TLR 307 ...... 10.7
Holden & Co v Crown Prosecution Service [1990] 2 QB 261 .... 11.67
Holmes v H Kennard & Son (a firm) (1984) 49 P & CR 202, 128 Sol Jo 854, [1984]
    LS Gaz R 363 .... 8.59, 8.66
Holt v Payne Skillington [1996] 02 LS Gaz R 29, 77 BLR 51, 140 Sol Jo LB 30, [1996]
    PNLR 179, CA 1.11, 1.24
Homsy v Murphy (1996) 73 P & CR 26, CA 3.37, 8.107
Hopkins v MacKenzie [1995] 6 Med LR 26, 23 BMLR 132, [1994] 45 LS Gaz R 38,
    [1995] PIQR P 43, 138 Sol Jo LB 222, CA 5.35, 5.36
Horsfall v Haywards (a firm) [1999] 1 FLR 1182, [1999] Fam Law 383, 143 Sol Jo
    LB 66, [1999] Lloyd's Rep PN 332, CA 3.43, 9.5, 9.21
Housing Loan Corpn plc v William H Brown [1999] Lloyd's Rep PN 185, CA 7.84
Howard (RP) Ltd v Woodman Matthews & Co [1983] Com LR 100, [1983] BCLC 117,
    133 NLJ 598 .... 1.8, 8.42, 8.94
Hughes v Kingston upon Hull City Council [1999] 2 All ER 49, [1999] 2 WLR 1229,
    [1998] 44 LS Gaz R 36, 143 Sol Jo LB 54 .... 11.52
Hunter v Chief Constable of West Midlands Police [1982] AC 529, [1981] 3 All ER 727,
    [1981] 3 WLR 906, 125 Sol Jo 829, HL 10.15, 10.16, 10.19

PARA

Hurlingham Estates Ltd v Wilde & Partners [1997] 1 Lloyd's Rep 525, [1997] STC 627,
    [1997] NLJR 453 .... 1.6, 2.6, 2.7, 9.13
Hussey v Eels [1990] 2 QB 227, [1990] 1 All ER 449, [1990] 2 WLR 234, [1990]
    1 EGLR 215, [1990] NLJR 53, [1990] 19 EG 77, CA 3.44, 3.45

I

Inder Lynch Devoy & Co v Subritzky [1979] 1 NZLR 87, CA 3.33, 3.35
Inter-Leisure Ltd v Lamberts [1997] NPC 49 .... 3.18, 3.19, 3.55, 8.55, 8.85, 8.89
Interallianz Finance AG v Independent Insurance Co Ltd [1997] EGCS 91 ..... 7.94, 7.96
Italia Express, The. See Ventouris v Mountain, The Italia Express

J

J (a minor), Re (25 March 1997, unreported), CA 11.42, 11.48
Jaffray v Marshall [1994] 1 All ER 143, [1993] 1 WLR 1285, [1993] 15 LS Gaz R 39: 4.57
Johnson v Agnew [1980] AC 367, [1979] 1 All ER 883, [1979] 2 WLR 487, 39 P &
    CR 424, 123 Sol Jo 217, 251 Estates Gazette 1167, HL 3.48
Johnson v Bingley Dyson & Furey [1995] NPC 27, [1997] PNLR 392 .... 2.8, 2.14,
                                                              2.33, 8.83, 8.87
Johnson v Gore Wood & Co [1998] NPC 151, CA 1.8
Johnson v Perez (1988) 82 ALR 587 .... 3.34, 3.48, 10.55
Jolliffe v Charles Coleman & Co (1971) 219 Estates Gazette 1608 .... 8.95, 8.99

K

K v P (J, third party) [1993] Ch 140, [1993] 1 All ER 521, [1992] 3 WLR 1015 ..... 6.22
Kelley v Corston [1998] QB 686, [1997] 4 All ER 466, [1998] 3 WLR 246, [1998]
    1 FCR 554, [1998] 1 FLR 986, [1998] Fam Law 399, [1997] NPC 111, [1997]
    NLJR 1276, CA 10.47
Kelly v Cooper [1993] AC 205, [1992] 3 WLR 936, [1994] 1 BCLC 395, [1992] 43
    LS Gaz R 30, PC 4.30, 4.35, 10.66
Kelly v South Manchester Health Authority [1997] 3 All ER 274, [1998] 1 WLR 244: 11.17
Kennedy v KB van Emden & Co (1996) 74 P & CR 19, [1996] 16 LS Gaz R 31,
    140 Sol Jo LB 99, [1996] PNLR 409, sub nom Kennedy v Emden [1997] 44 EG
    201, CA 3.58, 8.55, 8.79
Kenyon-Brown v Banks & Co (5 June 1998, unreported) 2.14, 8.4
Kershaw v Whelan [1996] 2 All ER 404, [1996] 1 WLR 358, [1995] TLR
    695 .... 12.27, 12.28, 12.30
Kershaw v Whelan (No 2) (1997) 141 Sol Jo LB 37 .... 5.75
Kilroy v Kilroy [1997] PNLR 66, CA 11.46, 11.54
King v Hawkins & Co (1982) Times, 28 January 3.33, 8.53
Kingsnorth Trust Ltd v Tizard [1986] 2 All ER 54, [1986] 1 WLR 783, 51 P & CR 296,
    130 Sol Jo 244, [1985] LS Gaz R 1231 .... 8.61
Kitchen v Royal Air Forces Association [1958] 2 All ER 241, [1958] 1 WLR 563, 102
    Sol Jo 363, CA 3.19, 9.17, 10.49, 10.50
Knapp v Ecclesiastical Insurance Group plc and Smith [1998] Lloyd's Rep IR 390,
    [1998] PNLR 172, CA 5.22, 5.36
Knightley v Johns [1982] 1 All ER 851, [1982] 1 WLR 349, [1982] RTR 182, 126 Sol Jo
    101, CA 3.39
Konigsberg (a bankrupt), Re, ex p Trustee v Konigsberg [1989] 3 All ER 289,
    [1989] 1 WLR 1257, [1990] Fam Law 94, 133 Sol Jo 1337, [1989] NLJR
    1302 .... 12.16, 12.18, 12.19
Kotowich v Petursson [1994] 3 WWR 669 .... 8.58
Koufos v C Czarnikow Ltd, The Heron II [1969] 1 AC 350, [1967] 3 All ER 686,
    [1967] 3 WLR 1491, [1967] 2 Lloyd's Rep 457, 111 Sol Jo 848, HL 3.28
Kumar v AGF Insurance Ltd [1998] 4 All ER 788, [1999] PNLR 269 .... 7.99

L

LR v Witherspoon [1999] Lloyd's Rep PN 401, CA 10.20, 10.22
Ladenbau (G & K) (UK) Ltd v Crawley and de Reya (a firm) [1978] 1 All ER 682,
    [1978] 1 WLR 266, 121 Sol Jo 356 .... 2.19, 3.36, 8.52, 8.53, 8.77, 8.78
Lake v Bushby [1949] 2 All ER 964, 94 Sol Jo 82 .... 8.4, 8.53
Lakha & Booth, Re (6 November 1998, unreported), CA 11.58
Landall v Dennis Faulkner & Alsop [1994] 5 Med LR 268 .... 10.47
Layzell v Smith Morton & Long [1992] 1 EGLR 169, [1992] 13 EG 118 .... 8.80
Letang v Cooper [1965] 1 QB 232, [1964] 2 All ER 929, [1964] 3 WLR 573, [1964]
    2 Lloyd's Rep 339, 108 Sol Jo 519, CA 5.79
Lillicrap v Nalder & Son (a firm) [1993] 1 All ER 724, [1993] 1 WLR 94, [1992] NLJR
    1449, CA 12.14, 12.15, 12.25, 12.26, 12.28, 12.29
Linaker v Keith Turner & Ashton Garland J (5 November 1998, unreported) 2.33, 8.7
Liverpool (No 2), The. See Enterprises of Panama Inc, SS, Liverpool (Owners) v Ousel
    (Owners), The Liverpool (No 2)
Liverpool City Council v Irwin [1977] AC 239, [1976] 2 All ER 39, [1976] 2 WLR 562,
    74 LGR 392, 32 P & CR 43, 13 HLR 38, 120 Sol Jo 267, 238 Estates Gazette 879,
    963, HL 2.1
Livingstone v Rawyards Coal Co (1880) 5 App Cas 25, 44 JP 392, 28 WR 357, 42 LT
    334, HL 3.1
Lloyds Bank Ltd v EB Savory & Co [1933] AC 201, 102 LJKB 224, 38 Com Cas 115,
    [1932] All ER Rep 106, 49 TLR 116, 44 Ll L Rep 231, sub nom Savory & Co v
    Lloyds Bank Ltd 148 LT 291, HL 6.14
Locabail (UK) Ltd v Bayfield Properties Ltd [1999] 20 LS Gaz R 39 .... 10.67
Locke v Camberwell Health Authority [1990] 1 Med LR 253, [1990] NLJR 205; revsd
    [1991] 2 Med LR 249, [1990] NLJR 205, CA 2.7, 2.11, 11.47
London and South of England Building Society v Stone [1983] 3 All ER 105,
    [1983] 1 WLR 1242, 127 Sol Jo 446, [1983] LS Gaz R 3048, 267 Estates Gazette
    69, CA 3.41
London, Chatham and Dover Rly Co v South Eastern Rly Co [1893] AC 429, 58 JP 36,
    63 LJ Ch 93, 1 R 275, 69 LT 637, HL 3.60, 3.61, 7.68
Lubrizol Ltd v Tyndalls (8 April 1998, unreported) 11.19
Lynne v Gordon Doctors and Walton (a firm) (1991) 135 Sol Jo LB 29 .... 9.15

M

McCormick v Grogan (1869) LR 4 HL 82, 17 WR 961, 4 App Cas 82 .... 4.18
McCullagh v Lane Fox & Partners Ltd (1995) 49 Con LR 124, [1996] 1 EGLR 35,
    [1996] 18 EG 104, [1995] EGCS 195, [1996] PNLR 205, CA: 1.21, 1.25, 1.26, 8.35
McElroy Milne v Commercial Electronics Ltd [1993] NZLR 39, NZCA 3.10, 3.28,
    3.35, 8.85, 8.91
McFarlane v Wilkinson [1996] 1 Lloyd's Rep 406; on appeal [1997] 2 Lloyd's Rep 259,
    [1997] PNLR 578, CA 10.8, 10.47
McGahie v Union of Shop Distributive & Allied Workers 1966 SLT 74 .... 5.8
McLeish v Amoo-Gottfried & Co (1993) 10 PN 102, 137 Sol Jo LB 204 .... 10.64
McLellan v Fletcher (1987) 3 PN 202, [1987] NLJ Rep 593 .... 9.15
McManus Developments Ltd v Barbridge Properties Ltd [1992] EGCS 50, [1992] NPC
    49, [1996] PNLR 431, CA 8.53
McNamara v Martin Mears & Co (1982) 127 Sol Jo 69 .... 10.53, 10.54, 10.60, 10.61
Macgregor, The. See British Fame (Owners) v Macgregor (Owners), The Macgregor
Madden v Quirk [1989] 1 WLR 702, [1989] RTR 304, 133 Sol Jo 752, [1989] 26 LS
    Gaz R 36 .... 6.21
Madley v Cousins Coombe [1997] EGCS 63 .... 8.8
Maes Finance Ltd v AL Phillips & Co (1997) Times, 25 March 6.4
Maes Finance Ltd v Leftleys [1998] PNLR 193; affd (1998) Times, 13 November, CA: 12.13
Mahoney v Purnell [1996] 3 All ER 61, [1997] 1 FLR 612, [1997] Fam Law 169 .... 8.25
Mainwaring v Goldtech Investments Ltd (1991) Times, 19 February, CA 11.70
Malyon v Lawrence Messer & Co [1968] 2 Lloyd's Rep 539, 112 Sol Jo 623: 10.58, 10.64
Manzanilla Ltd v Corton Property and Investments Ltd [1997] 3 FCR 389, CA: 11.6, 11.18
Markes v Coodes [1997] PNLR 252 .... 5.65
Marrinan v Vibart [1963] 1 QB 528, [1962] 3 All ER 380, [1962] 3 WLR 912, 106
    Sol Jo 649, CA 10.42

PARA

Massey v Midland Bank plc [1995] 1 All ER 929, [1995] 1 FCR 380, 27 HLR 227,
    sub nom Midland Bank plc v Massey [1994] 2 FLR 342, [1994] Fam Law 562,
    [1995] NLJR 180n, CA 8.18
Mathew v Maughold Life Assurance Co Ltd (1984) 1 PN 142; revsd (1987) 3 PN 98,
    CA 5.25
Mathew v TM Sutton Ltd [1994] 4 All ER 793, [1994] 1 WLR 1455, [1994] NLJR
    1278, [1994] CCLR 140 .... 4.66
Matlock Green Garages Ltd v Potter Brooke-Taylor & Wildgoose (13 November 1996,
    unreported) 3.28, 3.31, 8.97
Matrix-Securities Ltd v Theodore Goddard (a firm) [1998] STC 1, [1997] NLJR 1847,
    1998 PNLR 290 .... 1.3, 2.7, 2.11
Maynard v West Midlands Regional Health Authority [1985] 1 All ER 635, [1984]
    1 WLR 634, 128 Sol Jo 317, [1984] LS Gaz R 1926, 133 NLJ 641, HL 2.13
Mean v Thomas [1998] 05 LS Gaz R 30, [1998] EGCS 2 .... 2.32
Melton v Walker and Stranger (1981) 125 Sol Jo 861 .... 5.19
Merc Property Ltd, Re (1999) Times, 19 May 11.6, 11.17
Mercantile Building Society v Mitchell Dodds & Co [1993] NPC 99, CA 8.53, 8.73
Mercantile Credit Co Ltd v Fenwick [1997] NPC 120; [1999] 2 FLR 110, [1999] Lloyd's
    Rep PN 408, 143 Sol Jo LB 74, CA 7.34, 7.35, 7.107, 8.24, 8.26
Michael v Hart & Co [1901] 2 KB 867, 70 LJKB 1000, 50 WR 154, 85 LT 548,
    17 TLR 761; on appeal [1902] 1 KB 482, 71 LJKB 265, 50 WR 308, 86 LT 474,
    18 TLR 254, CA; affd sub nom Hart & Co v Michael (1903) 89 LT 422, HL .. 4.58
Midland Bank plc v Cameron, Thom, Peterkin & Duncans 1988 SLT 611 .... 8.42
Midland Bank plc v Cox McQueen (a firm) [1999] 1 FLR 1002, [1999] Fam
    Law 310, [1999] NLJR 164, [1999] EGCS 12, [1999] Lloyd's Rep PN 223,
    CA 1.2, 7.15, 7.35, 7.51, 7.52, 7.109, 10.4
Midland Bank plc v Serter (1995) 71 P & CR 264, [1995] 3 FCR 711, [1995] 1 FLR 1034,
    [1995] Fam Law 481, 27 HLR 647, 4 Bank LR 227, CA 8.18
Midland Bank Trust Co Ltd v Hett, Stubbs and Kemp (a firm) [1979] Ch 384, [1978] 3 All
    ER 571, [1978] 3 WLR 167, 121 Sol Jo 830 .... 1.8, 1.9, 1.10, 2.2, 2.23,
                                               2.24, 5.11, 5.13, 5.14, 5.15
Miliangos v George Frank (Textiles) Ltd [1976] AC 443, [1975] 3 All ER 801,
    [1975] 3 WLR 758, [1975] 2 CMLR 585, [1976] 1 Lloyd's Rep 201, 119 Sol Jo
    774, HL 3.48
Miller (Ron) Realty Ltd v Honeywell, Wotherspoon and Beedell (1992) 46 CLR 239,
    4 OR (3d) 492; on appeal (1993) 16 OR (3d) 255 .... 2.28
Mood Music Publishing Co Ltd v De Wolfe Publishing Ltd [1976] Ch 119, [1976]
    1 All ER 763, [1976] 2 WLR 451, 119 Sol Jo 809, CA 12.12
Moody v Cox and Hatt [1917] 2 Ch 71, 86 LJ Ch 424, 61 Sol Jo 398, 116 LT 740,
    CA 4.33, 4.34, 4.38, 8.5
Moore (DW) & Co Ltd v Ferrier [1988] 1 All ER 400, [1988] 1 WLR 267, 132 Sol Jo 227,
    [1988] 10 LS Gaz R 45, [1987] NLJ Rep 1013, CA 5.2, 5.15, 5.16, 5.20
Morrell v Morrell (1882) 7 PD 68, 46 JP 328, 51 LJP 49, 30 WR 491, [1881-5] All ER
    Rep 642, 46 LT 485 .... 9.11
Morris v Wentworth-Stanley [1999] 2 WLR 470, [1999] 1 FLR 83, [1998] 39 LS Gaz R 34,
    142 Sol Jo LB 258, CA 6.20
Mortgage Corpn v Halifax (SW) Ltd (1998) Times, 15 July, [1999] 1 Lloyd's Rep PN
    159 .... 3.64, 7.69, 7.88
Mortgage Express Ltd v Bowerman & Partners [1995] QB 375, [1996] 2 All ER 836,
    [1995] 2 WLR 607, [1995] NPC 129, [1996] 1 EGLR 129, [1995] 12 LS Gaz R 34,
    [1996] 04 EG 126, [1996] PNLR 62, CA 2.14, 2.38, 7.2, 7.39, 7.40,
                                          7.41, 7.42, 7.44, 7.52, 7.53,
                                               7.54, 12.7, 12.8
Mortgage Express Ltd v Newman & Co [1996] PNLR 603 .... 2.34, 6.4
Mount v Barker Austin [1998] PNLR 493, CA 3.16, 10.50
Muller v Linsley & Mortimer (a firm) [1995] 03 LS Gaz R 38, 139 Sol Jo LB 43, [1996]
    1 PNLR 74, CA 12.33
Murphy v Young & Co's Brewery plc and Sun Alliance and London Insurance plc
    [1997] 1 All ER 518, [1997] 1 WLR 1591, [1997] 1 Lloyd's Rep 236, CA ... 11.68
Murray v Lloyd [1990] 2 All ER 92, [1989] 1 WLR 1060, 21 HLR 525, [1990]
    1 EGLR 274, [1989] NLJR 938 .... 8.55, 8.80

N

NRG Holding NV v Bacon & Woodrow (a firm). See Nederlandse Reassurantie Groep
    Holding NV v Bacon & Woodrow (a firm)
Nadreph Ltd v Willmett & Co (a firm) [1978] 1 All ER 746, [1978] 1 WLR 1537,
    122 Sol Jo 744 .... 3.47, 8.100
Nash v Eli Lilly & Co [1993] 4 All ER 383, [1993] 1 WLR 782, [1992] 3 Med LR 353,
    14 BMLR 1, CA 5.43, 5.44
Nash v Phillips (1974) 232 Estates Gazette 1219 .... 2.14, 8.4, 8.71, 8.77, 8.81
National Home Loans Corpn v Giffen, Couch & Archer (a firm) [1997] 02
    LS Gaz R 25, 141 Sol Jo LB 29; revsd [1997] 3 All ER 808, [1998] 1 WLR 207,
    [1999] Lloyd's Rep PN 483, CA 1.10, 2.32, 7.2, 7.29, 7.30, 7.38,
                                        7.47, 7.48, 7.50, 7.53
National Home Loans Corpn plc v Stevens & Co (2 June 1997, unreported) 7.22
National Westminster Bank v Beaton (1997) 30 HLR 99, [1997] EGCS 53, 74 P & CR
    D19, CA 1.8, 8.29
Nationwide Building Society v Balmer Radmore (a firm) [1999] 09 LS Gaz R 31,
    [1999] Lloyd's Rep PN 241, 143 Sol Jo LB 58, Times, 1 March 2.16, 2.34, 4.1,
                                        4.9, 4.20, 4.30, 4.34, 4.44,
                                        4.45, 4.51, 4.52, 6.6, 7.2,
                                        7.3, 7.7, 7.13, 7.18, 7.20,
                                        7.21, 7.22, 7.23, 7.25, 7.27,
                                        7.42, 7.44, 7.45, 7.51, 7.54,
                                        7.56, 7.57, 7.59, 7.75, 7.80,
                            7.83, 7.85, 7.100, 7.115, 10.11
Nationwide Building Society v Goodwin Harte [1999] Lloyd's Rep PN 338 .... 4.34
Nationwide Building Society v Mian (12 September 1997, unreported) 4.8
Nationwide Building Society v Richard Grosse [1999] Lloyd's Rep PN 348 ....
    ....4.34, 7.26, 7.115
Nationwide Building Society v Thimbleby & Co (16 December 1998, unreported), CA: 4.19
Nationwide Building Society v Thimbleby & Co [1999] Lloyd's Rep PN 359 ... 6.5, 7.100
Nationwide Building Society v Various Solicitors (No 2) (1998) Times, 1 May 12.9
Nationwide Building Society v Various Solicitors (No 3), [1999] PNLR 52, Times,
    1 March 7.2, 12.5, 12.8, 12.16, 12.21, 12.22
Nationwide Building Society v Yoga & Co (12 September 1997, unreported) 7.23
Nederlandse Reassurantie Groep Holding NV v Bacon & Woodrow (a firm) [1995]
    1 All ER 976, [1995] 2 Lloyd's Rep 77 .... 12.17, 12.26, 12.27, 12.28
Neighbour v Barker [1992] 2 EGLR 149, [1992] 40 EG 140, CA 2.27, 8.49, 8.63
Neill v Crown Prosecution Service (1996) 161 JP 153, [1997] COD 171 .... 11.57
Nelson v Nelson [1997] 1 All ER 970, [1997] 1 WLR 233, [1997] 02 LS Gaz R 26,
    [1997] NLJR 126, 141 Sol Jo LB 30, CA 7.109, 11.62, 11.63, 11.64
Nelson v Rye [1996] 2 All ER 186, [1996] 1 WLR 1378, [1996] FSR 313, [1996]
    EMLR 37 .... 5.71, 5.75
Nestlé v National Westminster Bank plc [1994] 1 All ER 118, [1993] 1 WLR 1260,
    CA 4.57
Nestle v National Westminster Bank plc (No 2) [1993] 1 WLR 1260, CA 4.40
Neushul v Mellish and Harkavy (1967) 111 Sol Jo 399, 203 Estates Gazette 27, 117
    NLJ 546, CA 2.37
New Zealand Shipping Co Ltd v AM Satterthwaite & Co Ltd [1975] AC 154, [1974]
    1 All ER 1015, [1974] 2 WLR 865, 118 Sol Jo 387, sub nom The Eurymedon
    [1974] 1 Lloyd's Rep 534, PC 8.38
Nielsen v Watson (1981) 125 DLR (3d) 326 .... 8.53, 8.79
Nikolaou v Papsavas, Phillips & Co (1988) 166 CLR 394, 82 ALR 617, 63 ALJR 69,
    HC of A 10.55
Nixon v Stephensons (3 April 1996, unreported) 2.36
Nocton v Lord Ashburton [1914] AC 932, 83 LJ Ch 784, [1914-15] All ER Rep 45,
    111 LT 641, HL 4.20, 4.22, 4.23, 4.24, 4.25,
                                         4.32, 4.38, 4.51, 4.52, 6.6
Nordstern Allgemeine Versicherungs AG v Internav Ltd [1999] 23 LS Gaz R 33, CA: 11.69
Northam Rock Building Society v Archer (31 July 1998, unreported) 8.23
Norwich and Peterborough Building Society v Steed (No 2) [1993] Ch 116, [1993]
    1 All ER 330, [1992] 3 WLR 669, CA 8.62
Nyckeln Finance Ltd v Edward Symmons & Partners [1996] PNLR 245, CA 12.15

PARA

Nykredit Mortgage Bank plc v Edward Erdman Group Ltd (No 2) [1998] 1 All ER 305,
    [1998] 1 WLR 1627, [1998] 01 LS Gaz R 24, [1998] 05 EG 150, 142 Sol Jo
    LB 29, 75 P & CR D28, HL 3.7, 3.63, 5.3, 5.16, 5.17,
                                                            5.26, 5.28, 5.29, 5.30, 5.32, 5.34,
                                                            6.7, 7.71, 7.74, 7.77

O

O (a minor) (legal aid costs), Re [1997] 1 FCR 159, sub nom Re O (costs: liability of Legal
    Aid Board) [1997] 1 FLR 465, CA 11.20
O (a minor), Re [1994] 2 FCR 681, [1994] 2 FLR 842, [1994] Fam Law 670 ....   11.62
Oates v Anthony Pittman & Co (a firm) (1998) 76 P & CR 490, CA 3.58, 8.53, 8.73
Oates v Harte Reade & Co (a firm) [1999] 1 FLR 1221, [1999] Fam Law 383,
    [1999] Lloyd's Rep PN 215 ....   5.8
Oceanic Finance Co Ltd v Norton Rose (26 March 1997, unreported) 12.33
O'Donnell v Reichard [1975] VR 916 ....   3.14
Omega Trust Co Ltd v Wright Son & Pepper (1996) 75 P & CR 57, [1996] NPC 189,
    [1997] 1 EGLR 120, [1997] 18 EG 120, [1997] PNLR 424, CA ...   1.25, 1.27, 8.38
Omega Trust Co Ltd v Wright Son & Pepper (No 2) [1998] PNLR 337 ....   2.14
O'Rourke v Darbishire [1920] AC 581, 89 LJ Ch 162, [1920] All ER Rep 1, 64 Sol
    Jo 322, 123 LT 68, 36 TLR 350, HL 12.20, 12.22
Osman v United Kingdom [1999] 1 FLR 193, [1999] Fam Law 86, [1999] Crim LR 82,
    5 BHRC 293, Times, 5 November, ECtHR 10.9, 10.44
O'Sullivan v Management Agency and Music Ltd [1985] QB 428, [1985] 3 All ER 351,
    [1984] 3 WLR 448, 128 Sol Jo 548, CA 4.59, 4.61, 4.64, 4.66
Otter v Church, Adams, Tatham & Co [1953] Ch 280, [1953] 1 All ER 168, [1953]
    1 WLR 156, 97 Sol Jo 48 ....   3.16, 9.14
Owen v Fielding [1998] EGCS 110 ....   3.46, 8.53, 8.73

P

Pacific Colcotronis, The. See UBAF Ltd v European American Banking Corpn,
    The Pacific Colcotronis
Paffett v Trier (2 December 1994, unreported), CA 10.56
Pallant v Morgan [1953] Ch 43, [1952] 2 All ER 951, [1952] 2 TLR 813 ....   4.18
Paragon Finance plc v Freshfields [1999] 1 WLR 1183 ....   12.28, 12.30, 12.32, 12.33
Paragon Finance plc v Hare (1999) Times, 1 April 7.100
Paragon Finance plc v Thakerar & Co [1999] 1 All ER 400, 142 Sol Jo LB 243,
    CA 4.18, 4.19, 4.36, 5.67, 5.68, 5.72, 5.73,
                                                            5.75, 5.78, 5.80, 5.81, 5.84
Parker v Rolls (1854) 14 CB 691 ....   8.56, 8.70
Partington, Re, Partington v Allen (1887) 57 LT 654, 3 TLR 828 ....   9.23, 9.24
Patel v Hooper & Jackson [1999] Lloyd's Rep PN 1 ....   8.73, 8.76, 8.81
Peach Publishing Ltd v Slater & Co (a firm) [1998] BCC 139, 1998 PNLR 364, CA ..   1.23
Pelling v Bruce-Williams (16 December 1998, unreported) 11.56
Penn v Bristol and West Building Society [1996] 2 FCR 729, [1995] 2 FLR 938, [1996]
    Fam Law 28, [1995] 27 LS Gaz R 31, 139 Sol Jo LB 164; affd [1997] 3 All ER 470,
    [1997] 1 WLR 1356, [1997] 3 FCR 789, [1997] 18 LS Gaz R 32, [1997] EGCS 54,
    141 Sol Jo LB 105, CA 7.102, 7.103, 7.105, 8.7, 8.9, 8.42
Perrins v Bellamy [1899] 1 Ch 797, 68 LJ Ch 397, 47 WR 417, 43 Sol Jo 437, 80 LT 478,
    CA 4.14
Perry v Moysey [1998] PNLR 657 ....   5.54
Peyman v Lanjani [1985] Ch 457, [1984] 3 All ER 703, [1985] 2 WLR 154, 48 P &
    CR 398, 128 Sol Jo 853, CA 2.32, 8.63
Philex plc v Golban (t/a Capital Estates) [1994] Ch 205, [1994] 3 WLR 462, [1994]
    BCC 390, CA 11.29
Philips v Ward [1956] 1 All ER 874, [1956] 1 WLR 471, 100 Sol Jo 317, 4 BLR 142,
    CA 3.54
Phillips-Higgins v Harper [1954] 1 QB 411, [1954] 1 All ER 116, [1954] 2 WLR 117,
    98 Sol Jo 45; affd [1954] 1 QB 411, [1954] 2 All ER 51n, [1954] 2 WLR 782,
    98 Sol Jo 250, CA 5.67
Phosphate Sewage Co Ltd v Molleson (1879) 4 App Cas 801, HL 10.16

PARA

Pilbrow v Pearless De Rougemont & Co [1999] NLJR 441, sub nom Pearless de
    Rougemont & Co v Pilbrow 143 Sol Jo LB 114, CA 2.5
Pilkington v Wood [1953] Ch 770, [1953] 2 All ER 810, [1953] 3 WLR 522, 97 Sol
    Jo 572 .... 3.36, 3.41, 3.42, 8.58, 8.73, 8.77, 9.20
Pinnock v Wilkins & Sons (a firm) (1990) Times, 29 January, CA 3.62, 3.63
Piper v Daybell Court-Cooper & Co (1969) 210 Estates Gazette 1047 ..... 8.53, 8.73, 8.81
Platform Home Loans Ltd v Oyston Shipways Ltd [1996] 2 EGLR 110, [1996] 49 EG
    112, [1996] EGCS 146; on appeal [1998] Ch 466, [1998] 4 All ER 252, [1998]
    3 WLR 94, 13 PN 14, [1998] 01 LS Gaz R 26, [1998] 13 EG 148, 142 Sol Jo LB 46,
    CA; revsd [1999] 1 All ER 833, [1999] 2 WLR 518, [1999] NLJR 283, [1999] 13
    EG 119, [1999] EGCS 26, 143 Sol Jo LB 65, HL 3.64, 6.7, 6.9, 6.10, 6.12,
                                       7.62, 7.74, 7.81, 7.86, 7.88, 7.91
Playa Larga and The Marble Islands, The. See Empresa Exportadora de Azucar v
    Industria Azucarera Nacional SA, The Playa Larga and The Marble Islands
Port of Sheerness Ltd and Medway Ports Ltd v Brachers [1997] IRLR 214 .... 10.60, 10.61
Portman Building Society v Bond & Ingram [1998] CLY 320 .... 2.21, 2.24
Portman Building Society v Hamlyn Taylor Neck [1998] 4 All ER 202, 77 P & CR 66,
    [1998] 31 EG 102, 76 P & CR D16, CA 7.113
Portman Building Society v Royal Insurance plc [1998] PNLR 672, CA 12.10
President of India v La Pintada Cia Navigacion SA [1985] AC 104, [1984] 2 All ER 773,
    [1984] 3 WLR 10, [1984] 2 Lloyd's Rep 9, 128 Sol Jo 414, HL 3.60, 3.61, 7.68
Punford v Gilberts Accountants [1998] PNLR 763, CA 9.3, 9.4
Punjab National Bank v de Boinville [1992] 3 All ER 104, [1992] 1 WLR 1138, [1992]
    1 Lloyd's Rep 7, [1991] NLJR 856, CA 1.8, 1.21

R

R v Basra (Wasted Costs Order) [1998] PNLR 535, CA 11.57
R v Camden London Borough Council, ex p Martin [1997] 1 All ER 307, [1997]
    1 WLR 359, [1997] 3 FCR 659, [1997] 1 FLR 950, [1997] Fam Law 472 .... 11.19
R v Clinton [1993] 2 All ER 998, [1993] 1 WLR 1181, [1993] NLJR 471, CA 10.27
R v Graham and Oldham (29 June 1999, unreported) 10.64
R v Horsham District Council and West Sussex County Council, ex p Wenman [1994]
    4 All ER 681, [1995] 1 WLR 680, [1993] NLJR 1477, 159 LG Rev 365 ..... 11.40
R v Immigration Appeal Tribunal, ex p Gulsen [1997] COD 430 .... 11.19
R v Luton Family Proceedings Court, ex p R [1998] CLY 496, CA 11.47
R v Manchester Crown Court, ex p R (1999) Times, 15 February 12.16
R v Secretary of State for the Home Office, ex p Wong [1995] COD 331 .... 11.56
R v Westminster London Borough, ex p Geehan & Butler [1995] COD 204 .... 11.39
R v Wood Green Crown Court, ex p DPP [1993] 1 WLR 723 .... 11.58
Radford v de Froberville [1978] 1 All ER 33, [1977] 1 WLR 1262, 35 P & CR 316,
    121 Sol Jo 319, 7 BLR 35 .... 3.40, 8.80
Raineri v Miles [1981] AC 1050, [1980] 2 All ER 145, [1980] 2 WLR 847, 41
    P & CR 71, 124 Sol Jo 328, HL 8.72
Rakusen v Ellis, Munday & Clarke [1912] 1 Ch 831, 81 LJ Ch 409, [1911] 13 All ER
    Rep 813, 106 LT 556, 28 TLR 326, CA 10.72
Rama v Millar [1996] 1 NZLR 257, PC 4.44, 4.46
Rastin v British Steel plc [1994] 2 All ER 641, [1994] 1 WLR 732, CA 10.4
Rawlinson v Westbrook (1995) Times, 25 January, CA 2.21
Reaveley v Safeway Stores plc [1998] PNLR 526, CA 2.11, 11.47
Rees v Sinclair [1974] 1 NZLR 180, NZCA 10.45
Reeves v Thrings & Long (1995) 11 PN 32, [1996] PNLR 265, CA 2.35, 2.36, 2.37,
                                         3.55, 8.53
Reichel v Magrath (1889) 14 App Cas 665, HL 10.16
Rey v Graham & Oldham (9 June 1999, unreported) 10.64
Ricci v Masons (a firm) [1993] 2 EGLR 159, [1993] 37 EG 154 .... 8.94, 8.95, 8.96
Rich (Marc) & Co AG v Bishop Rock Marine Co Ltd, The Nicholas H [1996] AC 211,
    [1995] 3 All ER 307, [1995] 3 WLR 227, [1995] 2 Lloyd's Rep 299, [1995]
    31 LS Gaz R 34, [1995] NLJR 1033, 139 Sol Jo LB 165, HL 1.13
Richards v Cox [1943] 1 KB 139, [1942] 2 All ER 624, 112 LJKB 135, 87 Sol Jo 92,
    168 LT 313, 59 TLR 123, 74 Ll L Rep 23, CA 2.5

PARA

Ridehalgh v Horsefield [1994] Ch 205, [1994] 3 All ER 848, [1994] 3 WLR 462, [1994]
  2 FLR 194, [1994] Fam Law 560, [1994] BCC 390, CA 2.2, 2.10, 2.11, 2.12,
                                                      11.3, 11.5, 11.6, 11.10, 11.13,
                                                    11.15, 11.16, 11.17, 11.22, 11.23,
                                                    11.26, 11.28, 11.29, 11.34, 11.35,
                                                11.36, 11.43, 11.47, 11.51, 11.53, 11.56
Roberts v J W Ward & Son (1981) 126 Sol Jo 120, CA 8.103
Robinson v Harman (1848) 18 LJ Ex 202, 1 Exch 850, [1843-60] All ER Rep 383,
  13 LTOS 141 ....   3.1
Robinson v Robinson (1851) 1 De GM & G 247, 21 LJ Ch 111, 16 Jur 255, 91 RR 73,
  18 LTOS 293 ....   4.57, 4.58
Rochefoucauld v Boustead [1897] 1 Ch 196, 66 LJ Ch 74, sub nom De la Rochefoucauld
  v Boustead 45 WR 272, 41 Sol Jo 156, 75 LT 502, 13 TLR 118, CA 4.18
Roe v Robert MacGregor and Sons Ltd [1968] 2 All ER 636, [1968] 1 WLR 925, 112
  Sol Jo 235, CA 10.8
Roker House Investments Ltd v Saunders [1997] EGCS 137 ....   3.54, 8.77, 8.90
Rondel v Worsley [1967] 1 QB 443, [1966] 1 All ER 467, [1966] 2 WLR 300,
  110 Sol Jo 90; on appeal [1967] 1 QB 443, [1966] 3 All ER 657, [1966]
  3 WLR 950, 110 Sol Jo 810, CA; on appeal [1969] 1 AC 191, [1967] 3 All ER
  993, [1967] 3 WLR 1666, 111 Sol Jo 927, HL 10.38, 10.39, 10.42
Ross v Caunters [1980] Ch 297, [1979] 3 All ER 580, [1979] 3 WLR 605, 123 Sol
  Jo 605 ....   1.28, 9.9, 9.16
Rothschild & Sons Ltd v Berenson [1995] NPC 107, 70 P & CR D45; on appeal
  [1997] NPC 15, CA 3.13, 8.39, 12.23, 15.29
Routestone Ltd v Minories Finance Ltd [1997] BCC 180, [1996] NPC 83, [1997] 1
  EGLR 123 ....   2.22, 2.24
Rowe v Turner, Hopkins & Partners [1980] 2 NZLR 550; revsd [1982] 1 NZLR 178 ..   6.3
Royal Bank of Scotland v Etridge (No 2) [1998] 4 All ER 705, [1998] 3 FCR 675,
  [1998] 2 FLR 843, [1998] Fam Law 665, [1998] 32 LS Gaz R 31, [1998] NLJR
  1390, 76 P & CR D39, CA 1.8, 8.14, 8.15, 8.18, 8.19,
                                                        8.22, 8.24, 8.28, 8.32
Royal Bank of Scotland plc v Etridge [1997] 3 All ER 628, [1998] 1 FCR 222,
  [1997] 2 FLR 847, [1998] Fam Law 24, CA 8.22
Rumsey v Owen, White and Catlin (1977) 245 Estates Gazette 225, CA 3.28, 3.35
Russell v Fraser (1980) 118 DLR (3d) 733 (BCCA) 9.11

S

S v M (wasted costs order) [1998] 3 FCR 665, Times, 26 March 11.15
Saddington v Colleys Professional Services [1995] EGCS 109, CA 8.23
Sainsbury (J) plc v Broadway Malyan [1999] PNLR 286 ....   6.20
Sampson v John Boddy Timber Ltd [1995] NLJR 851, CA 11.38
Sasea Finance Ltd (in liquidation) v KPMG [1998] BCC 216 ....   3.25
Sawrij v Lynx (Helping Abused Animals) Ltd (21 February 1997, unreported), CA ..   11.54
Scarfe v Adams [1981] 1 All ER 843, 125 Sol Jo 32, CA 8.53
Schuppan (a bankrupt), Re [1996] 2 All ER 664, [1997] 1 BCLC 211 ....   4.38
Scott Group Ltd v McFarlane [1978] 1 NZLR 553 ....   8.39
Seale v Perry [1982] VR 193 ....   9.9
Secured Residential Funding Ltd v Nationwide Building Society [1997] NPC 147 ....   7.98
Segelman, Re [1996] Ch 171, [1995] 3 All ER 676, [1996] 2 WLR 173 ....   9.5
Segenhoe Ltd v Atkins (1992) 29 NSWLR 569 ....   3.42
Selangor United Rubber Estates Ltd v Cradock (a bankrupt) (No 3) [1968] 2 All ER 1073,
  [1968] 1 WLR 1555, [1968] 2 Lloyd's Rep 289, 112 Sol Jo 744 ....   4.18
Shah v Singh [1996] 1 PNLR 83 ....   11.45
Shaw v Fraser Southwell (25 March 1999, unreported), CA 3.46, 8.55, 8.74
Shaw v Halifax (S W) Ltd [1996] PNLR 451, CA 3.49
Shearson Lehman Hutton Inc v Maclaine Watson & Co Ltd (No 2) [1990] 3 All ER 723,
  [1990] 1 Lloyd's Rep 441, [1990] NLJR 247 ....   3.63
Sheldon v RHM Outhwaite (Underwriting Agencies) Ltd [1996] AC 102, [1995] 2 All ER
  558, [1995] 2 WLR 570, [1995] 2 Lloyd's Rep 197, [1995] 22 LS Gaz R 41,
  [1995] NLJR 687, HL 5.66
Shore v Bedford (1843) 12 LJCP 138, 5 Man & G 271 ....   12.19
Siasati v Bottoms & Webb [1997] NPC 20, [1997] EGCS 22 ....   2.32, 8.55, 8.76

PARA

Silver v Morris [1995] 139 NSR (2d) 18, 397 APR 18 .... 2.6
Simaan General Contracting Co v Pilkington Glass Ltd (No 2) [1988] QB 758, [1988]
    1 All ER 791, [1988] 2 WLR 761, 132 Sol Jo 463, [1988] 11 LS Gaz R 44,
    [1988] NLJR 53, 40 BLR 28, CA 1.18
Simmons v Pennington & Son (a firm) [1955] 1 All ER 240, [1955] 1 WLR 183, 99 Sol
    Jo 146, CA 2.15, 2.28, 3.28, 3.29, 3.38, 8.83, 8.84
Simple Simon Catering Ltd v J E Binstock Miller & Co (1973) 117 Sol Jo 529, 228 Estates
    Gazette 527, CA 3.57, 8.55
Simpson v Grove Tompkins & Co (1982) 126 Sol Jo 347, (1982) Times, 17 May,
    CA 8.56, 8.72
Sindall (William) plc v Cambridgeshire County Council [1994] 3 All ER 932, [1994]
    1 WLR 1016, 92 LGR 121, [1993] NPC 82, CA 8.36
Smith v Claremont Haynes (1991) Times, 3 September 9.9
Smith v Eric S Bush [1990] 1 AC 831, [1989] 2 All ER 514, [1989] 2 WLR 790,
    87 LGR 685, 21 HLR 424, 17 Con LR 1, 133 Sol Jo 597, [1989] 1 EGLR 169,
    [1989] NLJR 576, [1989] 17 EG 68, 18 EG 99, HL 1.12, 1.13, 1.14, 1.25
Smith v Linskills (a firm) [1996] 2 All ER 353, [1996] 1 WLR 763, [1996] NLJR 209,
    140 Sol Jo LB 49, CA 10.18, 10.19, 10.23, 10.26, 10.29
Smith v Mansi [1962] 3 All ER 857, [1963] 1 WLR 26, 106 Sol Jo 876, 184 Estates
    Gazette 723, CA 8.4, 8.57
Smith New Court Securities Ltd v Scrimgeour Vickers (Asset Management) Ltd [1997]
    AC 254, [1996] 4 All ER 769, [1996] 3 WLR 1051, [1997] 1 BCLC 350, [1996]
    46 LS Gaz R 28, [1996] NLJR 1722, 141 Sol Jo LB 5, HL 3.3, 3.6, 3.22, 3.50,
                                                            3.51, 3.53, 7.100
Snipper v Enever Freeman & Co [1991] 2 EGLR 270 .... 3.33
Société Commerciale de Réassurance v ERAS (International) Ltd, Re ERAS EIL appeals
    [1992] 2 All ER 82n, [1992] 1 Lloyd's Rep 570, CA 5.9, 5.41
Society of Lloyd's v Kitson Environment Services Ltd (1994) 67 BLR 102 .... 12.33
Solicitor, a (wasted costs order No 1 of 1994), Re [1996] 3 FCR 365, [1996] 1 FLR 40,
    [1996] Fam Law 83, [1995] 28 LS Gaz R 40, 139 Sol Jo LB 157, CA 11.57
Somasundaram v M Julius Melchior & Co (a firm) [1989] 1 All ER 129, [1988] 1 WLR
    1394, [1989] 4 LS Gaz R 43, [1988] NLJR 253, CA 10.34
Sonardyne Ltd v Firth & Co [1997] EGCS 84 .... 3.54, 8.55, 8.80
South Australia Asset Management Corpn v York Montague Ltd [1997] AC 191,
    [1996] 3 All ER 365, [1996] 3 WLR 87, [1996] 2 EGLR 93, [1996] 32 LS Gaz R
    33, [1996] NLJR 956, [1996] 27 EG 125, 140 Sol Jo LB 156, HL 3.2
Spector v Ageda [1973] Ch 30, [1971] 3 All ER 417, [1971] 3 WLR 498, 22 P & CR
    1002, 115 Sol Jo 426 .... 4.26, 4.38, 8.5
Spencer-Ward v Humberts [1995] 1 EGLR 123, [1995] 06 EG 148, CA 5.44
Spikins v Wickham & Fine (18 November 1998, unreported) 4.28
Spiro v Glencrown Properties Ltd [1991] Ch 537, [1991] 1 All ER 600, [1991] 2 WLR
    931, 62 P & CR 402, [1990] NPC 90, 134 Sol Jo 1479, [1991] 1 EGLR 185,
    [1990] NLJR 1754, [1991] 02 EG 167 .... 8.101
Spring v Guardian Assurance plc [1995] 2 AC 296, [1994] 3 All ER 129, [1994]
    3 WLR 354, [1994] ICR 596, [1994] IRLR 460, [1994] 40 LS Gaz R 36, [1994]
    NLJR 971, 138 Sol Jo LB 183, HL 1.12
Stanton v Callaghan [1998] 4 All ER 961, [1999] 2 WLR 745, [1998] 33 LS Gaz R 33,
    [1998] 28 LS Gaz R 32, [1998] NLJR 1355, [1999] BLR 172, [1998] EGCS 115,
    142 Sol Jo LB 220, CA 10.43
Stathams (Wasted Costs Order), Re, Banks v Woodall Duckham Ltd [1997] PIQR P 464,
    CA 11.43
Stephenson v Garnett [1898] 1 QB 677, 67 LJQB 447, 46 WR 410, 78 LT 371, CA . 10.16
Stinchcombe and Cooper Ltd v Addison, Cooper, Jesson & Co (1971) 115 Sol Jo
    368 .... 8.54, 8.63, 8.71
Stovold v Barlows [1995] NPC 154, [1995] 40 LS Gaz R 22, [1995] EGCS 155,
    139 Sol Jo LB 218, [1996] PNLR 91, CA 3.21
Strover v Harrington [1988] Ch 390, [1988] 1 All ER 769, [1988] 2 WLR 572, 56
    P & CR 302, 132 Sol Jo 416, [1988] 1 EGLR 173, [1988] 09 EG 61 .... 8.52, 8.53
Suleman v Shahsavari [1989] 2 All ER 460, [1988] 1 WLR 1181, 57 P & CR 465,
    [1989] 1 EGLR 203, [1988] NLJR 241, [1989] 09 EG 69 .... 7.103
Sullivan v West Yorkshire Passenger Transport Executive [1985] 2 All ER 134, CA .. 2.21
Summit Financial Group Ltd v Slaughter & May (12 March 1999, unreported) 2.5
Sutherland v Public Trustee [1980] 2 NZLR 536 .... 9.6, 9.11

PARA

Swindle v Harrison [1997] 4 All ER 705, [1997] PNLR 641, CA 3.6, 4.25, 4.27,
4.38, 4.43, 4.45, 4.49, 7.61
Swingcastle Ltd v Alastair Gibson (a firm) [1991] 2 AC 223, [1991] 2 All ER 353,
[1991] 2 WLR 1091, 135 Sol Jo 542, [1991] 1 EGLR 157, [1991] 21 LS Gaz R 34,
[1991] NLJR 563, [1991] 17 EG 83, HL 3.61, 6.7, 7.62, 7.63
Sykes v Midland Bank Executor and Trustee Co Ltd [1971] 1 QB 113, [1970] 2 All ER
471, [1970] 3 WLR 273, CA 2.28, 2.35, 3.11, 3.15, 8.8, 8.55
Symphony Group plc v Hodgson [1994] QB 179, [1993] 4 All ER 143, [1993] 3 WLR
830, [1993] 23 LS Gaz R 39, [1993] NLJR 725, 137 Sol Jo LB 134, CA 11.68

T

TSB Bank plc v Marshall, Marshall and Rodgers [1998] 2 FLR 769, [1998] Fam Law 596,
[1998] 39 EG 208 ....   8.31
Tabarrok v EDC Lord & Co (1997) Times, 14 February, [1997] PNLR 491, CA 5.23
Target Holdings Ltd v Redferns (a firm) [1994] 2 All ER 337, [1994] 1 WLR 1089,
CA; revsd [1996] AC 421, [1995] 3 All ER 785, [1995] 3 WLR 352, [1995]
31 LS Gaz R 36, [1995] NLJR 1164, 139 Sol Jo LB 195, HL 4.1, 4.6, 4.7,
4.12, 4.16, 4.39, 4.40, 4.48,
4.50, 4.53, 4.54, 4.57,
7.2, 7.114
Taylor v Warners (21 July 1987, unreported) 8.10
Teasdale v Williams & Co (1983) 269 Estates Gazette 1040, 133 NLJ 105, CA ..   8.94, 8.98
Tennant Radiant Heat Ltd v Warrington Development Corpn [1988] 1 EGLR 41, [1988]
11 EG 71, CA 6.3
Thake v Maurice [1986] QB 644, [1986] 1 All ER 497, [1986] 2 WLR 337, 129 Sol Jo 894,
[1986] LS Gaz R 123, [1986] NLJ Rep 92, CA 1.2
Thorpe v Chief Constable of Greater Manchester Police [1989] 2 All ER 827, [1989]
1 WLR 665, 87 LGR 537, 133 Sol Jo 750, [1989] NLJR 467, CA 12.11, 12.12
Titanic Investments Ltd v Macfarlanes [1997] NPC 105; on appeal (3 December 1998,
unreported), CA 3.18, 3.19, 8.103, 8.104
Tito v Waddell (No 2) [1977] Ch 106, [1977] 3 All ER 129, [1977] 2 WLR 496, 121
Sol Jo 10 ....   5.71
Tolstoy-Miloslavsky v Lord Aldington [1996] 2 All ER 556, [1996] 1 WLR 736,
[1996] 01 LS Gaz R 22, 140 Sol Jo LB 26, CA 11.2, 11.6, 11.28,
11.30, 11.61, 11.68, 11.70
Tomkinson v First Pennsylvania Banking and Trust Co [1961] AC 1007, [1960] 2 WLR
969, sub nom Re United Railways of Havana and Regla Warehouses Ltd [1960]
2 All ER 332, 104 Sol Jo 466, HL 4.55
Tonitto v Bassal (1992) 28 NSWLR 564 ....   8.103
Trans Trust SPRL v Danubian Trading Co Ltd [1952] 2 QB 297, [1952] 1 All ER 970,
[1952] 1 Lloyd's Rep 348, 96 Sol Jo 312, [1952] 1 TLR 1066, CA 3.60, 3.61
Transportation Agency v Jenkins (1972) 223 Estates Gazette 1101 ....   8.55, 8.76
Trusted v Clifford Chance (17 May 1999, unreported) 9.5
Tunbridge v Buss Murton & Co (1997) Times, 8 April 5.64
Turner Page Music v Torres Design Associates Ltd (1998) Times, 3 August,
CA 11.6, 11.39
Twinsectra Ltd v Yardley (28 April 1999, unreported), CA 4.5

U

UBAF Ltd v European American Banking Corpn, The Pacific Colcotronis [1984] QB 713,
[1984] 2 All ER 226, [1984] 2 WLR 508, [1984] 1 Lloyd's Rep 258, [1984] BCLC
112, 128 Sol Jo 243, [1984] LS Gaz R 429, CA 5.26
UCB Bank plc v Halifax (SW) Ltd [1999] Lloyd's Rep PN 154 ....   5.32
Udall v Capri Lighting Ltd [1988] QB 907, [1987] 3 All ER 262, [1987] 3 WLR 465,
131 Sol Jo 443, [1987] LS Gaz R 1334, [1987] NLJ Rep 293, CA 11.65
Umeweni v J B Wheatley & Co (a firm) [1989] EGCS 150; on appeal [1990] EGCS 57,
CA 8.7
United Bank of Kuwait v Prudential Property Services Ltd [1995] EGCS 190, CA: 2.22, 2.24

PARA

V

Vanderpump v Skyes [1999] Lloyd's Rep PN 422 .... 7.58
Veasey v Millfeed & Co Ltd [1997] PNLR 100, CA 11.44
Ventouris v Mountain, The Italia Express [1991] 3 All ER 472, [1991] 1 WLR 607,
    [1991] 1 Lloyd's Rep 441, [1991] NLJR 236, CA 12.20
Victoria Laundry (Windsor) Ltd v Newman Industries Ltd [1949] 2 KB 528, [1949]
    1 All ER 997, 93 Sol Jo 371, 65 TLR 274, CA 7.67
Vimeira, The. See Aiden Shipping Co Ltd v Interbulk Ltd, The Vimeira
Virgin Management Ltd v De Morgan Group plc [1996] NPC 8, CA 1.10
Vyse v Foster (1872) 8 Ch App 309, 42 LJ Ch 245, 21 WR 207, 27 LT 774; affd (1874)
    LR 7 HL 318, 44 LJ Ch 37, 23 WR 355, 31 LT 177 .... 4.64

W

Wadsworth v Lydall [1981] 2 All ER 401, [1981] 1 WLR 598, 125 Sol Jo 309,
    CA 3.60, 3.61
Walker v Boyle [1982] 1 All ER 634, [1982] 1 WLR 495, 44 P & CR 20, 125 Sol Jo 724,
    [1982] LS Gaz R 954, 261 Estates Gazette 1090 .... 8.38, 8.54
Walker v Geo H Medlicott & Son [1999] 1 All ER 685, [1999] 1 WLR 727, [1999] 1 FLR
    1095, [1999] Fam Law 214, [1999] 01 LS Gaz R 24, CA 9.5, 9.6, 9.20, 9.21
Walker v Giffen Couch & Archer [1988] EGCS 64 .... 8.53
Walker v Hall [1984] FLR 126, [1984] Fam Law 21, 127 Sol Jo 550, [1983] LS Gaz R
    2139, CA 8.10
Wall v Lefever [1998] 1 FCR 605, CA 11.6, 11.7, 11.37, 11.51
Wallersteiner v Moir (No 2) [1975] QB 373, 508n, [1975] 1 All ER 849, [1975] 2 WLR
    389, 119 Sol Jo 97, CA 4.62
Walpole v Partridge & Wilson [1994] QB 106, [1994] 1 All ER 385, CA 10.8, 10.20
Walter (D) & Co Ltd v Neville Eckley & Co [1997] BCC 331 .... 11.41
Wapshott v Davies Donovan (a firm) (1995) 72 P & CR 244, [1996] PNLR 361,
    CA 3.56, 8.53, 8.77, 8.81
Warren v Warren [1997] QB 488, [1996] 4 All ER 664, [1996] 3 WLR 1129, [1997]
    1 FCR 237, [1996] 2 FLR 777, [1996] Fam Law 720, CA 11.6, 11.35
Watson v M'Ewan [1905] AC 480, 74 LJPC 151, [1904-7] All ER Rep 1, 42 SLR 837,
    93 LT 489, 7 F 109, 13 SLT 340, HL 10.42
Watts v Morrow [1991] 4 All ER 937, [1991] 1 WLR 1421, 23 HLR 608, [1991]
    2 EGLR 152, [1992] 1 LS Gaz R 33, 54 BLR 86, [1991] 43 EG 121,
    CA 3.54, 3.55, 3.57
Watts v Public Trustee for Western Australia [1980] WAR 97 .... 9.9
Webber v Gasquet Metcalfe and Watson (1982) 132 NLJ 665, 1982 Abr 2888 .... 8.10
Welsh Development Agency v Redpath Dorman Long Ltd [1994] 4 All ER 10, [1994]
    1 WLR 1409, 38 Con LR 106, [1994] 21 LS Gaz R 42, 67 BLR 1, CA .. 5.78, 5.82,
                                                                     5.83, 5.84
West Bromwich Building Society v Mander Hadley [1998] NPC 30, [1998] CLC 814,
    Times, 9 March, CA 5.76
West London Observer v Parsons (1955) 166 Estates Gazette 749 .... 8.102
Westdeutsche Landesbank Girozentrale v Islington London Borough Council
    [1996] AC 669, [1996] 2 All ER 961, [1996] 2 WLR 802, 95 LGR 1, [1996]
    NLJR 877, 140 Sol Jo LB 136, HL 4.63, 7.69
Western Trust & Savings Ltd v Travers & Co (a firm) (1996) 75 P & CR 200, [1997]
    PNLR 295, CA 3.8, 3.43
Westlake v Bracknell District Council [1987] 1 EGLR 161 .... 5.63
Westlake v J P Cave & Co [1998] NPC 3 .... 3.46
Whelton Sinclair (a firm) v Hyland [1992] 2 EGLR 158, [1992] 41 EG 112, CA: . 1.7, 1.9,
                                                             1.24, 8.42, 8.94, 8.95
White v Jones [1995] 2 AC 207, [1993] 3 All ER 481, [1993] 3 WLR 730, [1993]
    23 LS Gaz R 43, [1993] NLJR 473, CA; affd [1995] 2 AC 207, [1995] 1 All
    ER 691, [1995] 2 WLR 187, [1995] 3 FCR 51, [1995] NLJR 251, 139 Sol Jo LB 83,
    HL 1.12, 1.14, 1.15, 1.18, 1.21,
                                                     1.28, 1.29, 7.105, 8.7, 8.43,
                                                     9.2, 9.3, 9.6, 9.7, 9.8,
                                                     9.9, 9.16, 9.25, 9. 26
Whittingham v Crease & Co (1978) 88 DLR (3d) 353, [1978] 5 WWR 45 .... 9.9, 9.17

PARA

Williams v Natural Life Health Foods Ltd [1998] 2 All ER 577, [1998] 1 WLR 830,
    [1998] 1 BCLC 689, [1998] BCC 428, [1998] 21 LS Gaz R 37, [1998] NLJR 657,
    142 Sol Jo LB 166, HL 1.12, 1.16
Williams and Glyn's Bank Ltd v Boland [1981] AC 487, [1980] 2 All ER 408,
    [1980] 3 WLR 138, 40 P & CR 451, 124 Sol Jo 443, [1980] RVR 204, HL 8.21
Wilsher v Essex Area Health Authority [1987] QB 730, [1986] 3 All ER 801,
    [1987] 2 WLR 425, 130 Sol Jo 749, [1986] LS Gaz R 2661, [1986] NLJ Rep
    1061, CA; revsd [1988] AC 1074, [1988] 1 All ER 871, [1988] 2 WLR 557,
    132 Sol Jo 418, [1988] 15 LS Gaz R 37, [1988] NLJR 78, HL 2.25, 3.14
Wilson v Bloomfield (1979) 123 Sol Jo 860, CA 8.35
Wintle v Nye [1959] 1 All ER 552, [1959] 1 WLR 284, 103 Sol Jo 220, HL 9.11
Wong (Edward) Finance Co Ltd v Johnson, Stokes and Master [1984] AC 296, [1984]
    2 WLR 1, 127 Sol Jo 784, PC 2.14, 2.17, 6.14, 8.64, 8.65, 8.68
Woodford & Ackroyd (a firm) v Burgess (1999) Times, 1 February, CA 2.21
Woodward v Wolferstans [1997] NPC 51 .... 8.43
Worldwide Corpn Ltd v GPT Ltd (2 December 1998, unreported), CA 10.5
Wroth v Tyler [1974] Ch 30, [1973] 1 All ER 897, [1973] 2 WLR 405, 25 P & CR 138, 117
    Sol Jo 90 .... 3.29

Y

Yager v Fishman & Co and Teff and Teff [1944] 1 All ER 552, CA 8.102
Yardley v Coombes (1963) 107 Sol Jo 575 .... 3.16, 10.55, 10.58
Yeoman v Ferries 1967 SLT 332 .... 3.16
Yonge v Toynbee [1910] 1 KB 215, 79 LJKB 208, [1908-10] All ER Rep 204,
    102 LT 57, 26 TLR 211, CA 11.63
Yorkshire Dale Steamship Co Ltd v Minister of War Transport, The Coxwold [1942]
    AC 691, [1942] 2 All ER 6, 111 LJKB 512, 86 Sol Jo 359, 167 LT 349, 58
    TLR 263, 73 Ll L Rep 1, HL 3.22
Young v Clifford Chance (21 December 1995, unreported) 1.20, 1.24
Young v Purdy [1997] 1 FCR 632, [1996] 2 FLR 795, [1997] Fam Law 93, [1997]
    PNLR 130, CA 1.9, 3.22, 3.23, 3.24, 3.38
Young v Robson Rhodes (1999) Times, 11 May 10.71

Z

Zamet v Hyman [1961] 3 All ER 933, [1961] 1 WLR 1442, 105 Sol Jo 911, CA 8.15
Zwebner v Mortgage Corpn Ltd [1997] NPC 42, [1997] PNLR 504; affd [1998] EGCS
    104, [1998] PNLR 769, CA 1.2, 2.4, 7.35

PART 1

General Principles

CHAPTER 1

The solicitor's duties in contract and tort

A DUTIES IN CONTRACT

1 Introduction

1.1 The relationship of solicitor and client is primarily a contractual one and, as with any contractual relationship, a solicitor's retainer is governed by the terms of the contract agreed with his or her client. It is common practice for solicitors to set out in an engagement letter the express terms of their remuneration and the procedure for complaints[1] but it is relatively uncommon for solicitors to set out precisely the nature and scope of the work to be undertaken.[2] Indeed often it will be impossible to do so. For this reason, claims for professional negligence are mainly concerned with the standard of reasonable care to be expected of a reasonably competent solicitor judged against the backdrop of the practice commonly adopted by the profession. Nevertheless because the relationship between solicitor and client is primarily a contractual one, any consideration of a solicitor's retainer must begin with the express terms agreed between the parties.

1   See The Solicitors Practice Rules 1990, r 15, *The Guide to the Professional Conduct of Solicitors* (6th edn, 1996) ('*The Guide*'), ch 13 passim.
2   It is common practice for commercial lenders to issue standard form instructions to solicitors and the nature and extent of some of the terms are considered in chapter 7. Less commonly, large institutions and commercial clients also have standard instructions to solicitors.

1.2 If the solicitor undertakes an express obligation, he may be sued for a breach of that obligation in contract whether or not the court would characterise that breach of contract as a failure to take reasonable care, and there is no reason in principle why the client should not instruct the solicitor to undertake more onerous obligations than the common law would normally impose.[1] By accepting instructions to act in a particular matter, however, a solicitor does not guarantee the outcome of the transaction on which his client is about to embark and in general the court will require very clear words before it will construe his instructions in those terms.[2] In *Barclays Bank plc v Weeks, Legg & Dean*[3] a solicitor acting for a purchaser gave his client's bank an undertaking to apply the bank's funds solely for the purpose of acquiring a good marketable title to the property which his client was about to purchase. The undertaking was construed by the court as an undertaking to apply those funds for the purpose of acquiring a title which 'a reasonably competent solicitor acting with proper skill and care would accept as a good marketable title'. To construe the undertaking otherwise would impose a greater duty to the bank than the solicitor owed to his client and would require him in effect to guarantee the title to the property. The same approach was adopted in *Midland Bank plc v Cox McQueen*.[4] In that case the solicitor agreed to carry out a bank's instructions to 'act on our behalf by obtaining the signatures of' a husband and wife to a number of documents. The bank's instructions also contained a request to 'explain the implications of our mortgage form'. The wife never signed the documents because the husband had her impersonated by an employee of his. Because of the duty to explain the Court of Appeal held that the obligation to obtain the wife's signature was not absolute but 'better suited to a requirement to exercise a reasonable standard of care'. In reaching this conclusion the court gave the following general guidance for the construction of legal instructions, particularly from commercial clients:[5]

'If commercial institutions such as banks wish to impose an absolute liability on members of a profession they should do so in clear terms so that the solicitors can appreciate the extent of the obligations which they are accepting. Frequently this sort of task is undertaken by small firms of solicitors who are already finding it difficult to remain viable. This is partly because they are heavily burdened by the costs of insurance. If they are to be liable for very substantial sums of damages as a result of the fraud of customers of the bank which they cannot prevent, then either they will have to withdraw from providing those services or they will have to charge for their services at a rate which is very different from that which was charged here. Neither result is in the interests of the banks or their customers or the public. The result is not in the interests of the banks' customers as they will not benefit from the explanation of the transaction from a member of the legal profession who is qualified to give an explanation. It is not in the interests of banks as they will have to pay higher fees which they may or may not seek to recover from their customers. It is not in the interests of the public because it is important that legal services are readily available and this will not be the case if small firms are unable to survive. Unless the language used in a retainer clearly has this consequence, the courts should not be ready to impose obligations on solicitors which even the most careful solicitor may not be able to meet.'

1   See eg *Bristol and West Building Society v Kramer* (1995) Independent, 26 January and *Zwebner v The Mortgage Corporation Ltd* (18 June 1998, unreported), CA.
2   See *Greaves & Co (Contractors) Ltd v Baynham Meikle & Partners* [1975] 1 WLR 1095, CA in which Lord Denning said this at 1100D: 'The surgeon does not warrant that he will cure the patient. Nor does the solicitor warrant that he will win the case.' See also the House of Lords in the same case to the same effect in (1978) 11 BLR 29 at 49–52 and *Thake v Maurice* [1986] QB 644 at 687–8, CA holding that a strict duty will be imposed on a professional only in 'special circumstances'.
3   [1998] 3 WLR 656 at 669G–671A, CA.
4   [1999] Lloyd's Rep PN 223.
5   Per Lord Woolf MR. *Zwebner v The Mortgage Corporation Ltd* unreported, 18 June 1998, CA was distinguished on a number of specific grounds which are considered in chapter 7. On the general question of construction the court considered that it should not be given a wide application.

1.3   Absent express instructions the law will not impose on a solicitor a duty to achieve a particular result. This is nicely illustrated by *Matrix Securities Ltd v Theodore Goddard*[1] in which the defendants, a firm of solicitors and a barrister, were instructed by the plaintiff with the aim of obtaining tax clearance for a particular scheme. Tax clearance was obtained and then successfully challenged by the Inland Revenue on the grounds essentially of non-disclosure. It was argued that 'if reasonable skill and care could have achieved a letter which, if replied to favourably, would stand no risk that the Revenue would revoke that reply, then each defendant was bound to achieve that result and is in breach of duty and liable for the fact that it was not achieved'.[2] The judge rejected this argument stating:[3]

'I hold that the duty ... was to exercise such skill and care as a reasonably competent practitioner in the relevant sector of the profession would have done with a view to securing such a clearance. I do not accept that their duties were to secure a clearance which was 100% reliable, or to do so if the exercise of reasonable skill and care could achieve such a thing. That formulation turns the common law position set out in *Saif Ali*[4] by Lord Diplock on its head. Instead of imposing legal liability on the professional only if he does that which no reasonably competent member of the relevant profession or part of the profession would have done in the same situation, he would be rendered liable for breach of duty if he omitted anything which any one of the reasonably competent members of the relevant group or class would have done, even if, as might be the case in an area involving judgment between different choices, the steps that a number of reasonably competent members of the profession would reasonably have taken would be incompatible with each other. That is not the law.'

1   [1998] PNLR 290 (Lloyd J).
2   [1998] PNLR 290 at 318D.
3   [1998] PNLR 290 at 321E–G.
4   See chapter 2, para 2.2.

1.4   Apart from the express terms agreed between the parties, the principal term implied by the law into the contract of retainer is that the solicitor should take reasonable care in providing legal services. Chapter 2 is devoted to exploring the standard to be expected of a solicitor to comply with this obligation. There is no difference between the content of this obligation which is imposed by the Supply of Goods and Services Act 1982, s 13, and the general tortious duty of care considered below. The only practical difference between the two duties is that caused by the different limitation periods in contract and tort. That difference is considered and explored in chapter 5.

1.5   Again, it is unusual for a solicitor to seek to restrict liability to his client for the consequences of a breach of duty and in particular to restrict or exclude liability for the consequences of negligence.[1] If a solicitor is instructed to act in relation to 'business done, whether as solicitor or advocate, in or for the purposes of proceedings begun before a court or before an arbitrator appointed under the Arbitration Act 1950', any agreement to exclude liability for negligence or to relieve him from 'any responsibility to which he would otherwise be subject as a solicitor' is void.[2]

1   The Council of the Law Society has stated that it is 'not acceptable' for solicitors to exclude liability: see *The Guide* at 12.09. Although this statement does not have the force of law, it inevitably makes the burden of showing that an exclusion clause is reasonable a very difficult one: see para 1.27. See also the Council's statement at (1987) 84 LSG at 1545.
2   Solicitors Act 1974, ss 59, 60(5) and 87. The definition of a 'contentious business agreement' quoted in the text expressly excludes non-contentious probate business as defined by Supreme Court Act 1981, s 128.

1.6   There is no statutory provision preventing a solicitor from excluding liability in relation to other business. However, such a term will have to satisfy the provisions of the Unfair Contract Terms Act 1977 and, possibly, the EC Directive on Unfair Terms in Consumer Contracts.[1] A detailed discussion of the effect of both the statute and the directive are outside the scope of this book, but it is likely that both will apply to a standard engagement letter sent by a solicitor to his client. It is also unlikely that the court will uphold a standard term under which a solicitor purports to exclude liability for negligence or breach of fiduciary duty or breach of trust. Further, in *Hurlingham Estates Ltd v Wilde & Partners*[2] Lightman J held, albeit obiter, that a limitation imposed by a solicitor upon his clients without their 'fully informed consent' would not be binding upon them. No authority was cited in support of this finding and it remains to be seen whether this obiter dictum will be followed.

1   Brought into force by SI 1994/3159. The statutory instrument leaves some uncertainty about the contracts to which it is to apply. It probably applies to all contracts (within the terms of the directive) made after 31 December 1994.
2   [1997] STC 627 at 633c–e.

2 Formation and duration of the retainer

1.7 Although it is quite common for a solicitor to ask his client to sign an engagement letter, a solicitor may be instructed to act and undertake to do so in the most casual of circumstances. In *Whelton Sinclair v Hyland*[1] it was held that a telephone call by the plaintiff to an unidentified person (who might have been a secretary or receptionist) brought a retainer into existence. The recipient of the telephone call did no more than tell the client that she would inform the partner who had acted for the client before and that 'he would get on with it'.[2]

1   [1992] 2 EGLR 158, CA.
2   The question whether the unidentified recipient of the call had authority to bind the firm (whether actual or ostensible) was not argued.

1.8 The circumstances in which a solicitor may be taken to have assumed a duty of care to a third party in tort are examined in section 4[1] and one rationalisation of the narrow range of circumstances in which such a liability is imposed is that the relationship between the solicitor and the third party is closely analogous or akin to a contract. There may be circumstances, however, in which a genuine contract may be implied between the solicitor and a party who is not the direct source of his instructions. It is not uncommon for a solicitor to be held to have acted for a number of parties where he carries out work for the benefit of a number of individuals or, in a commercial context, for directors or shareholders of a company client personally. According to Oliver J in *Midland Bank Trust Co Ltd v Hett, Stubbs and Kemp*:[2]

> '[A] retainer will be presumed if the conduct of the parties shows that the relationship of solicitor and client has in fact been established between them.'

In such circumstances a collateral contract may genuinely be implied between the solicitor and persons or bodies other than the individual from whom the solicitor receives instructions, and it is no answer for the solicitor to argue that he has not been instructed by, or on behalf of, the claimant expressly. A recent example is *Harris v Nantes and Wylde*[3] in which it was held arguable that a solicitor who had been instructed by one trustee alone (the wife) also undertook to act for the other trustee (the husband). In each of three recent decisions considered in detail in chapter 8, *Barclays Bank plc v Thomson*,[4] *National Westminster Bank v Beaton*[5] and *Royal Bank of Scotland v Etridge (No 2)*,[6] it was also held that a solicitor engaged by a lender to give independent advice to a potential mortgagor was the agent of the mortgagor and not of the lender itself. In those cases, the person giving the instructions may not be the 'client' at all. Finally, there are also cases in which the defendant is found to owe a duty of care in tort to someone so closely connected with the client or on whose behalf the solicitor undertook the work that he or she is entitled to the benefit of the solicitor's advice, despite the absence of a contract.[7]

1   Paras 1.12–1.27.
2   [1979] Ch 384 at 396D (Oliver J), citing *Groom v Crocker* [1939] 1 KB 194 at 222, CA. At 396A the judge stated: 'Who actually paid the bill, however, does not, I think, matter.'
3   [1997] NPC 7, CA.
4   [1997] 4 All ER 816, CA.
5   (1998) 30 HLR 99, CA.
6   [1998] 4 All ER 705, CA.
7   See eg *Foster v Crust* [1986] BCLC 307 (Staughton J) and *R P Howard Ltd v Woodman Matthews & Co* [1983] BCLC 117 (HHJ Finlay QC), where a duty to renew a lease was owed in tort to the shareholder of the company tenant. In *Christensen v Scott* [1996] 1 NZLR 273 a duty was found to be owed to director/shareholders guaranteeing a company's debts, but see now *Johnson v Gore, Wood & Co* [1998] NPC 151, CA, in which the approach in *Christiansen v Scott* was disapproved. For an analogous example outside the solicitors'

profession see *Punjab National Bank v de Boinville* [1992] 3 All ER 104 at 114g–116g, CA
where a contract was implied between an insurance broker and a third party bank (as well as
a duty of care in tort). The courts have also shown a willingness to ignore the corporate veil
in claims for negligent misstatement: see *Esso Petroleum Co Ltd v Mardon* [1976] QB 801 at
821E, 829H and 833H, CA.

1.9   If a solicitor wishes to decline instructions he owes a duty to the potential client
to inform him immediately.[1] And once he agrees to act for a client it is an implied term
of the contract that he may terminate the retainer only on reasonable notice.[2] In
Underwood, Son & Piper v Lewis,[3] it was held that the retainer of a solicitor who
accepted instructions to act on behalf of a client in litigation gave rise to an entire
contract which the solicitor could only terminate on reasonable notice. But the
retainer will not continue indefinitely. In the normal case it will be relatively easy to
identify the time when the solicitor's retainer is terminated (the date on which he
closes his file or renders a final bill), and it is well accepted that there is no such thing
as a 'general retainer' in the sense that a solicitor may be obliged to continue to act
for a client indefinitely without instructions.[4] It is therefore a question of fact when
the retainer was terminated. In the context of limitation it is often argued that a solicitor
who accepts instructions to act for a client comes under a continuing duty either to
put right a mistake or to inform his client that it has been made. In *Bell v Peter Browne
& Co*[5] it was held that a solicitor who had failed to register appropriate entries at the
Land Registry on behalf of his client had a continuing duty to his client in contract.
According to Mustill LJ:

> 'Certainly, a solicitor may have a continuing retainer from his client and no doubt
> there are retainers which require the solicitor to be constantly on watch for new
> sources of potential danger and to take immediate steps to nip them in the bud.'

Whether or not the solicitor's retainer continues in this way will depend on the precise
circumstances. But the question whether the retainer continues should be carefully
distinguished from the question when the solicitor committed a breach of retainer and
the cause of action accrued.

1   *Whelton Sinclair v Hyland* [1992] 2 EGLR 158 at 161B–C, CA.
2   See *The Guide* at 12.10 and *Young v Purdy* [1997] PNLR 130, CA where there was no appeal
    against the finding of the judge that the summary termination of a retainer by the solicitor was
    wrongful.
3   [1894] 2 QB 306, CA. It was applied in *Young v Robson Rhodes* [1999] Lloyd's Rep PN 641
    (Laddie J) where forensic accountants were held to be in repudiatory breach of contract for
    declining to act further when their firm merged with the defendants. There is some suggestion
    in the latter that the solicitor must also have 'good cause' before the retainer can be terminated.
4   *Midland Bank Co Ltd v Hett, Stubbs and Kemp* [1979] Ch 384 at 402G–H (Oliver J) .
5   [1990] 2 QB 495 at 512G, CA. See chapter 5, paras 5.12 and 5.23.

B   DUTY OF CARE IN TORT

1   Duty to the client

1.10   In *Midland Bank Co Ltd v Hett, Stubbs & Kemp*[1] Oliver J held that a solicitor owed
a concurrent duty of care to his client independently of his contractual obligations and
his decision has now been approved by the House of Lords in *Henderson v Merrett
Syndicates*.[2] The nature of the solicitor's duty was explained by him as follows:[3]

> 'The extent of his duties depends upon the terms and limits of [the] retainer and
> any duty of care to be implied must be related to what he is instructed to do.

Now no doubt the duties owed by a solicitor to his client are high, in the sense that he holds himself out as practising a highly skilled and exacting profession, but I think that the court must beware of imposing upon solicitors—or upon professional men in other spheres—duties which go beyond the scope of what they are requested or undertake to do. It may be that a particularly meticulous and conscientious practitioner would, in his client's general interests, take it upon himself to pursue a line of inquiry beyond the strict limits comprehended by his instructions. But that is not the test. The test is what the reasonably competent practitioner would do having regard to the standards normally adopted in his profession.'

The point was reemphasised by Peter Gibson LJ in *National Home Loans Corpn v Giffen, Couch & Archer*[4] where he summarised the relevant authorities as follows:

'As Oliver J said in *Midland Bank Trust Co Ltd v Hett, Stubbs and Kemp* [1979] Ch 384, 402, in relation to the duties of a solicitor to a client by whom he has been retained: "The extent of his duties depends upon the terms and limits of that retainer and any duty of care to be implied must be related to what he is instructed to do." Donaldson LJ stated in *Carradine Properties Ltd v D J Freeman & Co* (1982) 126 Sol Jo 157; Court of Appeal (Civil Division) Transcript No 60 of 1982 in relation to the solicitor's duty of care to his client that:

"the precise scope of that duty will depend, inter alia, upon the extent to which the client appears to need advice. An inexperienced client will need and will be entitled to expect the solicitor to take a much broader view of the scope of his retainer and of his duties than will be the case with an experienced client."

That statement was cited with approval by this court in *Virgin Management v De Morgan Group plc* [1996] NPC 8, CA.'

1   [1979] Ch 384.
2   [1995] 2 AC 145 at 190B.
3   At 402G–403B.
4   [1998] 1 WLR 207 at 213G–H, CA.

1.11   Whilst these authorities suggest that it is generally true to say that the nature and scope of the duty in tort assumed by the solicitor will be determined by the terms of the retainer agreed with the client, it has been held by the Court of Appeal that the duty in contract and duty in tort are not precisely the same. In *Holt v Payne Skillington*[1] it was held that in principle a professional (in this case an agent and valuer) may owe a more extensive duty of care in tort than he does under the terms of his contractual retainer.

1   (1996) 77 BLR 51 at 73B–H, CA. It may be that this was no more than a pleading point.

2   Duty to third parties

(a)   Hedley Byrne *liability*

1.12   Although in historical terms the development of the liability is comparatively recent, it is now well settled that one person may be liable to another for economic loss suffered as a consequence of a negligent misstatement or negligent advice despite the absence of any contractual relationship between them. In *Hedley Byrne & Co Ltd v Heller & Partners Ltd, Smith v Eric S Bush, Caparo Industries plc v Dickman, Henderson v Merrett Syndicates, White v Jones, Spring v Guardian Assurance plc* and

Williams v Natural Life Health Foods Ltd[1] the House of Lords explored and clarified the nature and scope of this liability. As the nature of liability was explored, a difference in approach could be detected in a number of the cases and although this difference did not lead to a different result in many situations, it was not a linguistic or theoretical difference.[2]

1 [1964] AC 465, [1990] 1 AC 605, [1990] 2 AC 605, [1995] 2 AC 145, [1995] 2 AC 207, [1995] 2 AC 296 and [1998] 1 WLR 830 respectively. In *Merrett* the House of Lords also stressed that liability will be imposed as much for a failure to provide information or advice as for negligent misstatement or for the negligent provision of services: see [1995] 2 AC 145 at 181F.

2 See the discussion of disclaimers in para 1.25 for a factual situation in which the approach adopted is of practical importance.

1.13 In *Smith v Bush* and *Caparo*[1] a threefold test of foreseeability, proximity and reasonableness coupled with reasoning by analogy with decided cases was favoured. According to Lord Bridge in *Caparo*:[2]

'What emerges is that, in addition to the foreseeability of damage, necessary ingredients in any situation giving rise to a duty of care are that there should exist between the party owing the duty and the party to whom it is owed a relationship characterised by the law as one of "proximity" or "neighbourhood" and that the situation should be one in which the court considers it fair, just and reasonable that the law should impose a duty of a given scope upon the one party for the benefit of the other. But it is implicit in the passages referred to that the concepts of proximity and fairness embodied in these additional ingredients are not susceptible of any precise definition as would be sufficient to give them utility as practical tests, but amount in effect to little more than convenient labels to attach to the features of different specific situations which, on a detailed examination of all the circumstances, the law recognises pragmatically as giving rise to a duty of care of a given scope. Whilst recognising, of course, the importance of the underlying general principles common to the whole field of negligence, I think that the law has now moved in the direction of attaching greater significance to the more traditional categorisation of distinct and recognisable situations as guides to the existence, the scope and the limits of the varied duties of care which the law imposes.'

1 The majority of the House of Lords also adopted the same formulation in *Marc Rich & Co v Bishop Rock Marine Co Ltd* [1996] AC 211. See also *Goodwill v British Pregnancy Advisory Service* [1996] 2 All ER 161, CA.

2 [1990] 2 AC 605 at 617H–618C.

1.14 In *Merrett,* however, the House of Lords rediscovered the idea or concept of an assumption of responsibility for giving advice or providing services which had appeared to be the cornerstone of liability in *Hedley Byrne*. Lord Goff gave a strong lead that this ought to be adopted as the principle underlying the imposition of a duty of care. He stated:[1]

'In subsequent cases concerned with liability under the *Hedley Byrne* principle in respect of negligent misstatements, the question has frequently arisen whether the plaintiff falls within the category of persons to whom the maker of the statement owes a duty of care. In seeking to contain the category of persons within reasonable bounds, there has been some tendency on the part of the courts to criticise the concept of "assumption of responsibility" as being "unlikely to be a helpful or realistic test in most cases" (see *Smith v Eric S Bush* [1990] 1 AC 831, 864–865 per Lord Griffiths; and see also *Caparo Industries v Dickman* [1990] 2 AC 605, 628 per Lord Roskill). However, at least in cases such as the present, in which the same problem does not arise, there seems to be no reason why recourse should not be had to the concept, which appears after all to have been adopted, in one form or another, by all of their Lordships in *Hedley Byrne* [1964] AC 465 ... Furthermore, especially in a context concerned with a liability which may arise under a contract or in a situation "equivalent to contract", it must be expected that an objective test will be applied when asking the question whether, in a particular case, responsibility should be held to have been assumed by the defendant to the plaintiff: see *Caparo Industries v Dickman* [1990] 2 AC 605, 637, per Lord Oliver of Aylmerton. In addition, the concept provides its own explanation why there is no problem in cases of this kind about liability for economic loss; for if a person assumes responsibility to another in respect of certain services, there is no reason why he should not be liable in damages to that other in respect of economic loss which flows from the negligent perform-ance of those services. It follows that, once the case is identified as falling within the *Hedley Byrne* principle, there should be no need to embark upon any further enquiry whether it is "fair just and reasonable" to impose liability for economic loss—a point which is, I consider, of some importance in the present case. The concept indicates too that in some circumstances, for example where the undertaking to furnish the relevant services is given on an informal occasion, there may be no assumption of responsibility; and likewise that an assumption of responsibility may be negatived by an appropriate disclaimer.'

1   [1995] 2 AC 145 at 180G–181E.

1.15   A majority of the House of Lords in *White v Jones* also favoured the same test. According to Lord Browne-Wilkinson:[1]

'[T]he special relationship is created by the defendant voluntarily assuming to act in the matter by involving himself in the plaintiff's affairs or by choosing to speak. If he does so assume to act or to speak he is said to have assumed responsibility for carrying through the matter he has entered upon.'

It is also clear from the speeches in *White v Jones*, however, that the term 'assumption of responsibility' and similar expressions are not being used solely to describe situations in which there was direct communication between the claimant and the defendant or the defendant had agreed by words or conduct to act for the claimant (even on a gratuitous basis).[2] Nor is the term being used to describe the state of mind of the defendant who consciously assumes a legal liability to the claimant.[3]

1   [1995] 2 AC 207 at 274G.
2   This is clearest from Lord Nolan's example of the car driver assuming responsibility to other road users at 293H.
3   See per Lord Browne-Wilkinson [1995] 2 AC 207 at 273G–274B.

1.16   This left open the possibility that there might be cases in which it was enough for the defendant to give advice or perform services in the knowledge or expectation that a third party would rely upon him to be fixed with a duty of care unless he clearly disclaimed responsibility. The development of a tortious liability in this way was sometimes criticised on the basis that extending the concept 'assumption of respon-sibility' to such wide bounds denuded it of meaning and undermined it as a practical test.[1] Despite such criticisms the debate about which test has primacy can now be regarded as settled. In *Williams v Natural Life Health Foods Ltd*[2] Lord Steyn, with whom the other members of the House of Lords agreed, affirmed the primacy of the assumption of responsibility principle:

'It is clear, and accepted by counsel on both sides, that the governing principles are stated in the leading speech of Lord Goff of Chieveley in *Henderson v Merrett Syndicates* [1995] 2 AC 145. First, in *Henderson's* case it was settled that the assumption of responsibility principle enunciated in *Hedley Byrne & Co Ltd v Heller & Partners Ltd* [1964] AC 465 is not confined to statements but may apply to any assumption of responsibility for the provision of services. The extended *Hedley Byrne* principle is the rationalisation of a technique adopted by English law to provide a remedy for the recovery of damages in respect of economic loss caused by the negligent performance of services. Secondly, it was established that once a case is identified as falling within the extended *Hedley Byrne* principle, there is no need to embark on any further inquiry whether it is "fair just and reasonable" to impose liability for economic loss: p 181. Thirdly, and applying *Hedley Byrne*, it was made clear that

> "reliance upon [the assumption of responsibility] by the other party will be necessary to establish a cause of action (because otherwise the negligence will have no causative effect) ..." (p 180).

Fourthly it was held that the existence of a contractual duty of care between the parties does not preclude the concurrence of a tort duty in the same respect.'

He also confirmed that the basis of liability is purely objective and not based on any assessment of the state of mind of the defendant:[3]

> 'The touchstone of liability is not the state of mind of the defendant. An objective test means that the primary focus must be on things said or done by the defendant or on his behalf in dealings with the plaintiff. Obviously, the impact of what a defendant says or does must be judged in the light of the relevant contextual scene. Subject to this qualification the primary focus must be on exchanges (in which term I include statements and conduct) which cross the line between the defendant and the plaintiff.'

In approaching any claim brought by a third party against a professional for the provision of advice or services (or the failure to provide them) this guidance must be applied.

1   See eg Barker 'Unreliable Assumptions in the Modern Law of Negligence' (1993) 109 LQR 461 and Powell *Professional & Client: The Duty of Care* in Birks (ed) *Wrongs and Remedies in the Twenty-First Century* (1996) 49 at 62–3.
2   [1998] 1 WLR 830 at 834E–H, HL.
3   [1998] 1 WLR 830 at 835F–G.

(b)   Claims against solicitors

1.17   Where a solicitor is the defendant it is unlikely that he or she will be able to show that the damage suffered by the claimant was unforeseeable or that there was insufficient proximity between them in the sense either that the defendant was unaware of his existence or identity or that the action or advice given by the defendant was not causally connected with the loss suffered. In almost all cases the claim will concern either a transaction or a piece of litigation in which the parties affected are finite and their interests known. The difficulty for the court in deciding whether to impose liability will be that the defendant was not retained by the claimant and was in all likelihood acting for someone else. The principal issue between the parties is likely to be whether it was reasonable for the claimant to rely on the defendant (and he did so) and whether either expressly or by his conduct the defendant led the claimant to believe that he could do so.

1.18   It will not be easy for a claimant to satisfy the court on this issue. It is not an automatic bar to a claim that the defendant was not retained by the claimant but retained by somone else. In *Merrett* itself it was held that managing agents at Lloyd's owed a duty of care in tort not only to those Names who had contracted with them directly (as members' agents) but also to Indirect Names with whom they had no contract. Lord Goff also stated:[1]

'I for my part cannot see why in principle a party should not assume responsibility to more than one person in respect of the same activity.'

But he later and crucially added:[2]

'I wish however to add that I strongly suspect that the situation which arises in the present case is most unusual; and that in many cases in which a contractual chain comparable to that in the present case is constructed it may well prove to be inconsistent with an assumption of responsibility which has the effect of, so to speak, short circuiting the contractual structure so put in place by the parties. It cannot therefore be inferred from the present case that other sub-agents will be held directly liable to the the agent's principal in tort. Let me take the analogy of the common case of the ordinary building contract, under which main contractors contract with the building owner for the construction of the relevant building and the main contractor sub-contracts with sub-contractors and suppliers ... [I]f the sub-contracted work or materials do not in the result conform to the required standard, it will not ordinarily be open to the building owner to sue the sub-contractor or supplier direct under the *Hedley Byrne* principle, claiming damages from him on the basis that he has been negligent in the performance of his functions. For there is generally no assumption of responsibility by the sub-contractor or supplier direct to the building owner, the parties having so structured their relationship that it is inconsistent with any such assumption of responsibility.'[3]

1   [1995] 2 AC 145 at 195C.
2   [1995] 2 AC 145 at 195G–196F, citing *Simaan General Contracting Co v Pilkington Glass Ltd (No 2)* [1988] QB 758 at 781, CA.
3   See also the dissenting speech of Lord Mustill in *White v Jones* [1995] 2 AC 207 at 279B–G where this point is particularly strongly articulated.

1.19   In *Gran Gelato Ltd v Richcliff Ltd*[1] Sir Donald Nicholls V-C held that a solicitor acting for a landlord owed no duty of care to a potential tenant in respect of pre-contract inquiries which were inaccurate. Directing himself by the test formulated in *Caparo*, which then had ascendancy, he held that it would not be reasonable to impose a duty on the solicitor to a potential purchaser in respect of the work he had undertaken to carry out for the vendor. He stated:

'[C]aution should be exercised before the law takes the step of concluding that, in any particular context, an agent acting within the scope of his authority on behalf of a known principal, himself owes to third parties a duty of care independent of the duty of care he owes to his principal. There will be cases where it is fair, just and reasonable that there should be such a duty. But, in general, in a case where the principal himself owes a duty of care to the third party, the existence of a further duty of care, owed by the agent to the third party, is not necessary for the reasonable protection of the latter. Good reason, therefore, should exist before the law imposes a duty when the agent already owes to his principal a duty which covers the same ground and the principal is responsible to the third party for his agent's shortcomings. I do not think that there is good reason for such a duty in normal conveyancing transactions.'

1   [1992] Ch 560 at 571D–E.

1.20 It is not easy from a comparison between *Merrett* and *Gran Gelato* to identify the exceptional reasons why the managing agents in the former were held to be liable to the Names whilst the solicitor in the latter was not liable to the tenant purchaser. Moreover, Sir Donald Nicholls V-C ultimately decided the latter on the basis that there was no good reason to impose a duty, which makes the decision questionable in the light of *Merrett* and the subsequent authorities. In *Merrett* the contracts between the parties were regulated by a bye-law and there was a continuing relationship between the Names, the members' agents and the managing agents in which the managing agents were writing business ultimately for the benefit of the Names. In *Gran Gelato* there was a single transaction in which the solicitors gave answers to a party bargaining at arm's length in circumstances where the answers were tendered on behalf of the vendor and not the solicitor personally. Nevertheless the judge rejected the argument that to impose a duty of care to a purchaser on a solicitor would, in every case, expose him to a potential conflict of interest.[1] The point of distinction may simply be that in answering the pre-contract inquiries, the defendants in *Gran Gelato* did not give any personal assurance or undertaking to the plaintiff that the answers were accurate and that the case of a solicitor acting for his client in a transaction is more closely analogous to the building sub-contractor, where the parties should not look behind the contractual relationship.[2]

1   [1992] Ch 560 at 571B–D. Evans *Lawyers' Liabilites* (1996) ch 4 (pp 44–57) examines the potential justifications for the decision without identifying any which he considers to be particularly convincing.
2   This was the conclusion reached by Popplewell J in *Young v Clifford Chance* (21 December 1995, unreported). This may not provide an entirely satisfactory justification for the decision in *Gran Gelato* because the answer to the pre-contract inquiry was a legal one, the vendor owed to the purchaser a duty of disclosure and both vendor and purchaser were relying in a real sense on the vendor's solicitors.

1.21 Although *Gran Gelato* was cited with approval by Lord Goff in *White v Jones*[1] there is a doubt whether it would be upheld in the Court of Appeal. It was the subject of further analysis by Hobhouse LJ in *McCullagh v Lane Fox & Partners Ltd*[2] who suggested that unless it was confined to a special rule applicable to solicitors in conveyancing transactions, it was inconsistent with the decision of the Court of Appeal in *Punjab National Bank v de Boinville*.[3] The majority of the court, Sir Christopher Slade and Nourse LJ, found it unnecessary to consider this point. But in *First National Commercial Bank plc v Loxleys*[4] the Court of Appeal accepted, at the strike out stage, that there was sufficient uncertainty in the authorities to make it arguable that a solicitor owed a duty of care to a third party purchaser for the accuracy of pre-contract inquiries and that a disclaimer would be ineffective to prevent that duty arising. The question of when a solicitor is liable to a potential purchaser for the answers to pre-contract enquiries is considered in detail in chapter 8.[5]

1   [1995] 2 AC 207 at 256D.
2   [1996] 1 EGLR 35 at 44G–J, CA.
3   [1992] 3 All ER 104, CA.
4   [1997] PNLR 211, esp at 215B–C.
5   At paras 8.35–8.38.

(c)   'Stepping outside the solicitor's role'

1.22 In *Gran Gelato*[1] the judge recognised that there would be cases in which a duty of care to a third party would be imposed on a solicitor. He characterised those instances as cases in which the solicitor steps outside his role as solicitor for the client and assumes 'a direct responsibility' to the third party. This notion appears to offer the most constructive rationalisation of a solicitor's liability to non-clients. In *Al-Kandari v J R Brown & Co*² a solicitor in a matrimonial case who had agreed to hold a defendant's passport (which was also the passport of his two children, who were the subjects of a custody dispute) to the order of the court was held liable to the plaintiff personally for releasing the passport to an official of the Kuwaiti embassy and failing to attend the following day when the defendant himself obtained the passport and abducted his children. The solicitor was held liable on the basis that 'in voluntarily agreeing to hold the passport to the order of the court the solicitors had stepped outside their role as solicitors for the client and accepted responsibilities towards both their client the plaintiff and the children'. This is, therefore, a good example of a situation in which a solicitor voluntarily assumes a personal responsibility to the plaintiff. The test whether the defendant had 'stepped outside his role' was applied again in *Abrams v Abrams*.³ It was held that a solicitor acting for one party in litigation owed no duty⁴ of care in respect of representations made to the other party in that litigation.⁵

1   [1992] Ch 560 at 571G–572B.
2   [1988] QB 665 at 672D, CA.
3   [1996] PNLR 129 (Gage J).
4   The decision on this issue was strictly obiter because he found that the representations alleged by the plaintiff had not been made and that the representations actually made were not false: see [1996] PNLR 129 at 134–6.
5   Compare *ADT Ltd v BDO Binder Hamlyn* [1996] BCC 808 (May J), a claim made against auditors in which the inquiry was virtually identical.

1.23   In *N M Rothschild & Sons Ltd v Berensons*¹ the defendant solicitors, who were acting for a purchaser, were held to owe a duty of care to the plaintiff for the accuracy of certain statements contained in a request for funds although the defendant was not retained by the plaintiff and there was no direct communication between them. The defendants did not act for the plaintiff but for the proposed mortgagee, CFL, to whom the plaintiff provided finance under a revolving credit facility. The plaintiff did not see or receive the funds request which contained the negligent statements. The request was addressed to Barclays Bank plc, the lead bank under the credit facility, which had no direct contractual relationship with the defendants either. But once the defendants knew of the mortgagee's financing arrangements, even in general terms, they either knew or clearly should have known that the primary purpose of the funds request and the certifications which they were required to give on the document was to enable CFL to draw on the credit facility provided by, amongst others, the plaintiff. Saville LJ stated that it should have been 'self-evident to any reasonably competent solicitor ... that all those lending would be doing so on the basis that the solicitors had provided to Barclays Bank a true and accurate Funds Request'. In this case the defendants' role included the provision of a clean report on title to the plaintiff and the other syndicate members and obviously so.²

1   [1995] NPC 107, [1997] NPC 15, CA.
2   See also *Allied Finance and Investments Ltd v Haddow & Co* [1983] NZLR 22 which was very similar on its facts. It was cited by Nicholls V-C in *Gran Gelato* as a 'stepping outside' case: see [1992] Ch 560 at 572A–B. These two cases are considered further in chapter 8, at paras 8.39–8.41. These two cases might also be compared with *Peach Publishing Ltd v Slater & Co* [1998] PNLR 364, CA, where an accountant was held not liable to the purchaser of a company for confirming directly to the purchaser the accuracy of certain management accounts where the *purpose* for which the statement was required was to obtain a warranty from the vendor.

1.24   The clearest indication that a solicitor has stepped outside his original retainer and undertaken a responsibility to the plaintiff is where there are direct discussions or communications between the solicitor and the third party. Even if a contract could not be implied in those circumstances, eg because there is no consideration, the court would be likely to impose a duty of care if the third party informed the solicitor that he was relying on the solicitor's advice and the solicitor accepted this.[1] But where there is no direct contact between the solicitor and the third party at all the following are some of the factors which may indicate whether a duty of care should be imposed:

(a) the extent to which the solicitor is aware of the existence and identity of the third party and the nature of his interests;

(b) the extent to which the interests of the third party are the same as the interests of the client and the existence of any actual or potential conflict between them;[2]

(c) whether the third party has instructed his own solicitors and, if so, their role and the extent of their participation in the transaction or litigation;

(d) the nature of the contractual relationship (or potential relationship) between the client and the third party and the extent to which that relationship is consistent or inconsistent with the existence of a direct duty of care;

(e) the nature of the information and advice provided to the third party or the actions undertaken by the solicitor and relied upon by him;

(f) the purpose for which the solicitor supplied the information or advice or undertook the work and the purpose for which the third party made use of it; and

(g) the existence and terms of any disclaimer.

1   The nature and context of the discussions would plainly be relevant to any assumption of responsibility but duties of care outside contract have been imposed in the most informal of circumstances: compare *Whelton Sinclair v Hyland* [1992] 2 EGLR 158, CA, *Holt v Payne-Skillington* (1996) 77 BLR 51, CA and *ADT v BDO Binder Hamlyn* [1996] BCC 808 (May J).

2   In *Young v Clifford Chance* (21 December 1995, unreported) it was held that the client and third party had a community of interest but not an identity of interest. Accordingly the potential for conflict must be genuine.

(d)   Exclusion of liability

1.25   As indicated, one important question in determining whether a solicitor has undertaken a duty of care is whether he disclaims any responsibility to the third party for the consequences of the inaccuracy of information provided or advice tendered. In *Smith v Bush*[1] it was held both that the Unfair Contract Terms Act 1977 (UCTA) applied to a disclaimer of liability made by a valuer to a potential purchaser, with whom he had no direct contractual relationship, and that the disclaimer could not negative the existence of a duty of care so that the defendant could escape the provisions of UCTA 1977.[2] In *Henderson v Merrett Syndicates*,[3] however, it was suggested that an appropriately worded disclaimer might be effective to prevent a duty of care arising at all. The point was then considered in *McCullagh v Lane Fox & Partners Ltd*[4] where it was held that a disclaimer given by an estate agent to the purchaser of a property marketed by him was effective to negative the existence of a duty of care. In both that case and in *Omega Trust Co Ltd v Wright Son & Pepper*[5] it was accepted that a disclaimer would be effective to negative the existence of a duty of care only if it satisfied the test of reasonableness prescribed by UCTA 1977, s11(3).[6] Finally, in *First National Commercial Bank Plc v Loxleys*,[7] a strike-out case in the context of answers to pre-contract inquiries, this issue was raised again. It was argued that it was illogical to permit the court to take into account a disclaimer at the stage of deciding whether a duty of care arose if the disclaimer could be held unreasonable under UCTA 1977. It was nevertheless held arguable that a disclaimer ought to be taken into account when deciding whether the vendor's solicitor owed a duty of care to the plaintiff for inaccurate answers, and the Court of Appeal made no attempt to resolve the illogicality or to resolve the question whether UCTA 1977 could be avoided altogether by a suitably worded disclaimer.

1   [1990] 1 AC 831, at 848D and 861D.
2   See UCTA 1977, ss 1(1), 2(2), 11(3) and 13(1). It is clear that UCTA 1977 was intended to apply the test of reasonableness to a notice purporting to disclaim a common law duty of care. Little or no time has been spent on the meaning of the word 'notice'. The EC Directive on Unfair Terms in Consumer Contracts (referred to in para 1.06) is of no application in this context because it applies only to contractual terms.
3   [1995] 2 AC 145 at 181D–E.
4   [1996] 1 EGLR 35, CA. The decision was obiter because a majority held that no duty arose in any event.
5   [1997] 18 EG 120, CA.
6   In *McCullagh v Lane Fox & Partners Ltd* the whole court appeared to accept that UCTA 1977 would apply to any disclaimer which assisted the defendant to negative the existence of a duty of care. Both Sir Christopher Slade and Nourse LJ considered that no duty of care would have arisen absent the disclaimers and they dealt with this point only very briefly.
7   [1997] PNLR 211, CA, decided before *Omega* but after *McCullagh v Lane Fox & Partners Ltd* which was cited to the court.

1.26   In the absence of clear authority on this point, it is suggested that there is no real illogicality and that the two stage approach adopted by Hobhouse LJ in *McCullagh v Lane Fox & Partners Ltd*[1] ought to be adopted. First, the disclaimer is not to be construed as a contractual provision but to be treated 'as one of the facts relevant to answering the question whether there has been an assumption of responsibility' by the defendant for the relevant statement. The court must ask whether a reasonable person would understand that the defendant was assuming responsibility for the statement in the light of both the disclaimer and all other relevant facts. If the court concludes that, as a consequence of the disclaimer, the defendant owed no duty of care to the plaintiff, the court must nevertheless go on to consider whether the defendant is precluded from relying on the disclaimer by the Act.

1   [1996] 1 EGLR 35 at 45F–M, CA.

1.27   If UCTA 1977 applies, it is an open question whether a disclaimer of liability made to a third party would be held reasonable. The following factors were identified in *Omega Trust Co Ltd v Wright Son & Pepper*[1] as relevant to the reasonableness of a disclaimer:

(i)   the burden of satisfying the reasonableness of the disclaimer rests upon the defendant;

(ii)   the court should assess the relative bargaining strengths of the parties;

(iii) whether it would be reasonably practicable for the third party to have obtained the relevant information or advice for himself;

(iv) whether to provide the information or advice was 'a straightforward, easily duplicated task'; and

(v)   the practical consequences of the disclaimer.

On this last point, Henry LJ stated:

'At this moment it is necessary to look at the purpose of the disclaimer. The first and obvious purpose of the disclaimer, as obtained by construction of the document, is to limit the assumption of responsibility to Omega and to no one else. It was clearly entered into to assure clarity, to assure transparency and to assure certainty. The valuer was entitled to do all that could be done to prevent himself having to fight a difficult law suit as to whether he owed a duty to an unknown lender. If his disclaimer had been complied with by either Omega or by the bank, that would have been his position. If his document had been complied with and consent from him had been sought, he could, had he wished, have declined to assume the additional responsibility ... Against this the bank submits that this is simply an uncovenanted benefit to the valuer and it would be unreasonable to let him rely on it. Unreasonable because, had in fact they asked permission of him, he would have granted permission. As to whether he would have granted permission or not we will never know because he was never asked. Certain it was that no fee was paid to him and that he would have been entitled to a fee had permission been sought of him.'

On this basis the disclaimer was held lawful. The same reasoning will apply to most disclaimers given by a professional to a party who is not his client but seeks to rely upon his work if that party party could have obtained his own advice or instructed his own solicitors. Even if UCTA 1977 applies to a disclaimer given by a solicitor to a third party, the disclaimer is likely to be effective unless there are exceptional circumstances.

1   [1997] 18 EG 120, CA.

(e)   *An exception:* White v Jones

1.28   In *Ross v Caunters*[1] it was held at first instance that a solicitor engaged by a testator owed a duty of care to a potential beneficiary in the preparation and execution of a will. In *White v Jones*[2] the House of Lords confirmed by a majority of three to two that a solicitor did indeed owe such a duty to carry out a client testator's wishes promptly and to prepare a new will for execution. Although the members of the majority each drew comfort from the existing law, it appears that the imposition of liability in such a case should be regarded more as an anomalous exception to the principle upon which a duty of care will be imposed rather than as a development or extension of that principle. Lord Goff considered that *Ross v Caunters* could not be justified on existing principles but was prepared to 'fashion a remedy to fill a lacuna in the law'. Lord Browne-Wilkinson agreed that the case did not fall within the existing categories of relationship to which the law attaches a duty of care but that it was appropriate to develop a novel category of negligence on the basis that there was a close analogy with existing categories of special relationship giving rise to a duty of care.[3] And in *Carr-Glynn v Frearsons*[4] the Court of Appeal has recently confirmed that the duty of care owed by a solicitor to a disappointed beneficiary should be regarded as an exceptional one.

1   [1980] Ch 297 (Sir Robert Megarry V-C).
2   [1995] 2 AC 207.
3   [1995] 2 AC 207 at 267H–268F, 274E–275E and 292F–295D. Lord Nolan, who agreed with Lord Goff, did not address the novel features of the case. It may be that he would not have imposed a duty of care in every case of a disappointed beneficiary and considered that the involvement and reliance of the beneficiaries in the process of drawing up the will was important, if not critical.
4   [1999] 2 WLR 1046, esp at 1054C–F, CA.

1.29   The nature and scope of the exception are considered further in chapter 9. At this point it is worth noting briefly what was so exceptional about the duty owed to the White family. The case of the disappointed beneficiary is exceptional for two principal reasons. First, reasonable reliance is central to the imposition of a duty of care and in almost all other cases it will be necessary to show that the claimant relied on the solicitor either directly or indirectly.[1] In *White v Jones*,[2] by contrast, it was held that reliance is not an essential ingredient of liability. If it were necessary for the beneficiary to establish reliance he would not be able to do so, for he cannot be said to rely on the testator's solicitor in any relevant sense at all. He may know about the will and its contents and he may be relying upon the testator to leave some part of the estate to him. But the testator is free to change his mind at any time thereafter and the beneficiary cannot be said to have relied upon the solicitor (as opposed to the testator) to confer a benefit upon him. Secondly, where a solicitor acts negligently in the preparation or execution of a will there will be no liability to anyone at all unless a duty of care to the disappointed beneficiary is imposed. Because the testator's will takes effect on death he suffers no loss himself during his lifetime as a consequence of his solicitor's negligence. His estate suffers no loss either because, however much his wishes have been frustrated, the net assets in the estate remain the same. If the solicitor owes no duty to the disappointed beneficiary and the individual to whom he did owe duties and who relied on his expertise has suffered no loss, a solicitor would escape liability for his negligence altogether. It was for this particular reason that the House of Lords imposed a duty of care and there is a strong public policy element in it.[3]

1   See *N M Rothschild & Sons Ltd v Berenson* [1997] NPC 15, CA (referred to in para 1.23) for an example of 'indirect reliance'. In that case no one from the plaintiff *read* the report on title which was submitted to the lead bank, Barclays. But the plaintiff would not have permitted CFL to draw down the credit facility without it.

2   See Sir Donald Nicholls V-C in the Court of Appeal [1995] 2 AC 207 at 221H–222B and Lord Browne-Wilkinson at 272D–G. Lord Goff suggests at 262C that it may be a requirement in the normal case. But compare his views in *Henderson v Merrett Syndicates* [1995] 2 AC 145 at 180E–F.

3   See [1995] 2 AC 207 at 268E and 276D. See also Stapleton 'Duty of Care: Peripheral Parties and Alternative Opportunities for Deterrence' (1995) 111 LQR 301 esp at 324–6.

CHAPTER 2

Breach of duty

A   THE STANDARD OF CARE

1   Introduction

2.1   Rarely is there any need to make a distinction between the standard of care to be expected of a solicitor in complying with his contractual obligations and that imposed by the law of tort. Although it is not suggested that the approach should be different, it is as well to remember that the source of the contractual duty is the implication of a term. According to Lord Wilberforce in *Liverpool County Council v Irwin*:[1]

> 'My Lords if, as I think, the test of the existence of the term is necessity the standard must not surely exceed what is necessary having regard to the circumstances. To imply an absolute obligation to repair would go beyond what is a necessary legal incident and indeed would be unreasonable. An obligation to take reasonable care to keep in reasonable repair and usability is what fits the requirements of the case. Such a definition involves—and I think rightly—recognition that the tenants themselves have their responsibilities. What it is reasonable to expect of a landlord has a clear relation to what a reasonable set of tenants should do for themselves.'

This statement has equal relevance to the contractual relationship between a solicitor and his client. The solicitor's contract of retainer imposes a duty to achieve a standard of reasonable conduct. As stated, the extent of the duty also depends on what a reasonable client should do for himself.

1   [1977] AC 239 at 256G dealing with the obligation to repair.

2.2   A solicitor will be liable in negligence if he fails to achieve the standard of the reasonably competent practitioner. This standard has been defined, variously, as follows:

> '[W]here you get a situation which involves the use of some special skill or competence, then the test as to whether there has been negligence or not is not the test of the man on the top of the Clapham omnibus, because he has not got this special skill. The test is the standard of the ordinary skilled man exercising and professing to have that special skill; it is well established law that it is sufficient if he exercises the ordinary skill of an ordinary competent man exercising that particular art.'[1]

> 'The test is what the reasonably competent practitioner would do having regard to the standards normally adopted in his profession.'[2]

> 'Those who hold themselves out as qualified to practise other professions, although they are not liable for damage caused by what in the event turns out to have been an error of judgment on some matter upon which the opinions of reasonably informed and competent members of the profession might have differed, are nevertheless liable for damage caused by their advice, acts or omissions in the course of their professional work which no member of the profession who was reasonably well-informed and competent would have given or done or omitted to do.

No matter what profession it may be, the common law does not impose on those who practise it any liability for damage resulting from what in the result turn out to have been errors of judgment, unless the error was such as no reasonably well-informed and competent member of that profession could have made.'[3]

1   *Bolam v Friern Hospital Management Committee* [1957] 1 WLR 582 at 586, McNair J, formally approved in eg *Greaves & Co (Contractors) Ltd v Baynham Meikle* above at 1101F and *Eckersley v Binnie* [1988] 18 CLR 1 at 79, CA ('applied and approved time without number', per Bingham LJ).
2   *Midland Bank Trust Co Ltd v Hett, Stubbs and Kemp* [1979] Ch 384 at 403 (Oliver J), cited with approval recently in *Martin Boston & Co v Roberts* [1996] PNLR 45 at 50, CA.
3   *Saif Ali v Sydney Mitchell & Co* [1980] AC 198 at 218D–E and 220D per Lord Diplock. See also *Ridehalgh v Horsefield* [1994] Ch 205 at 233C–D, CA.

2   The standard of reasonable competence

(a)   Level of expertise

2.3   There is obviously no ideal norm of a solicitor with certain qualifications and experience against which the court can measure the conduct of a defendant. There are a number of specific functions carried out by a solicitor's firm for which qualification as a solicitor is a statutory requirement[1] but many, often more mundane tasks, will be carried out by unqualified staff, possibly trainees, legal executives or para-legals. Once a solicitor is qualified then, subject to certain ongoing educational standards required by the Law Society, he or she may continue to practise by renewing his or her practising certificate.[2] It is noteworthy that a solicitor is not entitled to practise as a principal without three years' experience.[3]

1   See Solicitors Act 1974, ss 20–25.
2   See the Practising Certificate Regulations 1995 and *The Guide to the Professional Conduct of Solicitors* (6th edn, 1996) ('*The Guide*') at 2.05. Even if a solicitor fails to renew his or her practising certificate annually, he will not automatically lose the benefit of his expired certificate: see Solicitors Act 1974, s 14.
3   See the Solicitors Practice Rules 1990, r 13(1) and *The Guide* at 2.06.

2.4   In *Freeman v Marshall & Co* Lawton J held that an unqualified surveyor with limited experience had to satisfy the standard of a trained surveyor,[1] but many clients would not expect every aspect of the work which they entrust to their solicitor to be carried out by a fully qualified member of staff[2] and there is no decision of an English court which requires that where legal work is properly delegated to an unqualified employee (whether a trainee solicitor or a legal executive), that employee must meet the standard of care to be expected of a fully qualified solicitor. Again, there is no decision which requires that a fully qualified solicitor must have a minimum level of experience. The standard of care which the court will require of a firm and its employees will, therefore, depend entirely on the circumstances.

1   (1966) 200 Estates Gazette 777. See also *Baxter v Gapp* [1938] 4 All ER 457 (Goddard LJ at first instance).
2   See *Zwebner v Mortgage Corpn Ltd* [1997] PNLR 504 at 512D–513D (Lloyd J) (affirmed on appeal [1998] ECGS 104, [1998] PNLR 769, CA), for a factual description of the use of unqualified staff. The judge refused to find that in completing a report on title (which required signature by a qualified solicitor) for a commercial lender an unqualified conveyancing assistant committed a breach of fiduciary duty.

2.5   In most cases the difficulty in identifying the standard of care is probably more apparent than real. The standard which the court will require the solicitor to achieve will depend on a number of issues such as the nature of the task which the solicitor was engaged to perform, the expertise or experience professed by him or her to the client, the nature of the mistake made (whether a point of law or not), the relevance of any advice sought or received from counsel and any relevant body of practice or rules of conduct. If the client insists on being represented by a fully qualified solicitor, it will be a breach of duty if he is not.[1] But where the level of expertise required is not addressed by the parties, the choice of personnel is left with the defendant. There is no reason why simple tasks cannot be delegated to an inexperienced trainee. In more complex situations, however, it may be negligent to entrust work to an individual who is insufficiently skilled or experienced to undertake it competently, whatever level of expertise the client is prepared to accept.[2]

1   In *Pearless De Rougemont & Co v Pilbrow* [1999] 143 Sol Jo LB 114, CA, it was held to be a repudiatory breach of contract for a firm to provide the services of a legal executive where a qualified solicitor was promised. (It was not a negligence claim but a claim by the firm for unpaid fees.)
2   See *Richards v Cox* [1943] 1 KB 139, CA (solicitor's clerk) and *Summit Financial Group Ltd v Slaughter & May* (12 March 1999, unreported) where the judge held that the defendants were negligent because the drafting of a complicated document was split between two departments without one person assuming overall responsibility and the tax lawyer dealing with it was only very recently qualified and inexperienced.

2.6   It may also be negligent for a firm or a fully qualified individual to undertake work which calls for particular expertise where the individual defendant or firm has insufficient experience in the relevant field. For instance, it may be negligent for a firm to take on the drafting of a deed of trust or settlement if it is unable to give tax advice on the consequences of the deed. In *Hurlingham Estates Ltd v Wilde & Partners*[1] Lightman J held that a solicitor who had 'next to no knowledge of tax law and was quite unqualified to give tax advice' was negligent in failing to appreciate the application of s 34 of the Income and Corporation Taxes Act 1988, advise the client of the potential exposure to a tax charge and to structure a commercial agreement to avoid it.

1   [1997] STC 627. Compare *Silver v Morris* (1995) 139 NSR (2d) 18 where the opposite result occurred.

2.7   Where the nature of the retainer requires the services of a legally qualified solicitor, the standard of the reasonably competent practitioner requires a reasonable level of experience and knowledge on the part of the defendant. It is not unreasonable for a client to expect a firm or an individual to meet a standard which is no lower than that of the solicitor in general practice with a reasonable period of experience behind him judged at the date on which the cause of action accrued. As for the nature of that experience, the description 'general practice' begs the question. In *Duchess of Argyll v Beuselinck*[1] Megarry J left open the question whether the standard of care to be expected of a solicitor is that of the average solicitor or whether a higher standard is required if he or she is an expert in a particular field.[2] Despite the absence of authority on this point, we consider that the appropriate yardstick is the level of expertise to be expected of a solicitor practising in the area or areas in which the defendant practises. A solicitor with a predominantly commercial practice should be judged by the standard of his or her peers whereas a High Street firm whose practice consists, for the most part, of domestic conveyancing and general litigation, should be judged by the standards of an experienced practitioner of that type. The decision of Morland J in *Locke v Camberwell Health Authority*[3] at first instance supports this distinction. The judge held that a litigation solicitor in a medical negligence case was not required to have 'the specialised expertise of a partner in a firm specialising in medical negligence work' but rather that of a solicitor 'engaged in litigation in general practice'. But if the solicitor holds himself out as having certain expertise which is greater than that normally to be expected of the reasonably competent solicitor and the retainer requires a solicitor with that expertise, the court will usually require him to demonstrate it.[4]

1   [1972] 2 Lloyd's Rep 172 at 185 col 1.
2   The point was also left open in *Martin Boston & Co v Roberts* [1996] PNLR 45 at 50E, CA.
3   [1990] NLJR 205, affirmed at [1991] 2 Med LR 249.
4   See *Elcano Acceptance Ltd v Richmond, Richmond, Stambler & Mills* (1989) 68 OR (2d) 165 at 177b where the test applied was the 'reasonably competent solicitor engaged in commercial practice'; *Hurlingham Estates Ltd v Wilde & Partners* [1997] STC 627 at 634d where Lightman J applied the test of 'any reasonably competent solicitor practising in the field of conveyancing or commercial law'; and *Matrix-Securities Ltd v Theodore Goddard* [1998] PNLR 290 where Lloyd J used 'such skill and care as a reasonably competent solicitor in the relevant sector of the profession'. Compare for accountants and Lloyd's managing agents, *Henderson v Merrett Syndicates* [1996] PNLR 32 at 37C (Cresswell J).

(b)   Level of fees

2.8   It has been suggested from time to time that if a solicitor charges a low level of fees, eg, to carry out a basic conveyancing service, the standard of care which the law should impose on him or her should be commensurately lower.[1] In *Johnson v Bingley, Dyson & Furey*[2] expert evidence was admitted to show that in 'cut price conveyancing' a solicitor would not necessarily communicate with his client in person. The judge found that if true, this was regrettable but it did not affect the liability of the defendants. This case is, therefore, some authority for the proposition that the standard of care to be expected of a professional in relation to a particular engagement should be the same whatever level of fees he or she charges for that piece of work.

1   See *Duchess of Argyll v Beuselinck* [1972] 2 Ll Rep 172 at 183 col 1. No comment was made on this issue in *Boston v Roberts* [1996] PNLR 45, CA.
2   [1997] PNLR 392 at 406G–407C (Mr Benet Hytner QC).

(c)   Knowledge of the law

2.9   According to Bingham LJ in *Eckersley v Binnie:*[1]

'[A] professional man should command the corpus of knowledge which forms part of the professional equipment of the ordinary member of his profession. He should not lag behind other ordinary assiduous and intelligent members of his profession in knowledge of new advances, discoveries and developments in his field. He should have an awareness as an ordinarily competent practitioner would of the deficiencies in his knowledge and the limitations on his skill. He should be alert to the hazards and risks inherent in any professional task he undertakes to the extent that other ordinarily competent members of the profession would be alert. He must bring to any professional task he undertakes no less expertise, skill and care than other ordinarily competent members of his profession would bring, but need bring no more. The law does not require of a professional man that he be a paragon, combining the qualities of polymath and prophet.'

A similar view had also been taken in Canada in *Central Trust Co v Rafuse*[2] where it was stated that:

'[A] solicitor must have sufficient knowledge of the fundamental issues or principles of law applicable to the particular work he has undertaken to enable him to perceive the need to ascertain the law on the relevant points.'

Because the defendant should have realised when it was necessary to research a point or take counsel's advice it will rarely be a defence that the defendant failed to identify a point of law which would have affected the advice which he or she would have given, the document which he or she would have drafted or the course of action which was adopted.

1 [1988] CLR 1 at 79, CA. See also *Henderson v Merrett Syndicates* [1996] PNLR 32 at 35 (Cresswell J).
2 (1986) 31 DLR (4th) 481.

2.10 Where on the other hand the defendant identifies the point but fails to reach the right answer after adequate consideration, the court is far less likely to find negligence.[1] Again if the defendant identifies the point but is unable to provide full advice (either by his own researches or by instructing counsel) because of the urgency to take action, it is unlikely that the court would find that he or she was negligent.

1 See *Ridehalgh v Horsefield* [1994] Ch 205 at 244B–F, CA.

(d) Reliance on counsel's advice

2.11 In general it is a good answer to a claim for negligence that the defendant relied upon the advice of counsel.[1] In *Locke v Camberwell Health Authority*[2] the Court of Appeal laid down the following guidelines:

'(1) In general, a solicitor is entitled to rely upon the advice of counsel properly instructed.

(2) For a solicitor without specialist experience in a particular field to rely on counsel's advice is to make normal and proper use of the Bar.

(3) However, he must not do so blindly, but must exercise his own independent judgment. If he reasonably thinks counsel's advice is obviously or glaringly wrong, it is his duty to reject it.'

In *Matrix-Securities Ltd v Theodore Goddard*[3] the plaintiffs brought an action against both solicitors and counsel for failure to obtain a tax clearance which was itself the subject of proceedings which reached the House of Lords. The judge held that neither defendant was liable. In relation to the solicitors he accepted as a general proposition that a solicitor is required to bring his own expertise to bear on the issue. But he held that there was no distinction in principle between a general practitioner and a specialist (in this case in tax) and applied the guidance in *Locke*. He concluded[4] that:

'[I]t is only a solicitor's duty to differ from it [counsel's advice] at that time and to give separate advice or to record reservations separately to the client if there was an important point on which the solicitor regarded Counsel's advice as being seriously wrong.'

1 The case usually cited for this proposition is *Davy-Chiesman v Davy-Chiesman* [1984] Fam 48, CA.
2 [1991] 2 Med LR 249 at 254, expressly approved in *Ridehalgh v Horsefield* [1994] Ch 205 at 237G, CA and *Reaveley v Safeway Stores plc* [1998] PNLR 526, CA. In *Ridehalgh* it was added that 'the more specialist the nature of the advice, the more reasonable it is likely to be for a solicitor to accept it and act on it'.
3 [1998] PNLR 290 (Lloyd J).
4 [1998] PNLR 290 at 323A–B.

(e) Failure to obtain counsel's advice

2.12 In *Ridehalgh v Horsefield*[1] the appellant solicitors acted in both the preparation and advocacy of a case which took two days in the county court but proceeded on the wrong basis. The resulting confusion generated a number of further hearings and appeals. Sir Thomas Bingham MR stated:

> 'The solicitors do not appear to have approached the case in a careless way. There is nothing to contradict their statements that the textbooks they consulted did not give a clear answer to their problem. They could not be expected to bring the expertise of specialist counsel to the case. Nor could they reasonably be expected to be remunerated for prolonged research. We do not think their error was one which no reasonably competent solicitor in general practice could have made.'

This dictum offers some support for the converse proposition that a solicitor is not always obliged to consult counsel on points of law, even where the answer to the question is not straightforward. But the case in question was a possession action in the county court which a solicitor in general practice would usually be able to conduct without any specialist advocacy training or a wide experience. It will not take much, however, for a solicitor to come under a duty to offer his client the opportunity of instructing counsel. Further examples of cases concerned with counsel's advice are considered in chapters 10 and 11.

1   [1994] Ch 205 at 244C, CA.

3   The relevance of professional standards and practice

2.13   In *Bolam v Friern Hospital Management Committtee*[1] McNair J directed the jury that it would not be right to find a professional guilty of negligence where he had acted in accordance with a practice accepted as proper by a responsible body of medical men skilled in a particular art even if another body of opinion took the contrary view. The correctness of the *Bolam* test was not challenged for thirty years until in *Bolitho v City and Hackney Health Authority*[2] the House of Lords was invited to overrule it. The House declined to do so and whilst recognising that the court is not bound to accept expert evidence unless it is reasonable, Lord Browne-Wilkinson concluded:[3]

> 'I emphasise that, in my view, it will seldom be right for a judge to reach conclusions that views genuinely held by a competent medical expert are unreasonable. The assessment of medical risks and benefits is a matter of clinical judgment which a judge would not normally be able to make without expert evidence. As the quotation from Lord Scarman makes clear,[4] it would be wrong to allow such assessment to deteriorate into seeking to persuade the judge to prefer one of two views both of which are capable of being logically supported. It is only where a judge can be satisfied that the body of expert opinion cannot be logically supported at all that such opinion will not provide the bench mark by reference to which the defendant's conduct falls to be assessed.'

1   [1957] 1 WLR 582 at 587.
2   [1998] AC 232.
3   [1998] AC 232 at 242C–E.
4   In *Maynard v West Midlands Regional Health Authority* [1984] 1 WLR 634 at 639, HL.

(a)   The relevance of rules of conduct

2.14   The benchmark of the solicitors' profession is its own rules of conduct, the Solicitors Practice Rules 1990, which are amended and updated from time to time and published in *The Guide to the Professional Conduct of Solicitors*. Neither the rules nor the other provisions of *The Guide* have the force of law or give rise to a claim in negligence.[1] But a failure to comply with either the rules or *The Guide* will carry very substantial weight. In *Omega Trust Co Ltd v Wright Son & Pepper (No 2)*[2] the judge stated that *The Guide* was the 'starting point' in considering whether the defendants had been negligent and in *Mortgage Express Ltd v Bowerman*[3] Sir Thomas Bingham MR relied upon annex 24L of *The Guide* in rejecting the submission that a solicitor owed no duty to pass on certain information.[4] The court will also pay regard to views expressed or endorsed by the Law Society.[5]

1   See *Johnson v Bingley, Dyson & Furey* [1997] PNLR 392 (Benet Hytner QC) at 407E–G. The judge considered that a failure to comply gave rise to a prima facie case which could have been rebutted by demonstrating that the guidance did not apply in the instant case. See also *Kenyon-Brown v Banks & Co* (5 June 1998, unreported) (Peter Leaver QC).
2   [1998] PNLR 337 at 347D–E (Douglas Brown J). The decision of the Court of Appeal striking out the valuer's claim shortly before trial is considered in chapter 1, para 1.25.
3   [1996] 2 All ER 836 at 842a–d.
4   For further examples see also *Nash v Phillips* (1974) 232 Estates Gazette 1219 (Foster J) at 1222 col 2 and the discussion of *The Guide* in para 2.33 and chapter 8, paras 8.7–8.9.
5   See the quotation from Millett LJ's judgment in *Bown v Gould & Swayne* set out in para 2.15. In *Edward Wong* the Privy Council was heavily influenced by a report of a subcommittee of the Hong Kong Law Society which was critical of Hong Kong style completions: see 306F–307G. In *G & K Ladenbau v Crawley & De Reya* [1978] 1 WLR 266 Mocatta J also relied upon a warning in the Law Society Gazette: see 278H–279D.

2.15   By contrast, however, there are virtually no reported examples of cases in which the court's decision has turned on the view taken by a body of the profession, as expressed by an expert solicitor.[1] The reason for this may be that given by Millett LJ in *Bown v Gould & Swayne*[2] (where what was in issue was conveyancing practice):

'Two hundred and fifty years later the practice of investigating title has settled down sufficiently to be well established and recorded in the textbooks. If it is necessary to assist the judge to understand the proper machinery for the deduction and investigation of title, the proper way to do it is to cite the textbooks such as Emmett, Farrand, Williams and Dart, if necessary supplemented by Law Society opinions. In fact, this is a straightforward case in which I doubt that even such references would be necessary.'

In relation to litigation and the other specialist heads of practice considered in Part 2 of this book, an analysis of the individual cases shows that there is rarely a difference of opinion as to the proper practice to be adopted.

1   See *Jackson and Powell on Professional Negligence* (4th edn, 1997) pp 4–60. The only modern authority cited is that of *Simmons v Pennington* [1955] 1 WLR 183, CA, discussed in para 2.28. In that case, no expert evidence was given, and the question whether the defendant's reply to a preliminary inquiry in a standard form had had the effect of repudiating a contract for sale had already been once to the Court of Appeal: see Hodson LJ at 188. More recently, in *Esterhuizen v Allied Dunbar Assurance plc* [1998] 2 FLR 668 (Longmore J), the judge held that a lay will-writer was negligent by relying on the practice of solicitors.
2   [1996] PNLR 130 at 137A, CA.

2.16   In those rare cases where it is argued that the routine practice or procedure adopted by an individual solicitor is negligent, it ought to be relevant to that issue whether that same practice is also adopted by a substantial body of the profession. Genuine issues of conveyancing practice may arise even in the age of registered land. For example, questions whether and when it is reasonable or safe for a solicitor to accept another solicitor's undertaking are primarily questions of practice upon which an expert may genuinely be able to assist the court.[1] To take a more specific example, where it is alleged in a lender's context that a solicitor ought to have been aware of a substantial price differential on a sub-sale it may be relevant to consider whether, as a matter of practice, the sub-vendor would usually reveal the price under the head contract in satisfying the sub-purchaser's solicitors on title.[2] Again, the question whether a solicitor ought to give general advice to his client before contract may turn on the practice which the profession currently adopts (or adopted at the time of the alleged negligence).[3] Despite the absence of many concrete examples from the authorities, we consider that where a solicitor does adopt a practice which is also adopted by a substantial body of his or her profession, there should be no finding of negligence unless, in accordance with *Bolitho*, the practice cannot be defended on a logical basis.

1   See chapter 8, paras 8.65–8.69.
2   See, for consideration of this specific point, *Nationwide Building Society v Balmer Radmore* [1999] Lloyd's Rep PN 241.
3   This is an issue considered in chapter 8, paras 8.46–8.51. See also *Brenner v Gregory* (1972) 30 DLR (3d) 672 in which this precise issue arose.

2.17   Having said this, the court will be less reluctant in cases concerning solicitors' or barristers' negligence than in medical cases to make the judgment that a professional practice is negligent and cannot be defended. This is because the court is uniquely placed to form an opinion about the legitimacy or reasonableness of a standard practice adopted by lawyers, whilst it must to a greater or lesser extent rely on expert evidence in assessing a medical practice. *Edward Wong Ltd v Johnson, Stokes & Master*[1] is one of those rare cases, in which the court has found negligent a practice observed by the profession or a significant part of it. In that case the Privy Council held that a purchaser's solicitor in Hong Kong who paid the purchase price directly to the vendor's solicitor against an undertaking to provide documents of title was negligent when the vendor's solicitor absconded with the money, even though this practice was commonly followed in Hong Kong. Lord Brightman stated, in delivering the judgment of the Board:[2]

> 'As already indicated, the prevalence of the Hong Kong style of completion is established beyond a peradventure. It is particularly well adapted to the conditions in Hong Kong. It has obvious advantages to both solicitors and their clients. Their Lordships intend to say nothing to discourage its continuance. However, in assessing whether the respondents fell short of the standard of care which they owed towards the appellants, three questions must be considered: first, does the practice, as operated by the respondents involve a foreseeable risk? If so, could that risk have been avoided? If so, were the respondents negligent in failing to take avoiding action?'

Having answered the first two questions affirmatively, Lord Brightman then said this:[3]

> 'The risk inherent in the Hong Kong style of completion as operated in the instant case being foreseeable, and readily avoidable, there can only be an affirmative answer to the third question, whether the respondents were negligent in not foreseeing and avoiding that risk ... Their Lordships wish to add that they do not themselves attach blame to Miss Leung for the calamity which occurred. In entrusting the vendor's solicitor Mr Danny Liu with the whole of the money she was merely following the normal practice of her firm, and she had never been instructed to act otherwise in such a case or to take any special precautions.'

If therefore a practice is inherently negligent because it involves a risk to the client which is both reasonably foreseeable and easily avoidable, it is no defence for the defendant to rely upon the fact that it has been adopted either by a substantial body of his profession or, indeed, by the whole profession.

1   [1984] AC 296.
2   [1984] AC 296 at 306E–F.
3   [1984] AC 296 at 308G–309A.

2.18   A further, albeit less striking example, is provided by *Elcano Acceptance Ltd v Richmond, Richmond, Stambler & Mills.*[1] In that case the defendant had drafted a number of promissory notes for the plaintiff which contained an interest provision, which was defective for a highly technical reason. This came to light when the promisor took the point, although the action was later settled. The defendant's expert witnesses stated that this was a completely novel defence and that no commercial lawyer would have checked or considered the relevant statute in question. O'Leary J accepted the plaintiff's evidence but stated that 'even if all the solicitors called to testify had given the same opinion as those called by the defendants' he would still have concluded that the defendant had been negligent.[2]

1   (1989) 68 OR (2d) 165.
2   (1989) 68 OR (2d) 165 at 177g–178e. See also *Deeny v Gooda Walker* [1994] CLC 1224 in which Phillips J was not prepared to accept that because a significant number of underwriters were prepared to write 'spiral business' in the market, that was evidence of what constituted reasonable skill and care.

2.19   Again, unlike the medical profession, there will rarely be a genuine difference of opinion between expert witnesses about the practice to be adopted by a solicitor in a given case. In *G & K Ladenbau Ltd v Crawley and de Reya*[1] the judge was not prepared to accept that 'two equally well-established schools of practice' had emerged by the time the act complained of had taken place. Instead he preferred to accept the evidence of the plaintiff's expert as laying down, so far as possible, 'a general rule of useful guidance'. Where, however, the evidence is that two (or even more) practices have genuinely been established and adopted, the court ought to find that the defendant has not been negligent if the court is also satisfied that the practice was not itself negligent.

1   [1978] 1 WLR 266 at 288H (Mocatta J).

4   The relevance and admissibility of expert evidence

2.20   If it is rare that a case gives rise to issues about compliance with a particular practice or the competence of a solicitor who adopts it, there should be little need for expert evidence. For it is only in those cases that the practice of a significant body of the profession is genuinely relevant. Until very recently, however, there was a tendency for parties to seek to adduce expert evidence to criticise or defend the conduct of the defendant almost as a matter of routine. For a time judges were prepared to admit this evidence if the parties wished to adduce it. But, of late, the Court of Appeal has firmly disapproved of this tendency and the courts' desire to limit the calling of expert evidence is now enshrined in the Civil Procedure Rules themselves. Furthermore, as this trend has developed, it has become more difficult (and rightly in our view) to obtain leave to adduce expert evidence in the field of solicitors' negligence than it has in cases in other fields.

(a)   Jurisdiction

2.21   This tendency to admit expert evidence was, in part, due to a concern about the court's ability to exclude an expert's report at the interlocutory or interim stage.

Until recently there was Court of Appeal authority that the court had no power under RSC Ord 38 to exclude an expert's report prior to the trial of the action where a party applied in advance for leave to adduce expert evidence.[1] The practical consequence of this was to encourage expert evidence. Where a direction for expert evidence was made at the behest of one party, the opposing party would inevitably go to the trouble and expense of instructing an expert and, given that both parties had their expert evidence available, the trial judge would be reluctant to exclude it whatever weight he or she ultimately attached to it. In *Bown v Gould & Swayne*,[2] however, the Court of Appeal held that it had jurisdiction to disallow an expert's report where the court held a pre-trial review. This decision was affirmed in the recent case of *Woodford & Ackroyd v Burgess*[3] on the wider ground that the court had an inherent jurisdiction or a general power under RSC Ord 33, r 3 to exclude expert evidence at the interim stage. This position has now been codified in the Civil Procedure Rules.[4] The tendency to exclude unnecessary expert evidence at the interim stage is likely, therefore, to gather pace.

1   See *Sullivan v West Yorkshire Passenger Transport Executive* [1985] 2 All ER 134, CA and *Rawlinson v Westbrook* (1995) Times, 25 January, CA.
2   [1996] PNLR 130, followed by Mr Michael Crystal QC in *Portman Building Society v Bond & Ingram* [1998] CLY 320.
3   [1999] Lloyd's Rep PN 231, CA.
4   Rule 35.4: 'No party may call an expert or put in evidence an expert's report without the court's permission.' Rule 35.1 provides that 'Expert evidence should be restricted to that which is reasonably required to resolve the proceedings.' See, also, the judgment of Clarke LJ in *Woodford & Ackroyd v Burgess* [1999] Lloyd's Rep PN 231 at 236.

(b)   The scope of expert evidence generally

2.22   The relevance of evidence of a particular practice is dealt with above and, although rarely deployed in cases involving solicitors, has always been admissible in professional negligence cases where genuinely relevant to an issue in the action. But is an expert confined to giving evidence of this nature or can he give his opinion on whether he considers that the defendant was negligent or has made a mistake which no reasonably competent professional would have made? Prior to the passing of the Civil Evidence Act 1972 (CEA) it was an open question whether a witness could give evidence on the 'ultimate question', ie the issue which the court had to decide.[1] Whatever the right answer at common law the Act abolished the rule and in a proper case expert evidence can now be received on the very question which the judge has to decide.[2] What is a proper case? In *United Bank of Kuwait v Prudential Property Services Ltd*[3] it was held that an expert banker was entitled to state his opinion on the question whether the plaintiff had been guilty of contributory negligence. In reaching this conclusion, the Court of Appeal emphasised that there is no category of expert evidence which is automatically admissible or inadmissible. The 'overriding principle' is whether the evidence is 'helpful in assisting the Court to reach a fully informed decision'. It may be unnecessary to call evidence relating to a professional practice in simple cases and the court may not be able to reach an informed decision on critical issues of fact without the guidance of an expert in others.[4] The same approach was adopted by Jacob J in *Routestone Ltd v Minories Finance Ltd*,[5] where the evidence in question was that of a specialist valuer about marketing a property. It is, therefore, open to the court to admit or exclude the opinion of an expert, either at the interim stage or at trial, even though the expert passes comment on the competence of the defendant.

1   See *Cross & Tapper on Evidence* (8th edn, 1995) pp 552–3.
2   See *Glaverbel SA v British Coal Corpn* [1995] RPC 255 at 276, lines 15–29, CA.

3   [1995] ECGS 190, CA.
4   Evans LJ, transcript at p 7.
5   [1997] BCC 180, esp at 188E–190F.

(c)   Solicitor experts

2.23   Although expert opinion evidence can be admissible as a matter of law on the question whether the defendant was negligent where the defendant is engaged in another profession, English courts have been very reluctant to allow one solicitor to give evidence criticising or defending the conduct of another solicitor. The reasons for this were explained by Oliver J in *Midland Bank Trust Co Ltd v Hett, Stubbs and Kemp*:[1]

> 'I heard the evidence of a number of practising solicitors. Mr Harman modestly contented himself with calling one; but Mr. Gatehouse—mindful, no doubt, of what is said to be divine preference for big battalions—called no less than three. I must say that I doubt the value, or even the admissibility of this sort of evidence, which seems to be becoming customary in cases of this type. The extent of the legal duty in any given situation must, I think, be a question of law for the court. Clearly, if there is some practice in a particular profession, some accepted standard of conduct which is laid down by a professional institute or sanctioned by common usage, evidence of that can and ought to be received. But evidence which really amounts to no more than an expression of opinion by a particular practitioner had he been placed hypothetically and without the benefit of hindsight, in the position of the defendants, is of little assistance to the court; whilst evidence of the witnesses' view of what, as a matter of law, the solicitor's duty was in the particular circumstances of the case is, I should have thought, inadmissible, for that is the very question which it is the court's function to decide.'

This approach was expressly approved by the Court of Appeal in *Bown v Gould & Swayne*,[2] where Simon Brown LJ said this:

> 'Each of the seven respects in which the appellant's first affidavit sought to contend that expert evidence would assist the court proves, on analysis, to involve either a question of law or a question of fact. None of those matters can sensibly be regarded as inviting a view as to "some practice in [the solicitors'] profession, some accepted standard of conduct ... laid down ... or sanctioned by common usage."
>
> I entirely share the view of the judge below that, on the contrary, the evidence here sought to be adduced falls foul of Oliver J's dictum. It would amount to no more than an expression of opinion by the expert, either as to what he himself *would have done*, which could not assist, or as to what he thinks *should have been done*, which would have been the very issue for the judge to determine.'

1   [1979] Ch 384 at 402B–E.
2   [1996] PNLR 130 at 135B–D.

2.24   In *Bown v Gould & Swayne* the Court of Appeal was plainly of the view that expert solicitor evidence would rarely be of genuine assistance to the court, whether technically admissible or not. Unfortunately, the effect of the Civil Evidence Act 1972 was not considered either by Oliver J in *Midland Bank Trust Co Ltd v Hett, Stubbs and Kemp* or by the Court of Appeal in *Bown*.[1] In *Portman Building Society v Bond & Ingram*[2] it was argued that both decisions were per incuriam because they failed to take into account the fact that CEA 1972, s 3 had made expert evidence on the ultimate question admissible. This argument was 'unhesitatingly rejected' by the judge on the grounds that Oliver J's decision was unaffected by the CEA 1972. The evidence of an expert is irrelevant to the legal test to be applied which is solely within the province of the court and of little or no assistance in deciding questions of fact.[3] Whether it is to be regarded as a rule of evidence or a rule of practice, it now seems settled that leave to adduce expert evidence will not be given in solicitors' negligence cases unless that evidence goes to a professional practice and that practice is genuinely relevant to an issue in the action.

1   Neither *United Bank of Kuwait plc v Prudential Property Services* [1995] ECGS 190, CA nor *Routestone Ltd v Minories Finance Ltd* [1997] BCC 180 (Jacob J) were cited.
2   [1998] CLY 320.
3   See also *Re Barings plc (No 4)* [1998] All ER(D) 669 (Parker J), a case concerned with investment banking, where the same argument was raised and rejected.

5   Errors of judgment and slips

2.25   There are many dicta to the effect that the court will not punish an error of judgment and that if, with the benefit of hindsight, a decision taken by a solicitor turns out to have been wrong, this will not of itself justify a finding of negligence. The standard was defended by Bingham LJ in *Eckersley v Binnie*[1] on the following basis:

'[I]t is easy and tempting to impose too high a standard in order to see that the innocent victims of the disaster are compensated by the defendants' insurers. Many would wish that the right to recovery in such cases did not depend on proof of negligence. But so long as it does, defendants are not to be held negligent unless they are in truth held to have fallen short of the standards I have mentioned.'

In *Wilsher v Essex Area Health Authority*[2] Mustill LJ stated to the same effect:

'The risks which actions for professional negligence bring to the public as a whole, in the shape of an instinct on the part of the professional man to play for safety, are serious and are now well recognised. Nevertheless, the proper response cannot be to temper the wind to the professional man. If he assumes to perform a task, he must bring to it the appropriate care and skill. What the courts can do, however, is to bear constantly in mind that, in those situations which call for the exercise of judgment, the fact that in retrospect the choice actually made can be shown to have turned out badly is not itself a proof of negligence; and to remember that the duty of care is not a warranty of a perfect result.'[3]

1   (1988) 18 CLR 1 at 79, CA.
2   [1987] QB 730 at 747A–C, CA.
3   See also the passage from the speech of Lord Diplock in *Saif Ali v Sydney Mitchell & Co* [1980] AC 198 at 218D quoted in para 2.27 and, most recently, *Martin Boston & Co v Roberts* [1996] PNLR 45 at 50E, CA.

2.26   However difficult the process is, the court must also apply the appropriate standard without the benefit of hindsight. According to Megarry J in *Duchess of Argyll v Beuselinck*:[1]

'In this world there are few things that could not have been better done if done with hindsight. The advantages of hindsight include the benefit of having a sufficient indication of which of the many factors are important and which are unimportant. But hindsight is not a touchstone of negligence.'

1   [1972] 2 Lloyd's Rep 172 at 185 col 1 (Megarry J).

2.27   What will the court characterise, without hindsight, as an error of judgment rather than as negligence? Where a solicitor in drafting or advising on a will or a lease fails by mistake to include an important provision which the client wished to have included or to which the other negotiating party would have agreed without question, it is not appropriate to describe such a mistake as an error of judgment. Such a description is appropriate only where the defendant takes a step or gives advice to his client whilst taking a risk which he or she considers remote but which later material-ises.[1] If the court considers that the defendant was justified in taking or ignoring the risk, he or she will not be found negligent. But if the risk was unjustifiably high the defendant will nevertheless be found negligent even though it may have been consciously considered. *Martin Boston & Co v Roberts*[2] illustrates the distinction well. In that case the defendants acted for a firm of surveyors in a claim brought against them by a former client, which was a limited company. They were found negligent for accepting an offer by the plaintiff to provide security for costs by means of a personal guarantee from an individual without insisting on some form of security to back the guarantee (eg a charge or restriction on property). In correspondence, the plaintiff's solicitors had indicated that the guarantor owned freehold property in which there was equity of £65,000. The third party later defaulted on the guarantee and by the time of enforcement had recharged the property a number of times. It was argued on appeal that the court had imposed too high a standard of care. A majority of the Court of Appeal rejected this submission on the basis that the risk of the third party charging the property, if free to do so, was both clearly and obviously foreseeable and also avoidable, and in those circumstances the solicitors ought to have protected their client's position by insisting on some form of security or at least obtaining the client's instructions to take this risk.[3]

1   For a conveyancing example of an error of judgment which was not negligent see *Neighbour v Barker* (1992) 40 EG 140, CA.
2   [1996] PNLR 45, CA.
3   See Simon Brown LJ at 52A–G and Henry LJ at 56E–F and 57D. Ward LJ dissented on the basis that this was 'an error of judgment': see 60D–E. He considered that the defendants were justified in taking the view that the application for security might not succeed. Both Simon Brown and Henry LJJ considered it a wholly obvious case: see 54C and 55G.

2.28   The majority of claims for negligence involve not errors of judgment but routine mistakes. A more lenient attitude to such mistakes can be detected in the cases before the development and expansion of the tort of negligence in *Hedley Byrne*.[1] In *Simmons v Pennington*[2] a solicitor's clerk answered a requisition on title in a standard form but because of the circumstances of the case, inadvertently gave the purchaser an opportunity to rescind, which was taken. Denning LJ described this as 'a mistake' and 'one of those misadventures or misfortunes which sometimes happen even in the best conducted businesses'. A different attitude has been adopted since *Hedley Byrne*. Where an isolated mistake is made by an otherwise blameless solicitor of unimpeachable reputation and experience, a mistake which any professional is bound to make in the course of his practice, this will nevertheless be characterised as negligence. In *Sykes v Midland Bank Executor and Trustee Co Ltd*[3] the mistake in issue was described thus by Salmon LJ:[4]

'Reluctant though I am to find any negligence against a dead man who enjoyed the highest professional reputation I feel driven to the conclusion that Mr Rignall was negligent in overlooking this clause and failing to bring it to his clients' attention. The comon law, of course, recognises no degrees of negligence, but I should like to say that, in my view, the degree of blame in the present case was slight. It was the sort of negligence many a competent professional man many have committed on some isolated occasion in the course of his career.'[5]

In *Ron Miller Realty Ltd v Honeywell, Wotherspoon and Beedell*[6] it was expressly argued that the mistake made by the defendant would have been made by most lawyers but, even though the judge accepted this, the defendants were found to be negligent.

1   [1964] AC 465.
2   [1955] 1 WLR 183, esp at 186–7 and 189, CA. As late as 1955 Hodson LJ was applying *Fletcher & Son v Jubb, Booth & Helliwell* [1920] 1 KB 275 and the test of 'crassa negligentia'.
3   [1971] 1 QB 113, CA.
4   [1971] 1 QB 113 at 126E.
5   See also *Creech v Mayorcas* (1966) 198 Estates Gazette 1091 esp col 2, in which Pennycuick J had 'formed a high opinion' of the solicitor and considered the slip 'an understandable one' but nevertheless found the defendants negligent.
6   (1992) 4 OR (3d) 492, varied (1993) 16 OR (3d) 255.

2.29   In an article called 'The Reasonableness of Lawyers' Lapses'[1] Lord Hoffmann identified the increasing, insurance-driven, willingness of the courts to find solicitors in non-contentious work negligent without the attribution of any moral fault.[2] This book is not the occasion to discuss the desirability or long-term consequences of this development.[3] It is worth noting, however, that the attitude to slips, particularly in a conveyancing context, appears to be less indulgent than the approach taken to errors of judgment, particularly in a litigation context.

1   (1994) 10 PN 6.
2   See also Evans *Lawyers' Liabilites* (1996) ch 1.
3   In the property finance field the Court of Appeal is currently having to wrestle with the consequences because the profession is self-insuring and these claims have generated escalating premiums profession-wide. On the one hand, the courts must be seen to encourage uniformly high standards even in the context of often routine services for flat fees. On the other hand, those very circumstances suggest that in many cases of negligence, there can be no 'fault' in a traditional sense.

B   THE EXTENT OF THE DUTY TO ADVISE

1   Introduction

2.30   In every case where an allegation of negligence is made against a solicitor, the court may need to have recourse to the materials explored in the previous parts of this chapter in deciding whether he or she fell below the accepted standard. However, whether a finding of negligence is finally made, particularly in those cases where it is said that the advice given on a particular occasion was inadequate, will depend on the circumstances of the particular case. In *Duncan v Cuelenaere, Beaubier, Walters, Kendall & Fisher*[1] the court provided this helpful guidance:

'The test to be applied where a solicitor's negligence is alleged will depend on various circumstances: the sophistication of the client; the experience and training of the solicitor; the form and nature of the client's instructions; the specificity of those instructions; the nature of the action or the legal assignment; the precautions one would expect a solicitor, acting prudently and competently, to take; the course of the proceeding or assignment; and the influence of other factors beyond the control of the client and the adviser.'

1   [1987] 2 WWR 379 at 382.

2.31   In Part 2 of this book we attempt to organise and classify the particular duties of a solicitor in common, specific situations. In this section, we address one particular issue of general application, the extent to which a solicitor ought to advise his client and, in particular, the extent to which a solicitor ought to advise his client about the wisdom of the particular transaction which he proposes to enter.

2 The nature of the client

2.32 A solicitor's duty is to advise his client in terms which are appropriate to his own understanding and experience. According to Bingham LJ in *County Personnel (Employment Agency) Ltd v Pulver:*[1]

'It seems obvious that legal advice, like other communication, should be in terms appropriate to the comprehension and experience of the particular recipient. It is also, I think, clear that in a situation such as this the professional man does not necessarily discharge his duty by spelling out what is obvious. The client is entitled to expect the exercise of a reasonable professional judgment. That is why the client seeks advice from the professional man in the first place. If in the exercise of a reasonable professional judgment a solicitor is or should be alerted to risks which might elude even an intelligent layman, then plainly it is his duty to advise the client of these risks or explore the matter further.'

Thus the extent of the duty to advise will depend, as one would expect, on the identity and abilities of the client.[2] To take a simple example, if the client is foreign or unable to speak English, the solicitor may have to ensure that any document which he is required to sign is translated for him and that wider and more basic explanations are given. In *Siasati v Bottoms & Webb*[3] it was held that a solicitor owed a duty to explain the nature and scope of all of the obligations which the client was undertaking to clients whose knowledge of English was so limited that they needed to communicate with the solicitor through an interpreter. It was also held that the solicitor ought to have put the advice in writing. Where the client is a company or skilled in commercial matters, it will be far less onerous for a solicitor to discharge his or her duty.[4]

1   [1987] 1 WLR 916 at 922D, CA.
2   This approach was also adopted in *Carradine Properties Ltd v D J Freeman & Co* [1989] 5 Const LJ 267, CA, esp at 271 and 272. See also the part of the judgment of Donaldson LJ which is not reported in the above report but cited by Peter Gibson LJ in *National Home Loans Corpn v Giffen, Couch & Archer* [1998] 1 WLR 207 at 213H. The decision is now reported in full at [1999] Lloyd's Rep PN 483.
3   Mr Geoffrey Brice QC [1997] EGCS 22. See also *Donmez v Barnes* [1996] EGCS 129 and *Peyman v Lanjani* [1985] Ch 457 at 480B, CA.
4   See eg *Mean v Thomas* [1998] EGCS 2 (Stephen Tomlinson QC) where P was an experienced builder who purchased a property at auction subject to covenants in the property register. D advised that it was for P to satisfy himself that there was no obstacle to development but did not have an opportunity to examine the title before the auction. D was held not liable.

2.33 There is no duty imposed upon a solicitor either as a matter of general law or by the Solicitors Practice Rules 1990 to see and interview his client personally. Where instructions are communicated by a third party, eg a family member or friend, *The Guide*[1] gives the following guidance:

'Where instructions are received from a third party a solicitor should obtain written instructions from the client that he or she wishes the solicitor to act. In any case of doubt the solicitor should see the client or take other appropriate steps to confirm instructions.'

In *Johnson v Bingley, Dyson & Furey*[2] a solicitor was held negligent for failing to comply with a predecessor of this provision in a case of doubt. Obviously if a solicitor acts for more than one person and fails to take instructions from each of them, he runs the risk that his instructions are incorrectly transmitted, he is acting without authority or that one or more of the clients is inadequately advised.[3] But where the client is an experienced businessman, and the solicitor's advice can be dealt with by telephone, fax and letter, there should be no obligation to meet the client face to face.[4]

1   At 12.04.
2   [1997] PNLR 392 (Benet Hytner QC). See also *Linaker v Keith Turner & Ashton* Garland J (5 November 1998, unreported).
3   See chapter 8, paras 8.7–8.9.
4   See *Hallmark Finance Insurance Brokers Ltd v Fraser & Beatty* (1990) 1 OR (3d) 641 at 647f–g.

3   The nature of the advice

(a)   Advice generally

2.34   A solicitor is obliged to advise, not simply to pass on information. In *Mortgage Express Ltd v Newman*[1] Carnwath J stated:

'If the solicitors' duty is to draw attention to matters which might affect the value of the security, it must be their duty to do so in terms which draw attention to the reason for taking that view. It cannot be sufficient simply to pass the information across, perhaps by telephone.'

In *Nationwide Building Society v Balmer Radmore*[2] the judge applied the standard of a solicitor writing a letter of advice to an intelligent layman. He also stated that the solicitor was obliged to give reasons for his advice.

1   [1996] PNLR 603 at 611B–C.
2   [1999] Lloyd's Rep PN 241 at 270 (Blackburne J).

2.35   Where a solicitor is instructed to draw up or advise on a legal document, however, this does not mean that he or she is bound to read out every clause in the contract or lease to ensure that the client understands it. There must be an exercise of professional judgment in deciding which provisions to draw to the client's attention[1] and it seems obvious that the more unusual the provision, the more important it is to point it out.[2] Further it may not be enough simply to point out unusual or unexpected provisions. It may also be necessary to spell out their legal consequences. For example, prior to the Landlord and Tenant (Covenants) Act 1995, a relatively sophisticated client might not have understood that in executing and taking a long lease of premises, he was contractually bound to perform the covenants in the lease and, in effect, to guarantee the performance of any successor in title, although the concept of original tenant liability was and is commonplace to a lawyer.

1   See *Reeves v Thrings & Long* [1996] PNLR 265 at 275E–F per Sir Thomas Bingham MR, CA.
2   See *Sykes v Midland Bank* [1971] 1 QB 113 at 124B and 130F, CA.

(b)   Advice on commercial matters

2.36   The traditional principle is that a solicitor is not obliged to advise his client about the wisdom of the transaction which he is about to enter. According to Melford Stevenson J in *Bowdage v Harold Michelmore & Co,*[1] in which the plaintiff client, who had granted an option on her land to a third party at a very low price, claimed damages against the defendant solicitors for failing to advise her not to grant the option:

> '[A] solicitor who acted for a client in relation to the sale of land could not be said, in the absence of specific instructions, to undertake the duty of advising the client whether the transaction was from the client's view a prudent one. The defendants were never asked to advise the plaintiff about the value of the land and neither the nature of the transaction nor the lack of experience on her part imposed a duty to do so.'

This general approach was supported by the Court of Appeal more recently in *Reeves v Thrings & Long*[2] and by the Privy Council in *Clarke Boyce v Mouat*:[3]

> 'When a client in full command of his faculties and apparently aware of what he is doing seeks the assistance of a solicitor in the carrying out of a particular transaction, that solicitor is under no duty whether before or after accepting instructions to go beyond those instructions by proffering unsought advice on the wisdom of the transaction. To hold otherwise could impose intolerable burdens on solicitors.'

In general, therefore, a solicitor is under no duty to advise a client that what is proposed in general is imprudent nor to spell out the commercial consequences of any of the particular elements of the transaction.[4]

1   (1962) 106 Sol Jo 512.
2   [1996] PNLR 265 at 275E per Bingham LJ, at 279C per Simon Brown LJ and at 285A per Hobhouse LJ, CA. Unusually, the court reached different conclusions about whether the solicitor ought to have advised further, largely according to the differing weight they attached to parts of the evidence and the judge's findings of fact.
3   [1994] 1 AC 428 at 437D–E.
4   A good example of where the line is drawn is *Haigh v Wright Hassall & Co* [1994] EGCS 54, CA. See also *Nixon v Stephensons* (3 April 1996, unreported) (Mr John Martin QC).

2.37   This general approach can only be adopted, however, with important qualifications. First, and most obviously, the defendant may be specifically instructed to advise on the commercial consequences of the proposed transaction. To take a common example, it is now common practice for a bank to engage a separate firm of solicitors to advise a potential guarantor/mortgagor for their customer's debts of the nature of the transaction which is proposed. It is the function of the solicitor to point out to the client the 'manifest disadvantages' of the transaction.[1] Secondly, there may be circumstances in which it is so obvious to the solicitor that what the client proposes is improvident that the solicitor is obliged to give further advice.[2] Thirdly, and perhaps most importantly, it is not always easy to distinguish between legal and commercial advice, particularly where what is in issue is the implication of a specific clause or provision in a legal document.[3] At one extreme, any changes in the document have the potential to generate a commercial effect. Giving advice about a legal document inevitably requires the adviser to form a view about (a) those clauses which are complex or unusual and likely to require explanation and (b) those clauses which are sufficiently important in commercial terms to merit detailed discussion.[4] A solicitor's duty must be to point out the legal consequences of important clauses or provisions sufficiently forcefully and in layman's terms so that the client can appreciate their commercial significance.[5] This is, after all, one of the functions of legal advice. A good example of the fineness of the distinction is a rent review clause. A client may be attracted by the current rent of commercial premises and the inducements which the landlord is offering but may not see the implications of the rent review clause which, say, requires a review after five years to a headline rent. It may be unnecessary to say to some clients (but not others) that the rent will change after five years because this is obvious[6] but it will be necessary to explain the implications of the clause and the way in which the new market rent is to be calculated. This is legal advice although it will also have commercial consequences. Plainly the client cannot weigh up the commercial advantages of a low rent at the beginning of the term against the risk that the rent will increase substantially unless he or she fully understands the way in which the rent review clause operates. Moreover, rent review clauses are often drafted in standard terms which an experienced solicitor will understand but his client may not.

1   See chapter 8, paras 8.11–8.33.
2   See the facts of *Neushul v Mellish & Harkavy* (1967) 111 Sol Jo 399, CA (where the client was described as "rushing into an unwise, not to say, disastrous adventure'). The solicitors had given business advice, however, and had a conflict.
3   Bingham LJ rejected the distinction in *Pulver* [1987] 1 WLR 916 at 924A, CA.
4   In *Hallmark Finance Insurance Brokers Ltd v Fraser & Beatty and McNairn* (1990) 1 OR (3d) 641 Dunnet J drew what may also be a helpful distinction between 'business components' of the transaction and 'legal provisions': see 646d–f. (The clause in issue was a purchase formula.) The solicitor will not advise his client that he has inserted the purchase price in the contract because this will be assumed. Where, therefore, the solicitor simply transfers commercial terms from an exchange of letters or an oral agreement, it may well be unnecessary to draw attention to them in the completed document.
5   *Reeves v Thrings & Long* [1996] PNLR 265, CA is concerned with precisely this issue but no real ratio decidendi can be extracted from the case. Sir Thomas Bingham MR plainly did not believe that this had been done: see 277. Simon Brown LJ was satisfied that the plaintiff was aware of the legal position but was not concerned whether he understood the commercial implications: see 280G–281A. Hobhouse LJ did not fully address this issue. He stated at 288D that 'provided that a solicitor uses language which would lead a reasonable person in the position of the solicitor to believe that his advice was being understood, and there is no evidence that the solicitor should reasonably have observed that his advice was not being understood, the solicitor has discharged his duty.'
6   See the facts of *Forbouys v Gadhavi* [1993] NPC 122 (John Chadwick QC).

2.38   Finally, although the decision of the Court of Appeal in *Mortgage Express Ltd v Bowerman*[1] is always considered in the context of the liability of solicitors to institutional lenders (and thus is considered in this book in chapter 7) it is again authority for the proposition that a solicitor owes a duty to give advice which is wider than merely legal and which is of commercial significance.

1   [1996] 2 All ER 836, CA.

CHAPTER 3

Damages at common law

A   GENERAL PRINCIPLES

1   Damages in contract and tort

3.1   Before the increase in claims against solicitors and valuers generated by the collapse of the property market in the late 1980s and early 1990s, it was accepted that compensatory damages against a professional (whether in contract or tort)[1] were limited by the three principles of causation, remoteness and mitigation. These principles were most clearly explained by Sir Thomas Bingham MR in *Banque Bruxelles Lambert SA v Eagle Star*:[2]

'So the question arises: to what damage is the lender entitled against the negligent valuer? The general answer given by authority is clear. If the claim is in contract, it is given by Parke B in *Robinson v Harman* (1848) 1 Exch 850, 855:

"The rule of the common law is, that where a party sustains a loss by reason of breach of contract he is, so far as money can do it, to be placed in the same situation, with respect to damages, as if the contract had been performed."

If the claim is in tort the answer is given by Lord Blackburn in *Livingstone v Rawyards Coal* (1880) 5 App Cas 25, 39:

"I do not think that there is any difference of opinion as to its being a general rule that, where any injury is to be compensated by damages, in settling the sum of money to be given for reparation of damages, you should as nearly as possible get at that sum of money which will put the party who has been injured, or who has suffered, in the same position as he would have been if he had not sustained the wrong for which he is now getting his compensation or reparation."

It is not suggested that for present purposes there is any practical difference between these two tests.

In *British Westinghouse Electric and Manufacturing Co Ltd v Underground Electric Rlys Co of London Ltd* [1912] AC 673, 688–689, Viscount Haldane LC said:

"In order to come to a conclusion on the question as to damages thus raised, it is essential to bear in mind certain propositions which I think are well established. In some of the cases there are expressions as to the principles governing the measure of general damages which at first sight seem difficult to harmonise. The apparent discrepancies are, however, mainly due to the varying nature of the particular questions submitted for decision. The quantum of damage is a question of fact, and the only guidance the law can give is to lay down general principles which afford at times but scanty assistance in dealing with particular cases. The judges who give guidance to juries in these cases have necessarily to look at their special character, and to mould, for the purposes of different kinds of claim, the expression of general principles which apply to them, and this is apt to give rise to an appearance of ambiguity. Subject to these observations I think that there are certain broad principles which are quite well settled. The first is, that as far as possible, he who has proved a breach of a bargain to supply what he contracted to get is to be placed, so far as money can do it, in as good a situation as if the contract had been performed. The fundamental basis is thus compensation for pecuniary loss naturally flowing from the breach; but this first principle is qualified by a second, which imposes on a plaintiff the duty of taking all reasonable steps to mitigate the loss consequent on the breach, and debars him from claiming any part of the damage which is due to his neglect to take such steps. In the words of James LJ in *Dunkirk Colliery Co v Lever* (1878) 9 Ch D 20, at p 25, 'The person who has broken the contract is not to be exposed to additional cost by reason of the plaintiffs not doing what they ought to have done as reasonable men, and the plaintiffs not being under an obligation to do anything otherwise than in the ordinary course of business.' As James LJ indicates, this second principle does not impose on the plaintiff an obligation to take any steps which a reasonable and prudent man would not ordinarily take in the course of his business. But when in the course of his business he has taken action arising out of the transaction which action has diminished his loss, the effect in actual diminution of the loss he has suffered may be taken into account even though there was no duty on him to act."

These unimpeachable statements of principle are the necessary point of departure in considering any novel issue of damages in contract or tort not involving fraud or intentional wrongdoing. But their practical application calls for observance of other rules. An injured claimant may be compensated only for loss which is held, on investigation of the facts, to have been effectively caused by the breach. He may not be compensated for losses which—though caused by the breach—are too remote, as being outside the reasonable contemplation of the parties at the relevant time as a consequence of the breach. And there are certain heads of damage which, even if they satisfy the tests already listed, are treated by law as irrecoverable: the innocent victim of a breach of contract cannot, for example, be compensated in the ordinary way for the anguish or vexation he suffers as a result of the breach, however direct and foreseeable these consequences may be.'

1   As the quotation in the text indicates, there is no real distinction between contract and tort in this field. But this is not because damages in contract and tort are the same but because the obligation is identical under each regime, ie a duty to take reasonable care, and the function of damages to place the claimant in the position in which he would have been had the defendant exercised such care. This 'performance' based approach has been criticised by some commentators: see Stapleton 'The Normal Expectancies Measure in Tort Damages' 113 LQR 257 at 260.

2   [1995] QB 375 at 401H–403C, CA.

3.2   The application of these traditional principles was questioned by Lord Hoffmann in the same case when it reached the House of Lords:[1]

'The Court of Appeal began its judgment, at pp 401–402 with the citation of three well known cases ... stating the principle that where an injury is to be compensated by damages, the damages should be as nearly as possible the sum which would put the plaintiff in the position in which he would have been if he had not been injured. It described this principle, at p 403, as "the necessary point of departure."

I think that this was the wrong place to begin. Before one can consider the principle on which one should calculate the damages to which a plaintiff is entitled as compensation for the loss, it is necessary to decide for what kind of loss he is entitled to compensation.'

The Court of Appeal was prepared to accept that a defendant should be liable for all losses which were not excluded by the traditional limiting principles. The House of Lords by contrast was not prepared to accept that a defendant should be liable for all losses, however foreseeable, resulting from a transaction if they were caused by events beyond the control of either party. Lord Hoffmann identified another, and logically prior, inquiry which must be carried out before the claimant will recover damages:[2]

'A plaintiff who sues for breach of a duty imposed by the law (whether in contract or tort or under statute) must do more than prove that the defendant failed to comply. He must show that the duty was owed to him and that it was a duty in respect of the kind of loss which he has suffered.'

Accordingly, the loss must also be attributable to the defendant's breach of duty in the sense that it was the direct and identifiable consequence of the breach and within the scope of the duty which should have been but was not performed. We call this the principle of 'attributable loss'—brief discussion of the principle appears in section 3 of this chapter[3] and is developed in greater detail in chapter 7.

1   Sub nom *South Australia Asset Management Corpn v York Montague Ltd* [1997] AC 191 at 210G–211B. In keeping with the official law reports the case is referred to here as *BBL v Eagle Star* or *BBL.*
2   [1997] AC 191 at 211G–H.
3   Paras 3.7–3.10.

3.3   It is clear, however, that Lord Hoffmann did not intend the traditional analysis to be abandoned altogether and his speech has not been interpreted in this way. In *Smith New Court Securities Ltd v Scrimgeour Vickers (Asset Management) Ltd*,[1] which was decided after *BBL v Eagle Star*, Lord Steyn, who embraced the decision in *BBL*, stated:

'It is now necessary to consider separately the three limiting principles which, even in a case of deceit, serve to keep wrongdoers' liabilities within practical and sensible limits. The three concepts are causation, remoteness and mitigation. In practice the inquiries under these headings overlap. But they are distinct legal concepts.'

1   [1997] AC 254 at 283C and 284G. See also Otton LJ in *Bristol and West Building Society v Mothew* [1998] Ch 1 at 25A–D, CA.

2   Damages for misrepresentation

3.4   Before examining the principles which limit the recoverability of damage in detail, it is necessary to refer briefly to the treatment of damages for misrepresentation. Where the claimant's claim is for common law deceit, it is sufficient for him or her to show that the defendant's statement induced the course of conduct which caused the loss and it is unnecessary to show that if properly informed or advised, he or she would have acted differently. According to Hobhouse LJ in *Downs v Chappell*:[1]

'In general, it is irrelevant to inquire what the representee would have done if some different representation had been made to him or what other transactions he might have entered into if he had not entered onto the transaction in question.'

1   [1997] 1 WLR 426 at 441B–C, CA.

3.5   Whilst *Downs v Chappell* was a case in deceit, the point was directly applied to claims for negligent misstatement against solicitors by Millett LJ in *Bristol and West Building Society v Mothew*:[1]

'Where a client sues his solicitor for having negligently failed to give him proper advice, he must show what advice should have been given and (on a balance of probabilities) that if such advice had been given he would not have entered into the relevant transaction or would not have entered into it on the terms he did. The same applies where the client's complaint is that the solicitor failed to give him material information ...

Where, however, a client sues his solicitor for having negligently given him incorrect information, the position appears to be different. In such a case it is sufficient for the plaintiff to prove that he relied on the advice or information, that is to say, he would not have acted as he did if he had not been given such advice or information. It is not necessary for him to prove that he would not have acted as he did if he had been given the proper advice or the correct information. This was the position in *Downs v Chappell*.'

1   [1998] Ch 1 at 11B–D, CA. This does appear to be part of the ratio decidendi of the decision.

3.6   In *Downs v Chappell* the vendor of a business and his accountant falsified financial information about a bookshop in selling it to the plaintiffs and the plaintiffs clearly relied on this information in judging whether to buy it. The judge found that the true financial position, whilst worse, would not have influenced the plaintiff's decision to buy and they would have gone ahead. On this basis he awarded nominal damages. The Court of Appeal reversed his finding and awarded the plaintiffs all the losses flowing from their investment in the business.[1] It hardly lay in the mouths of the defendants (who had deliberately misrepresented the accounts) to argue that their misrepresentations had no significance in law. In *Swindle v Harrison*[2] Hobhouse LJ explained the decision in *Downs*:

'In conclusion, I would add a footnote about the statement in *Bristol and West Building Society v Mothew (t/a Stapley & Co)* [1996] 4 All ER 698 at 705–706, [1997] 2 WLR 436[3] at 443 that *Downs v Chappell* [1996] 3 All ER 344, [1997] 1 WLR 426 was authority for the proposition, and bound to hold, that it was sufficient to succeed in the tort of negligence for a plaintiff to prove that the defendant had made a negligent misrepresentation on which he, the plaintiff, had relied and that it was irrelevant what representation the defendant would have made if he had been careful. That was not in fact the decision in *Downs v Chappell*. In that case, the negligent accountant had purported to verify figures for a business at a time when he had no basis to confirm any figures at all (see [1996] 3 All ER 344 at 349, [1997] 1 WLR 426 at 431). The accurate figures were then unknown and the accountant should have said so. If he had said so, the plaintiff would not have purchased the business. The figures used by the judge were not produced for at least another 16 months, by which time the plaintiff had long since bought the business and become committed to the losses which formed the subject-matter of the action. The court in *Downs v Chappell* reversed the judge on this point because he had based his decision on the later, irrelevant, figure (see [1996] 3 All ER 344 at 351–352, [1997] 1 WLR 426 at 433).'

In many cases the defendant's breach of duty can be characterised as a failure to advise, a breach of contract and as a misrepresentation, and in most of those cases it will make little difference whether the question to be answered is whether the defendant's misrepresentation induced the claimant's conduct or whether he or she would have acted differently if the truth had been known. But there may be cases where the choice of question is a critical one. In such cases—which are likely to be lenders' claims[4]—it remains to be seen whether the distinction made in *Mothew* will survive Hobhouse LJ's 'footnote' in *Swindle v Harrison*. No justification was given in *Mothew* for extending the treatment of causation in deceit to claims of negligence based on misrepresentation and the introduction of a different test into an already complex area may produce little more than confusion. This distinction has not been observed traditionally and it is not drawn in the discussion below.

1   [1997] 1 WLR 426 at 443G–444H Hobhouse LJ introduced a 'qualification' to fraud damages which reflected the concern that damages might compensate the plaintiffs not for the consequences of the tort but for the consequences of market forces and their own misjudgment. On the facts this did not influence the outcome, but the approach was disapproved by Lord Steyn in *Smith New Court Securities Ltd v Scrimgeour Vickers Ltd* [1997] AC 254 at 283B–G.
2   [1997] 4 All ER 705 at 728g–j, CA.
3   Now reported at [1998] Ch 1.
4   Where the solicitor usually completes a report on title making certain standard representations to the lender. It is explored further in that context.

3   Attributable loss

3.7   The difficulty posed by the plaintiff's losses in *BBL* was that the defendant's valuation was simply one element in a sophisticated transaction which involved a number of risks. Having elected to take these risks the lender became locked into a venture and acquired security which then fell in value as a consequence of market forces wholly unconnected with the valuation. As Phillips J noted at first instance:[1]

'Where a party is contemplating a commercial venture which involves a number of heads of risk and obtains professional advice in respect of one head of risk before embarking on the venture, I do not see why the negligent advice in respect of that head of risk should, in effect, make the adviser the underwriter of the entire venture.'

Lord Hoffmann, when commenting later on *BBL* in *Nykredit Mortgage Bank plc v Edward Erdman Group Ltd*,[2] said:

'The principle approved by the House was that the valuer owes no duty of care to the lender in respect of his entering into the transaction as such and that it is therefore insufficient, for the purpose of establishing liability on the part of the valuer, to prove that the lender is worse off than he would have been if he had not lent the money at all. What he must show is that he is worse off as a lender than he would have been if the security had been worth what the valuer said.'

It seemed—and seems—unjust that the plaintiff should have been able to recover damages for risks which were part and parcel of its own lending decision, even though it would not have lent (or would not have lent so much) if the valuation had been accurate and both parties could foresee a fall in the market if not the extent of it.

1   [1995] 2 All ER 769 at 806j–807a.
2   [1998] 1 WLR 1627 at 1638D, HL.

3.8   In order to recover damages, therefore, one must begin by identifying the risk or danger against which the claimant sought to protect himself by engaging the defendant. This exercise may result in the defendant escaping liability altogether— as in *Caparo Industries plc v Dickman*[1]—because there is no duty of care. In other cases the exercise may result in the court identifying a particular risk or danger against which the defendant should have protected the claimant and placing a value on it.[2] This should not, however, disguise the fact that the exercise is much the same one:

'A duty of care which imposes upon the informant responsibility for losses which would have occurred even if the information which he gave had been correct is not ... fair and reasonable between the parties. It is therefore inappropriate either as an implied term of a contract or as a tortious duty arising from the relationship between them.'³

An example of this limiting principle is provided by the recent decision of *Europe Mortgage Co Ltd v GA Property Services Ltd*.⁴ In that case, the plaintiff lender claimed damages against the defendant valuer for a negligent valuation. The loss alleged by the plaintiff was not, however, the loss on possession and sale of the mortgaged property but the reduced price which it had been forced to accept for the loan on the sale of its mortgage book to a third party. Applying *BBL* the judge held that this loss was not within the scope of the valuer's duty of care which was limited to the shortfall in the security suffered by the plaintiff on repossession and sale. The defendant had been instructed to provide a valuation as a guide to how much the plaintiff would recover if it had resort to its security but no more.

1   [1990] 2 AC 605.
2   See the analysis of Phillips LJ in *Western Trust & Savings Ltd v Travers & Co* [1997] PNLR 295 at 300A–301C, CA. The case is considered under the head of mitigation below but it also contains a clear illustration of the working of this principle.
3   [1997] AC 191 at 214D.
4   (26 April 1999, unreported) (Moore-Bick J).

3.9   Thereafter it is necessary to consider the extent to which the defendant assumed responsibility to the plaintiff for the losses caused by the risk in question materialising. In the case of each of the defendants in *BBL* the House of Lords found that they were engaged to do no more than provide a piece of information, namely the value of a property on a particular day, and did not assume responsibility for the investment decision. They did not advise the plaintiffs on the creditworthiness of the borrowers or whether to make the loan; they did not advise on the amount which the plaintiffs should lend against the valuation; and they did not advise the plaintiffs on the amount of any provision which should be made against a fall in the market.¹ As a result they bore responsibility only for the amount by which they overvalued the security. Although the provision of information of this kind and the giving of advice both inevitably involve the exercise of professional skill, a professional adviser should only be taken to have assumed the wider responsibility if he or she is required to take reasonable care 'to advise someone as to what course of action he should take'.²

1   Much of the criticism of the decision centres on the—perhaps artificial—characterisation of a valuation as information rather than advice. But it should be borne in mind that at trial Phillips J made an express finding that the plaintiff did not rely on the valuer's valuation to provide any cushion against a fall in the market: see [1995] 2 All ER 769 at 806a–g.
2   *Bristol and West Building Society v Mothew* [1998] Ch 1 at 12E.

3.10   In the field of solicitors' negligence apart from lenders' claims it is more likely that the court will categorise the defendant's role as advice-giver rather than information-provider and the principle is unlikely to be invoked very often to limit recoverable damages. In *BBL* Lord Hoffmann distinguished and approved *McElroy Milne v Commercial Electronics Ltd*,¹ *County Personnel (Employment Agency) Ltd v Alan R Pulver & Co*² and *Hayes v James & Charles Dodd*,³ stating that they were cases in which 'the reasonably foreseeable consequences of the plaintiff's predicament are plainly within the scope of the duty'.⁴ The question arises why in these cases the further consequences did fall within the scope of the solicitor's duty. We suggest that the reason may be as follows. Unlike the valuer, the solicitor in these cases is not a mere reporter of market intelligence. Where, for instance, he or she is instructed to negotiate the terms of a lease or guarantee the role is an active and creative one. The solicitor is engaged to advise the client on the terms offered and to obtain, if possible, a desired result. If the desired result cannot be obtained, it will be the solicitor's obligation to advise the client of the proposed terms and whether to accept them. Even in a case like *Hayes v Dodd*[5] where the solicitor failed to report the existence of a right of way the defendants remained liable for the whole loss. Access was critical to the plaintiffs' business and the solicitor should have explained to the clients the consequences of the legal position which left them in no doubt what their options were. In lenders' claims by contrast the solicitor's duties are normally more limited and the subject of express terms. As a consequence, recovery in full (including market losses) remains possible in some cases, whilst in others the principle of attributable loss limits recovery quite severely. In this area of the law, therefore, the principle is of vital importance and its consequences are considered further in that context in chapter 7.

1   [1993] NZLR 39. This was a case of market fall but Lord Hoffmann stated that '[a]ll the reasonably foreseeable consequences of the situation were ... within the scope of the duty of care' [1997] AC 191 at 219D. The question whether movements in prices or values are too remote is considered in paras 3.33–3.36, where this case is dealt with in greater detail.
2   [1987] 1 WLR 916, CA.
3   [1990] 2 All ER 815, CA.
4   [1997] AC 191 at 218H and 219B–E. All of these cases are considered in chapter 8, paras 8.74, 8.76, 8.81 and 8.91. The argument was expressly raised in *Carter v TG Baynes & Sons* [1998] EGCS 109 (HHJ Prosser QC). The short report indicates that the defendants argued in reliance on *BBL* that they should not be liable for the fall in value of the plaintiff's property where development was prevented by a density covenant which the defendants failed to point out. The judge considered the case to be on all fours with *McElroy Milne*, as approved in *BBL*, and one in which the plaintiff's efforts were a reasonable response to extricate himself from his predicament.
5   [1990] 2 All ER 815, CA.

B   CAUSATION

1   How would the claimant have acted?

(a)   General

3.11   Where the defendant's wrongdoing consists of a positive act the question of causation is 'one of historical fact':[1] did the defendant's act cause the claimant's loss? Where the defendant's negligence is the failure to perform a particular act with a direct consequence, eg the failure to serve a notice or make an application, the connection between negligence and loss will also be clear. However, in many cases, the defendant's negligence involves giving misleading advice or failing to give advice. In those cases, the claimant will only recover substantial damages if the court is satisfied on a balance of probabilities that he or she would have acted on that advice and, if so, in a particular way which would have avoided the loss. In *Sykes v Midland Bank Executor & Trustee Co Ltd*[2] where the defendant failed to advise the plaintiffs about the terms of an underlease, the plaintiffs' evidence was that they would have executed the underlease in that form even if they had been properly advised. They recovered nominal damages only. Salmon LJ said this:[3]

> 'Nevertheless Mr Sykes was a remarkably candid witness. He, no doubt disappointingly, would not say that it would have made any difference had the proper advice been given ... At the end of his evidence it certainly appeared that in his

view it was as likely as not that the plaintiffs would have acted just as they did even if they had had proper advice about the effect of clause 2(xi) of the underleases.'

In *Sykes* the evidence was particularly (and unusually) unequivocal. In most cases, however, the question whether the advice would have made a difference to the claimant's conduct involves quite a sophisticated inquiry. In *Brown v KMR Services Ltd*,[4] Hobhouse LJ stated:

'The question of causation has to be approached on the basis of identifying first what specific advice he ought to have received and then what he has proved, on a balance of probabilities, would have been the consequence of his receiving such advice.'

1   *Allied Maples Group Ltd v Simmons & Simmons* [1995] 1 WLR 1602 at 1610A, CA.
2   [1971] 1 QB 113, esp at 124G–125E and 127B–H, CA.
3   [1971] 1 QB 113 at 127G–H.
4   [1995] 4 All ER 598 at 638d–e, CA, a Lloyd's Name suing a member's agent.

3.12   In most cases this question will depend purely upon the evidence of the claimant, although the court will inevitably wish to be certain that this evidence has not been coloured (whether consciously or unconsciously) with the benefit of hindsight. In *Allied Maples Group Ltd v Simmons & Simmons*[1] Stuart-Smith LJ stated:

'The plaintiff's own evidence that he would have acted to obtain the benefit or avoid the risk, while important, may not be believed by the judge, especially if there is compelling evidence that he would not. In the ordinary way where the action required of the plaintiff is clearly for his benefit, the court has little difficulty in concluding that he would have taken it. But in many cases the risk is not obvious and the precaution may be tedious or uncomfortable, for example the need to use ear-defenders in noisy surroundings or breathing apparatus in dusty ones ...

Although the question is a hypothetical one, it is well established that the plaintiff must prove on balance of probability that he would have taken action to obtain the benefit or avoid the risk. But again, if he does establish that, there is no discount because the balance is only just tipped in his favour.'

1   [1995] 1 WLR 1602 at 1610D and G–H.

(b)   The relevance of reliance

3.13   One critical piece of the jigsaw will be whether the claimant genuinely relied upon the advice given by the defendant. If the claimant took no notice of the advice he or she was given the court will be unlikely to conclude that the advice which should have been given would have made a difference. However, it may be that the chain of causation is more sophisticated than this. In *BBL v Eagle Star*[1] Phillips J found that the plaintiff had not relied upon the defendant's valuation in deciding whether to make a loan because the main purpose of obtaining the valuation was to satisfy Eagle Star, the plaintiff's indemnity insurers. The judge indicated, however, that he would have found the defendants liable if Eagle Star had relied upon the valuation (which they had not) because the plaintiff would not have entered the transaction without Eagle Star's agreement. In *NM Rothschild & Sons v Berensons*[2] the defendants were held liable to the plaintiff even though the plaintiff had not seen the certificate of title contained in the Funds Request and completed by the defendants because 'all those lending would be doing so on the basis that the solicitors had provided to Barclays Bank a true and accurate Funds Request'.[3]

1   [1995] 2 All ER 769 at 793h–796d.
2   [1997] NPC 15, CA.
3   Transcript, p 8 per Saville LJ.

(c)   The burden of proof

3.14   Despite the occasional suggestion to the contrary[1] it appears to be settled by *Wilsher v Essex Area Health Authority*[2] that the burden of proving the causal link between the defendant's act and the claimant's loss is squarely on the claimant. However, this does not necessarily mean that the claimant must call direct oral evidence to show what would have occurred. In *Cavendish Funding Ltd v Henry Spencer & Sons Ltd*[3] it was held that the plaintiff had relied upon the defendants despite the absence of direct evidence from the plaintiff as to what they would have done. The judge was able to reach this conclusion by inference from the agreed or unchallenged documents which were, in the instant case, the plaintiff's loan file, and the Court of Appeal upheld his finding.

1   See *Heywood v Wellers* [1976] QB 446 at 459, CA.
2   [1988] AC 1074.
3   [1998] PNLR 122, CA. In so doing the Court of Appeal followed *O'Donnell v Reichard* [1975] VR 916.

2   How would third parties have acted?

(a)   Loss of a chance generally[1]

3.15   It will be a rare case, as *Sykes* was, in which the claimant's conduct would have been completely unchanged if different and appropriate advice had been given. In some cases, the claimant satisfies the court that he or she would not have proceeded with the relevant transaction if that advice had been given. But in a substantial number of cases the court is more likely to find that the claimant would probably, and often through the medium of the defendants, have gone back to 'the other side' with proposals to deal with the point. In such cases it is rare that either party to the litigation will be in a position to call evidence about how those proposals would have been met. In *Allied Maples* Stuart-Smith LJ (with whom Hobhouse LJ agreed) resolved this difficulty by formulating the following principle: where the claimant's loss depends on showing what a third party would have done if the defendant had given the appropriate advice, the claimant will succeed if there is a substantial chance that the third party would have acted so as to avoid the loss.[2] The court will then quantify damages by discounting the damages to reflect the percentage chance that the loss would have been avoided.

1   The loss of chance cases discussed below are considered in the context of causation because the issues which arose were closely bound up with the conduct of the plaintiff. In the litigation cases discussed in chapter 10, paras 10.48–10.62 the issue is more properly how to assess damages. *McGregor on Damages* (16th edn, 1997) pp 246-256 considers these cases under the rubric 'Certainty of Damage'.
2   [1995] 1 WLR 1602 at 1611B and 1618H.

3.16   A 'substantial chance' in this context means something more than merely speculative. In *Allied Maples* the majority of the Court of Appeal rejected the submission that the court should only award damages where the chance that the third party would have acted in the plaintiff's favour exceeded 50%,[1] but would not lay down any percentage as the lower threshold. Indeed a number of the loss of chance cases involving litigation against solicitors have produced awards of less than 50%.[2] Furthermore even if the claimant establishes not only that there was a substantial chance but also a real probability that the third party would have acted in the way predicted—measured, say, as a 75% likelihood—the court must still discount damages by 25% to reflect the less likely outcome.[3]

1   [1995] 1 WLR 1602 at 1612G–1614D. See also *Mount v Barker Austin* [1998] PNLR 493, esp at 497E–498E, CA.
2   See, eg, *Yardley v Coomes* (1963) 107 Sol Jo 575 (33%) and *Yeoman v Ferries* 1967 SLT 332 (33%).
3   See *Allied Maples* [1995] 1 WLR 1602 at 1614G. See also *Otter v Church, Adams, Tatham & Co* [1953] Ch 280 (Upjohn J) where the damages were discounted by 10% to reflect a relatively improbable outcome. This case is not a reliable guide, however, for the reason stated by Stuart–Smith LJ in *Allied Maples* at 1612C.

(b)   Evaluation of the chance: commercial negotiations

3.17   Although in many cases it may be relatively straightforward to predict a finding that there was a substantial chance of a different outcome, it is often more difficult to predict how the court will evaluate the chance. In *Allied Maples* there was a difference of opinion about the inferences which the court could draw about the conduct of the third parties. Hobhouse LJ stated:[1]

'Negotiations may depend on the will of the parties and neither party was under any obligation at that stage to agree anything. But it is unrealistic to treat the outcome of further negotiation between the commercial parties as arbitrary and wholly unpredictable.'

Millett LJ, who dissented, did not consider that the outcome of commercial negotiations could be considered in the same light as, for example, the likelihood that a husband would have changed his will in favour of his wife. He stated:[2]

'The outcome would then have depended on Gillow's perception of the relative strengths of the parties' bargaining positions, the extent of the risk which they were being asked to assume and the effect on the deal if they refused. These are all subjective matters; none of them is known and none can be inferred.'

In the event it was unnecessary for the Court of Appeal to evaluate the chance.

1   [1995] 1 WLR 1602 at 1620G.
2   [1995] 1 WLR 1602 at 1624F.

3.18   In three recent cases the court has been called upon to consider the outcome of negotiations with a third party in detail. In *Inter-Leisure Ltd v Lamberts*[1] where the defendants, who were acting for the landlord plaintiff, had inserted an upwards downwards rent review clause in a lease when they should have inserted an upwards only provision, the judge had to evaluate two chances: first, whether the tenant would have agreed to an upwards only rent review clause; and, secondly, whether the tenants would have exercised a break option in the lease available for the first three years in the event that the upwards only rent review clause had been inserted.[2] Neither side called the evidence of the tenants on either issue. But the judge was able to find on the available evidence that there was a 75% chance that the tenants would have agreed to an upwards only clause and a one third chance that they would not have exercised the break option, leaving a 50% chance that the plaintiff would have had a lease with an upwards only rent review clause after three years. In *Titanic Investments Ltd v MacFarlanes*[3] where the defendants, acting for the plaintiff vendors, had agreed to a price formula for the exercise of a number of options without instructions, the judge found that, despite the absence of any direct oral evidence from the purchaser, '[t]he parties would have most probably agreed a short extension of time to permit further urgent negotiations to take place' and 'I do not find that there was any substantial chance that [the purchaser] would walk away from the options'. Finally, in *Hartle v Laceys*[4] the defendant solicitors negligently indicated to their client's neighbours that they had failed to register a restrictive covenant with the consequence that their client, the plaintiff, lost an opportunity to sell the property free of the covenant. The principal question for the Court of Appeal was whether there was a substantial chance that the plaintiff would have completed a sale before registration and this turned on four different contingencies: when the neighbour would have registered, whether planning permission could have been obtained, whether the plaintiff would have sold to one interested party or whether he would have sold to anyone else. After a detailed analysis of the evidence on each contingency, Ward LJ found that there was a 60% chance that a sale would have been achieved. It is noteworthy that all of the relevant parties gave evidence: the plaintiff, the neighbour and the potential purchasers. Unlike the judge in *Inter-Leisure Ltd v Lamberts* Ward LJ made no attempt to quantify the chance of each contingency.

1   [1997] NPC 49.
2   On the first review date when the tenants could still have exercised the break clause, the rent was reviewed down by approximately £50,000 per annum.
3   [1997] NPC 105, CA. This point was not argued on appeal (3 December 1998, unreported), CA.
4   [1999] Lloyd's Rep PN 315, CA.

3.19   In each of the three cases, there were a range of possible outcomes. In *Inter-Leisure* the judge accepted that even if the tenants had exercised the break clause after three years, the plaintiff would have been left with a freehold which was more valuable than the reversion to a defective lease. Whatever the actions of the third parties, the plaintiff would have been better off to some extent. Because he had found that there was a 50% chance that the plaintiff would have had a lease with an upwards only rent review clause and a 50% chance that they would have had vacant possession, he awarded to the plaintiff damages to reflect *both* contingencies: first, 50% of the difference between the value of the reversion with a good lease and its value with the lease as granted and, secondly, 50% of the difference between the vacant possession value of the property and the value with the lease as granted.[1] In *Titanic Investments*, by contrast, the judge found that there were, again, two likely outcomes. Instead of calculating damages on each basis and then discounting each by the percentage chance, the judge calculated damages on the following basis:[2]

> 'In this case I have thought it right to examine in some detail what seem to me to be the two most likely outcomes, that is success in resumed negotiations between the parties to arrive at a fixed price and (less probably) reference to an expert. Having done so I must take a broad view and arrive at a figure at some appropriate mean or median point within the range of possibilities, with no further discount because the particular outcome was only a chance; other comparable chances would lie on either side, cancelling each other out.'

In *Hartle v Laceys,* where there was range of possible sales between £350,000 and £410,000, the court also adopted a final figure (after deduction of legal and estate agent's fees) of £360,000. Ward LJ stated:[3]

> 'We have found that Mr Hartle lost the chance of selling his property before the market slumped. We have decided that he had a real chance of selling for £375,000, that being our valuation of the price which would have been agreed between a willing vendor—Mr Hartle—and a willing purchaser in the market conditions of the day. Had such a sale taken place, only the net proceeds would have enured for his benefit and so the estate agent's and solicitor's costs fall to be deducted. Making some estimate of those and perhaps rounding down, I assess the net proceeds of the lost sale to be £360,000. That is my starting point. The parties are at liberty to calculate a more precise figure but I do not encourage it.'

The approach adopted in the latter two cases is analogous to that adopted by the Court of Appeal in *Kitchen v Royal Air Forces Association*,[4] in which the basis on which damages for the loss of an opportunity to pursue potentially successful proceedings was considered. It is suggested that neither approach is necessarily wrong. Some cases may lend themselves to one form of analysis rather than the other. Where there are one or two potential outcomes each of which places the claimant in a better position, the former approach will lead to more accurate compensation. Where, however, there are a number of contingencies and a number of outcomes, it seems more suitable to assess the chances globally.

1   A similar approach was adopted on one particular element of damages in *Blue Circle Industries plc v Ministry of Defence* [1998] 3 All ER 385, CA. See Simon Brown LJ at 414d–415b.
2   Transcript, pp 32–3.
3   [1999] Lloyd's Rep PN 315 at 329, col 2.
4   [1958] 1 WLR 563, CA considered in chapter 10.

3.20   Finally, in *Hartle v Laceys* the Court of Appeal also considered whether the amount which the plaintiff actually achieved from the sale of the property should be deducted from the amount which he would, or might have achieved, before the 40% reduction was made or after the discount. They concluded that this amount should be deducted *before* any discount was applied, thereby increasing the amount of damages. This conclusion was reached on the basis that what the court was really being called upon to value was the chance that the plaintiff might achieve a better price than he actually did:

> 'Look at it another way. When Miss Chaplin lost the opportunity to participate in Mr Hicks' beauty contest, there was nothing left for her. She had lost the only chance she would ever have had of winning the prize. Having lost the chance, she was left with nothing. Mr Hartle did not lose everything when he lost this sale. He lost the chance of the sale but he did not lose the property itself. He retained the chance to sell it at some indeterminate time for some indeterminate price. He lost the chance of getting the excess of a over b but his chance of getting a – b was only 60% and so he should only recover 60% of it'.[1]

1   Per Ward LJ, [1999] Lloyd's Rep PN 315 at 330, col 1.

(c)   Evaluation of the chance: other cases

3.21   In *Stovold v Barlows*[1] the defendants acted for a vendor. On 13 September 1989 a secretary failed to check whether the purchaser's solicitors were on the DX and sent the title deeds to the wrong firm altogether. As a consequence the purchaser withdrew and bought another property. As luck would have it the purchaser looked at the property which he ultimately bought on 15 September 1989 when he was told that the deeds had not arrived. In evidence he said that he would probably not have gone to see it otherwise. The plaintiff vendor claimed the difference between the price agreed with this first purchaser and the price for which the property was ultimately sold. The question of damage turned, therefore, on two questions: first, whether the deeds would have arrived by post on 15 September 1989 and, secondly, whether the purchaser would still have gone to look at the second property in any event. The Court of Appeal held that there was a 50% chance that the purchase would have gone ahead and the plaintiff recovered 50% of the price reduction.[2] In *First Interstate Bank of California v Cohen Arnold & Co*[3] it was found that but for the defendants' negligence, the plaintiff bank would have begun to market its security two months earlier than it did in a falling market. The judge found that 'his best estimate' was that the property would have been sold for £3m. He awarded damages without evaluating the chance that this price would not be achieved and discounting it. The Court of Appeal ruled that there was a two thirds chance that this price would be achieved and discounted damages accordingly. The critical factor was the uncertainty of the market at the time and the speed at which it was falling.[4] This is an odd case, as Sedley J recognised.[5] In the normal case the court will be able to make reliable findings about market values. But in this case, market conditions were so volatile that the judge felt unable to do so.

1   [1996] PNLR 91, CA.
2   The trial took place before *Allied Maples* had been decided and there had been no expert evidence about the probabilities of a postal delivery on 15 September 1989.
3   [1996] PNLR 17, accountant's negligence.
4   See [1996] PNLR 17 at 25D, 30F–31C and 31F.
5   [1996] PNLR 17 at 31D–E.

3   Wider causes

3.22   There are cases in which the connection between the act or omission of the defendant and the ultimate loss of the claimant is even more tenuous, depending not on the vital intervention of a third party but on the correspondence of a number of events, of which the negligence of the defendant is only one. In a number of cases the court has found that although the negligence of the defendant played a part in the loss suffered and, indeed, the loss might not have occurred without it, the negligence did not cause the loss in law but was merely the occasion for its occurrence. It is not easy to identify the relevant test which should be applied nor the significant factors which will determine whether the conduct of the defendant was the cause or the occasion of the claimant's loss. A number of formulations of the relevant test have been tried.[1] But in *Galoo Ltd v Bright Grahame Murray*[2] the Court of Appeal declined to lay down any formal or detailed guidance, preferring to rely on the exercise of common sense.[3] In *Young v Purdy*[4] Leggatt LJ found 'the test of applying judicial common sense an unsure guide'. In *Smith New Court Securities Ltd v Scrimgeour Vickers (Asset Management) Ltd*[5] Lord Steyn stated:

> '[A]s yet, it seems to me that no satisfactory theory capable of solving the infinite variety of practical problems has been found. Our case law yields few secure footholds. But it is settled that at any rate in the law of obligations causation is to be categorised as an issue of fact. What has further been established is that the "but for" test although it often yields the right answer, does not always do so. That has led judges to apply the pragmatic test whether the condition in question was a substantial factor in producing the result. On other occasions judges assert that the guiding criterion is whether in common sense terms there is a sufficient causal connection: see *Yorkshire Dale Steamship Co Ltd v Minister of War Transport* [1942] AC 691, 706, per Lord Wright. There is no material difference between these two approaches. While acknowledging that this hardly amounts to an intellectually satisfactory theory of causation, that is how I must approach the question of causation.'

Despite these expressions of dissatisfaction, causation remains, as Lord Steyn indicated, a pragmatic test based upon the exercise of commonsense.

1   See *Clerk & Lindsell on Torts* (17th edn, 1995) ch 2 passim.
2   [1994] 1 WLR 1360, CA.
3   At 1370A–B, citing *Chitty on Contracts* (26th edn, 1989) Vol 2 at 1128–9 and 1375A.
4   [1997] PNLR 130 at 138B, CA.
5   [1997] AC 254 at 284H–285A.

3.23   The period of time between negligence and loss, the number of intervening events and their importance, the actions of third parties and the conduct of the claimant himself all appear to be relevant in determining whether negligent conduct should be considered an effective cause of loss. In *Young v Purdy* the defendants, who were acting as the plaintiff's solicitors in claims for ancillary relief against her husband, wrongfully refused to continue acting for her and the plaintiff took over the conduct of the litigation herself. She filled in a form incorrectly and then remarried. As a consequence of this combination of circumstances she lost her right to claim ancillary relief for herself. It was held that if the defendants had not terminated their retainer, the loss would not have occurred, but that the termination of the retainer was not the cause of the plaintiff's loss in law. In *Barnes v Hay*[1] by contrast, the defendants were held liable in the following circumstances: they acted for the plaintiff, who had occupied premises informally for some time, in his negotiations for a formal lease; terms were all but agreed when the plaintiff refused to sign and held out for further amendments; as a consequence no lease was ever signed and the rights of the plaintiff remained uncertain; the premises were sold and the new landlord commenced proceedings for possession; after summary judgment was refused him, the landlord took more direct action, interfering with the plaintiff's business and harassing him until he vacated the premises. The plaintiff claimed damages against the defendant for failing to warn him of the legal consequences of his failure to agree terms and to obtain a formal lease in the negotiations some years earlier.[2] It was found that the plaintiff would have executed a lease on the terms offered if he had been so advised and the defendants were held liable both for the plaintiff's losses during this period and his lost profits despite the tenuous connection and the lapse of time between the negligent conduct and the subsequent loss.

1   (1988) 12 NSWLR 337, CA.
2   Negligence was admitted on an agreed basis but it is not clear from the report what occurred after the sale. It appears from p 344 that the new landlord would probably have granted the lease if steps had been taken immediately. It is also not clear whether negotiations had even been broken off and whether the defendants were continuing to act at this time. If so, the causal nexus appears much stronger.

3.24   In each of these cases the loss suffered by the plaintiff was the product of a complicated combination of events which occurred well after the negligent conduct complained of. In *Barnes v Hay*,[1] however, these events, although complicated, all seemed to follow from the initial failure to warn the plaintiff to formalise his rights. They were also well beyond his control. His new landlord would not have attempted to obtain possession had the plaintiff's rights been formalised and registered and had he not failed to obtain possession in those proceedings, the landlord would not have attempted to obtain possession another way. By contrast, in *Young v Purdy*,[2] the plaintiff herself had opportunities to avoid the loss which she could have taken easily.

1   (1988) 12 NSWLR 337, CA.
2   [1997] PNLR 130, CA.

(a)   Trading losses

3.25   In *Galoo* the Court of Appeal affirmed the decision of the judge at first instance that auditors could not be liable to a client for negligently auditing its books where the only direct consequence of the negligence was that the company continued to trade but thereafter incurred substantial trading losses.[1] Although the plaintiff companies would not have been able to trade if the auditors had qualified their audit opinions (because they would have been put into liquidation) there was no evidence that the negligence of the auditors had any causal connection with the losses later incurred. The specific complaint was that they had failed to discover that the stock of the companies had been fraudulently overstated and even if the stock had been accurately stated, the companies would still have made the losses.[2] This decision is, therefore, direct authority for the proposition that a defendant will not be liable for trading losses incurred by a company or business where the negligence in question simply enabled the company or business to keep trading.

1   [1994] 1 WLR 1360 at 1369–1375, CA.
2   See also *Alexander v Cambridge Credit Corpn* (1987) 9 NSWLR 310, CA and, more recently, *Bank of Credit and Commerce International (Overseas) Ltd v Price Waterhouse (No 3)* (1998) Times, 2 April (Laddie J), transcript, para 66: 'The conclusion can be expressed in alternative ways. The defendants' duty of care did not extend this far. This is not the kind of damage from which they had to take care to hold Holdings harmless. Alternatively, the pleaded losses were not caused by the breaches alleged. They were caused by continued trading.' In *Sasea Finance Ltd v KPMG* [1998] BCC 216 (Collins J) the court refused to strike out a virtually identical claim against an auditor for clearance of a dividend which should not have been declared. This point was overlooked in *Galoo*.

3.26   Where, however, there is a direct connection between the negligent conduct and the subsequent trading or business losses, those losses, or some part of them, ought to be recoverable by the claimant.[1] In *British Racing Drivers' Club v Hextall Erskine & Co*[2] solicitors were found liable for failure to advise the board of the plaintiff company that a joint venture agreement for the acquisition of shares had to be approved by the company in meeting because one of the directors was interested in the contract. When the transaction was eventually put to the company at an extraordinary general meeting, the members refused to approve the contract and the plaintiff company took steps to rescind it. After proceedings were commenced the company settled the litigation by reselling the shares to the interested director for £2.1m less than it had paid for them. It was argued that the loss suffered by the company was caused not by the negligence of the defendants but by the poor commercial judgment of the board. *Galoo* was distinguished on the basis that there was a 'very close relationship between the defective advice given and the particular transaction which gave rise to the loss'.[3] There are three striking features about this case: first, having failed to seek the approval of the shareholders before the contract and failed to obtain retrospective approval, the board had no option but to take steps to extricate the plaintiff from the contract as best it could; secondly, the judge did not accept that the ultimate price obtained was a poor one but found that 'it was difficult in retrospect to understand how they can have regarded a price of £5.3m[4] as appropriate given the financial information before them'; and, thirdly, the interested director repurchased the shares for £3.2m, which the judge found to be a reasonable settlement for the company.[5] It was hard to argue that this was simply commercial misjudgment when the director could repurchase the shares at a price substantially lower than that at which the board, of which he was a member, had agreed to sell them.

1   In *Galoo* there was no claim that any of the subsequent losses were caused by defects in the company, eg systems and controls, which the auditors ought to have discovered.
2   [1996] 3 All ER 667 (Carnwath J).
3   [1996] 3 All ER 667 at 682h.
4   The original price.
5   [1996] 3 All ER 667 at 682c and 683j–684g. The case was decided prior to *BBL* in the House of Lords. Nevertheless Carnwath J found at 681f that the loss 'was within the reasonable scope of the dangers against which it was the solicitor's duty to provide protection'. This seems right. Ds should have protected P against the danger that the board would make a contract with a director

of substantial personal benefit to him without the agreement of the company in meeting. Having discovered the contract and elected to rescind it, the substantial risk—which materialised—was that the company would be unable to rescind. It was also clearly an advice case.

3.27   Where the court is not prepared to hold that the whole of the loss was directly caused by the defendant's negligence but at the same time cannot identify or isolate part of it as the direct product of the tort, it may be prepared to find that the defendant's negligence caused a percentage or fraction of the loss. In *British & Commonwealth Holdings plc v Quadrex Holdings Inc*[1] the defendant merchant bank was held liable to the plaintiff for misrepresentation as to the financial standing of a company which the plaintiff acquired. The misrepresentation caused the plaintiff to keep the company when it would have chosen to sell it immediately had it known the truth. For a number of extraneous reasons, including the mismanagement of the company and economic forces, it declined in value until it was worthless. The Court of Appeal held by a majority that the defendant was liable for a proportion of the loss. According to Beldam LJ:[2]

'Precisely to what extent the various causes contributed to the final catastrophic result may be difficult to quantify but the contribution must have been distinct. This is important for the existence of a concurrent cause for the same loss would not relieve Samuel Montagu of liability for the whole of the loss; but to hold them responsible for the intransigence and mismanagement because it operated during the same period would be to hold them liable for loss which they have not caused. The mere fact that it is not arithmetically possible to apportion loss between a period when it would be reasonable to regard Samuel Montagu's negligent misstatement as the predominant or effective cause and the period when the mismanagement of the company had become by far the more effective and the predominant cause seems to me to be no bar to a commonsense division of the loss.'

The defendant was found liable for two thirds of the decline in value of the target company.

1   (10 April 1995, unreported), CA.
2   Transcript at 143A–D.

C   REMOTENESS OF DAMAGE

1   Foreseeability of damage

(a)   Contract and tort contrasted

3.28   A defendant's failure to perform a professional service to his client is, primarily, a breach of contract and the classic formulation of the test of remoteness is that stated by Alderson B in *Hadley v Baxendale*:[1]

'We think the proper rule in such a case as the present is this: where two parties have made a contract which one of them has broken, the damages which the other party ought to receive in respect of such a breach of contract should be such as may fairly and reasonably be considered either arising naturally, ie according to the usual course of things, from such breach of contract itself, or such as may reasonaby be supposed to have been in the contemplation of both parties at the time they made the contract, as the probable result of the breach of it.'[2]

There are clear differences between the test for remoteness of damage in contract and that in the tort of negligence, not least that the question of reasonable foreseeability is tested at the moment of contracting in one and at the moment of damage in the other. Damages, to be recoverable in contract, must either be considered as arising naturally or within the reasonable contemplation of the parties at the date on which the contract was made but, according to Lord Reid in *Koufos v C Czarnikow Ltd*, the position in tort is as follows:[3]

> 'The defendant will be liable for any type of damage which is reasonably foreseeable as liable to happen even in the most unusual case, unless the risk is so small that a reasonable man would in the whole of the circumstances feel justified in neglecting it.'

In professional negligence cases it has usually been unnecessary for the courts to distinguish between the two forms of action and reported cases show that they have tended not to do so.[4] Where a single test has been adopted, it has usually been the test of remoteness in contract.[5] But it should be recognised that the ability to frame an action in both contract and tort does give the plaintiff the option of the more generous rule of remoteness in tort in that rare case where damage would be too remote in contract. In practical terms the form of action is only likely to affect the outcome where the defendant acquires signficant knowledge between the date of instructions and the date of breach.[6]

1   (1854) 9 Exch 341 at 354–5.
2   For the subsequent refinements of the rule and discussion of the level of probability required, see *McGregor on Damages* (16th edn, 1997) pp 243 et seq.
3   [1969] 1 AC 350 at 385. For a full discussion of this point, see *McGregor on Damages* (16th edn, 1997) at pp 161-3.
4   See eg the quotation from *BBL* in para 3.1, *Brown v KMR Services Ltd* [1995] 4 All ER 598 at 620f–621j and 641j–643f, CA and *McElroy Milne v Commercial Electronics Ltd* [1993] NZLR 39, CA per Cooke J.
5   See eg *Simmons v Pennington* [1955] 1 WLR 183 at 187, CA, *Rumsey v Owen, White and Caitlin* (1977) 245 Estates Gazette 225, CA and *Matlock Green Garages Ltd v Potter Brooke-Taylor & Wildgoose* (13 November 1996, unreported) (Wright J), all considered below.
6   There appears to be no reported decision which has turned on this difference.

(b)   Type and extent

3.29   The requirement of reasonable foreseeability (whether in contract or tort) does not require the claimant to show that the defendant knew or ought to have known the precise nature or details of the damage or the precise way in which it was suffered, or the full extent of the loss. It is sufficient for the claimant to show that the defendant either did or should have foreseen that the kind or type of loss in question was not unlikely to occur. In *Banque Keyser Ullmann SA v Skandia (UK) Insurance Co Ltd*[1] Slade LJ considered it unnecessary that there should be:

> '[F]oresight of the manner and means by which the particular loss was caused or the extent of the loss suffered.'[2]

Thus in *Brown v KMR Services Ltd*, where Lloyd's names sued members' agents for failure to advise them about the character of high risk syndicates of which they were members, and those syndicates had made unprecedented losses, it was argued that the defendants should only be liable for the scale of losses which could reasonably have been foreseen for the syndicates in question. This argument was rejected and the defendants were held liable for all losses however unforeseeable their scale or extent.[3] In *Simmons v Pennington*[4] by contrast, where the defendants were found negligent in failing to advise the plaintiff to mitigate his loss by selling the subject property pending the determination of legal proceedings, the defendants were not liable to compensate the plaintiff for the loss of his premises through fire. The market value of the premises did not go down and it was not reasonably foreseeable either that the plaintiff would fail to insure or that the premises would burn down.

1   [1990] 1 QB 665 at 767E, CA, cited with approval by Staughton LJ in *British & Commonwealth Holdings plc v Quadrex Holdings Inc* (10 April 1995, unreported) CA, transcript 125C.
2   See, to the same effect, *BBL v Eagle Star* [1995] QB 375 at 405D–G, CA, part of which is quoted in para 3.1.
3   See also *Wroth v Tyler* [1974] Ch 30 (Megarry J) at 60G–61A. Increase in house prices was foreseeable but not the steep increase which took place.
4   [1955] 1 WLR 183, CA.

3.30   It is not always easy to define—or even identify—particular types of losses where, as is usually the case, the claimant's losses are all financial. The loss suffered by the plaintiff in *Simmons v Pennington* was obviously of a different type from that which could have been reasonably foreseen, ie physical rather than financial damage, but in most cases such a clear cut distinction is not possible. In *British & Commonwealth Holdings plc v Quadrex Holdings Inc*, Staughton LJ stated:[1]

'I can find very little guidance as to what constitutes a kind or type; in the nature of things no more precise definition is to be expected. It is up to the judge to determine on the facts whether the requirement is satisfied ... Mr Stadlen for British & Commonwealth proposes, as the relevant type or kind in this case, financial loss ... Mr Newman for Samuel Montagu proposes, as a type or kind, reduction in the price obtainable for [certain companies] through a general fall in the market level of value for such companies. He defines the type or kind more narrowly, although he still leaves room for some unexpected developments within his framework. Who is right? In my opinion the law does not answer this question. It is a matter for the judge to decide, which test fairly compensates British & Commonwealth for their loss.'

1   Transcript at 124G–125A, 125F–G, 126A (10 April 1995, unreported), CA.

3.31   A good example of the pragmatic approach to different 'types' of financial loss which perhaps Staughton LJ had in mind is provided by *Matlock Green Garages Ltd v Potter Brooke-Taylor & Wildgoose*[1] in which the plaintiff claimed damages against the defendant for failure to renew a tenancy of a garage and filling station under the Landlord and Tenant Act 1954, Pt II. The plaintiff recovered damages for losing the garage. But as a consequence of the plaintiff's loss of this one site, it also had to close two related businesses, a body shop and a vehicle recovery service, both of which were undertaken from different premises. Wright J stated:

'While the Defendant firm of solicitors carried on practice in Matlock, and may perhaps be taken to have known that the business of the Plaintiff company was not restricted to the service station and garage located on the Matlock Green sites, there is no evidence before me and I do not consider that I would be justified in assuming that the Defendants had any knowledge, whether at the time of the contract or at the time of its breach, of the detailed inter-relationship between the various elements of the Plaintiffs' business, still less the extent to which, as it is claimed, the continued commercial viability of any of the elements of the Plaintiffs' business depended upon the continuing existence of other parts thereof.'

Given this indication that the court will not bracket or pigeon-hole types of financial loss into fixed categories, only one or two types of loss call for special mention.

1   Transcript at 18–19 (13 November 1996, unreported).

(c) Market changes

3.32 Whether or not they can be attributed to the defendant's breach of duty, increases or decreases in price or cost due to market forces which the claimant is forced to bear as a direct consequence of the defendant's negligence, however unexpected, are ordinarily treated as within the contemplation of the parties. The reason for this was given by Sir Thomas Bingham MR in *BBL v Eagle Star*:[1]

'[I]t has not been argued that L's claim for any part of his loss, including that part attributable to the fall in the property market, is too remote. The reason is obvious. L and V know, as everyone knows, that in any market prices may move upwards or downwards. That is the essence of a market. No one in recent times has expected property prices to remain stable over a prolonged period. It was plainly foreseeable that if, on the strength of an overvaluation by V, L entered into a mortgage transaction he would not otherwise have entertained, his risk of loss would be increased if the market moved downwards or reduced if it moved upwards.'

1   [1995] QB 375 at 405F, CA.

3.33 Increases in market prices have been considered in a number of cases. In *Inder Lynch Devoy & Co v Subritzky*[1] it was held that the plaintiff was not entitled to recover the increased building costs of his new property (which were due to a lack of local builders and a building boom) from the defendants, whose negligence caused a substantial delay in completing the sale of his property. Such losses were held to be too remote notwithstanding that the defendants knew of the plaintiff's intention; that building costs were a matter of public knowledge; and that a direct causal link was found between the defendants' breach and the plaintiff's loss. In *King v Hawkins & Co*[2] by contrast, where the plaintiff also sought to recover increased building costs, these costs were held to be recoverable. And in *Snipper v Enever Freeman & Co*[3] where the defendants failed to serve a notice under the Leasehold Reform Act 1967 within time and the plaintiff took steps to mitigate her loss by obtaining an extended lease, damages were assessed on the date when she had obtained the lease and was first able to sell her property. Sheen J stated:

'Between 1983 and 1990 the ravages of inflation have reduced the purchasing power of the pound sterling. This is reflected in higher prices. In my judgment it would be wrong in principle and unjust to assess the plaintiff's damages by calculating the loss at July 1983 [when the breach occurred] and then subtracting from that figure the benefit obtained from the steps in mitigation expressed in pounds which have lost much of their value. There should be only one date on which damages are assessed.'

1   [1979] 1 NZLR 87, CA. The correctness of the decision is in doubt: see para 3.35.
2   (1982) Times, 28 January (Mars Jones J).
3   [1991] 2 EGLR 270 at 271J (Sheen J).

3.34 A distinction may need to be drawn, however, between genuine market movements and the effect of inflation. In *Endhill Pty Ltd v Grasso, Searles & Romano*[1] the plaintiff sought damages for the delayed acquisition of a property. The difference in prices was caused purely by inflation and the diminishing value of money. The plaintiff could point to no other loss (eg increased borrowing costs or consequential losses such as loss of interest or finding the deposit) and recovered nominal damages only.[2]

1   [1993] 2 Qd R 136. See also *Johnson v Perez* (1988) 82 ALR 587.
2   See also chapter 8, para 8.72 and note 4.

3.35   Where the effect of a fall in the market is within the scope of the defendant's duty, the court may also have to consider whether such a fall is too remote. In *Rumsey v Owen, White and Caitlin*[1] the Court of Appeal held that it was not. As a consequence of the defendant's negligent advice, the plaintiff agreed to sell three shops with vacant possession in order to set up a factory. He could not obtain vacant possession because his tenants had security of tenure and he should have been advised to sell the properties subject to the tenancies. Because he could not obtain possession immediately, the plaintiff entered into an agreement with the purchaser to give vacant possession at a later date or to repurchase the properties. When he was unable to give vacant possession again, he was obliged to repurchase the properties when they were worth only half the original sale price. He could not complete the repurchase and damages were awarded to the purchaser against him. The Court of Appeal awarded the plaintiff not only the difference between the amount which he could have got for the three shops if he had sold them subject to the tenancies (ie the diminution in value of the properties) but also the damages which he was obliged to pay to the purchaser and which reflected the unexpected collapse in their value. Again, in *McElroy Milne v Commercial Electronics Ltd*[2] the defendant's negligent failure to obtain a guarantee left the plaintiff, who was the developer of a custom-built property, with a less saleable asset and delayed its sale until the market had collapsed. The New Zealand Court of Appeal chose to follow *Rumsey* and not their own decision in *Subritzky*.[3] Hardie Boys J stated:[4]

> '[I]t was plainly foreseeable that the failure to obtain the guarantee at the contract stage left the respondent vulnerable to a change of heart by Studio [the proposed guarantor]; and that its absence at the marketing stage was very likely to cause both delay in finding a purchaser and a reduction in the price that could be obtained; and further, that delay at that later stage left the respondent vulnerable to the vagaries of the market itself. Thus on any view of likelihood, the delay in selling, and the fall in market price occurring because of it, were reasonably foreseeable consequences of this contractual breach.'

1   (1977) 245 Estates Gazette 225, CA.
2   [1993] NZLR 39 at 53, line 11 to 56, line 12. The decision is also considered in chapter 8, para 8.91.
3   [1979] 1 NZLR 87, CA.
4   [1993] NZLR 39 at 45, lines 28–35.

(d)   Special contracts

3.36   In the normal case a defendant solicitor will not be liable to a claimant who loses the benefit of a particular contract as a consequence of his or her negligence unless the solicitor either did or ought to have had the contract in contemplation: see *Pilkington v Wood*.[1] Thus a defendant will not usually be liable to his client for the loss of a profit on resale of property unless he or she knew that the property had been acquired for resale. In a number of cases damages on this basis have been refused[2] but in *G & K Ladenbau (UK) v de Reya*[3] where there was an express finding that the solicitor should have foreseen that a loss on resale was likely, damages for the delay and increased costs on resale were awarded.

1   [1953] Ch 770 (Harman J). This appears to mirror the development of contracts for the sale of land rather than the sale of goods or commercial contracts: see *Diamond v Campbell-Jones* [1961] Ch 22 (Buckley J).
2   See chapter 8, para 8.77.
3   [1978] 1 WLR 266, esp at 289C–F (Mocatta J). See, generally, chapter 8, para 8.77, where the precise circumstances of the case are considered further.

3.37 Having said this, it may be that the court will accept that the price under the special contract which the claimant had lost is persuasive evidence of the value of the property at the date of breach. In *Homsy v Murphy*[1] the Court of Appeal held that the court could take into account a special interest purchaser, to whom the plaintiff proposed to sell the property, in assessing the open market value of a property at the date of breach. In the instant case the plaintiff had a purchaser not only for the land he had contracted to purchase but also his own land at a price which reflected the marriage value of the two interests. The defendant would have known of the existence of that interest and could have foreseen that the marriage of the two would increase their value, even if he was unaware of the purchaser's existence. Hobhouse LJ stated:

'The question of remoteness has to be determined by reference to the type of loss or damage, not its quantum. Provided that the loss is within the contemplation of the parties, it does not matter that its amount may be greater than expected ... Here, as previously explained, the loss was of a type which was within the reasonable contemplation of the parties. That Mr Graf was prepared to pay so much over the odds does not affect the position unless it shows that he was not a commercial purchaser of those premises but some collateral benefactor of Mr Homsy. The evidence was clearly that Mr Graf would have been a bona fide commercial purchaser, albeit a special interest purchaser. Therefore his interest is properly to be taken into account in assessing the value of the freehold in 1988/9.'

1   (1996) 73 P & CR 26, CA. This case is not concerned with negligence but with the breach of a contract for the grant of an option.

2 Intervening acts

3.38 The expression 'novus actus interveniens' is usually used to describe a supervening or intervening event of such significance that it breaks the chain of causation, whether the event is an act by a third party, an act of the plaintiff or a natural event. In claims against solicitors it is rare to find the conduct of a third party or of the plaintiff described in this way, although a number of cases, which are dealt with elsewhere in this chapter, lend themselves to this alternative analysis.[1]

1   See *Young v Purdy* and *Simmons v Pennington* (paras 3.23 and 3.29), and *Hitchens v Higgens & Bacchus* (para 3.43), all concerned with the conduct of the plaintiff. Compare also *British Racing Drivers' Club v Hextall Erskine & Co* (para 3.26), where the conduct of the plaintiff did not break the chain of causation.

3.39 Where there is an act of a third party or of the claimant himself following the defendant's wrong which contributes to the loss suffered, the court is likely to find that it has broken the chain of causation between a defendant's negligence and the claimant's loss if the act was tortious or unreasonable.[1] The question often has to be addressed where the claimant is faced with litigation brought by a hostile third party as a consequence of, or after, the defendant's negligence. The claimant may have no choice and be faced with an implacable third party. In both *Barnes v Hay*[2] and *Connor & Labrum v Regoczi-Ritzman*[3] the conduct of third parties in pursuing court proceedings, even to an unsuccessful conclusion, did not break the chain of causation because it was the solicitor's duty to protect the client against litigation and within his or her contemplation that a failure to give appropriate advice before a transaction might expose the client to the risk of litigation.

1   See, eg *Knightley v Johns* [1982] 1 WLR 349, CA (tortious conduct of third party in personal injury case) *Banque Kayser Ullmann v Skandia Insurance Co* [1991] 2 AC 249 at 279G–280B

(fraud of third party in insurance claim) and *Dixon v Rigby, Golding & Co* (13 March 1995,
unreported) CA (fraudulent conduct of solicitor's employee) noted by Jackson and Powell
Professional Negligence (4th edn, 1997) at 4–189, note 28.
2   (1988) 12 NSWLR 337, CA considered in para 3.23.
3   (1995) 70 P & CR D41–3 (Robert Walker J).

D   MITIGATION OF DAMAGE

3.40   The duty which requires a claimant in both contract and tort to take all
reasonable steps to mitigate the loss suffered as a consequence of the defendant's
breach of duty[1] is merely a reflection of the general compensatory principle. Not only
have courts sometimes approached the reasonableness of the claimant's subsequent
conduct as a question of causation or remoteness, as indicated above, but the
reasonableness of the reaction of the claimant to the breach of duty by the defendant
can also be a critical factor in determining the date on which damages fall to be
assessed,[2] an issue which is considered immediately below. In professional negligence claims the reasonableness of the claimant's conduct tends to be characterised
most commonly as a question of mitigation where the point at issue is whether the
claimant ought to have commenced or continued proceedings against another party
to reduce or recover his loss before turning to pursue the defendant.

1   The classic formulation of the duty by Viscount Haldane LC in *British Westinghouse Electric
and Manufacturing Co Ltd v Underground Electric Rlys Co Of London Ltd* [1912] AC 673
at 688–689 is quoted at para 3.1.
2   See eg *Radford v de Froberville* [1977] 1 WLR 1262 at 1258, in which Oliver J stated that
the rationale behind the rule in sale of goods lay 'in the inquiry—at what date could the plaintiff
reasonably have been expected to mitigate the damages by seeking an alternative performance
of the contractual obligation'.

1   Further litigation

3.41   In *London and South of England Building Society v Stone*,[1] a valuer's case,
Stephenson LJ summarised the principles on which the court would act:

'[The defendant] must prove it was reasonable and when the court has to decide
that question of fact, the [plaintiff's] conduct in not taking steps to reduce the
loss will not be weighed in nice scales at the instance of the party who has
occasioned the loss: see what Lord Macmillan said of the plaintiff's conduct in
taking positive steps to reduce his loss in *Banco de Portugal v Waterlow & Sons*
[1932] AC 452, 506. I bear in mind the illustrations given in *McGregor on
Damages* 14th ed (1980) paras 234–241, of which Mr Twigg relies on paras 236,
238, 239 and 240; and I accept these principles as establishing by authority and
applicable to this case: (1) a plaintiff need not take the risk of starting an uncertain
litigation against a third party, for which *Pilkington v Wood* [1953] Ch 770 is
authority and that includes litigation which may be reasonably certain to result
in judgment for the plaintiff but there is no certainty that the judgment will be
satisfied; (2) a plaintiff need not take steps to recover compensation for his loss
from parties who, in addition to the defendant, are liable to him, for which *The
Liverpool (No 2)* [1963] P 64 is authority. There the other party was a tortfeasor,
unlike the borrowers in this case; but (3) a plaintiff need not act so as to injure
innocent persons, and (4) need not prejudice its commercial reputation.
For both (3) and (4) *Banco de Portugal v Waterlow & Sons Ltd* [1932] AC 452
is authority; (3) is illustrated also by *James Finlay & Co Ltd v Kwik Hoo Tong*

Handel Maatschappij [1929] 1 KB 400 where this court held that buyers were entitled to refuse to enforce their legal rights against a sub-buyer, thereby wiping out their loss on the contract to purchase from the defendant, but injuring their commercial reputation.'

The defendant must satisfy the court that the claimant should have commenced and proceeded with litigation against another party, that those proceedings would have succeeded and a judgment could have been enforced. If the claimant has the benefit of advice from counsel, particularly leading counsel, that he should not pursue a claim, it is highly unlikely that the court would take a different view. Further, even if the claimant could reasonably have proceeded against another professional, eg a valuer or an accountant, *The Liverpool (No 2)* referred to by Stephenson LJ above remains good authority for the proposition that this is no defence to recovery in full by the claimant who is entitled to choose his defendants.

1   [1983] 1 WLR 1242 at 1262–3, CA.

3.42   In *Pilkington v Wood*[1] a purchaser of land brought proceedings against his solicitor when the title turned out to be defective and the defendants contended that the purchaser should have mitigated his loss by suing the vendor on an implied covenant of title. Harman J held[2] that:

'[T]he so-called duty to mitigate does not get so far as to oblige the injured party, even under an indemnity, to embark on a complicated and difficult piece of litigation against a third party.'

London and South of England Building Society v Stone and *Pilkington v Wood* were both followed in *Segenhoe Ltd v Atkins,* which provides an interesting illustration of the principle.[3]

1   [1953] Ch 770.
2   [1953] Ch 770 at 777. For the facts, see chapter 8, para 8.58. It is questionable whether the defect in title would now be found to give rise to a 'complicated and difficult piece of litigation' (even if the issue were to arise again). On the facts, it seems clear that the plaintiff would have been entitled to a declaration and an indemnity against the vendor.
3   [1990] ACSR 691, (1992) 29 NSWLR 569. Claim by company to recover dividends paid to shareholders as a consequence of accountants' negligence held to be too uncertain. P relied on a statement in *Halsbury* (adopted in both *Pennington* and *Palmer)* which Ds contended was wrong. The judge found that support for the position in *Halsbury* was 'far from overwhelming'. Nevertheless he held that P was not obliged to pursue either individual shareholders or the single largest shareholders, whose dividend was A$484,476. It is thought that it is hardly unreasonable to require a plaintiff to test a proposition in *Halsbury* with this sum at stake.

3.43   On the other hand these cases were distinguished in *Western Trust & Savings Ltd v Travers & Co Ltd,* where the plaintiff lender had taken no steps to seek possession of a mortgaged property before turning its attention to the defendants. The litigation in question was 'no more than a possession action with which the plaintiffs in this case were well familiar and which would have been a necessary step whether or not there were defects in the security'.[1] The submission that the court should 'attach significance' to the fact that the defendants would not offer an indemnity or take an assignment of the plaintiffs' rights was also rejected. Phillips LJ stated:[2]

'In my judgment these matters have very little relevance. It is for the court to decide what should or should not reasonably have been done by the plaintiffs in the circumstances of the case not for the defendants or their solicitors.'

In that case it was so clear that the plaintiff should have taken possession proceedings that the offer of indemnity was unnecessary. It is suggested that there will be cases, especially where the claimant is unable to fund the litigation, where the offer of an indemnity will be highly material. Again, in *Hitchens v Higgens & Bacchus*[3] the plaintiffs were found to have acted unreasonably because they had not commenced proceedings for specific performance of a contract which later went off. Finally, in *Walker v Geo H Medlicott & Son*[4] it was held that a plaintiff beneficiary had failed to mitigate his loss by commencing proceedings for rectification of a will before commencing proceedings against the solicitor who drafted it. Although the general principle quoted in para 3.42 was accepted, it was held[5] that where a claimant claims that a solicitor has failed to record a testator's instructions adequately, a claim for rectification should usually be brought before, or instead of, a claim for negligence. This is because the evidence in both actions will be virtually identical.

1   [1997] PNLR 295 at 303G, CA.
2   [1997] PNLR 295 at 304D.
3   NLD 17 July 1997, CA. The short report suggests that the Court of Appeal might have taken a different view of a legal issue to Giles J in *Segenhoe*. The contract specified that P would produce a root of title dating from 1911 when Ps could only do so from 1930. The court found that P could have obtained specific performance despite the contractual provision.
4   [1999] 1 WLR 727, CA. The case is discussed in detail in chapter 9, paras 9.6 and 9.20. Compare *Horsfall v Haywards* [1999] Lloyd's Rep PN 332, CA (considered in para 9.21), where it would not have been worth bringing rectification proceedings.
5   [1999] 1 WLR 727 at 738H–739H, 741E–742H and 743H–744G.

2   Consequential benefits

3.44   A different problem arises when the claimant actually receives a benefit as a consequence of the defendant's breach of duty. This usually occurs where the claimant establishes that he would not have purchased property or entered the transaction in question if he had been properly advised. In those circumstances the court must decide whether the defendant can take the benefit of everything which flows from the transaction including benefits which the claimant has obtained for himself either by good fortune or by his or her own skill and hard work. In *Hussey v Eels*[1] which was applied in *Gardner v Marsh and Parsons*[2] it was held that the plaintiff who had purchased a defective property in reliance on the defendant's misrepresentation was not obliged to give credit for the profit which he had made by obtaining planning permission and selling to a developer and that the negligence which caused the loss did not cause the profit. In *Gardner*, as a consequence of the plaintiffs' negotiations, the landlord repaired their flat some years after purchase and cured the defect which the defendant surveyor had failed to notice. In both cases the plaintiff recovered the difference between the price paid for the property and its market value if its true condition were known at the date of acquisition.

1   [1990] 2 QB 227.
2   [1997] 1 WLR 489 (Peter Gibson LJ dissenting).

3.45   In both cases, statements of principle were avoided. In *Hussey v Eels*[1] Mustill LJ determined the question in this way:

> 'To my mind the reality of the situation is that the plaintiffs bought the house to live in, and did live in it for a substantial period. It was only after two years that the possibility of selling the land and moving elsewhere was explored, and six months later still that this possibility came to fruition. It seems to me that when the plaintiffs unlocked the development value of their land they did so for their own benefit, and not as part of a continuous transaction of which the purchase of land and bungalow was the inception.'

In *Gardner,* Hirst LJ followed this approach finding as follows:[2]

'In my judgment, having regard to the intervening events and to the long interval of time, the repairs executed in 1990 were not part of a continuous transaction of which the purchase of the lease as a result of Mr Dyson's negligence was the inception. Furthermore these repairs undertaken by Guidedale [the landlord] at the plaintiff's insistence were res inter alios acta and therefore collateral to Mr Dyson's negligence.'

Pill LJ was influenced by the fact that the defendants would not have been entitled to take the benefit of any market increase in the value of the property after acquisition and that if the plaintiffs had wished to sell it at any time before the repairs were done, they would have suffered a loss. He stated:[3]

'In my judgment the present case, on its facts, is on the *Hussey v Eels* side of the line ... Years after the defendant's negligence, the freeholders performed their obligation to the plaintiffs under a contract which the plaintiffs had negotiated with them. That had the effect of rectifying the damage resulting from the defendants' negligence. The benefit came by reason of the performance of a contractual obligation by a third party. The plaintiff had to undertake protracted negotiations with that third party and other third parties, the other tenants in the building. Before that obligation was performed by the freeholder, there was considerable lapse of time in the course of which the plaintiffs, because of the structural defect, were unable to sell the property which they wished to do so in 1988. In my judgment, the facts relied upon as affecting the measure of damages are too remote to be taken into consideration and, on the facts, the judge was entitled to find for the plaintiffs as he did.'

1   [1990] 2 QB 227 at 241D, cited by both Hirst and Pill LJJ in *Gardner* at 500B and 514A. The decision was also followed in *Blue Circle Industries plc v Ministry of Defence* [1998] 3 All ER 385, CA where the defendant was not entitled to take the benefit of the plaintiff's decision to wait and sell in a more favourable market.
2   [1997] 1 WLR 489 at 503H.
3   [1997] 1 WLR 489 at 514C–F.

3.46   In both of these cases, neither of which involved solicitors, the court adopted the diminution in value rule or the valuation method applied at the date of transaction.[1] The courts have shown a greater willingness to depart from this method of assessment in cases of solicitors' negligence, although in four similar cases it has been applied. In *Westlake v J P Cave & Co,*[2] a claim against a solicitor for failure to give adequate advice to a client joining a partnership to develop land, Ebsworth J followed the approach in *Hussey v Eels* and assessed damage at the date on which the plaintiff advanced money to his partner to purchase the land and, therefore, first suffered loss. She ignored the fact that the plaintiff later acquired part of the land and obtained planning permission to develop it. The same approach was also taken in *Owen v Fielding*[3] in which the defendants had failed to advise the plaintiffs about rights of common. They were awarded the difference between the price paid and the actual value of the land at date of purchase. Steel J ignored the profit made by the plaintiffs when they later divided the land, obtained planning permission for another house and eventually sold both properties. In *Shaw v Fraser Southwell*[4] the facts were similar to, albeit stronger than, *Gardner,* and the principle was applied.

1   In *Gardner,* there was evidence that the plaintiffs wished to sell in 1988 at the height of the market before the defect was cured. Perhaps the true measure of damage should have been the difference between the price which was lost and the value at the date of sale.
2   [1998] NPC 3.
3   [1998] EGCS 110.
4   (25 March 1999, unreported), CA.

3.47 Even if the court is satisfied that a benefit formed part of a continuous transaction beginning with the defendant's negligence, the claimant must also show that the benefit goes to the same loss.[1] In one case only has this issue arisen directly for decision. In *Nadreph Ltd v Willmett & Co*[2] the defendant's negligent advice to the plaintiff landlord caused the tenant to vacate the holding and claim compensation for disturbance under the Landlord and Tenant Act 1954, Pt II. The plaintiff did, however, recover possession and was able to make use of the premises. The court held that the defendant was entitled to set off against the compensation the value of having vacant possession of the premises.[3]

1   This was accepted by the whole court in *Gardner* [1997] 1 WLR 489.
2   [1978] 1 All ER 746 (Whitford J).
3   The reasons why Whitford J reached this conclusion are not easy to discern. Two factors were: first, the subsequent occupation arose in the ordinary course of the plaintiff's business: see 751g; and, secondly, the defendant's negligence was the direct cause of the tenant vacating: see 752g.

E   DATE OF ASSESSMENT

1   The breach date rule and beyond

(a)   The date of breach

3.48 The traditional date for assessing damages in contract and tort is the date of the breach of duty in question. This date was and is particularly suited to claims involving the sale of goods where non-delivery or delivery of defective goods will coincide with the claimant's opportunity to accept them or to reject them and look for an alternative means of performance. Although the practice of assessing damages at the date of breach had a long history,[1] in two modern decisions the House of Lords elevated the practice to the status of a rule which was only to be departed from 'if to follow it would give rise to injustice'.[2]

1   '"[T]he breach-date rule" has a long history, possibly, but I think not clearly, extending back to the Year Books' per Lord Wilberforce in *Miliangos v George Frank (Textiles) Ltd* [1976] AC 443 at 459F.
2   *Miliangos* [1976] AC 443 at 468. The citation is from Lord Wilberforce's speech in *Johnson v Agnew* [1980] AC 367 at 401C. The High Court of Australia took a similar line in *Johnson v Perez* (1988) 82 ALR 587. The case is of particular interest because it was a claim of solicitor's negligence. The plaintiffs' claims for personal injury were struck out for want of prosecution. When the claims against the solicitors were heard 10 years later the effect of inflation would have reduced substantially the awards which they would have received (even taking into account interest). By a majority the court affirmed the traditional rule. Damages were assessed at the date on which the actions were dismissed for want of prosecution. Mason CJ concurred that the appropriate date was the date of breach but thought that the appropriate date was the date on which the actions should have been heard.

(b)   The date of transaction

3.49 In a claim for the sale of defective goods the date of breach is usually the date of sale, ie when the seller contracts to deliver the goods and transfer property in them to the buyer, the buyer contracts to pay the price and the transfer of risk takes place. In a claim for defective advice against a professional the date of breach does not necessarily coincide with the date on which the claimant acts in reliance on it, suffers damage or has an opportunity either to mitigate the loss or obtain an alternative performance. But the time lapse between the date of a surveyor's report or a solicitor's letter and the date on which the claimant acts on it will in most cases be a matter of days and of little or no significance. In professional negligence cases in the 1980s and early 1990s the breach date rule was generally applied on the basis that the date of breach and the date on which the claimant becomes committed to the transaction were, for all practical purposes, one and the same. But the fact remains that the court cannot assess damages at the date of breach if the claimant has not entered the transaction at that date, and the facts of *Shaw v Halifax (SW) Ltd*[1] neatly illustrate the point. In that case the defendant valuer valued the property at £37,000 in June 1988 when it was only worth £32,000. In August 1988 the plaintiffs exchanged contracts to buy it for £42,000. By this time the true value had appreciated by £5,000 and the property was genuinely worth £37,000. It was argued that the plaintiffs had suffered no loss because by the time the plaintiffs bought the property it was worth what the defendants had said it was worth. This argument was rejected on the grounds that the plaintiffs had been entitled to rely on the report two months later when they paid what they believed to be the market price of the property given the rise in the market between the date of report and the date of purchase. If the breach date rule had been applied strictly, it would have been impossible to assess loss because the plaintiffs had not committed themselves to the purchase at that date or nominal damages would have been awarded because when they later purchased the property it had the higher value.

1   [1996] PNLR 451.

3.50   *Smith New Court Securities Ltd v Scrimgeour Vickers (Asset Management) Ltd*[1] clarified the law. In *BBL* Lord Hoffmann had stated[2] that there was no general principle that damages were to be assessed at the date of breach although it represented a prima facie rule in relation to sale of goods. Then in *Smith New Court*[3] Lord Browne-Wilkinson stated that the old nineteenth century cases which had established the breach date rule could no longer be treated as laying down 'a strict and inflexible rule'. He continued:

> 'In many cases, even in deceit, it will be appropriate to value the asset acquired as at the transaction date if that truly reflects the value of what the plaintiff has acquired. Thus, if the asset acquired is a readily marketable asset and there is no special feature (such as a continuing representation or the purchaser being locked into a business that he has acquired) the transaction date rule may well produce a fair result. The plaintiff has acquired the asset and what he does with it thereafter is entirely up to him, freed from any continuing adverse impact of the defendant's wrongful act. The transaction date has one manifest advantage, namely that it avoids any question of causation. One of the difficulties of either valuing the asset at a later date or treating the actual receipt on realisation as being the value obtained is that difficult questions of causation are bound to arise. In the period between the transaction date and the date of valuation or resale other factors will have influenced the value or resale price of the asset. It was the desire to avoid these difficulties of causation which led to the adoption of the transaction date rule.'

Lord Steyn agreed that in general the date of transaction 'would be a practical and just date to adopt'.[4]

1   [1997] AC 254.
2   [1997] AC 191 at 220H.
3   [1997] AC 254 at 266C.
4   [1997] AC 254 at 284B.

(c)   The flexible approach

3.51   The citation from Lord Browne-Wilkinson's speech above shows, however, that the date of transaction is not to be elevated into an inflexible rule either. In *Smith New Court* Lord Steyn stressed that it is only prima facie the right date and will usually only be appropriate (if at all) when what he described as 'the valuation method' of assessing damages is adopted. He used this term—which we adopt—to describe what had been commonly known as 'the diminution in value rule'. The new term indicates that it should no longer be accorded rule status but is merely a method of assessing damages which may or may not be appropriate to any particular case.

2   The valuation method

3.52   What Lord Steyn labelled the valuation method originally became known as the diminution in value rule following the decision of the Court of Appeal in *County Personnel v Alan R Pulver & Co*[1] (although it had been steadily applied before that case). It was explained in these terms by Browne-Wilkinson LJ (as he then was):

'The diminution in value rule is concerned with a case where the client has purchased for a capital sum a property having a capital value. Such client thinks it has certain features which render it more valuable. Due to the shortcomings of his professional adviser he is not aware of the fact that it lacked these features.'

1   [1987] 1 WLR 916 at 927F–G.

3.53   From this description it is clear that the valuation method of assessing damages is particularly suited to cases where the claimant has acquired a capital asset such as land or property and it is in the context of conveyancing and real property that it has been applied most frequently in solicitors' negligence cases. If applied at the date of transaction the method often provides a just and convenient way of assessing damages which avoids the difficulties which Lord Steyn later identified in *Smith New Court*. A brief consideration of the conveyancing cases discussed in chapter 8, however, will show that it has never been applied with the same regularity in solicitors' cases as it has in claims against surveyors.[1] Some additional qualifications need to be made therefore about the applicability of the valuation method.

1   See Jackson and Powell *Professional Negligence* (4th edn, 1997) at 3–128 and footnote 39.

3.54   First, in order to recover more than nominal damages, the claimant must show that he would have acted differently if the defendant had complied with his duty. The valuation method has generally been applied where the evidence of the claimant has been either that there would be no transaction or that there would have been some renegotiation, whether of price or terms. But it may be that this was no more than a default or fall-back position. In *Watts v Morrow*[1] Ralph Gibson LJ stated:

'The decision in *Phillips v Ward* was based upon that principle: in particular, if the contract had been properly performed the plaintiff either would not have bought, in which case he would have avoided any loss, or, after negotiation, he would have paid the reduced price. In the absence of evidence to show that any other or additional recoverable benefit would have been obtained as a result of proper performance, the price will be taken to have been reduced to the market price of the house in its true condition because it cannot be assumed that the vendor would have taken less.'

The decision of the Court of Appeal in *Allied Maples Group Ltd v Simmons & Simmons*[2] is illustrative of an increasing willingness on the part of the courts to undertake a more sophisticated analysis of the causative effects of negligent conduct, and in the light of this willingness this fall-back assumption may be made less and less. The valuation method may be appropriate if it can be shown that the transaction would never have proceeded at all. In contrast the method may be inappropriate if the causative effect of the defendant's negligence was that the claimant lost a chance to negotiate a price reduction or some other benefit which can be quantified with reasonable certainty.[3]

1   [1991] 1 WLR 1421 at 1435A–B, CA. Both *Watts v Morrow* and *Phillips v Ward*, which is reported at [1956] 1 WLR 471, CA, are surveyors' cases.
2   [1995] 1 WLR 1602, CA.
3   For two recent examples see *Roker House Investments Ltd v Saunders* (Alliott J, 22 October 1997), briefly reported in [1997] EGCS 137 and *Sonardyne Ltd v Firth & Co* [1997] EGCS 84 (Curtis J).

3.55   Secondly, to begin with it was often assumed without argument that the valuation method or diminution in value rule should be applied at the date of breach. Lord Steyn's comments suggest that it should continue to be applied either at that date or at the date of transaction and not otherwise. We suggest that this generalisation should be treated with some caution. In some recent cases it has been suggested that the valuation method need not necessarily be applied in conjunction with the breach date rule or at the date of transaction but at other dates if more appropriate. The point was left open by Ralph Gibson LJ in *Watts v Morrow*[1] and Sir Thomas Bingham MR would have applied the valuation method at the date on which the defect came to light in *Reeves v Thrings & Long*.[2] As Lord Steyn has said, the valuation method is particularly suitable when coupled with assessment at the date of transaction. This is because the claimant is free to deal with the asset after that point in time and fairness dictates that he or she should take the risk of market movements or inflation or of depreciation in value. But in the light of the flexible approach to be taken to assessment, there may be a greater willingness in the future to divorce the valuation method from the date of transaction, particularly where the claimant does not discover the defect and have the opportunity to remedy it until some time later or becomes locked into the transaction and is unable to extricate himself at all.[3] Again where the values in question fluctuate radically depending on market movements, application of the rule at the date of transaction may seem a random or arbitrary means of assessing compensation and a more representative date might be selected.

1   [1991] 1 WLR 1421 at 1437H–1438B, CA.
2   [1996] PNLR 265 at 278D. See also *Connor & Labrum v Regoczi-Ritzman* (1995) 70 P & CR D41–3 in which Robert Walker J applied the valuation method at the date of trial when the property in question remained unsold; and *Inter-Leisure v Lamberts* [1997] NPC 49 (Michael Harvey QC): damages assessed at the date on which the plaintiffs should reasonably have taken steps to mitigate their loss.
3   See *Blue Circle Industries plc v Ministry of Defence* [1998] 3 All ER 385, CA. The valuation method was applied at the date when the plaintiff ceased to be locked into the asset and became able to sell. See Aldous LJ at 400h–401c. For a brief summary of the complicated facts of this case see para 3.65. (Damages were also discounted for the chance that the plaintiff would have been unable to sell. Damages for stigma were also awarded.)

3.56   The flexible approach was called into question in *Wapshott v Davies Donovan & Co*[1] in which the Court of Appeal upheld the first instance decision of the master to assess damages by applying the valuation method at the date of breach. Two couples who owned flats in a building part of which stood on land to which they had no title, had been awarded the difference between the purchase price of their respective properties and their actual value at the date of breach. Because of the defect in title the actual value of the properties was found to be valueless on that date although the relevant land was later bought in. The plaintiffs submitted that damages should be assessed in accordance with the valuation method but not at the date of breach but at the date when the defect first became apparent to them. It became apparent because they had found purchasers when values had increased substantially and both sales fell through as a direct consequence of the title defect. This submission was rejected because the court found that there was no reason to depart from what was described as the normal rule.[2] The decision appears to be right, although for two reasons which were not articulated in the judgments: first, loss of profit on resale is normally too remote;[3] secondly, it was common ground that if properly advised neither couple would have purchased their properties at all. On this basis there would seem to be no justification for awarding a loss based on the increase in value of the properties. The case should not be seen, therefore, as authority for the wide proposition that the valuation method can *only* be applied at the date of breach or the date of transaction.

1   [1996] PNLR 361, CA.
2   Two points are also worth noting: First, Ds submitted that each flat with its defect in title ought to have been given a substantial value to reflect the fact that the defect in title could be cured and that a speculative purchaser would have paid between 30–50% of its open market value. This submission was rejected on the facts because at the time of the purchase the possibility of curing the defect seemed too remote. Secondly, the court noted that interest had been awarded on a generous basis at first instance to reflect the increase in property prices: see 375E. This award was not disturbed.
3   See para 3.36 and chapter 8, paras 8.77–8.78.

3.57   Thirdly, the valuation method has been applied most commonly in cases concerned with the acquisition of property subject to a physical or legal defect or incumbrance. The reason for using the valuation method is that it appears to put the claimant simply and clearly in the position which he or she would have occupied if the defendant had performed his or her duty. In a simple case where the claimant would not have made the acquisition at all, the measure of damage is the difference between the price actually paid by the claimant for the property believing that the advice which he or she had received was accurate and its true market value subject to the defect or incumbrance.[1] From time to time slightly different formulations have been used,[2] comparing the value of the property without the defect and its actual value subject to the defect. In most cases a formulation of this kind produces exactly the same result because the price paid by a purchaser who was unaware of the defect is the best guide to the value of the property without it. But if the claimant has struck a good bargain and the value of the property without the defect would have been much more, he or she should not recover this additional sum, for this would be loss of bargain damages and only appropriate for breach of warranty. For example, if the claimant purchased a property for £100,000 subject to a public right of way which the defendant failed to identify, and the existence of the right of way would have made it worth £75,000, the claimant should recover £25,000. The fact that the open market value of the property on the assumption that there was no right of way was £125,000 should make no difference. It should also make no difference that the claimant had bought the property to sell on and make a profit. Again, it should make no difference that the claimant had informed the defendant both of the true value and of his intention. For the purpose of the assessment is to put the claimant in the position he would have been in if he had not entered the transaction, not to compensate him for loss of the bargain he hoped to make once he had acquired it. A comparison between the value of the property in its actual condition and its value in the condition in which it ought to have been can, if care is not taken, confuse the contractual and tortious measures.[3]

1   See *Simple Simon Catering Ltd v Binstock Miller & Co* (1973) 228 Estates Gazette 527, CA, per
    Lord Denning: 'In those cases it was the difference between the price actually paid for the property
    on the basis that the advice was good and the price at which it could be bought as it was in fact.'
2   'The measure of damages is the difference, put broadly, between its actual value and the value
    it would have had had it possessed the features which he thought it had' per Browne-Wilkinson
    LJ in *Pulver* at 927G; '[t]he proper measure of damage was the difference in money between the
    value of the property in the condition described and its value as it should have been described'
    per Ralph Gibson LJ in *Watts v Morrow* [1991] 1 WLR 1421 at 1430A, CA. The issue in *Watts*
    was whether the appropriate measure of damage was diminution in value or cost of repair.
3   As in *Ford v White* [1964] 1 WLR 885 (Pennycuick J).

3.58   The valuation method has barely been discussed in lenders' cases and the
principles on which damages are awarded in such cases are given separate treatment.[1]
In chapter 8,[2] we have attempted to classify and explain the real property and
conveyancing cases—in which the valuation method has been more often, if not
consistently, applied—in a way which draws out their factual similarities and
explains why it has or has not been used. It should be noted that this is not a
classification which is adopted by the courts or advanced elsewhere. Often a departure
from the valuation method is justified purely on the basis that an alternative measure
of damage reflects more accurately the overriding compensatory principle.[3]

1   See chapter 7.
2   Paras 8.71–8.80.
3   See eg *Kennedy v Van Emden* [1996] PNLR 409 at 414A and 417G, CA. In *Oates v Anthony
    Pittman & Co* (1998) 76 P & CR 490, CA, Sir Brian Neill (giving the judgment of the court)
    adopted a similar, albeit rather simpler, classification to that adopted by us in chapter 8, paras
    8.71–8.80.

3.59   As a footnote to this discussion, the decision of Phillips J in *Deeny v Gooda
Walker Ltd*[1] shows that the court has—and may in special cases where future losses
are claimed, exercise—a discretion not to assess damages at the date of trial but
postpone further assessment until the future losses have been suffered and can be
quantified.

1   [1995] 1 WLR 1206.

F   INTEREST AT COMMON LAW

1   Interest as damages

3.60   Where a debtor commits a breach of contract by failing to repay a debt on time
but his creditor has not commenced proceedings for its recovery by the time of
payment, there is a special rule that a creditor may not bring an action for damages
under English law to recover interest for being kept out of the money. This rule has
been applied consistently (if reluctantly), despite the fact that it is difficult to defend
in principle. Furthermore the rule has long been understood to apply not only to an
action for the recovery of interest for late payment of a debt but also to damages at
common law generally where what the claimant has lost or incurred is interest on
money.[1] More recently an exception to this rule has been developed whereby a
claimant may recover a sum to compensate for lost interest or interest charges incurred
either as a consequence of a failure to meet a payment obligation or a breach of contract
generally where he or she is able to prove that the loss in question is 'special damage'.
The term in this context means damage falling within the second limb of the rule in
Hadley v Baxendale, ie damage which was in the direct contemplation of the parties

at the time when the plaintiff retained the defendant rather than damage arising in the normal course. Again this artificial distinction has not been defended with any real enthusiasm but it has been recognised at the highest level.[2] In the field of solicitors' negligence at least it seems to be accepted that a claimant may recover as special damage any additional interest charges or the cost of additional borrowings incurred or made necessary by the defendant's breach of duty where the defendant was aware of the plaintiff's indebtedness and this knowledge was specifically pleaded.[3]

1   See *London, Chatham and Dover Rly Co v South Eastern Rly Co* [1893] AC 429 affirmed in *President of India v La Pintada Compania Navigacion SA* [1985] AC 104. The suggestion by Denning and Romer LJJ in *Trans Trust SPRL v Danubian Trading Co Ltd* [1952] 2 QB 297 at 306–7, CA that the rule did not apply generally to awards of damages was rejected by Lord Brandon in *La Pintada* as obiter dicta: see 124F–125E.
2   See *Wadsworth v Lydall* [1981] 1 WLR 598, CA, approved in *La Pintada* at 127A–C and *The Lips* [1988] AC 395 at 423H.
3   See *Hartle v Laceys* [1999] Lloyd's Rep PN 315 at 327–92, CA, cited in *Blue Circle Industries plc v Ministry of Defence* [1998] 3 All ER 385 at 416c–g, CA; and *Birmingham Midshires Mortgage Services Ltd v Phillips* [1998] PNLR 468 (HHJ Bromley QC).

3.61   It also appears to be open to the claimant to recover as special damages the interest which he can prove he would have made if he had received and then invested the money at the proper time.[1] By the same token the claimant would have to plead and prove that the defendant knew that the money which he would have received would be used for investment purposes.

1   See *Swingcastle Ltd v Gibson* [1991] 2 AC 223 at 237A–B. In *Swingcastle* the plaintiff recovered the principal debt from the mortgagor and sought compensation for the loss of interest from the defendants. The 'special damage' point was never explored.

2   Statutory interest

3.62   By statute the court also has a discretion to award simple interest on damages for all or part of the period between the date on which the cause of action arose and the date of judgment or, if payment is made before judgment, the date of payment.[1] In *Pinnock v Wilkins & Sons*[2] the Court of Appeal by a majority confirmed that damages for professional negligence against a solicitor would normally carry interest at the judgment rate from the date on which the cause of action accrued by analogy with the provisions of the Rules of the Supreme Court concerned with default judgments.[3] No special features were identified by the court in selecting the judgment rate as the appropriate rate of interest and the case remains some authority for the proposition that the court should continue to consider the judgment rate as the appropriate rate for an award of interest on damages in tort. In *Watts v Morrow*,[4] however, Bingham LJ stated that interest at judgment rate should be avoided.

1   Supreme Court Act 1981, s 35A and County Courts Act 1984, s 84.
2   (1990) Times, 29 January, CA.
3   Nicholls and Fox LJJ, Ralph Gibson LJ dissented. He would have applied STIA or Special Account rates.
4   [1999] 1 WLR 1421 at 1446, CA.

3.63   In recent years it has become the trend to award interest either at base rate or at base plus 1% or a similar percentage, following the usual practice in the Commercial Court.[1] In *Nykredit Mortgage Bank plc v Edward Erdman Group Ltd*[2] a rate of 0.4% above LIBOR was agreed between the parties and the House of Lords cast no doubt on the appropriateness of this rate. In *Birmingham Midshires Mortgage Services Ltd v*

Phillips[3] it was agreed that the appropriate statutory rate was the LIBOR three month rate. *Pinnock v Wilkins & Sons*[4] is inconsistent with this trend although it should be remembered that the plaintiff was a private individual and there was no evidence about what he would have done with the money. It is unlikely to be followed in most cases.

1 See, eg *BBL v Eagle Star* [1995] 2 All ER 769 at 817j–818a per Phillips J, applying *Shearson Lehman Hutton Inc v Maclaine Watson & Co Ltd* [1990] 3 All ER 723 (Webster J) at 732–3.
2 [1997] 1 WLR 1627 at 1635B.
3 [1998] PNLR 468 (HHJ Bromley QC).
4 (1990) Times, 29 January, CA: see para 3.62.

3.64 In *Platform Home Loans Ltd v Oyston Shipways Ltd*[1] Morritt LJ suggested that in complex claims, particularly where there was also a claim to interest as damages, interest should be the same whatever the basis on which it was awarded. The claim for interest (including the rate) was remitted to the trial judge for further consideration and unfortunately the Court of Appeal was not called upon to comment on the adoption of any particular rate or approach to assessment.[2] If the suggestion in *Platform* is followed and the court is not constrained to award judgment rates, it is rare that a different approach will be called for whether the court is awarding interest as damages or under the section (even though the court has an undoubted discretion under the statute). The claimant may need to plead and prove interest as special damage only where he or she has incurred exceptional rates of interest or would have earnt interest at those rates but for the defendant's wrong. This leaves the question of compond interest. In *Hartle v Laceys*[3] and *Birmingham Midshires Mortgage Services Ltd v Phillips*[4] the court refused to award a commercial lending subsidiary the compound rates which it had incurred by borrowing money from its parent company because there was no evidence that it was within the second limb of the rule in *Hadley v Baxendale* and within the reasonable contemplation of the defendants. The plaintiff was awarded simple interest at the rate mentioned above pursuant to Supreme Court Act 1981, s 35A. In *The Mortgage Corporation v Halifax (SW) Ltd*[5] by contrast it was held that compound interest was recoverable because it was reasonably foreseeable. This was a valuer's negligence claim and the judge held that, because it was a claim in tort, the second limb of the rule in *Hadley v Baxendale* did not apply. It remains to be seen whether the Court of Appeal will uphold the decision. If it does, a claimant who wishes to recover compound interest instead of statutory interest will have to plead his claim in tort. Either way, the anomalies between contract and tort will continue to exist until removed by statute.[6]

1 [1998] 3 WLR 94 at 106E, CA.
2 [1998] 3 WLR 94 at 106H.
3 [1999] Lloyd's Rep PN 315 at 327–9, CA,
4 [1998] PNLR 468 (HHJ Bromley QC).
5 [1999] 1 Ll Rep (PN) 159 at 174–5 (HHJ Lawrie).
6 A detailed discussion of claiming interest as damages is found in chapter 7, paras 7.65–7.69 and 7.74.

3.65 The only other example of a case in which the difference has proved critical is provided by the decision of the Court of Appeal in *Blue Circle Industries v Ministry of Defence*.[1] In that case the plaintiff's land was wrongfully contaminated with radioactive waste by the defendant and a sale of the land in April 1993 went off. The plaintiff was awarded the difference between the amount for which the land would have been sold in April 1993 (£10m) less its value 18 months later when the contamination had been cleared (£4m).[2] The argument about interest turned not on the date from which interest was to run or the rate which was to be applied but rather the amount which ought to carry interest. The plaintiff also argued that during the

18-month period during which it had been locked into the land it should be entitled to recover interest on the whole price in April 1993 (£10m) and not just on the net amount of the damages award (£6m). Given the sums involved this made a significant difference. At first instance Carnwath J accepted the defendants' argument that throughout this period the land had some residual value and interest should only be awarded on the lower figure. The Court of Appeal rejected this argument but refused to award damages on the higher figure for a different reason. The plaintiff had not pleaded a claim for this sum as special damage but had only claimed interest under the statute and on the true construction of Supreme Court Act 1981, s 35A there was no jurisdiction to award interest on this basis at all. The court may only award interest on *'all or any part of the debt or damages in respect of which judgment is given'*; and judgment had not been given for the higher figure (£10m) but only the lower (£6m).[3] This could be significant in pleading terms. In cases where a claimant is locked into an investment as a consequence of the defendant's negligence, he must claim interest as damages if he wishes to recover compensation for loss of the use of his money between the date of breach and resale. In lenders' claims it has been common currency to claim interest as damages for some time. The practice has not been so widespread in other cases.

1   [1998] 3 All ER 385, CA.
2   The tort in question was breach of statutory duty under Nuclear Installations Act 1965, s 7. The facts set out in the text have been simplified slightly. In fact part of the award was discounted by 25% for the chance that the sale would not have taken place. Various items of special damage were also awarded.
3   See Simon Brown LJ [1998] 3 All ER 385 at 415c–417a.

CHAPTER 4

Claims in equity

A THE RELEVANCE OF EQUITY

1 Introduction

4.1 Claims for equitable compensation for breach of trust came into vogue after the Court of Appeal's decision in *Target Holdings Ltd v Redferns*[1] as claims by lenders against solicitors increased. The effect of that decision was widely perceived to be that, if the client could show a breach of duty on the part of the solicitor, it could obtain summary judgment for all its losses without the need to comply with common law rules of causation and remoteness and without facing reductions for contributory negligence or failure to mitigate the loss. Understandably, this was attractive to claimants. This perception was corrected by the House of Lords' decision in the same case[2] but by the time it came to be reported, it had fuelled enormous interest in equitable claims. Claimants began routinely to make claims for breach of trust and breach of fiduciary duty against solicitors in addition to claims for negligence. Because of this it became necessary for the Court of Appeal to examine the extent of liability for breach of trust and breach of fiduciary duty in *Bristol and West Building Society v Mothew*.[3] In the light of this decision and the subsequent decision of Blackburne J in *Nationwide Building Society v Balmer Radmore*[4] the law can now be regarded as reasonably settled. Pleaders contemplating proceedings against solicitors must now, therefore, consider whether such allegations are properly justifiable and whether they provide any practical advantage over claims for breach of contract or negligence.[5]

1   [1994] 1 WLR 1089, CA.
2   [1996] AC 421.
3   [1998] Ch 1.
4   [1999] Lloyd's Rep PN 241.
5   See Millett 'Equity's Place in the Law of Commerce' (1998) 114 LQR 214 at 217: '[P]laintiffs and their advisers have discovered the apparent advantages of alleging breach of trust or fiduciary duty, with the result that a statement of claim is considered to be seriously deficient if it does not contain inappropriate references to these concepts which are often scattered throughout the pleadings with complete abandon.'

4.2 Nevertheless, the interest in equitable claims generated by these decisions still remains and that interest dictates the need for this chapter in a book about negligence. This chapter, therefore, considers claims against solicitors on the grounds of breach of trust and breach of fiduciary duty. Claims for breach of trust arise where a solicitor, who is entrusted with client monies or other trust property, deals with them in breach of his authority. Claims for breach of fiduciary duty arise where a solicitor fails to comply with his obligations as a fiduciary, such as the duty of confidence or the duty to be loyal. Genuine claims for breach of trust or fiduciary duty will continue to overlap with liability at common law in a number of cases but the principles which apply are different both as to liability and as to remedy.[1] These are often difficult and technical areas and it is not possible to provide a full survey of the law of equity in this book. But what can be attempted is a discussion which focuses upon the sort of claim against a solicitor which arises at the same time as a claim for negligence.

1   See Millett (1998) 114 LQR 214 at 225: 'It is misleading to speak of breach of trust as if it were the equitable counterpart of breach of contract at common law; or to speak of equitable compensation for breach of fiduciary duty as if it were common law damages masquerading under a fancy name.'

B   BREACH OF TRUST

1   Express, implied and resulting trusts

(a)   Express trusts

4.3   A large part of the traditional work of a solicitor in the nineteenth and early twentieth centuries consisted of acting as a trustee. The terms of the solicitor's authority, his powers and duties were—and remain today—governed by the express terms of his appointment and the relevant legislation which assisted in the construction or amplification of trust powers and duties.[1] A breach of trust:

> 'may be deliberate or inadvertent; it may consist of an actual misappropriation or misapplication of the trust property or merely of any investment or other dealing which is outside the trustees' powers; it may consist of a failure to carry out a positive obligation of the trustees or merely of a want of care on their part in the management of the trust property; it may be injurious to the interests of the beneficiaries or be actually to their benefit.'[2]

Unlike the law of obligations considered in the remainder of this book, the duties of a trustee do not principally depend upon him or her acting in accordance with a general standard set by the court. Whether a particular act, omission or course of dealing will amount to a breach of trust will turn on the terms of the trust deed or other instrument of the trustee's appointment. Some of the obligations of the trustee will be strict and some will require the trustee to exercise reasonable care. But, as a matter of general law, a trustee may owe a beneficiary neither:

> 'I accept the submission made on behalf of [the plaintiff] that there is an irreducible core of obligations owed by the trustees to the beneficiaries and enforceable by them which is fundamental to the concept of a trust. If the beneficiaries have no rights enforceable against the trustees there are no trusts. But I do not accept the further submission that these core obligations include the duties of skill and care, prudence and diligence. The duty of the trustees to perform the trusts honestly and in good faith for the benefit of the beneficiaries is the minimum necessary to give substance to the trusts, but in my opinion it is sufficient.'[3]

1   Codified for the most part in the 1925 legislation.
2   See *Armitage v Nurse* [1998] Ch 241 at 251A–B per Millett LJ, CA.
3   [1998] Ch 241 at 253H–254A.

4.4   In contrast again to the law of contract or tort, the purpose of a remedy awarded by a court of equity is not necessarily to compensate the claimant for a loss which he or she has suffered. Equitable remedies were, and are, necessarily elastic. The claimant in a 'trust' action may be a beneficiary who believes that a trustee is not acting in his or her best interests but it may be the trustee himself.[1] Moreover, the first aim of beneficiaries who are concerned about the conduct of their trustees is usually to obtain information about the way in which trust affairs have been conducted. The traditional remedies provided by a court of equity to a beneficiary against a trustee who refused to answer his questions was to order an account to be taken of the way in which trust property had been dealt with. Following the taking of the accounts or inquiries, the beneficiary might be entitled to further relief either individually or on behalf of all of the beneficiaries. The nature of the relief and its relationship with compensation and damages are considered in more detail below.

1   See eg *Finers v Miro* [1991] 1 WLR 35, CA.

(b)   Implied or resulting trusts

4.5   Recent decisions have tended to focus on the more informal trust where the solicitor receives and holds money on behalf of his client without express appointment or a trust deed and usually pending the completion of a transaction on which the client has embarked. But the same principles should apply. There has never been very much doubt that a solicitor holds money or property on trust in these circumstances[1] and the terms on which a solicitor holds a client's money are now governed by the Solicitors Accounts Rules 1991.[2] Rule 7 provides as follows:

'There may be drawn from a client account—

(a)   in the case of client's money—

(i)   money properly required for a payment to or on behalf of a client;

(ii)   money properly required in full or partial reimbursement of money expended by the solicitor on behalf of the client;

(iii) money drawn on the client's authority;

(iv) money properly required for or towards payment of the solicitor's costs where there has been delivered to the client a bill of costs or other written intimation of the amount of the costs incurred and it has thereby or otherwise in writing been made clear to the client that money held for him or her is being or will be applied towards or in satisfaction of such costs; and

(v)   money which is transferred into another client account;'[3]

Plainly a payment out of a client account without the authority of the client and in breach of Rule 7 of the Solicitors Accounts Rules will amount to a breach of trust. There is far more difficulty in establishing the other duties of the solicitor trustee under an implied or resulting trust or, perhaps more precisely, breach of which terms of the contractual retainer also amount to a breach of trust. The difficulty is identifying the scope of the solicitor's authority and what breaches of his retainer will bring his authority to deal with the client's money to an end.

1   See *Burdick v Garrick* (1870) 5 Ch App 233 at 240 and 243, CA and *Brown v IRC* [1965] AC 244 for client monies. See also *Twinsectra Ltd v Yardley* (28 April 1999, unreported), CA for the effect of undertakings to hold or apply funds. Whether the trust in question is an implied or resulting trust matters little for present purposes. Where precise definition is necessary see Millett 'Restitution and Constructive Trusts' (1998) 114 LQR 399 at 401. A resulting trust arises 'whenever legal title has been transferred to another and the person who provided it did not intend to pass the whole beneficial interest to the recipient'. See also *Westdeutsche Landesbank Girozentrale v Islington London Borough Council* [1996] AC 669 at 708
2   Dated 16 July 1991. They came into effect on 1 June 1992.
3   Rule 7(b) deals with 'trust money' which is defined by rule 2(1) as money held by a solicitor which is not client's money but which is subject to a trust of which the solicitor is a trustee: ie where the individual solicitor is a trustee of the trust but the trust is not a client of the firm. Rules 7(c) and (d) deal with specific situations with which we are not concerned.

4.6   The law on this issue appears principally in Lord Browne-Wilkinson's speech in *Target*[1] and Millett LJ's judgment in *Bristol and West Building Society v Mothew*.[2]

In the former Lord Browne-Wilkinson made clear that, although a solicitor did hold his client's money on trust, the nature of the trust was different from a traditional trust and that not every duty owed by the solicitor was a trust obligation. The solicitor held the lender's money on a bare trust and Lord Browne-Wilkinson said that this was[3]

> '[B]ut one incident of a wider, commercial transaction involving agency. In the case of moneys paid to a solicitor by a client as part of a conveyancing transaction, the purpose of that transaction is to achieve the commercial object of the client, be it the acquisition of property or the lending of money on security. The depositing of money with the solicitor is but one aspect of the arrangements between the parties, such arrangements being for the most part contractual. Thus, the circumstances under which the solicitor can part with money from client account are regulated by the instructions given by the client: they are not part of the trusts on which the property is held. I do not intend to cast any doubt on the fact that moneys held by solicitors on client account are trust moneys, or that the basic equitable principles apply to any breach of such trust by solicitors. But the basic equitable principle applicable to breach of trust is that the beneficiary is entitled to be compensated for any loss he would not have suffered but for the breach.'

1   [1996] AC 421 at 428. Each of the other law lords agreed with him.
2   [1998] Ch 1 at 22D to 24D, CA.
3   [1996] AC 421 at 436B–D.

4.7   This passage suggests that arguments to the effect that the terms of the trust are the same as the terms of the solicitor's contract, so that any breach of contract automatically amounts to a breach of trust, are wrong. In the case of money paid by a purchaser or a lender, the purpose of the arrangement is presumably to be taken as the acquisition of an asset or the lending of money on security. The question which arises is this: if it is wrong to suppose that any breach of contract amounts to a breach of trust, what does amount to a breach of trust? In *Target*, the defendants had admitted breach of trust, and so strictly speaking the House of Lords did not need to deal with that issue. Lord Browne-Wilkinson did, however, set out the basis of the concession, and it looks from his judgment as if he considered that it had been properly made. The facts of *Target* were very briefly as follows. A was selling a property to B for £775,000; B was then to sell it to C for £1.25m; and C was to sell it to D for £2m. The defendant solicitors acted for each of B, C and D, so they knew of the price increase. The lenders, Target, agreed to lend D £1.706m on the understanding that D was purchasing the property for £2m. Of the sum of £1.706m, £1.525m was to be used for the purchase of the property, and the rest for payment of various insurance premiums. Target did not know of the previous contracts. Target instructed Redferns, the defendants, as their solicitors. Target paid the £1.525m to Redferns without giving any express instructions as to its release. Before D had purchased the property or executed charges in favour of Target, Redferns paid £1.525m of Target's money to B. This was the sum which C owed B to purchase the property. There was common ground as to the basis on which Redferns had acted in breach of trust. First, it was agreed that Redferns 'had implied authority to pay the money to or to the order of [D] when the property had been conveyed to [D] and [D] had executed charges in Target's favour'.[1] Further, it was agreed that Redferns acted in breach of trust when they paid away Target's money 'to a stranger who had no contractual relationship with [D] and before completion of the purchase by [D] or the mortgages by [D] to Target'.[2]

1   [1996] 1 AC 421 at 429A.
2   [1996] 1 AC 421 at 429H.

4.8   Strictly speaking anything said as to liability for breach of trust in *Target* is obiter. But we can summarise the basis of the parties' agreement, which the House of Lords appears to have accepted was correctly made, in the following way. The solicitor holds the client's money on a bare trust for the purpose of facilitating the commercial purpose of the transaction, which, in *Target*, was to obtain a valid security over the property which it understood the borrower to be purchasing. His trust obligations depend upon the authority which the court will imply into the retainer to part with his client's money. The court is likely to hold that the terms of the solicitor's authority—and his duty as trustee—are that he may not part with the client's money except to the payee identified by the client or to whom the client is indebted and, where the solicitor is acting on an acquisition or disposal, only upon receipt of the assets, money or documents of title for which the client has bargained.[1]

1   In the case of a mortgage this will be that (a) the property has been conveyed to the borrower, and (b) the borrower has executed a valid charge in favour of the lender. If there is an endowment mortgage, it will probably be a breach of trust to fail to obtain an assignment of the policy: see *Nationwide Building Society v Mian* (12 September 1997, unreported) (Chadwick J).

4.9   Millett LJ considered the matter further in *Bristol and West Building Society v Mothew*.[1] He said that the solicitors held the lender's money[2]

'... in trust for the [client] but with the [client]'s authority (and instructions) to apply it in the completion of the transaction of purchase and remortgage of the property. Those instructions were revocable but, unless previously revoked, the defendant was entitled and bound to act in accordance with them.'

In *Mothew* the lender made an argument to the effect that its instructions to the solicitor were to be construed as making the solicitor's authority to complete the transaction conditional upon his having complied with all his obligations to the lender; thus, as he had failed to comply with all those obligations, it was said that he had no authority to complete; hence, when he did complete, he did so without authority and in breach of trust. Millett LJ rejected this argument. While it was possible that a lender could adopt instructions which would have this effect, the result would be very inconvenient: 'it would in my judgment require very clear wording to produce so inconvenient and impractical a result' because 'no solicitor could safely accept such instructions, for he could never be certain that he was entitled to complete'.[3] Millett LJ added that the defendant's authority to apply the mortgage money in completion of the purchase 'was not vitiated by the misrepresentations for which he was responsible but of which he was unaware'.[4] These dicta were applied in *Nationwide Building Society v Balmer Radmore*[5] in which it was a held that a solicitor who released a mortgage advance before he complied with his express instructions to confirm the purchase price of the property did not commit a breach of trust. It was also held that he had not committed a breach of trust by agreeing with the vendor's solicitors that payment of the balance of the purchase price could be deferred without taking his lender client's instructions. There was nothing in the latter's instructions to indicate that the advance could only be released if the balance of the price was paid at the same time. The practical effect of these decisions is that a failure to comply with a term of the retainer or the making of a negligent misrepresentation will not determine a solicitor's authority to release funds unless there is an express term to that effect, and in the usual case a failure to exercise reasonable care in carrying out the other terms of the retainer, whether it is investigating title or advising the client about the terms of a contract, will not amount to a breach of trust.

1   [1998] Ch 1.
2   [1998] Ch 1 at 22E.

3   [1998] Ch 1 at 22B–C.
4   [1998] Ch 1 at 22D.
5   (1999) Sol Jo LB 58 (Blackburne J).

(c) Fraudulent or dishonest breach of trust

4.10 In *Mothew* it was a term of the defendant solicitor's instructions that he should report any proposal that the purchaser might arrange a second mortgage. The report on title also required him to confirm that the balance of the purchase price was being provided by the purchaser personally without resort to further borrowing. He was told that the borrower intended to leave a sum of £3,350 outstanding to another lender after completion and that it would be secured by a second charge. He failed to report this to the plaintiff and gave the confirmation requested. It was accepted that this failure was in breach of contract but there was no allegation of dishonesty or bad faith, and Millett LJ said that 'on the [lender]'s pleaded case the defendant must be taken to have known the facts at one time but to have forgotten or overlooked them so that they were not present in his mind when he came to complete his report to the society'.[1] In the context of the breach of trust he said this:

> 'The defendant knew that he was a trustee of the money for the [lender]; but he did not realise that he had misled the [lender] and could not know that his authority to complete had determined (if indeed it had). He could not be bound to repay the money to the [lender] so long as he was ignorant of the facts which had brought his authority to an end, for those are the facts which are alleged to affect his conscience and subject him to an obligation to return the money to the [lender].'[2]

It was unnecessary, therefore, for the court to consider what the position would have been if a fraudulent, dishonest or deliberate breach of trust had been alleged.

1   [1998] Ch 1 at 15G.
2   [1998] Ch 1 at 23G–H.

4.11 If the defendant had known that the report on title was misleading when he completed it, the plaintiff could have recovered damages for deceit at common law. But this would also have been a fraudulent breach of trust, which Millett LJ himself defined in *Armitage v Nurse*:[1]

> 'The expression "actual fraud" in clause 15 is not used to describe the common law tort of deceit. As the judge appreciated it simply means dishonesty. I accept the formulation put forward by Mr Hill on behalf of the respondents which (as I have slightly modified it) is that it
>
> > "connotes at the minimum an intention on the part of the trustee to pursue a particular course of action, either knowing that it is contrary to the interests of the beneficiary or being recklessly indifferent whether it is contrary to their interests or not".
>
> It is the duty of the trustee to manage the trust property and deal with it in the interests of the beneficiaries. If he acts in a way which he does not honestly believe is in their interests then he is acting dishonestly. It does not matter whether he stands or thinks he stands to gain personally from his actions. A trustee who acts with the intention of benefiting persons who are not the objects of the trust is not the less dishonest because he does not intend to benefit himself.'

1   [1998] Ch 241 at 251D–G. The judge was defining 'actual fraud' for the purpose of a trustee exemption clause.

4.12   It is hard to think of a stronger example of a trustee intentionally or recklessly disregarding his beneficiary's interests than a fraudulent misrepresentation. But, as Millett LJ was at pains to point out, the notion of a fraudulent or dishonest breach of trust is not co-terminous with a common law action for deceit. In *Alliance & Leicester Building Society v Edgestop*[1] it was held that a solicitor who knew that his borrower client had made fraudulent misrepresentations to his lender client but concealed this fact from his client was liable for breach of trust. This knowledge made it apparent to the solicitor that the transaction was wholly different from the transaction which the lender client had intended to authorise and, accordingly, vitiated the solicitor's authority to release the money. The judge stated:[2]

> 'The case against them is put in various ways but the principal cause of action relied upon is misapplication of the society's funds. It is said that upon receipt of the money from the society, the solicitors held it in trust to apply it in accordance with the society's instructions and subject thereto in trust for the society. The society's instructions authorised the money to be advanced for the purposes of the purchases set out in the instructions and not for some materially different transactions. It also required that the society should, before completion, be notified of matters which ought reasonably to have been brought to its attention. The solicitors knew or ought to have known that the true nature of the transactions had been concealed from the society and I think that there can be no doubt that if the facts known to the solicitors had been brought to the attention of the society before completion it would not have made any of the advances.'

1   (18 January 1991, unreported) (Hoffmann J). The decision was approved but distinguished by the House of Lords in *Target* [1996] AC 421 at 439B–D.
2   At 3G–4C of the transcript.

(d)   Deliberate breach of trust

4.13   *Edgestop* was a strong case. There was no doubt that the borrower was fraudulent or that the solicitor was aware of this fact and party to a criminal conspiracy.[1] In a passage in *Bristol and West Building Society v Mothew*,[2] however, Millett LJ drew a distinction between a dishonest and an intentional breach of fiduciary duty and that distinction taken with the remarks which he made about breach of trust and which we have quoted in para 4.10 have been taken to mean that a solicitor who releases his client's money in the knowledge that he has committed a breach of duty is guilty of a breach of trust even though his conduct cannot be characterised as dishonest or fraudulent, even in the extended sense.

1   The judge's use of the phrase 'knew or ought to have known' should not be taken as authority for the proposition that a solicitor who *ought* to have known that his client was fraudulent but did not was in breach of trust. But if this is what he intended, it appears to have been obiter dictum in the light of his findings of fact and will not stand with the comments made by Millett LJ in *Mothew* discussed below.
2   [1998] Ch 1 at 19E, CA.

4.14   The deliberate but innocent breach of trust is familiar to trust lawyers and in *Armitage v Nurse*[1] Millett LJ said this immediately before setting out the test quoted in para 4.11:

> 'By consciously acting beyond their powers (as, for example, by making an investment which they know to be unauthorised), the trustees may deliberately commit a breach of trust; but if they do so in the interest of the beneficiaries their conduct is not fraudulent. So a deliberate breach of trust is not necessarily

fraudulent. Hence the remark famously attributed to Selwyn LJ by Sir Nathaniel Lindley MR in the course of argument in *Perrins v Bellamy* [1899] 1 Ch 797, 798: "My old master, the late Selwyn LJ used to say 'The main duty of a trustee is to commit *judicious* breaches of trust'".

In that case the distinction was relevant to the terms of an exemption clause in a trust deed. The distinction may also be relevant to the measure of compensation or to the court's decision to relieve a trustee from the consequences of his breach of trust.[2] But a conscious, if innocent, breach of duty by a solicitor will not automatically elevate a claim for negligence or breach of contract into a claim for breach of trust. This turns on the terms of the solicitor's authority to release the money or property. Where it is necessary to imply a term, the court might well distinguish between the release of funds after an inadvertent breach of duty and the release of funds by a solicitor after a conscious or deliberate breach of duty.[3] But it will depend on the precise wording of the instructions and the nature of the breach.

1   See *Armitage v Nurse* [1998] Ch 241 at 251D, CA.
2   Although it is hard to believe that the court would excuse a 'judicious' breach of trust nowadays where the trustee had time to apply to the court for directions. See *Phipps v Boardman* [1965] Ch 992 per Lord Denning MR, CA.
3   The terms of the retainer will make it clear what steps the solicitor has to take prior to completion. Although the parties will not be taken to have intended that the solicitor's authority will be determined by an inadvertent failure to carry all of them out, it is clearly arguable that the parties cannot sensibly intend that the solicitor may complete when he knows that he has failed to comply with his instructions. This was not, however, the view of Millett in 'Equity's Place in the Law of Commerce' (1998) 114 LQR 214.

4.15   The important point is that *Mothew* is not authority for the proposition that a conscious or deliberate breach of his instructions makes a solicitor liable for breach of trust in circumstances where the court would not consider his conduct dishonest. Moreover, there is a real danger of over-elaboration here. It will be a rare case indeed where a solicitor who knows that he has not complied with the terms of his retainer will release funds or transfer property without his client's instructions but nevertheless with the intention of furthering his interests. It will be even more rare that a claimant will be in a position to plead or prove this precise state of mind years after a routine transaction has taken place.

4.16   In most cases, therefore, it will be rare that a claimant has the ammunition to plead or establish a breach of trust of this nature unless he also has the ammunition to establish an *Edgestop* type breach of trust at the same time. And in most of those cases, the claimant may also be able to plead and prove a claim for deceit. The only obvious advantage in advancing a claim for breach of trust will be in those cases where the defendant has made no positive representation to him but has concealed information which he knows it is in the claimant's interests to have when he releases the money. This was in fact the case in both *Target* and *Edgestop*.[1]

1   The terms of the report on title in *Target* were not set out by Lord Browne-Wilkinson in his recital of the facts at [1996] AC 421 at 428-30. The reports did in fact contain no representations as to the price of the property or the identity of the vendor.

2   Constructive trusts

4.17   The label 'constructive trust' has come to represent a basket of remedies for a number of widely differing factual situations. Liability to account as a constructive trustee is commonly imposed where there is an imperfect gift or transfer of property;

where an agent intermeddles in trust affairs; where a third party receives trust property from a trustee or fiduciary in breach of trust; and where a third party is an accessory to a breach of trust or fiduciary duty. The relationship of solicitor and client will not usually give rise to a constructive trust and the principles upon which liability is imposed in any of these given situations are, for the most part, outside the scope of this book.[1]

1   Reference should be made to the standard textbooks and articles on these topics: Oakley *Constructive Trusts* (3rd edn, 1997); Underhill and Hayton *Law Relating to Trusts and Trustees* (15th edn, 1995) pp 42–4, 345–432; *Snell on Equity* (29th edn, 1990) pp 175–197. See also Millett 'Tracing the Proceeds of Fraud' (1994) 107 LQR at 71 and 'Restitution and Constructive Trusts' (1998) 114 LQR 399.

4.18   That said, the liability of a solicitor to his client as constructive trustee was recently considered by the Court of Appeal in *Paragon Finance plc v DB Thakerar & Co*,[1] where the facts were similar to *Target* and *Edgestop* and the defendant solicitors had been involved in a series of fraudulent transactions. Each of them involved a sub-sale in which there was a substantial price rise on the second transaction; in each case the amount of the mortgage advance which the borrower was obtaining from the plaintiff lender was substantially in excess of the price payable by the sub-vendor to the original vendor. The defendant solicitors failed to report these matters. The plaintiff lender had pleaded breach of contract, negligence, and breach of fiduciary duty, although no intentional breach had been alleged. It then sought leave to amend to allege that the defendant was liable to the plaintiff as a constructive trustee of the advance monies outside the normal six year limitation period for breach of trust. The question for the court was whether this claim was statute-barred. Millett LJ, with whom the other judges in the Court of Appeal agreed, analysed the different types of constructive trust in a passage which merits quoting at length:[2]

> 'Regrettably, however, the expressions "constructive trust" and "constructive trustee" have been used by equity lawyers to describe two entirely different situations. The first covers those cases already mentioned, where the defendant, though not expressly appointed as trustee, has assumed the duties of a trustee by a lawful transaction which was independent of and preceded the breach of trust and is not impeached by the plaintiff. The second covers those cases where the trust obligation arises as a direct consequence of the unlawful transaction which is impeached by the plaintiff.
>
> A constructive trust arises by operation of law whenever the circumstances are such that it would be unconscionable for the owner of property (usually but not necessarily the legal estate) to assert his own beneficial interest in the property and deny the beneficial interest of another. In the first class of case, however, the constructive trustee really is a trustee. He does not receive the trust property in his own right but by a transaction by which both parties intend to create a trust from the outset and which is not impugned by the plaintiff. His possession of the property is coloured from the first by the trust and confidence by means of which he obtained it, and his subsequent appropriation of the property to his own use is a breach of that trust. Well known examples of such a constructive trust are *McCormick v Grogan* (1869) 4 App Cas 82 (a case of a secret trust) and *Rochefoucauld v Boustead* [1897] 1 Ch 196 (where the defendant agreed to buy property for the plaintiff but the trust was imperfectly recorded). *Pallant v Morgan* [1953] Ch 43 (where the defendant sought to keep for himself property which the plaintiff trusted him to buy for both parties) is another. In these cases the plaintiff does not impugn the transaction by which the defendant obtained

control of the property. He alleges that the circumstances in which the defendant obtained control make it unconscionable for him thereafter to assert a beneficial interest in the property.

The second class of case is different. It arises when the defendant is implicated in a fraud. Equity has always given relief against fraud by making any person sufficiently implicated in the fraud accountable in equity. In such a case he is traditionally though I think unfortunately described as a constructive trustee and said to be "liable to account as constructive trustee". Such a person is not in fact a trustee at all, even though he may be liable to account as if he were. He never assumes the position of a trustee, and if he receives the trust property at all it is adversely to the plaintiff by an unlawful transaction which is impugned by the plaintiff. In such a case the expression "constructive trust" and "constructive trustee" are misleading, for there is no trust and usually no possibility of a proprietary remedy; they are "nothing more than a formula for equitable relief": *Selangor United Rubber Estates v Cradock* [1968] 1 WLR 1555 at p 1582, per Ungoed-Thomas J.

The constructive trust on which the Plaintiffs seek to rely is of the second kind. The Defendants were fiduciaries, and held the Plaintiffs' money on a resulting trust for them pending completion of the sub-purchase. But the Plaintiffs cannot establish and do not rely upon a breach of this trust. They allege that the money which was obtained from them and which otherwise would have been subject to it was obtained by fraud and they seek to raise a constructive trust in their own favour in its place.'

1   [1999] 1 All ER 400, CA.
2   [1999] 1 All ER 400 at 408–409.

4.19   The reasons why the plaintiffs in *Paragon* sought to amend to plead a constructive trust of the second kind rather than a breach of the implied or resulting trust of the *Target* or *Edgestop* kind are obscure.[1] The relevance of the distinction drawn between the two types of constructive trust is considered in relation to limitation periods elsewhere in this work.[2] For present purposes, however, the question is whether the solicitor's liability to account as a constructive trustee will arise in circumstances any different from those which give rise to a claim of deceit at common law or a claim of dishonest or fraudulent breach of trust of the kind discussed above. This is unlikely. Millett LJ said that the plaintiff's amendments were:[3]

'[B]ased on the same factual allegations as the common law claims for fraud and conspiracy to defraud. The equitable jurisdiction which the plaintiffs invoke is thus the concurrent jurisdiction. The new claims are not different causes of action (which is historically a common law concept) but merely equitable counterparts of the claims at common law.'

If this second type of constructive trust arises simply as equity's response to the same facts which, at common law, would amount to deceit or conspiracy to defraud, then the advantage in pleading them will arise only in relation to matters such as limitation. But in fact, it appears that there is no advantage in advancing the claim in this alternative way. Indeed it may be that there is a distinct disadvantage in alleging a constructive trust against a solicitor in these circumstances.[4]

1   The amendment is not quoted in full in the text of the judgment although it is summarised by Millett LJ: [1999] 1 All ER 400 at 407. The application was heard by Chadwick J at first instance on 4 June 1997 and after both *Target* and *Mothew* had been fully reported. In *Nationwide Building Society v Thimbleby & Co* (16 December 1998, unreported), CA the Court of Appeal allowed an amendment outside the six year period to plead a fraudulent breach of trust of the *Edgestop* kind.

2   See chapter 5, paras 5.70–5.74.
3   [1999] 1 All ER 400 at 406.
4   In *Re Bell's Indenture* [1980] 1 WLR 1217 Vinelott J held that a solicitor's partnership was
    not vicariously liable for the liability of one of its partners as an accessory to a breach of trust.
    In *Agip (Africa) Ltd v Jackson* [1991] Ch 547, CA it was held without argument that one partner
    in a firm of accountants was liable for the assistance of his partner in a breach of trust. In *Dubai
    Aluminium Co v Salaam* (1998) Times, 4 September (Rix J), the judge held that the partners
    in a firm of solicitors were vicariously liable pursuant to Partnership Act 1890, s 10. The matter
    remains in doubt but if the earlier decision is upheld a firm may have a defence to a claim where
    the individual partner (who is unlikely to have cover) does not.

C   BREACH OF FIDUCIARY DUTY

1   Introduction

4.20   The blurring of the distinction between a breach of fiduciary duty and a breach
by a fiduciary of a duty of care is largely historical. In *Nocton v Lord Ashburton*[1] the
House of Lords awarded compensation in equity for a solicitor's failure to advise his
client at a time when the common law gave no remedy for negligent misstatement
causing economic loss. That deficiency was remedied by the decision of the House
of Lords in *Hedley Byrne & Co Ltd v Heller & Partners Ltd*[2] and since then the problem
addressed in *Nocton v Lord Ashburton* has largely become the province of the
common law. In some jurisdictions, most notably New Zealand, the analytical
difficulty of distinguishing between a solicitor's duties at common law and his or her
fiduciary duties has been resolved by expanding the scope of equitable obligations
and awarding equitable compensation on much the same basis as at common law.[3] In
England, however, this approach has not been adopted. In *Henderson v Merrett
Syndicates Ltd*[4] Lord Browne-Wilkinson drew a distinction between the breach by a
fiduciary of his obligations of skill and care and a breach by him of his fiduciary
obligations. The point was taken up and applied by the Court of Appeal in *Bristol and
West Building Society v Mothew,*[5] in which Millett LJ pointed out that:

> '[T]he expression "breach of fiduciary duty" is properly confined to those duties
> which are peculiar to fiduciaries and the breach of which attracts legal conse-
> quences differing from those consequent upon the breach of other duties.'

Thus, not every breach of duty by a fiduciary should be described as a breach of
fiduciary duty and, although fiduciaries owe contractual duties and duties to act with
reasonable skill and care, these duties are not peculiar to fiduciaries. This section is,
therefore, concerned with the special duty of loyalty owed by a solicitor to his client
and enforced in equity.[6]

1   [1914] AC 932.
2   [1964] AC 465.
3   See, in particular, *Day v Mead* [1987] 2 NZLR 443. See also the survey by Blackburne J in
    Nationwide Building Society v Balmer Radmore [1999] Lloyd's Rep PN 241 at 279–282.
4   [1995] 2 AC 145 at 204D–206G.
5   [1998] Ch 1 at 16C, CA.
6   A solicitor also owes his client a duty of confidentiality. Unlike the duty of care this duty arises
    out of the relationship of trust and confidence rather than the provision of skilled services.
    Nevertheless it is protected as much by implied terms in the contract as it is by the intervention
    of equity. It is not considered further in this chapter although various aspects of the duty are
    considered in chapter 7 in relation to lenders, and see also chapter 10, para 10.66. See *Prince
    Jefri Bolkiah v KPMG* [1999] 2 WLR 215, HL and Millett 'Equity and the Law of Commerce'
    (1998) 114 LQR 214.

4.21   A solicitor is a fiduciary in the same way as an agent or a company director because of the relationship of trust and confidence between him and his client. The client is entitled to assume that the solicitor is always acting in his interests and that he will put those interests first. When a conflict arises between the solicitor's personal interest and his duty to the client or between his duties to two different clients, equity is quick to protect the vulnerability of the client both to the competing interests of the solicitor and to the interests of the solicitor's other clients.[1] For the most part equity protects the client's interests by imposing a strict duty of disclosure on the solicitor without proof of dishonest or deliberate conduct or proof of fault. Indeed, where the fiduciary's own interests are concerned equity requires that the solicitor should never act for a client where he has a personal interest in the outcome unless he can show that the transaction is fair and that he has made full disclosure. But even if the solicitor makes full disclosure at the outset of the relationship, he has a continuing obligation of good faith. If he is guilty of a breach of this obligation or of bad faith in the course of the retainer, he will also be liable in equity.

1   See Millett 'Equity's Place in the Law of Commerce' (1998) 114 LQR 215, esp at 222.

2   Conflict of interest and duty

4.22   Any consideration of the fiduciary duties owed by a solicitor to his client must begin with *Nocton v Lord Ashburton*.[1] The plaintiff, Lord Ashburton, sued his solicitor, Nocton, to recover the amount of a mortgage advance which he had made to two developers, Douglas and Holloway, to develop a property in Church Street, Kensington. Nocton had originally owned the property with Lord Ashburton's brother, Alexander Baring, and they had sold it on to the developers. The agreement was conditional on the developers obtaining a loan for £60,000 and the vendors themselves making a further loan of £20,000 on the security of a second charge. Nocton wrote to Lord Ashburton asking whether he would be prepared to make a loan to Douglas and Holloway. Despite Nocton's partners warning him of the risk that the security might be inadequate and reminding him of Nocton's interest in the property, Lord Ashburton lent them £65,000. A year later, Nocton wrote to him again asking him to release part of the security to enable the developers to obtain further finance. He failed to inform Lord Ashburton that the effect of the release was to advance the second charge of Nocton and Baring to a first charge and benefit Nocton personally to the tune of £15,000. When the developers defaulted, the remaining security was wholly inadequate and Lord Ashburton commenced proceedings against Nocton. He sought a declaration that Nocton had improperly advised him in relation to making the advance for his own ends. He also sought a declaration that in relation to the release Nocton 'allowed [him] to believe that he was advising the plaintiff independently and in good faith and in [his] interests'.[2]

1   [1914] AC 932. For the background to the case and some explanation for what may have been a surprising result see Gummow 'Compensation for Breach of Fiduciary Duty' in Youdan (ed) *Equity Fiduciaries and Trusts* (1989) at 57–91.
2   [1914] AC 932 at 939.

4.23   Neville J treated the claim as an action in deceit and dismissed it. The Court of Appeal dismissed the appeal in relation to the taking of the original mortgage (because of the warnings given by Nocton's partners) but found that Nocton had been guilty of fraud in relation to the release of the first mortgage. They ordered an inquiry as to damages and an interim payment of £3,789. The House of Lords affirmed the Court of Appeal's order but on different grounds. Viscount Haldane LC stated as follows:[1]

'I have read the evidence of the appellant and, although it is obviously unreliable evidence, it leaves on my mind the same impression that it left on that of the learned judge who heard it, that the solicitor did not consciously intend to defraud his client, but largely owing to a confused state of mind, believed that he was properly joining with him and guiding him in a good faith.

I cannot, therefore, treat the case, so far as it is based on intention to deceive, as made out. But where I differ from the learned judges in the Courts below is as to their view that, if they did not regard deceit as proved, the only alternative was to treat the action as one of mere negligence at law unconnected with misconduct. This alternative they thought was precluded by the way the case had been conducted. I am not sure that, on the pleadings and on the facts proved, they were right even in this ... There is a third form of procedure to which the statement of claim approximated very closely, and that is the old bill in Chancery to enforce compensation for breach of a fiduciary obligation ...

My Lords, it is known that in cases of actual fraud the Courts of Chancery and of Common Law exercised a concurrent jurisdiction from the earliest times. For some of these cases the greater freedom which, in early days, the Court of Chancery exercised in admitting the testimony of parties to the proceedings made it a more suitable tribunal. Moreover, its remedies were more elastic. Operating in personam as a Court of conscience it could order the defendant, not indeed in those days, to pay damages as such, but to make restitution, or to compensate the plaintiff by putting him in as good a position pecuniarily as that in which he was before the injury.

But in addition to this concurrent jurisdiction, the Court of Chancery exercised an exclusive jurisdiction in cases which, although classified in that Court as cases of fraud, yet did not necessarily import the element of dolus malus. The Court took it upon itself to prevent a man from acting against the dictates of conscience as defined by the Court to grant injunctions in anticipation of injury, as well as relief where injury had been done ...

My Lords, I have dealt thus fully with this distinction because I think that confusion has arisen from overlooking it. It must now be taken as settled that nothing short of proof of a fraudulent intention in the strict sense will suffice for an action of deceit. This is so whether a Court of Law or a Court of Equity, in the exercise of concurrent jurisdiction, is dealing with the claim ... But when fraud is referred to in the wider sense in which the books are full of the expression used in Chancery in describing cases which were within its exclusive jurisdiction, it is a mistake to suppose that an actual intention to cheat must always be proved. A man may misconceive the extent of the obligation which a Court of Equity imposes on him. His fault is that he has violated, however innocently because of his ignorance, an obligation which he must be taken by the Court to have known, and his conduct has in that sense always been called fraudulent, even in such a case as a technical fraud on a power. It was thus that the expression "constructive fraud" came into existence. The trustee who purchases the trust estate, the solicitor who makes a bargain with his client that cannot stand, have all for several centuries run the risk of the word fraudulent being applied to them. What it really means in this connection is not moral fraud in the ordinary sense, but breach of the sort of obligation which is enforced by a Court that from the beginning regarded itself as a Court of conscience.

When, as in the case before us, a solicitor has had financial transactions with his client, and has handled his money to the extent of using it to pay off a mortgage made to himself, or of getting the client to release from his mortgage a property over which the solicitor by such release has obtained further security for a mortgage of his own, a Court of Equity has always assumed jurisdiction to scrutinise his action. It did not matter that the client would have had a remedy in damages for breach of contract.'

1   [1914] AC 932 at 945–6, 952 and 958.

4.24   The speech of Lord Dunedin also makes it clear that the jurisdiction to give relief in equity was derived from the relationship between the plaintiff and the defendant and the potential or actual conflict between their interests which made it fraudulent or unconscionable for the defendant not to act or speak out despite the finding made by Neville J:[1]

'If then we turn to the solicitor's position, we may look at it in two aspects, which is not to look at two different things but to look at the same thing from two different points of view. He has contracted to be diligent; he is negligent. Law will give a remedy. It may well be that if a bill had been filed with a bald statement to the effect above, there might have been a demurrer for want of equity ... But from the other point of view he may have put himself in a fiduciary position, and that fiduciary position imposes on him the duty of making a full and not a misleading disclosure of facts known to him when advising his client. He fails to do so. Equity will give a remedy to the client. This it does quite apart from the doctrine of *Derry v Peek* for in that case there was no fiduciary relationship and the action had to be based on the representation alone.'

1   [!914] AC 932 at 964–5.

4.25   The law was recently restated by Mummery LJ in *Swindle v Harrison*:[1]

'The decision of the House of Lords in *Nocton v Ashburton* is the seminal case, although, as Lord Devlin observed in *Hedley Byrne & Co Ltd v Heller & Partners Ltd* [1963] 2 All ER 575 at 604, [1964] AC 465 at 520, "it is not easy to determine exactly what it decided." That is a common characteristic of pathbreaking cases: it may take a generation or more to work out the ramifications of broad statements of legal principle. It is possible to extract from the speeches the following principles relevant to this appeal. (1) A solicitor stands in a fiduciary relationship with his client. (2) A solicitor who enters into a financial transaction with his client is under a fiduciary duty, when advising his client, to make full disclosure of all relevant facts known to him. (3) Liability for breach of fiduciary duty is not dependent on proof of deceit or negligence. Equity imposes duties in special relationships above and beyond the minimum legal duties to be honest and to be careful. Fiduciary duties rest on the idea of trust and of conduct offensive to conscience. (4) The equitable remedies available for breach of fiduciary duty are "more elastic" than the sanction of damages attached to common law fraud and negligence.'

The facts of the case itself show that the duty of a solicitor to make full disclosure is strict when he proposes to enter into a transaction with his client. The plaintiffs were a firm of solicitors who sought to enforce a charge against their client, the second defendant. Her son, the first defendant, persuaded her to purchase a restaurant and she had agreed to put up her house as security for a loan from the bank. A further loan from the brewery was also required. Once contracts were exchanged and a deposit of £44,000 had been paid, the brewery refused to lend the defendants the balance required to complete. The plaintiffs lent it to them themselves by drawing on a loan facility which they had with their own bank. The venture was disastrous and mother and son lost everything which they had put into the restaurant. The judge found that the plaintiffs were acting in breach of fiduciary duty because they failed to disclose that they were making a profit of 2.5% and £1,000 on the loan and in failing to disclose that they knew that the brewery needed satisfactory references before lending the balance. The argument on causation is considered below but the judge's conclusion when he asked himself what advice other solicitors would have given was as follows:[2]

> 'I can only imagine that they would have been astounded at the offer being made by the plaintiffs in the circumstances and that with full knowledge of the circumstances they would have said "Grab it". It was, after all, a lifeline for them. There is no evidence that a better offer could have been obtained elsewhere. The alternative was to forfeit the deposit.'

1 [1997] 4 All ER 705 at 731h–732a–c.
2 Set out by Evans LJ at 711e–f.

4.26 The facts of *Spector v Ageda*[1] by contrast demonstrate why there is a need for a strict standard which is met only by full and candid disclosure. In that case the plaintiff, a solicitor, sought to enforce a mortgage against the defendant, who was her client and to whom she had lent money. The claim failed both because the transaction was tainted with illegality and because the plaintiff had failed to advise the defendant properly. The money was lent by the plaintiff to repay a loan made by the plaintiff's sister who was an unlicensed moneylender and the rate of interest in the original loan agreement had also been tampered with by the plaintiff herself, who was then acting for her sister. The plaintiff knew that this agreement was unenforceable but she lent the money to the defendant to pay it off. The judge found that the earlier illegalities tainted the later agreement between the parties despite the fact that it was valid in point of form. He also found that the plaintiff was in breach of her duty to the defendant.[2] He said this:[3]

> '[T]he solicitor must be remarkable indeed if he can feel assured of holding the scales evenly between himself and his client. Even if in fact he can and does, to demonstrate to conviction that he has done so will usually be beyond possibility in a case where anything to his client's detriment has occurred. Not only must his duty be discharged but it must manifestly and undoubtedly be seen to have been discharged. I abstain from any categorical negative: the circumstances of life are of such infinite variety. But I can at least say that in all ordinary circumstances a solicitor ought to refuse to act for a person in a transaction to which the solicitor is himself a party with an adverse interest; and even if he is pressed to act after his refusal, he should persist in that refusal. Nobody can insist on an unwilling solicitor acting for him, at all events when there is a conflict of interest.'

1 [1973] Ch 30 (Megarry J).
2 He stated that the plaintiff was guilty of a 'plain breach of duty'. Given the plaintiff's knowledge, she was probably guilty both of negligence and a breach of fiduciary duty. The judge's remarks as quoted in the text above appear to have been directed to the latter.
3 [1973] Ch 30 at 47E–F.

3 Conflict of duty and duty

4.27 The position becomes more complex where the solicitor has no personal interest in the transaction but undertakes to act for more than one client whose interests may potentially conflict with each other and, consequently, the solicitor's duties to each of them. In *Bristol and West Building Society v Mothew*[1] where the Court of Appeal was asked to consider the position of a solicitor acting for two clients, lender and borrower, Millett LJ set out the relevant duties of the solicitor:

'The principal is entitled to the single-minded loyalty of his fiduciary. This core liability has several facets. A fiduciary must act in good faith; he must not make a profit out of his trust; he must not place himself in a position where his duty and his interest may conflict; he may not act for his own benefit or the benefit of a third person without the informed consent of his principal. This is not intended to be an exhaustive list but it is sufficient to indicate the nature of fiduciary obligations. As Dr Finn pointed out in his classic work *Fiduciary Obligations* (1977) p 2, he is not subject to fiduciary obligations because he is a fiduciary; it is because he is subject to them that he is a fiduciary.'

He then analysed the fiduciary obligations owed by a solicitor to each of his clients and we adopt the terms which he used in his judgment: the 'double employment rule', the 'duty of good faith', the 'no inhibition principle' and the 'actual conflict' rule.[2]

1   [1998] Ch 1 at 18A–C, CA, approved by a differently constituted Court of Appeal in *Swindle v Harrison* [1997] 4 All ER 705 at 716h–j and 720a–c.
2   [1998] Ch 1 at 18J to 20G.

(a)   The double employment rule

4.28   The double employment rule usually comes into play at the outset of the retainer when a solicitor is contemplating taking instructions from a client whose interests may conflict with the interests of another of his or her clients. The rule requires that the solicitor may not act for two principals whose interests may come into conflict with each other unless he or she obtains the informed consent of each client and a failure to comply with the rule also constitutes a breach of fiduciary duty without proof of fault or bad faith.[1] In *Clark Boyce v Mouat*[2] Lord Jauncey set out the rule in the following terms:

'There is no general rule of law to the effect that a solicitor should never act for both parties in a transaction where their interests may conflict. Rather is the position that he may act provided that he has obtained the informed consent of both to his acting. Informed consent means consent given in the knowledge that there is a conflict between the parties and that as a result the solicitor may be disabled from disclosing to each party the full knowledge which he possesses as to the transaction or may be disabled from giving advice to one party which conflicts with the interest of the other. If the parties are content to proceed upon this basis the solicitor may properly act.'

In that case the defendant acted for both the plaintiff and her son in relation to a mortgage granted by the plaintiff to secure the son's borrowings. The defendant advised her that her position as guarantor was substantially different to that of her son as the recipient of the loan. He also advised her to take independent advice and told her that he could arrange it with a local solicitor. On three occasions in total he raised the question of independent advice.[3] It was held that the defendant was not in breach of fiduciary duty by continuing to act for the plaintiff and without revealing that her son's own solicitor had refused to act.[4]

1   See *Mothew* [1998] Ch 1 at 19A: 'Breach of the rule automatically constitutes a breach of fiduciary duty.'
2   [1994] 1 AC 428 at 435F–H.
3   See [1994] 1 AC 428 at 433A–C and 433G.
4   See also *Spikins v Wickham & Fine* (18 November 1998, unreported) (Peter Leaver QC) for another example where the court held that informed consent had been given.

4.29   Obviously, the precise nature of the information which it is necessary for the solicitor to disclose will depend on the circumstances of the case but the following is a useful rule of thumb:

> 'For the client to make an informed decision, the lawyer must reveal the existence of the multiple representation. The lawyer must disclose whether there is a regular and continuing relationship with any of the clients, and in these circumstances, the lawyer must recommend that the client obtain independent representation ... The lawyer must disclose the implications of a joint retainer to the confidentiality of information passing between a lawyer and a client. The lawyer must also discuss the consequences of any unresolvable conflict of interest developing during the retainer.'[1]

The double employment rule is plainly relevant when a solicitor agrees to act for lender and borrower or vendor and purchaser and the disclosure requirements in each of those cases are considered elsewhere in this work.[2]

1   See Perell *Conflicts of Interest in the Legal Profession* (1995) pp 90–1.
2   See chapter 7, paras 7.54–7.56 and chapter 8, para 8.01–8.06.

4.30   The rule is not, however, mechanistically applied. Even if the solicitor fails to give any sort of warning, consent may be implied. In *Kelly v Cooper*[1] the plaintiff, who was selling his house in an exclusive neighbourhood of Bermuda, sued the defendant, his estate agent, for failing to reveal to him that she was also acting for the vendor of the next door property and that the purchaser wanted them both to create a 'family compound'. The Privy Council found that this information would have been directly relevant to the price negotiations. However the action failed. Lord Browne-Wilkinson stated:[2]

> 'In a case where a principal instructs as selling agent for his property or goods a person who to his knowledge acts and intends to act for other principals selling property or goods of the same description, the terms to be implied into such agency contract must differ from those to be implied where an agent is not carrying on such general agency business. In the case of estate agents, it is their business to act for numerous principals; where properties are of a similar description, there will be a conflict of interest between the principals each of whom will be concerned to attract potential purchasers to their property rather than that of another. Yet, despite this conflict of interest, estate agents must be free to act for several competing principals otherwise they will be unable to perform their function. Yet it is normally said that it is a breach of an agent's duty to act for competing principals. In the course of acting for each of their principals, estate agents will acquire information confidential to that principal. It cannot sensibly be suggested that an estate agent is contractually bound to disclose to any one of his principals information which is confidential to another of his principals. The position as to confidentiality is even clearer in the case of stockbrokers who cannot be contractually bound to disclose to their private clients inside information disclosed to the brokers in confidence by a company for which they also act. Accordingly, in such cases there must be an implied term of the contract with such an agent that he is entitled to act for other principals selling competing properties and to keep confidential the information obtained from each of his principals.'

In *Mothew* itself informed consent was implied. There was no formal invitation by the solicitor to the lender to consider whether it wished to instruct the solicitor to act for both the lender and borrower.[3]

1   [1993] AC 205, PC.
2   [1993] AC 205 at 214B–D.
3   [1998] Ch 1 at 19B and C: 'It [the society] knew the defendant was acting for the purchasers when it instructed him. Indeed that was the very reason why it chose the defendant to act for it.' 'Its decision to forward the cheque for the mortgage advance to the defendant and to instruct him to proceed was based on false information but its earlier decision to employ the defendant despite the potentially conflicting interest of his other client was a fully informed decision.' See also *Nationwide Building Society v Balmer Radmore* [1999] Lloyd's Rep PN 241 at 260–264.

4.31   By contrast, there may be circumstances in which it is impossible for the solicitor to act for both parties even with the informed consent of both parties. Such circumstances will be extreme and there is no reported instance in English law. In Canada, however, in *Davey v Woolley*,[1] it was held that a firm of solicitors, which acted for three different parties (including a company in which a partner in the firm was personally interested) on the sale of a business, had committed a breach of fiduciary duty by accepting instructions from all three parties and no answer that each of the clients had signed a release acknowledging the joint retainer and the partner's personal interest.

1   (1982) 35 OR (2d) 599 (Ontario Court of Appeal). The leading judgment was delivered by Wilson JA (as she then was).

(b)   The duty of good faith

4.32   As stated in para 4.27, when once a solicitor accepts instructions from two clients with competing interests, each one is entitled to his single–minded loyalty. But it does not follow from this that because a solicitor is retained by two clients, any breach of retainer or negligence is a breach of fiduciary duty. Although the passage from Viscount Haldane's speech in *Nocton v Lord Ashburton* quoted above demonstrates that equity has historically extended the description of fraud or bad faith to conduct which the court considered 'against the dictates of conscience', something genuinely amounting to bad faith must be shown. As Millett LJ put it in *Mothew*:[1]

> 'The various obligations of a fiduciary merely reflect different aspects of his core duties of loyalty and fidelity. Breach of fiduciary obligation, therefore, connotes disloyalty or infidelity. Mere incompetence is not enough. A servant who loyally does his incompetent duty is not unfaithful and is not guilty of a breach of fiduciary duty.'

Because it is essentially a jury question, it is hard to define exactly what amounts to a breach of this duty and it is best demonstrated by example. S is asked to act for two clients, C1 and C2, and obtains the informed consent of each of them. A direct conflict of interest then arises: C1 gives S information which S considers relevant to his retainer from C2 and which he feels obliged to report. He asks C1 whether he may reveal this information and C1 refuses. S is obliged to withdraw and should cease to act for both parties.[2] Because C1 is an established client, S does not do so and, faced with the choice whether to disobey C1 and reveal what he has learnt to C2 or to ignore his duty to C2, he chooses to remain silent and not to reveal the information to C2. The information given to him by C1 does not demonstrate that C1 is guilty of any impropriety in his dealings with C2. It is confidential and price-sensitive information which C1 wishes to keep secret but might be relevant to C2's decision to proceed with the transaction.[3] In this example, S is guilty of a breach of fiduciary duty to C2. The critical ingredient of C2's claim is that S recognises the conflict of interest but chooses to act in C1's interests and against the interests of C2. As Millett LJ put it in *Mothew*[4] (emphasis added):

'Even if a fiduciary is properly acting for two principals with potentially conflicting interests he must act in good faith in the interests of each and must not act *with the intention* of furthering the interests of one principal to the prejudice of those of the other ... I shall call this "the duty of good faith". He must not allow the performance of his obligations to one principal to be influenced by his relationship with the other. He must serve each as faithfully and loyally as if he were his only principal.

Conduct which is in breach of this duty *need not be dishonest but it must be intentional. An unconscious omission which happens to benefit one principal at the expense of the other does not constitute a breach of fiduciary duty*, though it may constitute a breach of the duty of skill and care. This is because the principle which is in play is that the fiduciary must not be inhibited by the existence of his other employment from serving the interests of his principal as faithfully and effectively as if he were the only employer. I shall call this the "no inhibition principle".'

If S had been unaware of his duty to report information to C2 or of the conflict of interest, C2's claim would have been in negligence only. This was the case in *Mothew* itself, the facts of which are set out above.

1   [1998] Ch 1 at 18F.
2   See *The Guide to the Professional Conduct of Solicitors* (6th edn, 1999) at 15.03.
3   See Scrutton LJ's example of the flaw in title quoted below. For certain defects in title, this example still holds good. Indeed C1 may be wholly unaware of the flaw in title until advised by S himself.
4   [1998] Ch 1 at 19D–G.

4.33   Furthermore in this example it is no defence to a claim by C2 that S was obliged by his instructions from C1 to keep the information confidential. This Millett LJ described as 'the actual conflict rule':[1]

'Finally, the fiduciary must take care not to find himself in a position where there is an *actual* conflict of duty so that he cannot fulfil his obligations to one principal without failing in his obligations to the other ... If he does, he may have no alternative but to cease to act for at least one and preferably both. The fact that he cannot fulfil his obligations to one principal without being in breach of his obligations to the other will not absolve him from liability. I shall call this "the actual conflict rule".'

In *Moody v Cox and Hatt*[2] the plaintiff bought a public house and some cottages from the defendants, who were trustees of an estate. They were also solicitors and acted for both the plaintiff and as solicitors of the trust. The first defendant who conducted the negotiations on behalf of the trust failed to reveal the existence of certain valuations which would affect the price. Although this was in certain respects a conflict of interest and duty case, the Court of Appeal treated it as a conflict of duties case.[3] At first instance, Younger J found that the failure to reveal the valuations was a breach of fiduciary duty. He made no finding that the defendants were in breach of contract or that Cox made misrepresentations to the plaintiff.[4] The Court of Appeal upheld his judgment. Scrutton LJ said this:[5]

'It seems to me the full duty to disclose was on Hatt.[6] How did he perform it? Again I take Cox's own evidence. Part of the subject-matter of the contract was some cottages. Cox had had a valuation made within a month or two of valuing those cottages at £160 a cottage. He sold them to Moody at £225 a cottage. He did not tell Moody of the valuation; and in his evidence, moreover, he stated as follows: "I did say the cottages were worth £225; I knew that they were not worth it because I had been advised they were worth a good deal less. I knew the value of the

Marquis of Granby had depreciated since the probate valuation; I did not tell him the amount of the probate valuation". A man who says this admits in the plainest terms that he is not fulfilling the duty which lies upon him as a solicitor acting for a client. But it is said that he could not disclose that information consistently with his duty to his other clients, the cestuis que trust. It may be that a solicitor who tries to act for both parties puts himself in such a position that he must be liable to one or the other, whatever he does. The case has been put of a solicitor acting for vendor and purchaser who knows of a flaw in the title by reason of his acting for the vendor, and who, if he discloses that flaw in the title which he knows as acting for the vendor, may be liable to an action by his vendor, and who, if he does not disclose the flaw in title, may be liable to an action by the purchaser for not doing his duty as solicitor to him. It will be his fault for mixing himself up in a transaction in which he has two entirely inconsistent interests, and solicitors who try to act for both vendors and purchasers must appreciate that they run a very serious risk of liability to one or the other owing to the duties and obligations which such curious relation puts upon them.'

1   [1998] Ch 1 at 19G–H.
2   [1917] 2 Ch 71, CA.
3   See Lord Cozens-Hardy MR at 81 and Warrington LJ at 84–5.
4   See the findings at first instance at 74–5. The Court of Appeal might have made different findings on the evidence quoted above: see Lord Cozens-Hardy MR at 80: 'This being what I can call nothing else but a lie uttered'. It is, therefore, a strong case. But liability was based purely on non-disclosure.
5   [1917] 2 Ch 71 at 91.
6   As Cox's principal. Although both were trustees, Cox was not a qualified solicitor and Hatt was the sole principal of the firm.

4.34   In *Nationwide Building Society v Richard Grosse & Co* and *Nationwide Building Society v Goodwin Harte*,[1] where twelve sample cases were heard at the same time, the judge was prepared to conclude that two solicitors consciously put their borrower client's interests before those of their lender client. In the first case, the critical factor from which the judge was prepared to draw this conclusion was that the solicitor had submitted a clean report on title at a time when he had taken no steps whatever to investigate title at all. In that case the solicitor elected to give evidence.[2] In the second case, where the solicitor elected not to give evidence, the judge was also prepared to make a finding of breach of fiduciary duty.[3] In that case, the judge found that on the basis of his admitted knowledge the solicitor must have known that his borrower client was defrauding his lender client and, in the absence of evidence from the solicitor, the judge felt entitled to conclude that his failure to disclose the relevant information to the plaintiff was 'conscious, deliberate and in bad faith'. Both these and *Moody v Cox and Hatt* were strong cases.[4] In *Bristol and West Building Society v Fancy and Jackson*[5] by contrast the judge was not willing to infer, in the absence of evidence, that the solicitor's conduct had been deliberate.

1   [1999] Lloyd's Rep PN 348 and [1999] Lloyd's Rep PN 338 (Blackburne J).
2   [1999] Lloyd's Rep PN 348 at 355–6: 'The clear picture which emerged from [his] evidence was of someone who paid little regard to the Society's interests. He returned an unqualified report on title without caring whether what he was saying in it was true or not.'
3   [1999] Lloyd's Rep PN 338 at 345.
4   The evidence quoted by Scrutton LJ in the passage from *Moody v Cox and Hatt* [1917] 2 Ch 71 at 91, CA quoted above indicates the sort of evidence from which the court will draw the inference of deliberate breach.
5   [1997] 4 All ER 582 at 613g and 614d–e (Chadwick J): 'I should not draw an inference of dishonesty against a solicitor without cogent evidence; evidence which, in effect, compels me to reach that conclusion.'

4.35 Finally, it is important to bear in mind that a conflict of duties does not automatically arise simply because a solicitor's duty to one client involves him acting against the interests of the other. If the solicitor has obtained the informed consent of both clients, each accepts in general terms that the solicitor must be permitted to carry out the instructions of the other. But the client may also agree that the solicitor is entitled to reveal information which he might otherwise prefer to be kept secret or, as in *Kelly v Cooper*, that the solicitor's duty of disclosure to him should be circumscribed. In *Mothew* there was no conflict of duties when they were properly analysed:

> 'In the present case the judge evidently thought that the defendant was in breach of both the duty of good faith and the actual conflict rule. In *Bristol and West Building Society v May, May & Merrimans*[1] he said:
>
> > "There can be no doubt that the requirement of unconscionable conduct is present where a solicitor who is acting for both borrower and lender misrepresents to the lender some fact *which he knows, or must be taken to know*, will or may affect the lender's decision to proceed with the loan. In those circumstances, the solicitor *is abusing his fiduciary relationship with one client, the lender, to obtain an advantage for his other client, the borrower.* It is as much 'against the dictates of conscience' for a solicitor *knowingly to prefer the interests of one client over those of another client* as it is for him to prefer his own interests over those of his client." (My emphasis.)
>
> I respectfully agree: but no such allegation is made in this case.'

As to the actual conflict rule, the judge said:[2]

> 'First, in *Mothew* the "agent" was a fiduciary who put himself in a position in which his duty to the lender *was* in conflict with the interests of his other client, the borrower.' (My emphasis.)
>
> I do not accept this. By instructing him to act for them, the purchasers must be taken to have authorised the defendants to complete the report without which the mortgage advance would not have been forthcoming; and to complete it truthfully. The defendant was required by the society to report on the purchaser's title as well as to confirm the absence of any further borrowing. The two stood in exactly the same case. The defendant would not have been in breach of his duty to the purchasers if he had disclosed the facts to the society any more than if he had reported a defect in their title.
>
> This proposition can be tested by considering what the defendant's position would have been if he had acted for the purchasers and another solicitor had been instructed to act for the society. He would have been required to deduce the purchaser's title to the satisfaction of the society's solicitor, and to confirm to him that no further borrowing or second charge was in contemplation. His duty to the purchasers would have required him to ascertain the facts from them and to report them to the society. Unless they told him the facts and instructed him to lie to the society, instructions which he would have been bound to refuse, his duty to the purchasers would not inhibit him in providing full and truthful information to the solicitor acting for the society.'[3]

The nature of the information which a solicitor acting for both borrower and lender is free to disclose to each of his clients is considered further in chapter 7. For present purposes the important point is that before it can be said that a conflict of duties arises, the solicitor's implied authority to disclose information must be considered.

1   [1996] 2 All ER 801 at 817–818.
2   [1996] 2 All ER 801 at 832.
3   [1998] Ch 1 at 20A–G.

(c) Conclusion

4.36 Apart from the duty of good faith, fiduciary duties are strict. In order to show a breach of the fiduciary duty of good faith, the claimant must establish a conflict of duties. If there has been adequate disclosure at the outset and no breach of the double employment rule, this will turn on the express or implied terms of the solicitor's retainer from each client. If the terms of the consent are to be implied from the nature of the transaction and the relationship between the two clients, this is best tested by considering what the defendant would have been impliedly authorised by C1 to reveal to another solicitor acting for C2. If, properly analysed, there is a genuine conflict of duties, the claimant will also have to show that the defendant was aware of this and preferred the interests of C1 to the interests of C2. Finally, if such a claim is to be advanced at all a breach of the duty of good faith must be clearly pleaded. It is not enough to allege a breach of fiduciary duty. The claimant must plead and prove that the solicitor committed a deliberate or intentional breach of duty amounting to bad faith.[1] When the fiduciary duties of a solicitor are understood in this way, it will be seen that the scope for an additional remedy in equity is fairly circumscribed. If a solicitor lies to his client, the remedy is a claim in deceit. If he assists one client to defraud another without making fraudulent misrepresentations himself, he may be liable for conspiracy to defraud at common law. If he is trusted with the money and property of one client and transfers it to another, he will be liable for breach of trust if the circumstances of the transfer are outside his authority or if he acts dishonestly. It is only if he fails to carry out the instructions of one client on the instructions of the other or in the knowledge that he cannot comply with the instructions of both, that a breach of fiduciary duty is properly made out.

1   See *Paragon Finance v D B Thakerar & Co* [1999] 1 All ER 400 at 404–6.

D   COMPENSATION IN EQUITY

1   Introduction

4.37 The remedies available for a breach of trust or a breach of fiduciary duty are far more varied than an order for compensation, the nearest equivalent to common law damages. The remedy sought or ordered will turn on the nature of the complaint, the identity and interest of the complainant and the circumstances existing at the date of the order. Where the complaint is exploitation of trust property for personal gain, the usual remedy will be an account of profits. Where the complaint is damage to the trust, the remedy will depend on the circumstances. It might turn on whether the trust has come to an end; if the trust is continuing, the defaulting trustee is likely to be removed. That might be a sufficient remedy in itself. But he may also be ordered to restore trust property or, where his conduct has caused damage through unauthorised or negligent investments, to compensate the trust for the consequential losses. If the trust has been wound up and the deficiencies come to light on the taking of a final account, the trustee may be ordered to compensate the beneficiaries directly rather than to reconstitute the fund. Where an order for compensation is made in these circumstances, the analogy between equity and common law is at its closest.

4.38 One of the predominant purposes of the intervention of equity for breach of fiduciary duty is prophylactic. Its rules were developed, no doubt, for the purpose of policing trustees or, as Lord Dunedin put it in *Nocton v Lord Ashburton*,[1] 'to keep persons in a fiduciary capacity up to their duty'. For instance, the double employment rule is designed to ensure that actual conflicts do not arise rather than to provide compensation for injuries suffered. As a consequence, claims based upon breach of this duty are rare. If a client learns that his solicitor is acting for another client with conflicting interests and wishes him not to, he will withdraw his own instructions or, less likely, apply for an injunction to prevent the firm from continuing to act.[2] If the fiduciary fails to make full disclosure, his principal's primary remedy is rescission of the transaction into which he has been induced to enter.[3] Finally, the remedy for a breach of fiduciary duty will often be tailored to meet the circumstances of the case. In *Spector v Ageda*[4] the solicitor's breach of fiduciary duty was a defence to a claim brought by her to enforce the charge which her client had executed. The charge was held to be unenforceable.[5] Where compensation is awarded by the court for misappropriation or misapplication of trust property, the form of the relief granted by the court is an order for an account to be taken, to surcharge and falsify the account, and to require the fiduciary or trustees to make compensation for any losses discovered on the taking of the account. But this is not simply a matter of form. The account is struck at the date of judgment and the defaulting trustees or fiduciary will be orderd to restore the missing trust property or compensate the trust for its misapplication.[6]

1   [1914] AC 932 at 963.
2   As in *Re Schuppan (a bankrupt)* [1996] 2 All ER 664 (Robert Walker J) and *McPherson v Thompson* (15 December 1998, unreported) (Judge Havery QC).
3   This may be appropriate not only in conflict of interest and duty cases. This was the relief obtained in *Moody v Cox and Hatt* [1917] 2 Ch 71.
4   [1973] Ch 30 (Megarry J).
5   In *Swindle v Harrison* [1997] 4 All ER 705, CA the plaintiff solicitors orginally sought and obtained an order for possession but the charge appears to have been rescinded by agreement: see 726g–h per Hobhouse LJ. If this is right, Mrs Harrison achieved the primary relief to which she was entitled. The judge did not make a declaration in these terms. He simply dismissed the claim for want of prosecution.
6   See the discussion in *Target Holdings v Referns* [1996] AC 421 in Millet 'Equity's Place in the Law of Commerce (1998) 114 LQR 214 and Oakley 'Chancery Bar Association Seminar: Equity's Place in the Law of Commerce' February 1998.

4.39   The nature and extent of equitable compensation were set out in *Canson Enterprises Ltd v Broughton & Co*[1] by McLachlin J:

'What is the ambit of compensation as an equitable remedy? Proceeding in trust, we start from the traditional obligation of a defaulting trustee, which is to effect restitution to the estate. But restitution in specie may not always be possible. So equity awards compensation in place of restitution in specie, by analogy for breach of fiduciary duty with the ideal of restoring to the estate that which was lost through the breach.

The restitutionary basis of compensation for breach of trust was described in *Ex p Adamson* (1878) 8 Ch D 807 at 819:

"The Court of Chancery never entertained a suit for damages occasioned by fraudulent conduct or for breach of trust. The suit was always for an equitable debt or liability in the nature of a debt. It was a suit for the restitution of the actual money or thing, or value of the thing, of which the cheated party had been cheated."

It has been widely accepted ever since. As Professor Davidson states in his very useful article "The Equitable Remedy of Compensation",[2] "the method of calculation [of compensation] will be that which makes restitution for the value of the loss suffered from the breach ..."

In summary, compensation is an equitable monetary remedy which is available when the equitable remedies of restitution and account are not appropriate. By analogy with restitution, it attempts to restore to the plaintiff what has been lost as a result of the breach, ie the plaintiff's loss of opportunity. The plaintiff's actual loss as a consequence of the breach is to be assessed with the full benefit of hindsight. Foreseeability is not a concern in assessing compensation, but it is essential that the losses made good are only those which, on a common sense view of causation, were caused by the breach. The plaintiff will not be required to mitigate, as the term is used in law, but losses resulting from clearly unreasonable behaviour on the part of the plaintiff will be adjudged to flow from that behaviour, and not from the breach. Where the trustee's breach permits the wrongful or negligent acts of third parties, thus establishing a direct link between the breach and the loss, the resulting loss will be recoverable. Where there is no such link, the loss must be recovered from the third parties.'

As this analysis shows, equitable compensation was originally available where, on the taking of the account, the defaulting trustee or fiduciary was unable to restore the trust property in question. As financial markets and institutions became more sophisticated, the courts of equity developed technical rules for the valuation of property and assessment of capital and income losses. Those technical rules which still apply on the taking of an account are outside the scope of this work and reference should be made to the standard textbooks on this topic.[3] But as the duties and liabilities of fiduciaries became extended in other ways, equitable compensation also became available where the remedies of restitution and account were inappropriate. Where the complaint is that the fiduciary caused loss by placing himself in a position of conflict or failed to disclose information to his principal, the court is faced with many of the same issues which arise at common law. It is in this situation that the analogy with common law damages is at its closest. What follows is a discussion of these issues and a comparison with the common law rules discussed earlier in this work.

1   (1991) 85 DLR (4th) 129 at 157e–h and 163e–h. The seven judges concurred in the result. McLachlin J, with whom L'Heureux-Dube J concurred, were the minority. The speech was, however, expressly approved by Lord Browne-Wilkinson in *Target Holdings Ltd v Redferns* [1996] AC 421 at 438D–439B.
2   (1982) 13 Melbourne ULR 349 at 351.
3   For a full discussion of the 'account' cases as opposed to the 'non-account' cases see Parker and Mellows (ed Oakley) *The Modern Law of Trusts* (7th edn, 1998) ch 24 at pp 679ff.

2   Causation

4.40 In *Target Holdings Ltd v Redferns*[1] the House of Lords affirmed that it was necessary for a beneficiary seeking equitable compensation to establish a causal connection between the breach of trust and the loss suffered.[2] In fact, the issues raised by the case did not really involve causation at all but rather the nature of the remedies available for breach of trust and the time at which loss should be assessed. The precise points in issue were whether it was open for a solicitor trustee, who had paid away a lender's funds prematurely and without the client's authority, to argue that he had made good the loss since the date of breach by getting in the security or whether the lender, who with the benefit of hindsight did not want the security, was entitled to restitution of the mortgage advance in full despite the solicitor trustee's subsequent actions. The Court of Appeal[3] had held that the lender beneficiary was entitled to an order for restitution of the mortgage advance despite the solicitor's later conduct. The House of Lords reached the opposite conclusion and held, first, that a beneficiary was not automatically entitled to restitution of the trust fund for a breach of trust and, secondly, that compensation in equity falls to be determined at the date of trial in the light of all the circumstances then known. The solicitor had belatedly got in the security and, because he had done so, it was arguable that the lender had suffered no loss as a consequence of the breach.[4]

1   [1996] AC 421.
2   There was existing authority to this effect: see *Nestle v National Westminster Bank plc (No 2)* [1993] 1 WLR 1260 and *Re Miller's Deed Trusts* (1978) 75 LSG 454 (Oliver J).
3   [1994] 1 WLR 1089, CA.
4   The issue arose on the plaintiff's application for summary judgment and an interim payment. In fact the House of Lords restored the order of Warner J for conditional leave to defend and an interim payment on the grounds that there was a 'high probability' that the plaintiff would establish that the transaction would not have gone ahead if the money had not been released early.

4.41   Nevertheless, Lord Browne-Wilkinson, with whom the other members of the House agreed, did make the following general observation:[1]

> 'Equitable compensation for breach of trust is designed to achieve exactly what the word compensation suggests: to make good a loss in fact suffered by the beneficiaries and which, using hindsight and common sense, can be seen to have been caused by the breach.'

1   [1996] AC 421 at 439B.

(a)   The conduct of the claimant

4.42   In chapter 3[1] we considered the position of a claimant seeking damages at common law. In an article[2] published shortly after the Court of Appeal had delivered judgment in *Target,* Mr JD Heydon QC suggested that the decision might be justified on the basis of the principle expressed by Lord Thankerton in *Brickenden v London Loan & Savings Co,*[3] where he said this:

> 'When a party holding a fiduciary relationship, commits a breach of his duty by non-disclosure of material facts, which his constituent is entitled to know in connection with the transaction, he cannot be heard to maintain that disclosure would not have altered the decision to proceed with the transaction because the constituent's action would be solely determined by some other factor, such as the valuation by another party of the property proposed to be mortgaged. Once the court has determined that the non-disclosed facts were material, speculation as to what course the constituent, on disclosure, would have taken is not relevant.'

This statement suggested that there was a marked difference between equity and the common law, at least in relation to claims based on the tort of negligence. This was because there was a presumption of loss in favour of a beneficiary claiming in equity and it was unnecessary for him to establish that he would have acted differently if the fiduciary had fulfilled his duty.

1   Paras 3.4–3.6 and 3.11–3.15.
2   'Causal Relationships Between a Fiduciary's Default and a Principal's Loss' (1994) 110 LQR 328.
3   [1934] 3 DLR 465 at 469, PC.

4.43   *Brickenden* was a case of conflict of interest and duty. A solicitor acted for both borrower and lender but failed to disclose to the lender, which was a company, that its loan was to be used (in part) to repay him personally. When the borrower defaulted, the plaintiff sought to recover the loan from the solicitor himself. By the time of trial the relevant officer of the plaintiff company was dead and the defendant refused to give evidence, placing the plaintiff in some difficulty.[1] Given the facts of the case it was in some doubt whether Lord Thankerton's dictum should be treated as having the status of principle. Moreover, the decision was not cited to the Court of Appeal in *Target* and because of the way the argument developed, it was unnecessary for the House of Lords to look at the case or consider the point.[2] Nevertheless, in both *Bristol and West Building Society v May, May & Merrimans*[3] and *Swindle v Harrison*[4] *Brickenden* was relied upon in support of the general proposition that it was unnecessary for a principal to establish that he would have avoided the loss if the trustee or fiduciary had not committed the breach of duty. In neither case was the dictum accepted without qualification and after both decisions it still remained unclear whether the principle, if principle there was, had survived *Target;* and, if so, whether it applied beyond cases where the trustee or fiduciary was guilty of fraud or bad faith; and whether it made a difference that the fiduciary was guilty of a positive misrepresentation rather than non-disclosure.

1   See [1933] 3 DLR 168 cited by Blackburne J in *Nationwide Building Society v Balmer Radmore* [1999] Lloyd's Rep PN 241 at 273–4.
2   The case was cited in the plaintiff's printed case but not the subject of oral argument in the House of Lords.
3   [1996] 2 All ER 801.
4   [1997] 4 All ER 705.

4.44   The issue was finally considered by Blackburne J in *Nationwide Building Society v Balmer Radmore*,[1] where, after a comprehensive review of all the authorities, the judge said this:

> 'I take the view that, except where the fiduciary has acted dishonestly or in bad faith (or its equivalent), the correct approach to equitable compensation for breach of fiduciary duty is to assess what actual loss, applying common sense and fairness, has resulted from the breach having regard to the scope of the duty which was broken. I am also of the view that nothing in the authorities compels me to disregard any inference which, on the evidence, can properly be drawn as to what would have happened if the fiduciary had performed his duty. Failing any such evidence, however, the beneficiary is entitled to be put in the position he was in before the breach occurred. This assumes that he can show that the breach was causally relevant to the course of action which has given rise to his loss in the sense that, but for the breach of duty, the beneficiary would not have acted in the way which has caused his loss.'

In the light of this conclusion it is probable now that the court will apply the same test in evaluating the claimant's own conduct whether the claim is one for negligence or for breach of trust or breach of fiduciary duty unless dishonesty is expressly alleged.

1   [1999] Lloyd's Rep PN 241 at 278. The relevant passages in each of the earlier decisions and in *Target* are set out and analysed in full at 272–279. For this reason the passages in question are not cited here. The judge also relied on *Rama v Millar* [1996] 1 NZLR 257, PC and *Ata v American Express Bank Ltd* (26 June 1998, unreported), CA referred to in paras 4.46 and 4.47.

4.45   Although it seems unlikely that the defendant's counterclaim would have succeeded on either test, *Swindle v Harrison*[1] provides one of the few examples in which a claim for equitable compensation has failed on this ground. There was no challenge to the judge's finding that Mrs Harrison would have accepted the loan from the plaintiff firm of solicitors even if full disclosure of the benefits which the firm was taking had been made to her.[2] Evans LJ concluded as follows:

> '[T]he prima facie measure of [her] loss is the amount by which she is worse off now than she would have been if those breaches had not occurred. The failure to disclose cannot be said to have led to the making of the loan, even on a "but for" basis, precisely because disclosure of the true facts would not have affected her decision to accept it. Since she would have accepted the loan and completed the purchase, even if full disclosure had been made to her, she would have lost the value of the equity in her home in any event. She cannot recover damages or compensation for that loss, in my judgment, except on proof either that the plaintiffs acted fraudulently or in a manner equivalent to fraud or that she would not have completed the purchase if full disclosure had been made ie if the breach of duty had not occurred. She cannot do either, and in my judgment her claim for damages must fail.'[3]

1   [1997] 4 All ER 705.
2   See Evans LJ [1997] 4 All ER 705 at 713d–f.
3   [1997] 4 All ER 705 at 718f–j. The fraud exception was only mentioned by Evans LJ. Blackburne J, however, considered that the approach was 'consistent with the views' of all of them: see *Nationwide Building Society v Balmer Radmore* [1999] Lloyd's Rep PN 241 at 278.

4.46   The facts of *Rama v Millar*,[1] which provides another example, were more complex. The parties set up a partnership to trade in swaps. In order to provide capital, the defendant took out a loan facility from the Bank of New Zealand on which he alone was personally liable. When the parties faced a major loss, the defendant settled his liability to the bank by assigning certain partnership claims to it without the consent of the plaintiff and against his known wishes. The plaintiff commenced proceedings for breach of fiduciary duty. The Privy Council found that in a position of deadlock, it was a term of the partnership that the defendant was entitled to 'proceed to settle the matter without further delay unless Mr Millar was able and willing to provide a financial indemnity to Mr Rama'.[2] Because Mr Millar was unable to show that he would have been able to do so, his claim also failed.[3]

1   [1996] 1 NZLR 257.
2   [1996] 1 NZLR 257 at 261 lines 25–35, per Lord Nicholls.
3   It was common ground that he was entitled to recover a commitment fee of NZ$70,000, which the Privy Council did not disturb, although it is hard to see why, in the light of the above finding, Rama was entitled to recover anything at all: see 260 and 262, lines 3–8.

(b)   The conduct of third parties

4.47   In chapter 3[1] we considered the cases in which the court has approached the conduct of third parties at common law by valuing the claimant's chance of achieving a different outcome. In *Rama v Millar* the New Zealand Court of Appeal had awarded judgment on the basis that the partnership could have achieved a much better settlement if the defendant had acted in good faith. Lord Nicholls said this:[2]

> 'There is another difficulty with the conclusion of the Court of Appeal. The partners were in a strong bargaining position against the BNZ but in a weak position against IHD and PB Finance. The terms of settlement which the Court of Appeal regarded as realistic involved no contribution from the BNZ but a significant contribution from IHD or PB Finance, or both of them. Despite the terms of the letter of 17 August and with all respect to the Court of Appeal, it must be highly questionable whether in practice a speedy settlement could have been effected on these terms.'

In the light of the finding that Mr Rama was entitled to settle the claims in a position of deadlock, it was unnecessary for the Board to consider how best to evaluate the prospect that settlement might have been achieved on more advantageous terms and, if so, whether the basis of assessment should be the same as the evaluation of a chance at common law. It is unlikely that the court is *bound* to adopt this approach in the light of the authorities discussed above, and what little judicial sentiment there is suggests that it is more likely that the court will simply assess loss on a broad commonsense basis. As Rix J put it at first instance in *Ata v American Express Bank Ltd*:[3]

'In the first place the element of causation and the need for a plaintiff to prove his loss are emphasised. Secondly, the element of hindsight is used not to enable a plaintiff to demand favourable assumptions in his favour, but to enable the court to evaluate in the round what has happened and what, if anything, the plaintiff has in fact lost by the breach of trust complained of. Thirdly, the need for common-sense is underlined.'

In *Guerin v R*[4] (considered in para 4.50) where equitable compensation was assessed by reference to the plaintiffs' lost opportunity to exploit their land for development the judge, whose decision was upheld by the Supreme Court of Canada, arrived at 'a "global" figure: a considered reaction based on the evidence, the opinions, the arguments and, in the end, his own conclusions of fact'.

1   Paras 3.15–3.21.
2   [1996] 1 NZLR 257 at 261, lines 46–53.
3   (26 June 1998, unreported), CA.
4   (1984) 13 DLR (4th) 321 at 332.

(c)   Causation in fact

4.48   There also appears to be a real difference between the position at common law and in equity in relation to causation in fact. At common law, it is not enough for the claimant to show that the defendant's breach of duty was the occasion for his loss. He must establish that it was an effective or dominant cause: see chapter 3.[1] According to McLachlin J in *Canson Enterprises Ltd v Broughton & Co*,[2] the position in equity is as follows:

'The requirement that loss flow from the breach also assists in determining responsibility for the acts of strangers or third parties. If the breach permits a third party to take an unlawful advantage causing loss to the plaintiff, the fiduciary will be liable because there is a causal link between the breach and the loss. This was the case in *Caffrey v Darby*, where a trustee whose neglect permitted another to abscond with trust property was held liable for that loss. Where, on the other hand, the plaintiff suffers loss as a result of the act of a third party after the fiduciary's obligation has terminated and the plaintiff has taken control of the property, the result will be otherwise.'

In *Caffrey v Darby*[3] trustees failed to get in certain trust property which was left in the hands of a beneficiary. The beneficiary committed the property to a third party who went bankrupt and the assets were seized. The trustees were held liable. Sir William Grant MR said:[4]

'[I]f they have been guilty of negligence, they must be responsible for any loss in any way to the property: for whatever may be the immediate cause, the property would not have been in a situation to sustain that loss, if it had not been for their negligence. If they had taken possession of the property, it would not have been in his possession. If the loss had happened by fire, lightning or any other accident, that would not be an excuse to them, if guilty of previous negligence.'

The decision was followed by Lord Cottenham in *Clough v Bond*[5] and both were cited with approval by Lord Browne-Wilkinson in *Target*.[6]

1 Paras 3.22–3.27.
3 (1991) 85 DLR (4th) 129 at 163c–e.
3 (1801) 6 Ves 488, 31 ER 1159.
4 (1801) 6 Ves 488 at 496 and 31 ER 1159 at 1162. In the English Reports the decision is attributed to Lord Eldon.
5 (1838) 3 My & Cr 490.
6 [1996] AC 421 at 434E: 'Even if the immediate cause of the loss is the dishonesty or failure of a third party, the trustee is liable to make good that loss to the trust estate if, but for the breach, the loss would not have occurred.'

4.49 Liability is not unlimited, however. In *Canson*, the defendant solicitors acted for the plaintiffs, two joint venture companies, in relation to their purchase of development land. The proposal was put to them by an agent, to whom they agreed to pay a 15% commission if the deal was completed. The defendant solicitors also acted for the vendor of the property but failed to disclose to the plaintiffs that the vendor was a company formed by the agent solely to purchase the property and 'flip' it to the plaintiffs at an increase in price. It was common ground that if the plaintiffs had known this, they would not have bought the property. Following the purchase the plaintiffs proceeded with their development. It proved to be a disaster because of the negligence of their contractors, against whom they obtained judgment but were unable to recover in full. They then sued the defendants. The Supreme Court of Canada held that the defendants were liable for the amount of the secret profit made by the agent which the defendants had not reported to them but not liable for the failure of the development because of the negligence of the third parties. The solicitor had ceased to act by then and the plaintiffs were themselves responsible for choosing the engineers and pile-drivers whose negligence caused it to fail. Although the members of the court reached their conclusion by very different routes, all were agreed that the losses were not recoverable and both the majority and the minority emphasised the question of control. Where the trustee or fiduciary is in control of the relevant asset, a failure to protect it adequately will lead to liability. Where, however, the trustee and fiduciary has ceased to act in a fiduciary capacity, independent actions of third parties will break the chain of causation.[1] Stevenson J, who delivered a short judgment concurring with the result, put it most succinctly:[2]

> 'In my view a court of equity, applying principles of fairness, would and should draw the line at calling upon the fiduciary to compensate for losses arising as a result of the unanticipated neglect of the engineers and pile-driving contractor. The fiduciary had nothing to do with their selection, their control, their contractual or bonding obligations. It follows that I agree with the trial judge and the British Columbia Court of Appeal that these losses are too remote, not in the sense of failing the "but for" test but in being so unrelated and independent that they should not, in fairness, be attributed to the defendant's breach of duty.'

Swindle v Harrison can also be explained on the same basis. Mrs. Harrison's losses were caused by her choice to invest in a restaurant scheme proposed by her son which were unrelated to and independent of the plaintiffs' breach of fiduciary duty. Their involvement came to an end when the purchase was completed and their breaches of duty had nothing to do with the purchase itself. *Caffrey v Darby* is distinguishable because the defendants in that case were under a continuing duty to get in the trust estate which they failed to carry out.

1 See La Forest J (1991) 85 DLR (4th) 129 at 146b–f, McLachlin J at 164b–g.
2 (1991) 85 DLR (4th) 129 at 165e–g.

(d)   Remoteness of damage

4.50   In chapter 3[1] we considered remoteness of damage at common law. Again, there is clear authority that foreseeability of damage will not restrict recovery in equity in the same way.[2] At common law, damages for loss of profit on resale are usually irrecoverable.[3] But in *Guerin v R*[4] the Crown was authorised by a native American band to negotiate a lease of a golf club on its land on specific terms. In breach of its fiduciary duty to them the Office of Indian Affairs negotiated a lease on terms which were less advantageous than those authorised and on which the band would not have been prepared to contract.[5] They commenced proceedings for breach of fiduciary duty. The trial judge awarded damages not by reference to the value of the land subject to the authorised terms (which the golf club itself would not have accepted) but by reference to the increased development value of the land. The value of the land had escalated due to its development potential in a way that was wholly unforeseen at the date of breach and he awarded compensation of $10m. The Supreme Court of Canada upheld the award of damages on the basis that equitable compensation was a substitute for specific restitution and that the Crown was liable to restore its value however unforeseen the cost of replacement would be.[6] Accordingly, the band was awarded the lost opportunity of selling the land for residential development. The analogy with specific restitution is less than convincing in this context[7] but the award seems appropriate subject only to the issue of foreseeability. If the Crown had fulfilled its duty, no lease would have been concluded and the band would have been free to develop the land some years later when land values had increased. The development value of the land genuinely represented the band's loss. The wholly unforeseen escalation in land prices would have been a defence at common law but was not in equity.

1   Paras 3.28–3.39.
2   See *Canson Ltd v Broughton & Co* (1991) 85 DLR (4th) 129 at 162e–g, cited with approval by Lord Browne-Wilkinson in *Target Holdings Ltd v Redferns* [1996] AC 421 at 439G and 440A.
3   See chapter 3, para 3.36 and chapter 8, paras 8.77–8.78.
4   (1984) 13 DLR (4th) 321.
6   See Wilson J (1984) 13 DLR (4th) 321 at 355.
6   See Wilson J (1984) 13 DLR (4th) 321 at 365–7 and Dickson J at 334.
7   See Davies 'Causation, Foreseeability and Remoteness' in Youdan (ed) *Equity, Fiduciaries and Trusts* (1993) p 309. See also the analysis of McLachlin J in *Canson* (1991) 85 DLR (4th) 129 at 160d–g.

(e)   Contributory negligence and mitigation

4.51   In England the defence of contributory negligence is purely a statutory one and the Law Reform (Contributory Negligence) 1945 does not apply to a claim for breach of trust or breach of fiduciary duty. In *Day v Mead*,[1] however, the New Zealand Court of Appeal held that contributory negligence was available as a defence to a claim for breach of fiduciary duty by analogy with the equivalent statutory defence in New Zealand.[2] A majority of the Supreme Court of Canada in *Canson Enterprises Ltd v Broughton & Co*[3] agreed with the approach although the point did not arise for decision. In *Nationwide Building Society v Balmer Radmore*[4] Blackburne J had to consider whether the same approach should be applied by an English court. In deciding that contributory negligence was not a defence to a claim of breach of fiduciary duty in English law, the judge recognised that English courts take a narrower view of the conduct which amounts to a breach of fiduciary duty than courts in New Zealand and Canada. He said this:[5]

'The kind of fiduciary duty with which I am concerned in these twelve cases is, as Mr Patten pointed out, one in which, following *Mothew*,[6] a breach must be intentional. The fiduciary cannot be unconsciously disloyal. The betrayal of trust inherent in the breach is necessarily a disloyal act. This feature which, following *Mothew*, is how English law regards breach of fiduciary duty, appears to be different from (and more stringent than) what needs to be shown in New Zealand and Canada. In *Day v Mead* Sir Robin Cooke P (at page 447) quoted with approval the trial judge's findings in relation to breach of fiduciary duty including his observation that the defendant solicitor had "acted quite innocently". In his judgment in *Canson Enterprises Ltd v Broughton & Co* La Forest J (at page 150) referred to the fact that the New Zealand Court of Appeal "agreed that Mead, *though he acted quite innocently,* was, having regard to the circumstances, in breach of fiduciary duties ..." (my emphasis). The "measure of duty" is not, therefore, the same.

In English law contributory negligence has never been a defence to an intentional tort: in such cases the 1945 Act has no application. By parity of approach I can see no good reason why equity, concerned as Lord Dunedin remarked in *Nocton v Lord Ashburton* [1914] AC 932 at page 963 "... to keep persons in a fiduciary capacity up to their duty", should adopt a less rigorous approach.

I therefore take the view that where, in order to establish a breach of fiduciary duty, it is necessary to find that the fiduciary was consciously disloyal to the person to whom his duty was owed, the fiduciary is disabled from asserting that the other contributed, by his own want of care for his own interests, to the loss which he suffered flowing from the breach. To do otherwise, as Gummow J pointed out in his article in "Equity, Fiduciaries and Trusts",[7] risks subverting the fundamental principle of undivided and unremitting loyalty which is at the core of the fiduciary's obligations. In his article he pointed to the "unwisdom of entangling the already complex law as to fiduciary duties with notions of contributory negligence."'

1   [1987] 2 NZLR 443.
2   The breach of duty was a failure to advise the plaintiff to take independent advice before investing in a company of which the defendant was a director and shareholder. The judge found that the defendant was innocent and there were no findings of negligence at common law.
3   (1991) 85 DLR (4th) 129 at 151–2, per La Forest J.
4   [1999] Lloyd's Rep PN 241.
5   [1999] Lloyd's Rep PN 241 at 281–2.
6   [1998] Ch 1.
7   See para 4.22, note 1.

4.52   Again, according to the traditional view, a principal or beneficiary who is the victim of a breach of fiduciary duty or breach of trust is under no duty to mitigate his loss. This view was expressed by McLachlin J in *Canson*:[1]

'[W]hile a plaintiff will not be required to act in a reasonable and prudent manner as might be required in negligence or contract, losses stemming from the plaintiff's unreasonable actions will be barred. This is also sound policy in the law of fiduciary duty. In negligence and contract the law limits the actions of the parties who are expected to pursue their own best interest. Each is expected to continue to look after their own interests after a breach or tort, and so a duty of mitigation is imposed. In contrast, the hallmark of fiduciary relationship is that the fiduciary, at least within a certain scope, is expected to pursue the best interest of the client. It may not be fair to allow the fiduciary to complain when the client fails forthwith to shoulder the fiduciary's burden. This approach to mitigation accords with the basic rule of equitable compensation that the injured party will be reimbursed for all losses flowing directly from the breach. When a plaintiff, after due notice and opportunity, fails to take the most obvious steps to alleviate his or her losses, then we may rightly say that "the plaintiff has become the author of his own misfortune." At this point, the plaintiff's failure to mitigate may become so egregious that it is no longer sensible to say that the losses which followed were caused by the fiduciary's breach. But until that point, mitigation will not be required.'

In *Nationwide Building Society v Balmer Radmore*[2] Blackburne J adopted the same approach:

'This does not mean that the conduct of the person to whom the fiduciary duty is owed is irrelevant. There comes a point, following breach of fiduciary duty, where the loss is too remote from the breach to be said to be a loss flowing from it (as exemplified in *Canson Enterprises Ltd v Broughton & Co*) or where the claimant's own conduct comes into play as a factor determining the loss which he can recover.'

It is clear, therefore, that the conduct of the claimant must be so unreasonable that it breaks the chain of causation. Although there is no direct authority on this point, consider the facts of *Nocton v Lord Ashburton*.[3] Lord Ashburton chose to lend money a second time despite a clear warning from Nocton's partners, yet this conduct did not prevent recovery.

1   (1991) 85 DLR (4th) 129 at 162e–g.
2   [1999] Lloyd's Rep PN 241 at 282.
3   [1914] AC 932; see para 4.22.

4.53   In chapter 3[1] we considered the duty of a claimant at common law to mitigate his loss by commencing or pursuing litigation against third parties. Whatever the precise limits of the duty to mitigate a breach of trust or fiduciary duty, it is clear that in equity a claimant 'is not required to engage in hazardous litigation in order to mitigate his loss'.[2]

1   Paras 3.40–3.44
2   *Target Holdings Ltd v Redferns* [1996] AC 421 at 440B per Lord Browne-Wilkinson discussing *Bishopsgate Investment Management Ltd v Maxwell (No 2)* [1994] 1 All ER 261.

3   Measure of compensation

4.54   Although they may often correspond, the measure of compensation in equity is not exactly the same as an award of damages at common law. The function of damages at common law, even in a claim for fraud, is primarily compensatory. It is to compensate the claimant, so far as it is possible in money terms, for the defendant's breach of duty. Compensation in equity is primarily restitutionary. Its function is usually to compensate the claimant in money terms for the deprivation of a particular asset or the defendant's inability to restore it. In *Target Holdings Ltd v Redferns*[1] Lord Browne-Wilkinson stated that the basis upon which it is to be assessed as follows:

'The quantum is fixed at the date of judgment at which date, according to the circumstances then pertaining, the compensation is assessed at the figure then necessary to put the trust estate or the beneficiary back into the position it would have been in had there been no breach.'

1   [1996] AC 421 at 437D.

4.55 The difference can be illustrated quite easily where compensation is limited to the loss of a particular asset. At common law damages will ordinarily be assessed by reference to values current at the date of breach or date of transaction.[1] In equity, it is the trustee's duty to repay to the fund or the beneficiaries the amount which would be required to buy in the same asset at judgment together with any interest or income lost. If the relevant asset has increased in price by the date of judgment, this is a risk which the trustee must take. In *Re Dawson*[2] the executors of the deceased's estate had funds in both Australia and New Zealand. One of the trustees allowed £4,700 to be paid of the New Zealand assets for investment in Australia. A third party absconded with the money and the question was whether the defaulting trustee should restore the money by reference to the currency rate at the date of breach (which favoured him), or by reference to the currency rate at the date of judgment (which favoured the beneficiaries). It was held that the rate prevailing at the date of judgment should be applied.[3] Street J stated:[4]

> '[T]he distinction between common law damages and relief against a defaulting trustee is strikingly demonstrated by reference to the actual form of relief granted in equity in respect of breach of trust. The form of relief is couched in terms appropriate to require the defaulting trustee to restore to the estate the assets of which he deprived it. Increases in market values between the date of breach and the date of recoupment are for the trustee's account: the effect of such increases would, at common law, be excluded from the computation of damages: but in equity a defaulting trustee must make good the loss by restoring to the estate the assets of which he deprived it notwithstanding that market values have increased in the meantime. The obligation to restore to the estate the assets of which he deprived it necessarily connotes that, where a monetary compensation is paid in lieu of restoring assets, that compensation is to be assessed by reference to the value of the assets at the date of restoration and not at the date of deprivation. In this sense the obligation is a continuing one and ordinarily, if the assets are for some reason not restored in specie, it will fall for quantification at the date when recoupment is to be effected, and not before.'

The fund was situated in New Zealand and would have remained there had there been no breach of trust. The beneficiaries were not penalised for the fall in the value of the Australian dollar and the trustee was obliged to purchase sufficient New Zealand pounds and pay sufficient interest to make good the deficiency in the fund.

1 See chapter 3, paras 3.48–3.58. This is not an invariable rule.
2 [1966] 2 NSWR 211.
3 At the date of the decision the common law rule was that a creditor of a foreign debt had to convert it at the date on which the debt fell due: *Re United Railways of Havana* [1961] AC 1007. This is not, of course, the position at common law now. It is not clear what the prevailing position was in New South Wales at the time the case was decided.
4 [1966] 2 NSWR 211 at 215 lines 13–27.

4.56 Where a trustee's breach of duty results in the loss or destruction of an asset and the asset is real property or a stable investment, the amount which must be restored to the trust or beneficiaries should be relatively easy to establish, as *Re Dawson* demonstrates. Where, however, equitable compensation is awarded for a breach of duty which does not involve particular assets but, say, non-disclosure of information, or where the assets of the trust can be freely traded and are perpetually fluctuating in value, the amounts which the principal or trustee is obliged to restore are difficult to determine and the analogy with specific restitution is not particularly helpful.

4.57 In *Robinson v Robinson*[1] the Court of Appeal considered a claim against a trustee where he had an option of investing in different funds. Lord Cranworth stated:[2]

'Where a man is bound by covenants to do one of two things, and does neither, in an action by the covenantee, the measure of damage is in general the loss arising by reason of the covenantor having failed to do that which is least not that which is most beneficial to the covenantee: and the same principle may be applied by analogy to the case of a trustee failing to invest in either of two modes equally lawful by the terms of the trust.'

In *Guerin*,[3] however, the Supreme Court of Canada adopted an entirely different approach. Wilson J stated:

'Just as it is to be presumed that a beneficiary would have wished to sell his securities at the highest price available during the period they were wrongfully withheld from him by the trustee (see *McNeil v Fultz* (1906) 38 SCR 198), so also it should be presumed that the band would have wished to develop its land in the most advantageous way possible during the period covered by the unauthorized lease. In this respect also the principles applicable to determine damages for breach of trust are to be contrasted with the principles applicable to determine damages for breach of contract. In contract it would have been necessary for the band to prove that it would have developed the land; in equity a presumption is made to that effect.'

Despite the authority of *Robinson v Robinson*, the approach in *Guerin* was initially preferred by English courts and the decision was treated as authority for the proposition that in valuing trust assets or opportunities, all presumptions are to be made against the trustee and in favour of the beneficiary.[4] Accordingly, it was to be presumed that assets would be sold or realised at their highest value and at the most opportune time.

1   (1851) 1 De GM & G 247.
2   (1851) 1 De GM & G 247 at 257.
3   (1984) 13 DLR (4th) 321 at 367.
4   See *Jaffray v Marshall* [1993] 1 WLR 1285 (Nicholas Stewart QC) at 1290E–1293C. The case was disapproved by the House of Lords in *Target Holdings Ltd v Redferns* [1996] AC 421 at 440E–F. See also *Nestle v National Westminster Bank plc* [1993] 1 WLR 1260 at 1268C–1267A, CA per Dillon LJ. *Robinson v Robinson* was not cited in the former. In the latter, Dillon LJ considered it 'flawed'.

4.58   The position was made even more confused by uncertainty about the relevant rule to be applied at common law. In *Michael v Hart*[1] the plaintiff sued the defendant stockbroker for selling shares in breach of contract. Wills J found as follows:

'[I]t seems to me that the plaintiff is entitled to all the advantages that would have been his or that might have been his if the contract had been carried out. Amongst those advantages was the right to sell the shares whenever he chose during the period over which the transactions were to run, and at different times different prices might have been realised. No doubt the plaintiff would in fact never have realised the best prices that ruled during the period. But I think I am right in saying that the Courts have never allowed the improbability of the plaintiff's obtaining the highest prices to be taken into consideration for the purpose of reducing damages. The defendants are wrongdoers, and every presumption is to be made against them. In my opinion the plaintiff is entitled to the highest prices which were obtainable during the period during which he had the option of selling.'

In *Ata v American Express Bank Ltd*[2] the Court of Appeal had to consider both lines of authority and whether presumptions were to be made against a wrongdoer at common law or in equity. The court reached the conclusion that no presumptions were to be made in either jurisdiction, overruled *Michael v Hart* and approved *Robinson v Robinson*, and held as follows:[3]

'Thus in a claim for equitable compensation it is necessary to prove loss and causation. Accordingly, the judgment of Wills J in Michael v Hart cannot be supported even if confined to claims for equitable compensation for breach of trust or fiduciary duty.'

The position can now be stated with greater certainty: the measure of damages at common law and measure of compensation in equity are quantified by the same principles. Although there is no prima facie rule that damages are to be assessed either at the date of breach or by reference to the valuation method, the plaintiff must establish on the evidence precisely what loss he would have avoided if there had been no breach of trust or fiduciary duty. Where the loss arises because of the failure to buy or sell an asset, the plaintiff must prove when and at what price the asset would have been bought or sold in order to recover compensation.

1   [1901] 2 KB 867. The common law was not consistent either, however: see *The Playa Larga* [1983] 2 Lloyd's Rep 171.
2   (1998), Times, 26 June, CA.
3   Transcript at 23. Although *Nestle* was cited, no mention was made of Dillon LJ's criticism of *Robinson v Robinson*.

4   Interest

(a)   History of the equitable jurisdiction

4.59   There is no power to award interest at common law and the jurisdiction to award interest on damages is statutory only. Courts of equity, however, have always awarded interest under their inherent jurisdiction. In the nineteenth century when rates of interest were very stable, the court usually awarded interest at a rate of 4%. Where, however, special circumstances existed the court would either award interest at the higher rate of 5% or award compound interest. The special circumstances usually involved the trustee himself making a profit from the trust. At the same time the court had a power to award interest on the return of money or investments when making an order for rescission. Where the contract was induced by a fraud, a higher rate would again be applied.[1]

1   See the analysis of Dunn LJ in *O'Sullivan v Management Agency and Music Ltd* [1985] QB 428 at 449E–458B, CA.

4.60   The principle and practice of the nineteenth century, as they applied to a solicitor trustee, are conveniently set out in *Burdick v Garrick*[1] where simple interest at 4% was awarded. Lord Hatherley LC said this in overruling the award of compound interest made at first instance:[2]

'I cannot, however, think the decree correct in directing half-yearly rests, because the principle laid down in the case of the *A-G v Alford* 4 De GM & G 843, appears to be the sound principle, namely, that the court does not proceed against an accounting party by way of punishing him for making use of the plaintiff's money by directing rests, or payment of compound interest, but proceeds upon this principle, either that he has made, or has put himself into such a position as that he is to be presumed to have made, five percent, or compound interest, as the case may be. If the court finds it is stated in the bill, and proved, or, possibly (and I guard myself upon this part of the case), if it is not stated, but admitted on the face of the answer, without any statement on the bill, that the money received had been invested in an ordinary trade, the whole course of decision has tended to this, that the court presumes that the party against whom relief is sought has made the amount of profit which persons ordinarily do make in trade, and in those cases the court directs rests to be made. But how does the case stand here? There is no charge made in the bill of any employment of this money which would produce compound interest; there is an admission in the answer that one of the trustees, being engaged with his co-partner in a solicitor's business, has paid into the common account of the firm portions of this fund. But then it must not be forgotten that a solicitor's business is not such a business as I have described; it is not one in which they could make compound interest on the money embarked, or in which half-yearly rests, or yearly rests, as the case may be, would be made in making up the account. A solicitor's profit arises from the time and the labour which he is engaged. There is nothing like compound interest obtained upon the money employed by a solicitor. On the contrary, he is out of pocket for a considerable period by those moneys which he expends, and upon which he receives no interest, for, possibly, three or four years. It appears to me, therefore, that no case arises here in which you could say that a profit has been made, or necessarily is to be inferred, and consequentially that there has to be an error committed in directing compound interest.'

The award, whether of simple or compound interest and whether at the higher or lower rates, was intended to be compensatory and not punitive, and the basic principle upon which compound rather than simple interest was awarded was that the defendant should not profit personally from the use of the plaintiff's assets to which he had no right.

1   (1870) 5 Ch App 233 at 241.
2   (1870) 5 Ch App 233 at 241.

4.61   The practice prevailed well into the twentieth century. In the 1970s the practice of awarding fixed rates of interest disappeared. In *Bartlett v Barclays Trust Co Ltd (No 2)*[1] Brightman LJ awarded interest at the court's short term investment rate:

'I turn now to the question of interest. It is common ground that interest can be claimed on the compensation which is found due. Dispute only arises on the rate of interest to be charged. In former days a trustee was as a rule charged only with interest of 4 per cent unless there were special circumstances. The rate seems to have prevailed as the general rule until recent years. The defendant has helpfully supplied the court with a table of bank and minimum lending rates and bank deposit rates. Between 1963, the year in which the Old Bailey scheme began, and the present day there have been nearly 80 changes of bank rate of minimum lending and nearly 70 changes in Barclays Bank deposit rate. The bank or minimum lending rate during this period has varied between 4 per cent and 17 per cent and the deposit rate has varied between two per cent and 15 per cent. In these days of huge and constantly changing interest rates (the movement being usually upwards so far) I think it would be unrealistic for a court of equity to abide by the modest rate of interest which was current in the stable times of our forefathers.

In my judgment, a proper rate of interest to be awarded, in the absence of special circumstances, to compensate the beneficiaries and trust funds for non-receipt from a trustee of money that ought to have been received is that allowed from time to time on the courts' short-term investment account, established under section 6(1) of the Administration of Justice Act 1965.'

In the past the special account rate has been lower than commercial rates although the difference is not now significant.[2] In any event, in *O'Sullivan v Management Agency and Music Ltd*,[3] where there were no special circumstances either, the court awarded interest at a rate of 1% above the bank minimum lending rate. The position, therefore, at common law and in equity, absent special circumstances, is now very much the same.

1   [1980] Ch 515 at 546G–547B.
2   See *The Supreme Court Practice* (1998 ed) Vol 1 at 6/L/12 (pp 60–1).
3   [1985] QB 428, CA.

4.62   *Wallersteiner v Moir (No 2)*[1] was a case of special circumstances, where the plaintiff and defendant to the counterclaim had been guilty of a number of breaches of his fiduciary duties as a director of a public company. The court awarded interest at 1% above the minimum bank lending rate with yearly rests. The basis on which the award was made was as follows:[2]

> 'Dr Wallersteiner was at all material times engaged in the business of finance. Through a complex structure of companies he conducted financial operations with a view to profit. The quarter million pounds assistance which he obtained from the two companies in order to finance the acquisition of the shares meant that he was in a position to employ the money or its capital equivalent in those operations. Though the truth is unlikely ever to be fully known, shrouded as it is by the elaborate corporate structure within which Dr Wallersteiner chose to operate, one may safely presume that the use of the money (or the capital it enabled him to acquire) was worth to him the equivalent of compound interest at commercial rates with yearly rests, if not more.'

1   [1975] QB 373, 508n.
2   At 406E–G, per Scarman LJ. See also Buckley LJ at 398E–399A. Lord Denning MR would have awarded interest both for this reason and on a wider basis which is not supported by the authorities: see 388B–H.

4.63   In *Westdeutsche Landesbank Girozentrale v Islington London Borough Council*[1] where the House of Lords refused to award compound interest on a claim for money had and received at common law, Lord Browne–Wilkinson said this:[2]

> '[I]n the absence of fraud equity only awards compound (as opposed to simple) interest against a defendant who is a trustee or otherwise in a fiduciary position by way of recouping from such a defendant an improper profit made by him. It is unnecessary to decide whether in such a case compound interest can only be paid where the defendant has used trust moneys in his own trade or (as I tend to think) extends to all cases where a fiduciary has improperly profited from his trust.'

The usual rule can now be stated as follows: in the absence of fraud, compound interest will only be awarded where the defendant has profited personally from the breach of trust or fiduciary duty and an account of profits is sought. Where fraud is alleged and proved, the court may award compound interest.

1   [1996] AC 669.
2   [1996] AC 669 at 702D–E. The entire House agreed with the traditional limits of the equitable jurisdiction. A minority, Lords Goff and Woolf, would have extended the jurisdiction to award compound interest to a claim for money had and received at common law.

(b)   Compound interest

4.64   *Burdick v Garrick* still accurately represents the law. Thus, in the absence of fraud, a solicitor should not ordinarily be charged with compound interest unless he makes a personal profit from the trust.[1] Equitable fraud is, however, wider than deceit at common law:

> 'In equity the term "fraud" embraces not only actual fraud but certain other conduct which falls below the standards demanded by equity, and is known as constructive fraud, one of the examples of which is a transaction which has been procured by undue

influence, or where one party is in breach of a fiduciary duty to another. As Fox LJ said in the course of argument, it is questionable whether it is morally worse to obtain a benefit by making a statement known to be false, or to obtain the same benefit by taking advantage of a confidential or fiduciary relationship.'[2]

The jurisdiction obviously extends to cases where the solicitor has acted dishonestly or in bad faith or taken advantage of the solicitor–client relationship to further his or her own interests. It is not clear whether an English court would extend the principle to breaches of trust or breaches of the duty of good faith which, although deliberate or intentional, are not characterised as fraudulent or dishonest. In *Re Dawson*[3] Street J held that a deliberate breach of trust took it into the category of special circumstances:

> 'The Court's jurisdiction in selecting the appropriate rate of interest is exercisable solely for compensatory purposes. Although orders for interest may in some cases appear to have the effect of penalising defaulting trustees, the Court does not, in ordering interest and in selecting a rate, attempt in any way to impose a punishment upon the defaulter (*Vyse v Foster* (1872) 8 Ch App 309, at p 333). The practice of imposing a higher rate in the second class of case is based upon a requirement that the defaulter compensate the estate at the mercantile rate. The lesser rate of four per cent applied in the first class of case is a special rate which represents some concession in favour of the trustee: the assessment is made by reference to interest considered to be obtainable on authorized trustee investments rather than on the higher mercantile rate.
>
> There can be little doubt but that the breach of trust committed by Percy Stewart Dawson belongs to the higher category and not to the lower, or four per cent. It was a deliberate and wilful act the purpose of which was to deprive the estate of the moneys in question; and its intended manner of implementation involved illegalities according to the law of the country where this part of the estate was then situated. It does not appear to me to lie in the mouth of Percy Stewart Dawson to seek some more favourable terms of recoupment than would have been imposed had his wrongful purpose in fact been achieved and the money safely reached the hands of the company. It would be taking too lenient a view of the breach to classify it as being amongst those cases in which four per cent is regarded as the proper rate to apply.'

Ultimately the question is always one of discretion but if this also represents the law in England, then compound interest is available against a solicitor who is guilty of a deliberate or intentional breach of trust or fiduciary duty. But because the purpose of the award is compensatory and not punitive, we consider that the plaintiff must always satisfy the court that he would have earned compound interest on the fund or had to pay compound interest as a consequence of being kept out of the assets.[4]

1   See *Guardian Ocean Cargoes Ltd v Banco do Brasil (No 3)* [1992] 2 Lloyd's Rep 193 (Hirst J) at 198 col 2: 'Thus, as shown in *Burdick's* case, compound interest would be inappropriate in the case of a solicitor trustee who was not engaged in an investment business.'

2   *O'Sullivan v Management Agency and Music Ltd* [1985] QB 428 at 455C–D, per Dunn LJ. This statement seems too wide if it suggests that *every* breach of fiduciary duty entitles the principal to claim compound interest.

3   [1966] 2 NSWR 211 at 218–9. See at 212–3 for the precise facts which Street J considered to give rise to a 'clear and deliberate breach'. It is clear that the trustee was prepared to evade exchange controls. He was not, however, seeking to further his own interests against those of the trust but the interests of the beneficiaries as a whole. He was dead by the time of the action.

4   Compound interest may also be awarded where the trustee has failed to comply with his duty to invest in particular interest-bearing securities or a specific fund: see Underhill and Hayton *Law Relating to Trusts and Trustees* (15th edn, 1995) p 840. The loss suffered by the trust

in such cases is the accumulation of capital year on year. Unless the solicitor is charged with breach of an express trust, these cases are unlikely to be relevant.

(c)   The appropriate rate

4.65   The appropriate rate will turn on what the plaintiff could have expected to earn and is a matter of evidence. In *Guardian Ocean Cargoes Ltd v Banco do Brasil (No 3)*[1] Hirst J accepted expert evidence of available rates in New York and ordered 1% above the New York prime rate. He declined, however, to follow the prevailing commercial practice in New York where three-monthly rests were usual and preferred 'to adhere strictly to the *Wallersteiner* formula, and award yearly rests'. In *El Ajou v Dollar Land Holdings plc (No 2)*[2] Robert Walker J awarded interest at the base rate from time to time of one of the London clearing banks. He stated that 'the rate of interest should mirror, so far as possible, the income which the plaintiff might have earned had the principal sum been paid to him in March 1988'. He also declined to award rests any more frequently than yearly.

1   [1992] 2 Lloyd's Rep 193 at 199 col 1.
2   [1995] 2 All ER 213 at 224e–j.

(d)   Account of profits

4.66   Where the solicitor is the recipient of the funds in question and makes use of them himself, it may be more appropriate for the court to order an inquiry. In *Mathew v T M Sutton Ltd*[1] Chadwick J set out some helpful guidance in identifying the correct rate or rates of interest to be applied where the fiduciary or trustee is the recipient of the trust monies:

> 'The question in the present case is whether interest should be awarded at a rate which is linked to some independent commercial rate (say, bank rate or the rate allowed on the short term investment account) or whether I should order an inquiry for the purpose of ascertaining what use was made by the defendant of the money which it held as a fiduciary and what return was made by the defendant upon it.
>
> In my view this is an appropriate case for an inquiry. It would have been open to the defendant to place the surplus proceeds of sale upon an interest bearing account—distinct from any account in which it held its own money—to await the outcome of any claim made by the permanent trustee. If that had been done— and, as it seems to me, that is what should have been done—the defendant would have been accountable for the interest earned on that account. No more and no less. If that was not done, then it must (at the least) be likely that the defendant used the surplus in its business. That business includes the lending of money at rates which have been equal to, or in excess of, 3 per cent per month. If the defendant was, in fact, able to and did obtain a return equivalent to 3 per cent per month on what (on this hypothesis) was the plaintiff's money, I can see no reason why the plaintiff should be required to accept a lesser return.'

Accordingly, the plaintiff is entitled to an inquiry, if appropriate, to establish what profit the trustee or fiduciary made from the use of the money and to recover the profit actually made.[2]

1   [1994] 1 WLR 1455 at 1462E–H.
2   Subject possibly to the defendant's expenses and reasonable remuneration: see *O'Sullivan v Management Agency and Music Ltd* [1985] QB 428 at 458D–F.

CHAPTER 5

Limitation

A INTRODUCTION

5.1 Limitation issues often arise in claims against solicitors. As to the substantive law, it is necessary to distinguish between claims at common law, and those in equity. Sections B and C of this chapter consider claims at common law, including the statutory extensions to limitation periods contained in Limitation Act 1980 (LA), ss 14A and 32. Section D considers claims in equity: for breach of trust and breach of fiduciary duty. Section E considers two procedural issues: in particular, the principles which apply if the claimant seeks leave to amend to add a new cause of action after expiry of the limitation period. Limitation is a complex subject, and the Law Commission is currently considering wholesale reform.[1]

1 Law Commission Consultation Paper No 151 'Limitation of Actions' (1998).

B CLAIMS AT COMMON LAW

1 Introduction

5.2 It is helpful to consider the courts' approaches to the various issues which arise in relation to limitation in general terms before considering specific points. It is now clear that solicitors owe their clients concurrent duties in both contract and the tort of negligence, and that a client may rely upon either cause of action if it provides a more favourable regime as to limitation.[1] Except where the claimant's action includes a claim for damages for personal injuries,[2] the limitation period in both contract and the tort of negligence is six years from the date on which the cause of action accrued, unless an extension applies under the Limitation Act 1980.[3] In contract the cause of action accrues at the date of the breach of duty and in the tort of negligence it accrues when the negligence first causes legally recoverable loss. The loss caused in solicitors' negligence cases is almost always economic rather than physical loss. It may often be the case that the claimant is unaware that he or she has suffered economic loss due to the error of his solicitor until more than six years after the solicitor's breach of duty. If the causes of action in both contract and negligence accrued at the date of the original breach of duty, this could lead to the potential unfairness that the claimant's action would be statute-barred even though he could not reasonably have brought an action within the time limit.[4]

1 *Henderson v Merrett Syndicates Ltd* [1995] 2 AC 145, 185F–H, 191 C–D, discussed at para 1.14.
2 See para 5.6.
3 LA 1980, ss 5 and 2, respectively.
4 Bingham LJ adverted to this problem in *DW Moore & Co Ltd v Ferrier* [1988] 1 WLR 267 at 279.

5.3 Parliament's answer to this problem is contained in LA 1980, s 14A, which is headed 'special time limit for negligence actions where facts relevant to cause of action are not known at date of accrual'. In theory at least, the question of when the cause of action accrues is one of principle which depends on the general rules of contract and negligence law, as they apply to solicitors. This must be kept distinct from the questions introduced by section 14A, which were designed by Parliament to deal with the potential unfairness mentioned in the last paragraph. Thus, even if the application of principle leads to a result which appears unfair to the claimant it is, at least in negligence, still open to the claimant to rely upon s 14A. There is no need for the court to strain the common law principles stating when a cause of action accrues, in order to deal with this potential injustice to claimants.[2]

1 See paras 5.39–5.59.
2 See the speech of Lord Nicholls of Birkenhead in *Nykredit Mortgage Bank plc v Edward Erdman Group Ltd (No 2)* [1997] 1 WLR 1627, HL, at 1630H–1631A.

5.4 In addition, where the claimant has been guilty of fraud or deliberate conceal- ment, there is a further provision for extension of the limitation period, in LA 1980, s 32. This is also discussed below.[1] Section 32 will apply, inter alia, in all cases where the claimant is able to rely upon the tort of deceit.

1 See paras 5.60–5.69.

5.5 The issues which will be considered in this part are, first, cases in which a limitation period of only three years applies; and secondly, the date on which the cause of action accrues in contract and the tort of negligence. In section C the statutory extensions to the limitation period under LA 1980, ss 14A and 32 are examined.

2 Personal injuries: claims in which a limitation period of only three years applies

5.6 The effect of section 11 of the Limitation Act 1980 is that, in relation to actions in either contract or tort to which s 11 applies, the limitation period is only three years. The three years is measured either from the date on which the cause of action accrued, or from the claimant's 'date of knowledge', as defined in LA 1980, s 14, if that provides a later date. The effect of s 14 is considered below in relation to s 14A, which contains a similar extension to the limitation period. Leaving that aside for the moment, the question arises as to which claims fall within the scope of s 11.

5.7 Limitation Act 1980, s 11(1) provides:

'This section applies to any action for damages for negligence, nuisance or breach of duty (whether the duty exists by virtue of a contract or of provision made by or under a statute or independently of any contract or any such provision) where the damages claimed by the plaintiff for the negligence, nuisance or breach of duty consist of or include damages in respect of personal injuries to the plaintiff or any other person.'

The Court of Appeal considered this provision in *Bennett v Greenland Houchen & Co*.[1] The plaintiff had left his employer and begun work for a rival employer, in 1988. The former employer sought to enforce restrictive covenants against the plaintiff, who retained the defendant solicitors to act for him. The action was compromised. Nearly six years later, the plaintiff sued the solicitors alleging that their negligence and breach of contract had caused him both financial loss and clinical depression. The question was whether the action came within the scope of s 11, so that the limitation period was only three years rather than six. The Court of Appeal held that it did. Depression counted as personal injury for these purposes.[2] Both Otton and Peter Gibson LJJ emphasised that s 11 applies to claims which 'include' claims for damages in respect of personal injury. One of the plaintiff's pleaded claims was for damages for personal injury, in the form of depression. Thus the action did include a claim for damages for personal injury, and so it was statute-barred.

1   [1998] PNLR 458, CA.
2   By LA 1980, s 38, personal injury is defined to include 'any disease and impairment of a person's physical or mental condition'.

5.8   Thus the effect of pleading a claim for damages for depression was that the plaintiff's whole claim was held to be statute-barred, including the claim for damages for financial loss alone. But if the plaintiff had simply claimed financial loss, then s 11 would not have applied and the limitation period would have been six years so that the claim would not have been statute-barred. In the later case of *Oates v Harte Reade & Co*,[1] Singer J held that *Bennett* applied, so that the plaintiff's claim for both financial loss and physical injury was statute-barred. The plaintiff sought to escape the effect of this by abandoning the claim for damages in respect of physical injury. The judge held that he had discretion to allow the proposed amendment, but declined to exercise it in the plaintiff's favour, on the basis that it would deprive the defendant of a cast-iron limitation defence. It is submitted that this refusal to exercise the discretion in the plaintiff's favour was harsh. There was no suggestion that the abandonment would prejudice the defendant in any respect other than the loss of the limitation defence. The defendant had taken the point on limitation only at a late stage. If the plaintiff had not sought damages in respect of physical injury then the defendant would have had no limitation defence to the financial aspect of the claim. Thus the plaintiff's decision to seek damages in respect of physical injury gave the defendant an unexpected windfall, in the form of a defence which would not otherwise have been available. In cases where the point arises more than three but fewer than six years after the accrual of the cause of action, it may be different: here, the claimant may still be able to begin again with the financial aspect of the claim. But where the matter is not determined until more than six years after accrual of the cause of action, so that the claimant cannot bring alternative proceedings, the effect of these cases is to give solicitors a defence based upon pure technicality.[2] On the other hand, it is unlikely that s 11 will apply in cases where the claim is based on a failure to advise as to legal entitlement to a category of benefits to which the claimant is entitled only if he suffers injury in the course of his work. This is a claim for damages for negligent advice rather than for damages for personal injury, even though the claimant is entitled to damages only if he has suffered personal injury, because the entitlement to benefit would have been dependent upon such injury.[3]

1   [1999] Lloyd's Rep PN 215 (Singer J).
2   Although it may be possible to pursue the personal injury aspect of the claim pursuant to LA 1980, s 33.
3   *Gaud v Leeds Health Authority* (1999) Times, 14 May, CA. Compare *McGahie v Union of Shop Distributive & Allied Workers* 1996 SLT 74, per Lord Fraser at 75, cited with approval by Aldous LJ in a different context in *British & Commonwealth Holdings plc v Barclays Bank plc* [1996] 1 WLR 1 at 8F–9C, CA.

3   Contract

5.9   As stated above, in contract, the cause of action accrues on the date when the breach of contract occurred, and the claimant then has six years in which to commence proceedings. In most cases it will not be of great importance that the limitation period in contract has expired, because, as mentioned above, the claimant will be able to sue on a concurrent duty in tort, which may provide a later a limitation period, and will also, unlike the claim in contract, allow the claimant to seek to rely upon LA 1980, s 14.[1]

1   *Société Commerciale de Réassurance v ERAS Ltd* [1992] 2 All ER 82n, CA.

5.10   There is, however, one point of potential interest in relation to the limitation period in contract.[1] This was raised in cases which arose before LA 1980, s 14A had come into force. The argument is, essentially, that where a solicitor has acted negligently, after his negligence he is subject to a continuing duty to advise his client that he has acted negligently. This duty continues until the date when the client's claim in respect of the original negligence becomes statute-barred, and breach of this further duty is itself actionable. If this argument were correct, then a solicitor who was negligent in 1980 would have a continuing duty to warn the client of his own negligence. That duty would be in force until 1986, whereupon the solicitor could presumably be sued in the following six years, until 1992, for failure to warn that he had previously acted negligently. In this way the limitation period would effectively run for 12 rather than six years, and possibly ad infinitum. Thus, it is unlikely that arguments of the type set out in this paragraph are correct.

1   For further commentary see Evans *Lawyers' Liabilities* (1996) at 189–191.

5.11   An alternative approach succeeded in *Midland Bank Trust Co Ltd v Hett, Stubbs and Kemp*.[1] In 1961 Mr Green's father granted him an option to purchase a farm. Mr Green engaged the defendant solicitors, who negligently failed to register the option. In 1967 Mr Green's father conveyed the farm to his wife. This had the effect of rendering the unregistered option worthless, so its value was lost due to the failure to register it. Mr Green's executors commenced an action against the defendants in 1972. Oliver J held that the action in contract was not statute-barred: as the solicitors kept the option and were consulted about it over the years, they had a continuing obligation to register it, which was terminated only after conveyance of the farm.

1   [1979] Ch 384 (Oliver J).

5.12   The Court of Appeal considered this approach in *Bell v Peter Browne & Co*.[1] In that case, the plaintiff contacted the defendant solicitors in 1977 following the breakdown of his marriage. Pursuant to the plaintiff's instructions, the defendants prepared a transfer of the former matrimonial home to the plaintiff's wife, which he executed in 1978. But the defendants negligently failed to protect the plaintiff's continuing interest in the house, which was that he should receive one sixth of the proceeds of sale. They should have prepared a trust deed to that effect, and registered a caution. In 1986 the plaintiff's wife told him that she had sold the former matrimonial home and spent all the proceeds. Thus the effect of the defendants' negligence was that the plaintiff had lost the one sixth interest in the proceeds of sale which he ought to have had. He issued a writ against the solicitors in August 1987.

1   [1990] 2 QB 495, CA.

5.13   The Court of Appeal held that the cause of action in contract had accrued at the date of the original failure, 1978, and rejected a continuing duty argument. Nicholls LJ accepted that there might be

'... exceptional cases where, on the true construction of the contract, the defaulting party's obligation is a continuing contractual obligation. In such cases the obligation is not breached once and for all, but it is a contractual obligation which arises for performance day after day, so that on each successive day there is a fresh breach. A familiar example of this is the usual form of repairing clause in a tenancy agreement ...'

But he distinguished *Hett, Stubbs and Kemp* on the basis that, there, the solicitors continued to have dealings with their client in respect of the unregistered option, whereas in *Bell* there was no evidence that the defendants had had any further contact with the plaintiff after the conclusion of his divorce proceedings, so that there was no continuing contractual obligation.[1] Beldam LJ too considered that there was only one breach of contract.[2] Like Nicholls LJ, Mustill LJ considered it possible that a solicitor could have a continuing obligation, as part of his retainer, 'to be constantly on watch for new sources of potential danger, and to take immediate steps to nip them in the bud'. But there was no express duty to that effect in *Bell*, and Mustill LJ thought it 'impossible to imply such a strange obligation from the mundane facts of the present case'.[3] Thus there was only one breach of contract.

1   See [1979] Ch 385 at 501D–H.
2   See [1990] 2 QB 495 at 509D–E.
3   See [1990] 2 QB 495 at 512G–513B.

5.14   To conclude, while it is possible that a solicitor's contract of retainer may contain a continuing obligation to check whether he has made errors and put them right, unless such a term of the retainer is express, the court is unlikely to hold that there is an implied term to this effect, unless the facts are similar to those of *Hett, Stubbs and Kemp*, where the solicitors continued to deal in some way with the option after their initial failure to register it.

4   The tort of negligence

5.15   In the tort of negligence, the cause of action accrues when the defendant's negligence first causes the claimant loss. The cases in relation to lenders' claims, litigation, and the loss of benefits under a will, give rise to special problems and for this reason merit separate treatment.[1] In general, however, the relevant type of loss for these purposes is the loss for which the claimant claims compensation in his or her statement of case. As mentioned,[2] in solicitors' negligence cases the loss claimed is usually economic loss. Problems have arisen in cases where the solicitor's negligence has exposed the claimant to a risk of loss, for example by failing to register an option which would prevent a third party from selling his property to persons other than the claimant, but the event the subject of the risk does not actually take place for several years. In such a case, there are two principal candidates for the date when the loss is suffered:

(i)   the date of the initial negligence, which gave rise to the risk; or

(ii) the date when the event of which there was a risk actually took place: in our example, the date when the property was actually sold.

The argument in favour of (ii) is that the event which is the subject of the risk might never occur. For instance, in *Hett, Stubbs and Kemp*[3] Mr Green's father might not have sold the farm to his wife, and so might not have deprived Mr Green of the opportunity to buy the farm. If the risk does not occur, the argument runs, the claimant has suffered no loss; so there is no loss unless and until the event actually occurs. Against this is the argument that, as soon as there is a risk of an untoward event happening, the presence of the risk itself causes the claimant loss, because a risk of something untoward happening is in principle capable of being valued. The value of the risk depends on the likelihood of the event happening and the amount of damage which will be suffered if it does occur. Thus, at time (i), the claimant has suffered loss in the amount of the value of the risk. As Bingham LJ has observed, attaching a money value to a possible future contingency is something which judges do[4]

'... every day in awarding claimants damages for the risk of epilepsy, the risk of osteoarthritis, the risk of possible future operations, the risk of losing a job and so on. The valuation exercise is, of course, different, but the difference is one of subject matter, not of kind.'

1   See sections 5, 6 and 7 below respectively.
2   See para 5.2.
3   Para 5.11.
4   *D W Moore & Co Ltd v Ferrier* [1988] 1 WLR 267 at 280B–C, CA.

5.16   In most cases where the solicitor is retained to deal with property or contracts, other than those where the claimant is to obtain security, the cause of action accrues at the time when the claimant becomes legally obliged to proceed with the original transaction. The reason is as follows. As the cause of action in negligence accrues when damage is first caused, the starting point is to consider what counts as 'damage' in the context of claims for economic loss. Delivering the leading speech in the recent case of *Nykredit Mortgage Bank plc v Edward Erdman Group Ltd (No 2)*,[1] Lord Nicholls of Birkenhead approved a passage in the earlier case of *Forster v Outred & Co*[2] in which it was said that, for these purposes, damage meant

'... any detriment, liability or loss capable of assessment in money terms and it includes liabilities which may arise on a contingency, particularly a contingency over which the plaintiff has no control; things like loss of earning capacity, loss of a chance or bargain, loss of profit, losses incurred from onerous provisions or covenants in leases.'

Once it is accepted that damage can include exposure to the risk of an event over which the claimant has no control, it is possible to hold that damage is caused as soon as the claimant is exposed to that risk, even if the event does not occur until later. This is on the basis set out in the last paragraph. The court assesses the amount of the risk in the manner identified by Bingham LJ.[3] But note that, if the value of the contingency is so low that only nominal damages would be awarded shortly after the date of the negligence, then the cause of action may be said to accrue later: see the discussion of *Moore v Ferrier*.[4] The position may, however, be different in lenders' cases.[5]

1   [1997] 1 WLR 1627, HL.
2   [1982] 1 WLR 86 at 94, CA.
3   See para 5.15.
4   [1988] 1 WLR 267; see para 5.22.
5   See paras 5.26ff.

5.17   Cases in which damage was held to have accrued at the time of completion of the original, negligently prepared legal document, even though the risk to be guarded against did not occur until later, form a line of authority which begins with *Forster v Outred*. Lord Nicholls approved these cases in *Nykredit*, even though he held that a different approach was correct on the facts of *Nykredit* itself. The facts of these cases will be considered here.[1]

1   Evans (see para 5.10, note 1) deals with these cases in more detail, but note that he was writing before the House of Lords' decision in *Nykredit*.

5.18   In *Forster v Outred & Co*,[1] the court had to proceed on the following assumptions of fact. The plaintiff's son asked her to sign a mortgage, secured on her home, to assist him in his business. The plaintiff believed that the mortgage would provide only temporary security for a bridging loan; that her son would soon obtain a permanent mortgage from elsewhere; and that, when this happened, the mortgage over her home would be terminated. In fact, the mortgage covered all present and future liabilities of her son and was unlimited in time. The defendant solicitors failed to explain this to the plaintiff. If they had explained it, she would not have signed the mortgage. Having held that damage for these purposes could include contingent damage (see above), the court concluded that the plaintiff had suffered damage when she entered into the mortgage deed, rather than later when the mortgagee made a demand under the mortgage, because she had encumbered her interest in the house and subjected it to a liability which might mature according to events wholly outside her control. In other words, the damage was encumbering the property so that there was a risk of a demand being made on the mortgage, which the plaintiff would have to meet.

1   [1982] 1 WLR 86.

5.19   *Forster* was followed in *Melton v Walker and Stanger*.[1] The solicitors' negligence was in the drafting of an agreement as to who should pay capital gains tax in the event of the sale of a farm. Due to their negligence in drafting it, when the farm was sold some years after the date of the agreement, the plaintiff had to pay more capital gains tax than she would have done if the agreement had been properly drafted. The court held that the cause of action accrued when the agreement was signed, and not when the farm was sold or the plaintiff was assessed for capital gains tax on the sale. Similarly, in *Baker v Ollard and Bentley*,[2] the defendants negligently failed to ensure that, on 12 April 1973, the plaintiff obtained security of tenure of the first floor of a house. The Court of Appeal held that the plaintiff suffered loss on 12 April 1973, even though, at that date, the quantum of her damages could be assessed only by considering the attitude of Mr and Mrs B who had the power to seek possession of the first floor, but did not in fact do so until December 1973. The plaintiff should have had security on 12 April 1973, and she did not. It did not matter that the risk of eviction at that date depended upon a contingency.

1   (1981) 125 Sol Jo 861, Nourse J.
2   (1982) 126 Sol Jo 593, CA.

5.20   Again, in *D W Moore & Co Ltd v Ferrier*,[1] on 1 July 1971 the plaintiff insurance brokers signed a contract with one Fenton, whereby he became a director and shareholder of the first plaintiff. The contract contained a restrictive covenant relating to Fenton. The defendant solicitors prepared the agreement for the plaintiffs and represented to them that it would prevent Fenton from working as an insurance broker within 15 miles of King's Lynn for three years from the date on which he ceased to be a director of or employed by the first plaintiff. In fact, however, the restrictive covenant did not take effect when Fenton ceased to be an employee or director. The plaintiffs did not discover this until 1980, when Fenton sought to change employment. The Court of Appeal held that the plaintiffs had suffered loss in 1971 when they signed the agreement, because, at that date, they had a worthless restrictive covenant; thus, at that date, they were subjected to the risk that Fenton would leave and do what the restrictive covenant was supposed to prevent him from doing. Neill LJ pointed out that:[2]

> 'a valid restrictive covenant, if it is not personal solely to the covenantee, can be assigned to the purchaser of the goodwill of a business. To my mind, it does not require evidence to establish that such a covenant has some value, particularly when it is given in the context of a broking business where personal contacts may be of particular importance.'

He added that, as in *Baker*,[3] it did not matter that, prior to the date of Fenton's departure, the assessment of damages would depend on his likely future attitude. Although this went to the assessment of damages, it did not mean that, before Fenton's departure, the plaintiffs had suffered no damage at all.

1 [1988] 1 WLR 267, CA.
2 [1988] 1 WLR 267 at 277A-B.
3 (1982) 126 Sol Jo 593, CA: see para 5.19.

5.21 Bingham LJ's approach was similar. On the assumptions which the court had to make, it was 'clear beyond argument that from the moment of executing each agreement the plaintiffs suffered damage because instead of receiving a potentially valuable chose in action they received one that was valueless'. He dealt with the argument that, at the outset, the loss was minimal, as follows:[1]

'If the quantification of the plaintiffs' damage had fallen to be considered shortly after the execution of either agreement, problems of assessment would undoubtedly have arisen. It might have appeared that Mr Fenton was unlikely to leave, taking much of the first plaintiff's business with him, to establish a competing business. If so, the plaintiffs' damage would have been assessed at a modest figure. But the risk of his so doing could not have been eliminated altogether, and so long as there was any risk that one of the first plaintiff's two directors might leave, taking much of the first plaintiff's business with him, to establish a competing business, there must necessarily have been a depressive effect on the value of the first plaintiff's business and on that of the second and third plaintiffs' derivative interests.'

1 [1988] 1 WLR 267 at 279H–280B, CA.

5.22 Further, Bingham LJ suggested a test of whether damage had been caused. The defendants were certainly in breach of contract. If, shortly after the breach, the plaintiffs had sued in contract, would they have recovered more than nominal damages? If they would, then damage had also been caused for purposes of the tort of negligence; not if not. There is some doubt as to whether this approach should be regarded as a general test for assessing whether damage has been caused for the purposes of the tort of negligence.[1] In any event, the point is that, although risks of loss which are contingent can amount to loss for these purposes, the risk must have at least some substance to it. If the risk is so low as to be de minimis, then loss is not suffered when it arises. It follows that, unless the facts of a case are on all fours with existing authorities, defendants may wish, in applications on this basis, to consider adducing evidence to show that the risk to which the claimant had been subjected had a considerable value at an early date, and claimants may wish to adduce evidence showing the opposite. On the other hand, in taking that approach, parties must be careful not to place themselves in a position where, if the action is not held to be barred by the Limitation Act 1980, they will have substantially weakened their case for trial.

1 In the recent insurance brokers' case of *Knapp v Ecclesiastical Insurance Group plc* [1998] PNLR 172, CA Hobhouse LJ found it a helpful test (182), but Buxton LJ did not consider that this passage in Bingham LJ's judgment had been intended to be used as a test of general application in cases of this kind (190). Butler-Sloss LJ did not express a view on the point.

5.23 The last leading solicitors' case in this line of authority is *Bell v Peter Browne & Co*, the facts of which were considered above in relation to contract.[1] In short, in 1978 the defendant solicitors negligently failed to ensure that the plaintiff's interest in his former matrimonial home was protected when he transferred it to his wife. The Court of Appeal held that the plaintiff suffered loss in 1978 when the transfer took effect without him having the formal protection of his interest in the proceeds of sale which he ought to have had. The extent of his loss depended on the attitude of his former wife. Before she sold the house, there must have been uncertainty as to those intentions. Nicholls LJ applied Bingham LJ's test. If the plaintiff had sued in 1980, before sale of the house, his damages might have been low, but not nominal: 'he would have been entitled at least to recover from the defendants the cost incurred in going to other solicitors for advice on what should be done and for their assistance in lodging the appropriate caution.'[2] Beldam LJ said that, due to the negligence, the plaintiff's interest was clearly less valuable in 1978 than it would have been if there had been no negligence.[3]

1　See para 5.12. See also *Tabarrok v EDC Lord & Co* [1997] PNLR 491, CA. P alleged negligence by D solicitors in allowing him to become a surety for his company's obligations under a lease. It was alleged inter alia that D had given P negligent advice as to the schedule of dilapidations to the lease. The Court of Appeal held that the cause of action accrued on the date when the lease was executed, rather than the later date when the company defaulted. On the facts, if P's allegations were correct, then, had he sued D at the date of execution of the lease, he would have recovered more than nominal damages because his obligations would already have been more onerous than they ought to have been.

2　[1990] 2 QB 495 at 503G.

3　[1990] 2 QB 495 at 510F.

Purchasers' cases: date of exchange or date of sale?

5.24　In the recent case of *Byrne v Hall Pain & Foster*,[1] flat-buyers sued their surveyors for professional negligence in the provision of the valuation report on which they had relied to purchase the flat. The question arose as to whether the cause of action had accrued at the date when they exchanged contracts to purchase the flat, or when the transaction completed. The Court of Appeal held that the former was the correct date: on exchange, the plaintiffs became irrevocably committed to purchasing the lease of the flat, which, due to the defendants' negligence, was in a worse condition than they believed it to be. Thus, at the time of exchange of contracts, the plaintiffs had suffered some detriment capable of valuation in money terms, and so the cause of action accrued. Cases where the plaintiff is a lender, which are considered in the next section, were distinguished: there, as will be seen, the plaintiff's loss depended in part on the borrower's performance of his covenant, and so different principles applied. It might be added that, in lenders' cases, the lender is not generally irrevocably committed to the transaction until completion, because its standard terms generally permit it to withdraw from the transaction at any time prior to completion. It is likely that the reasoning in *Byrne* would apply equally to an action brought by a purchaser of an interest in real property against solicitors who had negligently reported on title: the cause of action would probably accrue on exchange of contracts rather than at completion.

1　[1999] Lloyd's Rep PN 147, CA.

5.25　To conclude, this line of authority suggests that in cases where the claimant's loss is, at the outset, dependent upon a contingency which is not within the control of the claimant and which may or may not occur, then damage is suffered as long as the value which can be assigned to the risk, or to the consequences of the negligence, immediately after the claimant is legally obliged to enter the transaction or agreement, is more than nominal. Where the contingency is within the control of the claimant however, it is likely that damage will not be suffered, and the cause of action will not accrue, until the time when it becomes impossible for the claimant to act to avoid loss.[1] The line of cases considered in this section must, however, be distinguished from lenders' cases in which, as a result of the negligently executed transaction, the claimant obtains benefits in the form of security. Those are considered next.

1   See Evans *Lawyers' Liabilities* (1996) p 182, citing Leonard J's treatment of limitation in relation to the accountants in *Mathew v Maughold Life Assurance Co Ltd* (1985) 1 PN 142, approved in passing by the Court of Appeal in the same case at (1987) 3 PN 98, 107.

5   Lenders' cases: *Nykredit*

5.26   The leading case in this category is now the House of Lords' decision in *Nykredit Mortgage Bank plc v Edward Erdman Group Ltd (No 2)*.[1] This was the House's judgment on interest payable in those cases which remained from the *BBL*[2] decision. Although in *Nykredit* the lenders were suing valuers rather than solicitors, the same principles are likely to apply to lenders' claims against solicitors.[3] The question before the House was what interest should be awarded on damages. As statutory interest could be awarded only from the date when the cause of action arose, this raised the question of when the lenders' cause of action had arisen. The House acknowledged that its decision on this point would be relevant not only to claims for interest, but also to questions of limitation.[4] It is submitted that *Nykredit* should be regarded as authoritative in relation to when the cause of action arises, as well as in relation to interest.

1   [1997] 1 WLR 1627. As Lord Hoffmann observed, at [1997] 1 WLR 1639D, the House of Lords' decision was in accordance with the Court of Appeal's earlier decisions in *UBAF Ltd v European American Banking Corpn* [1984] QB 713 and *First National Commercial Bank plc v Humberts* [1995] 2 All ER 673.
2   *Banque Bruxelles Lambert SA v Eagle Star Insurance Co Ltd* [1997] AC 191, HL. See further chapter 7.
3   See para 7.75.
4   [1997] 1 WLR 1627, per Lord Nicholls at 1630A–B and Lord Hoffmann at 1638B. Lord Hoffmann said that although for purposes of interest the question under Supreme Court Act 1981, s 35A was when the cause of action 'arose', whereas for limitation under the Limitation Act 1980 it was when the cause of action 'accrued', in his view the two words had the same meaning.

(a)   The basic comparison

5.27   The principal speech was delivered by Lord Nicholls. He considered the question of when the cause of action accrued in a case where, as a result of negligent advice, property was acquired as security. The question was when the lender first sustained loss. The loss was economic rather than physical in character. At the moment after the lender had made the advance, it was not certain that it would suffer financial loss, because (i) the borrower might not default, and, even if he did, (ii) the security might be sufficient to cover the amount of the borrower's debt.

5.28   In assessing when loss was suffered, the court had to consider the appropriate *measure* of loss. In cases where, had there been no negligence, the lender would not have entered into the transaction,[1]

'... a professional negligence claim calls for a comparison between the plaintiff's position had he not entered into the transaction in question and his position under the transaction. That is the basic comparison. Thus, typically in a case of a negligent valuation of an intended loan security, the basic comparison called for is between (a) the amount of money lent by the plaintiff which he would still have had in the absence of the loan transaction, plus interest at a proper rate, and (b) the value of the rights acquired, namely the borrower's covenant and the true value of the overvalued property.'

In the rest of his speech Lord Nicholls referred to this formula as 'the basic comparison'. In order to determine when the lender first suffered a loss, it was necessary to apply the basic comparison to the facts of the case.

1   [1997] 1 WLR 1631E–F. Lord Nicholls did not deal with the position in cases where, had there been no negligence, the lender *would* still have entered into the transaction. Normally these are cases where, absent negligence, the lender would have lent less. Thus it might be said that the cause of action accrues as at the date of completion, because the lender had, at that date, lent more than it would have done. But the logic of *Nykredit* probably means that this approach is wrong: even if the lender is caused to lend more than it should have done, it may suffer no loss, because the borrower may repay all he owes. So, even in this type of case, it is probably necessary to assess the date when the cause of action accrues by reference to the basic comparison.

5.29   How should the basic comparison be applied? Lord Nicholls accepted that this might raise difficulties in obtaining evidence, but these difficulties were not difficulties in principle.[1] In other words, the *type* of evidence required was clear; the problem might be in actually obtaining it. As to this evidence, at any given time, it should be possible to obtain figures for part (a) of the basic comparison, namely, the amount of the advance plus interest at a proper rate. As to the appropriate rate of interest, see the discussion of basic loss in chapter 7.[2] Similarly, it should be possible to obtain a retrospective valuation giving the value of the security. It might be more difficult to value the borrower's covenant. On this, Lord Nicholls said:[3]

'Ascribing a value to the borrower's covenant should not be unduly troublesome. A comparable exercise regarding lessees' covenants is a routine matter when valuing property. Sometimes the comparison will reveal a loss from the inception of the loan transaction. The borrower may be a company with no other assets, its sole business may comprise redeveloping and reselling the property, and for repayment the lender may be looking solely to his security. In such a case, if the property is worth less than the amount of the loan, relevant and measurable loss will be sustained at once. In other cases the borrower's covenant may have value, and until there is default the lender may presently sustain no loss even though the security is worth less than the amount of the loan. Conversely, in some cases there may be no loss even when the borrower defaults. A borrower may default after a while but when he does so, despite the overvaluation, the security may still be adequate.'

1   [1997] 1 WLR 1627 at 1632B–C.
2   See para 7.64.
3   [1997] 1 WLR 1627 at 1632C–E.

5.30   Lord Nicholls went on to reject the notion that the cause of action could not arise until the property had been sold. It was wrong to suggest that loss could not be suffered until then:[1]

'… no accountant or prospective buyer, viewing the loan book of a commercial lender, would say that the shortfall in security against outstanding loans to defaulting borrowers did not represent a loss to the lender merely because the securities had yet to be sold.'

On the facts of *Nykredit*, the borrower defaulted at once and its covenant was worthless. The amount lent always exceeded the value of the security. Thus the cause of action accrued at or about the time of the transaction.[2]

1   [1997] 1 WLR 1627 at 1633B.
2   [1997] 1 WLR 1627 at 1635A–B.

5.31   The effect of this is that, where the borrower defaults and disappears without assets at once and the security was always worth less than the advance, the cause of action accrues almost immediately. On the other hand, where the borrower defaults but the value of the security is sufficient to cover the amount of the advance plus interest and costs of repossession, no loss is suffered and so the cause of action does not accrue, unless perhaps there is a delay in sale during which time the amount of the advance plus interest comes to exceed the value of the security.

(b)   Can the cause of action accrue before the borrower has defaulted?

5.32   More difficult is the question whether there are circumstances in which the cause of action can accrue before the borrower has defaulted. In principle, according to Lord Nicholls, there may be:[1]

> 'An alternative ... possibility is that the cause of action does not arise until the lender becomes entitled to have recourse to the security. I am not attracted by this, as a proposition of law. This suggestion involves the proposition that, until then, as a matter of law, the lender can never suffer loss, and the lender can never issue his writ, whatever the circumstances. That does not seem right to me. This proposition, like the date of realisation submission, loses sight of the starting point: that the lender would not have entered into the transaction had the valuer given proper advice. If the basic comparison shows a loss at an earlier stage, why should the lender have to wait until the borrower defaults before issuing his writ against the negligent valuer?'[2]

Lord Nicholls had already observed that there might be cases where the borrower's covenant had value so that until there was default there would be no loss even though the security was worth less than the amount of the advance. But by rejecting the notion that no cause of action could accrue until the borrower defaulted, he implicitly accepted that there could be circumstances in which, although the borrower had not defaulted, the basic comparison showed a loss. Presumably this would have to be on the basis that a commercial valuer, looking at the borrower's covenant, would regard it as being of low value even though the borrower had not yet defaulted. Perhaps the valuer might know that the borrower was about to go bankrupt. In practice, however, and, it is submitted, in most cases, the basic comparison will not show a loss until the borrower has defaulted. Lord Nicholls accepted this:[3]

> 'I recognise that in practice the basic comparison may well not reveal a loss so long as the borrower's covenant is performing satisfactorily. For this reason there is little risk of a lender finding his action statute-barred before he needs to resort to the deficient security. But it would be unwise to elevate this practical consideration into a rigid rule of law.'

Presumably it would be unwise because it would rule out the possibility of evidence as to, for example, the borrower's impending financial nemesis. Note that Lord Hoffmann's approach on this, as on the other points, was similar to Lord Nicholls's:[4]

> 'The lender may be able to show that the rights which he has acquired as lender are worth less in the open market than they would have been if the security had not been overvalued. But I think that this would be difficult to prove in a case in which the lender's personal covenant still appears good and interest payments are being duly made.'

1   [1997] 1 WLR 1627 at 1633E–G.
2   Compare Mummery LJ's obiter remarks in *UCB Bank plc v Halifax (SW) Ltd* [1999] Lloyd's Rep PN 154 at 158.
3   [1997] 1 WLR 1627 at 1633E–G.
4   [1997] 1 WLR 1627 at 1639B–C.

5.33   Future cases may explore the extent to which defendants can succeed in showing that loss was suffered before the borrower defaulted. Another issue which requires clarification is the extent to which loss may be suffered if the borrower has defaulted to some degree, but is still making sporadic payments and claiming that he will be able to pay his debts in due course. Presumably a commercial valuer would assess such a borrower's covenant as being worth less than that of a non-defaulting borrower, but more than that of a borrower who had disappeared leaving no assets. It is conceivable that a new breed of experts who value borrowers' covenants will spring up. The question which the court will have to consider will be not simply whether the covenant of a sporadic payer is worth less than that of someone who always pays on time; rather, the question will be whether the covenant of the sporadic payer has a value which, when added to the value of the security, is worth less than the amount of the advance plus unpaid interest. It will be necessary not simply to value the borrower's covenant on a scale comparing it to other borrowers' covenants, but to express its value in a figure which can fairly be compared to the amount of the advance plus interest. In practice, it will be hard for defendants to show that the cause of action arose prior to, say, the commencement of possession proceedings, unless they can find experts who are able to provide such valuations. It remains to be seen whether they will be able to do so.

(c)   Comparison between the last two categories of case

5.34   We have suggested that, in considering limitation in tort, lenders' cases be placed in a different category from other cases. It is clear that Lord Nicholls did not consider there to be any inconsistency in this approach.[1] In most cases, as we have seen, the court is prepared to consider a risk of future loss and to hold that loss has occurred when the value of that risk is more than nominal; usually, this will occur at the time of the transaction or negligence in question. The difference in a lender's case is that the lender need not call upon the defendant valuer or solicitor for damages until the borrower proves unable to pay. Thus, there may be negligence by a solicitor which causes the lender no loss, according to the basic comparison, because the borrower continues to pay. Applying the basic comparison, lenders are unlikely to suffer loss until, at the earliest, it becomes plain that the borrower will default. It is the added element of the borrower's covenant which introduces the need for the basic comparison in lenders' cases, and means that a different approach is required to the question of when loss is first suffered. This leads in turn to a different approach to limitation.

1   See *Nykredit* [1997] 1 WLR 1627 at 1633H.

6   Loss of litigation

5.35   Where the claimant sues his solicitor for the loss of litigation, in the sense of negligently having allowed his claim to be struck out for want of prosecution, the cause of action accrues on the date on which the claim is actually struck out. This is the effect of the Court of Appeal's decision in *Hopkins v Mackenzie*.[1] The plaintiff claimed that he had been injured in the course of an operation in February 1979. He instructed solicitors to sue for medical negligence in April 1981, and they issued a writ on 24 February 1982.

The claim was ultimately struck out for want of prosecution on 4 February 1986. The plaintiff issued a writ against his solicitors on 27 January 1992. The question was whether the cause of action in tort had arisen more than six years before, in other words, prior to 27 January 1986. The plaintiff conceded that, by February 1984, there was a plain and obvious risk that the action would be struck out. Thus, if a plain and obvious risk of striking out had counted as damage for the purposes of the tort of negligence, then this would have occurred in February 1984 and the action would have been statute-barred. Saville LJ accepted that, at this stage, the value of the claim might have been diminished, in the sense that the settlement value might have been reduced due to the risk of striking out.[2] He considered, however, that this did not count as damage for the purposes of limitation in tort, because the plaintiff was not suing for compensation for a risk of his claim being struck out, but rather was suing for the actual striking out; thus the damage did not occur until the claim was actually struck out.

1   [1995] 6 Med LR 26.
2   [1995] 6 Med LR 26 at 30.

5.36   As Hobhouse LJ observed in the recent case of *Knapp v Ecclesiastical Insurance Group plc,*[1] it is hard to reconcile the decision in this case with the authorities discussed in the first category of cases concerning limitation in tort,[2] where it has been held that a more than minimal risk of loss occurring *is* sufficient to amount to loss so as to give rise to a cause of action in tort, and that it is wrong to suppose that no damage occurs until the event of which there is a risk actually occurs. Nevertheless, unless overruled, *Hopkins* remains the law.

1   [1998] PNLR 172, CA, 187D–E. See also Evans's criticism: *Lawyers' Liabilities* (1986) pp 186–189.
2   See paras 5.15–5.25.

7   Loss of benefits under a will

5.37   In *Bacon v Howard Kennedy,*[1] the defendant solicitors had negligently failed to carry out X's instructions to draft a will whereby he left his estate to the plaintiff. The plaintiff sued the defendants for negligence. The question was whether the plaintiff's cause of action accrued when the defendants ought to have drafted the will, in which case the claim was statute-barred, or when X died, in which case it was not. The judge opted for the latter date. It was argued that, in accordance with cases such as *Forster v Outred,*[2] the plaintiff suffered a loss in the sense of a risk that he would receive nothing, as soon as the defendants had negligently failed to draft the will. The judge's rejection of this may be justified on the basis that it is an essential part of the cause of action that the testator has died,[3] because, until that time, the defendant's negligence will not have caused the plaintiff any loss. This is because, had there been no negligence, the testator could have revoked the part of the will leaving property to the plaintiff at any time until his or her death. Thus, until the testator has died, it will always be an open question whether, before death, the testator might have removed the plaintiff from the will. Further, until the testator has died, if the defect in the will is discovered, it can be remedied.[4]

1   [1999] PNLR 1, HHJ Bromley QC sitting as a Deputy High Court Judge.
2   [1982] 1 WLR 86, CA: see para 5.18.
3   *Evans* p 181. Mr Evans was also successful counsel for the plaintiff in *Bacon.*
4   The negligent solicitor might be liable for the cost of doing this, but this would be principally liability to the testator not potential beneficiaries under the will.

C   STATUTORY EXTENSIONS TO THE LIMITATION PERIOD

5.38   Sections 14A and 32 of the Limitation Act 1980 contain statutory extensions of the normal limitation period, in cases to which they apply. These are complicated provisions, and it is not possible to consider every aspect of them.[1] We shall, however, attempt to concentrate upon issues which particularly concern solicitors' cases.

1   See McGee *Limitation Periods* (3rd edn, 1998) and Oughton, Lowry and Merkin, *Limitation of Actions* (1998).

1   Limitation Act 1980, s 14A

5.39   Section 14A was added to the Limitation Act 1980 to deal with cases where the defendant did not know of the facts relevant to the cause of action at the time when it accrued. As mentioned at the start of this chapter, given that loss in solicitors' negligence cases is usually economic, it is quite possible that the claimant, through no fault of his own, may not realise that he has suffered loss until more than six years after the accrual of the cause of action. A number of the cases considered above demonstrate this.[1] Under normal principles, such claims would be statute-barred. The purpose of s 14A is to remedy that injustice.[2]

1   See paras 5.15–5.25.
2   See the Twenty-Fourth Report of the Law Reform Committee (Latent Damage) (1984).

5.40   The effect of LA 1980, s 14A is that, in cases to which it applies, if six years have passed since the accrual of the cause of action, the claimant has an alternative possible limitation period in which to sue. The alternative period is three years from the 'starting date', as defined in s 14A, but subject to a longstop of 15 years from the act or omission which is alleged to constitute negligence.[1]

1   LA 1980, s 14B.

(a)   Scope of s 14A

5.41   Section 14A applies only to claims where the cause of action is the tort of negligence, and not to breaches of contract, even if the breach alleged is a failure to act with reasonable skill or care.[1] This means that, where it is alleged that a solicitor has failed to act with reasonable skill and care, which is actionable in either contract or tort, a claimant wishing to take advantage of s 14A should abandon the claim in contract. Section 14A does not apply to cases to which LA 1980, s 32(1)(b) applies,[2] that is, cases of farud, deliberate concealment or mistake. A different extension to the limitation period applies in those cases.[3]

1   *Société Commerciale de Reassurance v ERAS (International) Ltd* [1992] 2 All ER 82n, CA.
2   LA 1980, s 32(5).
3   See paras 5.60ff.

(b)   The 'starting date'

5.42   The provisions defining what counts as the starting date, from which the claimant has three years in which to issue a writ, are complex and require to be quoted in full:

'(5)   For the purposes of this section, the starting date for reckoning the period of limitation under subsection (4)(b) above is the earliest date on which the plaintiff or any person in whom the cause of action was vested before him first had both the knowledge required for bringing an action for damages in respect of the relevant damage and a right to bring such an action.

(6)   In subsection (5) above "the knowledge required for bringing an action for damages in respect of the relevant damage" means knowledge both—

(a)   of the material facts about the damage in respect of which damages are claimed; and

(b)   of the other facts relevant to the current action mentioned in subsection (8) below.

(7)   For the purposes of subsection (6)(a) above, the material facts about the damage are such facts about the damage as would lead a reasonable person who had suffered such damage to consider it sufficiently serious to justify his instituting proceedings for damages against a defendant who did not dispute liability and was able to satisfy a judgment.

(8)   The other facts referred to in subsection (6)(b) are—

(a)   that the damage was attributable in whole or in part to the act or omission which is alleged to constitute negligence; and

(b)   the identity of the defendant; and

(c)   if it is alleged that the act or omission was that of a person other than the defendant, the identity of that person and the additional facts supporting the bringing of an action against the defendant.

(9)   Knowledge that any acts or omissions did or did not, as a matter of law, involve negligence is irrelevant for the purposes of subsection (5) above.

(10)   For the purposes of this section a person's knowledge includes knowledge which he might reasonably have been expected to acquire—

(a)   from facts observable or ascertainable by him; or

(b)   from facts ascertainable by him with the help of appropriate expert advice which it is reasonable for him to seek;

but a person shall not be taken by virtue of this subsection to have knowledge of a fact ascertainable only with the help of expert advice so long as he has taken all reasonable steps to obtain (and, where appropriate, to act on) that advice.'

Various aspects of this definition of the starting date will be commented upon.

(c)   Burden of proof

5.43   If the writ is not issued within six years of the date when the cause of action accrued, the onus is on the claimant to plead and prove that the starting date is a date within the three years preceding issue of the writ. If the defendant wishes to allege that the starting date is a date prior to the three years immediately preceding issue of the writ, then the onus is on the defendant to prove this.[1] Presumably, in a case of this type, if neither party succeeds in satisfying the onus of proof, the claimant should lose the claim because he or she has failed to show that s 14A prevents the operation of the ordinary limitation period.[2]

1   *Nash v Eli Lilly & Co* [1993] 1 WLR 782 at 796H, CA. That case concerned the provisions of Limitation Act 1980, s 14 but that provision is analogous to s 14A and cases on s 14 are helpful in construing s 14A: see the Court of Appeal's judgment in *Hallam-Eames v Merrett Syndicates Ltd* [1996] 7 Med LR 122.
2   Compare *Campbell v Meacocks* [1995] NPC 141, CA (per Otton LJ).

(d)   Actual knowledge

5.44   Leaving aside the provisions relating to constructive knowledge,[1] what degree of certainty in the plaintiff's mind counts as (actual) knowledge for the purposes of s 14A(6)? In *Spencer-Ward v Humberts*,[2] Sir Thomas Bingham MR quoted and applied an observation of his predecessor Lord Donaldson of Lymington MR in the case of *Halford v Brookes*:[3]

> 'The word has to be construed in the context of the purpose of the section, which is to determine a period of time within which a plaintiff can be required to start any proceedings. In this context "knowledge" clearly does not mean "know for certain and beyond possibility of contradiction". It does, however, mean "know with sufficient confidence to justify embarking on the preliminaries to the issue of a writ, such as submitting a claim to the proposed defendant, taking legal and other advice and collecting evidence." Suspicion, particularly if it is vague and unsupported, will indeed not be enough, but reasonable belief will normally suffice. It is probably only in an exceptional case such as *Davis v Ministry of Defence*[4] that it will not, because there is some other countervailing factor.'

Although *Halford v Brookes* concerned s 14, it was helpful by way of analogy in interpreting s 14A, and indeed Sir Thomas Bingham MR, with whom the other judges agreed, applied this test to hold that, on the facts of *Spencer-Ward*, the plaintiffs had knowledge within the meaning of the section at a time when they wrote a letter to their former surveyors which was couched in terms similar to a letter before action.

1   See para 5.56.
2   [1995] 1 EGLR 123, CA.
3   [1991] 1 WLR 428 at 443E, CA. He also quoted a passage from *Nash v Eli Lilly & Co* to similar effect.
4   [1985] LS Gaz 3265, CA. Lord Donaldson dealt with the facts of that case at 442–3.

(e)   Knowledge 'that the damage was attributable in whole or in part to the act or omission which is alleged to constitute negligence' (s 14A(8))

5.45   The meaning of this phrase is the most difficult aspect of interpreting s 14A. The basic question is: what facts, or kinds of facts, must the claimant know in order for time to start running under s 14A? Constructive knowledge is dealt with below;[1] for the moment we shall consider only actual knowledge. Knowledge that acts or omissions did or did not amount to negligence in law is irrelevant.[2] Problems arise in cases where the defendant argues that the claimant knew all the material *facts* at the time when the cause of action accrued, and that the reason the claimant did not commence proceedings within the limitation period was simply due to ignorance of the *law*, namely the law of negligence showing that there was a cause of action, which has to be ignored. On the face of it this could give rise to the same injustice which the enactment of s 14A was intended to prevent, namely, claimants finding that their claims have become statute-barred before they could reasonably have brought proceedings to enforce them.

1   See para 5.56.
2   LA 1980, s 14A(9).

5.46   The Court of Appeal dealt with the issue in *Hallam-Eames v Merrett Syndicates Ltd*.[1] Various Names at Lloyd's sued their active underwriter, managing agents and members' agents on the basis that the writing of various policies had been negligent because the liability to which members of the relevant syndicates were thereby exposed was potentially enormous, and the defendant underwriter did not have the material on which he could have formed any reasonable view of what that liability was likely to be. Delivering the judgment of the court, Hoffmann LJ referred to a previous Court of Appeal decision in relation to s 14, *Dobbie v Medway Health Authority*,[2] which he summarised as follows:[3]

'In *Dobbie* the plaintiff was admitted to hospital for the removal of a lump in her breast. The surgeon who excised the lump formed the view that it was cancerous and removed the breast. Afterwards on microscopic examination the lump turned out to be benign. She knew shortly after the operation that the breast had been removed before the microscopic examination but was not advised until 17 years later that it might have been negligent to do so. Again this court held that she knew enough at the earlier stage to satisfy section 14(1)(b).'

In relation to s 14A(8), Hoffmann LJ said that it was not sufficient simply that the plaintiff knew that his damage had been caused by an act or omission of the defendant. In addition,[4]

'... the act or omission of which the plaintiff must have knowledge must be that which is causally relevant for the purposes of an allegation of negligence. There may be many acts, omissions or states which can be said to have a causal connection with a given occurrence, but when we make causal statements in ordinary speech, we select on common sense principles the one which is relevant for our purpose. In a different context it could be said that a Name suffered losses because some members' agent took him to lunch and persuaded him to join Lloyd's. But this is not causally relevant in the context of an allegation of negligence.

It is this idea of causal relevance which various judges of this court have tried to express by saying ... that one should

"... look at the way the plaintiff puts his case, distil what he is complaining about and ask whether he had in broad terms knowledge of the facts on which that complaint is based." (Hoffmann LJ in *Broadley* [1994] 4 All ER 439).

If one asks on common sense principles what Mrs Dobbie was complaining about, the answer is that the surgeon had removed a healthy breast. It would in our view be a seriously incomplete statement of her case to say that it was simply that the surgeon had removed her breast. This is not a matter of elaborating detail by requiring knowledge of precisely how he had come to the act complained of, such as this court rejected in *Broadley*. It was part of the essence of her complaint. Nor is it requiring knowledge of fault or negligence. The court's emphatic rejection of such a requirement is entirely consistent with characterising the act complained of (and of which knowledge was therefore required) as the removal of a healthy breast ...

If one asks what is the principle of common sense on which one would identify Mrs Dobbie's complaint as the removal of a healthy breast rather than simply the removal of a breast, it is that the additional fact is necessary to make the act something of which she would prima facie seem entitled to complain. She was suspected of having a cancerous lump and if this had been the case, the removal of her breast would not have been a matter for complaint ...

The plaintiff does not have to know that he has a cause of action or that the defendant's acts can be characterised in law as negligent or as falling short of some standard of professional or other behaviour. But, as Hoffmann LJ said in *Broadley*, the words "which is alleged to constitute the negligence" serve to *identify* the facts of which the plaintiff must have knowledge. He must have known the facts which can fairly be described as constituting the negligence of which he complains.'

1   [1996] 7 Med LR 122.
2   [1994] 1 WLR 1234.
3   [1996] 7 Med LR 122 at 125.
4   [1996] 7 Med LR 122 at 126.

5.47   The court went on to consider what, on the facts of *Hallam-Eames*, should be regarded as the facts which fairly constituted the negligence of which the Names complained. Those facts were not simply the writing of the relevant policies or certification of accounts, because[1]

> 'these facts in themselves do not amount to acts of which the Names would even *prima facie* be entitled to complain. It is necessary to add the allegation that the run off policies and RTCs exposed the names to potentially huge liabilities and that the certified accounts attributed values to IBNRS, none of which were in fact capable of reasonable quantification.'

1   [1996] 7 Med LR 122 at 126.

5.48   Thus the correct approach to LA 1980, s 14A(8) is to ask what facts can fairly be described as constituting the negligence of which the claimant complains. It appears that those facts include not only the facts that the claimant has suffered loss, or that there is a causal link of some kind between the defendants and that loss; for s 14A(8) to be satisfied, it is also necessary that the claimant know facts which show the defendant's error, even though he need not know that those facts give rise to a cause of action in law.[1]

1   The Court of Appeal considered the issue further in *Forbes v Wandsworth Health Authority* [1997] QB 402, a case on s 14. It appears that the majority, Stuart-Smith and Evans LJJ, applied *Hallam-Eames*.

5.49   As Hoffmann LJ made clear in the passages quoted above, for the purposes of s 14A(8) it is necessary to distinguish between:

(i)   knowledge that, on the facts known to the claimant, he has a cause of action in negligence. This is irrelevant.

and

(ii)   the relevant knowledge, namely, knowledge of facts which, to a lawyer, constitute the essence of the factual basis of the claimant's claim in negligence: in *Dobbie*, the fact that the surgeon had removed a breast which in fact was healthy and did not require removal; or, in *Hallam-Eames*, the fact that the underwriters caused the Names to be exposed to liabilities which were potentially enormous, when the underwriters did not have the material on which they could have formed any reasonable view of what the liability was likely to be. Similarly, in the later case of *Forbes v Wandsworth Health Authority*,[1] Evans LJ characterised the fact that was relevant for the purposes of the equivalent part of LA 1980, s 14 as being the fact[2]

> 'that there was, as is now alleged, a lost opportunity to prevent the injury which [the plaintiff] later suffered.'

1   [1997] QB 402, CA.
2   One might say that part of the difficulty in applying s 14A(8) arises because the 'facts' which are relevant for the purposes of that subsection include elements of judgmental or evaluative propositions about how defendants *ought* to have behaved. But, at least in everyday speech, we do not always describe statements about 'how X *ought* to have behaved' as facts. Although it relates to matters well beyond the scope of this book, those interested in this point may wish to look at Mackie's discussion of 'is' and 'ought' in *Ethics: Inventing Right and Wrong* (1977) at p 64.

(f) Cases where the negligence alleged is an error of law

5.50   Reference has already been made to the basic injustice at which LA 1980, s 14A was aimed, namely, the danger that a claimant's claim might become statute-barred through no fault of his own. The provision that knowledge that an act or omission constitutes negligence is irrelevant for the purpose of s 14A gives rise to a danger that that aim might not be achieved: the claimant might not sue within the limitation period simply due to ignorance that he had a cause of action. The cases considered above seek to ensure that, though knowledge that acts constitute negligence is irrelevant, nevertheless the potential injustice is avoided, because the knowledge required to start time running under s 14A involves knowledge of all the factual issues which are required to constitute the cause of action, in the way set out in the last paragraph. In the examples quoted there, a claimant who knew the facts which the court characterised as necessary to start time running under s 14A would be likely to realise that there was a potential claim, or at least that there was something to complain about which had caused the claimant damage. Thus the potential injustice was avoided.

5.51   It is submitted that, in cases where the negligence alleged is essentially an error of law, there is a danger that the potential injustice may not be averted. Solicitors' negligence cases will often fall into this category. The problem is that, in this type of case, when one applies Hoffmann LJ's test of asking what the claimant is essentially complaining about, the answer will be: an error of law. If it is actionable at all, the error of law will, by definition, amount to negligence. But s 14A(9) provides that knowledge that acts or omissions did or did not involve negligence is irrelevant for the purposes of s 14A. The key point about which the claimant would have had to have known in order to realise that he should bring proceedings will be that advice given by lawyers contained an error of law; without this knowledge the claimant could not reasonably be expected to sue within the limitation period; yet this knowledge is irrelevant for the purposes of s 14A, so ignorance of it will not assist a claimant in using s 14A to extend the limitation period.

5.52   Two cases illustrate the possibility of injustice. In *HF Pension Trustees Ltd v Ellison*,[1] the plaintiffs were successors of the trustees of an occupational pension scheme called the FMC scheme. In May 1989 the FMC trustees sought advice from a solicitor experienced in pension matters as to whether they could transfer a surplus in their scheme to another scheme. The solicitor advised the FMC trustees that they had power to do so and on 17 November 1989, in reliance upon that advice, the FMC trustees made transfers totalling £18.44m. Various pensioners complained about the transfers to the Pensions Ombudsman, who found in a determination dated 11 October 1995 that the transfers were in breach of trust. On 12 July 1996 Knox J upheld that decision.[2] On 17 October 1997 the plaintiffs issued a writ against the solicitor for negligent advice in 1989, seeking repayment of any sums transferred which could not be recovered, and the costs of dealing with the question of the validity of the transfers. The primary limitation period had expired and the question was whether s 14A could assist the plaintiffs. Jonathan Parker J held that it could not.[3] The material facts for the purposes of s 14A were that the solicitor had advised that the transfers be made, and that they had been made in reliance upon his advice. The plaintiffs had known these facts from the outset. They had not known that the solicitor's advice was negligent, but that was a matter of law which had to be ignored.

1   (1999) Times, 5 March (Jonathan Parker J).

2   His decision is reported at [1997] 1 All ER 862.
3   Applying Judge Paul Baker QC's decision in *Bradstock Trustee Services Ltd v Nabarro Nathanson* [1995] 1 WLR 1405.

5.53   On the facts of *Ellison*, there may have been no injustice. The limitation period probably expired at earliest in November 1995, six years after the transfer. By that time the plaintiffs must have known about the decision of the Pensions Ombudsman dated 11 October 1995, and so they could presumably have issued writs against the defendant before expiry of the limitation period. But the effect of the judge's reasoning, though legally quite correct, could easily produce injustice in other cases, for the reasons stated in para 5.51: in other cases, the claimant might know all the material *facts* at the outset, but there might be nothing to alert him to the possibility that his solicitor's advice was negligent until after expiry of the primary limitation period. On the judge's reasoning, s 14A would not assist such a claimant. It is submitted that this is a flaw in the wording of s 14A.

5.54   A similar issue arose in *Perry v Moysey*.[1] The plaintiff was considering entering into contracts of employment with two companies. His accountant, the defendant, advised him that it would be acceptable if the contracts provided for him to receive net salaries of £1,080 per month, index-linked. In reliance upon that advice, he entered into contracts on that basis in 1989. In September 1994 the companies were advised that the contracts were in breach of Companies Act 1985 (CA), s 311 in that it was unlawful for a director to be paid remuneration net of income tax. The plaintiff discovered that he was liable to substantial sums in tax. He issued a writ in 1997, after expiry of the primary limitation period.[2] Judge Jack QC held that the plaintiff was entitled to rely upon s 14A. As to the argument that the only matter of which the plaintiff had been unaware was a matter of law, namely the effect of s 311, which could not assist him for the purposes of s 14A, he said:[3]

> 'The damage which Mr Perry has suffered is a liability to account for tax either to the revenue or the companies in respect of payments received by him up to September 1994, and the reduction of his payments thereafter. Both situations, namely that relating to the period up to September 1994 and that thereafter, are matters of fact: he owes more money; he is receiving less. They come about by the operation of s 311, which is a matter of law; but the effect of the section's operation is to give rise to factual situations. Subsection (9) is not relevant to these considerations because it relates on the present facts to whether or not Mr Perry knew or did not know that an omission by Mr Moysey to consider s 311 would be negligent.'

1   [1998] PNLR 657 (Judge Jack QC sitting as a deputy High Court judge).
2   The primary limitation period expired on 2 January 1995, six years after the plaintiff had entered the contracts. Thus it is possible that he could have issued a writ in the period between September 1994 when the problem was discovered, and January 1995, but unclear whether he realised the need to do so during that period. Of course, this issue is irrelevant to the issue the court had to decide.
3   [1998] PNLR 657 at 660G–661B.

5.55   In *Ellison*,[1] Jonathan Parker J distinguished *Perry* on the basis that, in the latter, the plaintiff did not know of his damage, namely liability to pay the revenue, until years after the initial negligence, whereas in the former the plaintiffs knew of the damage, namely the transfers, at the outset. This is not wholly convincing. One might say that in both cases it was new facts which caused the plaintiffs to realise they should sue: in *Ellison* it was probably the decision of the Pensions Ombudsman and in *Perry* it was the advice given to the company as to the effect of CA 1985, s 311. In both cases, this new matter, although a fact, arose essentially from a realisation that an error of law had been made. On that basis, in both cases LA 1980, s 14A should not have been applied, but, in both cases, a refusal to apply it would probably have led to an element of injustice of the very kind against which s 14A was intended to protect. If this approach is correct, then it is to be hoped that the Law Commission will have the opportunity to consider the reform of s 14A in its forthcoming report.

1 (1999) Times, 5 March; see para 5.52.

(g) Constructive knowledge

5.56 It is clear from LA 1980, s 14(10) that constructive knowledge of the claimant of the relevant facts will suffice, if he does not have actual knowledge. The decision of the majority of the Court of Appeal in *Forbes v Wandsworth Health Authority*[1] suggests that individual characteristics of the claimant in question should not be taken into account in assessing whether the claimant had constructive knowledge, and that the court will not be particularly slow to hold that a reasonable claimant should have sought advice which would have given him knowledge of his claim.

1 [1997] QB 402 at 420H–421A.

5.57 Although the question of what it was reasonable for the claimant to have done is essentially one which will depend on the facts in each case, *Henderson v Temple Pier Co Ltd*,[1] another case on s 14 rather than s 14A, is a further example of the court taking a fairly firm view to the effect that a claimant ought to have acted earlier to find out the relevant knowledge. The plaintiff claimed to have slipped and fallen when walking down a gangway leading to a ship which was moored at Temple Pier in London. She was intending to visit a bar on the ship. The accident occurred in January 1993. She instructed solicitors in February 1993 but they did not commence proceedings until April 1997.[2] The Court of Appeal held that it was no defence that the plaintiff had entrusted her action to solicitors. Insofar as they provided legal advice as to whether the facts in issue constituted negligence, this was irrelevant (s 14A(9)). Insofar as they provided factual advice which assisted the claim, such as helping to identify the owner of the ship on which the plaintiff had sustained injury, this was information which was ascertainable by the plaintiff herself without the need for legal expertise. Thus she was unable to rely upon her appointment of solicitors. In the context of s 14A, the effect of this would be that the facts which the solicitors had delayed in finding out were facts which came under s 14A(10)(a): the fact was not one 'ascertainable only with the help of expert advice', so the plaintiff could not rely on having taken reasonable steps to obtain expert advice, within the meaning of the end of s 14A(10).

1 [1998] 1 WLR 1540, CA.
2 It would therefore appear that the plaintiff had an action against her solicitors for loss of the litigation: see chapter 10.

5.58 HHJ Fox-Andrews QC considered the provisions of s 14A in the context of a lender's claim against solicitors in *Abbey National plc v Forsyths*.[1] The plaintiff operated various departments with different functions. In the judge's view,[2]

> '... it is unreasonable and therefore unrealistic to consider that in the absence of special circumstances the knowledge of a person in one department can be regarded as the knowledge of a person in another department or that the totality of that knowledge is to be regarded as the knowledge of the society.'

On the facts of the case, however, he went on to hold that, on receipt of a letter which indicated unusual circumstances surrounding the transaction, the plaintiff should then have acted to gather together all its knowledge, whereupon it would have had the relevant knowledge for the starting date to be reached.[3] See also *Finance for Mortgages Ltd v Farley*,[4] where Kay J considered when the starting date occurred in a claim by a lender against a valuer in relation to a negligent overvaluation. If the lender had acted prudently, it would have repossessed the property by 31 January 1991 and obtained valuations which revealed the overvaluation by March 1991. Thus the lender ought to have known the relevant facts to start time running by the end of March 1991.

1　(11 June 1997, unreported) (Official Referees' Business).
2　At p 26 of the transcript.
3　HHJ Bowsher QC reached a similar conclusion in *Birmingham Midshires Building Society v Infields* (20 May 1999, unreported) (Technology and Constuction Court). See also para 5.68.
4　[1998] PNLR 145.

(h)　Knowledge in relation to separate causes of action

5.59　Where a claimant has sufficient knowledge to start time running under s 14A in relation to *one* cause of action against a solicitor, this does not start time running in relation to separate causes of action, even if they arise out of the same defendant's handling of the same transaction on behalf of the same claimant. Thus, in *Birmingham Midshires Building Society v JD Wretham*[1] the plaintiff, a lender, had known sufficient facts to start time running in relation to a claim that the defendant solicitors had failed to report to it the true purchase price of the property. The plaintiff also claimed that, in breach of duty, the solicitors had failed to report to the lender that the property was subject to a demolition order. The judge held that this gave rise to a separate cause of action, so that the plaintiff's knowledge, for s 14A purposes, of the claim in relation to the purchase price did not start time running in relation to the claim concerning the demolition order.

1　[1999] Lloyd's Rep PN 133 (Technology and Construction Court).

2　Limitation Act 1980, s 32[1]

5.60　Section 32 of the Limitation Act 1980 extends the limitation period in cases of fraud, deliberate concealment, or mistake. The section provides:

'(1)　Subject to subsections (3) and (4A) below, where in the case of any action for which a period of limitation is prescribed by this Act, either—

(a)　the action is based upon the fraud of the defendant; or

(b)　any fact relevant to the plaintiff's right of action has been deliberately concealed from him by the defendant; or

(c)　the action is for relief from the consequences of a mistake;

the period of limitation shall not begin to run until the plaintiff has discovered the fraud, concealment or mistake (as the case may be) or could with reasonable diligence have discovered it.

References in this subsection to the defendant include references to the defendant's agent and to any person through whom the defendant claims and his agent.

(2)　For the purposes of subsection (1) above, deliberate commission of a breach of duty in circumstances in which it is unlikely to be discovered for some time amounts to deliberate concealment of the facts involved in that breach of duty.

(3)   Nothing in this section shall enable any action—

(a)   to recover, or recover the value of, any property; or

(b)   to enforce any charge against, or set aside any transaction affecting, any property;

to be brought against the purchaser of the property or any person claiming through him in any case where the property has been purchased for valuable consideration by an innocent third party since the fraud or concealment or (as the case may be) the transaction in which the mistake was made took place.

(4)   A purchaser is an innocent third party for the purposes of this section—

(a)   in the case of fraud or concealment of any fact relevant to the plaintiff's right of action, if he was not a party to the fraud or (as the case may be) to the concealment of that fact and did not at the time of the purchase know or have reason to believe that the fraud or concealment had taken place; and

(b)   in the case of a mistake, if he did not at the time of the purchase know or have reason to believe that the mistake had been made.

(4A)   Subsection (1) above shall not apply in relation to any time limit prescribed by section 11A(3) of this Act or in relation to that time limit as applied by virtue of section 12(1) of this Act.

(5)   Sections 14A and 14B of this Act shall not apply to any action to which subsection (1)(b) above applies (and accordingly the period of limitation referred to in that subsection, in any case to which either of those sections would otherwise apply, is the period applicable under section 2 of this Act).'

1   McGee *Limitation Periods* (3rd edn, 1998) ch 20; Oughton, Lowry and Merkin *Limitation of Actions* (1998) pp 57–73.

5.61   The effect of this section is helpfully summarised by Oughton, Lowry and Merkin:[1]

'Accordingly, there are three exceptional cases in which the ordinary limitation periods laid down by the Act are suspended. These are:

(a)   the action is based upon the fraud of the defendant; or

(b)   any fact relevant to the plaintiff's right of action has been deliberately concealed from him by the defendant; or

(c)   the action is for relief from the consequences of a mistake.

In all such cases the period of limitation does not begin to run until the plaintiff has discovered the fraud, concealment or mistake or could with reasonable diligence have discovered it.'

It is helpful to consider in turn the provisions relating to fraud, deliberate concealment, mistake, and constructive knowledge.

1   *Limitation of Actions* (1998) p 58.

(a)   Fraud

5.62   The claimant has to show that the action 'is based upon the fraud of the defendant'. In order to show this, he must be relying upon a cause of action which is based upon fraud, such as an action in deceit, or an action claiming the rescission of a transaction brought about by fraud; conversion, for example, is not such an action, because the defendant's fraud is not an essential element of the cause of action.[1]

1   *Beaman v ARTS Ltd* [1949] 1 KB 550, CA. This case considered identical wording in the Limitation Act 1939. See also *GL Baker Ltd v Medway Building and Supplies Ltd* [1958] 1 WLR 1216.

(b)   Deliberate concealment

5.63   There are a number of points on deliberate concealment. LA 1980, s 32(2) provides that deliberate commission of a breach of duty in circumstances in which it is unlikely to be discovered for some time amounts to deliberate concealment. Further, it is likely that reckless concealment would be held to amount to deliberate concealment for the purposes of s 32.[1] Problems arise in relation to a solicitor who negligently fails to realise that he has acted in breach of duty toward his client, and fails to tell the client that he has acted in breach of duty because he does not realise that he has. In the light of a decision of the Court of Appeal reached as we prepared for press,[2] it is possible that all that the claimant need show is that the conduct of the solicitor which amounted to concealment was done deliberately, and not that the solicitor had any awareness that he had breached his duty or that he was concealing a breach of duty from the client. If that is the position, it might mean that claimants would be able to rely upon s 32A more readily than in the past, and could do so to escape the complexities of s 14A. In the absence of a full transcript, however, it is impossible to comment further.

1   See *Westlake v Bracknell District Council* [1987] 1 EGLR 161 at 163J–K (Mr PJ Cox QC sitting as a Deputy High Court Judge).
2   *Brocklesby v Armitage & Guest* 9 July 1999, NLD, CA.

5.64   In the recent case of *Tunbridge v Buss Murton & Co*,[1] Laddie J declined to strike out an allegation of deliberate concealment by defendant solicitors. It was alleged that the solicitors had negligently drafted a debenture, that there had been occasions when the defendants had had to re-consider the debenture, and that, on re-considering the debenture, competent solicitors would have realised the error they had made. The judge held that this was a sufficient plea of deliberate concealment: if, at trial, the court accepted these allegations, it might then be able to infer that the defendants had themselves realised their own earlier error; if the court was able to make that inference, then it was likely that it would be able to make the further inference that the defendants' failure to report such knowledge to the plaintiff had been due to a deliberate decision to conceal the information.

1   (1997) Times, 8 April.

5.65   The issue also arose in *Markes v Coodes*.[1] The defendant solicitors acted for the plaintiff on his purchase of a workshop in 1987. In 1991 British Gas, who owned neighbouring land, wrote to the defendants and made clear that the workshop had been built over land which was subject to a right of way in their favour. This was indeed the position. The defendants had negligently failed to report the existence of the right of way to the plaintiff in 1987. The defendants sent the plaintiff a copy of British Gas's letter, but they did not explain that its effect was to show that they themselves had been negligent. The defendants effectively conceded that they had deliberately concealed matters relevant to the plaintiff's right of action from him, and the judge agreed.[2]

1   [1997] PNLR 252 (HHJ Thompson sitting as a deputy High Court judge).
2   See [1997] PNLR 252 at 261F–G.

5.66   Note that, where the concealment on which the claimant relies occurs after the accrual of the claimant's cause of action, s 32(1)(b) nevertheless applies to that subsequent concealment, so that time starts to run only after the claimant has, or could with reasonable diligence have, discovered the deliberate concealment.[1] Thus, if a solicitor acts negligently in 1990, and at that time does not deliberately conceal the negligence from his client, but then re-considers the issue in 1992 and does deliberately conceal it from the client, the six year limitation period starts to run in 1992 rather than 1990.

1   *Sheldon v RHM Outhwaite (Underwriting Agencies) Ltd* [1996] AC 102, HL. This was a 3–2 decision of the House. See Oughton, Lowry and Merkin at pp 67–9 for criticism.

(c)   Mistake

5.67   Extension of the limitation period on the basis that the action is 'for relief from the consequences of a mistake' may be granted only if the mistake in question is an essential element of the cause of action, in which case it should be pleaded in the statement of claim.[1]

1   *Phillips-Higgins v Harper* [1954] 1 QB 411, Pearson J. The case was decided in relation to the equivalent provision of the Limitation Act 1939, but the wording of that provision was identical to s 32(1)(c).

(d)   Constructive knowledge

5.68   In the types of case to which LA 1980, s 32 applies, time begins to run from the date on which the claimant either has actual knowledge of the fraud, deliberate concealment or mistake, or 'could with reasonable diligence have discovered it'. In the recent case of *Paragon Finance plc v DB Thakerar & Co,*[1] the Court of Appeal considered the meaning of these words. Millett LJ, with whom the other judges agreed, said:[2]

> 'The question is not whether the plaintiffs *should* have discovered the fraud sooner, but whether they *could* with reasonable diligence have done so. The burden of proof is on them. They must establish that they *could not* have discovered the fraud without exceptional measures which they could not reasonably have been expected to take. In this context the length of the applicable period of limitation is irrelevant. In the course of argument May LJ observed that reasonable diligence must be measured against some standard, but that the six year limitation period did not provide the relevant standard. He suggested that the test was how a person carrying on a business of the relevant kind would act if he had adequate but not unlimited staff and resources and were motivated by a reasonable but not excessive sense of urgency. I respectfully agree.'

1   [1999] 1 All ER 400, CA.
2   [1999] 1 All ER 400 at 418b–d.

5.69   In cases of fraud, the question will be when the claimant, with reasonable diligence, could have discovered 'the facts which are necessarily relied upon to justify the allegation of fraud' which is pleaded, as opposed to when the claimant could reasonably have concluded that he or she had been a victim of fraud. Similarly, in relation to deliberate concealment, the question will be when the claimant, acting with reasonable diligence, could have discovered 'those facts sufficient to constitute or complete the particular cause of action ... the acid test cannot be wider than those facts which were relied upon to support the pleas made in the Points of Claim'.[1]

1   *Comphania de Seguros Imperio v Heath (REBX) Ltd* (30 March 1999, unreported) (Langley J), at pp 58 and 59 of the transcript.

D   CLAIMS IN EQUITY

1   Breach of trust

5.70   The relevant parts of Limitation Act 1980, s 21 provide as follows:

'21   Time limit for actions in respect of trust property

(1)   No period of limitation prescribed by this Act shall apply to an action by a beneficiary under a trust, being an action:—

(a)   in respect of any fraud or fraudulent breach of trust to which the trustee was a party or privy; or

(b)   to recover from the trustee trust property or the proceeds of trust property in the possession of the trustee, or previously received by the trustee and converted to his use.

...

(3)   Subject to the preceding provisions of this section, an action by a beneficiary to recover trust property or in respect of any breach of trust, not being an action for which a period of limitation is prescribed by any other provision of this Act, shall not be brought after the expiration of six years from the date on which the right of action accrued.'

By virtue of LA 1980, s 38, the words 'trust' and 'trustee' have the same meanings as set out in the Trustee Act 1925; by Trustees Act 1925, s 68(17), 'trusts' include implied and constructive trusts.

5.71   On the face of it, therefore, the effect of s 21 is that there is a limitation period of six years for all breaches of trust except those which fall within the exceptions set out in s 21(1), so that, by s 21(1)(a), there is no limitation period for fraudulent breaches of trust. But this proposition must be heavily qualified. First, dicta of Sir Robert Megarry V-C in *Tito v Waddell (No 2)*[1] suggest that breaches of the rules that a trustee must not sell trust property to himself, or that a trustee must deal fairly with trust property and must not prejudice the interests of the beneficiaries, are not breaches of trust within the meaning of s 21. This would suggest that no limitation period applies to them, though they would be capable of being barred by acquiescence or laches.[2]

1   [1977] 3 All ER 129 at 246–8, dealing with Limitation Act 1939, s 19 which was in similar terms to s 21.
2   *Nelson v Rye* [1996] 1 WLR 1378. Subsequently disapproved on a different point: see para 5.75.

5.72   Secondly, in relation to constructive trusts, the Court of Appeal considered the question of the constructive trusts to which s 21 applies, in detail, in *Paragon Finance plc v DB Thakerar & Co.*[1] Note that, for procedural reasons, the court was concerned only with the question of whether the defendants' contentions were reasonably arguable, rather than with whether they were necessarily correct.[2] Thus, strictly speaking, the ratio is simply that those contentions are reasonably arguable. But it is submitted that the depth of analysis contained in Millett LJ's judgment renders the court's view highly persuasive.[3]

1   [1999] 1 All ER 400.
2   For an explanation of why this was, see paras 5.82ff.
3   Further, Langley J applied it in *Comphania de Seguros Imperio v Heath (REBX) Ltd* (30 March 1999, unreported).

5.73 Millett LJ set out the distinction between two wholly different situations in which the court would impose a constructive trust. The distinction is discussed in chapter 4.[1] It is between:

(i) cases where the constructive trustee receives the claimant's property in circumstances in which the court will genuinely imply a trust, and

(ii) cases in which there is 'accessory liability', that is, a third party has been guilty of a fraudulent breach of trust and the defendant has received trust property or been an accessory to the breach.

The effect of the Court of Appeal's decision in *Paragon* is that Limitation Act 1980, s 21 applies to trusts in category (i) but does not apply to 'trusts' in category (ii). Nevertheless, category (ii) trusts should be treated for limitation purposes in the same way as fraud at common law. Further, it is doubtful whether category (ii) constructive trusts should properly be called constructive trusts, since it leads to potential confusion with category (i), and the nature of category (ii) is more of a device to justify the imposition of a remedy than a circumstance that is truly akin to the traditional trust. Millett LJ's judgment sets out 10 reasons, based both on statutory interpretation and principle, supporting these conclusions. Perhaps the critical factor is that, in category (ii) cases, the trust is imposed pursuant to a jurisdiction in equity which is concurrent with the common law jurisdiction for fraud; a limitation period does apply to claims at common law; thus, the court of equity applies the same limitation period by analogy.

1   At paras 4.17–4.19.

5.74   Does this mean that the limitation period for category (ii) cases is six years from the breach of trust, or, by analogy with claims at common law, six years from the date when the claimant could with reasonable diligence have discovered the fraudulent breach of trust?[1] In principle, given that the rationale for category (ii) cases being beyond s 21 is that equity should apply the same limitation as applies at common law, one might argue that the appropriate limitation period for category (ii) cases would be the same as applies in relation to fraud at common law, that is, six years from the date on which the claimant could with reasonable diligence have discovered the fraudulent breach of trust.

1   Cf LA 1980, s 32.

2   Breach of fiduciary duty

5.75   The Limitation Act 1980 does not contain a limitation period in relation to breaches of fiduciary duty. Thus the question arises whether they are exempt from any limitation period. The Court of Appeal considered an application for leave to amend to allege intentional breach of fiduciary duty in *Paragon*.[1] The application was rejected. If there was a claim for breach of fiduciary duty, it was subject to the same arguable limitation defence as was the claim to amend to allege a breach of a constructive trust in category (ii), which was dealt with in the last section.[2] The point appears to be that a claim for breach of fiduciary duty in the sense of a solicitor concealing from a lender information which tends to show that the transaction in question is fraudulent is a claim where, if the court takes any step, it will be to impose a remedy in circumstances analogous to common law fraud; thus the same principle applies as applies in relation to category (ii) constructive trusts: it is arguable that the court will apply a limitation period by analogy with common law fraud. On the other hand, there may be no limitation period in relation to claims for breach of fiduciary duty which amount to interference with trust property, and are not analogous to category (ii).[3]

1   [1999] 1 All ER 400. It expressly overruled *Nelson v Rye* [1996] 1 WLR 1378, and impliedly overruled *Kershaw v Whelan (No 2)* (1997) 141 Sol Jo LB 37, which was not cited.
2   At para 5.73.
3   See for example *Coulthard v Disco Club Mix Ltd* [1999] 2 All ER 457 (Mr Jules Sher QC sitting as a deputy High Court judge).

E   PROCEDURAL POINTS

1   Protective writs

5.76   Under the Rules of the Supreme Court, the Court of Appeal held that it would generally amount to an abuse of process to issue a writ in order to escape the expiry of a limitation period, in circumstances where the plaintiff had no intention to proceed with the action unless sued by a third party.[1] It seems most unlikely that a less rigorous attitude will prevail under the Civil Procedure Rules 1998.[2]

1   *West Bromwich Building Society v Mander Hadley & Co* (1998) Times, 9 March, CA.
2   Part 1.1(2)(d) makes ensuring that cases are dealt with expeditiously part of the overriding objective.

2   Amendment to add new causes of action after expiry of the limitation period

5.77   Although the discussion which follows deals with authorities in relation to the former rules of court, part 17.4 of the Civil Procedure Rules 1998 employs similar wording to the old RSC Ord 20 r 5, and Limitation Act 1980, s 35 remains unchanged, so it seems likely that reference may still need to be made to the authorities on the previous rules, which are discussed here. Nevertheless, in reading this section it is important to bear in mind that the position will not necessarily be the same under the new regime.

5.78   The Court of Appeal dealt with this topic, in the context of claims against solicitors under the Rules of the Supreme Court, in *Paragon Finance plc v DB Thakerar & Co,*[1] which helpfully set out the preceding law, as well as developing a number of aspects of it. Where the claimant seeks leave to amend after the expiry of any relevant limitation period, the following questions arise.[2] First, does the proposed amendment add a new cause of action to the pleading? If it does not, then leave will generally be granted, subject to costs. If it does, then leave should not be granted unless the claimant can show that either:

(i)   the defendant does not have a reasonably arguable case on limitation which would be prejudiced by allowing the amendment; or

(ii) the new cause of action arises out of the same, or substantially the same, facts as a cause of action in respect of which the claimant has already claimed relief.

These points will be discussed in turn.

1   [1999] 1 All ER 400.
2   See *Paragon* [1999] 1 All ER 400 at 404e–g, *Welsh Development Agency v Redpath Dorman Long Ltd* [1994] 1 WLR 1409, CA, and *Darlington Building Society v O'Rourke James Scourfield & McCarthy* [1999] Lloyd's Rep PN 33, CA.

(a)   What counts as a new cause of action?

5.79   In *Letang v Cooper*,[1] Diplock LJ said that:

> 'A cause of action is simply a factual situation the existence of which entitles one person to obtain from the court a remedy against another person.'

Commenting on this passage in *Darlington Building Society v O'Rourke James Scourfield & McCarthy*,[2] Sir Ian Glidewell, with whom the other judges agreed, said

> 'Where ...the claim is based on a breach of duty, whether arising from contract or in tort, the question whether an amendment pleads a new cause of action requires comparison of the unamended pleading with the amendment proposed in order to determine:
>
> > (a)   whether a different duty is pleaded;
> >
> > (b)   whether the breaches pleaded differ substantially; and where appropriate
> >
> > (c)   the nature and extent of the damage of which complaint is made.
>
> ... In my view where an amendment pleads a duty which differs from that pleaded in the original statement of claim it will, or certainly will usually, raise a new cause of action. If there is no allegation of a different duty but different facts are alleged to constitute a breach of the duty it is more difficult to decide whether a new cause of action is pleaded.'

1   [1965] 1 QB 232 at 242–3, CA.
2   [1999] Lloyd's Rep PN 33 at 36.

5.80   An example of the pleading of a different duty appears in *Paragon*.[1] The plaintiffs sought to amend to allege that acts of the defendant solicitors which they had previously contended were merely negligent were, in the alternative, intentional breaches of duty on the part of the solicitors. The Court of Appeal held that this amounted to pleading a new cause of action. Another case in which the court held that two separate causes of action arose out of solicitors' handling of the same transaction was *Birmingham Midshires Building Society v JD Wretham*.[2]

1   [1999] 1 All ER 400.
2   [1999] Lloyd's Rep PN 133, Technology and Construction Court, discussed at para 5.59.

5.81   As to whether the addition of different facts amounts to a new cause of action, in *Paragon*, Millett LJ said that the selection of the material facts to define a cause of action 'must be made at the highest level of abstraction'.[1] Merely adding particulars will not count as adding a new cause of action.

1   [1999] 1 All ER 400 at 405g.

(b)   Can the claimant show that the defendant does not have a reasonably arguable case on limitation which will be prejudiced by the new claim?

5.82   The effect of the Limitation Act 1980, s 35(1) and (2) is that, if leave to amend is granted to add or substitute a new cause of action, the new cause of action is treated for limitation purposes as if it had been pleaded in a separate action which had been commenced on the same date as the original proceedings. Thus, if leave to amend is granted to allow a cause of action to be included after expiry of the limitation period in relation to that cause of action, then the defendant will lose the benefit of his accrued limitation defence, and will be unable to rely upon limitation as a defence at all. This would be unfair, unless the claimant can show that the cause of action arises out of the same or substantially the same facts as have already been pleaded. The latter is a ground for permitting the amendment (see below). But leaving that aside for the moment, and assuming that the claimant cannot show that the new cause of action arises out of the same or substantially the same facts, the court's approach is as follows. If the claimant can show that the defendant does not have a *reasonably arguable* defence to the new cause of action, on limitation, then the amendment is allowed. But if the claimant cannot show this, then leave to amend is not granted.[1] The effect of this is that, if the defendant has a reasonably arguable defence to the new cause of action, then, if the claimant wishes to proceed with its new cause of action, it must commence fresh proceedings, in which limitation may be tried as a preliminary issue.

1   *Welsh Development Agency v Redpath Dorman Long Ltd* [1994] 1 WLR 1409.

5.83   In judging whether it has been shown that granting leave to amend would deprive the defendant of a reasonably arguable limitation defence, the amendment is treated as being made at the date when the pleading is amended, which will be not earlier than the date when the application for leave to amend is *granted*, rather than, for example, the date when the summons seeking leave to amend was first issued or served.[1]

1   *Welsh Development Agency v Redpath Dorman Long Ltd* [1994] 1 WLR 1409.

(c)   Does the cause of action arise out of the same or substantially the same facts as those which are already pleaded?

5.84   The court's power to give leave for an amendment, after expiry of the limitation period, if it arises from the same or substantially the same facts as those already pleaded derives from Limitation Act 1980, s 35(4) and (5) and, now, Part 17.4 of the Civil Procedure Rules 1998. The issue of what counts as the same or substantially the same facts is substantially a matter of impression.[1] In cases where the proposed amendment seeks to introduce a claim of intentional wrongdoing where none was made before, *Paragon*[2] suggests that the amendment should not be said to arise out of the same or substantially the same facts.

1   *Welsh Development Agency v Redpath Dorman Long Ltd* [1994] 1 WLR 1409.
2   [1999] 1 All ER 400.

CHAPTER 6

Contributory negligence and contribution

A CONTRIBUTORY NEGLIGENCE

1 Introduction

6.1 Both contributory negligence and claims for contribution are issues of general application in actions at common law. While, in relation to each issue, there are some solicitors' cases which we discuss, to some extent it is necessary to consider cases from other areas of professional negligence in order to see how the principles operate. So, in this chapter, we discuss cases which go beyond solicitors' negligence.

2 Ambit

6.2 Apportionment for contributory negligence on the part of the claimant is becoming increasingly important in solicitors' negligence actions. The statutory basis for reductions on account of contributory negligence is the Law Reform (Contributory Negligence) Act 1945, s 1(1), which provides:

'where any person suffers damage as a result partly of his own fault and partly of the fault of any other person or persons a claim in respect of that damage shall not be defeated by reason of the fault of the person suffering the damage but the damages recoverable in respect thereof shall be reduced to such an extent as the court thinks just and equitable having regard to the claimant's share in responsibility for the damage.'

There is no doubt that the defence is available in actions based only upon negligence.[1] The position in relation to other varieties of claim is discussed next.

---

1   By s 4, fault is defined as 'negligence, breach of statutory duty or other act or omission which gives rise to liability in tort or would, apart from this Act, give rise to the defence of contributory negligence'.

(a) Contract

6.3 There was for some time doubt as to whether the Act applied to claims in contract as well as tort. This was resolved by the Court of Appeal's decision in *Forsikringsaktieselskapet Vesta v Butcher*.[1] The court approved Hobhouse J's analysis, which was that, in considering application of the Act to contractual claims, it was necessary to divide such claims into three categories:[2]

'(1) Where the defendant's liability arises from some contractual provision which does not depend on negligence on the part of the defendant.

(2) Where the defendant's liability arises from a contractual obligation which is expressed in terms of taking care (or its equivalent) but does not correspond to a common law duty to take care which would exist in the given case independently of contract.

(3) Where the defendant's liability in contract is the same as his liability in the tort of negligence independently of the existence of any contract.'

The Court of Appeal held that the Act did apply to category 3 cases, such as *Butcher* itself, but indicated that it did not apply to category 1 or 2 cases. O'Connor LJ cited with approval the dictum of Prichard J in the New Zealand case of *Rowe v Turner, Hopkins & Partners*[3] that 'the Contributory Negligence Act cannot apply unless the cause of action is founded on some act or omission on the part of the defendant which gives rise to liability in tort'.[4] The rationale for this approach is that, in a case where the defendant's liability to the claimant is the same in tort as in contract, as for example in an employer's liability case, the defendant may take advantage of arguments as to contributory negligence if he is sued in tort, and it would be unfair if he could not do the same if sued in contract.[5] On the other hand, the terms of the contract may, exceptionally, provide for the exclusion of liability for contributory negligence, in which case the Act will not apply.[6] Further, even in category 1 and 2 cases, it may be possible to argue that there should be a reduction in damages on the ground that the defendant caused only part of the loss.[7] But where the duty which has been broken is solely contractual, that is, would not have existed independently of the contract, or where there is breach of a strict contractual duty, contributory negligence has no application.

1   [1989] AC 852, [1988] 2 All ER 43, approving Hobhouse J's decision at first instance, [1986] 2 All ER 488. The Court of Appeal's decision was affirmed without discussion of the contributory negligence point by the House of Lords, [1989] AC 852. See also *Barclays Bank plc v Fairclough Building Ltd* [1995] QB 214, CA.
2   [1986] 2 All ER 488 at 508f–g.
3   [1980] 2 NZLR 550.
4   [1989] AC 852 at 866C.
5   See [1986] 2 All ER 488 at 509d–e (Hobhouse J) and [1989] AC 852 at 860H–861A (O'Connor LJ).
6   Cf [1986] 2 All ER 488 at 510j.
7   See *Tennant Radiant Heat Ltd v Warrington Development Corpn* [1988] 1 EGLR 41, CA.

6.4   The more negligent a claimant is, the keener he or she will be to show that the case falls into category 1 or category 2 so that contributory negligence will not run. The point has arisen in particular in relation to lenders' claims against solicitors and valuers. In *Bristol & West Building Society v Kramer & Co*,[1] the defendant solicitor was in breach of an instruction in the retainer providing that 'any matters which might prejudice the Society's security or which are at variance with the Offer of Advance should be notified to the Society immediately they become known.' The defendant argued that the Society was contributorily negligent in lending on insufficient information as to the value of the security and the status of the borrower. Blackburne J held that any contributory negligence was irrelevant as the claim was for breach of a strict duty, commenting that the

> 'obligation [in the retainer] is dependent on the knowledge of the matters in question and is not in any way dependent upon negligence on the part of the defendant firm. The fact that [the solicitor] was negligent (as distinct from deliberate) in overlooking his obligation to inform the Society of what he knew does not convert his obligation into one that is *dependent* on negligence.'

But Carnwath J declined to follow this approach, on slightly different wording of the solicitors' instructions, in *Mortgage Express Ltd v Newman*[2] and *Alliance & Leicester v Wheelers*.[3] Further, it is probably inconsistent with Sir Richard Scott V-C's decision in *Maes Finance Ltd v A L Phillips*[4] and Chadwick J's approach in *Bristol and West Building Society v Fancy and Jackson*.[5] The plaintiff did not seek to rely upon *Kramer*, even though the judge was Blackburne J, in the recent case of *Nationwide Building Society v Balmer Radmore*.[6] It is doubtful whether *Kramer* would today be followed in any case which was not on all fours with it.

1   (1995) Times, 6 February (Blackburne J).
2   [1996] PNLR 603, 612.
3   (23 January 1997, unreported).
4   (1997) Times, 25 March.
5   [1997] 4 All ER 582.
6   [1999] Lloyd's Rep PN 241.

(b)   Fraudulent and negligent misrepresentation

6.5   In *Alliance & Leicester Building Society v Edgestop Ltd*[1] Mummery J held that damages for deceit could not be reduced for contributory negligence. The plaintiff alleged that the defendant had fraudulently overvalued a property to induce it to make a loan to the purchaser. The defendant claimed that the plaintiff had been contributorily negligent in that it had not followed its own checking and approval procedures and should have realised that the borrowers would be unable to service the loan. The apportionment legislation was regarded as inapplicable as it had never been a defence to deceit prior to the legislation. Blackburne J reached the same conclusion, after thorough consideration of the authorities, in the solicitors' case of *Nationwide Building Society v Thimbleby & Co.*[2] By contrast, in *Gran Gelato Ltd v Richcliff (Group) Ltd*[3] it was held that the legislation did apply to claims for *negligent* misrepresentation under the Misrepresentation Act 1967, s 2(1) even though the wording of the section expressly equated liability under the section to that which would result 'had the misrepresentation been made fraudulently'.

1   [1993] 1 WLR 1462.
2   [1999] Lloyd's Rep PN 359.
3   [1992] Ch 560, CA.

(c)   Fiduciary duty

6.6   Commonwealth authority has suggested that the common law apportionment regime may be applied by analogy to breach of a fiduciary duty.[1] But this is not the position in England, at least in cases of deliberate breach of fiduciary duty: in the recent case of *Nationwide Building Society v Balmer Radmore* Blackburne J said:[2]

> 'In English law contributory negligence has never been a defence to an intentional tort: in such cases the 1945 Act has no application. By parity of approach I can see no good reason why equity, concerned as Lord Dunedin remarked in *Nocton v Lord Ashburton* [1914] AC 932 at page 963 "to keep persons in a fiduciary capacity up to their duty" should adopt a less rigorous approach.
>
> I therefore take the view that where, in order to establish a breach of fiduciary duty, it is necessary to find that the fiduciary was consciously disloyal to the person to whom his duty was owed, the fiduciary is disabled from asserting that the other contributed, by his own want of care for his own interests, to the loss which he suffered flowing from the breach.'

Thus the position in relation to deductions for contributory negligence for breaches of fiduciary duty appears to be similar to that in relation to misrepresentation, considered in the last paragraph: if intentional disloyalty is a necessary element of the breach of fiduciary duty then deductions for contributory negligence may not be made, but if mere negligence is sufficient to found the claim then they may be. Thus there is a symmetry between the position at law and in equity.

1   *Day v Mead* [1987] 2 NZLR 443, NZCA; *Canson Enterprises Ltd v Broughton & Co* (1991) 85 DLR (4th) 129, SCC.
2   [1999] Lloyd's Rep PN 241 at 281.

(d)   Lenders' cases[1]

6.7   In *Platform Home Loans Ltd v Oyston Shipways Ltd*,[2] the House of Lords had to consider how the 1945 Act applied to a lenders' case. Although the defendant was a surveyor, similar principles are likely to apply in solicitors' cases. In order to understand the decision, it is necessary to understand the distinction between basic and attributable loss, which is discussed in chapter 7.[3] In summary, the *basic loss* is the amount of the claimant's loss calculated by taking the amount of the advance, plus the cost, in interest payments, to the lender of funding that advance, but less the amount of the payments made by the borrower and the net proceeds of sale of the property if it has been repossessed and sold.[4] The *attributable loss*, in a valuer's case, is the difference between the valuation of the property which the valuer in fact gave, and the correct valuation at the time. The notion of attributable loss was introduced by the House of Lords' decision in *BBL*.[5] In a claim by a lender against a valuer, if the basic loss exceeds the attributable loss then damages are limited to the amount of the attributable loss, plus statutory interest; if the basic loss is less than the amount of the attributable loss, then the claimant recovers damages in the amount of the basic loss.

1   See further chapter 7.
2   [1999] 2 WLR 518, HL. See Murdoch [1999] 08 EG 168, Russell and Coffin [1999] 2 PNLRev 1, Charlwood (1999) 143 Sol Jo 456.
3   See paras 7.62 ff and 7.70ff.
4   See *Swingcastle Ltd v Alastair Gibson* [1991] 2 AC 223, HL and *Nykredit Mortgage Bank plc v Edward Erdman (No 2)* [1997] 1 WLR 1627, per Lord Nicholls of Birkenhead at 1631–1632.
5   *Banque Bruxelles Lambert SA v Eagle Star Insurance Co Ltd* [1997] AC 191, HL. See chapter 7 for the application of these principles in solicitors' cases.

6.8   In *Platform* the basic loss was £611,000 and the attributable loss £500,000. Thus, leaving aside deductions for contributory negligence, the effect of *BBL* was that damages were limited to £500,000 plus interest. The trial judge assessed contributory negligence at 20%. The first question was whether s 1(1) of the 1945 Act applied at all. This depended on whether the plaintiff had suffered 'damage partly as a result of its own fault and partly as a result of the fault of' the defendant.[1] The lenders argued that 'damage' for these purposes meant only the attributable loss; only the defendant and not the lender had caused this part of the damage; thus this damage was not suffered 'partly due to the fault of the plaintiff', and so s 1(1) did not apply at all. The House of Lords rejected this argument. The 'damage' to which s 1(1) referred was the basic loss and not simply the attributable loss. The fault of both parties had contributed to this damage. Thus the Act applied, but on the basis set out in the next paragraph.

1   See the wording of s 1(1) at para 6.2.

3   Application

(a)   Lenders' cases

6.9   The next issue which the House of Lords considered in *Platform Home Loans*[1] was whether the 20% reduction in damages for contributory negligence should be made from the basic or the attributable loss. The basic loss was £611,000 and the attributable loss £500,000. Thus, if the reduction was made from the basic loss it would give a figure of £489,000 in damages and if it was made from the attributable loss it would give £400,000. The House held that the reduction should be made from the basic loss, reversing the Court of Appeal which had deducted it from the attributable loss. Lords Lloyd of Berwick and Hope of Craighead each agreed with the speeches of both Lords Millett and Hobhouse of Woodborough. In Lord Hobhouse's view, in cases where damages were reduced due to the *BBL* measure, the reduction to the amount of the attributable loss was a reduction in damages which was made for reasons similar to those justifying a reduction for contributory negligence.[2] Hence to make a deduction of 20% from the attributable loss on account of contributory negligence[3]

> '... in effect makes the same deduction twice over. The [*BBL*] principle already involves an exercise of attribution in relation to the extent of the defendants' responsibility for the plaintiffs' actual loss.'

1   [1999] 2 WLR 518.
2   [1999] 2 WLR 518 at 536A.
3   [1999] 2 WLR 518 at 536C–D.

6.10   Lord Millett reached the same conclusion. He added, obiter, that a different result might be appropriate in cases where the plaintiff lender's negligence had contributed directly to the overvaluation. In cases of that type, it might be appropriate to apply the reduction for contributory negligence to the attributable loss as well as the basic loss.[1] Lord Hobhouse did not make this distinction. Further, it is not strictly binding, but it must be of considerable persuasive weight.[2]

1   [1999] 2 WLR 518 at 539C–D.
2   Lords Lloyd of Berwick and Hope of Craighead both agreed with Lord Millett's speech, but they also agreed with the speech of Lord Hobhouse, who did not make this distinction, so it is unclear whether they supported the existence of the exception to which Lord Millett adverted.

6.11   It is submitted that whether one considers *Platform* to have been correctly decided depends upon whether, like Lord Hobhouse, one considers that the *BBL* reduction in damages performs essentially the same function as reductions on account of contributory negligence. If the two devices perform the same function then plainly it amounts to double counting to make the same reduction twice. It is thought, however, that these two mechanisms in truth perform quite different roles. The question of whether the court should make a reduction in damages on account of contributory negligence depends principally upon whether the claimant has behaved in a way which was negligent and contributed to the basic loss. It is easy to imagine cases where either there is say a 50% reduction for contributory negligence of the claimant but no reduction on account of *BBL*, or reduction on account of *BBL* but no reduction for contributory negligence. That is because the facts required to give rise to the two types of reduction are quite different. Once this proposition is accepted, it is submitted that to make separate reductions on account of both contributory negligence and *BBL* is, in general, the right approach. It does not involve double counting, because the rationales of the two different types of reduction are different. Imagine a case where the basic loss is £200,000, the attributable loss £100,000, there is contributory negligence of 50% and the claimant's negligence did not contribute to the overvaluation. On the House of Lords' principle, the deduction for contributory negligence must be made from the basic and not the attributable loss. Thus damages are £100,000 (50 % of £200,000). But this is exactly the same as they would have been, on the *BBL* measure, even if there had been no contributory negligence at all. So the effect of the House of Lords' decision is that there may be cases where a claimant lender recovers the same amount whether his contributory negligence is 0 or 50%. This seems unfair.

6.12   On the other hand, Lord Millett criticised the result of the Court of Appeal's approach in the following terms:[1]

'Instead of awarding the appellant damages of £489,398, representing the 80% of the overall loss of £611,748 which was not attributable to its own fault, as the judge had done, it reduced the award to £400,000, being 80% of the respondents' overvaluation of £500,000. The remarkable consequence is that, if the award stands, the appellant will bear more than one third of a loss for which it was only 20% to blame.'

It is submitted, however, that what this amounts to is a criticism of the decision in *BBL* itself. If, on the facts of *Platform*, there had been no contributory negligence at all, the effect of *BBL* would have been that the lender would itself have had to bear the difference between the basic and the attributable loss: thus the lender would have borne 18% of the basic loss[2] in a case where it was not to blame at all. The result to which Lord Millett referred is remarkable only if one considers that a reduction in damages on account of *BBL* is either intended to serve the same purpose as a reduction for contributory negligence, or intrinsically unjustifiable. We have suggested that the former proposition cannot be supported. The latter, a direct attack on the decision in *BBL*, is something which the House of Lords did not openly consider in *Platform*. Yet it appears that what underlies the decision of the majority is a feeling that reductions in damages on the basis set out in *BBL* may be unfair. This nettle was grasped only in the speech of the dissenter, Lord Cooke of Thorndon. In his view, as long as *BBL* stood, deductions for contributory negligence had to be made from the attributable rather than the basic loss, but he added:[3]

'If any anomalies or inequities be thought to arise from approaching the present case in this way, they will be attributable to the limit of a valuer's duty of care, and consequent liability, imposed by your Lordships' House in the *Banque Bruxelles* and *Nykredit* decisions, which your Lordships were not asked to reconsider on this occasion.'

On this approach, either *BBL* provides a sound principle, in which case it justifies a reduction in addition to reductions for contributory negligence, or it does not, in which case the House of Lords should have decided not to follow it. For the moment, however, the position is as set out in *BBL* and *Platform*.

1   [1999] 2 WLR 518 at 537F–G.
2   £111,000 divided by £611,000.
3   [1999] 2 WLR 518 at 524G–H.

(b)   Negligence of the claimant's employees

6.13   If the claimant would have been vicariously liable for the conduct of another for the purpose of a claim brought by a third party then, in principle, it would seem that such conduct should be imputed to the claimant for the purpose of establishing contributory negligence. Thus the negligence of an employee, agent or director may be imputed to the employer, principal or company. Where, however, where the defendant is in breach of a duty to check that the employee, agent or director has acted carefully and properly, then it may be anomalous to impute to the claimant the very improper conduct which the defendant was supposed to report or prevent. In *British Racing Drivers' Club Ltd v Hextall Erskine & Co*[1] Carnwath J refused to impute to the plaintiff company the negligence of its directors so as to allow the defendant solicitors to plead contributory negligence. The solicitors had failed to advise the plaintiff's board that Companies Act 1985, s 320 required the transaction contemplated by the plaintiff to be approved by its members because the transaction involved a director. As the purpose of s 320 was 'to ensure that, in relation to a major transaction involving a director, the directing mind and will of the company would not be the board of directors unsupervised by the general meeting' it followed that 'for the defendants now to rely on directors' negligence as that of the company would be wholly inconsistent with the statutory scheme'.[2] In contrast, in *Daniels v Anderson*[3] the New South Wales Court of Appeal did impute the conduct of a director to the plaintiff company in the context of an action against auditors for failing to give adequate warnings of poor records and internal controls. In *Daniels*, however, the relevant conduct of the director was his failure to act on the inadequate warnings that were given by the auditors and it may be argued that where the contributory conduct consists of a failure to respond to warnings, it should be imputed to the claimant company.

1   [1996] 3 All ER 667. See also *Henderson v Merrett Syndicates Ltd (No 2)* [1996] PNLR 32, where Cresswell J held that the allegedly negligent conduct of Lloyd's agents should not be imputed to the plaintiff Names who were suing the defendant auditors for negligently failing to detect the agents' failures when drawing up the close of year accounts. To impute the agents' conduct to the Names, in order to found a plea of contributory negligence, would make 'a nonsense of the purpose for which the auditors were employed'.
2   [1996] 3 All ER 667 at 682. For criticism see Bartlett 'Attribution of contributory negligence' (1998) 114 LQR 460.
3   (1995) 37 NSWLR 438, NSWCA.

(c) Fault

6.14 What test determines what counts as 'fault' on the part of the claimant for the purposes of the Act? A tension has emerged, at least in relation to lenders' cases, between two different approaches.[1] In *Banque Bruxelles Lambert SA v Eagle Star Insurance Co Ltd*,[2] Phillips J accepted the submission that the plaintiff lender's conduct had to be judged against the standard of a reasonably competent merchant bank at the time. Thus, the test was related to how a reasonably competent member of the profession in question would have behaved at the relevant time. The difficulty with this approach is that there may be cases where the court considers that a practice was negligent even though it was one which respected members of a profession did adopt at the time.[3] In *Birmingham Midshires Mortgage Services v David Parry & Co*[4] the lender did not require any proof of the existence or level of the borrower's earnings, other than a signed assurance from the borrower himself. Sir John Vinelott explained, in a passage which was strictly obiter, that:[5]

> 'evidence of the way in which other businesses are conducted is not a reliable guide to the question whether a business was conducted prudently—that is whether it took reasonable care to protect itself against the risk of loss. There may be good commercial reasons which lead those engaged in a business enterprise to take risks, pressure of competition or a desire to break into a new market.'

Thus he considered that a standard of prudence was more appropriate. This tension will arise principally in cases where it is accepted on all sides that a particular practice was regarded as acceptable by the relevant profession at the material time, but the defendant still contends that it amounted to contributory negligence. It may be that the reason why there appears to be no authority which conclusively resolves the issue is that, in practice, it will rarely arise: if both parties call expert evidence, the experts usually disagree, or, if they agree, it is rare for a party to feel able to submit that his expert was wrong.

1   For criticism and discussion, see Hugh Evans's helpful article, 'Contributory Negligence by Lenders' (1998) 14 PN 43.
2   [1995] 2 All ER 769 at 821e–f.

3   Cf *Lloyds Bank Ltd v EB Savory & Co* [1933] AC 201, HL (as to the practice of bankers) and
    Edward Wong Finance Co Ltd v Johnson, Stokes and Master [1984] AC 296, PC (as to the
    practice of solicitors).
4   [1996] PNLR 494 at 518. Although the case was appealed [1997] NPC 153, CA, this point
    did not have to be dealt with on appeal.
5   See [1996] PNLR at 516A–B.

(d)   Basis of reduction in damages

6.15   The Act empowers the court to reduce the claimant's damages 'to such an extent
as the court thinks just and equitable having regard to the claimant's share in
responsibility for the damage'. Determining the amount of the reduction is 'essentially an exercise of judgment on matters of fact and degree' and one where an
appellate court 'will only interfere if it regards it as plainly wrong or where the judge
can be shown to have taken into account some immaterial matter or to have overlooked
some material matter'.[1] Reductions vary considerably with the evaluation of the facts.
Thus, a range of percentage reductions, reaching as high as 90%, have been made in
relation to awards of damages to lenders to take account of risky lending practices.[2]
The principle is that the court will have regard to the questions of the blameworthiness and the causative potency of the parties' respective faults.[3] A striking
example of this weighing-up is in the inter-defendant apportionment in *Downs v
Chappell*[4] where the court assessed damages between a fraudulent vendor and a
negligent accountant at 50/50, as the causative potency of the accountant's negligence was greater than that of the vendor's more blameworthy fraud.

1   *Griffin v Mersey Regional Ambulance* [1998] PIQR P34 at 38, CA, per Simon Brown LJ.
2   See further chapter 7, paras 7.81ff.
3   *Davies v Swan Motor Co (Swansea) Ltd* [1949] 2 KB 291.
4   [1997] 1 WLR 426, CA. The issue concerned claims for contribution rather than contributory
    negligence, but the test which the court applies is essentially the same: see the next section.

B   CONTRIBUTION

1   Scope

6.16   Contribution claims are governed by the Civil Liability (Contribution) Act
1978 which provides that 'any person liable in respect of any damage suffered by
another person may recover contribution from any other person liable in respect of
the same damage (whether jointly with him or otherwise)'. The Act applies whatever
the basis of liability.[1] Hence, a tortfeasor may claim from another who is liable only
in contract or equity for the same damage. In *Friends' Provident Life Office v Hillier
Parker May & Rowden*[2] surveyors who were alleged to have *negligently* authorised
payment by the plaintiff client of unjustified claims made by a developer were able
to bring a contribution claim against the developer on the ground that the developer
could also be liable to the plaintiff under a *restitutionary* claim for money paid under
a mistake of fact.

1   See Civil Liability (Contribution) Act 1978, s 6(1).
2   [1997] QB 85, CA.

6.17   But the Act is limited to cases in which B and C are liable for the same damage,
and to be liable for the same damage both B and C must be liable to the same person,
A. Further, it is necessary to take care in formulating the precise nature of the damage

for which each party is liable. In *Birse Construction Ltd v Haiste Ltd*,[1] A, a water authority, appointed B, a contractor, to undertake the design and construction of a storage reservoir. B appointed C as consulting engineers for the design. A also appointed D, one of its own employees, to act as supervising engineer. Thus C had a contract with B but not A or D, and D had a contract with A, but not B or C. The reservoir proved defective. A sued B for damage caused in not having a properly completed reservoir at the expected time. B settled A's claim by agreeing to construct a new reservoir at B's own expense. B then issued proceedings as plaintiff seeking an indemnity from C who, in turn, claimed contribution from D. D sought a determination from the court as to whether he could be liable in respect of the 'same damage' as C: he contended that he could not, so that the Act would not apply and C could not obtain contribution from D even if it made out its case on the facts. The Court of Appeal accepted D's contention. D was potentially liable to A for A's damage, and C was potentially liable to B for B's damage, but D and C were not liable for the same damage, because A's damage was different from B's damage: A's damage was 'not having a completed properly working reservoir at the time that [A] expected', while B's damage was 'having to construct a second reservoir as a result of their compromise with A'. Although both types of damage could 'speaking loosely' be said to be essentially the defective condition of the reservoir and the need to replace it, the Court of Appeal considered that s 1 required a more precise analysis of the different types of damage.[2] This case shows the need for careful consideration of both the exact nature of the damage in question in contribution proceedings and of which duties were owed by who to whom.

1   [1996] 1 WLR 675, CA.
2   Per Sir John Wood, [1996] 1 WLR at 680F–G.

6.18   Provided that both B and C are liable to the same person for the same damage, a contribution claim may be brought even if they are liable to a differing extent. Thus, it is likely that a solicitor liable for a lender's entire loss could bring a contribution action against a valuer liable only to the extent of the overvaluation.

6.19   The Act further provides that, where B has reached a bona fide settlement with A, there is no need for B to prove his own liability in order to claim contribution from C, *provided that* 'he would have been liable assuming that the factual basis of the claim against him could be established'.[1] Thus, in order to obtain contribution from C, B does not need to prove *the facts* which A alleged against him, but does have to show that A's claim against him was good *in law*. In *Dubai Aluminium Co Ltd v Salaam*,[2] a solicitor called Amhurst was sued on the basis that he had dishonestly assisted in a breach of trust; his innocent partners were sued on the basis that they were vicariously liable for Amhurst's breaches. Amhurst and his partners settled with the plaintiff. Rix J had to consider whether Amhurst's innocent partners could seek contribution from other parties to the action. This turned on whether, assuming the facts pleaded against the innocent partners to be true, they would have been liable in law to the plaintiff. If the pleaded facts were true, then Amhurst himself was liable for dishonest assistance in breaches of trust. But Rix J had to go further, and consider whether, on that assumption, the innocent partners would have been liable for those acts on the part of their partner. This was principally a question of law. He held that they would have been liable, pursuant to Partnership Act 1890, s 10, which could impose vicarious liability for assistance in breaches of trust, if they were done within the ordinary course of the partner's business.[3] Hence the innocent partners were entitled to seek contribution.

1   Civil Liability (Contribution) Act 1978, s 1(4). Note that s 1(2) also provides that a person
     who 'has ceased to be liable in respect of the damage in question' may claim a contribution
     provided he was liable 'immediately before he made or was ordered or agreed to make the
     payment in respect of which the contribution is sought'. In order to claim under s 1(4), B does,
     of course, need to show that *C* is or would have been liable to A.
2   Rix J (1998) Times, 4 September, but see also the transcript.
3   But in *Re Bell's Indenture* [1980] 1 WLR 1217 Vinelott J held that a solicitors' partnership
     was not vicariously liable for the liability of one of its partners as an accessory to a breach of
     trust. See further chapter 4, para 4.19.

6.20   If B settles with the claimant A, then the provision referred to in the last
paargraph prevents B from having to prove, in contribution proceedings against C,
his *liability* to A. But, in the proceedings against C, he must still prove that the
quantum of his settlement with A was reasonable. Section 1 of the Act[1]

> '... does not affect the right of the person from whom contribution is being sought
> [C] to assert that the person claiming contribution [B] paid too much or that in
> assessing contribution the party liable to contribute [C] should not be required
> to pay compensation for elements of the payment for which that person [C] could
> never have been held liable had he been sued directly.'

Further, although payments of interest in B's settlement with A do count as
damages in respect of which there may be contribution under the Act, it seems that
payments of A's costs do not, so that there can be no claim for contribution in
respect of the latter.[2]

1   *J Sainsbury plc v Broadway Malyan* [1999] PNLR 286, per HHJ Humphrey Lloyd QC at
     321A–B. Letters in square brackets added.
2   *J Sainsbury plc v Broadway Malyan* [1999] PNLR 286 at 333–4 and 334–6.

6.21   Where a judgment on the merits between C and A has held C not liable, that
judgment is conclusive against B, and C is protected from a contribution claim.[1]
Where there are joint debtors, if A settles against one (B), without expressly reserving
the right to pursue the others (C and D), then he is likely to find that the doctrine of
accord and satisfaction prevents him from pursuing C and D.[2] In this case, although
in general a settlement between A and B provides B with no protection from a claim
for contribution from C, A will be prevented from proceeding against C and thus there
will be no loss in respect of which C can claim contribution from B. Where C has been
held not liable or has ceased to be liable to A because of the expiry of the limitation
period relating to A's claim, C is not protected against a contribution claim. B may
bring a contribution claim against C within two years from the date when his own
liability to A was determined by settlement or judgment.[3]

1   Civil Liability (Contribution) Act 1978, s 1(5).
2   *Morris v Wentworth-Stanley* (1998) 142 Sol Jo LB 258, CA.
3   Limitation Act 1980, s 10.

2   Application

6.22   The Act provides that the amount of the contribution recoverable shall be 'such
as may be found by the court to be just and equitable having regard to the extent of
that person's responsibility for the damage in question'.[1] The application of this test
is a matter for the trial judge to determine on the facts and appeal courts must not
interfere unless the decision of the judge was unreasonable in the light of the
evidence.[2] As a result, regrettably, there is little authority as to the principles to be
followed when apportioning responsibility. Perhaps the only principle to be

established clearly is that the test 'involves a consideration not only of the causative potency of a factor, but also of its blameworthiness'.[3] In *Downs v Chappell*,[4] the trial judge had indicated that, if he had held the two defendants liable, he would have held them equally responsible for the plaintiff's damage. The Court of Appeal allowed the plaintiff's appeal and held that the defendants were liable for the loss. Thus it was necessary to consider the appeal in relation to contribution. The second defendants contended that the trial judge had erred as he had given too little weight to his finding that the first defendants had been fraudulent whereas they, the second defendants, had been only negligent. Hobhouse LJ, with whom the other judges agreed, rejected this. The extent of a person's 'responsibility', within the meaning of the Act, depended upon both causative potency and moral blameworthiness. The judge was entitled to find that, although the first defendants were fraudulent and therefore more blamewor-thy, the second defendants' conduct had more causative effect, so that each had equal responsibility overall.

1   Civil Liability (Contribution) Act 1978, s 2(1).
2   *The Macgregor* [1943] AC 197 at 200, HL, per Lord Wright.
3   *Davies v Swan Motor Co (Swansea) Ltd* [1949] 2 KB 291, CA, and, for this Act, see *Madden v Quirk* [1989] 1 WLR 702 at 707.
4   [1997] 1 WLR 426 at 445B–H, CA.

6.23   Whereas, in relation to contributory negligence, apportionment between claimant and defendant may not be made if the defendant has been fraudulent,[1] a dishonest defendant may claim contribution from a fellow tortfeasor under the Civil Liability (Contribution) Act 1978.[2] In *K v P*,[3] Ferris J held that, even if its elements were made out, the maxim *ex turpi causa non oritur actio* could be no bar to a claim for contribution. On the other hand, where there is a claim for contribution by parties who are themselves innocent, and liable only vicariously for the wrongs of another, should the court take account of their innocence? In *Dubai Aluminium Co Ltd v Salaam*,[4] Rix J accepted that innocent but vicariously liable parties stood in the same position as those for whom they were liable so far as causative potency was concerned, and might also do so where the plaintiff's claim was based on negligence. But he held that in a case such as *Dubai*, where the parties seeking contribution were themselves innocent but were vicariously liable for the *fraud* of their partner, the court could take account of their innocence in assessing the amount of contribution that should be based on blameworthiness as opposed to causative potency. The innocence would not provide them with a complete indemnity, but it would be one of the factors which the court took into account in weighing up the amount of contribution which it was just and equitable to order.

1   See para 6.5.
2   See for example *Downs v Chappell* [1997] 1 WLR 426.
3   [1993] Ch 140.
4   (1998) Times, 4 September (Rix J), discussed at para 6.19.

C   INTERRELATION OF CONTRIBUTORY NEGLIGENCE AND CONTRIBUTION

6.24   Section 2(3) of the Civil Liability (Contribution) Act 1978 provides that where B's liability to A is, or would have been, limited by a reduction for contributory negligence or a limitation of damage clause, that limit caps the amount of the contribution payable by B to C. Thus, in the situation where a solicitor is liable to a lender for the whole of the lender's loss, but a valuer is liable only to the extent of the overvaluation, then if the valuer's liability to the lender was limited by a limitation clause, the valuer's liability to make contribution to the solicitor could not exceed the amount which the lender would have recovered from the valuer after application of the limitation clause. The solicitor might argue that s 2(3) does not refer to limits to the valuer's liability imposed by the House of Lords' decision in *BBL*[1] but it is thought that, if the valuer's liability to the lender were limited in that way, it could not be just and equitable for the court to order the valuer to pay by way of contribution more than he would have had to pay to the lender directly.

1   See para 6.7.

6.25   The Act does not indicate whether, in cases where B's liability is limited by contributory negligence or a limitation clause, courts should apportion loss between defendants first and then cap B's contribution on the basis of the contributory negligence or limitation clause, or cap first and then apportion within the cap. In our example, imagine that the claimant lender's total loss was £100,000 and the court considered that the positions of the solicitor and the valuer deserved equal apportionment of the lender's loss. Should the court take the full loss of £100,000, attribute £50,000 to the solicitor and £50,000 to the valuer, and *then* consider whether the valuer's portion exceeded the amount at which it would have been limited by contributory negligence or a limitation clause? Alternatively, should the court assess the amount at which the valuer's liability would have been assessed bearing in mind the limitation clause or contributory negligence (say £50,000), and then make a further reduction on account of contribution? In our example, the latter approach would lead to reducing the valuer's liability by half, to £25,000. It is thought that, in principle, the latter approach is fairer, at least to the valuer, who, on the first approach, might in practice receive no additional reduction in damages on account of being liable to make contribution as to only 50%.

PART 2

Specific Claims

CHAPTER 7

Lenders' claims

A   CONTRACT AND THE TORT OF NEGLIGENCE

1   Introduction and summary of the key issues

7.1   In the years following the recession and property crash of the early 1990s, residential mortgage lenders such as banks and building societies suffered enormous losses due to the default of borrowers to whom they had lent, usually in cases where the property on which they had taken security was repossessed but sold at a price which was insufficient to pay off the sums owing pursuant to the loan. In many cases they sought to recover their losses from solicitors who had acted for them in arranging their mortgages. The ensuing litigation has led to a large number of decisions as to the solicitors' liability, which have developed the principles which apply in the law of contract, tort, fiduciary duties and trusts, and provided material for two new sets of law reports.[1] Many of the cases concern transactions which took place in the early 1990s before lenders were fully aware of the likely extent of the decline in the property market, and the nature of sub-sale fraud.[2] As the 1990s proceeded, they became more familiar with both. It seems likely that the enormous volume of cases in this area will decline: actions based on the events of the early 1990s are likely to be statute-barred, and it is likely that by the mid-1990s lenders were more aware of the danger of large losses, and reduced their lending accordingly. But there will still be litigation, and it is thought that the principles to be applied have now become relatively clearly settled. In particular, we refer to what are likely to be the main battlelines between lenders and solicitors in future, at para 7.3.

1   Those practising in this area will wish to have regard to both: Sweet and Maxwell's Professional Negligence Law Reports (PNLR) and the recently introduced Lloyd's Law Reports Professional Negligence (Lloyd's Rep PN).
2   See para 7.12 for definitions of sub-sales.

7.2   In this chapter we concentrate in particular on two decisions in the Chancery Division in relation to managed lists of actions. In 1995, the court effectively consolidated a large number of actions brought by the Bristol and West Building Society against solicitor defendants. Chadwick J's final judgment, concerning eight individual actions, is reported as *Bristol and West Building Society v Fancy and Jackson*[1] (hereafter *Fancy and Jackson*). In 1997, a similar practice was adopted in relation to actions brought by the Nationwide Building Society against various solicitor defendants. Blackburne J's judgment on all issues other than mitigation and assessment of loss was handed down on 1 February 1999; most of it is reported as *Nationwide Building Society v Balmer Radmore*[2] and thus it is referred to hereafter as *Balmer Radmore*. The consolidation of actions enabled the court to deal with the issues in more detail than might have been possible on hearing only one action, and to produce more wide-ranging judgments. This is why we deal principally with those decisions, together with the leading judgments which they apply, namely those of the Court of Appeal in *Mortgage Express Ltd v Bowerman & Partners*,[3] *Bristol and West Building Society v Mothew*[4] and *National Home Loans Corpn plc v Giffen Couch & Archer*[5] and the House of Lords in *Target Holdings Ltd v Redferns*[6] and *Banque Bruxelles Lambert SA v Eagle Star Insurance Co Ltd*[7] (hereafter *BBL*).

155

1   [1997] 4 All ER 582. The same judge gave judgment on a large number of applications for
     summary judgment in *Bristol and West Building Society v May, May & Merrimans* [1996] 2
     All ER 801, but that decision has to be treated with some care as the Court of Appeal criticised
     some aspects of it in *Bristol and West Building Society v Mothew* [1998] Ch 1.
2   [1999] Lloyd's Rep PN 241.
3   [1996] 2 All ER 836.
4   [1998] Ch 1.
5   [1998] 1 WLR 207.
6   [1996] AC 421.
7   [1997] AC 191. This case is also known as *SAAMCo*, which is an abbreviation of the name
     of the first plaintiff, in the appeal in the House of Lords.

Key issues

7.3   Although we comment below on a number of features of *Balmer Radmore*, it is
thought that, for practical purposes, the two most important points which arise out of
the case are these. First, in cases where the lender proves only breach of contract or
negligence against the solicitor, the effect of *Balmer Radmore* was greatly to increase
the benchmark for awards of contributory negligence against claimant lenders. This
is dealt with at para 7.81. But secondly, in cases where the lender succeeds in showing
deliberate breach of fiduciary duty against the solicitor, there will be no deduction
for contributory negligence, no matter how negligent the lender was in making the
offer of advance. Thus, it is thought that in future claims lenders will be keen to show
deliberate breach of fiduciary duty, while solicitors will seek to avoid such findings,
and to emphasise the contributory negligence of the lender. What is required to show
breach of fiduciary duty is discussed in chapter 4[1], and in section E of this chapter.[2] In short,
something close to dishonesty on the part of the solicitor is required.

1   Paras 4.20ff.
2   Paras 7.114ff.

7.4   This chapter begins with a brief discussion of the roles of lenders and solicitors
in the typical mortgage transaction, and the basic mechanism of a sub-sale fraud. This
need be read only by those unfamiliar with this type of claim. We then deal with claims
in contract and the tort of negligence: breach of the express terms of the solicitor's
retainer, breach of implied terms, causation and the application of *BBL*, interest,
contributory negligence, mortgage indemnity guarantees, mitigation, contribution,
and claims by multiple lenders. Next are considered other claims at common law: those
based on fraud, breach of warranty of authority, and actions for money had and
received. Finally we refer briefly to equity, which is dealt with fully in chapter 4.

7.5   It should be stated at the outset that decisions as to breaches of express terms are likely
to turn on the precise wording of the express terms of the particular claimant lender;
similarly, claims for breaches of warranties made in reports on title will turn on the wording
of the particular lender's report on or certificate of title. Thus a decision on the express terms
of lender A may not be determinative of liability on similar facts under the different terms
of lender B. On the other hand, as will be seen in section 2, in many cases lenders' express
instructions and reports on title are worded similarly. Further, this problem may be of less
importance after 1 October 1999, when the final version of the Law Society's Practice Rule
6(3) is due to come into effect.[1] That rule, which applies when solicitors act for both lender
and borrower in the same transaction, is designed to be used in conjunction with the
Lenders' Handbook, which is a set of standard mortgage instructions which a number of
major lenders have agreed to adopt. But those terms will govern only cases which relate
to work carried out on or after 1 October 1999, and, even then, will not govern cases in
which the lender has not adopted the handbook.

1   See [1999] Law Society's Gazette 6 May at 38.

7.6   In order to understand the issues in lenders' claims, it is necessary to understand the ways in which lenders normally deal with mortgage applications and solicitors normally deal with residential conveyancing when acting for both lender and borrower, and the nature of sub-sale frauds. These points are considered in the next paragraphs, and need not be read by those who are already familiar with them.

2   Roles of the lender and solicitor[1]

7.7   A typical transaction might proceed as follows. A prospective house-buyer ('the borrower') applies to a mortgage lender ('the lender') for a mortgage in order to buy a property ('the property'). Normally the borrower will not apply for a mortgage until he or she has agreed a price for the sale, subject to contract, although this need not necessarily be the case. In deciding whether to lend money to the borrower, the lender considers essentially two issues: first, the value of the property which is to be taken as security for the loan, and secondly, the ability of the borrower to make the repayments required. The latter will be referred to as the value of the borrower's covenant: the borrower covenants with the lender to make the repayments.

1   For a helpful statement of the procedure followed by the Nationwide Building Society in the period 1989 to 1991, which is typical of many, see *Balmer Radmore* [1999] Lloyd's Rep PN 241 at 247–251.

(a)   Value of the security

7.8   The lender will take a first legal charge over the property which should enable it to take possession of, and sell, the property in the event of the borrower defaulting. Hence the lender must consider the value of the property, and the proportion of the valuation which the borrower wishes to borrow. In order to determine the value, a building society must commission and receive a written valuation report from a competent valuer.[1] A bank will normally do so too. Pausing there, this means that in all claims by lenders against solicitors, the solicitors must consider whether the valuer who prepared the valuation report was negligent, and, if so, whether contribution proceedings should be instituted.[2] Once the lender has received the valuation report, it must consider how much the borrower wishes to borrow. This proportion is known as 'loan to value' or 'LTV'. For instance, if a property is valued at £100,000 and the borrower wishes to borrow £75,000, then the LTV is 75%. The lender will have written lending criteria which are likely to set out the maximum percentage of the valuation, or LTV, which it is prepared to lend. Some lenders lend up to 75% of the value of the property, others 90%, and others have in the past lent 100%. Lending more than 75% LTV in a market where property prices are known to be falling and after little scrutiny of the borrower's finances may well constitute contributory negligence.[3] Much of the discussion of liability below considers the circumstances in which solicitors who discover information which casts doubt on the value which the lender believes the property to have ought to report such information to the lender. Put briefly, they generally do have an obligation to do so.

1   Building Societies Act 1986, s 13.
2   See para 7.92.
3   See para 7.85.

(b)   Value of the borrower's covenant

7.9   The second issue is whether the borrower will be able to afford to make the repayments required in order to finance the proposed loan. Questions are generally asked on the mortgage application form relating to this issue. Two broad categories of loan should be considered. First, in the ordinary case the lender will undertake what are known as 'status checks', in other words enquiries as to the borrower's creditworthiness. Various checks are made by different lenders; again, the precise steps which a particular lender takes will depend on the terms of that lender's mortgage criteria. They may include seeking: a banker's reference; a reference from the borrower's landlord, if the borrower is renting his or her accommodation, or from the previous lender, if it is charged; a search with a credit reference agency to determine whether, for instance, there are any unpaid county court judgments in the borrower's name; in the case of an employee, an employer's reference; in the case of a self-employed person, three years' accounts and possibly an accountant's reference; or a search of the electoral roll to see whether the borrower is recorded as living at the address given in the mortgage application form. The lender may also interview the borrower to satisfy itself of the truth of his or her answers. The extent to which a particular claimant lender has undertaken such enquiries is likely to be relevant in determining whether it has been contributorily negligent. As we shall see below, in general it is doubtful whether solicitors have any implied duty to report matters which they discover which are relevant only to the borrower's ability to pay.

7.10   An alternative approach is for a lender to rely almost entirely on the value of the property as security for the loan, and therefore to make no, or limited, investigation of the borrower's finances. Depending on their precise terms, loans made on this basis may be known as 'non-status' loans, if the lender has not investigated the borrower's financial status at all, or 'self-certifying loans', where the lender has relied upon the borrower's own statement as to his or her means. It appears that loans of these two varieties have led to more losses for lenders than other loans, and that they have become rarer. We discuss the circumstances in which lending on such a basis might amount to contributory negligence below.[1]

1   See para 7.88.

7.11   Once the lender is satisfied as to both the value of the security and the borrower's ability to pay, it makes an offer of advance, and generally issues written instructions to solicitors at the same time. Normally the same solicitors act for both lender and borrower. The written instructions incorporate the express terms of the lender's retainer of the solicitors. The solicitors are normally required to submit to the lender a report on title. The precise terms of the report depend on the requirements of the particular lender, though the solicitors are always required to state something to the effect that the title to be charged is good and marketable and may safely be accepted by the lender as security. The report on title is generally the principal document in which the solicitors report information to the lender. If the lender receives a report on title which raises no concerns about the transaction then it will normally proceed to forward the advance money to the solicitors so that the transaction may be completed. The lender will expect to be provided by the solicitors with an enforceable and valid first legal charge over the property after completion. We consider the nature of the solicitors' duties further below.

3 Sub-sales, back to back sales and direct payments

7.12 Most cases involve allegations of the following type. A sells a property to B, and then B sells it on to C. The sales from A to B and from B to C take place on the same day. A sells to B for say £100,000, and B sells exactly the same property to C for, say, £150,000.[1] In most cases, the property market is in fact falling at the time. C's mortgage lender is unaware of the sale from A to B, and may lend, say, £120,000 on C's supposed purchase from B for £150,000. If B and C are in league, then the sale from B to C may be a device to deceive C's lender. B and C can use £100,000 of C's lender's money to pay off A, and retain the remaining £20,000 while they disappear into the ether. B and C may inform their respective solicitors that there is no need for payment of a deposit, or even of any of the balance of £50,000, because C has paid the £50,000 directly to B. The key point is that the price at which B is selling to C (£150,000) is a sham: the true value of the property is the price at which A is selling to B (£100,000), but C's lender must be deceived into believing the true value to be £150,000. This is why, from the lender's point of view, knowledge of the price at which A is selling to B may be very helpful in detecting the fraud and withdrawing from the transaction. It is also why both the lender and the solicitor may also wish to blame the surveyor who has presumably valued the property at £150,000 rather than £100,000.

1   This device may be referred to as either a 'back to back' transaction or a sub-sale, depending on the nature of the contractual framework. In a back to back transaction, A has a contract to sell to B and B has a separate contract to sell to C. In a sub-sale, A has a contract with B which requires him to transfer the property directly to C.

7.13 The cases suggest that, in the early 1990s, frauds of this type occurred on a considerable scale. The extent to which solicitors realised the risk of such fraud is considered below.[1] In particular, the question arises of the extent to which solicitors should have realised that sub-sales with price uplifts were taking place, and should have reported them to lenders. The effect of the recent judgment in *Balmer Radmore*[2] is that solicitors often should have realised this risk and reported it to lenders.

1   See paras 7.38ff.
2   [1999] Lloyd's Rep PN 241.

7.14 One might ask why fraudsters thought it necessary to enter into such an elaborate series of transactions in order to defraud mortgage lenders. Our example assumes that A is honest and the sale from A to B is at the market price of £100,000. It would of course be possible for a fraudster, B, to purchase the property for £100,000 and tell his lender that the price was £150,000. But this would require the involvement of a dishonest solicitor who was willing to tell his lender client a blatant lie as to the price at which the property was being bought. The advantage of the sub-sale mechanism is that C does not require a dishonest solicitor in order to ensure that his lender does not find out the full story of the transactions. As long as C's solicitor either fails to find out the price of the sale from A to B, or does not trouble to ask himself whether it is a matter which should be reported to C's lender, the transaction may proceed without the lender knowing of it. Thus the transaction may proceed without C needing to find a dishonest solicitor. This was perhaps the reason for its apparent popularity as a fraudulent device.

4   Liability for breach of express contractual terms

7.15   Solicitors acting for lenders do so pursuant to a contractual relationship. In considering solicitors' liability to lenders, the first question is therefore whether they have acted in breach of the express terms of the contract. The second question, which we consider in the next section, is whether the solicitors have acted in breach of implied terms or the duty of care in negligence. As indicated above,[1] points of construction of a particular lender's terms often turn on the precise wording of the instructions, so that authority as to the construction of one lender's instructions may be of little help in construing another lender's instructions.[2] It is, however, possible to detect general approaches to construction in relation to specific issues which commonly arise in lenders' claims. This is what we attempt to do here.

1   See para 7.5.
2   See *Midland Bank plc v Cox McQueen* [1999] Lloyd's Rep PN 223, CA.

(a)   Incorporation into the contract of the terms upon which the lender relies[1]

7.16   The first issue is what the express terms of the contract are. As mentioned above, the lender normally sends formal instructions to the solicitor whom it wishes to act for it. Normally, this solicitor has been nominated by the borrower. The instructions will purport to incorporate the terms of the lender's general instructions to solicitors, and may also add some further instructions which apply to the particular transaction in question. In some cases the solicitor writes back and formally accepts the terms of the lender's retainer; here, there is no difficulty in concluding that the lender has retained the solicitor and that the express terms of the contract include the terms of the lender's general instructions to solicitors, and any special instructions mentioned in the lender's letter to the solicitor.

1   See generally Chadwick J's discussion in *Fancy and Jackson* [1997] 4 All ER 582, 603h–605d.

7.17   In other cases, there is no formal acceptance of retainer, but the solicitor acts as if he or she were instructed by the lender and, in particular, fills in the lender's report on title and sends it to the lender, thereby requesting payment of the advance moneys. The report on title normally contains a declaration which the solicitor must sign, stating, inter alia, that all requirements of the lender's express instructions to the solicitor have already been, or will by the time of completion have been, satisfied; it may also state that there is nothing adverse to report. In cases of this type, the court is likely to infer that the solicitor has accepted the lender's terms by conduct.[1] But, even if it will not, as long as the solicitor signs the report on title, it would appear that he or she is warranting that the terms of the lender's instructions have been, or will by the time of completion have been, complied with.[2] It is hard to see how a solicitor who signed such a declaration, without qualification, and returned it to the lender, could argue that he or she was not liable for failing to ensure that he or she complied with the declaration. Hence, even if strictly speaking the lender's general or special instructions to solicitors have not been incorporated into the contract, it is likely that the solicitor will be liable for failure to comply with them.

1   'The society's offer to retain the solicitor, contained in the solicitor's letter, is one which, again prima facie, can be accepted by conduct.' *Bristol and West Building Society v May, May & Merrimans* [1996] 2 All ER 801 per Chadwick J at 809g.
2   In the case of Bristol and West Building Society's standard documents, see *Fancy and Jackson* [1997] 4 All ER 582 at 605a–d.

7.18 Although the document in which the solicitor is obliged to report matters to the lender is normally the report on title, the solicitor's instructions will often be construed to import a continuing obligation to report any matters which the lender ought to know up until the completion of the transaction.[1]

1   See, for example, *Balmer Radmore* [1999] Lloyd's Rep PN 223 at 252.

(b)   Categories of breach of express term

7.19 In the remainder of this section we consider five categories of allegations of breach of express term on which lenders commonly rely in this type of case. The first concerns failing to report circumstances suggesting that the true purchase price was not the price stated in the offer of advance. The second relates to special conditions requiring confirmation that the borrower intended to reside in the property. The third concerns requirements that the borrower's existing mortgages be redeemed before completion; the fourth, obligations to report material changes in the borrower's circumstances; and the fifth, the requirement to ensure that the lender receives adequate security for its loan. Finally, we draw some conclusions on the correct approach to construing express terms of the solicitor's retainer.

(c)   Failing to report circumstances suggesting that the true purchase price was not the price stated in the offer of advance

7.20 The nature of a sub-sale fraud combined with a direct payment was summarised in paras 7.12–7.14. A large percentage of the cases decided in both *Fancy and Jackson*[1] and *Balmer Radmore*[2] concerned failure to report matters of these kinds. In only one of those cases had the lender incorporated a term in its instructions which expressly required that solicitors report sub-sales to it.[3] In the other cases, the obligation to report sub-sales, as opposed to direct payments, arose from the solicitors' implied rather than express duties.

1   [1997] 4 All ER 582.
2   [1999] Lloyd's Rep PN 241.
3   This was *Colin Bishop*. The lender was the Cheshunt Building Society, which was subsequently taken over by the Bristol and West. The defendant solicitors claimed that the requirement to report sub-sales applied only to sales where there was only one transfer document, executed by each of the various vendors and purchasers. For example, if A was selling to B who was selling to C on the same day, the defendant's case was that this arrangement was a sub-sale only if each of A, B and C executed the same transfer document. If there were two separate transfer documents, one relating to the sale from A to B and the other to the sale from B to C, then this was not a sub-sale. Chadwick J rejected that argument: see [1997] 4 All ER 582 at 609g. Either type of transaction was a sub-sale which had to be reported to the Cheshunt, under its standard terms. Hence the solicitors were held liable.
4   See paras 7.38ff.

7.21 In relation to direct payments, however, the obligation could arise pursuant to the express terms of the retainer, in the following way. In *Fancy and Jackson*, Bristol and West's solicitors' instructions required that the solicitor report to Bristol and West any discrepancy in the details shown in the offer of advance. Those details included the purchase price. Further, in signing the report on title the solicitor had to confirm that the details of the transaction accorded exactly with the particulars in the offer of advance, including the purchase price. The general nature of the solicitor's obligation, in Chadwick J's analysis, was as follows.[1] First, a solicitor who knew that the true purchase price payable by the purchaser/borrower to the vendor was not the purchase price stated in the offer of advance could not properly sign and return the report without qualification. Secondly, a solicitor who signed and returned the report and request without qualification was, at the least, warranting to the lender that he had made those enquiries (if any) which a competent solicitor, acting reasonably, would make in order to satisfy himself that the purchase price stated in the offer of advance was the true purchase price to be paid by the purchaser/borrower to the vendor, and that, in light of those enquiries, he knew of no reason why he could not give the unqualified confirmation to which he had put his signature. Thus, a solicitor who signed the report on title in circumstances where either he had not made such reasonable enquiries, or he had made them and they suggested that the true purchase price was different from that stated in the offer of advance, would be in breach of duty.

1   [1997] 4 All ER 582 at 605e–f. Blackburne J's approach in *Balmer Radmore* was similar.

(d)   Allowances

7.22   This raises the question as to what circumstances should have caused a reasonably careful solicitor to conclude that the purchase price might not be that stated in the offer of advance. The Law Society's Guidance on Mortgage Fraud, first published on 30 November 1990, stated:

> 'Solicitors acting contemporaneously for a buyer and a lender should consider their position very carefully if there is any change in the purchase price, or if the solicitors become aware of any other information which they would reasonably expect the lender to consider important in deciding whether, or on what terms, it would make the mortgage advance available. In such circumstances the solicitors' duty to act in the best interests of the lender would require them to pass on such information to the lender ... Solicitors must not withhold information relevant to a transaction from any client and for a lender this includes not only straightforward price reductions but may also include other allowances (eg for repairs, payment of costs, the inclusion of chattels in the price and incentives of the kind offered by builders such as free holidays and part-subsidisation of mortgage payments) which amount to a price reduction and which would affect the lender's decision to make the advance. Solicitors should not attempt to arbitrate on whether the price change is material but should notify the lender.'

This guidance reflected what was probably already standard practice among conveyancing solicitors by December 1990.[1] Thus allowances of the kinds referred to by the Law Society should have been reported to lenders at this time. In *Balmer Radmore*, Blackburne J considered that an agreement by the vendor to pay the purchaser's costs and expenses of the purchase would amount to a price reduction which should be reported, though if the vendor supplied the purchaser with a free structural survey it would not.[2] Further, in *National Home Loans Corpn plc v Stevens & Co*,[3] the lender's documents were similar to Bristol and West's and the solicitor did have an express obligation to report changes in the purchase price. The price stated in the contract and the offer of advance was £62,650, but surveyors' reports suggested that the purchaser would have to carry out significant repairs, and for that reason the vendor agreed to an 'allowance' of £3,000 on the purchase price. In other words, although the sum stated in the contract remained at £62,650, the sum which the purchaser actually had to pay the vendor was only £59,650. The solicitor considered that the £3,000 would genuinely be spent on repairs, was an 'allowance' rather than a reduction in price, and therefore did not have to be reported. The Deputy Recorder held that there had been a reduction in price, so that the solicitor had acted in breach of duty in failing to report it to the lender. As to causation, however, he held that if the reduction had been reported, the lender would simply have reduced the advance by £297.50, so damages were £297.50 plus interest.

1   See *Balmer Radmore* [1999] Lloyd's Rep PN 241 at 265.
2   *Balmer Radmore* [1999] Lloyd's Rep PN 241 at 265.
3   A decision of Mr John Tackaberry QC sitting as a Deputy Recorder on Official Referee's Business (2 June 1997, unreported).

(e)   Direct payments

7.23   Lenders commonly allege a duty on the part of solicitors acting for them to report that part of the purchase price of the property has been paid directly from the purchaser to the vendor, without passing through the hands of either party's solicitor, and that the solicitor has not taken steps to check whether the payment was in fact made. The expert evidence in *Fancy and Jackson* showed that in the vast majority of cases the whole of the price payable on the purchase of domestic property passed through the bank account of the purchaser's solicitor.[1] Thus it was unusual for money to pass directly from purchaser to vendor rather than via solicitors. Addressing the issue in *Balmer Radmore*, Blackburne J said this:[2]

'The failure of the solicitor to obtain verification of a direct payment leaves open the possibility that vendor and purchaser/borrower were misrepresenting the position, that, in truth, no payment had been made and that the true price being paid for the property was the contract price less the direct payment; in short, that the assertion of a direct payment was intended to conceal a price reduction. This possibility, if accurate, meant that vendor and purchaser/borrower were together engaged in a fraud on the Society, representing dishonestly that the price to be paid for the property was £x whereas, in truth, it was £x less the amount of the direct payment. The purpose of such dishonesty could only be to induce the Society, supported by a valuation overstating the true value of the property, into making the advance in the belief that the overall price paid was indeed £x.

There arrived a time when the device of the so-called direct payment, where unverified, came to be recognised by solicitors as one of the badges of mortgage fraud. This, together with a recognition of other indications of mortgage fraud, led in March 1991 to the publication by the Law Society of the so-called "Green Card" warning on mortgage fraud. It included, among one of the signs to watch for in cases of mortgage fraud, "a deposit paid direct—a deposit, perhaps exceeding a normal deposit, paid direct or said to be paid direct, to the seller".

In his evidence, Mr Ward[3] accepted that, after the publication of the Green Card warning, there was what he described as a "fairly absolute" requirement on solicitors to report to the lender an unverified claim by the borrower to have made a direct payment.'

Thus, although none of the cases in either *Fancy and Jackson* or *Balmer Radmore* concerned a failure to report an unverified direct payment after receipt of the Law Society's Green Card, it would appear that such a failure would amount to a breach of duty.[4]

1   See [1997] 4 All ER 582 at 605g–h.
2   [1999] Lloyd's Rep 241 PN at 266.
3   The defendants' solicitor expert.
4   There might be doubt as to the position in the period March to May 1991, when the Green Card was in the course of being sent to all solicitors. In *Nationwide Building Society v Yoga & Co* (12 September 1997, unreported) Chadwick J said, in setting aside judgement in default: '... the appreciation of mortgage fraud and the way in which it might be perpetrated had begun

to be recognised in the solicitors' profession by, at the latest, November 1990. But I am not persuaded that it is unarguable that a sole practitioner—as this defendant was—would or ought to have appreciated these points in March 1991.'

7.24   The position is less clear cut in relation to transactions which were completed prior to March 1991. Until then, there had been no warning to solicitors from the Law Society that direct payments were a badge of mortgage fraud, nor was there a general perception amongst solicitors to that effect.[1] In *Fancy and Jackson*, Chadwick J's approach was as follows. In the period prior to March 1991, unless there were exceptional circumstances, a solicitor whose borrower client told him of a direct payment had the following obligation. He had to obtain confirmation from the vendor's solicitor in advance of completion that the vendor would give a full receipt for the supposed purchase price in the transfer. Even if the solicitor failed to do that, however, he would act reasonably if the transfer did in fact contain a receipt in those terms. It appears that by a 'receipt', the judge was referring to the statement in the transfer of what the purchase price had been. So, if the price stated in the transfer was the same as the price stated in the offer of advance, then the lender's solicitor would not be liable for failing to report a direct payment, unless there were exceptional circumstances.[2] The facts of the *Fancy and Jackson* case itself are an example of this. The transaction took place at the end of 1989. The purchase price was £175,000 and there was a direct payment of £25,000, which the solicitor failed to report to the lender. But the transfer contained a receipt for the full amount of the purchase price and was stamped accordingly; the judge concluded that there was nothing other than the fact of the direct payment itself which ought to have led to the conclusion that the vendor and purchaser were colluding in a dishonest scheme to deceive the lender. He held that there had been no breach of duty in failing to report the direct payment.[3]

1   *Fancy and Jackson* [1997] 4 All ER 582 at 606f–j.
2   See [1997] 4 All ER 582 at 605j–606b.
3   [1997] 4 All ER 582 at 607a–e.

7.25   In *Balmer Radmore*, Blackburne J quoted this part of Chadwick J's judgment and said that he agreed, but then went on to add a gloss the effect of which would appear to be that, in most cases, the solicitors *would* have an obligation to report an unverified direct payment, even prior to March 1991:[1]

> 'Any solicitor on being informed that his client has made a direct payment is likely in most cases to want to know why. As Chadwick J pointed out, in the vast majority of cases the whole of the purchase price passed through the solicitor's hands so that a direct payment was sufficiently unusual to warrant an explanation. Unless it was obvious to the solicitor that the claim to have made a direct payment was false, and therefore that his client was engaged in some fraudulent transaction, the solicitor would first seek an explanation from his client. If, having sought an explanation and having no proof of payment beyond his client's assertion (coupled, no doubt, with an acceptance by the vendor that a direct payment had indeed been made), the solicitor remains doubtful, he might consider that, although not able to conclude that he was acting for a dishonest client, the circumstances were such that he could not confirm that the stated purchase price was indeed the price. In that case his obligation would be to report the matter to the Society, stating the facts as he understood them, including whatever steps he had taken to establish whether the payment had in truth been made, and explaining why, in the circumstances, he felt unable to confirm that the stated price was indeed the price to be paid.

I am inclined to think, however, that the problem is more apparent than real. Any solicitor of reasonable competence, aware of his duty to notify the Society of a possible discrepancy in the purchase price, who was told by his borrower client of a direct payment but who entertained a doubt whether the payment had been made, would surely say to the client: "I need to be able to inform the Society that the contract price is indeed the price that is being paid. When the price passes entirely through my hands I can do that. But I cannot do so as regards the payment which you tell me you have paid the vendor direct. Please get your bank to confirm the payment to me." If the client were unable to furnish evidence of payment and if there was no convincing explanation for the absence of evidence, the solicitor would be entitled to conclude that his client was involved in a fraudulent transaction and, having come to that conclusion, he would have no choice but to cease acting. At the very least he would be obliged to report that he was unable to confirm the price stated on his instructions.'

Although in general he considered that direct payments should have been reported, on the facts of the individual cases which Blackburne J had to decide, there were two cases, involving direct payments of relatively small amounts, in which he held that the mere fact that there had been a direct payment was not, taken on its own, something which ought to have been reported.[2]

1   *Balmer Radmore* [1999] Lloyd's Rep PN 241 at 267.
2   See the decisions in *Borm Reid* and *Adams Delmar*: at the time of writing these parts of the *Balmer Radmore* judgment have not been reported and reference must be made to the transcript.

7.26   Thus, in relation to the period prior to March 1991, it is necessary to look at the facts of each individual case to see whether the matters of which the solicitor was, or should have been, aware were sufficiently suspicious to give rise to a duty to report to the lender. For example, in *Richard Grosse*,[1] one of the *Balmer Radmore* decisions, the stated purchase price was £660,000. There were back-to-back transfers with a price increase from £477,000 to £660,000, an increase of 38% in March 1990, and a supposed direct payment of £66,000. The lender was advancing £594,000, so the difference between the purchase price and the amount of the advance was exactly the amount of the supposed direct payment, which meant that the borrower did not need to pay anything toward the purchase price through his solicitors. The direct payment was supposedly made at a time when the borrower had not even exchanged contracts to buy the property, and when the intermediate vendor had proved no title in the property. The solicitor knew that the borrower had originally been dealing with the head vendor, who was willing to sell for £477,000, but had only later decided to buy from the intermediate vendor, who was ostensibly profiting from the uplift in price. Blackburne J held that the solicitor was in no position to confirm that £660,000 was the price of the property, and was under a duty to report the suspicious nature of the transaction to the lender.

1   [1999] Lloyd's Rep PN 348.

(f)   Resident borrower

7.27   In *Birmingham Midshires Mortgage Services Ltd v David Parry & Co*,[1] the Court of Appeal had to consider the following argument. The solicitor's instructions required him to ensure that the general and special conditions specified in the offer of advance were 'complied with and brought to the [borrower]'s attention on or before completion'. General condition 4 provided that the borrower must '... personally reside in the property within 30 days of completion'. The lender contended that the solicitor either did know, or ought to have known, that the borrower did not intend personally to occupy the property within 30 days of completion, and that the terms quoted required the solicitor to inform the lender of this, which he had failed to do. The court disagreed. It construed these terms as requiring the solicitor to bring the terms of general condition 4 to the borrower's attention, 'and to report to the plaintiffs knowledge on his part that [the borrower] does not intend to comply with the condition'. Thus the solicitor would be in breach of duty if he had actual knowledge that the borrower did not intend to reside in the property at all, and had not reported this to the lender. But[2]

> 'There is no obligation imposed on [the solicitor] to check with [the borrower] that he intends to reside in the property personally or to report to the plaintiffs facts relating to [the borrower]'s current or past residence. [The solicitor] was entitled to assume, in the absence of information to the contrary, that [the borrower] intended to comply with the terms of the offer of advance which he had accepted ... Without the benefit of hindsight a reasonably competent solicitor would have been entitled to take the view that the available information about the circumstances and actions of [the borrower] was consistent with an intention on his part to use [the property] as a secondary residence; that would constitute "personal residence" within general condition 4. There was no condition in the offer of advance that [the borrower] should reside in [the property] as his only or primary residence.'

1   [1997] EGCS 150, CA.
2   Transcript p 21. Blackburne J applied this on the facts of the case of *Balmer Radmore* itself: see the transcript of that case.

(g)   *Redemption of existing mortgages before completion*

7.28   A further point arose in *Parry*.[1] The solicitors' instructions contained a term that the borrower's 'existing mortgages must be redeemed on or before completion of this advance'. It was argued that this term required redemption not only of existing mortgages secured over the property which was to be charged to the lender, but also of charges over other properties which the borrower owned. Read literally, the term would have applied to other charges. But the Court of Appeal construed the term in the context that the borrower was not required, by the terms of the offer of advance, to redeem mortgages over other properties, and on the basis that it is not generally part of the solicitor's duty to report matters relating to the borrower's financial position.[2] Thus the lender's argument was rejected.

1   [1997] EGCS 150, CA.
2   See paras 7.47ff for the solicitor's duties in relation the borrower's financial position.

(h)   *Obligation to report material changes in circumstances*

7.29   In *National Home Loans Corpn v Giffen Couch & Archer*,[1] the lender contended that when, after their instruction by the lender, the defendant solicitors learnt that the borrowers were under threat of legal proceedings from their previous lender, this amounted to a material change of circumstances which ought to have been reported to the lender. By paragraph 6 of the lender's report on title the solicitors certified that 'We are not aware of any material change in the applicant's circumstances subsequent to the date of the offer of loan'. Peter Gibson LJ, delivering the only reasoned judgment, said that this would naturally lead the defendant solicitors to believe that, subject only to a clear bankruptcy search being obtained, the lender was satisfied that the borrowers' circumstances at the date of the offer of advance made them suitable borrowers.[2] Peter Gibson LJ rejected the argument that knowledge that the borrowers were under threat of legal proceedings constituted a material change in circumstances. It was the existence of the arrears that was material; the additional information that the previous lenders might be proposing to commence possession proceedings on the basis of those arrears was not a material change of circumstances, and need not have been reported.[3]

1   [1997] 3 All ER 808, CA. This case is discussed in more detail in paras 7.47ff.
2   See [1997] 3 All ER 808 at 814b, CA.
3   See [1997] 3 All ER 808 at 816e–f, CA.

(i)   Failing to obtain proper security on completion

7.30   The primary function of a solicitor acting for a lender in a standard transaction is to ensure that the lender obtains a valid and effective first charge on the property, which requires in particular that the charge is over good and marketable title.[1] Chadwick J elaborated on this in *Bristol and West Building Society v May, May & Merrimans*:[2]

> '... in signing and returning the report on title, the solicitor warrants or represents that his principal obligation under the contract has been performed—"I/We have investigated the title of this property and report that I/We consider the title to be good and marketable and that it may be safely accepted by the society."
>
> It is, I think, beyond argument that a solicitor who had not investigated title at all or who had not investigated the particular matters which the solicitor's instructions require to be investigated—see, in particular, para 4 (searches), para 5 (vacant possession and rights of persons in occupation) and para 7 (leasehold securities)—would be in breach of his contract with the society if he were to sign and return the report on title without qualification. Alternatively, by returning the report on title without qualification, he would be in breach of warranty or guilty of misrepresentation. So, also, the solicitor would be in breach of his contract with the society if he had failed to exercise the required degree of care and skill in carrying out his investigation. Further, the solicitor would be in breach of contract, breach of warranty or guilty of misrepresentation, if he were to sign and return the report on title without qualification in circumstances where, having made a full investigation of the title, he did not consider the title to be good and marketable. Yet further, he would be in breach of contract if, having made a full investigation of title, he were to sign and return the report on title without qualification in circumstances in which a reasonable conveyancing solicitor, exercising the required degree of care and skill, could not have reached the conclusion that the title was good and marketable on the material available.'

1   See *National Home Loans Corpn plc v Giffen, Couch & Archer* [1997] 3 All ER 808 at 813f–g, CA.
2   [1996] 2 All ER 801 at 809h–810c.

7.31   Further, in the *Fancy and Jackson* case itself, Chadwick J held that solicitors who did not have an official search certificate from the Land Registry at the time of completion acted in breach of duty. They had not investigated title properly before completion. Again, in *Alliance & Leicester Building Society v Wheelers*,[1] the lender's instructions to the defendant solicitors contained a term which read 'Completing solicitors to be satisfied that all the necessary planning, byelaw and statutory consents are in force and suitable for the use of the property as offices'. The solicitors wrote to the lender saying that there was planning permission for use of the property as B1 office use. This was incorrect. The permitted use was D1, as a surgery. For that reason summary judgment was granted against the solicitors.[2]

1   (23 January 1997, unreported), Ch D.
2   Further, for a discussion of 'shared ownership' schemes, see *Halifax plc v Gould and Swayne* [1999] PNLR 184, CA, although all the court had to do was conclude that the solicitors had an arguable defence to the allegations of negligence.

(j)   Forms of undertaking agreed between banks and the Law Society

7.32   In *Barclays Bank plc v Weeks Legg & Dean*,[1] the Court of Appeal considered three cases relating to a solicitor's undertaking to a lender that the lender's money would be used only for the purpose of obtaining 'good marketable title' to the property in question. In each case, the solicitor had provided an undertaking in a form agreed between banks and the Law Society.[2] It is important to recognise that these were not standard lenders' cases, because, with one small exception, the bank did not instruct the solicitors to act for it in the transaction; it did not ask the solicitors to provide a report on title or to advise in relation to any aspect of the transaction; and the solicitors were not paid by the bank for their services.[3] Millett LJ, with whom the other judges agreed, said that, as the undertaking was designed to stand alone as the only communication passing between the solicitor and the bank, the scope of the solicitor's obligations was determined exclusively by the terms of the undertaking.[4] It follows that there would be no room for implied contractual obligations, or a duty of care in tort, which went beyond the express terms of the undertaking. This distinguishes cases based on such an undertaking from the standard case which we consider below.[5]

1   [1998] 3 WLR 656, CA.
2   The undertaking now appears as form no 3 at annex 25C to *The Guide to the Professional Conduct of Solicitors* (7th edn, 1996). It reads:
     'Undertaking by Solicitor
     To send Deeds/Land Certificate to Bank on completion of a purchase, the Bank and/or the Customer having provided the purchase monies.   TO BARCLAYS BANK PLC
     If you provide facilities to my/our client   ... for the purchase of the Freehold/Leasehold property ....
     I/We undertake: (a) that any sums received from you or your customer for the purpose of this transaction will be applied solely for acquiring a good marketable title to such property and in paying any necessary deposit legal costs and disbursements in connection with such purpose. The purchase price contemplated is £... gross and with apportionments and any necessary disbursements is not expected to exceed £... (b) after the property has been acquired by ... and all necessary stamping and registration completed to send the Title Deeds and/or Land Certificates and documents to you and in the meantime to hold them to your order.'
3   See [1998] 3 WLR 656 at 665H–666A.
4   [1998] 3 WLR 656 at 666D–E.
5   See paras 7.38ff.

7.33   By the express terms of the undertaking, the solicitors agreed that the bank's money would be applied solely for obtaining a 'good marketable title'. Millett LJ said:[1]

> 'The obligation of a vendor is to deduce sufficient title to the property which he has contracted to sell. The expression "good marketable title" describes the quality of the evidence which the purchaser is bound to accept as sufficient to discharge this obligation. It says nothing about the nature or extent of the property contracted to be sold to which title must be deduced. The expression is a compendious one which describes the title and not the property. It is used in contradistinction to "a good holding title", by which is meant a title which a willing purchaser might reasonably be advised to accept, but which the court would not force on a reluctant purchaser.'

In the first case, the land in question was purchased subject to a special condition that it was subject to a right of way in favour of an adjoining owner. The Court of Appeal held that this did not mean that the solicitors were wrong to state that title to the property was good and marketable: an unwilling purchaser could have been forced to buy the land. The fact that the right of way rendered the land less valuable than the lender bank had thought was irrelevant to the question of whether there was good marketable title to it. Although the case turns on construction, one might observe that the effect of the bank's argument was that the solicitors' obligations were similar to those which they would have had if they had supplied a report on title, even though the solicitors had been paid nothing by the bank and had not supplied a report on title. In that context, it is perhaps unsurprising that the bank's contentions were rejected.

1   [1998] 3 WLR 656 at 668B–C.

(k)   Forged signatures on charges

7.34   Various cases concern the liability of solicitors who agree with a lender to ensure that specific persons sign a charge in favour of the lender, but then find that the signature of one of those persons on the charge has been forged. If it is found that the solicitors failed to act with reasonable care to ensure that the right people signed the charge then they are likely to be found liable. Further, if the same solicitors act for both lender and borrowers, then the solicitors may be liable to the lender for breach of warranty of authority.[1] But can lenders argue that, even if the solicitor, acting with reasonable skill and care, would not have detected the forgery, the solicitor is still liable to the lender? In other words, can it be said that the solicitor's obligation to the lender is a strict one, to ensure that the correct people sign the charge, so that the solicitor is liable if the wrong people sign, even though he or she took reasonable skill and care?

1   See paras 7.101ff. In the context of a guarantor who claims that her signature has been obtained by undue influence, the Court of Appeal has held that solicitors acting only for the lender have a duty to take reasonable steps to ensure that a guarantor is advised by either the borrower's solicitor or an independent solictor: *Mercantile Credit Co Ltd v Fenwick* [1999] Lloyd's Rep PN 408.

7.35   In *Zwebner v The Mortgage Corpn Ltd*,[1] the report on title which the lender's solicitors signed contained an undertaking that all appropriate documents would be 'properly executed' on completion. Mr Zwebner was borrowing money from the lender on the security of a house which he owned jointly with Mrs Zwebner, so it was necessary for Mrs Zwebner to sign the mortgage. In fact her signature was forged. The Court of Appeal held that the solicitors' obligation to ensure that the wife signed the mortgage deed was a strict one, so that it would have been breached even if the solicitors had acted with reasonable care. But in *Midland Bank plc v Cox McQueen*,[2] Lord Woolf MR, with whom the other judges agreed, distinguished *Zwebner*. The solicitors had agreed to ensure that a wife signed a charge for a lender, but her signature was forged. The points of distinction were that in *Cox* the solicitors merely certified that the wife had signed, rather than undertaking, and merely agreed that she would sign, rather than stating that the charge would be 'properly' executed. But Lord Woolf added:[3]

'In my judgment the decision in *Zwebner* should not be given a wide application. To do so would ignore the wider consequences of our decision. If commercial institutions such as banks wish to impose an absolute liability on members of a profession they should do so in clear terms so that the solicitors can appreciate the extent of their obligation which they are accepting. Frequently this sort of task is undertaken by small firms of solicitors who are already finding it difficult to remain viable. This is partly because they are heavily burdened by the costs of insurance. If they are to be liable for very substantial sums of damages as a result of the fraud of the customers of the bank which they cannot prevent, then either they will have to withdraw from providing these services or they will have to charge for their services at a rate which is very different from that which was charged here. Neither result is in the interests of the banks or their customers or the public. The result is not in the interests of the banks' customers as they will not benefit from the explanation of the transaction from a member of the legal profession who is qualified to give that explanation. It is not in the interests of banks as they will have to pay higher fees which they may or may not seek to recover from their customers. It is not in the interest of the public because it is important that legal services are readily available and this will not be the case if small firms are unable to survive. Unless the language used in a retainer clearly has this consequence, the courts should not be ready to impose obligations on solicitors which even the most careful solicitor may not be able to meet.'

1   [1998] PNLR 769, CA.
2   [1999] Lloyd's Rep 223 PN, CA.
3   [1999] Lloyd's Rep 223 PN at 229. See also *Mercantile Credit Co Ltd v Fenwick* [1999] Lloyd's Rep PN 408, CA.

7.36   The Court of Appeal reached a similar conclusion, interpreting a solicitor's obligation to ensure that the lender obtained good marketable title, in *Barclays Bank plc v Weeks Legg & Dean*.[1] Strictly speaking, decisions on construction all turn on the precise documents in issue, so that authorities do not greatly assist in interpreting documents with slightly different words. But the rationale which Lord Woolf set out in the passage quoted is not of such limited application.

1   [1998] 3 WLR 656.

(l)   Conclusion in relation to construction of express terms of the retainer

7.37   Without abandoning the warnings already given as to the value of authority in construing contractual documents, some brief conclusions may be ventured. In all the categories set out above apart from the first, there is now authority at Court of Appeal level opposing a strict literal construction of the terms of the solicitor's duties, and tending to read such duties in a way which confines them to acting with reasonable skill and care. In the first category, the court's tendency is to construe the express terms in a relatively broad way, so as to require, for example, the reporting of direct payments in cases where the written terms of the contract do not expressly refer to these. But it can be argued that even this approach mirrors the court's construction of the solicitor's implied duties, because, as we shall see in the next section, those implied duties to act with reasonable skill and care have been interpreted to require the solicitor to report, for example, sub-sales with price uplifts in a falling property market.

5   Liability for breach of implied contractual terms and in the tort of negligence

7.38   Section 13 of the Supply of Goods and Services Act 1982 implies into the solicitor's contract of retainer a term that the solicitor must act with reasonable skill and care. This standard is generally treated as imposing the same standard as the duty which the solicitor owes the client in the tort of negligence, to act with reasonable skill and care. The question is the extent to which, in the absence of breach of an express contractual term, the court will hold that a solicitor acting for a lender has failed to act with such skill or care. It is helpful to consider the information, which it is alleged there is an implied duty to report, as falling into two categories: information relating to the value of the property which is to be taken as security for the loan, and information relating to the value of the borrower's covenant.[1] In summary, in the first category there generally will be an implied duty to report, and in the second there will not. In this section we consider these two categories in turn. We then look at two further possible limitations on the duty to report information.

1 See paras 7.7ff, and *National Home Loans Corpn plc v Giffen Couch & Archer* [1997] 3 All ER 808 at 815j, CA.

(a) Implied duty to report matters relevant to the value of the security

7.39 In *Mortgage Express Ltd v Bowerman & Partners*[1] (*'Bowerman'*), the facts were as follows. On 21 November 1990 the plaintiff lender sent a letter instructing Mr Gilroy of the defendant solicitors to act for the plaintiff in relation to the proposed purchase by a Mr Hadi of a flat in Queensway, London for £220,000, with a loan of £180,150 from the plaintiff. The letter included a valuation of the property in the sum of £199,000, and it was apparent that the plaintiff's loan was based on this valuation. Mr Gilroy then agreed to act on Mr Hadi's behalf and discovered that the proposed vendor was a Mr Arrach. On 26 November 1990 Mr Gilroy learnt that in fact Mr Arrach had not yet purchased the property: he was due to purchase it from a Mr Rasool for £150,000, and simultaneously to sell it on to Mr Hadi for £220,000, an increase of nearly 50% in price. Mr Gilroy was concerned that Mr Hadi might be paying too much, and that the valuation of £199,000 might be incorrect, and so he warned Mr Hadi of the price at which Mr Arrach was purchasing. Mr Gilroy also knew that Mr Rasool had purchased the property only a few days earlier on 2 November 1990, that the London property market was not rising at the time, and suspected that Mr Rasool's purchase had been at a sum lower than £150,000. He did not report any of this information to the plaintiff lender in his report on title or by other means. The transaction completed, Mr Hadi made only one mortgage payment before defaulting, and the plaintiff repossessed the property and sold it at a loss.

1 [1996] 2 All ER 836, CA.

7.40 The judge found that, in failing to report such matters to the plaintiff, the defendant had breached its duty to the plaintiff. The Court of Appeal upheld that conclusion. Sir Thomas Bingham MR said:[1]

> 'A client cannot expect a solicitor to undertake work he has not asked him to do, and will not wish to pay him for such work. But if in the course of doing the work he is instructed to do the solicitor comes into possession of information which is not confidential and which is clearly of potential significance to the client, I think that the client would reasonably expect the solicitor to pass it on and feel understandably aggrieved if he did not.
>
> I would accordingly reject the submission originally made on behalf of the solicitors as to the narrow ambit of the duty, as the judge did, and accept, as I understand her to have done, the submission of Mortgage Express. That was that *if, in the course of investigating title, a solicitor discovers facts which*

a reasonably competent solicitor would realise might have a material bearing on the valuation of the lender's security or some other ingredient of the lending decision, then it is his duty to point this out.'

Millett LJ, concurring, said:[2]

'It might be thought ... that the question which the judge should have asked herself was: "Would a solicitor of ordinary competence have regarded the information that Mr Arrach was paying only £150,000 for the flat as throwing doubt on the valuation of £199,000?" That, however, would not, in my opinion, be an accurate formulation of the question. Mr Gilroy was not a valuer and it was not his responsibility to doubt a professional valuation. *The question which the judge had to ask herself was whether a solicitor of ordinary competence would have regarded the information in question as information which might cause the plaintiffs to doubt the correctness of the valuation which they had obtained.'* [Emphasis added.]

Schiemann LJ agreed with both judgments.

1   [1996] 2 All ER 836 at 842d–f, CA.
2   [1996] 2 All ER 836 at 845e–g, CA.

7.41   The relevant information in *Bowerman* was information which a solicitor of ordinary competence would have regarded as information which might cause the lender to doubt the correctness of the valuation which it had obtained. Sir Thomas Bingham MR formulated the implied duty as going further, and relating not only to information of that kind, but also to information which might have a material bearing on 'some other ingredient of the lending decision'. It will be suggested below[1] that, in light of later authority, it is doubtful whether the implied duty extends to this second type of information. For the moment we concentrate on the first type: information which a solicitor of ordinary competence would have regarded as information which might cause the lender to doubt the correctness of the valuation which it had obtained. For brevity we refer to this as the '*Bowerman* valuation duty'.

1   Paras 7.52–7.53.

7.42   Considering *Bowerman* in *Balmer Radmore*, Blackburne J said that he accepted the defendants' submission that[1]

'... in considering whether a solicitor acting for a lender is subject to a *Bowerman* type duty, the correct approach is to examine the terms of the retainer and then consider what implied obligations, if any, there are to accompany the expressed ones. Having said that, however, I am inclined to think that the *Bowerman* duty is a species of obligation which the court will ordinarily imply, or find present, where a solicitor acts for a lender in a mortgage transaction except to the extent that to do so would be inconsistent with the express terms of the engagement or with the surrounding circumstances of the relationship.'

He did not consider that the terms of Nationwide's instructions were inconsistent with the existence of such a duty, and concluded:[2]

'... a solicitor retained by the Society on the terms of its standard printed conditions was obliged to report to it information obtained by him in the course of investigating title or preparing for completion which was not confidential and which a solicitor of ordinary competence would have regarded as information which might cause the Society to doubt either the correctness of the valuation which, as the solicitor would know, it had obtained or the bona fides of the borrower. It is not necessary for me to express any view on whether the duty extended to a requirement to report information discovered by him which might affect some other ingredient of the Society's lending decision.'

1   [1999] Lloyd's Rep 241 PN at 258.
2   [1999] Lloyd's Rep 241 PN at 259.

7.43 Two points should be noted on this formulation. First, even in cases where there is an implied duty to report, it is subject to two further restrictions: it relates only to information which (i) the solicitor obtains in the course of investigating title or preparing for completion, and (ii) the solicitor is not prevented from reporting by obligations of confidentiality owed to the borrower. These limitations also appear in the passage quoted from Sir Thomas Bingham above. We consider them further below.[1] Secondly, as to the scope of the duty, note that it extends beyond information which the solicitor of ordinary competence would have regarded as information which might cause the lender to doubt the correctness of the valuation:[2] on Blackburne J's formulation, it relates also to information which the same solicitor would have regarded as information which might cause the lender to doubt the bona fides of the borrower. It is thought that the latter is a more controversial proposition. Again, we consider this further below.[3]

1   Paras 7.54–7.56.
2   Which we have called the *Bowerman* valuation duty.
3   Paras 7.52–7.53.

7.44 Leaving those points aside for the moment, what is the extent of the *Bowerman* valuation duty? The effect of *Balmer Radmore* is that, in cases where the property market was falling, the duty is likely to extend to a duty to report sub-sales or back to back transactions in which there was a price uplift that was anything other than minimal. For example, in *ATM Abdullah*, the defendant solicitor failed to report a back-to-back transaction in autumn 1991 where there was a price increase from £54,000 to £63,000, an uplift of 17%, but the head vendor was a mortgagee in possession. Blackburne J held the solicitor liable. Property prices were falling at the time. Although a reasonably competent solicitor might have thought that the explanation for the price rise was that the head vendor was a mortgagee in possession selling at a discount,[1]

> '... he would have been mindful that whereas he had no particular expertise in matters of valuation, the Society did have access to persons who possessed such expertise. In these circumstances he would surely not have taken upon himself to conclude that the explanation for the uplift in price was indeed because the head sale was by a mortgagee in possession.
>
> In my view, a reasonably competent solicitor would not have speculated on the reasons for the uplift but would have reported the matter to the Society as being information which might cause the Society to doubt the correctness of the £63,000 valuation which it had obtained of which, having received a copy, Mr Abdullah was aware. £54,000 was almost £6,000 less than the amount of the Society's offer of advance.'

It did not, however, follow that the lender recovered the whole of its loss on the transaction. The judge held that, if this information had been reported, it would still have lent to the borrower, but would have lent £2,800 less than it did lend, so damages were £2,800 plus interest.

1   This was one of the cases decided as part of *Balmer Radmore*, but as yet has not been reproted. See pp 473–4 of the *Balmer Radmore* transcript.

7.45   It is no excuse that, before completion, the defendant solicitor did not know the amount of the price increase. In investigating title to registered land, he ought to find out who the registered owner is. In the case of a sub-sale, it will not be the party from whom the borrower is buying ('the intermediate vendor'), so the solicitor will know that a sub-sale or back to back transaction is involved. Before completing the transaction, the solicitor ought to insist upon seeing a copy of the contract between the registered owner and the intermediate vendor, in order to be sure that the intermediate vendor can make title. It is possible that, before exchange of contracts, the intermediate vendor might supply the borrower with a copy of his own contract with the registered owner from which the price had been blanked out, so as to prevent the borrower from finding out the amount of the intermediate vendor's profit. But, after exchange and before completion, it would not matter if the borrower found this out, so the intermediate vendor's solicitors could not refuse to make available an unexpurgated copy of his contract. Thus, before completion, the solicitor acting for the lender and borrower ought to know the amount of the price uplift.[1] If exchange of contracts and completion on both transactions were due to take place on the same day, the borrower's solicitor would not know the price at which the intermediate vendor was buying, but the transaction would be so unusual that the solicitor would have an obligation to explain its nature to the lender.[2]

1   See *ATM Abdullah* in the *Balmer Radmore* judgment: pp 458–482 of the transcript.
2   See *Balmer Radmore* [1999] Lloyd's Rep PN 241 at 269.

7.46   A similar duty may apply in relation to a remortgage. If a borrower purchases a property for £120,000 and then obtains an offer of re-mortgage a few days later in the sum of £134,000, the solicitor acting for the lender offering the re-mortgage ought to find out the amount of the earlier purchase and realise that it casts doubt on the second lender's valuation, since the second lender's valuation must state that the property was worth at least the amount of the advance, £134,000, and thus considerably more than the amount at which the property had been purchased a few days earlier.[1]

1   See *Littlestone & Cowan* in the *Balmer Radmore* judgment: pp 340–362 of the transcript.

(b)   Generally no implied duty to report matters relevant to the creditworthiness of the borrower

7.47   In general there is no implied duty on solicitors to report to lenders matters which relate only to the creditworthiness of the borrower, and not to the value of the security, though of course there may be an express duty of this kind, and there may be cases where the solicitors' instructions would be construed to include such a term by implication. This emerges from the Court of Appeal's decision, subsequent to *Bowerman*, in *National Home Loans Corpn plc v Giffen, Couch & Archer ('Giffen')*,[1] confirmed by the Court of Appeal in *Birmingham Midshires Mortgage Services Ltd v David Parry & Co*.[2]

1   [1998] 1 WLR 207, [1997] 3 All ER 808, CA.
2   [1997] ECGS 150, CA.

7.48   In *Giffen*, a Mr Choudhry borrowed from the Halifax Building Society to purchase 224 Buckingham Road, Bletchley ('the property'). On 30 June 1988 Mr Choudhry transferred title to the property into his own and his wife's names, and Mr and Mrs Choudhry ('the borrowers') remortgaged the property to a company known as Western Trust, using part of the advance to pay off the Halifax. In February 1989 the borrowers wanted to remortgage the property again. They were introduced to the plaintiff by an intermediary. They applied to the plaintiff for a remortgage in an application form dated 10 February 1989. In the application form they stated inter alia that they had never at any time been in arrears by more than one month with any existing or previous loan and had never had any county court judgment recorded against them. On 5 April 1989 the plaintiff offered the borrowers an advance, and on the same day instructed the defendants, solicitors, to act for them 'in the preparation of a mortgage with any other appropriate documents in accordance with the Notes for Guidance and the documents provided'. The plaintiff sent the defendants its Instructions to Solicitors and Licensed Conveyancers, and instructed them to report on title on the plaintiff's standard form. On 31 May 1989 the defendants submitted a report on title to the plaintiff. Completion, using the plaintiff's money, took place on 9 June 1989. The borrowers quickly fell into arrears and the plaintiff sold the property as mortgagee in possession on 13 April 1992, leaving a shortfall on the borrowers' account.

7.49　The plaintiff lender's case was as follows. By 17 May 1989, the defendants had discovered that there were arrears of over £4,000 on the borrowers' mortgage with Western Trust, and that there was a danger of Western Trust commencing legal proceedings to repossess the property. The defendants did not report these pieces of information to the plaintiff. In particular, they did not refer to them in their report on title dated 31 May 1989. The plaintiff claimed that the defendants ought to have reported such information to it, and that, by failing to do so, the defendants were in breach of their implied contractual duty and duty of care owed to the plaintiff.

7.50　The Court of Appeal disagreed. Peter Gibson LJ, with whom the other two judges agreed, set out five factors which were relevant to determining the scope of the defendants' duties:[1]

'(1) The instructions from the plaintiff required the defendants to act for the plaintiff "in the preparation of a mortgage ... in accordance with the Notes for Guidance and the documents provided." Any solicitor of ordinary competence and experience would realise that the defendants' primary function was to make sure that the plaintiff received a valid and effective first mortgage on the property, and that required in particular that the plaintiff should receive a good and marketable title. The approval of the title by the defendants was an express condition of the loan.

(2) The plaintiff, an experienced commercial lender, provided its own detailed printed instructions to the solicitors. Those instructions specified the particular matters on which the plaintiff required to be advised. This made clear, for example, that the investigation of title should go beyond ordinary conveyancing matters, but extended to matters which might affect the valuation put upon the property. To give another example, they were required to advise if any information suggested that the property was not to be the principal residence of [the borrowers] for the sole continuing occupation of them and their family. The plaintiff provided its own form of a report on title which stated precisely what the solicitor was required to certify. In these circumstances, whatever the position in other cases with differing circumstances, there is limited room here for treating the scope of the duty of care as extending to require the solicitor to take action which has not been expressly required by the plaintiff in its instructions.

(3) Subject to para 6 of the report on title, the only action which the defendants were instructed to take relating to the financial circumstances of [the borrowers] was twofold: to do a bankruptcy search and to report on any matter revealed by the search.

(4) The plaintiff did not send a copy of the application by [the borrowers] to the defendants, and there is no evidence that they knew any of its contents.'

Pausing there, the relevance of this was that the defendants could not have known that the information which they had as to the arrears demonstrated that the borrowers had lied to the plaintiff on the application form.

'(5) Further, the report on title, in requiring the defendants to certify that they were not aware of any material change in the circumstances of [the borrowers] subsequent to the date of offer of loan, would naturally lead the defendants to believe that, subject only to a clear bankruptcy search being obtained, the plaintiff was satisfied that the circumstances of [the borrowers] at that date were such that they were appropriate borrowers. The defendants did not know what inquiries, if any, had been made by the plaintiff. Mrs Butler, a legal executive who was employed by the defendants and who ... dealt with the matter for them, presumed that the plaintiff would have sought a reference from Western Trust.'

The presence of the fifth factor is probably not a necessary condition for concluding that there is no implied duty to report matters relevant to creditworthiness.[2]

1   See [1997] 3 All ER 808 at 813f–814c.
2   See *Birmingham Midshires Mortgage Services Ltd v David Parry & Co* [1997] ECGS 150, CA.

7.51   Blackburne J distinguished *Giffen* in *Balmer Radmore* on the following bases:[1]

'The question in that case was whether the solicitor should have reported certain information which cast doubt on the borrowers' ability to pay. The information was of a kind which it would be reasonable to suppose the plaintiff would have obtained from other sources. The instructions were held, where matters of creditworthiness were concerned, to be of very limited scope. The decision does not seek to limit the scope of the duty to report where, as here, the information relates to matters going to the value of the property and therefore to the adequacy of the security or where, as here, the information derives from an investigation of title and therefore from matters which it is the business of the solicitor to investigate and not that of the Society or of others on its behalf.'

Thus we have suggested a distinction, in the nature of the implied duties which the court will ordinarily imply, between, first, matters which a solicitor would normally discover in the course of his or her investigation of title on behalf of the lender, which are relevant to the value of the security, and secondly, matters going to the credit-worthiness of the borrowers, which the solicitor could normally expect that the lender would find out itself, and which a solicitor acting only for the lender and not the borrowers would probably not discover. There will normally be an implied duty to report information which falls into the first category, but no implied duty to report information which falls into the second category. The approach of limiting solicitors' duties to those within the solicitor's core function is similar to that taken in *Midland Bank plc v Cox McQueen*.[2]

1   *Balmer Radmore* [1999] Lloyd's Rep PN 241 at 258.
2   Para 7.35.

(c)   Conclusion on the Bowerman *duty*

7.52   At paras 7.41 and 7.43, we raised the question of whether *Bowerman* should be interpreted to give rise to a duty which went beyond what we called the *Bowerman* valuation duty. We defined the *Bowerman* valuation duty as being an implied duty to report information which a solicitor of ordinary competence would have regarded as information which might cause the lender to doubt the correctness of the valuation. Further, on Blackburne J's formulation of the duty,[1] the obligation is to report information discovered in the course of investigating title or preparing for completion.[2] It is clear that a duty of this kind will normally be implied into the solicitor's instructions. The question is whether the implied duty which the court will normally imply as a result of *Bowerman* should go further, and encompass, as Sir Thomas Bingham suggested in *Bowerman*,[3] a duty to report information which a solicitor of ordinary competence would have regarded as information which might cause the lender to doubt 'some other ingredient of the lending decision'.

1 See para 7.42.
2 This is subject to an exception which we consider at para 7.56.
3 See the passage quoted at para 7.40.

7.53 It is likely that this broader duty would be inconsistent with the subsequent decision in *Giffen*. In *Giffen*, the Court of Appeal distinguished *Bowerman* on five bases. The key points were that information as to creditworthiness did not relate to title or the adequacy of the security, or to any other matter on which the defendant solicitors were instructed to advise. Peter Gibson LJ pointed out that Millett LJ had decided *Bowerman* on a narrower basis than Sir Thomas Bingham MR, stating that the reportable information appeared on the face of the vendor's title, and thus was information which the defendant solicitors would have discovered in the course of investigating title. It is thought that, in order to be consistent with *Giffen*, it is necessary to construe the duty arising out of *Bowerman* as being confined to what we have called the *Bowerman* valuation duty.[1] This may still be a broad duty, since many matters may be relevant to the value of the property, and in particular information suggesting sub-sale frauds generally will be relevant to value. If, however, one were to construe the *Bowerman* duty as extending, for example, to a duty to report all matters suggesting bad faith of the borrowers, then one might have difficulty in explaining why the plaintiff lost in *Giffen*: the information as to arrears in that case might be seen as being information which suggested that the borrowers were acting in bad faith and knew that they would never be able to repay the lender.

1 Para 7.41.

(d) Implied waiver of confidentiality of the borrower in the instant transaction

7.54 The implied duty, arising out of *Bowerman*, is subject to two limitations: first, it is limited to information which is not confidential; secondly, it is generally limited to information which the solicitor discovers in the course of doing the work which he is instructed to do on behalf of the lender, which is principally investigating title and preparing for completion.[1] We consider the second limitation below. As to the first, what counts as confidential information for these purposes? The question is likely to arise where, as is normally the case, the same solicitor acts for both lender and borrower. Blackburne J set out the position, in relation to information which the solicitor has learnt in the course of handling the transaction for which the borrower seeks a loan from the lender, in *Balmer Radmore* as follows:[2]

'In *Bowerman*, Millett LJ said this (at page 844j):

"A solicitor who acts for more than one party to a transaction owes a duty of confidentiality to each client, but the existence of this duty does not affect his duty to act in the best interests of the other client. All information supplied by a client to his solicitor is confidential and may be disclosed only with the consent, express or implied, of his client. There is, therefore, an obvious potentiality for conflict between the solicitor's duty of confidentiality to the buyer and his duty to act in the best interests of the mortgage lender.

No such conflict, however, arose in the present case. It is the duty of a solicitor acting for a purchaser to investigate the vendor's title on his behalf and to deduce it to the mortgagee's solicitor. He has the implied authority of his client to communicate all documents of title to the mortgagee's solicitor."

In *Mothew*,[3] he said this (at page 20d):

"By instructing him to act for them, the purchasers must be taken to have authorised the defendant to complete the report without which the mortgage advance would not have been forthcoming; and to complete it truthfully. The defendant was required by the society to report on the purchasers' title as well as to confirm the absence of any further borrowing. The two stood in exactly the same case. The defendant would not have been in breach of his duty to the purchasers if he had disclosed the facts to the society any more than if he had reported a defect in their title."

This proposition can be tested by considering what the defendant's position would have been if he had acted for the purchasers and another solicitor had been instructed to act for the society. He would have been required to deduce the purchasers' title to the satisfaction of the society's solicitor, and to confirm to him that no further borrowing or second charge was in contemplation. His duty to the purchasers would have required him to ascertain the facts from them and to report them to the society. Unless they told him the facts and instructed him to lie to the society, instructions which he would be bound to refuse, his duty to the purchasers would not inhibit him in providing full and truthful information to the solicitor acting for the society.

The answer to the first question, therefore, lies in ascertaining what it is that the solicitor is obliged by his instructions to report on to the lender: the implied authority to disclose covers all matters to which the instructions relate. By naming his own solicitor to act also for the society, which occurred in each of the twelve cases before me, the borrower must therefore be taken to have authorised the solicitor to complete the report on title and make whatever disclosures were necessary to enable the solicitor to comply with the society's instructions, without which the mortgage advance would not be forthcoming, and to complete the report on title truthfully.'

1   See the formulations of Sir Thomas Bingham MR at para 7.40 and Blackburne J at para 7.42.
2   [1999] Lloyd's Rep PN 241 at 261.
3   *Bristol and West Building Society v Mothew* [1998] Ch 1, CA.

7.55   It is therefore unlikely that confidentiality owed to the borrower, in relation to the instant transaction, will be a bar to the solicitor reporting to the lender. On Blackburne J's formulation, where a borrower names his own solicitor to act also for the lender, he impliedly authorises the solicitor to disclose to the lender any matters, concerning the instant transaction, which it is necessary to disclose in order to comply with the lender's instructions. Thus, if a piece of information needs to be reported in order to comply with the lender's instructions, the borrower will be taken to have impliedly authorised such disclosure, even if the information is confidential, so confidentiality will be no bar to disclosure.

(e)   Information learnt from other transactions

7.56   The second limitation on the implied duty to report information, arising out of *Bowerman*, was that the duty generally related only to information which the solicitor discovered in the course of doing the work which he was instructed to do on behalf of the lender. This is principally investigating title and preparing for completion. Thus, there is generally no implied duty to report information which the solicitor knows from other sources, for instance, from working for the borrower client on other unrelated transactions.[1] But the position is different where the information which the solicitor knows from other sources, taken with the information which he has in relation to the lender's transaction, provides the solicitor with strong evidence of fraud. In that case, any confidentiality of the borrower's is overridden,[2] and the solicitor will have an implied duty to report to the lender both the information, and the reason why he is reporting it, namely, that it leads him to suspect fraud.[3]

1   *Bristol and West Building Society v Baden Barnes Groves & Co (No 1)* (26 November 1996, unreported) (Chadwick J).
2   *Darlington Building Society v O'Rourke James Scourfield & McCarthy* [1999] Lloyd's Rep PN 33, CA.
3   See Blackburne J's decision in *Vanderpump & Sykes*, part of the *Balmer Radmore* judgment: [1999] Lloyd's Rep PN 422.

6   Causation

7.57   In contract and the tort of negligence, the test of causation applied to lenders' cases turns on whether, if the solicitors had reported the matters which they ought to have reported, the lender would have made the advance which it in fact made. This is a question of fact which turns on the judge's assessment of the particular lending officer in question. The response of the lending officer would depend in part on the terms in which the solicitor made the report of the relevant information. In *Balmer Radmore*, Blackburne J said that the solicitor ought to have reported as if he or she were writing to an intelligent layman.[1] But his decisions in the individual cases suggest that his approach was rather that the solicitor should assume that he was writing to a layman who needed potential difficulties spelt out in the clearest possible way, which is perhaps not wholly unfair, since, in relation to contributory negligence, he found that the lender's employees did not generally think about applications in a careful or critical way. The judge held that the solicitor's duty was not merely to report the bare facts which ought to be passed to the lender, but also the reason why they were being reported. Thus, in a case where the lender was offering to advance £134,000 by remortgage and the solicitor had a duty to report that the property had been purchased a few days earlier for only £120,000, the solicitor's duty was[2]

> 'to state in clear terms, preferably in a letter to the Society so that there could be no mistake about the matter, not simply the essential facts of the [borrowers]' earlier purchase (ie that it had occurred only three or so weeks earlier and had been for £120,000) but why he was reporting the matter (ie that the information might cast doubt on the valuation of the property which the Society would have obtained and without which it would not have been willing to advance £134,000). In my view it is not a sufficient discharge of that duty simply to report the bare facts and leave it to the recipient within the Society, whoever he or she might be, to guess what the reason is for the disclosure.'

1   [1999] Lloyd's Rep PN 241 at 270.
2   *Littlestone v Cowan*: see pp 351–2 of the transcript.

7.58   Again, in *Vanderpump & Sykes*, Blackburne J set out numerous matters which the defendant solicitor ought to have reported to the lender, including doubts as to the honesty of the transaction.[1] In that case, the lender's surveyor had expressed doubts about the honesty of the transaction, but it nevertheless proceeded with the advance. In Blackburne J's view, there was a critical difference in relation to causation between the society's surveyor expressing such doubts, and its solicitor, who also acted for the borrower, expressing the same doubts: even though the former had not caused the lender to withdraw from the transaction, the latter would have done. This shows that Blackburne J's view that, once a solicitor has a duty to report matters, he or she must spell them out in detail, may be crucial to causation: the more the solicitor has a duty to explain why he is reporting matters, the more likely it is that, had such a report been made, the lender would have withdrawn, even if, in other respects, its employees were unthinking or even careless.

1   [1999] Lloyd's Rep PN 422 at 440.

7.59   There are essentially three possible answers to the question of what the lender would have done if the solicitor had reported as he or she ought to have done. First, it might have made the same advance in the same amount. In that case, it can recover only nominal damages, and probably not costs.[1] Secondly, it might have lent to the same borrower but on a lower advance. In that case, its loss is the difference between the advance it in fact made, and the advance it would have made if there had been no breach of duty, plus interest.[2] Thirdly, it might not have lent at all. In that case, one moves to consider basic loss and the effect of *BBL*,[3] which we deal with below.

1   See *Alltrans Express Ltd v CVA Holdings Ltd* [1984] 1 WLR 394, CA.
2   See the *ATM Abdullah* decision in *Balmer Radmore* at pp 458–482 of the transcript.
3   [1997] AC 191, HL. This case is also known as *SAAMCo*, which is an abbreviation of the name of the first plaintiff, in the appeal in the House of Lords.

7.60   There is a final issue on causation. In *Bristol and West Building Society v Mothew*,[1] Millett LJ considered the Court of Appeal's decision in *Downs v Chappell*,[2] where Hobhouse LJ had delivered the only reasoned judgment. In summary, Millett LJ said that the effect of *Downs* was that the court had to distinguish between negligent acts of a solicitor, and negligent omissions. In the case of negligent acts, where the solicitor had negligently given the client incorrect advice or information, it was sufficient for the plaintiff to prove that he had relied on the advice or information, in the sense that he would not have acted as he did if he had not been given such advice or information. It was not necessary for the plaintiff to go further and prove that, if he had been given the correct advice or information, he would not have acted as he did. In other words, it appeared that, in relation to negligent acts, it was no defence on causation for the solicitor to prove that, had the lender been given the correct advice, it would in any event have proceeded with the advance. On the other hand, this was a defence on causation in relation to negligent omissions. This appeared to create a distinction of doubtful merit.

1   [1997] 2 WLR 436 at 442F–443H, CA.
2   [1997] 1 WLR 426, CA.

7.61   Three points may be made on this. First, Hobhouse LJ has since suggested that Millett LJ's interpretation of *Downs* was incorrect.[1] Secondly, in *Fancy and Jackson*, although Chadwick J heard full argument on *Downs*, *Swindle* and *Mothew*, he did not apply this distinction. In what may have been a reference to it, he did say that he did not find all the observations in each of the judgments in these cases easy to reconcile, and concluded that the correct approach was to proceed directly to applying what Lord Hoffmann had said as to scope of duty in *BBL*, without considering further glosses.[2] It would thus appear that this is now the correct approach, and it is to be hoped that the distinction set out in the last paragraph need not be considered further. Thirdly, even if this were not correct, note that, even in *Mothew*, the effect of Millett LJ's treatment of the next test, of scope of duty under *BBL*, was to reintroduce the question of what the lender would have done if it had been given the correct advice.[3]

1   See *Swindle v Harrison* [1997] 4 All ER 705 at 728g–j, CA.
2   See [1997] 4 All ER 705 at 620b.
3   See [1997] 2 WLR 436 at 444–5. This point is discussed further in the next section. For further criticism of what was formerly understood to be the effect of *Downs v Chappell*, see Tomlinson, Seitler and Grant *Property Finance Negligence: Claims Against Solicitors and Valuers* (1996) pp 77–78.

7   Basic loss

7.62   The decision of the House of Lords in *BBL* introduced a distinction, in cases to which it applies, between two kinds of loss. Although the case did not provide labels for these two types, we use here the terms basic loss and attributable loss. Attributable loss is the loss which is recoverable in accordance with the principles set out in *BBL*, which we consider below.[1] Basic loss was a term used by Lord Hobhouse in *Platform Home Loans Ltd v Oyston Shipways Ltd*.[2] He derived it from Lord Nicholls's definition of the 'basic comparison' which has to be made in a lender's case, and which we discussed in chapter 5.[3] The basic loss is assessed according to the principles set out in *Swingcastle Ltd v Alastair Gibson*.[4] This is a question of comparing the position which the lender is in fact in, with the position it would have been in if there had been no advance. Thus, it depends upon the nature of the evidence which the claimant provides as to what would have happened if the defendant had not been in breach of duty.

1   At paras 7.70ff. We take the term 'attributable' from *BBL*.
2   [1999] 2 WLR 518 at 526H, HL.
3   Paras 5.27ff.
4   [1991] 2 WLR 1091, HL.

7.63   In *Swingcastle*, the defendant valuer negligently overvalued the borrowers' property. In reliance on the valuation, the plaintiff lenders advanced money to the borrowers, secured by a mortgage. Under the terms of the loan, the borrowers were required to pay interest at the rate of 36.51% per annum, or 45.619% per annum in the event of default. The issue in the appeal was whether a lender who made a loan at a high rate of interest in reliance on a negligent valuation could recover, as part of his damages from the negligent valuer, interest at the contractual rate which the lender was entitled to be paid by the borrower and which remained outstanding at the termination of the transaction between the lender and the borrower. The House of Lords held that it could not. The valuers had not guaranteed that the borrowers would pay the money owing under the loan. The correct measure of loss was damages to put the lender in the position it would have been in if there had been no negligence. If there had been no negligence, the lender would not have entered into the transaction. Thus the lender was entitled to damages to compensate it for the difference between (i) the position it was in fact in, and (ii) the position it would have been in if there had been no transaction. It was up to the lender to provide evidence as to (ii), so that the court could make the necessary comparison. But what the lender could not do was claim from the valuer the interest calculated on the rates of 36.51 and 45.619% which the borrowers had failed to pay.

7.64   The amount claimed in each case will depend on the evidence which the lender provides as to the position it would have been in if there had been no transaction. In part this will depend on whether the money which was advanced was money which the lender already had in its possession, or was money it had to borrow. In the former case, the loss would be calculated by reference to what the lender would have done with the money if there had been no transaction. In *Fancy and Jackson*, for example, Chadwick J summarised the lenders' claim as to quantum of loss as follows:[1]

> 'The society quantifies [its] loss by adding to the principal sum lent the interest which would have been earned on an equivalent sum invested in the money market at London Inter-Bank Offered Rates (LIBOR) and deducting from the aggregate the interest and capital repayments (if any) actually made by the borrowers and the net recoveries (if any) from the realisation of the mortgaged property on sale.'

Presumably the lender's evidence was that, if there had been no transaction, it would have lent the money to others at LIBOR rates. On the other hand, the lender's evidence is often that the lender itself had to borrow the money which it advanced to the borrower. Thus part of the claim is for the cost to the lender of borrowing the money which formed the advance, since, if there had been no transaction, the lender would not have borrowed the money. But, in this case too, the evidence tends to be that the cost of funding should be calculated by reference to LIBOR plus or minus a small percentage. The claimant's calculation of its loss in an average case of this second kind might look like this:

			£
Advance			100,000
Cost to the lender of borrowing the amount of			
the advance (interest it has had to pay to borrow the £100,000)			20,000
			120,000
Less			
Borrowers' payments		5,000	
Sale price	80,000		
Less cost of sale (estate agents'			
and solicitors' fees)	3,000		
Net proceeds of sale	77,000	77,000	
Total deductions		82,000	
			82,000
Total claim			**38,000**

In principle, deductions for items such as solicitors' fees should be made at the date when the claimant paid the fee, so that interest on such a sum runs only from the date when the claimant suffered the loss. It should be emphasised that this calculation is merely an example of what might be claimed. In the next few paragraphs we consider the basis on which the court might agree that it was payable.

1   See [1997] 4 All ER 582 at 616e–f.

Interest

7.65 A number of issues arise in relation to interest. First, there is a question as to the rate at which interest should be awarded.[1] This tends to be agreed in lenders' cases. In principle, at least where interest is being awarded *as* damages rather than *on* damages (see below), it is thought that the right approach is to consider the rate at which the claimant actually suffered the loss. This will depend on the claimant's evidence, but, as mentioned above, in lenders' cases it will often be a small fraction above or below LIBOR.

1   See paras 3.60ff.

7.66 More difficult is the question whether lenders are entitled to claim interest on a compound rather than merely a simple basis in cases where the evidence shows that they have in fact suffered a loss calculated by reference to compound rather than simple interest. It is necessary to distinguish between interest *on* damages and interest *as* damages. A claim to interest *on* damages arises where the total amount of damages payable has already been calculated, and interest is payable on that total sum from a date prior to trial until trial. A claim to interest *as* damages arises where part of the damages claimed, and set out in the statement of case, is interest. In the example given in para 7.64, the claim to interest ought to be pleaded, and would then count as a claim for interest *as* damages. The power to award interest *on* damages in common law claims arises from Supreme Court Act 1981, s 35A, but that provision permits the award of only simple and not compound interest. For that reason, subject to an exception which arises in considering *BBL*,[1] lenders tend to frame their claims to interest in terms of interest *as* damages rather than interest *on* damages.

1   See para 7.74.

7.67 For reasons set out in chapter 3,[1] the court will award compound interest only if the case falls within the second limb of *Hadley v Baxendale*.[2] Thus the question is which cases fall within that second limb. Claims within the first limb are those which 'may fairly and reasonably be supposed as arising naturally, ie according to the usual course of things, from' the breach of contract in question, or 'such as may reasonably be supposed to have been in contemplation of both parties at the time they made the contract, as the probable result of the breach of it'.[3] Cases within the second limb are those where there are special circumstances, which were within the knowledge of the contract breaker at the time the contract was entered into, which are outside the ordinary course of things, and of such a kind that breach in those special circumstances would be likely to cause more loss.[4]

1   See para 3.60.
2   (1854) 9 Exch 341.
3   *Hadley v Baxendale* (1854) 9 Exch 341, quoted in *Hartle v Laceys* [1999] Lloyd's Rep PN 315, CA.
4   *Victoria Laundry (Windsor) Ltd v Newman Industries Ltd* [1949] 2 KB 528, CA.

7.68 It is thought that, in the ordinary lender's case, it is likely that the solicitor will be aware that, if he acts in breach of duty and the lender subsequently suffers loss due to the default of the borrower, the lender will suffer loss in the sense of interest calculated on a compound rather than a simple basis. This is because the solicitor, if he thought about the matter, would realise that, if there were no transaction, the lender would not have to obtain the money to form the advance. Thus he would realise that the lender's loss would be having to supply the money to form the advance. Further, he would realise that the source of the advance money must be either borrowing by the lender, or use of the lender's own money. If the lender has borrowed the money, it must pay interest on it, probably at a compound rate; and if the lender used its own money then, if there had been no advance, it would have lent it on some other basis and been paid interest, probably on a compound basis. Thus it is likely that the solicitor will realise that the consequence of a breach of duty on his part will be that the lender will suffer a loss of interest on a compound basis. But the key point is that in most cases the reason the solicitor will realise this will be his knowledge of how lenders fund their advances *in the ordinary course of business*; it is unlikely that any special circumstances of the particular case will draw the solicitor's attention to these matters. Thus it is likely that compound interest will be irrecoverable, because the case falls within the first rather than the second limb of *Hadley v Baxendale*. This may seem unfair to a lender which has proved foreseeable loss of compound interest. But this is an unfairness on which the House of Lords commented in 1893.[1] Parliament has since legislated on the issue, but has, it appears, chosen not to deal with this particular problem.[2]

1   *London, Chatham and Dover Rly Co v South Eastern Rly Co* [1893] AC 429.
2   See the analysis of Lord Brandon of Oakbrook in *President of India v La Pintada Cia Navigacion SA* [1985] AC 104, HL.

7.69   In *Birmingham Midshires Mortgage Services Ltd v Phillips*[1] HHJ Bromley QC sitting as a deputy High Court judge declined to award the plaintiff lender compound interest, because the defendant solicitor had not been cross-examined about what was within his contemplation at the time. On the other hand, in *Hartle v Laceys*,[2] which was not a lenders' case but did concern solicitors' negligence, the defendant solicitor knew that the plaintiff developer owed large sums to banks, knew the terms on which the banks were lending, which included monthly compounding, and knew that the plaintiff would be likely to use the sum which, absent negligence he ought to have obtained, to reduce that indebtedness. The reason why the solicitor was so well informed about the plaintiff's means was partly that he was acting for him in ancillary relief proceedings, and engaged in giving full and frank disclosure of the plaintiff's means. The Court of Appeal held that compound interest and bank charges were recoverable, as the case clearly fell within the second limb of *Hadley v Baxendale*.[3]

1   [1998] PNLR 468, Ch D, at 467E–F.
2   [1999] Lloyd's Rep PN 315, CA.
3   *Hartle* was distinguished in *The Mortgage Corpn v Halifax (SW) Ltd* [1999] 1 Lloyd's Rep PN 159 (HHJ Lawrie sitting as a deputy High Court judge), on the basis that the case was a surveyors' case and the defendants owed duties only in tort and not contract. Thus the test of remoteness in tort, rather than contract, applied. It is unlikely, however, that this approach would govern many solicitors' cases, as solicitors normally act for lenders pursuant to a contract. In any event, the decision may well be wrong: 'the power to award compound interest is not available at common law' per Lord Goff in *Westdeutsche Landesbank Girozentrale v Islington London Borough Council* [1996] AC 669 at 684, HL.

8   Attributable loss

7.70   Once the claimant has proved its case in breach of duty at common law, causation, and established the amount of the basic loss, the question arises of whether it can recover all the basic loss, or whether there should be a reduction on account of the principles in *BBL*.[1] *BBL* concerned three cases brought by lenders against valuers. We consider the effect of the decision first in relation to valuers, then in relation to interest, and finally in relation to solicitors.

1   [1997] AC 191, HL.

(a) BBL *and valuers*

7.71 Each of the cases considered in *BBL* concerned the assessment of damages where a valuer had negligently overvalued a property, and a lender had lent on the security of the property in reliance upon the overvaluation. The practical result of the decision in relation to valuers is that, other than in exceptional cases, the lender's damages are limited to the lower of :

(i) the basic loss, calculated as set out in the last section, and thus probably including compound interest as damages; and

(ii) the amount of the overvaluation.

In cases where (ii) is lower than (i), the lender will be entitled to simple interest on the amount of the overvaluation, from the date when the basic loss reaches the amount of the overvaluation.[1] Thus if the true value of the property was £100,000, and the valuer stated the value to be £150,000, then the amount of the overvaluation would be £50,000. The valuer cannot be liable to the lender in damages for more than the amount of the overvaluation. So in our example, the valuer could not be liable for more than £50,000 in damages, though simple interest would be added.

1　See *Nykredit Mortgage Bank plc v Edward Erdman Group Ltd (No 2)* [1997] 1 WLR 1627, HL.

7.72 The practical effect of this rule is to limit the damages which the lender can recover. Lord Hoffmann explained the rationale for the rule by reference to an example:[1]

> 'A mountaineer about to undertake a difficult climb is concerned about the fitness of his knee. He goes to a doctor who negligently makes a superficial examination and pronounces the knee fit. The climber goes on the expedition, which he would not have undertaken if the doctor had told him the true state of his knee. He suffers an injury which is an entirely foreseeable consequence of mountaineering but has nothing to do with his knee.'

Lord Hoffmann said that the doctor should not be liable for the injury. The reason was set out in the following principle:[2]

> 'that a person under a duty to take reasonable care to provide information on which someone else will decide upon a course of action is, if negligent, not generally regarded as responsible for all the consequences of that course of action. He is responsible only for the consequences of the information being wrong. A duty of care which imposes upon the informant responsibility for losses which would have occurred even if the information which he gave had been correct is not in my view fair and reasonable as between the parties. It is therefore inappropriate either as an implied term of a contract or as a tortious duty arising from the relationship between them.'

Hence the principle is that in cases where the defendant is sued for breach of a duty to provide information, the defendant is not liable for losses which would have occurred even if his information had been correct. Thus, in Lord Hoffmann's example, the doctor is not liable for the mountaineer's injury, which would have occurred even if the doctor's advice, that the mountaineer's knee was fit, had been correct. On the other hand, if the mountaineer's injury had been caused by his weak knee, so that the injury would *not* have occurred if the doctor's advice had been correct, then the doctor would be liable for the injury.

1　*BBL* [1996] 3 WLR 87 at 94F–G.
2　See *BBL* [1996] 3 WLR 87 at 95D–F.

7.73 Applying this test to valuers, Lord Hoffmann assessed the difference between the negligent valuation, and the true value of the property, at the date of the valuation. Taking the example above, £150,000 – £100,000 = £50,000. Lord Hoffmann then said that the consequences of the valuation being wrong were that the lender had less security than it thought, by the amount of the overvaluation.[1] So on our example, the lender had £50,000 less security than it thought. Damages were to be limited to that sum, in other words, to the extent of the overvaluation. The principle did not apply in three exceptional types of case. The first two exceptions were cases based on fraud[2] or breach of warranty.[3] The third was cases where the defendant was in breach of a duty to advise the claimant what course of action to take, rather than a duty to provide information. This third category does not normally apply in lenders' cases.

1   [1996] 3 WLR at 102G–H.
2   See para 7.99.
3   See para 7.101.

(b)   BBL *and interest*

7.74 How should interest be assessed in cases where the basic loss exceeds the amount of the attributable loss, so that there is a reduction in damages on account of *BBL*? Assuming that the claim for basic loss includes interest as damages, accumu-lating as loss which the lender has in fact had to pay but would not have done if there had been no breach of duty, the first step is to calculate when the amount of the basic loss reaches the level of the attributable loss. At that date, interest as damages ceases to be awarded, and the claimaint is entitled only to simple interest on the amount of the attributable loss, pursuant to Supreme Court Act 1981, s 35A, generally until trial.[1] Morritt LJ commented on the calculation of these figures in *Platform Home Loans Ltd v Oyston Shipways Ltd*:[2]

> 'I confess that I am greatly concerned at the time and expense which is likely to be incurred in carrying out these computations. So far as I can see if the interest representing the cost to [the lender] of the money lent to [the borrower] is the same as the interest awarded under s 35A Supreme Court Act 1981 then whatever the answers to these complicated enquiries[3] the same figure will be produced. In these circumstances I consider that the party requiring the full calculation to be made should pay for it unless it can be demonstrated that it made so significant a difference to the result as would justify the costs involved.'

But the calculations will be the same only if (i) there is no claim for compound, as opposed to simple, interest as part of the basic loss, and (ii) as in *Nykredit*, it is agreed that the appropriate rate for the award of interest under s 35A is the same as the rate claimed as part of the basic loss. Since lenders generally claim compound interest, it is doubtful whether this criticism will generally be valid.

1   See *Nykredit Mortgage Bank plc v Edward Erdman Group Ltd (No 2)* [1997] 1 WLR 1627, HL.
2   [1998] Ch 466. Although the Court of Appeal's decision was overturned by the House of Lords, the House did not need to comment this passage.
3   Ie as to the date when the cause of action accrued, calculated in the way set out above.

(c)   BBL *and solicitors*

7.75 It is clear from *Bristol and West Building Society v Mothew*[1] and *Fancy and Jackson*[2] that the principles in *BBL* apply to lenders' claims brought against solicitors as well as valuers. Their application, however, is more complex. We consider principally Chadwick J's analysis in *Fancy and Jackson*, which Blackburne J applied in *Balmer Radmore*.[3] It is necessary to consider three categories of case—those where:

(i) the lender's loss is not attributable to the breach of duty, so that only nominal damages flow from the breach;

(ii) the breach of duty was relevant only to the valuation of the property; and

(iii) if there had been no breach of duty, the lender would not have wished to make any advance to the borrower in question.

1   [1998] Ch 1, CA.
2   [1997] 4 All ER 582, CA.
3   [1999] Lloyd's Rep PN 241 at 271–272.

(i)   Loss not attributable to the breach of duty

7.76   In considering the facts of the *Fancy and Jackson* case itself, Chadwick J held that none of the basic loss was recoverable:[1]

> 'The defendants ought to have informed the society that they did not have an official search certificate. If they had done so, the society would not have authorised the advance—or, at least, would not have authorised completion on 6 October 1989. But the loss which the society has suffered as a consequence of making the advance on 6 October 1989 is not caused by the absence of an official search certificate on that day. The title to the property taken as security was not, in fact, defective. The society obtained what it intended to obtain when it decided to enter the transaction. The loss which occurred would have occurred in exactly the same way and to exactly the same extent if the defendants had had what, by implication, they represented they did have on 6 October 1989—namely a clear search certificate showing good title to the property.'

Putting the matter another way, although the solicitor's breach of duty was relevant to the quality of the title to the property which formed the lender's security, in fact the breach of duty did not reduce the value of that security, because there was no defect in the title. Thus, applying Lord Hoffmann's test in *BBL*, the lender would have suffered the same loss even if the information which the solicitor negligently supplied had been correct. For this reason, no loss was recoverable.

1   [1997] 4 All ER 582 at 621j–622a.

7.77   Similarly, in *Mothew*,[1] in breach of contract and negligently the defendant solicitor failed to report to the plaintiff lender that the borrowers, Mr and Mrs Towers, were not proposing to comply with an express condition of the advance which required that they provide the balance of the purchase money, apart from the lender's advance, without resort to further borrowing. The information which should have been reported was that the borrowers were arranging for an existing bank debt of £3,350 to be secured by a second charge on the property. Millett LJ said:[2]

> 'The society was told that Mr and Mrs Towers had no other indebtedness and that no second charge was contemplated. The existence of the second charge did not affect the society's security. The absence of any indebtedness to the bank would not have put money in the purchasers' pocket; it would merely have reduced their liabilities. Whether their liability to the bank affected their ability to make mortgage repayments to the society has yet to be established, but given the smallness of the liability its effect on the purchasers' ability to meet their obligations to the society may have been negligible. It may even be, for example, that the purchasers made no payments at all to the bank at the relevant time, and if

so it is difficult to see how any part of the loss suffered by the society can be attributable to the inaccuracy of the information supplied to it by the defendant. *It would have occurred even if the information had been correct.*' (Emphasis added.)

Thus, in cases where the lender would have suffered the same loss as it in fact suffered even if the information which the solicitor wrongly supplied had been correct, then only nominal damages should be awarded. Strictly speaking the test of causation which we considered above[3] is separate from the question of applying *BBL.*[4] Thus, on the facts of the *Fancy and Jackson* case Chadwick J found that, if there had been no breach of duty, the transaction would not have proceeded, at least in the way that it did, so that causation was made out; it was the application of *BBL*, rather than principles of causation, which produced the conclusion that only nominal damages should be awarded. In practice, however, it is possible that, where cases fall into this category, the court will first conclude that, had there been no breach of duty, then the lender would in any event have proceeded, and then go on to hold in the alternative that, even if the lender had proceeded, the loss was not attributable to the solicitor's breach of duty.[5]

1   [1998] Ch 1, CA.
2   [1997] 2 WLR 436 at 444H–445A.
3   At para 7.57.
4   See Lord Hoffmann's emphasis of this in *Nykredit*: [1997] 1 WLR 1627 at 1638F–G, HL.
5   Compare the accountants' negligence case of *Bank of Credit and Commerce International (Overseas) Ltd v Price Waterhouse (No 3)* (1998) Times, 2 April (Laddie J).

(ii)   Breach of duty relevant only to valuation

7.78   In *Colin Bishop*, another of the cases decided in *Fancy and Jackson*, the matters which the solicitor ought to have reported included a sub-sale in which the price increased by 33%. Chadwick J held that, had these matters been reported to the lender, they would not have caused it to conclude that the borrowers were people with whom it did not wish to do business,[1] but would have caused it to doubt its valuation. He held that the recoverable loss was 'the loss suffered by the society as a consequence of the [lender] taking a security which was less valuable than it thought', and added that 'the position seems to me indistinguishable from the valuer cases considered in [*BBL*] itself.'[2] On that basis, the measure of damages ought to be the difference between the amount of security which the lender thought it was obtaining, and the amount which it was in fact obtaining: the difference between the true value of the property at the date of the advance, and the value which the lender believed it to have. So if the lender thought it was obtaining security worth £150,000, but the true value was only £100,000, the measure of damages would be £50,000. This measure is not the same as taking the difference between the advance which the lender in fact made, and the advance which it would have made if it had known the true value, unless, in both cases, the lender would have lent 100% of the valuation. If, in our example, the lender was using an LTV ratio of 80%, then, as it believed the property to be worth £150,000, it would in fact have lent £120,000, whereas, if it had known that the true value was £100,000, it would have lent only £80,000, so the measure of loss would be £120,000 – £80,000 = £40,000, rather than the £50,000 produced by *BBL*. The measure which produced £40,000 would be the correct measure if the court concluded, in relation to the prior question of causation, that, had there been no negligence, the lender would still have made the advance, but in a lower amount.[3] Strictly speaking, the application of *BBL* is a different question to causation, which explains why the two measures are slightly different.

1   See para 7.80.
2   See [1997] 4 All ER 582 at 622j.
3   See para 7.59.

7.79 A result similar to *Colin Bishop* was reached in *Alliance & Leicester Building Society v Wheelers.*[1] The defendant solicitors confirmed to the lender that there was planning permission under category B1 for a block to be used as offices. The lender lent on the security of the block. It transpired that the solicitor had been wrong: the planning permission was for D1 use rather than B1 use. Carnwath J held that it was appropriate to apply *BBL*, and that the measure of loss was the difference between what the property would have been worth with the planning permission which the lender believed it to have, and its value with the planning permission which it in fact had.

1   (23 January 1997, unreported), Ch D.

(iii)   Lender would not have wished to make any advance to the borrower

7.80 In *Steggles Palmer*, a further case decided in *Fancy and Jackson*, Chadwick J considered various suspicious facts which the solicitors ought to have reported to the lender, but had not:[1]

'I have held that the defendants were in breach of duty in failing to notify the society that the transaction was by way of sub-sale; in failing to notify the society that they could not confirm that the borrower was to pay the balance of the purchase moneys from his own resources; and in breach of duty in failing to tell the society that they were also acting for the vendor. I have also held that if the society had known of those matters it would not have made the advance. But that is not, in my view, because the society would have been unwilling to lend what it did lend on the security of the property. In deciding how much to lend on the security of the property the society was relying on its own valuation; and there is no evidence that that valuation was wrong, or that it would have been affected by knowledge of the sub-sale or the relationship between vendor and purchaser. The reason why the society would not have made the advance is, in my view, because the society would have been unwilling to lend to that borrower in order to fund a purchase from that vendor. If the society had known what it should have known, *it would have decided that Mr Whittaker was a borrower to whom it did not wish to lend.* In those circumstances it seems to me fair, in accordance with Lord Hoffmann's test, that the defendants should be responsible for the consequences of the society not being in the position to take the decision which it would have taken if the defendants had done what they should have done. That is to say, the defendants should be responsible for the loss suffered by the society as a result of lending to Mr Whittaker. That, subject to questions of mitigation and contributory negligence, is the whole loss arising from the advance.' (Emphasis added.)

To summarise, had the solicitors reported the matters which they ought to have reported, the lender would have had such grave doubts as to the character of the borrower that it would not have wished to risk lending to him at all, presumably due to the risk of mortgage fraud. For that reason, the lender's loss could not be restricted to matters going to valuation, as in the previous category of case; instead, all the lender's basic loss on the transaction was attributable to the solicitor, and recoverable. Most of the individual cases decided in *Balmer Radmore*[2] provide further examples of cases which the court considered fell into this category. Lenders will of course wish to claim that most cases fall into this category, so that their damages are not limited by *BBL*, and solicitors will wish claim that most cases do not, so that damages *are* limited by *BBL*. Blackburne J was certainly not slow to hold that cases fell into this category.[3]

1   [1997] 4 All ER 582 at 622c–f.
2   [1999] Lloyd's Rep PN 241.
3   The judge dealt with the issue in relation to 11 of the 12 cases, though in some cases the view
     he expressed was not part of the ratio as he had already held that there was no breach of duty.
     He considered that eight of those 11 cases fell into this category.

9   Contributory negligence and mortgage indemnity guarantees

7.81   We have already considered, in chapter 6, the general principles which apply
to claims that damages be reduced on account of contributory negligence, as well as
the House of Lords' decision in *Platform Home Loans Ltd v Oyston Shipways Ltd*[1] that
deductions on account of contributory negligence should be made from the basic loss
rather than the attributable loss. We now turn to various matters which apply in
particular to lenders' claims. It must of course be borne in mind that allegations of
contributory negligence in particular cases turn on the facts of the individual case,
so that the value of authority is limited. Nevertheless, some trends may be observed.

1   [1999] 2 WLR 518.

7.82   Allegations of contributory negligence in lenders' claims tend to be of two
kinds. In cases where the valuer was an employee of the lender, there may be
allegations of negligence on the part of the valuer, for which the lender is liable.
Alternatively, there may be allegations that the lender acted negligently in the
scrutiny which it applied to the borrower's application for a mortgage or remortgage,
before making the offer of advance. We set out the broad nature of the enquiries which
lenders generally carry out, at paras 7.9 and 7.10.

7.83   Blackburne J dealt in detail with allegations of contributory negligence, both of
a generalised kind and in relation to particular cases, in *Balmer Radmore*.[1] His discussion
related to the conduct of the Nationwide Building Society in the period 1990–1991. He
found that, prior to March 1991, the society had provided inadequate training of its staff,
in particular in relation to the dangers of mortgage fraud. Commenting on the performance
of members of the society's staff in considering mortgage applications, he said:[2]

> 'With one or two notable exceptions ... I had the impression that, in general, the
> process was one of going through the motions of ticking off the boxes to see that
> the relevant information had been supplied and that, applying the relevant
> lending criteria, the valuation and income disclosed justified the loan applied
> for. There seemed to be very little critical evaluation of the information supplied
> looked at overall. For example, the fact that in *Richard Grosse & Co* the
> information available to the Society indicated that the applicant had written
> cheques which were dishonoured was either not noticed or simply ignored. On
> occasions procedures were simply ignored.'

In general the society did not interview applicants, but Blackburne J considered that[3]

> 'The utility of conducting an interview, at any rate in the case of new borrowers
> to the Society is, in most cases, obvious. It serves as a means of reducing the risk
> of fraud. Over and above that, in cases where the loan applied for is to be a high
> proportion of the value of the property offered by way of security (and the loan
> applied for is at or near the maximum allowed applying the Society's income
> criteria) then, unless the applicant's creditworthiness is clearly evident from the
> information supplied to the Society and there is no reason to doubt the accuracy
> of that information, the interview serves as a means of assessing whether the
> applicant is likely to be able to honour his commitments.'

1   [1999] Lloyd's Rep PN 241 at 282–299 for the general discussion.
2   [1999] Lloyd's Rep PN 241 at 288.
3   [1999] Lloyd's Rep PN 241 at 288.

(a)   Levels of deduction for contributory negligence

7.84   Writing about contributory negligence in lenders' claims in 1998, Hugh Evans[1] observed that

'With two exceptions, none of the reported cases have assessed contributory negligence at above 30 per cent. In the two exceptions, the remarks on contributory negligence were obiter, as the defendants were found not to be negligent.'

In relation to the twelve individual cases which Blackburne J had to decide in *Balmer Radmore*, he made reductions for contributory negligence on a percentage basis in ten.[2] In those ten cases, he made reductions for contributory negligence of 90% in one case, 75% in another, 66% in three cases, 50% in two cases, and in the three remaining cases of 40%, 30% and 20% respectively.[3] In no case did he hold that there was no contributory negligence. It will be seen that these levels of reduction are much higher than had been the norm in previous cases. Although the amount by which damages should be reduced on account of contributory negligence is essentially a question for the discretion of the judge on which authority does not bind, it is thought that after *Balmer Radmore* the courts are likely to assess contributory negligence on the part of lenders at considerably higher levels than had previously been the case.[4]

1   'Contributory Negligence by Lenders' (1998) 14 PN 43 at 47–8.
2   The other two cases were cases where, if there had been no negligence, the lender would still have lent. Here the contributory negligence was expressed by reference solely to the excessive LTV, and was capable of precise calculation rather than expression merely as a percentage. See *Adams Delmar* and *ATM Abdullah*, and para 7.86.
3   In two of these ten cases the deduction for contributory negligence was not made because the solicitor was also in breach of fiduciary duty: see paras 7.114ff.
4   See also *The Housing Loan Corpn plc v William H Brown* [1999] Lloyd's Rep PN 185, CA: the Court of Appeal refused to overturn a finding of 75% contributory negligence in a lender's action against a surveyor.

(b)   Excessive LTVs

7.85   A number of points arise in relation to allegations that lenders have advanced an excessive LTV,[1] for example, over 75% of the valuation of the property. In *Fancy and Jackson*,[2] Chadwick J set out a calculation on the following bases: interest rates of roughly 10%, no payments of interest by the borrower, a period of roughly two years to repossess and sell the property, sale at the amount of the valuation, and sale costs of 4%. On those figures, if a lender lent 75% of the valuation, then it would recover all its money and break even on repossession; if it lent more than this, it would lose out. He concluded that, to the extent that the lender's losses had been contributed to by its having lent more than 75% of the value of the property, this had been negligent and, to that extent, its losses must be reduced. Blackburne J considered this part of Chadwick J's judgment in *Balmer Radmore*. While he found force in the point he added:[3]

'I accept Mr Patten's submission that the Society was entitled to lend in excess of 75% LTV without additional security provided that the value of the property (ie the security offered) exceeded the amount of the loan.
    I also accept Mr Patten's submission that lending over 75% or 80% LTV is not per se negligent. Whether it is in any particular case must depend on the facts of that case. Thus, it would not, I think, be negligent to lend 95%,

or even 100%, LTV to a borrower with an impeccable borrowing record and a sufficient and secured source of income or where property values are rising. If, on the other hand, little or no scrutiny has been applied to the borrower's disclosed source of income or to his loan record and other financial commitments, or where property values are static or falling, it is difficult to see how a decision to lend 95% LTV or more can be prudent. It is no answer in such a case to maintain that, viewed overall, a policy of high LTV lending has proved profitable and that the risk of loss on any individual transaction will be more than offset by the profits made elsewhere and by the cushion against default provided by the SMA scheme.

The question therefore is whether, in the particular case, the decision to lend at the particular LTV was a prudent one.'

1   For 'LTVs' see para 7.8.
2   See [1997] 4 All ER 582 at 624e–h.
3   [1999] Lloyd's Rep PN 241 at 289–290.

7.86   One of the individual cases which Blackburne J had to decide was *ATM Abdullah*, which provides an example of his application of the principles quoted in the last paragraph. Of the lender's decision to lend on a 95% LTV, he said:[1]

'[The borrower] was just over 24. He had no known track record as an owner or tenant of property. Nothing was known of [the borrower]'s ability to handle a large loan or meet his financial obligations. The housing market was in decline. No one could say how long this would last and whether, in particular, property values would start moving up again. In my view the Society should not have advanced more than 75% of valuation.'

Thus, while there is no general rule that to lend on an LTV of over 75% is negligent, in cases where, at the time of the advance, the property market was falling and the borrower's creditworthiness had not been properly investigated, it is likely that it would be held negligent. Further, if the court does find that the LTV was excessive, it should calculate the precise amount by which the advance was too much, and reduce the basic loss by that precise amount.[2]

1   At pp 480–481 of the *Balmer Radmore* transcript.
2   See *Platform Home Loans Ltd v Oyston Shipways Ltd* [1999] 2 WLR 518, HL, per Lord Hobhouse at 528H–529A and Lord Millett at 537D.

7.87   Some lenders supplemented their security by taking a mortgage indemnity guarantee ('MIG'). A condition of the offer of advance was that the borrower paid a premium, which was deducted from the advance, to a third party insurance company. Under the terms of the MIG, if the borrower defaulted and the lender repossessed the property, the insurance company became liable to pay the lender a sum calculated by reference to, but lower than, the amount of the lender's shortfall after taking account of the net proceeds of sale of the property. It is generally not open to defendant solicitors to require that lenders give credit for the proceeds of such policies.[1] On the other hand, in answering a claim of negligence in lending on an LTV that was too high, it is not open to the lender to rely upon the fact that it has required the borrower to take out an MIG: 'the conduct is negligent or imprudent whether or not the [lender] has insured against consequential loss.'[2]

1   *Bristol and West Building Society v May, May & Merrimans (No 2)* [1997] 3 All ER 206, Chadwick J.
2   *Fancy and Jackson* at 625e–f.

(c) *Non-status lending*

7.88 In some cases, lenders made no or almost no enquiries as to the status or creditworthiness of the borrower, and instead relied solely on the value of the property as security. This procedure was inherently more risky, unless the lender adopted a considerably lower LTV than it would have done had it undertaken status checks. The question of whether this procedure was negligent depends, in any given case, on the LTV which was used, but also has to depend on the other facts of the case.[1]

1   See Jacob J's judgment at first instance in *Platform Home Loans Ltd v Oyston Shipways Ltd* [1996] 2 EGLR 110, and *The Mortgage Corpn v Halifax (SW) Ltd* [1999] 1 Lloyd's Rep PN 159, HHJ Lawrie sitting as a deputy High Court judge.

10   Mitigation

7.89 The issues which arise in relation to mitigation in lenders' cases were best summarised by Chadwick J in *Fancy and Jackson*:[1]

> 'The pattern of realisation in cases of this nature requires a number of sequential steps which may be summarised as follows. First, there is the society's decision to initiate the process of realisation following the borrower's default. Second, there is the issue of a summons for possession. Third, there is the order for possession. Fourth, there is the taking of possession. Fifth, there is the contract for sale. Sixth, there is completion of that contract. Delay in taking any of those steps will prolong the period between the borrower's default and the recovery of moneys advanced. Prolongation of that period will increase that element of the society's claim which is said to represent "lost interest" on the principal advanced. It may also have the effect, in a falling market, of reducing the amount for which the mortgaged property is sold; and so reducing the amount to be set against the claim for principal and lost interest. Accordingly, there are two questions to be considered: (i) whether there has been unreasonable delay by the society in taking any of the steps which had to be taken towards realisation in the particular case and (ii) whether that delay did, in fact, have the effect of reducing the amount for which the mortgaged property was sold.'

1   [1997] 4 All ER 582 at 623g–j.

7.90 Chadwick J then went on to consider those two questions in relation to the cases of *Steggles Palmer* and *Colin Bishop*. In each case, he set out the lender's progress, or lack of progress, in relation to each of the six steps set out in the quotation. The judge considered that there had been unreasonable delay, of, respectively, 42 months[1] and 30 months.[2] There is insufficient space to set out here the way in which those conclusions were reached, but it can be said that, in reaching them, the judge subjected the lenders' conduct to fairly severe scrutiny. In each case he concluded that the delay would not have altered the price at which the property was ultimately sold. He held in each case that there should be excluded from the plaintiffs' loss (i) lost interest and (ii) periodic outgoings, in relation to the periods which he had identified as being periods in which the lender delayed unreasonably.

1   This was not included in the All England Law Report. It is necessary to consider p 6 of the transcript (22 July 1997).
2   See p 10 of the transcript (22 July 1997).

7.91 The question arises whether deductions for failure to mitigate should be made from the basic loss figure or the attributable loss. We have already seen that, in relation to contributory negligence, the House of Lords has decided that the deduction should be made from the basic rather than the attributable loss.[1] It is thought that, for similar reasons, reductions for failure to mitigate should be made from the basic rather than the attributable loss.

1   See the discussion of *Platform Home Loans Ltd v Oyston Shipways Ltd* [1999] 2 WLR 518, HL, at paras 6.7ff.

11   Contribution

7.92   In chapter 6, we considered the principles which govern claims for contribution in general. In lenders' cases, solicitors sued by lenders should normally consider whether it is appropriate to seek contribution from valuers or, in cases where they were involved, from financial intermediaries. The principles on which valuers may be held liable are beyond the scope of this book. Those representing solicitors, however, will wish to consider the likelihood of successfully showing that valuers have acted negligently, and whether the valuer either was insured or is worth suing. Two lenders' cases in which the court had to consider contribution between solicitors and valuers were *Bristol and West Building Society v Christie*[1] and *Chelsea Building Society v Goddard & Smith*.[2] In each case, the court ordered the solicitors and the valuers to pay 50% of the damages each. Reference should be made to the transcripts for the facts.

1   [1996] EGCS 53 (HHJ Esyr Lewis QC), Official Referees' Business.
2   [1996] EGCS 157 (HHJ Overend sitting as a judge of the Queen's Bench Division).

12   Loans made by multiple lenders

7.93   Where large sums are lent in relation to commercial property transactions, the problem may arise that more than one lender has been involved in the transaction. The variety of possible sets of facts is in theory as diverse as the inexhaustible ingenuity of those who structure financial agreements, but reference may be made to a number of types of loan dealt with in the cases. It is helpful to distinguish between claims in contract and in tort.

(a)   Claims in contract

7.94   Where there are simply many lenders lending separate amounts, according to separate loan agreements, in relation to one transaction, and the solicitor is instructed by each lender individually, there should be no difficulty in each lender suing the solicitor in contract. If there was only one loan agreement, to which many lenders were parties, and the solicitor's report on title was addressed to all the lenders, then each of the lenders would probably have a cause of action either in contract or in tort on the basis that the solicitor owed each of the lenders a duty of care.[1]

1   Cf *Interallianz Finance AG v Independent Insurance Co Ltd* [1997] EGCS 91, Thomas J.

7.95   At first instance in *Banque Bruxelles Lambert SA v Eagle Star Insurance Co Ltd*,[1] Phillips J had to consider the position where, after completion of the transaction in which the defendant valuers had acted, the plaintiff lender, BBL, syndicated parts of the loan. In other words, parts of BBL's loan were transferred to third party lenders by novation. The third parties took parts of BBL's rights pursuant to the original transaction, and in return reimbursed BBL for part of the original loan. BBL contended that these subsequent agreements were *res inter alios acta*, which should not be taken into account in assessing BBL's damages, so that there should be no deduction from BBL's damages on the basis that some of the loss which BBL would otherwise have suffered on the transaction had been transferred to the third party lenders. Phillips J rejected this argument. The doctrine of *res inter alios acta* did not apply to allow BBL to claim loss which in fact had been suffered by the third parties. This conclusion was not challenged on appeal. The moral of this is presumably that in a similar case in future the third parties would have to consider bringing actions themselves. Although *BBL* was a valuers' case, it is likely that the same principles would apply in relation to solicitors.

1   [1995] 2 All ER 769 at 802g–j.

7.96   *BBL* was distinguished in *Interallianz Finance AG v Independent Insurance Co Ltd*.[1] As in *BBL*, at the time when the defendant valuers undertook their valuation, there was only one lender, Interallianz, who instructed them. The valuers were unaware of any plans to share the risk of the loan among different financial institutions. After the transaction had completed, Interallianz spread the risk of the loan by means of sub-participation agreements. These were different from the loan novations which had occurred in *BBL*. The effect of the sub-participation agreements was that, unlike in *BBL*, Interallianz remained the only party with a direct contractual relationship with the borrower. Under the sub-participation agreements, the sub-participators had no direct interest in the mortgage, and were not lenders to the borrower. Rather, they had a loan agreement with Interallianz, but the loan did not have to be repaid if the borrower defaulted. All that the sub-participators were entitled to were the amounts which Interallianz actually recovered under its mortgage with the borrowers. In fact, the sub-participation agreements reduced the amount of Interallianz's losses, because Interallianz had received funds from the sub-participators. But Thomas J held that sums received under those agreements were *res inter alios acta* which should be ignored in calculating Interallianz's loss, because

> '. . .they were not known to or contemplated by Allsop [the valuer], they were entered into before any loss was contemplated although after Allsop's breach of duty was in fact committed (but unknown to Interallianz), they did not arise out of Allsop's breach of duty and had nothing to do with Allsop's valuation.'

He added, however, that if Interallianz had entered into the agreements with knowledge of the alleged negligence, and they had been part of action taken in consequence of it, then benefits received pursuant to those agreements should have been taken into account. Further, in obiter dicta, Thomas J said that, if he were wrong that the proceeds of the sub-participation agreements should not be taken into account, in any event there was an implied term in the agreements that Interallianz should account to the sub-participators for any damages they received, and so, in any event, there should be no deduction from Interallianz's damages on account of the sub-participation agreements.

1   [1997] EGCS 91.

(b)   Claims in tort

7.97   If the third party provider of funds does not sue in contract, it may still have a claim in tort, as in *NM Rothschild & Sons Ltd v Berenson*.[1] Barclays Bank instructed the solicitor, and the request for funds was addressed to Barclays, but the funds were being provided by other banks. At the time when the solicitors were instructed, Barclays explained to them in general terms that it and other financial institutions would be providing the funds for the advance. The Court of Appeal held that, because this had been explained, it should have been self-evident to any reasonably competent solicitor that all those lending would be doing so on the basis that the solicitor had provided a true and accurate request for funds. Hence the solicitors owed a duty of care to the other lenders.

1   [1997] NPC 15, CA.

7.98   In *Secured Residential Funding Ltd v Nationwide Building Society*,[1] a valuers' case, the court held that the defendant valuers could not be liable in tort for losses suffered by a third party lender which had relied upon their valuation report. The judge held that the defendants could not be liable in tort to the third party unless they had in fact known that the third party was lending in reliance upon their report, or ought to have known this. He found that the defendants had not had either actual or constructive knowledge of the third party's involvement, and so the third party had no claim. As to constructive knowledge, he said that the defendants could not be held liable unless there was, at least, a 'high degree of probability' that someone other than the intended recipient of the valuation report would rely upon its contents.

1   A decision of Mr Daniel Brennan QC sitting as a Deputy High Court judge: [1997] NPC 147. See Coates and Evans-Tovey, 'Duty of care of professional advisers' (1998) 142 Sol Jo 60.

B   FRAUD

7.99   'Fraud is proved when it is shown that a false representation has been made (1) knowingly, or (2) without belief in its truth, or (3) recklessly, careless whether it be true or false.'[1] Solicitors are not insured in respect of dishonest or fraudulent acts or omissions which they themselves carry out, but innocent partners or employers of those who do such acts are insured.[2] Thus, even in cases where it lurks in the shadows, it is rare for fraud to be alleged against sole practitioners, as they would not be insured, and the claimant might find that the solicitor had insufficient assets to meet the claim. But this raises no difficulty in suing the partners or employees of allegedly dishonest solicitors.[3]

1   *Derry v Peek* (1889) 14 App Cas 337, per Lord Herschell at 374.
2   Solicitors' Indemnity Rules 1998, rule 14(f), and see *Abbey National plc v Solicitors' Indemnity Fund Ltd* [1997] PNLR 306, Steel J.
3   Compare *Kumar v AGF Insurance Ltd* [1999] PNLR 269, Thomas J.

7.100   If fraud is established, the claimant benefits from a more lenient limitation period,[1] a more favourable rule in relation to causation,[2] no risk of reductions in damages in respect of contributory negligence, even if the claimant was negligent,[3] and no reduction in damages on account of *BBL*. On the other hand, an allegation of fraud must be carefully pleaded.[4] In *Paragon Finance plc v Hare*,[5] Moore-Bick J struck out allegations of conspiracy to defraud against defendant solicitors. It was not enough simply to plead the primary facts: the plaintiff had to go further and set out clearly how those primary facts gave rise to the inference that the defendants were party to a conspiracy. Further, the court will not infer dishonesty or recklessness without cogent evidence which in effect compels such a conclusion.[6] Thus only the most serious of lenders' cases fall within this category.

1   See para 5.60.
2   *Smith New Court Securities Ltd v Scrimgeour Vickers (Asset Management) Ltd* [1997] AC 254, HL.
3   *Alliance and Leicester Building Society v Edgestop Ltd* [1993] 1 WLR 1462, Mummery J, and *Nationwide Building Society v Thimbleby & Co* [1999] Lloyd's Rep PN 359 (Blackburne J).
4   See para 11.2 of the *Practice Direction—Statements of Case*, which supplements CPR Part 16.
5   (1999) Times, 1 April (Moore-Bick J).
6   Per Blackburne J in *Vanderpump & Sykes*, one of the *Balmore Radmore* decisions, transcript p 413.

C BREACH OF WARRANTY OF AUTHORITY

1 Liability

7.101   In two fairly recent cases, claims for breach of warranty of authority have succeeded against solicitors who believed that they acted for both a husband and wife, but where in fact the wife's signature had been forged on various documents, she knew nothing of the transaction, and she had never given her authority to act to the defendant solicitors who assumed that they had such authority.

(a)   Solicitor purporting to act for the vendors: Penn v Bristol and West Building Society[1]

7.102   In *Penn*, Mr and Mrs Penn owned their home, subject to a mortgage to the Bradford & Bingley Building Society. Mr Penn's business ran into debt, and he decided to engage in a mortgage fraud to obtain the money to pay off the debts. The fraud involved a supposed sale of the property to a Mr Wilson, without Mrs Penn's knowledge. Mr Wilson borrowed £75,293 from the Bristol & West Building Society. That sum was paid to Mr Brill, a solicitor, who believed that he acted for both Mr and Mrs Penn. Mr Brill used £31,769.78 of the money to pay off the Bradford & Bingley, and paid the rest, at the direction of Mr Penn, to Barclays Bank. Unbeknown to Mr Brill, the money paid to Barclays was paid without Mrs Penn's knowledge or consent. When Mrs Penn discovered what had happened she brought proceedings against various parties.

1   [1997] 3 All ER 470, CA.

7.103   On appeal, the only issue of liability was whether Mr Brill, the solicitor who had believed himself to be acting for both Mr and Mrs Penn, was liable to the Bristol and West for breach of warranty of authority. The Court of Appeal held that he was, on the following basis. First, a solicitor who signed a contract purporting to act for his clients was liable for breach of warranty of authority if he did not have their authority to sign it.[1] The same applied on the facts of *Penn*, even though in *Penn* the conduct which amounted to a representation that the solicitor had the authority of both Mr and Mrs Penn went short of actually signing the contract. The conduct which the Court of Appeal considered amounted to a representation that Mr Brill had the authority of both clients to complete the transaction was as follows. The transaction proceeded in the usual way, with Mr Brill corresponding with solicitors who acted simultaneously for both the purchaser, Mr Wilson, and the building society, Bristol and West. During the course of that correspondence, Mr Brill believed himself to be acting for both Mr and Mrs Penn, and held himself out as being so authorised in all the pre-contract correspondence, negotiations and completion.[2] During the course of taking those steps, Mr Brill knew that the solicitors with whom he was dealing were acting for both the purchaser and the building society. Those solicitors were ultimately a firm called Gartons. It was conceded by Mr Brill's counsel that, had Mr Wilson not himself been a party to the fraud, he would have been able to rely upon Mr Brill's conduct toward Gartons as amounting to a warranty that Mr Brill had authority to act on behalf of both Mr and Mrs Penn.[3] That being the case, Waller LJ stated the principal issue on the appeal as being as follows.[4]

'... whether in circumstances where a solicitor is acting for a vendor, and negotiating on the vendor's behalf with a solicitor whom he knows to be acting on behalf not only of the purchaser but a building society, through whom the purchaser will be borrowing money to complete the purchase, the solicitor's warranty that he is duly authorised on behalf of the vendor is given not only to the purchaser but to the building society.'

1   *Suleman v Shahsavari* [1988] 1 WLR 1181 approved.
2   [1997] 3 All ER 470 at 473c, CA.
3   [1997] 3 All ER 470 at 477d, CA.
4   [1997] 3 All ER 470 at 472g–h, CA.

7.104   The Court of Appeal's answer was that the solicitor's warranty was indeed given not only to the purchaser but also to the lender. Waller LJ, with whom the other two judges agreed, set out the basis of the court's decision in this way:[1]

'During the negotiation, following which a number of documents were to be executed in order to bring the transaction to fruition, and in completing the transaction, Mr Brill knew that Gartons were also acting for the building society. He knew indeed that Gartons would be arranging the completion of the purchase including arranging for Mr Wilson to execute a mortgage so as to obtain from the building society the purchase price and secure the building society's interest in the house. Thus, he knew that Gartons, in their capacity as the solicitors for the building society, would be relying on his having the authority of Mrs Penn to bring the transaction to fruition, just as much as they were relying on the same as the purchaser's solicitor. What is more, Bristol and West through Gartons did rely on Mr Brill having the authority of Mrs Penn to bring the matter to fruition, in that having obtained from Mr Wilson execution of a charge, money was advanced and available for the purpose of completing the transaction. If at any stage Mr Brill had said he did not have the authority of Mrs Penn the result would have been that Bristol and West would have proceeded no further.'

He went on to say that it did not matter whether Mr Brill the solicitor had known the name of the building society in question; it was sufficient that he knew that a specific lender was involved.

1   [1997] 3 All ER at 477f–h.

7.105   The position of solicitors acting for husband and wife vendors, or other co-owners, thus appears to be as follows. In an ordinary transaction, such as occurred in *Penn*, the solicitor must ensure that he or she does indeed have the authority of all the vendors to act. If the vendors' solicitor fails to do so, and if it transpires that one client or another was unaware of the transaction and had not authorised the solicitor to act for him or her, then a lender who lends to the purchaser of the property, in reliance upon the belief that the vendors' solicitor had authority to act for all the vendors, has a claim for breach of warranty of authority against the vendors' solicitor, as long as

(i)   in correspondence and negotiations with the lender's solicitor, the vendors' solicitor did in fact hold himself out as acting for all the vendors, and

(ii)   the vendors' solicitor knew that a lending institution was intending to lend the purchasers money for the purchase. All that is necessary for liability is that the vendors' solicitor knew that a lending institution was involved; it need not be shown that he or she knew the identity of the particular lender in question.

Once the above has been shown, the vendors' solicitor will be liable for breach of warranty of authority. The correct legal analysis of this doctrine appears from *Penn*[1] to be a variety of collateral contract. The next question is what loss the lender can recover. This is considered below, after discussion of other categories of liability.[2]

1   [1997] 3 All ER at 477a.
2   Note that other issues may arise between the various parties in this type of case. The judge at first
     instance in *Penn* held that the solicitors owed a duty of care to the wife, even though they were
     not acting for her. See [1995] 2 FLR 938, and discussion of *White v Jones* [1995] 2 AC 207 in
     chapter 1, paras 1.12ff. Secondly, the lender providing an advance as a re-mortgage may have
     a claim to be subrogated to the rights of the previous lender, whose mortgage has been redeemed
     using the new lender's advance. Again, see the report of the decision at first instance.

(b)   Solicitor acting for the purchasers/borrowers, or for the lender

7.106   Will the court apply the decision in *Penn* to the following analogous case?
A husband and wife jointly own their matrimonial home. They apply to a new lender
for a re-mortgage. The husband appoints a solicitor who also acts for the lender on the
re-mortgage, but assumes, without checking, that he has the authority of the wife as
well as the husband. The husband provides the solicitor with a legal charge apparently
signed by both husband and wife. Only after the solicitor has disbursed the lender's
advance moneys does it become apparent that the wife knew nothing of the transaction
and that her signature has been forged.

7.107   In *Cooke & Borsay*, one of the cases considered in *Fancy and Jackson*,[1] Chadwick
J held that *Penn* did apply on these facts. He said that, if the lender and borrower had
instructed separate solicitors, the position of the solicitor acting for the *lender* would have
been as follows. If the borrowers' solicitor provided a mortgage deed which appeared to
have been signed by the borrowers, and witnessed, and there was nothing irregular on the
face of the document, then the *lender's solicitor* would be entitled to accept the document
without question, and would not act in breach of duty in doing so. But the reason for this,
following *Penn*, would be that the *lender's solicitor* would have an implied warranty,
provided by the *borrowers' solicitor*, to the effect that the borrowers' solicitor had the
authority of both borrowers to complete the mortgage by delivering the mortgage deed.
It is implicit in this that the *borrowers' solicitor* would, in those circumstances, be liable
to the lender for breach of warranty of authority if he did not have the authority of both
borrowers to complete. Chadwick J then said:[2]

> 'I can see no reason why the position should be different in the circumstances
> that the same solicitor acts for both lender and borrowers. I do not hold that
> the duty of the solicitor, as solicitor for the lender, is increased by the fact
> that he acts also for the borrowers; but, equally, I can see no reason why, as
> solicitor for the borrowers, he should not be taken to warrant to the lender that
> he is acting for them in the transaction with their authority. That does not,
> necessarily, mean that he is warranting that the signature on the mortgage
> deed is authentic; but it has much the same effect. Mr Borsay must be taken
> to have warranted to the society that the mortgage deed which he delivered
> on completion as solicitor for the borrowers was delivered with the authority
> of both Mr and Mrs Barton. If the deed had been delivered with the authority
> of Mrs Barton as security for the advance which was made by the society, the
> fact that it did not, in fact, bear her signature would be relatively unimportant.
> She would clearly be bound by its terms.'

Although *Cooke & Borsay* concerned a re-mortgage, it is hard to see any distinction in
principle in the case of an ordinary mortgage to husband and wife as borrowers. So it would
appear that there, too, a solicitor acting for the borrowers who failed to ensure that he had
the wife's authority, would be liable to the lender for breach of warranty of authority if in
fact he did not have the wife's authority, and the transaction proceeded but was
subsequently challenged by the wife.

1   [1997] 4 All ER 582.
2   See [1997] 4 All ER 582 at 613c–e. Compare *Mercantile Credit Co Ltd v Fenwick* [1999] Lloyd's Rep PN 408, CA.

7.108   The following conclusions may be drawn. First, where the borrowers are husband and wife, if the borrowers' solicitors provide the lenders' solicitors with a mortgage deed, apparently signed and witnessed by both borrowers, then, in the absence of exceptional circumstances, the lender's solicitors may proceed on the basis that both husband and wife have signed the deed. If this proves not to be the case, and if the wife had not authorised those who appeared to be solicitors for both borrowers, then the lender has a claim for breach of warranty of authority against the solicitors who appeared to act for both borrowers. Similarly, the lender may have a remedy against those who appeared to act for vendors who are husband and wife, if they provided a transfer document apparently signed by both vendors, in circumstances where the wife had not authorised them to act or signed the deed.

7.109   From the point of view of solicitors acting for husbands and wives, either as vendors or borrowers, it is essential that they ensure that they have the authority not only of the husband but also of the wife, if they wish to escape the risk of liability of this type. It is doubtful whether simply taking reasonable steps to ensure that the solicitors have authority to act would absolve them from liability: they probably have a defence only if they actually do have the wife's authority.[1] The effect of this is to place onerous obligations upon solicitors acting for husbands and wives.

1   See *Chitty on Contracts* (27th edn, 1994) at 31–093. But compare *Nelson v Nelson* [1997] 1 WLR 233 (see paras 11.62–11.64). It can be argued that the effect of the Court of Appeal's construction of the solicitor's warranty in that case was that the solicitor would be liable only for lack of reasonable care. Compare also *Midland Bank plc v Cox McQueen* [1999] Lloyd's Rep PN 223, CA (para 7.35).

2   Causation and measure of loss

7.110   As to causation of loss, it is unlikely that a lender which has proved liability for breach of warranty of authority will fail to establish that, but for the breach of duty, it would not have made the advance:[1]

> 'I think it beyond argument that no advances officer would authorise completion if he were told that the solicitor could not himself verify the signature of one of the borrowers for whom he was acting; and could not warrant that he had any instructions from that borrower.'

Similarly, in *Penn* the Court of Appeal rejected an appeal on the basis that the breach of warranty of authority had not caused the loss.

1   *Fancy and Jackson* at [1997] 4 All ER 582 at 617a–b.

7.111   How does *BBL*[1] apply to cases of breach of warranty of authority? In *Cooke & Borsay*, Chadwick J referred to Millett LJ's analysis of *BBL* in *Mothew*,[2] and said that the measure of damage was[3]

> '... the difference between the position which the society would have been in if the authority had been as warranted and the position that it is in in the absence of authority ... The loss in this case is the difference between the value of security over the whole property and the value of security over the husband's share only.'

1   [1997] AC 191, HL.
2   [1998] Ch 1, CA.
3   See [1997] 4 All ER 582 at 623a–b.

3 Contributory negligence and mitigation

7.112 Chadwick J held that contributory negligence was no defence to a claim for breach of warranty of authority.[1] As to mitigation of loss, he set out the facts and said:[2]

'In my view it is for the [lender] to establish that it has taken reasonable steps to recover the one half share in the property to which it is undoubtedly entitled. The [lender] has made no attempt to establish that it has taken any steps to that end. In these circumstances the [lender] should not recover damages in excess of the value of a one half share of the property—such value to be assessed at the date upon which, with reasonable diligence, it could have had proceedings for an order under section 30 of the Law of Property Act 1925 determined in the county court—together with interest on that amount from that date. I put that date at 1 March 1995, being some eight months from the discovery of the alleged forgery.'

Although each case turns on its own facts, this approach to assessing damages and interest is likely to be at the least highly persuasive in later cases.

1   In a passage which was edited out of the All England Law Report, but appears at page 14 of the transcript dated 22 July 1997.
2   This passage was edited out of the All England Law Report, although cf the reference at [1997] 4 All ER 582 at 624b. For the full passage, see pp 12–13 of the transcript dated 22 July 1997.

D   ACTIONS FOR MONEY HAD AND RECEIVED

7.113   In *Portman Building Society v Hamlyn Taylor Neck*,[1] the Court of Appeal struck out as hopeless a claim by a lender against solicitors brought as an action for money had and received. The lender sought to rely on this claim as, unlike its other claims, it was not statute-barred. For the purposes of the application, it had to be assumed that the lender's allegation, which was that it had paid the advance money to the solicitors under a mistake of fact caused by the solicitors, was correct. Millett LJ said that an action for money had and received was a claim for restitution for unjust enrichment. The action could not succeed because the solicitors had not been enriched at all: they had paid away the lender's money in accordance with the lender's instructions. Although those instructions were capable of being revoked, they had not been revoked, and continued to bind the solicitors. Thus the solicitors' defence was that they had properly accounted for the lender's money, in accordance with the lender's instructions. No action for money had and received would succeed unless the lender had revoked its instructions before the solicitors paid away the money. Thus, except in cases where the lender does expressly revoke the solicitor's instructions to pay the money to the borrowers, before the solicitor makes the payment, it is unlikely that actions by lenders for money had and received will succeed.

1   [1998] 4 All ER 202, CA.

E   EQUITY AND CONCLUSION

7.114   Equity is discussed in detail in chapter 4. In this section, we merely refer in broad outline to the issues which are most relevant in lenders' cases. Two types of claim in equity must be considered: breach of trust, and breach of fiduciary duty. It is unlikely that claims for breach of trust will figure largely in lenders' claims in the future, for two reasons. First, in *Target Holdings Ltd v Redferns*[1] the House of Lords indicated that, in relation to claims for breach of trust, the court applied a test of causation which was similar to the common law test.[2] Lenders could no longer argue that, once a breach of trust had been shown, they need prove only that a lending officer had read the report on title in order to be granted summary judgment for their entire basic loss, without having to prove what would have happened if the solicitor had not breached his duty.[3] Secondly, the discussion of breach of trust in *Mothew*[4] showed that it was harder for lenders to prove breach of trust than had previously been thought. The practical result of these two developments has been that lenders have viewed claims for breach of trust with considerably less enthusiasm than was previously the case: it is harder to prove the case, and when it is proved it does not necessarily lead to any benefit in relation to the test of causation which the court will apply, in comparison to a less exotic claim at common law.

1   [1996] AC 421, HL.
2   Per Lord Browne-Wilkinson, giving the only reasoned speech: [1996] AC 421 at 432E–G.
3   See paras 4.40ff.
4   [1998] Ch 1, CA and see para 4.09.

7.115   The position is, however, different in relation to claims for breach of fiduciary duty. As we mentioned at the start of this chapter,[1] it is likely that in future the key battleground will relate to such claims. That is because, following *Balmer Radmore*, it is likely that there will be large reductions for contributory negligence in claims in contract and the tort of negligence,[2] but there will be no such reductions in cases where the claimant is able to establish a breach of fiduciary duty which amounts to conscious disloyalty by the solicitor to the lender client.[3] Thus it will be in the interests of lenders to characterise solicitors' conduct as being in breach of fiduciary duty whenever possible. But references to breach of fiduciary duty should not be 'scattered throughout the pleadings with complete abandon'.[4] Further, in order to show intentional breach of fiduciary duty it is necessary to show a breach which is 'conscious, deliberate and in bad faith',[5] or a solicitor who returns a report on title either reckless, or not caring, whether it is true or false.[6] In most cases, this will be hard.[7]

1   See para 7.3.
2   See para 7.84.
3   See *Balmer Radmore* [1999] Lloyd's Rep PN 241 at 278 and para 4.44.
4   See 'Equity's Place in the Law of Commerce', Sir Peter Millett (1998) 114 LQR 214 at 217.
5   See para 4.34.
6   See *Nationwide Building Society v Richard Grosse* [1999] Lloyd's Rep PN 348 at 356 (Blackburne J).
7   Pleas of breach of fiduciary duty succeeded in only two out of 11 cases in *Balmer Radmore*; in the twelfth case there was a judgment in default for, inter alia, breach of fiduciary duty.

CHAPTER 8

Conveyancing

A ACTING FOR MORE THAN ONE PARTY

1 Acting for vendor and purchaser

8.1 Joint or multiple retainers may involve no conflict of interest but this is not always the case. It is fundamental to the solicitor's retainer that he must exercise his professional judgment solely for the benefit of the client and this can only be achieved if the solicitor is able to give undivided loyalty to that client and is not placed in a position where the interests of two clients may conflict or the loyalty to one client may inhibit or interfere with the loyalty to another. An obvious example of the danger of conflict is where a solicitor is instructed to act for both vendor and purchaser on the sale of land. Solicitors are permitted to act for both although to ensure that the danger is minimised guidelines have been provided by the Law Society. Rule 6 of the Solicitors' Practice Rules 1990 provides as follows:

'(1) (Transfers and Leases of Land)

A solicitor, or solicitors practising in associated practices, must not act for both seller and buyer on a transfer of land for value at arm's length, or for both lessor and lessee on the grant of a lease for value at arm's length, except as permitted by paragraph (2).

(2) (Exceptions)

A solicitor, or solicitors practising in associated practices, may act for both seller and buyer on a transfer of land for value at arm's length, or for both lessor and lessee on the grant of a lease for value at arm's length, if all the following conditions are satisfied:

(a)   no conflict of interest exists or arises; and

(b)   neither the solicitor, nor any solicitor practising in an associated company, is instructed to negotiate the sale of the property; and

(c)   the seller or lessor is not a builder or developer, selling or leasing as such; and

(d)   one or more of the following applies:

   (i)   both parties are established clients; or

   (ii)   on a transfer of land, the consideration is £10,000 or less; or

   (iii) there is no other solicitor or other qualified conveyancer in the vicinity whom either party can reasonably be expected to consult; or

   (iv) the parties are respectively represented by two associated practices or offices of the same practice ...

(e)   both parties give their written consent to the arrangement.'[1]

1   For discussion of sub-rules (3) and (4) as amended by the Solicitors Practice (Lender and Borrower) Amendment Rule dated 29 September 1998 see chapter 7.

8.2 These rules reflect the 'double employment' rule,[1] which provides that a fiduciary may not act for two clients with potentially conflicting interests without the informed consent of each client. A failure to comply with these rules, therefore, is likely to involve the solicitor in breach of an equitable duty to one or more clients, although it should be noted that in one respect practice rule 6 imposes a higher duty on the solicitor than that imposed on fiduciaries more generally. For it is only in certain circumstances *and* with the written consent of each client that the solicitor is permitted to act for both of them.

1   Discussed in chapter 4, paras 4.28–4.31.

8.3   One further word of caution is necessary, however. The fact that a solicitor has committed a breach either of practice rule 6 or the double employment rule will not of itself make him liable to a claim for compensation in equity. In order to recover the claimant will have to show that the breach of duty was truly causative of loss. If a solicitor does obtain clear and informed consent from each client in circumstances where he would still be in breach of rule 6 (eg because neither is an established client), or if he obtains the consent of neither in circumstances where that consent would undoubtedly have been forthcoming, it is likely that there will be no actionable breach of fiduciary duty.[1]

1   See *Clarke Boyce v Mouat* [1994] 1 AC 428.

8.4   On the other hand, the fact that a solicitor may have committed a technical breach of the double employment rule in acting for both vendor and purchaser or by the same token a breach of practice rule 6 may well be evidence of a breach of the common law duty of care to one or even both clients. Where there is a genuine conflict between the interests of each client[1] the conflict is bound to affect the way in which the solicitor discharges the duties to both clients. As Millett LJ stated in *Bristol and West Building Society v Mothew*:[2]

> 'An unconscious omission which happens to benefit one principal at the expense of the other does not constitute a breach of fiduciary duty, though it may constitute a breach of the duty of skill and care. This is because the principle which is in play is that the fiduciary must not be inhibited by the existence of his other employment from serving the interests of his principal as faithfully and effectively as if he were the only employer. I shall call this "the no inhibition principle".'

If a solicitor is unconsciously inhibited in the performance of his duty, he or she is more likely than not to commit a breach of the common law duty of care. A good example of such a case is *Goody v Baring*[3] in which a solicitor who acted for both vendor and purchaser was held liable to the purchaser for accepting what his vendor client told him and for failing to make adequate further inquiries before exchange of contracts.[4] As Danckwerts J stated:

> 'It is plain that the standard of skill and care required of a solicitor who acts for both parties on a sale and purchase is at least as great as that which would be required of a solicitor who acts for a purchaser alone.'

The fact that the defendant acted for both parties inhibited him in fulfilling this duty to the purchaser. Again, in *Nash v Phillips*[5] a solicitor was held liable in negligence for failing to inform his purchaser client that his vendor client had accepted a cash offer and was about to exchange contracts with a third party (for whom the solicitor was also acting).[6]

1   As in *Nash v Phillips* (1974) 232 Estates Gazette 1219 (Foster J). It is noteworthy that the judge found that there was an actual conflict of interest and a breach of what is now practice rule

6 because 'one [client] wished an early sale and the other wished to sell his house before he signed a contract', a common occurrence.

2   [1998] Ch 1 at 19E–G, CA.

3   [1956] 1 WLR 448.

4   He failed to make adequate inquiries about the rents receivable from the property and, in particular, to satisfy himself that they would not go down as a consequence of rents being registered under the Rent Restriction Acts.

5   (1974) 232 Estates Gazette 1219 (Foster J).

6   See also *Lake v Bushby* [1949] 2 All ER 964 (Pritchard J); *Smith v Mansi* [1963] 1 WLR 26 at 30, CA; and *Attard v Samson* (1966) 110 Sol Jo 249 (Phillimore J). For an example of a case where a breach of the double employment rule did not lead to liability at common law, see *Kenyon-Brown v Banks & Co* (5 June 1998, unreported) (Peter Leaver QC).

8.5   If the solicitor is one of the parties to the conveyancing transaction, the duty of the solicitor is all but absolute:[1]

'[I]n all ordinary circumstances a solicitor ought to refuse to act for a person in a transaction to which the solicitor is himself a party with an adverse interest; and even if he is pressed to act after his refusal, he should persist in that refusal. Nobody can insist upon an unwilling solicitor acting for him, at all events when there is a conflict of interest.'

1   *Spector v Ageda* [1973] Ch 30 (Megarry J) at 47G and *Moody v Cox and Hatt* [1917] 2 Ch 71, CA, considered in chapter 4, paras 4.26 and 4.33. In the latter, the defendant solicitors were parties to the transaction, although it was treated as a case of conflict of duties.

8.6   In this section we have been considering the situation where the solicitor has acted for both parties innocently either without either realising that there is a conflict of interest, or facing and dealing with that conflict properly. Where the solicitor is consciously aware that there is a conflict and chooses to prefer the interests of one client over the other or chooses to exploit his client by putting his own interests first, he commits a breach of fiduciary duty.[1]

1   This is considered in chapter 4, paras 4.32–4.35.

2   Obtaining the authority of the client or clients

8.7   A solicitor who acts only for one client must obtain that client's authority to act. If the solicitor is instructed on behalf of a client by a third party, then the solicitor must ensure that the third party has the client's authority to instruct him or her. The safest way to do this is to comply with paragraph 12.04 of *The Guide to Professional Conduct of Solicitors* (6th edn, 1996) ('*The Guide*') which provides:

'Where instructions are received from a third party a solicitor should obtain written instructions from the client that he or she wishes the solicitor to act. In any case of doubt the solicitor should see the client or take other appropriate steps to confirm instructions.'

In *Linaker v Keith Turner & Ashton*,[1] the plaintiff's wife instructed the defendant solicitors to act on behalf of the plaintiff and the lender in a transaction to remortgage the family home, legal title to which was registered only in the plaintiff's name. The defendants purported to act for the plaintiff in the transaction but the judge found that he had never authorised them to do so. He held that taking instructions from the plaintiff's wife was not sufficient to give the defendants ostensible or apparent authority to act. The defendants had not complied with the predecessor of paragraph 12.04 because, although they had taken his wife's instructions, they had neither obtained the plaintiff's written instructions to act nor seen him in person to do so.

Further, they had failed to comply with the lender's instructions to explain the mortgage deed to the plaintiff. The judge held that, for these reasons, the defendants had acted negligently and breached their duty of care to the plaintiff.[2] A similar decision was reached in *Al-Sabah v Ali*.[3] In that case, it was held that the defendants were negligent in relying on instructions from the plaintiff's agent and a power of attorney forged by him where the agent himself not only had an interest in the transaction but was a party to it. Again, the judge relied on paragraph 12.04 in deciding that the defendants had a duty to satisfy themselves that they had received proper instructions.[4] It appears, therefore, that in domestic conveyancing transactions, solicitors who receive instructions from a third party on behalf of a separate client ought to comply with paragraph 12.04 or they risk being found to have acted negligently if the client claims not to have given authority to the third party. Further, having obtained authority to act, similar principles are likely to apply at all stages of the transaction at which the solicitor requires the client's further instructions.[5]

1　(5 November 1998, unreported) (Garland J) and *Umeweni v JB Wheatley & Co* [1990] EGCS 57, CA (Bar Library Transcript 1990/272).
2　He held that, as the plaintiff had never given the defendants authority to act, there was no retainer, so the defendants could not owe the plaintiff any contractual duty. Instead, they owed the plaintiff a duty of care on the basis that he was plainly within their reasonable contemplation as being a person who would be affected by their actions. See *White v Jones* [1995] 2 AC 207, HL, discussed in chapter 1, paras 1.28 and 1.29, and *Penn v Bristol and West Building Society* [1995] 2 FLR 938 (HHJ Kolbert) at 947H–949G. (This point did not arise on the appeal in *Penn*: see [1997] 1 WLR 1356 at 1360F–G, CA.)
3　[1999] EGCS 11 (Ferris J).
4　The judge also held that the defendants were not entitled to rely on the ostensible authority of the agent.
5　See *Farrer v Copley Singletons* [1998] PNLR 22, CA considered in para 8.8.

8.8　Similarly, where a solicitor acts for a number of clients in the same transaction, the solicitor's

> 'contract of retainer is with each and every client; the duties of the solicitor are owed and must be discharged to each of them. It must follow that a solicitor is entitled to communicate with and take instructions from only one of several clients only if he has the authority of the other clients so to do ... From the point of view of [the solicitor] the authority might be actual, whether express or implied, or apparent; but in each case the authority must emanate from the alleged principals, not the alleged agent ...'[1]

In relation to domestic conveyancing, the practical consequence is that, in order to ensure that he or she has the authority of each client to act, the safest course is for the solicitor to comply with paragraph12.04 in respect of each one of the clients. Failure to do so may well amount to a breach of duty owed to the client whose authority was not obtained and it will not be sufficient to rely purely upon a statement from one client that he has the authority of the others to give instructions.[2] On the other hand, where a solicitor acts for a commercial partnership which consists of a substantial number of partners, the solicitor is not normally required to take the instructions of anyone but the partner who directly instructed him, because a partner in such a firm will normally have his partners' actual or ostensible authority to give instructions.[3]

1　*Farrer v Copley Singletons* [1998] PNLR 22, per Brooke LJ at 32G–33B, CA.
2　The source of the solicitor's duty may be a duty of care in tort, on the basis set out at para 8.7, note 2. Alternatively, the court may hold that the solicitor's conduct in acting for the client gave rise to an implied retainer, so that he owed the client a duty in contract to ensure that he or she had properly taken the client's instructions. See *Madley v Cousins Coombe* [1997] EGCS

63, QBD (commercial partners) and *Harris v Nantes and Wilde* [1997] NPC 7, CA (husband and wife). In the latter, much reliance was placed upon the facts that the co-owners were trustees, and that the defendants had acted for them both on the acquisition of the property. This is clear only from the transcript (30 January 1997) at p 10.

3 See *Sykes v Midland Bank Executor and Trustee Co Ltd* [1971] 1 QB 113 at 124B–D, 126D–E and 130F–G, CA. In *Madley v Cousins Coombe* [1997] EGCS 63 there were two partners but in *Sykes* there were only four. Although neither case was decided on the ground that the instructing partner in *Sykes* had the authority of his other partners whilst in *Madley* he did not, this is probably the true ground of distinction: see *Farrer* [1998] PNLR 22 where there were four co-owners but none had the authority of the others to give instructions. Further, in *Madley* there was a conflict between the interests of the two partners, which should have been apparent.

8.9 The consequences of a breach of duty by a solicitor who acts without the authority of one or more of his clients may depend on whether his actions or words are binding on them. A solicitor who acts on the instructions of one co-owner without the authority of the others warrants to third parties such as a purchaser or a lender that he or she has authority to act on behalf of all of the co-owners and may become liable to them for breach of that warranty in the event that his or her actions are not genuinely authorised: see *Penn v Bristol and West Building Society*.[1] But he does not usually have actual or ostensible authority to bind the clients themselves. In many cases, therefore, a breach of this duty will not yield substantial damages because the solicitor's actions will not divest the client of his or her interest in the property.[2] In *Al-Sabah v Ali*,[3] however, two properties were transferred under a forged power of attorney and charged to third party mortgagees. The judge held that, although he had the power to rectify the register, he would not do so against the innocent mortgagees. Accordingly, even though the defendants' acts did not bind the plaintiff as a matter of law, he had lost the properties as a consequence.[4]

1 [1997] 1 WLR 1356, CA, discussed further in chapter 7.
2 See *Penn v Bristol and West Building Society* [1995] 2 FLR 938 (HHJ Kolbert) at first instance at 947H–949G and 965A–C. There may be consequential losses. Mrs Penn was unable to obtain payment of her mortgage interest by the DSS because of the transaction which was at the centre of the dispute. It was held that she could recover such losses in principle and an inquiry was ordered.
3 [1999] EGCS 11 (Ferris J).
4 The judge awarded the difference between the values of the two properties in question and the amount required to discharge the mortgages. He also held that right of indemnity under the Land Registration Act 1925 could not be prayed in aid by the defendants. The Land Registry, as an insurer of last resort, was only obliged to indemnify the plaintiff *after* taking into account his right to damages from the defendants.

8.10 It is plainly the solicitor's duty to convey the property into joint names where he or she acts for joint purchasers.[1] It also the solicitor's duty to explain the consequences of the different forms of ownership to the clients, take their instructions on which form is suitable or appropriate (after taking into account their long term wishes) and carry this into effect by preparing an appropriate deed of trust.[2]

1 See the facts of *Webber v Gasquet, Metcalfe and Watson* (1982) 132 NLJ 665 (HHJ Judge Finlay QC).
2 See *Taylor v Warners* (21 July 1987, unreported) discussed by Jackson in *Conveyancing for Common Lawyers* delivered to the PNBA and *Walker v Hall* [1984] FLR 126 at 129E–F, CA.

3 Acting for mortgagors, mortgagees and sureties

8.11 A number of claims arise from the activities of solicitors in acting in relation to the execution of mortgages or charges over real property, where one of the mortgagors or sureties claims that he or she did not understand the charge which he or she signed, or that he or she signed it only after the application of undue influence.

Assume that a solicitor (S) is instructed by a lender (L) in relation to the making of a loan to the principal borrower (B1) on the security of a property which is already owned jointly by B1 and another (B2). B2 will often but not always be B1's spouse. B1 and B2 default on the mortgage, and L brings possession proceedings against them. B2 alleges that she signed the mortgage only after B1 had either misrepresented to her the nature of the transaction and document which she was signing, or exercised undue influence over her. On that basis she claims that L cannot enforce the mortgage against her. It is likely that L will have instructed a solicitor to advise B2 in relation to the effect of the mortgage before she signed it. It may have been the same solicitor as was acting for L on the transaction, or it may have been a different solicitor. In either case, L is likely to respond to B2's claim by saying that it had no notice of the alleged undue influence, because the solicitor was acting for B2. Both B2 and L may sue their solicitors. B2 may sue the solicitor who witnessed her signature to the transaction, for failing to carry out the duties he or she owed to her. If that solicitor was instructed by L to explain the effect of the mortgage to B2, then L may also sue that solicitor on a similar basis. If the same solicitor acted for both L and B2, then there may be the following claims: L v B1 and B2; L v S; and B2 v S.[1]

1   B2 may also sue B1 for undue influence, but B1 has often lost all assets and, for practical purposes, is not worth pursuing.

8.12   These various claims are likely to overlap as, for example, if L succeeds against B1 and B2 then it may be entitled to no damages from S. In these circumstances, it will usually be desirable for the actions to be consolidated and tried together. In order to consider the solicitor's position, it is first necessary to consider the action between L and B2.

(a)   Guarantors' or mortgagors' claims to set aside mortgages

(i)   Non est factum

8.13   Two types of claim are often made by guarantors or mortgagors who seek to escape the effect of the documents they have signed. The first is that the deed should be set aside on the basis of non est factum. Full discussion of this doctrine is outside the scope of this book.[1] In summary, however, the basis of the claim will be that B2 made a fundamental mistake as to the nature of the document which he or she was signing, so that he or she had no idea that it was a mortgage. The difficulty with a claim of this type for B2 is likely to be that the doctrine will not assist a party who was negligent in signing a document.[2] Normally L will have required that B2 sign in the presence of a solicitor whose duty it was to advise B2 of the effect of the deed. It is thought that, assuming a solicitor is present, then it will normally be negligent for B2 to sign without first asking the solicitor for at least some indication of the nature of the document which he or she is being asked to sign. If the solicitor does provide at least some explanation to the effect that it is a mortgage and of the nature of a mortgage, then it will be hard for B2 to show that his or her mistake as to the nature of the document was sufficiently fundamental to invoke the doctrine of non est factum.

1   See *Chitty on Contracts* (27th edn, 1994) at 5.032–5.036.
2   *Barclays Bank plc v Schwartz* [1995] CLY 2492, CA per Millett LJ, and *Hambros Bank Ltd v British Historic Buildings Trust and Din* [1995] NPC 179, CA.

(ii)   Undue influence

8.14   The second type of claim commonly made is that the deed is unenforceable by L because it was executed due to the undue influence of B1, or alternatively of a third party (T) who sought to borrow on the basis of security provided by B2.[1] Two broad issues arise: first, B2 must show that he or she signed the document due to the undue influence of B1 or T; secondly, B2 must show that L had notice of that undue influence, so that its mortgage is unenforceable because of it. The law in relation to undue influence, and the role of solicitors, in cases of this kind was exhaustively and helpfully explained by the Court of Appeal in *Royal Bank of Scotland v Etridge (No 2)*.[2] What follows is not a substitute for reading that case.

1   See eg *Credit Bank Nederland NV v Burch* [1997] 1 All ER 144, CA.
2   [1998] 4 All ER 705, CA. This landmark decision consisted of eight conjoined appeals in which a particularly strong Court of Appeal laid down numerous guidelines.

8.15   As to the first issue,

'Cases of undue influence are now classified in three categories. Class 1 consists of cases of actual (or express) undue influence. In these cases it is necessary for the complainant to prove affirmatively that she entered into the impugned transaction not of her own free will but as a result of actual undue influence exerted against her. Class 2 consists of cases of presumed undue influence. In these cases it is sufficient for the complainant to establish the existence of a relationship of trust and confidence between her and the wrongdoer of such a nature that it is fair to presume that the wrongdoer abused the relationship in procuring her to enter into the impugned transaction. Once such a relationship has been established, the burden shifts to the wrongdoer to prove that the complainant entered into the impugned transaction with her "full, free and informed thought" (*Zamet v Hyman* [1961] 3 All ER 933, [1961] 1 WLR 1442 at 1444 per Lord Evershed MR).

6. The necessary relationship can be established in either of two ways. Class 2A consists of certain well-known relationships which are by presumption of law irrebuttably treated as relationships of trust and confidence. Class 2B consists of other cases where the complainant establishes by affirmative evidence that she was accustomed to repose trust and confidence in the wrongdoer.'[1]

B1 and L will wish to show that B2 entered into the transaction by the exercise of his or her own free will, rather than due to undue influence. The most obvious way in which to do this is to show that B2 entered into the transaction after the nature and effect of it had been explained by an independent and qualified person who was fully informed of the material facts. The obvious candidate is a solicitor. Thus it was in this context that the Court of Appeal in *Etridge (No 2)*[2] began to consider the duties of a solicitor retained to advise B2. These are considered further below.[3]

1   *Etridge (No 2)* [1998] 4 All ER 705 at paragraphs 5 and 6 (all references are to the paragraph numbers in the judgment of the court).
2   [1998] 4 All ER 705. See at paragraphs 16 and 19.
3   At paras 8.21ff.

8.16   If B2 succeeds in establishing undue influence, the second issue is whether L had notice of it. As mentioned above, this is likely to be central to the assessment of damages in any claim against solicitors. If L had no notice, then its charge will be enforceable against B2 even if undue influence is proved. In this case, even if S acted in breach of duty to L,[1] L's damages against S are likely to be low or minimal. But B2 may have a claim against a solicitor who advised her in relation to the transaction. On the other hand, if L's claim to possession fails then B2 is unlikely to have such a claim against solicitors, but L may have a claim for failure either to ensure that B2 fully understood what she was signing, or, possibly, for failure to report unusual features of the transaction to L. Each of these possibilities is considered below.

1   See paras 8.23 and 8.31.

8.17   Whether L had notice of the undue influence depends upon how the transaction appeared, or should have appeared, to L. L may have had actual, imputed or constructive notice of the undue influence. If it had actual notice, through its employees, it will be unable to rely upon the charge. As to imputed notice, in *Halifax Mortgage Services Ltd v Stepsky*[1] it was held at first instance that S owed a duty to inform L of the facts which would have put it on notice that B1 had unduly influenced B2 to execute a mortgage. In the Court of Appeal the decision was reversed on the narrower ground that the information was acquired before S was instructed by L and could not be imputed to L when instructions were later given. Despite the fact that the defendants were instructed by L to report on title, the question of whether S was in breach of his retainer by failing to report material facts to L was not considered relevant to the question of whether L was fixed with knowledge.[2]

1   [1996] Ch 1 and 207 (Edward Nugee QC and CA).
2   See Morritt LJ [1996] Ch 207 at 214E–216F.

8.18   In *Etridge (No 2)*,[1] the Court of Appeal set out a number of guidelines which summarised the law on L's notice in these circumstances. Guidelines (3) and (4) concerned imputed notice:

'(3) When giving advice to the wife[2] the solicitor is acting exclusively as her solicitor: see *Serter*'s case[3] and *Thomson*'s case.[4] It makes no difference whether he is unconnected with the husband or the wife (see *Thomson*'s case) or is also the husband's solicitor (see *Serter*'s case, *Massey*'s case[5] and *Mann*'s case[6]) or that he has agreed to act in a ministerial capacity as the bank's agent at completion (see *Serter*'s case and *Stepsky*'s case[7]). Whoever introduces the solicitor to the wife and asks him to advise her, and whoever is responsible for his fees, the bank is entitled to expect the solicitor to regard himself as owing a duty to the wife alone when giving her advice (see *Thomson*'s case). If the solicitor accepts the bank's instructions to advise the wife, he still acts as her solicitor and not the bank's solicitor when he interviews her (see *Thomson*'s case).

(4) It follows that the bank is not fixed with imputed notice of what the solicitor learns in the course of advising the wife even if he is also the bank's solicitor. Such knowledge does not come to him in his capacity as the bank's solicitor: see *Stepsky*'s case.'

Thus it is most unlikely that L will be held to have imputed notice of any undue influence exercised in relation to B2.

1   [1998] 4 All ER 705 at paragraph 44.
2   The court assumed that the party we have called B1 was a husband and B2 a wife, but said that similar principles applied wherever there was an emotional relationship between co-habitees: see paragraph 4.
3   *Midland Bank plc v Serter* [1995] 3 FCR 711, CA.
4   *Barclays Bank plc v Thomson* [1997] 4 All ER 816, CA.
5   *Massey v Midland Bank plc* [1995] 1 All ER 929, CA.
6   *Banco Exterior Internacional v Mann* [1995] 1 All ER 936, CA.
7   [1996] Ch 1.

8.19   That leaves the question of constructive notice. Again, the Court of Appeal summarised the position in *Etridge (No 2)*.[1] If B2 is represented by a solicitor, L will normally have no constructive notice of any undue influence, because it is entitled to assume that the solicitor will have carried out his professional obligations to B2 properly, thus preventing any undue influence. If B2 does not approach L through a solicitor, it is normally sufficient if L has urged B2 to obtain independent legal advice prior to executing the charge. In most circumstances, therefore, even if B2 is able to make out undue influence, L will not be fixed with notice of it. The result will be that, in most cases, if undue influence is made out, L will still obtain possession, so any claim it may have against the solicitor who advised B2 before she signed the charge is likely to be low;[2] by the same token however, B2 *is* likely to have a claim against such solicitor, because she will have executed a charge in his presence, subject to undue influence, but will still lose her interest in the property because L will be able to enforce the charge against her.[3]

1 [1998] 4 All ER 705 at paragraph 44.
2 See para 8.31.
3 Para 8.23.

8.20 On the other hand, if the terms of the charge which B2 signed are plainly very substantially to her disadvantage, for instance if she guarantees a large liability for B1 of whom she is merely a junior employee rather than a co-habitee, then L may be fixed with knowledge of undue influence even if a solicitor has been involved.[1] In that case, B2 may have no claim against her solicitor, because the charge has been set aside, but L may claim that the solicitor has breached his or her retainer to it, by failing to explain the transaction fully to B2, to detect risks of undue influence, or even to report them to L. These issues are considered further below.

1 See *Credit Lyonnais Bank Nederland NV v Burch* [1997] 1 All ER 144, CA. Alternatively the court may set the transaction aside as an unconscionable bargain: see 153c–d, per Millett LJ.

(b) Acting for the guarantor

(i) Liability

8.21 In the terminology used above, B2 may be a co-habitee who either has both legal and beneficial interests in the property, or only a beneficial interest. In the former case B2 will be asked to sign the mortgage; in the latter, she will probably be asked to sign a form consenting to the mortgage and agreeing that any interest of hers will take effect subject to the mortgage.[1] But in either case there may be a risk that B1, at whose instance L's money is being borrowed, has applied undue influence to B2. The duty of S, a solicitor asked to advise B2 or witness her signature on the relevant legal document, is the same in either case. S may be instructed directly by B2. Alternatively, in the modern context S is often instructed by L, rather than by the client herself, to give independent legal advice to B2 in person, and S may look to L for his fees. For instance, to comply with the voluntary Code of Banking Practice lending institutions usually require an independent solicitor to witness a charge and to sign a certificate which states that the solicitor explained the nature of the transaction to B2 before it was executed. Although instructed by a third party and difficult to analyse in straightforward contractual terms, it is clear that it is S's duty to advise B2 and not to advise either L or B1.[2]

1 The purpose of this type of form is to prevent L being bound by an overriding interest of B2's in the property. See *Williams and Glyn's Bank Ltd v Boland* [1981] AC 487, HL.
2 See *Banco Exterior Internacional v Mann* [1995] 1 All ER 936 at 950a–d, CA, per Bingham MR and para 8.18.

8.22 In those circumstances S owes the same duty to B2 that he would owe to any client who had instructed him directly and paid his fees. The duty to explain the consequence of documents is considered in general in chapter 2. But in this context it is unlikely to be enough for S simply to explain the nature of the document to B2 and the consequences of default. The Court of Appeal recently gave the following direction about the extent of the solicitor's duty to a wife about to execute a guarantee charge in *Etridge (No 2):*[1]

'It is not sufficient to explain the documentation and ensure that she understands the nature of the transaction and wishes to carry it out ... His duty is to satisfy himself that his client is free from improper influence, and the first step must be to ascertain whether it is one into which she could sensibly be advised to enter if free from such influence. If he is not so satisfied it is his duty to advise her not to enter into it and to refuse to act further for her in the implementation of the transaction if she persists. In this event, whilst the content of the advice must remain confidential, he should inform the other parties (including the bank) that he has seen his client and given her certain advice, and that as a result he has declined to act further. He must in any event advise her that she is under no obligation to enter into the transaction at all and, if she still wishes to do so, that she is not bound to accept the terms of any document which has been put before her ..."

Compliance may also require S to make enquiries either of B1 or L about the extent of the borrowings or the standing of the principal debtor in order to assess and advise B2 whether the transaction is one which 'she could sensibly be advised to enter'.[2] If a solicitor fails to comply with these requirements, he is likely to be liable in negligence to B2. If B2 has retained him, this will be liability in contract; if S was retained purely by L to advise B2, it is likely that S will owe B2 a duty of care in tort.[3]

1   [1998] 4 All ER 705 at paragraph 19. The court overruled *Royal Bank of Scotland v Etridge (No 1)* [1997] 3 All ER 628, CA, one of the cases which had gone to the Court of Appeal at an interlocutory stage.
2   See *Credit Lyonnais Bank Nederland NV v Burch* [1997] 1 All ER 144 at 152a–b, CA.
3   See para 8.7, note 2.

(ii)   Damages

8.23   As indicated above, if L is fixed with notice of undue influence, B2's interest may be unaffected, so that B2 will have no claim against S.[1] But in most cases L will not be fixed with notice of undue influence. S will wish to show that B2's allegation of undue influence is false, or, alternatively, that even if S had acted with reasonable care B2 would still have signed the documents in question, so that B2 cannot prove causation of loss against S. If B2 is able to overcome both those hurdles, however, then B2 may have a claim to recover damages equal to the value of his or her interest in the charged property. Difficulties will arise if the property was charged prior to the loan by L to B1 or to B1 and B2. In those circumstances, L may have a right of subrogation in relation to the prior charge.[2] B2 will seek damages based upon a comparison between the actual position and what would have occurred if B2 had not agreed to the new charge over the property,[3] although S may be able to argue that the mere acceptance of a loan by B2 cannot amount to damage.[4] Where B2 has no legal interest in the property, but relies upon an interest under a constructive trust which arises by reason of, for example, contributions to the purchase price or mortgage instalments in respect of the property, valuation of B2's interest may be complex.[5]

1   It is conceivable that B2 might have a claim for damages if L obtained an order for sale pursuant to Trusts of Land and Appointments of Trustees Act 1996, s 14. See para 8.31.
2   See *Bowers v Bowers* (3 February 1987, unreported) (Hoffmann J) and *Boscawen v Bajwa* [1996] 1 WLR 328, CA.
3   See, eg *Harris v Nantes and Wilde* [1997] NPC 7 where substantial damages were awarded

at first instance. In related proceedings B2 appears to have obtained both a declaration that a transfer forged by B1 was not binding on him *and* an order that B1 account to him for the proceeds of sale. The loss alleged against the defendants appears to have been based on the fact that B2 could not recover this sum from B1.

4 See *Saddington v Colleys Professional Services* [1999] Lloyd's Rep PN 140, CA.
5 See further Oakley *Constructive Trusts* (3rd edn, 1997) pp 70–77. In the two most recent cases on the topic B2 did not recover substantial damages from S. In *Northern Rock Building Society v Archer* (31 July 1998, unreported), CA, B2 succeeded in setting aside the charge. Ds were found liable in negligence although no substantial damage was suffered as a consequence. In *Etridge v Pritchard Englefield* (28 April 1999, unreported), CA, Mrs Etridge's claim against her solicitors was dismissed despite her having failed in her defence against the Royal Bank of Scotland. The judge held that she would have executed the charge in any event and this was upheld by the Court of Appeal.

(c)   Acting for both mortgagors

8.24   S may also be instructed by B1 to act on behalf of both B1 and B2 and this often happens where B1 asks his or her solicitor to witness B2's execution of the charge. In *Etridge (No 2)*[1] the Court of Appeal indicated that they considered the practice of acting for both B1 and B2 to be perfectly permissible provided that there was no conflict between the interests of each client.[2] It will not always be easy for S to decide whether he can continue to represent both where B2 is being asked to charge his or her interest in the family home to secure the business debts of B1. The court gave the following guidance which they recognised that practitioners might find difficult to follow:

> 'It is also a matter for the solicitor's professional judgment whether he should himself advise the wife on the wisdom of the transaction, or invite her to obtain other advice, for example from the accountant to the business. In order to enable him to exercise his judgment, however, it will usually be necessary for the solicitor to inform himself of the circumstances of the proposed transaction, the amount of the existing indebtedness and of the new advance, and of the reasons for the new advance or the bank's request for additional security. He may also need to probe the stability of the marriage. This would need to be done with some sensitivity; but the wife should at least be warned that by entering the transaction she could be putting at risk the one substantial asset on which she could rely should the marriage come to grief.'

1 [1998] 4 All ER 705 at paragraph 25, CA.
2 See the facts of *Credit Lyonnais Bank Nederland NV v Burch* [1997] 1 All ER 144, CA and *Mercantile Credit Co Ltd v Fenwick* [1997] NPC 120 (Carnwath J) (upheld in CA, [1999] Lloyd's Rep PN 408) for good examples of the circumstances in which the conflict is soluble only by S declining to act for B2. In *Fenwick* S's advice to B2 was plainly inadequate. However, in that case B2 took the initiative and instructed her own solicitors whom she found through the Yellow Pages. This alone saved S from liability.

8.25   Where he reaches the conclusion that he cannot safely act for both clients S must advise B2 of the potential conflict and to obtain independent advice.[1] In the event that S continues to act for both B1 and B2 in those circumstances, he or she is likely to be in breach of duty to B2 for failing to fully explain the nature of the transaction.[2] As to damages in a claim by B2, the principles which apply are likely to be the same as set out above at para 8.23.

1 Paragraph 12.03 of *The Guide to the Professional Conduct of Solicitors* provides that S must see B2 alone. S must also give clear and unequivocal advice: see *Mahoney v Purnell* [1996] 3 All ER 61 at 93g–94f. If S continues to act, having given an inadequate warning, he will be liable in negligence to B2.
2 See, eg, *Atkins v Atkins* [1993] EGCS 54. Solicitors failed to explain to the plaintiff that the true purpose of the transaction was that she should provide security for the debts of her son.

(d)   Acting for the lender alone

8.26   In the normal course L itself owes no duty of care to either B1 or B2 and correspondingly, if S acts only for L and not for either B1 or B2, S owes B1 and B2 no duty of care either. Moreover, in discharging his duty to L, S is usually entitled to assume that B2 has received independent advice and is under no obligation to obtain written confirmation from B1's solicitor that he is acting for both B1 and B2 or, if not, that B2 has been independently advised.[1] Where both B1 and B2 are represented by separate solicitors it makes it extremely unlikely that any pressure placed on B2 will be 'undue'.[2]

1   See *Mercantile Credit Co Ltd v Fenwick* [1999] Lloyd's Rep PN 408, CA. See also the facts of *Bank of Baroda v Shah* [1988] 3 All ER 24.
2   *Fenwick* above is just such an example. B2 only received legal advice at all rather belatedly and on her own initiative.

(e)   Acting for the lender and the principal mortgagor (B1)

8.27   Where B1 instructs S to act as his or her own solicitors in relation to the transaction S's duties to B1 depend on the scope and terms of the retainer. One practical concern of the profession when accepting instructions to act for a mortgagor has now been laid to rest by the decision of the Court of Appeal in *Barclays Bank plc v Weeks Legg & Dean*.[1] A solicitor acting for a client who is proposing to grant a charge to a bank to secure an overdraft or commercial borrowings is often called upon by the bank to obtain his client's signature to the charge without payment. At the same time the solicitor gives a standard form undertaking which has been agreed between the Law Society and the bank to use the bank's money for the purpose of acquiring a good marketable title to the property. The Court of Appeal have now decided that where a solicitor gives this undertaking, procures that his client execute the charge and returns the title deeds to the bank he or she owes no duty to give further advice to the bank.[2] Moreover they also held that the terms of the standard undertaking require the solicitor to carry out no further investigation into title than he has carried out for or on behalf of his purchaser client.[3]

1   [1998] 3 WLR 656, CA at 660C–G and 672B–G.
2   The precise terms of the undertaking to apply the advance monies to obtain a good marketable title are considered in chapter 7, paras 7.32–7.33.
3   See [1998] 3 WLR 656 at 669G–671A and chapter 1, para 1.2.

(f)   Duty to the lender when acting for the lender and the guarantor (B2)

(i)   Liability

8.28   It seems likely that the Court of Appeal would not impose any positive duty on S to report information to L which might be relevant to L's decision to lend but which was learnt by S in the course of giving advice to B2.[1] Where S has been instructed *exclusively* to provide *independent* advice to B2 there ought to be no duty to report to L facts learnt in the course of giving that advice even although L is the source of S's instructions.[2]

1   See the passage from *Etridge (No 2)* [1998] 4 All ER 705, quoted at para 8.18.
2   Contrast *Halifax Building Society v Stepsky* [1996] Ch 1 and 207 (Edward Nugee QC reversed by CA on different grounds). The judge held that S owed L a duty to report that B1 intended to use L's advance to discharge a previous mortgage and repay his business debts whereas L had been told that the advance was required to acquire shares in a family business. Although it was a remortgage S was instructed to act on behalf of both L and B2 and submitted a report on title. This distinguishes it from the 'notice' cases considered in the passage referred to in note 1.

8.29 On the other hand, if S fails to ensure that B2 fully understands the nature of the document and consents to the transaction, it is possible that S may be in breach not only of a duty to B2 but also of the terms of the retainer from L. In *Connell v Odlum*[1] a husband engaged a solicitor to advise his wife on a pre-nuptial agreement whilst he himself was advised by other solicitors. His wife was later successful in having the pre-nuptial agreement set aside for undue influence. It was held that the solicitor owed a duty to the husband to ensure that he gave adequate advice to the wife. There is no directly comparable authority in England. But if S is instructed by L or B1 to ensure that B2 receives adequate advice and the advice given is inadequate, there seems to be no reason why either L or B1 should not recover damages for this failure if a loss is later caused by the inadequacy of the advice. If B2 succeeds in setting aside a charge on the grounds of undue influence, S may be liable to L notwithstanding that L instructed S to advise B2 exclusively. Moreover, if S certifies (usually on the charge itself) that he or she has fully explained the nature of the document to B2 or given independent advice or advised B2 to seek independent advice, S may be open to a claim of misrepresentation by L.[2]

1   [1993] 2 NZLR 257.
2   *National Westminster Bank plc v Beaton* (1998) 30 HLR 99 provides another good example. B2 was led to believe that the charge was both limited and intended to replace an earlier charge rather than to secure additional business borrowings. Despite S's knowledge of her misapprehension, L was not fixed with notice of undue influence and suffered no loss. It seems clear that S had failed to comply with the terms of the retainer and that the certificate was inaccurate.

8.30 Similarly, if S fails to obtain a consent form[1] from B2 in circumstances where B2 has an overriding interest, it is likely that S will have breached the terms of his or her retainer by L.

1   See para 8.21.

(ii)   Damages

8.31 If L is not fixed with notice of undue influence then any claim which it may have against S for damages is likely to be restricted to consequential damages caused by the delay in obtaining possession and any additional legal costs. If L is fixed with notice of undue influence as a consequence of a breach of duty by S, S will be liable to L for the net value of B2's interest in the security at the date on which it would have been sold[1] together with any consequential costs. These may, however, be substantial because B2 may be entitled to remain in the property unless and until an order for sale is made. When and whether an order for sale will be made turns on the proper construction of Trusts of Land and Appointment Trustees Act 1996, s 14. Prior to the passing of the Act, L's interests were likely to prevail in most circumstances and B2 had a limited ability to prevent an order being made.[2] The wording of the 1996 Act makes the position less clear.[3] If an order for sale *is* made then L will at least be able to recover B1's interest in the property.

1   See para 8.23 for possible problems in valuing this.
2   *Re Citro* [1991] Ch 142, CA.
3   According to *TSB Bank plc v Marshall, Marshall and Rodgers* [1998] 2 FLR 769 (county court), the position is unchanged. This is open to question.

(g)   *Acting for the lender and the mortgagors*

8.32 Finally, S may be instructed by B1 to act for B1 and B2 and then by L to act on its behalf. Given the greater sensitivity of the profession to conflicts of interest, this factual situation is likely to be the subject matter of claims far less frequently than it used to be.[1] Further, as from 1 April 1999 rule 6(3) of the Solicitors Practice Rules 1990 (as amended)[2] provides that a solicitor may only accept instructions from a lender which are limited to:

> '[A]dvising any other person required to sign any document supplied by the lender on the terms of that document or, if there is a conflict of interest between that person and the borrower, advising that person on the need for separate legal advice.'

1   In *Royal Bank of Scotland v Etridge (No 2)* [1998] 4 All ER 705 at paragraph 24, the Court of Appeal frowned on a solicitor acting for L and B2. They stated that it was 'obviously unwise' for S to act for B2 unless S was 'instructed to act for the bank only in a ministerial capacity at completion'.

2   By the Solicitors' Practice (Lender and Borrower) Amendment Rule dated 29 September 1998 and published in the Law Society Gazette on 21 October 1998.

8.33   The rule is to be welcomed because acting for all three parties could often give rise to the following and, often, acute difficulties: first, S might receive information from B2 which was inconsistent with what, to S's knowledge, B1 had told S or L; second, S might receive information from B2 or make observations from which a reasonable solicitor would conclude that B2 had been coerced or prevailed upon to execute the charge or transfer; and, third, S might fail to advise B2 in sufficiently clear or strong terms with the consequence that B2 executed a document without fully informed consent. Where S was in possession of information confidential to B1 when instructed by L, it was S's duty either to obtain B1's consent to reporting that information to L or to decline to act. If S continued to act he or she might be forced to choose between his duties to L or B1. If S had been instructed to report all material matters to L or to ensure that B2 gave his or her fully informed consent to the mortgage but failed to do so, S was in breach of the terms of the retainer from L.[1] If S reported the information to L, he was in breach of duty to B1. Finally, if B2 did not receive clear and adequate advice whether to execute the charge, S was in breach of duty to him or her as well.

1   See eg the facts of *Halifax Building Society v Stepsky* [1996] Ch 1 and 207 considered at paras 8.17 and 8.28 note 2.

4   Duties to third parties

8.34   As discussed in chapter 1 a solicitor ordinarily owes no duty to any party to a transaction for whom he does not act unless he 'steps outside' the terms of his retainer and voluntarily assumes responsibility to that third party. In the following circumstances, solicitors have been found liable to other parties when involved in a sale of land. In the context of conveyancing, this issue has generally arisen in two situations: firstly, in the context of replies given by a vendor's solicitor to pre-contract inquiries (often where the original client, who would inevitably be liable for a misrepresentation contained within them, is insolvent); and, secondly, in the context of certificates of title. These certificates are given by a vendor's solicitors directly to a purchaser or lender, usually in a commercial context and often as part of a wider due diligence exercise.

(a)   Pre-contract inquiries

8.35   There are two cases in which it has been held at first instance that a vendor's solicitor will not be held liable to a purchaser for errors made in answering pre-contract inquiries: *Gran Gelato Ltd v Richcliff (Group) Ltd*[1] and *Cemp Properties (UK) Ltd v Dentsply Research and Development Corpn Ltd*.[2] For reasons which are explored in chapter 1, paras 1.17–1.21, there remains a doubt whether a court at first instance or the Court of Appeal would be bound to follow them and in two cases it has been held arguable that a solicitor is liable to third parties for errors in inquiries: *Wilson v Bloomfield*[3] and *First National Commercial Bank plc v Loxleys*.[4] Nevertheless, in all but the most exceptional cases we consider that no duty of care would arise.[5]

1   [1992] Ch 560 (Sir Donald Nicholls V-C).
2   [1989] 2 EGLR 205, esp at 207 col 1 (Morritt J).
3   (1979) 123 Sol Jo 860, CA.
4   [1997] PNLR 211, CA.
5   See the suggestion of Hobhouse LJ in *McCullagh v Lane Fox & Partners* [1996] 1 EGLR 35, CA at 46J–K that a duty of care would be more likely to be imposed where the representation made concerned matters not included in the particulars of sale or not expected to be included in them. In the same way, a solicitor would be more likely to be liable in respect of additional inquiries or oral discussions outside normal conveyancing practice. This analysis is supported by *Computastaff v Ingledew, Brown Bennison and Garrett* (1983) 268 Estates Gazette 906 (McNeill J) in which the vendor's *agents* (rather than solicitors) were found liable for misinforming the purchaser's agents by telephone about the rateable value of a property after the same mistake had been made in pre-contract inquiries. Again, if the vendor's solicitor is personally requested to give a reply in relation to matters within his or her own knowledge and agrees to do so, this may found a duty of care: see the form of disclaimer discussed in para 8.37.

8.36   In the event that a solicitor is held to have owed a duty of care for a statement of fact contained in the reply to an inquiry the nature and effect of any representation contained in the reply will normally turn on the question and answer in issue. It is quite usual, however, for a vendor to answer questions about the existence of adverse rights and incumbrances 'Not so far as the vendor is aware' leaving the purchaser to make his own inquiries of third parties or to rely upon the documents of title with which he has been provided. It has been held that this reply:

> '[R]epresents not merely that the vendor and his solicitor had no actual knowledge of a defect but also that they have made such investigations as could reasonably be expected to be made by or under the guidance of a prudent conveyancer.'[1]

1   *William Sindall plc v Cambridgeshire County Council* [1994] 3 All ER 932 at 942e, CA.

8.37   It is also quite usual for the replies to pre-contract inquiries to contain a disclaimer. The standard form disclaimer contained in the current form of replies to pre-contract inquiries is as follows:

> 'These replies, except in the case of any enquiry expressly requiring a reply from the Vendor's solicitors, are given on behalf of the proposed Vendor and without responsibility on the part of his solicitors, their partners or employees. They are believed to be correct but the accuracy is not guaranteed and they do not obviate the need to make appropriate searches, enquiries and inspections.'

In *First National Commercial Bank v Loxleys*[1] it was held arguable that this disclaimer negatived the existence of a duty of care (subject to the effect of the Unfair Contract Terms Act 1977) although the issue was not finally resolved. There is no authority in which the effect of this disclaimer has been conclusively determined but we consider that it is likely to be sufficient to negative a duty of care to a purchaser on the part of the vendor's solicitor for a number of reasons:

(i)   The disclaimer does not purport to restrict the liability of the *vendor*, only that of his solicitors.

(ii) Replying to pre-contract inquiries is a voluntary process. The vendor is not obliged to answer them and, subject to the equitable duty of disclosure,[2] may refuse to do so. It is then for the purchaser to decide whether to make further inquiries himself or whether to take a risk.

(iii) The purchaser will invariably be represented by a solicitor. If the solicitor is unhappy with the replies given by the vendor, he may request additional inquiries and he may request the imprimatur of the vendor's solicitors personally.[3] If the vendor's solicitors refuse to answer, the purchaser is then faced with the same decision as before.

(iv) The disclaimer only extends to replies which the vendor's solicitor believes to be correct (although he or she might have been careless in researching the reply). It would not apply to replies which were carelessly given in the sense that the wrong answer was recorded or the solicitor did not turn his or her mind to the reply.

1   [1997] PNLR 211, CA.
2   The vendor has a duty to disclose defects in title which are latent but not patent. Whilst easy to state, it is not always very clear what amounts to a latent defect in title. This, of itself, encourages the vendor's solicitor to make as full a disclosure as possible. See, generally *Emmet on Title* (26th edn, looseleaf) Vol I at 4.026 et seq.
3   *Emmet* Vol I 1.021 suggests that the vendor's solicitor may be liable to the *vendor* if he or she fails to make adequate investigations to reply to the inquiries in a way which satisfies a (reasonable) purchaser. Given that the disclaimer is designed to protect the vendor's solicitors and not the vendor, the vendor will also have a right of indemnity against his own solicitor for inaccurate replies even if the solicitor owes no direct duty to the purchaser: see *Cemp Properties (UK) Ltd v Dentsply Research and Development Corpn Ltd* [1989] 2 EGLR 205 (Morritt J) at 207.

8.38   Again it is considered that a defendant firm of solicitors ought to be able to satisfy the court that a disclaimer in the form set out above would be reasonable for the reasons discussed by Henry LJ in *Omega Trust Co Ltd v Wright Son & Pepper*.[1] A limited disclaimer in the form quoted above should be distinguished from a provision in a contract of sale excluding liability for misrepresentation or purporting to prevent the purchaser asserting that he has entered into the contract in reliance on any representation contained in pre-contract inquiries. There is some doubt whether the vendor's solicitors could rely directly on such a contractual provision contained, as it is, in a contract between vendor and purchaser[2] and in *Walker v Boyle*[3] Dillon J held that such a provision was unreasonable and therefore void pursuant to Misrepresentation Act 1967, s 3 (as amended). Whilst there may be grounds for arguing that the term would not be unreasonable as between the vendor's solicitor and the purchaser, certainty dictates that the term ought to have the same effect whoever relies upon it.[4]

1   [1997] 18 EG 120 at 122–3, set out in chapter 1, para 1.27.
2   See *New Zealand Shipping Co Ltd v AM Satterthwaite & Co Ltd* [1975] AC 154.
3   [1982] 1 WLR 495 at 507A–508E.
4   However, see Hobhouse LJ in *McCullagh v Lane, Fox & Partners* [1996] 1 EGLR 35 at 46B, CA, indicating that it might not be fair just and reasonable for the court to impose liability on the vendor's solicitor in favour of a purchaser who agreed to this term with the vendor. The judgment also takes a very different attitude to standard terms and, for this reason as well casts doubt on the efficacy of *Walker v Boyle* (at least when a solicitor seeks to rely on such a provision).

(b)   Certificates of title

8.39   In *Allied Finance v Haddow & Co*[1] the solicitors of the purchaser of a yacht provided a certificate to a third party insurance company that the proposed mortgage of the yacht would be binding on the purchaser and that there were no other charges over the vessel. In fact a limited company was acquiring the yacht and the vendor had a lien over it for a part of the purchase price. The solicitor was held to owe a duty of care to the finance company. Cooke J stated:[2]

'That is a classic duty of care situation ... The proximity is almost as close as it could be, short of contract. Nor are there any sufficient negativing considerations. Far from disclaiming responsibility, the solicitor has virtually in terms accepted it. It would be strange if the law failed to impose a duty.'

Although *Haddow* was not cited in the judgments[3] the Court of Appeal reached a similar result in *N M Rothschild & Sons Ltd v Berensons*.[4] It is of note that the defendant firm was found liable not to the lead bank Barclays Bank plc, to whom the Funds Request (which contained the certificate) was addressed, but also to an individual bank in the consortium, Rothschild, which had agreed to provide the funds. In sophisticated transactions a firm of solicitors may be asked to provide certificates of title both to a purchaser or to a lender or to a syndicate of lenders. Both of these authorities suggest that an English court would impose a duty of care upon the solicitor who failed to exercise reasonable care in providing such certificates.

1   [1983] NZLR 22, which was cited with approval by Sir Donald Nicholls V-C in *Gran Gelato Ltd v Richcliff (Group) Ltd* [1992] Ch 560.
2   [1983] NZLR 22 at p 24, line 45 to p 25, line 2. See Richardson J to similar effect at p 30, lines 1–21.
3   Although it was relied upon by Knox J at first instance [1995] NPC 107. It should also be noted that *Anns v Merton London Borough Council* [1978] AC 728 and *Scott Group Ltd v McFarlane* [1978] 1 NZLR 553 were both relied upon. Neither is now regarded as good law in this country.
4   [1997] NPC 15, CA. The facts are set out in chapter 1, para 1.23.

8.40   As will be clear from the discussion of pre-contract inquiries[1] there is no decided authority on the question whether a disclaimer given by a solicitor to a third party would either negative the existence of a duty of care or, if it were necessary to do so, satisfy the test of reasonableness provided by Unfair Contract Terms Act 1977, s 11(3). In the context of certificates of title, it is suggested that the determination of these issues might be of some significance. For it is unlikely that in circumstances where a solicitor had been personally requested to verify legal issues for a potential purchaser or lender a blanket disclaimer of liability for negligence would be held to be reasonable, although a sufficiently clearly-worded disclaimer submitted to a purchaser who had the benefit of legal advice might very well negative any assumption of responsibility. For the present, at least, it would be prudent for a solicitor to assume that any disclaimer might be held unreasonable.

1   In paras 8.35–8.38.

8.41   It is far more likely that the court would uphold as reasonable a more limited disclaimer. For instance, if the certificate is a 'for your eyes only' certificate limited to named or identified parties, the court would be likely to follow *Omega* (where the disclaimer was of this kind) and limit the solicitor's liability to those parties so named unless express consent had been sought and obtained to extend the recipients. Again in a climate where very substantial claims have been made against professionals and where it might be very difficult indeed to predict the reliance which might be placed on a certificate of title or the losses which might be sustained as a consequence of it, the court might well be sympathetic to an express limitation of liability to the defendant's insurance cover or to a fixed amount.[1]

1   See *The Guide* at paragraph 12.09, which suggests that it would be acceptable for solicitors to limit their liability to *clients* to the limit of cover provided that the minimum level of cover is that required by the Solicitors' Indemnity Rules. It also states: '[T]he Council takes the view

that it may be reasonable in some circumstances for a solicitor to seek to limit or exclude altogether the liability he or she might otherwise incur to such persons [who are not his or her clients] under the [*Hedley Byrne*] principle'.

(c)   Miscellaneous cases

8.42   In very few cases apart from those discussed above has an English court been prepared to find that a solicitor who acts in relation to a conveyancing transaction owes a duty to anybody other than his client.[1] If a solicitor provides a reference in relation to the financial standing or honesty of his client either to a lender or another party, then it is suggested that he would come under a duty of care for the accuracy of the reference or the financial information provided in the same way as an accountant.[2] Apart from this example most of the cases in which a duty of care has been extended to a third party are cases in which the third party is intimately connected with the client or the client's personal or corporate alter ego.[3]

1   The extensive Commonwealth authorities are digested in Jackson and Powell *Professional Negligence* (4th edn, 1991) at paragraph 4–37 and footnotes 8–10.
2   See *Midland Bank v Cameron, Thom, Peterkin & Duncans* [1988] SLT 611. On the facts the solicitor was not held to have assumed responsibility for the accuracy of the statements.
3   See *R P Howard Ltd v Woodman Matthews* [1983] BCLC 117 (Staughton J) (duty to principal shareholder of client company both in contract and tort); *Foster v Crust* [1986] BCLC 307 (HHJ Finlay QC) (duty in tort to director guaranteeing corporate client's debts). *Jackson & Powell* (see note 1) at paragraph 4–28 refer to both *Whelton-Sinclair v Hyland* [1992] 2 EGLR 158 and *Penn v Bristol and West Building Society* [1995] 2 FLR 938 (HHJ Kolbert) as examples of liability without reliance. Both are considered elsewhere.

8.43   *Woodward v Wolferstans*[1] is a good example. The plaintiff's father instructed the defendant firm to act in relation to the acquisition and mortgage of a property on behalf of the plaintiff who was 22 years old. There was no contact between the plaintiff and the defendants and she did not rely upon them at all. It was held that they owed a duty of care to her because of the close relationship of proximity, but following *White v Jones*[2] the duty only extended to carrying out her father's instructions and not to advising her personally about the nature of the obligations which she had undertaken. It is not entirely clear why no contractual retainer came into existence. Even if the plaintiff gave no formal instructions to the defendants, she must have tacitly agreed for them to act on her behalf when she signed the documents and permitted them to be returned to the defendants.[3]

1   [1997] NPC 51 (Martin Mann QC).
2   [1995] 2 AC 207.
3   See chapter 1, paras 1.28 and 1.29. See also para 1.8 for the implication of a contractual retainer.

(d)   Damages

8.44   In *Haddow* the lender recovered from the borrower's solicitors the balance of the loan outstanding after the boat had been sold and apart from the question of interest, no issue was raised about damages in the appeal. No guidance can be derived from the cases about the quantum of damages to be recovered from a solicitor in the event that he or she is found liable to a third party. In lenders' cases where reliance is laid on a certificate of title to a security it seems only right that damages should be restricted to the amount by which the value would have been affected at the date of the certificate by analogy with valuers' cases. In other cases, the valuation method[1] is likely to be applied.

1   See chapter 3, paras 3.52–3.59.

B ACTING FOR THE PURCHASER

1 Duties before contract

(a) Introduction

8.45 The duty of a solicitor to give his or her client commercial advice is considered in chapter 2. As discussed there, a solicitor has in general terms no duty to inform his client that the purchase of property he is about to make will be unwise or prove to be commercially imprudent. However, because the purchase of land is complex, involving a number of professionals and a number of stages, a solicitor may well be obliged to give some advice with commercial implications. The precise nature of that advice is now considered. Whilst an attempt is made to generalise as much as possible, it should be noted that the advice which is required by the client will always depend on that individual. Even in the context of relatively straightforward residential conveyancing, the advice which will be required by a first-time buyer with no legal experience whatsoever may differ substantially from that required by a client who is moving house for the second or third time.

(b) Deposits, mortgages and surveys

8.46 Prior to exchange of contracts it is the solicitor's primary responsibility to explain to his or her client the terms of the contract and the consequences of an exchange. For instance, depending on the client it may be necessary to explain to him that on exchange he will be legally bound to purchase the property and that if he fails to complete the transaction, he will lose his deposit and may be liable for damages (or, if no deposit has been paid, liable for the deposit and damages). The more difficult question is whether the reasonably competent solicitor must go beyond this. In *Buckland v Mackesy*[1] it was held that a solicitor who had advised his client at an earlier stage to obtain a survey but knew at exchange of contracts that he had not obtained a survey and had no mortgage funding in place, owed no duty to his client to advise him not to exchange until he had obtained them. It was held that the solicitor discharged his duty in a telephone conversation, the defendant's evidence of which was as follows:[2]

> 'In that telephone conversation Mr Mackesy said "Buckland said 'Do you think that I should do this?' and I [Mackesy] said 'If you don't want to take some risks you don't get anywhere. It is only £100: if the worst comes to the worst we can get rid of it' and that Buckland said 'Well I don't want to lose £100'." Thereafter Buckland signed the contract.'

The plaintiff was a shopkeeper with no particular commercial experience and no great financial means. This case must be taken therefore as authority for the proposition that once a solicitor has stressed to his client the legally binding nature of the contract and its effect, he has no duty to satisfy himself that the client will be able to comply with the contract and if necessary to advise the client to not to exchange until able to do so. In particular, it must be taken as authority that a solicitor is not obliged to advise the client to obtain the results of a survey or a mortgage offer before exchange of contracts.

1   (1968) 208 Estates Gazette 968, CA.
2   (1968) 208 Estates Gazette 968 at 974 per Baker J.

8.47 In certain circumstances and with certain clients (usually businessmen or property developers) the courts have gone even further than *Buckland v Mackesy* and found that it is unnecessary for the solicitor to advise on the binding nature of a contract at all or the potential loss of a deposit. In *Aslan v Clintons*[1] Leonard J stated:

> 'There is no question of an obscure and unusual clause. It would be otiose for a solicitor to point out to a property dealer or to any business man that if he failed to observe the clear terms of a contract which he was on the point of signing, he would be at risk of a successful claim being brought against him.'

In *Haigh v Wright Hassall & Co*[2] the defendant firm gave a solicitor's undertaking to the vendor to pay the deposit and exchanged contracts even though the clients had been unable to raise the deposit. It was argued that they ought to have advised the clients not to exchange until they had raised the deposit and to have questioned them about the reason why they had been unable to do so. Had they done this, it would have been apparent that they had no mortgage offer and the defendants would have warned them not to proceed. It was held that the defendants owed no duty to warn the client not to exchange without the deposit (let alone the wider duty) because the client understood the legally binding nature of an exchange of contracts.

1   (1983) 134 NLJ 584.
2   [1994] EGCS 54, CA.

8.48   In *Buckland v Mackesy* the Court of Appeal found in favour of the defendant solicitor only very reluctantly and there are some features about the transaction which distinguish it from a normal purchase.[1] First, the deposit had been negotiated down to a figure of £100 (by Mackesy himself) and Buckland was plainly prepared to risk that sum. If the client were asked to pay the conventional deposit of 10% it might not be enough for the solicitor simply to point out the risk of its loss. Second, Buckland was advised by the second defendant, Watts (his surveyor), to wait until he had sold one of the flats which he owned before committing himself to the purchase. Third, it was accepted by the court that Mackesy did advise Buckland to get a survey and, as a consequence, he instructed Watts to provide one. Fourth, and finally, it appears from the report that the reason why Buckland was unable to complete was because his mortgagee's surveyor did not consider the subject property to be good security (and Watts was found liable for failing to carry out an adequate survey). Buckland, therefore, had made arrangements to obtain a mortgage and would, it seems, have got one in time to complete if it had not been for the additional survey carried out between exchange and completion.

1   See Harman LJ (1968) 208 Estates Gazette 968 at 969: 'A better solicitor might go further. I do not think that these professional men can be proud of their parts in this transaction'; Salmon LJ at 973: 'the plaintiff having fallen short, although not very far short, of establishing negligence'; and Baker J: 'I reach that conclusion without enthusiasm'.

8.49   It is suggested that if the Court of Appeal comes to reconsider the question of a solicitor's duties to advise his or her client before contract, it may well give the following paragraph of the Final Report of the Royal Commission on Legal Services 1979[1] (the Benson Commission) legal effect:

> 'It is at this point that the solicitor should discuss with his client all matters which the client should consider carefully before deciding whether to enter a binding contract, for example, the means of financing the transaction, the type of mortgage required, the necessity for mortgage protection, the names in which the property will be taken, matters relating to capital gains and capital transfer tax and the date required for completion. In general the solicitor will discuss whether the client is satisfied with the survey, has taken account of any proposed development in the neighbourhood and, in general, whether the property suits his requirements.'[2]

It requires no more than that the solicitor should run through this list with the client simply to direct his or her mind toward these issues or set them out in a standard form letter. The objection to this sort of practice appears to be threefold:

(i) that this is the thin end of a particularly difficult wedge;

(ii) that if a solicitor raises particular issues, substantial further work may be required the costs of which will be unacceptable to a majority of clients (and their lenders); and

(iii) that this would be an unwarranted (and, possibly, unwanted) interference by the solicitor in the client's business.

None of these objections seems particularly convincing and the authorities recognise that best practice is for the solicitor to give such advice.[3]

1   Cmnd 7648, Vol I, para 21.15 cited in *Emmet* Vol I at 1.007. The editors point out that, in broad terms, this is also the view of the Law Society and suggest that this legal result might be achieved because the profession holds itself out as providing a better service than it used to. Put another way, if a claimant could demonstrate that there has been a genuine change in general practice since *Buckland v Mackesy*, as supported by the Law Society, it would be open to the court not to follow it: see *Brenner v Gregory* (1972) 30 DLR (3d) 672 and *O'Connor v First National* [1991] IRLM 208 in which this point was taken. In the same way that medical practice does not stand still, neither should legal practice.

2   See also *Neighbour v Barker* [1992] 40 EG 140, CA at 144, per Scott LJ (advice pre-contract to have a survey described as 'strong and sensible advice'). One might also add to this list the need to advise the client to consider whether to be satisfied with a valuation report or whether to have a full structural survey.

3   In each of the cases cited in this paragraph, that was the case. If the solicitor does choose to advise in this situation, he or she will be liable for inaccurate advice. In *Collard v Saunders* (1972) 222 Estates Gazette 795 (Mocatta J) damages were awarded against the defendants for recommending an unqualified surveyor.

8.50   Where the client is proposing to acquire a special property, eg a freehold subject to a statutory tenancy or the fag end of a long lease in the hope of exercising the right to enfranchise under the Leasehold Reform Act 1967 (as amended), we suggest that—whatever the position more generally—a solicitor would be obliged in the process of explaining the legal position to recommend to his client to obtain specialist valuation advice if he or she had not already done so and to consider whether or not to obtain a structural survey.

8.51   Finally, there may be other reasons why the solicitor should advise his client about the legal effect and consequence of entering a binding contract. In *Attard v Samson*[1] the client assumed possession of the property and carried out extensive repairs in the expectation that a contract would be made. It never was. The defendant was negligent in failing to advise him of the risk which he was running in carrying out repairs before contract and in ensuring that a binding contract was made immediately.

1   (1966) 110 Sol Jo 249 (Phillimore J). The defendant acted for both parties and negligence was admitted.

(d)   Searches and inquiries

8.52   A solicitor is bound to satisfy himself or herself that the vendor has good title to the property to be sold and to make all necessary inquiries of the vendor to satisfy himself or herself that the property which the client wishes to acquire is free from any charges, encumbrances or adverse interests (other than those disclosed by the vendor and agreed to by the purchaser). The solicitor does not guarantee the title of the property but it is clear that the duty is not discharged simply by submitting to the vendor preliminary inquiries in the standard form. The solicitor is bound to ask additional inquiries where they are necessary.[1] If those replies turn out to be inconsistent with the information supplied already either by the vendor, his solicitors, the client or estate agents or they raise doubts about the accuracy of information provided or give rise to additional concerns, the solicitor has a duty to follow them up with the vendor's solicitors.[2] Again, the solicitor is bound to make all necessary inquiries of the local authority (the agreed standard form of which includes inquiries about the planning position) and where those searches give rise to doubts or additional concerns, the solicitor has a duty to follow them up as well.[3] The solicitor is not always bound to make a commons search in a densely built up area but should do so if it is vacant land or land which has not been built on.[4] If his or her inquiries reveal the existence of potential encumbrances, restrictions or adverse interests, the solicitor is bound to communicate that information to the client.[5]

1   *Goody v Baring* [1956] 1 WLR 448 esp at 453–48, CA.
2   *Computastaff Ltd v Ingledew Brown Bennison and Garrett* (1983) 268 Estates Gazette 906 (McNeill J), esp at 911 col 1.
3   See *Faragher v Gerber* [1994] EGCS 122 (HHJ Lachs). In *G P & P Ltd v Bulcraig and Davies* [1986] 2 EGLR 148 (John Gorman QC), appeal on damages at [1988] 1 EGLR 138, the judge held at 151A that a surveyor who made an oral inquiry as to the contents of the register might be obliged to follow it up depending on the answer. (The search was negative but as it happened the reply to the solicitor's search in writing revealed the existence of planning consent which turned out to be restrictive of user.) See *Emmet* Vol I at 1.031 et seq for the subject matter of local authority searches.
4   *G & K Ladenbau Ltd v Crawley v de Reya* [1978] 1 WLR 266 at 278F–H and 289A–C.
5   *Strover v Harrington* [1988] Ch 390 at 409H–410A (Sir Nicolas Browne-Wilkinson V-C). The solicitor has authority to receive all relevant information on the client's behalf and a positive duty to pass it on.

8.53   Although it is not intended to be an exhaustive list, defendant solicitors have been found liable or avoided liability for failure to make adequate searches or inquiries or advise their clients adequately about what was revealed in the following circumstances:

(i)   Boundaries and dimensions

Mercantile Building Society v JW Michell Dodds & Co: part of house not included in registered title, solicitors found liable for failure to check filed plan against agent's plan; *Wapshott v Davies Donovan & Co*: extension built over land owned by neighbour, solicitors found liable for failure to investigate title; *McManus Developments Ltd v Barbridge Properties Ltd*: fence three feet north of the boundary shown on the filed plan, solicitors found liable for failing to identify and point out the discrepancy after the neighbouring owner moved the fence; *Barclay-White v Guillaume & Sons*: solicitors found liable for failure to notice a discrepancy between estate agent's particulars and the filed plan of the property; *Nielsen v Watson*: driveway and garage excluded from property shown on the plan prepared by client's surveyor, solicitor found liable for failing to take instructions from client about the discrepancy.[1]

(ii)   Local authority searches

Lake v Bushby:[2] solicitor liable for failure to advise that no planning permission had been granted; *G & K Ladenbau Ltd v Crawley & de Reya*: solicitor liable for failure to make commons search; *GP & P Ltd v Bulcraig and Davies*: solicitor liable for failure to notice planning restrictions; *Raintree Ltd v Homes*: solicitor liable for failure to check currency of planning permission (which was due to expire between exchange and completion); *Oates v Pittman & Co:* solicitor liable for failure to find out that there was no planning permission for use as holiday-lets and of building regulation and fire prevention requirements if an application for a retrospective permission was to be made; *Faragher v Gerber*: solicitor liable for failure to follow up a reply to a local authority search which suggested that the purchaser should consult the LDDC; *Owen v Fielding*: solicitor liable for failure to make adequate commons search.[3]

(iii)   Rates and tenancies

Goody v Baring: solicitor liable for failure to establish whether rents of property liable to be reduced on certification under the Rent Acts; *Computastaff Ltd v Ingledew, Brown Bennison and Garrett*: solicitor liable for failure to ascertain the rateable value of the property.[4]

(iv)   Easements and restrictive covenants

Ford v White: solicitor liable for failure to advise on terms of restrictive covenant against building; *Piper v Daybell Court-Cooper & Co*: solicitor liable for failure to establish and advise on the existence of a right of way; *King v Hawkins & Co*: solicitor liable for failure to discover public highway; *Strover v Harrington*: solicitor should have advised that he had been told (contrary to the replies to inquiries) that the property had no mains drainage; *Walker v Giffen Couch & Archer*: solicitor liable for failure to discover existence of public footpath; *Hayes v Dodd*: solicitor liable for failing to establish that a workshop and maisonette had a right of way for two way traffic; *Reeves v Thrings & Long*: solicitor not liable for failing to explain that there was no secure right of way to a hotel car park; *Bittlestone v Keegan*: solicitor liable for failure to point out a covenant which prevented the owner from carrying out alterations; *Carvin v Dunham Brindley & Linn*: solicitor not liable for failure to advise purchaser that he should not be satisfied with a licence of drainage through an unadopted drain but acquire the freehold (or an easement); *Carter v TG Baynes & Sons*: solicitor liable for failure to notice covenant restrictive of development.[5]

1   [1993] NPC 99; [1996] PNLR 361; [1996] PNLR 431; [1996] EGCS 123; (1981) 125 DLR (3d) 326. In *Scarfe v Adams* [1981] 1 All ER 843 the Court of Appeal gave general guidance about the scale and dimensions of plans. It is suggested that if a solicitor failed to comply with this guidance (in preparing plans) or failed to make further inquiries where plans were not sufficiently detailed, this would be a breach of duty.
2   [1949] 2 All ER 964. The defendant was also retained by the vendor who told him, when he asked about the absence of planning permission, that he would 'make it right' for the plaintiff.
3   [1978] 1 WLR 266; [1986] 2 EGLR 148 (appeal on damages at [1988] 1 EGLR 138); (1984) 134 NLJ 453, CA, (1998) 76 P & CR 490, CA [1994] EGCS 122 and [1998] EGCS 110. *Emmet* Vol I at 1.042 et seq suggests that the standard form Oyez preliminary inquiries may be insufficient. It also discusses what obligations a vendor may have to disclose the terms of planning permissions. These issues are beyond the scope of this book but may have some bearing on whether adequate searches have been made.
4   [1956] 1 WLR 448 and (1983) 268 Estates Gazette 906. The facts of *Goody v Baring* are not likely to arise again in practice but it remains critical for purchasing landlord's solicitors to satisfy themselves about tenancies because of the Landlord & Tenant Act 1987.
5   [1964] 1 WLR 885; (1969) 210 Estates Gazette 1047; (1982) Times, 28 January; [1988] Ch 390; [1988] EGCS 64; [1990] 2 All ER 815; [1996] PNLR 265; [1997] EGCS 8; [1997] EGCS 90, CA and [1998] EGCS 109. In *Bittlestone v Keegan* [1997] EGCS 8 Sir John Vinelott stated that it was the solicitor's duty to point out the nature and effect of every restrictive covenant unless unenforceable.

(e)   Advice on the terms

8.54   It goes without saying that the solicitor must advise his client fully about the terms of the contract which he is about to enter. In *Walker v Boyle*[1] Dillon J gave the following guidance:

'It is, of course, the duty of a solicitor to advise his client about any abnormal or unusual term in a contract, but I think it is perfectly normal and proper for a solicitor to use standard forms of conditions of sale such as the National Conditions of Sale. I do not think he is called on to go through the small print of those somewhat lengthy conditions with a toothcomb every time he is advising a purchaser to draw to the purchaser's attention every problem which on a careful reading of the conditions might in some circumstance or other conceivably arise. I cannot believe that purchasers of house property throughout the land would be overjoyed at having some lengthy explanations of the National Conditions of Sale ritually foisted upon them.'

In *Stinchcombe and Cooper Ltd v Addison, Cooper, Jesson & Co*[2] Brightman J held that it was a solicitor's duty to inform the client 'of what was needed to obtain a conveyance of the land' in relation to a conditional contract which provided for completion 14 days after a building had been completed.

1   [1982] 1 WLR 495 at 507F–H.
2   (1971) 115 Sol Jo 368, a rather extreme example, because the solicitor failed to understand or point out that contracts had been exchanged at all.

(f)   Leasehold purchasers

8.55   When the client proposes to take the grant or assignment of a lease, one of the key functions of the solicitor will be to explain to the client the terms of the lease which the landlord proposes to grant or the assignor to assign. The solicitor will not be required to recite and explain mechanically every term of the lease, and those which should be mentioned and which ignored will inevitably be a question of judgment. Similar guidance to that quoted above was given by Bingham LJ in *County Personnel Ltd v Alan R Pulver & Co*[1] in the context of leases. Again without attempting to identify exhaustively the clauses upon which a solicitor should concentrate, solicitors have been found liable or escaped liability in the following cases concerned with the terms of leases:[2]

(i)   User clauses

Hill v Harris: solicitor liable for failure to establish that a headlease prohibited the use permitted by the underlease without the head landlord's consent; *Sykes v Midland Bank Executor and Trustee Co Ltd*: solicitor liable for failure to advise that user clause contained a prohibition qualified not only by the lessor's consent (such consent not to be unreasonably withheld) but also by the head landlord's consent and to discover that the headlease contained an absolute prohibition on change of use; *Transportation Agency Ltd v Jenkins*: solicitor liable for failure to advise an investor in a snack bar business that cooking was prohibited by the user clause; *Simple Simon Catering Ltd v Binstock Miller & Co*: solicitor liable for failure to advise a client who was proposing to use premises as a restaurant that there was a covenant to permit the landlord to share use of the kitchen.[3]

(ii)   Rent review clauses

County Personnel Ltd v Alan R Pulver & Co: solicitor liable for failure to advise about a clause which required a subtenant of part to pay a rent increased by the same percentage differential as under the headlease; *Forbouys v Gadhavi*: rent review due between exchange and completion, solicitor advised as to timing of the review but not liable for failing to advise against a sub-sale until the review had been determined;

Sonardyne Ltd v Firth & Co: solicitor liable for failure to point out that the new rent would take into account improvements carried out by the tenant; *Halifax Building Society v Grosse*: solicitor liable for failure to advise that rent review was linked to the headlease and that he could not obtain a copy of that lease; *Inter-leisure Ltd v Lamberts* and *Theodore Goddard v Fletcher King Services Ltd*: solicitors liable for failure to ensure that there was an upwards only clause.[4]

(iii)   Alienation clauses

Murray v Lloyd: solicitor liable for failure to advise that the consequence of a covenant against assignment in a residential lease was that if the assignment in a residential lease was taken in the name of the company, the landlord could refuse consent to assign to an individual and prevent enfranchisement, *Kennedy v Van Emden*: solicitor liable for failure to advise that it was illegal to charge a premium on assignment; *Siasati v Bottoms & Webb*: solicitor liable for failure to advise that a full repairing lease of a shop and residential premises (which were in poor condition) contained a covenant to charge the residential premises to the landlord and not to create any other mortgage or charge without the landlord's consent; *Shaw v Fraser Southwell*: solicitor liable for failure to advise that the alienation clause in the lease of a flat restricted assignment, transfer, subletting and parting with possession except to a limited company only for the purposes of use as a high class residence for the occupation of one family only.[5]

1   [1987] 1 WLR 916, CA at 923, quoted in chapter 2, para 2.32 where further consideration is given to this point.
2   It is noted that a number of these cases are concerned with the terms of the headlease and their operation on a sub-lease (which the new tenant's solicitors had not seen).
3   [1965] 2 QB 601 at 618B–C; [1971] 1 QB 113; (1972) 223 Estates Gazette 1101; (1973) 228 Estates Gazette 527.
4   [1987] 1 WLR 916; [1993] NPC 122; [1997] EGCS 84; [1997] EGCS 111; [1997] NPC 49; [1997] 32 EG 90. The latter two are 'landlord's' cases not tenants but also mentioned here for completeness sake. In *Pulver* it was accepted that the client was advised that the original rent would be increased in step with increases in the headlease but this was held to be inadequate.
5   [1989] 1 WLR 1060, [1996] PNLR 409, [1997] EGCS 22, (25 March 1999, unreported), CA. The first decision is one on damages not liability and the assignment was taken in the name of the company on the advice of the defendants for the purpose of avoiding tax. In the third there was also a finding that the defendant failed to advise the plaintiff about the onerous nature of the rent review clause.

2   Duties on exchange of contracts

8.56   When the solicitor has received instructions to enter a contract it follows that he or she is then under an obligation to do so in a binding form[1] with a person of full capacity[2] containing the terms agreed by the client[3] and within the time limit agreed with the vendor[4] and, if possible, simultaneously with the client's own sale.[5] In practice most difficulties with the form and execution of the contract will be generated by s 2 of the Law of Property (Miscellaneous Provisions) Act 1989 and the requirement that contracts of sale be signed by both parties and contain all of the terms which have been agreed. Issues arising on this section are outside the scope of this book.[6] However, mistakes such as that made in *Harrison v Battye*[7] where the contracts signed by each party were not in identical terms and the vendor's solicitor returned the purchaser's signed part rather than his own client's[8] are not untypical.

1   *Parker v Rolls* (1854) 14 CB 691 (Jervis CJ).
2   *Clarke v Milford* (1987) 38 DLR (4th) 139.

3   *Costa v Georghiou* (1983) 1 PN 201, solicitor failing to insert rent review clause in lease.
4   *Simpson v Grove Tompkins & Co* (1982) 126 Sol Jo 347, CA.
5   *Buckley v Lane Herdman & Co* [1977] CLY 3143 (HHJ Faye).
6   See *Emmet* at 2.036 et seq.
7   [1975] 1 WLR 58, CA.
8   The first mistake was held to be fatal to a binding contract but not the second. Absent estoppel, both would be held to be fatal now.

Exchange

8.57   The Law Society has provided formulae for exchanging contracts by telephone, telex and now by fax.[1] Each formula provides for undertakings to be given by solicitors to each other (and on behalf of their firms). A failure to abide by the terms of the formulae would in all probability be a breach of duty where that breach of duty involved the client in loss. There are also risks inherent in the use of the formulae to exchange contracts by telephone. The parties must trust each other to make what may be critical and complicated amendments to contracts, they are at the mercy of the post, and where deposit monies are to fund a deposit further down a chain the risks are obvious. A solicitor may have to draw a client account cheque for his client's deposit before he has received the money himself.[2] Where the solicitor acts for both parties, no exchange of contracts is necessary if both parties sign the same document.[3]

1   See *The Guide* Annex 25D.
2   See *Castle* 'Exchange of contracts by Formula B: some horror stories': LSG, 18 November 1986. See also *Colby* 'Rates of Exchange'[1998] 46 EG 180 for pitfalls in the electronic age.
3   *Smith v Mansi* [1963] 1 WLR 26, CA.

3   Duties post-contract

(a)   Searches and investigation of title

8.58   Traditionally the purchaser's solicitor investigates and considers the adequacy of title after exchange of contracts. In registered conveyancing the only search which is usually made by a solicitor is a Land Registry search affording priority to his or her client pending completion.[1] It is not usual to repeat inquiries or searches which have been carried out prior to exchange. However, in *Goody v Baring*[2] Danckwerts J. stated that it was still necessary for a solicitor to repeat the inquiries (if only in the form of requesting the vendor to confirm that the replies to inquiries remain correct) after contract and prior to completion.[3] Where searches are out of date, particularly a local land charges registry search, it may be that a solicitor should make a further search before completion. Where the solicitor is instructed after exchange, eg where the property is purchased at auction, it is likely that it would be found negligent not to carry out the standard searches especially if they gave grounds for rescission of the contract. Unregistered conveyancing is now rare but a solicitor may still be called upon to check title to land which is unregistered and then to make an application for first registration. This process would normally take place after exchange. In *Pilkington v Wood*[4], in which negligence was admitted, the defendant failed to notice that the vendor had acquired part of the subject property from the trustees of his father's will of whom he was one. It was argued that this was a technical breach of duty only but Harman J held that because the class of beneficiaries who could claim under the will was not closed, the purchaser obtained a defective title only and could be dispossessed.[5]

1   It is in fact more common today for a solicitor to carry out the search before exchange and now
     that the register is open there is no reason why he or she cannot do so. It is unlikely that a failure
     to carry out a search before contract is negligent provided that the purchaser is adequately protected.
2   [1956] 1 WLR 448 at 456.
3   The words used by the judge were 'requisitions and inquiries'. It is unlikely that he had in
     mind repeating local authority searches: compare *Kotowich v Petursson* [1994] 3 WWR 669,
     solicitor not liable for failure to establish the planning position *after* exchange.
4   [1953] Ch 770.
5   At 775. It is doubtful whether this would constitute a blot on the title to registered land because
     the purchaser would have no notice of the trusts.

(b)   Encumbrances

8.59   One important duty of the solicitor after exchange is to ensure that any encumbrances to which the sale is not intended to be subject are discharged and no further encumbrances are registered pending completion. In *Holmes v H Kennard & Sons*[1] the defendants were found liable for a failure to ensure that notice of a charge registered under the Matrimonial Homes Act 1967 was removed from the register of the subject property prior to completion. They had received a form 71 from the wife's solicitors but the Land Registry refused to accept this. It was in the wrong form and the wife's solicitors had no actual or ostensible authority to agree to the discharge of the charge. In the case of the simple residential house purchase where completion is agreed at 28 days after exchange it is usual for the client's interest to be protected solely by a priority search. In more complex cases it will be negligent if the solicitor fails to protect his client's priority either by registering a caution or insisting that it is a term of the contract that a notice or restriction be entered in the proprietorship register of the relevant title.[2]

1   (1984) 49 P & CR 202.
2   See, eg, *Bell v Peter Browne & Co* [1990] 2 QB 495, CA (failure to register caution to protect
     agreement to receive part of the proceeds of sale). Of course, the caution does not afford the
     client priority per se, only the right to be informed of a pending registration. The solicitor will
     have to take further steps to ensure that priority is maintained.

(c)   Conditions

8.60   It is axiomatic that the solicitor must satisfy himself or herself that any conditions which require to be satisfied before the purchase is completed are satisfied before completing. In *Creech v Mayorcas*[1] the defendant's clerk failed to ensure that the landlord's licence to assign was obtained before completing the assignment.

1   (1966) 198 EG 1091 (Pennycuick J).

(d)   Occupiers

8.61   By Land Registration Act 1925, s 70(1)(g) the rights of every person in actual occupation of the land are overriding interests and binding on a purchaser except where inquiry has been made of such persons and the rights have not been disclosed. Moreover, any right or interest of a person who goes into occupation prior to completion of the purchase will be binding as an overriding interest.[1] Finally a purchaser will be fixed with constructive notice of those rights which he could reasonably have discovered from an inspection of the property and inquiries of the occupier.[2] The standard form inquiries before contract ask about occupiers and if the replies disclose the existence of occupiers with potential rights, the solicitor would be at risk of a claim for negligence if he or she did not advise the purchaser to make further inquiries of the occupiers personally as to their rights in the property. Furthermore, it not infrequently occurs that a purchaser will agree to purchase a property, which is currently let, with vacant possession but on the vendor's assurance that the tenancy will be determined. Again, a solicitor would be at risk of a claim for negligence if he failed to advise the purchaser that there could be no guarantee that the tenant would quit and that the tenancy would continue to be binding.[3]

1   *Abbey National Building Society v Cann* [1991] 1 AC 56.
2   See *Kingsnorth Trust Ltd v Tizard* [1986] 1 WLR 783 and *Emmet* Vol I at 1.155.
3   Short of making the contract conditional on a deed of surrender, there appears to be no way of ensuring that vacant possession would be obtained on completion. The solicitor must, therefore, give appropriate advice.

8.62   In unregistered conveyancing the purchaser will be bound by rights which either come to his or her solicitor's notice or which ought to have come to the solicitor's notice if such inquiries and inspections which ought reasonably to have been made, had been made: see Law of Property Act 1925, s 199(1)(ii). Although registration of title is compulsory in England and Wales, this section will apply to conveyances or transfers on first registration. It also has effect in relation to the knowledge of a solicitor acquired in a registered conveyancing transaction where a question of notice arises.[1] Accordingly, if a solicitor fails to make reasonable inquiries in relation to rights to occupy land, his client may be bound by that failure despite the fact that neither client nor solicitor had actual knowledge of the rights being asserted.[2]

1   Most notably in undue influence cases: see the discussion in para 8.17. In *Barclays Bank plc v Boulter* [1998] 1 WLR 1 at 11B–D, CA, Mummery LJ confirmed that notice remains relevant where the land in question is registered. The issue may also arise in other circumstances: see, eg *Norwich and Peterborough Building Society v Steed (No 2)* [1993] Ch 116, CA. The question of notice may also arise in relation to certain issues concerning restrictive covenants. It should also be noted that the subsection only applies to knowledge which was acquired or which ought to have been acquired 'in the same transaction to which a question of notice to the purchaser arises': see *Halifax Mortgage Services v Stepsky* [1996] Ch 207, CA.
2   For circumstances in which it would be reasonable to make no further inquiries, see *Emmet* Vol I at 5.155 which provides a helpful distinction between an occupier's rights consistent with the documents disclosed to the purchaser (and his solicitors) and rights which are inconsistent with the documents.

(e)   Advice

8.63   The solicitor has no duty to repeat advice given prior to exchange of contracts once the client is bound.[1] *Neighbour v Barker*[2] illustrates the way in which the solicitor's duties may differ before contract and after. In that case the defendants advised the plaintiffs to have a survey before contract. This advice was not taken but after exchange of contracts the plaintiffs engaged a surveyor who reported that the property suffered from substantial defects. The defendants advised the plaintiffs to complete because they were bound. It later transpired that the plaintiffs had grounds for rescinding the contract. The defendants were found not to be liable for failing to advise the plaintiffs to explore ways of escaping from their obligations. However, in *Peyman v Lanjani*[3] a solicitor was found liable for failure to advise a purchaser that he had grounds for rescinding a contract. Where for instance time is of the essence it is incumbent on the solicitor to remind the client.[4]

1   See *Elland Developments Ltd v Smith* [1995] EGCS 141 (Rattee J).
2   [1992] 40 EG 140, CA.
3   [1985] Ch 457, CA at 478D–G.
4   See, eg, *Stinchcombe and Cooper Ltd v Addison, Cooper, Jesson & Co* (1971) 115 Sol Jo 368 (Brightman J).

4 Duties on completion

8.64 It is the solicitor's duty to complete the purchase on behalf of his client and this obligation involves ensuring that the client obtains title to the property.[1] In the case of the purchaser's solicitor this usually involves a tender of the purchase price (usually by telegraphic transfer or, less commonly now, banker's draft[2]) in return for the documents of title and a statutory receipt and discharge of any mortgage or legal charge. According to Lord Brightman in *Edward Wong Finance Ltd v Johnson, Stokes and Master*:[3]

> 'The normal method of completing a contract for the sale of land in England is for the purchaser's solicitor to deliver to the vendor's solicitor a draft for the balance of the purchase price in exchange for an executed grant of the land or interest in the land contracted to be sold; if the property is subject to a mortgage, the mortgagee will either be a party to the grant and will receive the whole or part of the purchase money by way of redemption; or he will execute a separate release of his charge in return for the redemption money; if the property to be purchased is to be financed by a new mortgage, the loan will be made against delivery of the executed grant and instrument of charge. In other words, the payment of money and perfection of title are simultaneous transactions. This procedure is merely a reflection of the common-sense principle that, in the absence of an agreement for credit, the purchase money is not handed over to the vendor or anyone else except in exchange for the delivery of the subject-matter of the sale, whether it be a loaf of bread or a parcel of land ...'

1   As opposed to mere possession, see *Dogma Properties Ltd v Gale* (1984) 136 NLJ 453 (Kilner Brown J) where the purchaser's solicitors purported to complete and released the purchase price but failed to obtain a good title.
2   See (1969) 66 LSG 406 and 761.
3   [1984] AC 296 at 303F–304A.

8.65 Despite this statement made only 15 years ago it is rare in the writers' experience for there to be a personal completion or for two drafts to be given by the purchaser's solicitors to the vendor's solicitor, one for the mortgagee and one for the vendor. More often than not completion takes place by post in accordance with the Law Society's Code for Completion by Post[1] whereby the purchaser's solicitor authorises the vendor's solicitor to act as his agent and then commit the documents to the post or document exchange. The workability of this code—if it is adopted—depends upon the purchaser accepting undertakings from the vendor's solicitors and, in particular, an undertaking from the vendor's solicitor that he has the authority of any mortgagee to receive that part of the purchase price which is necessary to discharge the charge. The soundness of the code has never been tested in the English courts but it does seem that it fails to address the criticisms of the 'Hong Kong completion' made in *Edward Wong Finance Ltd v Johnson, Stokes and Master*. In that case it was held negligent for a solicitor in Hong King to rely upon a standard undertaking from the vendor's solicitor to provide within 10 days the documents of title and a reassignment of the property by the vendor's bank (the equivalent of a receipt and discharge) when the vendor's solicitor, who had no authority to receive the mortgage monies, absconded with the purchase price. If the vendor's solicitor had been authorised to receive the purchase price, then the purchaser would have been entitled to a discharge of the charge and the risk of defalcation would have fallen on the bank. Lord Brightman also posed and answered this question:[2]

> 'Their Lordships turn to the question whether the risk could have been avoided in the instant case. The answer, in their Lordships' view is that it could readily have been avoided without in any way undermining the basic features of the Hong Kong style

of completion. For example, all that is needed in such a case is that the purchaser's or lender's solicitor should take reasonable steps to satisfy himself that the vendor's or borrower's solicitor has authority from his client to receive the purchase money or loan; and, in the case of property already subject to a mortgage which is to be discharged, so much of the purchase price or loan as is needed to discharge the prior mortgage could be paid by cheque or draft in favour of the mortgagee or his duly authorised agent, and not by a draft in favour of the vendor's solicitor.'

1   1984, revised 1996. Set out in Annex 25E of *The Guide*.
2   [1984] AC 296 at 307G–308B.

8.66   There is a real risk that the provisions of the Law Society's code do not contain sufficient safeguards to avoid, or minimise, the risk of fraud or defalcation. First, the code does not require the purchaser's solicitor to obtain confirmation from the lender itself that the vendor's solicitor has authority to give a receipt for the mortgage monies. In *Holmes v H Kennard & Son*[1] it was considered negligent for a solicitor to rely on a form signed by the vendor's solicitors without confirming that they had the authority to act and a representation by an agent as to his authority will not bind the principal unless that agent has authority to make the representation. The court could find that the solicitor acting for a purchaser who does no more than request the vendor's solicitor to confirm that he has the requisite authority has not taken reasonable steps to satisfy himself that the vendor's solicitor has that authority. Second, Lord Brightman indicated that the solicitor should also pay the balance of the mortgage debt by cheque or draft addressed directly to the lender. The Law Society's code does not require this.

1   (1984) 49 P & CR 202, CA. See para 8.59.

8.67   In the case of building society mortgages the vendor's solicitor will often give a standard form undertaking to discharge the mortgage and to supply the receipted mortgage or legal charge or Form 53 to the purchaser's solicitors once discharged. Again this practice which has also been endorsed by the Law Society suffers from the same deficiencies. It would not prevent a dishonest solicitor from taking the purchase price in circumstances where the purchaser could not insist on a discharge of the mortgage or charge.[1]

1   See *Emmet* Vol I at 11.079 for the form of undertaking and certain additional criticisms. The editors are of the view that accepting such an undertaking would lead to a finding of negligence: see 11.080.

8.68   In the vast majority of cases the use of either practice discussed above will involve no loss. It is possible that the court might find that it is not unreasonable for the purchaser's solicitor to rely upon an undertaking given by a firm consisting of more than one partner but not upon an undertaking given by a sole practitioner.[1] But this does not seem logical or fair.[2] It is more likely that the courts would either uphold it as reasonable or condemn the practice as a whole. Moreover, there may be other reasons why these practices are risky apart from the possibility that the vendor's solicitor is dishonest. The vendor's solicitor may have failed to get the authority of his client's mortgagee to give a receipt by an oversight; there may be confusion or delay whilst the lender prepares and dispatches the receipted charge or Form 53; and it may also be that the lender gives an inaccurate redemption statement which it then seeks to amend at the same time refusing to discharge the charge. In most cases this will lead to delay but no loss. However, if the vendor's solicitor has released some part of the purchase price to the vendor in the expectation that the charge would be discharged but it is not discharged, the purchaser may be unable to obtain title to the property at all or recover the purchase price from the vendor.[3]

1   As was the case in *Edward Wong Finance Ltd v Johnson, Stokes and Master* [1984] AC 296.
2   First, whilst it is true that the purchaser might have recourse to the indemnity insurance of the other
     partner or partners, this should not be a factor in determining whether it was negligent to rely on
     the undertaking. Second, even where there is more than one partner this is unlikely to have any
     effect on whether the firm has genuinely obtained authority. Third, although it does seem less likely
     that a dishonest solicitor could withdraw the purchase price from the firm's client account in a firm
     of more than one partner, this may not be strong enough to justify such an extreme distinction.
3   Consider the facts of *Boscawen v Bajwa* [1995] 4 All ER 769, CA.

8.69 If the parties' solicitors do not formally adopt the Law Society's code in
correspondence or, where there is a building society mortgage, the vendor's solicitor
does not give an undertaking to obtain a discharge, the purchaser's solicitor will
inevitably be found liable in negligence if he or she releases the purchase price but
fails to obtain title in reliance on the vendor's solicitor.[1] Again, if the vendor is a
solicitor and is representing himself, it could well be negligent to rely upon his
undertaking. Finally, if the vendor is not represented or not represented by a qualified
solicitor, it may be negligent for the purchaser's solicitor to adopt conventional
practice for exchange and completion of contracts for the sale of land.[2]

1   See *Dogma Properties Ltd v Gale* (1984) 136 NLJ 453 (Kilner Brown J).
2   See *The Guide* at 25.07 and Annex 25A which sets out a code for dealing with unqualified
     conveyancers and *Emmet* Vol I at 1.001 et seq. There appear to be no particular practical
     difficulties in dealing with a licensed conveyancer: see *The Guide* at 25.06.

8.70 A solicitor is at risk of a claim for negligence if he fails to have the relevant
transfer or instrument stamped as necessary[1] and he or she has a duty to retain and
preserve the relevant documents of title prior to registration.[2] By Land Registration
Act 1925, s 123(1) every conveyance of land, every grant or assignment of a lease for
a term of more than 21 years is void so far as regards the conveyance or grant of the
legal estate if no application is made to register it within two months of the date of
delivery of the relevant instrument. A solicitor who fails to apply to register his client's
purchase within that time will be negligent. It will also be negligent for a solicitor to
fail to deal with requisitions raised by the Land Registry either within the time specified[3]
or within a reasonable time. The solicitor must also understand and appreciate the
consequences of a failure to register. In *Hartle v Laceys*[4] the defendant, who was acting
for the plaintiff purchaser, was found liable for informing the vendor after completion that
a restrictive covenant given by his client had not been registered. He had failed to realise
that the covenant would be void against a subsequent purchaser and prevented his client
from taking the opportunity to sell on before the covenant was registered.

1   Compare *Parker v Rolls* (1854) 14 CB 691 (Jervis CJ).
2   Registration is now compulsory in all parts of England and Wales.
3   The consequence of a failure to do so may be that the Land Registry will cancel the application
     and, even if a fresh application is made, the purchaser will lose priority.
4   [1999] Lloyd's Rep PN 315, CA.

5   Damages

(a)   *Loss of opportunity to purchase*

8.71 If, as a consequence of the negligence of the defendant (D) the claimant (C)
loses the chance to buy a property, the appropriate measure of damage is likely to be
the difference between the purchase price at which C would have acquired the property
and its value at the date of contract: see *Nash v Phillips*[1] in which this measure of
damage was adopted subject to a 10% deduction for the risk that contracts would not

have been exchanged and the costs which would have been incurred. This case is perhaps better regarded as the application or modification of the usual principle on which loss of bargain damages are awarded for a breach of contract for the sale of land[2] rather than as an application of the valuation method. In *Stinchcombe and Cooper Ltd v Addison, Cooper, Jesson & Co*[3] where C had actually exchanged contracts but as a consequence of D's negligence the vendor (V) was able to rescind it C was awarded the difference between the purchase price and the value of the land at the date of rescission. In *Clarke v Milford*[4] in which Ds failed to obtain the sanction of the court to a sale by a minor and then to complete the purchase P recovered the purchase price which he had paid to V's guardian on the footing that he, as a minor, could never have been compelled to complete the contract. The complaint was that the purchase price could not be recovered. If no money had been paid by C to V it would follow that nominal damages would have been awarded and no damages for loss of purchase could have been recovered.

1   (1974) 232 Estates Gazette 1219 (Foster J). Damages for the cost of acquiring a more expensive substitute property were refused.
2   See *Emmet* Vol I at 7.020.
3   (1971) 115 Sol Jo 368 (Brightman J). The date of transaction might have been the more approriate date. There is no indication from the report that this was argued or would have made a difference.
4   (1987) 38 DLR (4th) 139.

(b)   Delayed purchase

8.72   Where D's negligence causes a delay in the purchase rather than the purchase to go off C ought to recover any consequential expenditure incurred. This would normally include the cost of additional accommodation, interest paid to V under the terms of the contract and general damages for inconvenience.[1] C may also incur additional finance costs which are in principle recoverable provided that they are not too remote. Where the negligent conduct causes C to lose a purchase at the original price but it is later acquired at a higher price, he or she ought to recover the difference between the price originally agreed and the market price of the property when finally acquired (usually the ultimate purchase price): see *Simpson v Grove, Tompkins & Co.*[2] However the market must be genuinely rising. In *Endhill Pty Ltd v Grasso, Searles & Romano*[3] it was held that an increase in price which C had agreed to pay after settling specific performance proceedings was irrecoverable because the increase in price simply reflected a decrease in the value of money[4] and not a genuine lost bargain.

1   There appears to be no direct authority but see, by analogy, *Bailey v Bullock* [1950] 2 All ER 1167, CA (solicitor's failure to obtain possession on behalf of landlord client) and *Raineri v Miles* [1981] AC 1050 at 1094H.
2   (1982) Times, 17 May, CA. In most cases, the market price at the later date will be the purchase price. In this case, it was held that the plaintiff had paid too much.
3   [1993] 2 Qd R 136.
4   This decision may need to be treated with some caution: it is not clear from the report what the negligence of the solicitors was; the delay was substantial and part of it caused by the plaintiff's decision to deal with other projects first.

(c)   Defective purchase (1): valuation method applied

8.73   In *Pilkington v Wood*[1] C was awarded the difference between the market value of the property with a good title and its value subject to a defect in title but no damages for improvements which C had carried out to the property. The purchase price was treated as the market value at the date of breach. In *Ford v White*[2] Pennycuick J rejected the submission that damages should be awarded on a warranty basis, ie the difference between the actual value of the property and the value which it would have had without the defect, and awarded as damages the difference between the purchase price and the market value of the property. Given that V had offered it for sale subject to the restrictions and at a market price (but D failed to notice this) damages were nominal. It was accepted by the judge that if, when C had learnt of the defect, he had attempted to sell, he might have recovered damages for his wasted expenditure.[3] In *Piper v Daybell, Court-Cooper & Co*[4] C recovered the difference between the price paid for the property and its market value at the date of purchase subject to a right of way. In *Collard v Saunders*[5] C was awarded the difference between the purchase price (representing market value of the property as it was assumed to be) and its value out of repair. In *Faragher v Gerber*[6] C was awarded the difference between the price paid and its value in the light of a proposed highway development to which D ought to have drawn her attention.[7] In *Wapshott v Davies Donovan & Co*[8] Cs were awarded the difference between the purchase price of the properties and their actual value at the date of breach despite the fact that they were locked into the properties by D's negligence and lost a purchaser at a higher price when the defect came to light. It was common ground that Cs would not have purchased the property. The award placed them in the position they would have been in if they had never bought and a generous award of interest compensated them for locking up their capital. In *Connor & Labrum v Regoczi-Ritzman*[9] Robert Walker J held that Cs were entitled to their expenditure on acquiring and improving the property (including mortgage interest) less its value at the date of trial because it remained unsold. He too refused to award the loss of profit on resale. In *Owen v Fielding*[10] Cs were awarded the difference between the price paid for the property and the value of the property subject to the rights of common which D had failed to identify. The judge found this to be 80% of the purchase price on the basis that Cs would have obtained a 20% discount at the date of purchase if they had known of the defect. D's submission that Cs' profits on resale should be taken into account were rejected.[11] In *Oates v Pittman & Co*[12] it was common ground that Cs were entitled to the difference between the price paid by Cs on the assumption that the property had planning permission for Cs' proposed use as holiday lets and its actual value at the date of purchase. The issue argued on the appeal was whether Cs were entitled to the profits which they would have earned from the holiday business and this claim was rejected. Cs were awarded the costs of obtaining a retrospective (albeit more limited) planning permission. In *Shaw v Fraser Southwell*[13] C was awarded the difference between the purchase price and the value of the property subject to an onerous alienation covenant. The small profit realised by C eight years after the purchase after he had taken a number of steps to extricate himself was considered too remote. Finally, in *Cygnet Health Care plc v Elletson & Co*[14] C was awarded the difference between the purchase price of the properties (three cottages) and their value subject to a planning condition restricting their use of three cottages subject to a planning condition restricting their use for agricultural workers. P was also awarded interest on their capital value and the cost of maintenance whilst the condition was being removed.[15]

1 [1953] Ch 770 (Harman J).
2 [1964] 1 WLR 885 (Pennycuick J).
3 At 888. P elected to stay. If the court had found that he would not have bought the property at all and he had sought to extricate himself, it is suggested that he could have recovered any loss on a resale.
4 (1969) 210 Estates Gazette 1047 (Nield J).
5 (1972) 222 Estates Gazette 795 (Mocatta J).
6 [1994] EGCS 122 (HHJ Lachs).
7 See also *Mercantile Building Society v J W Mitchell Dodds & Co* [1993] NPC 99, CA, where the rule also appears to have been applied.

8   [1996] PNLR 361, CA. See the discussion of this case at chapter 3, para 3.56.
9   (1995) 70 P & CR D41–3. The case is included in this classification because the judge expressly
     applied the valuation method albeit at the date of sale. It may be no more than a question of
     semantics but it is perhaps better regarded as an extrication case.
10   [1998] EGCS 110 (Steel J).
11   The profit was due to Cs' decision to apply for planning permission, subdivide the property
     and resell: see chapter 3, para 3.47. Damages for inconvenience were also refused.
12   (1998) 76 P & CR 490, CA.
13   (25 March 1999, unreported), CA.
14   (10 May 1999, unreported) (HH Judge Elizabeth Steel).
15   It appears that P would have purchased at the lower price rather than not purchased at all.
     Accordingly, the additional expenses were properly recoverable. Compare *Patel v Hooper
     and Jackson* [1999] Lloyd's Rep PN 1 at 7–8, CA.

(d)   Defective purchase (2): the extrication cases

8.74   In *County Personnel Ltd v Alan R Pulver & Co*[1] C was awarded the cost of
surrendering a lease with a defective rent review clause as the primary head of loss.
Two slightly different reasons were given by the court for departing from what the
court called the diminution in value rule and which we call the valuation method:
Bingham LJ considered that the rule would involve 'a somewhat speculative and
unreal valuation exercise intended to reflect the substantive negative value of this
underlease'. Sir Nicolas Browne-Wilkinson considered that the rule was inappropriate and that a rule concerned with capital diminution would be 'wholly artificial' for
a lease at a rack rent which had no capital value and would have had no capital value
even if the rent review clause had not been defective.[2]

1   [1987] 1 WLR 916 at 926C and 928A, CA. This figure also included arrears of rent due as
     a consequence of a rent review.
2   [1987] 1 WLR 916 at 926B and 927G–928A.

8.75   In *GP & P Ltd v Bulcraig and Davies*[1] a planning restriction was not discovered
until C had gone into receivership at which point the receiver surrendered the lease but
this time for value. Again it was found that C would not have taken the lease if properly
advised and it recovered all of its expenditure less the amount received on surrender. It
was common ground that C was obliged to give credit for the benefit of occupying the
premises for 18 months during which it had traded without interference until surrender. The
issue before the Court of Appeal was whether C was obliged to give credit at a rate equal
to a market rent or for rent at the very low rate negotiated by C itself.[2] It was held that C
had to give credit at the higher rate because it would not have received the benefit of a
low rent if it had not entered the transaction.

1   [1986] 2 EGLR 148 (John Gorman QC) and [1988] 1 EGLR 138, CA.
2   It was also common ground that C had to give credit for the value of the premises in their
     improved state since C recovered the capital cost of the improvements.

8.76   In *Hayes v Dodd*[1] Cs were awarded all of the costs incurred by them in the
acquisition, operation and resale of a workshop and maisonette with defective rights
of access over a six year period. The heads of loss included the cost of the lease of the
workshop, the freehold of the maisonette, the goodwill of the business and the plant,
rates, insurance, bank interest, travel costs and other costs. The reason given by
Staughton LJ for the departure from the diminution in value rule was that Cs would
not have bought if they had been properly advised, the case was not 'concerned with
a readily saleable commodity' and it took Cs, who were only able to trade for one year,
nearly six years from the date of purchase to dispose of their interest. Cs were, however,
required to give credit for the profit which they realised on resale of the maisonette.[2]

It was also held that the conduct of Cs was a reasonable response to the predicament in which they found themselves.[3] *Hayes v Dodd* was directly applied in *Siasati v Bottoms & Webb*.[4] Wasted expenditure was also awarded as the primary head of loss in *Transportation Agency Ltd v Jenkins*.[5] In *Patel v Hooper & Jackson*[6] the court distinguished *Hayes v Dodd* because Cs would have bought another property. They recovered the diminution in value together with their rent and expenses when they moved out of the property. They did not recover the mortgage payments because they would have incurred these anyway.

1   [1990] 2 All ER 815, CA.
2   [1990] 2 All ER 815 at 819g–820b and 822d–h. On the facts Cs were only required to give credit for 80% of the profit on resale.
3   See also *Bridgegrove v Smith* [1997] 2 EGLR 40, CA, a claim for misrepresentation brought by C against V in which it was held that although the term of the tenancy came to an end after six months, it was reasonable for C to remain in occupation on a monthly tenancy in an attempt to improve the business.
4   [1997] EGCS 22 (Geoffrey Brice QC).
5   (1972) 223 Estates Gazette 1101 (Kerr J) in which the judge drew up 'a balance of what the plaintiffs had in fact lost and gained'.
6   [1999] Lloyd's Rep PN 1.

(e)   Defective purchase (3): loss on resale

8.77   Normally C will not recover loss of profit on the resale of the property: see *Pilkington v Wood, Nash v Phillips, Wapshott v Davies Donovan & Co* and *Connor & Labrum v Regoczi-Ritzman*.[1] Where the property which was acquired was residential, as in each of these cases, this will usually be because the loss is too remote.[2] Where, however, D knew or ought to have known that C was intending to resell for profit, the court is likely to find that this profit was within the reasonable contemplation of the parties. In *G&K Ladenbau v de Reya*[3] where resale of the property was delayed by D's failure to identify rights of common over it, C was awarded the additional interest payable on the purchase price and also interest on the purchase price which would have been obtained. Mocatta J stated:

> 'The evidence of Mr Smith, a director of the plaintiff company, who went to see Mr Kaufmann of the defendants when the latter were originally instructed during Mr Franklyn's absence on holiday, was that Mr Kaufmann was told that the plaintiff's intention was to build a factory for shop fittings that would occupy an acre and develop the rest of the area and sell or let off the rest. In the light of these instructions, and in the state of the property market as it was then, the defendants should in my judgment have reasonably contemplated that if they failed to secure an unencumbered title for the plaintiffs without warning them of the defect, the damages the plaintiff would suffer were "not unlikely" to be the loss of a handsome profit on resale.'

In *Carter v TG Baynes & Sons*[4] where Ds failed to advise developer C of a density covenant C was awarded the difference between the value of the property when it would have been sold in 1991 and the price achieved in 1996 when a release of the covenant was obtained and increased borrowings as a consequence of the delay.

1   [1953] Ch 770 (Harman J), (1974) 232 Estates Gazette 1219 (Foster J), [1996] PNLR 361, CA and (1995) 70 P & CR D41–3 (Robert Walker J): see paras 8.71–8.73.
2   Consider also *Roker House Investments Ltd v Saunders* [1997] EGCS 137 (Alliott J) in which the loss on resale was ordered. The case is considered in *Vendors* at para 8.90. But this was a case where the property was an investment property and there was an express finding that if the defect had come to light it would have been cured.
3   [1978] 1 WLR 266 at 289C–F.
4   [1998] EGCS 109 (HHJ Prosser QC).

8.78   If C would not have purchased the property *at all* if properly advised, the overriding purpose of damages in tort should dictate that loss of profit on resale is irrecoverable however clear it was to D that C intended to resell. In *Pulver* the trial judge found that C would not have entered the lease with the defective rent review clause and C recovered the cost of surrendering the lease. C also claimed £17,000 for loss of a sale of the lease and the goodwill of its business. The case was remitted to the Master for an assessment of damages and Bingham LJ stated:[1]

> 'It must, however, be accepted on the findings of the deputy judge that if they had not been negligently advised the plaintiffs would not have entered into this underlease at all. This being so, damage cannot be assessed with reference to a specific gain which the plaintiffs could only have made if they had entered into this underlease, unless it be proper on the facts to conclude that properly advised, the plaintiffs would probably have been able to negotiate the grant of this underlease but without the offending clause. Even then the offer of £17,000 would call for closer scrutiny.'

In *Connor v Regoczi-Ritzman* the profit on resale was refused because it was a 'no transaction' case. In *Ladenbau v Crawley and de Reya* the judge made no specific finding either that C would have purchased the land in any event or, for that matter, that if Ds had acted with reasonable care, they could have obtained a release of the rights of common by the date on which C had originally intended to resell the property. However this seems implicit from the judgment. When C instructed new solicitors they were able buy in the rights and complete the resale within a four month period.[2]

1   *County Personnel Ltd v Alan R Pulver & Co* (1995) 70 P & CR D41 at 926E.
2   The short report in *Carter v TG Baynes & Sons* [1998] EGCS 109 does not indicate the basis on which lost profit on resale was awarded.

(f)   Defective purchase (4): cost of cure

8.79   In a number of cases the court has departed from the valuation method and awarded damages on what can best be described as a cost of cure basis. This measure of damage is most likely to be appropriate where C has mitigated his loss by curing the defect in question after the breach. In *Barclay-White v Guillaume*[1] C was awarded his out of pocket expenses but not the diminution in value of the property because it was later sold for current market value; in *Creech v Mayorcas*[2] where C took an assignment without the consent of the landlord, C was awarded £120 as the cost of obtaining a licence together with some consequential expenses; and in *Kennedy v Van Emden*[3] where the defect had been cured without inconvenience by the date of trial, C recovered nominal damages only.

1   [1996] EGCS 123 (HHJ Crawford QC). Cf *Nielsen v Watson* (1981) 125 DLR (3d) 326 where C was awarded the cost of buying in the missing strip of land together with out of pocket expenses.
2   (1966) 198 Estates Gazette 1091 (Pennycuick J).
3   [1996] PNLR 409, CA.

8.80   This measure may, however, also be appropriate where there is no available market for what C has lost. In *Murray v Lloyd*[1] C was advised by D to take the assignment of a lease for 15 years in the name of a company and so lost the opportunity to become a statutory tenant. She was awarded as damages the amount which it would cost to buy a similar tenancy which would carry such rights on termination. The judge stated:

> 'In my judgment, damages are to be assessed by reference to what it would cost the plaintiff to acquire what she has lost, ie the cost of acquiring similar rights of occupation on similar terms in similar alternative accommodation.'

The reason why the valuation method could not be applied was that the rights in question were personal and non-assignable and whilst unquestionably valuable could not be bought and sold on the open market.[2] To similar effect is *Layzell v Smith Morton & Long*[3] where D failed to serve a notice claiming a right to succession of a tenancy under the Agricultural Holdings Act 1986. C was awarded the cost of acquiring the freehold of a similar farm less the amount he would realise on a sale and leaseback of the farm on the terms of the original tenancy. In *Computastaff Ltd v Ingledew Brown Bennison and Garrett*[4] where C would not have taken a tenancy of the premises in question on the terms offered if it had been advised of their true rateable value, C was awarded the difference between the rates it expected to pay over the term and the rates which it actually had to pay.[5] The judge chose this measure purely for simplicity's sake but took comfort from the fact that the amount was close to that calculated by comparing the expenditure which C actually incurred with that which it would have incurred had it found cheaper premises. A similar approach was also taken in *Sonardyne Ltd v Firth & Co*[6] where C recovered the difference between the rent it would have paid if the rent review clause had disregarded tenant's improvements and the higher rent C was obliged to pay on review under the terms of the lease which did not contain this disregard. Curtis J found that the landlord would have agreed to disregard tenant's improvements on review if the point had been raised.

1 [1989] 1 WLR 106 (Mummery J).
2 See 1064D. Compare *Radford v de Froberville* [1977] 1 WLR 1262. The lack of an available market was one of the situations identified by Oliver J in which the cost of cure would be awarded.
3 [1992] 1 EGLR 169 (Schiemann J).
4 (1983) 268 Estates Gazette 906 (McNeill J).
5 Compare *Ford v White* [1964] 1 WLR 885 (Pennycuick J) and see chapter 3, para 3.58.
6 [1997] EGCS 84 (Curtis J).

(g) Damages for inconvenience

8.81 In *Hayes v Dodd*[1] the Court of Appeal refused to award damages for mental distress suffered as a consequence of D's breaches of duty where C acquired both a business and a residence and remained locked into them for a period of six years. In *Wapshott*[2] however they did award damages to Cs who had had children in 1988 and 1991 for the inconvenience and physical discomfort of living in a cramped and unsuitable flat between 1986 and 1992. The amount awarded was £3,000. In *Faragher v Gerber* C was awarded £6,000 for the physical inconvenience of a new highway development adjacent to the property.[3] In *Patel v Hooper & Jackson*[4] two plaintiffs were each awarded £2,000 for discomfort.

1 [1990] 2 All ER 815 at 823a–824c, CA.
2 [1996] PNLR 361 at 377D–379A, CA.
3 These are the most recent awards. Damages for physical inconvenience were also awarded in *Bailey v Bullock* [1950] 2 All ER 1167 (Barry J) and *Piper v Daybell* (1969) 210 Estates Gazette 1047 (Nield J) but not in *Nash v Phillips* (1974) 232 Estates Gazette 1219 (Foster J).
4 [1999] Lloyd's Rep PN 1.

C ACTING FOR THE VENDOR

1 Liability

(a) Contract races

8.82 Rule 6A of the Solicitors Practice Rules 1990[1] provides that where a solicitor is instructed by a vendor client to deal with more than one prospective buyer, he or she must disclose that decision to the solicitor acting for each prospective buyer by telephone or fax. If the vendor refuses to authorise such disclosure, the solicitor must immediately cease to act.[2] It would, therefore, be an implied term of the solicitor's retainer that he could terminate the retainer in these circumstances. Whether a breach of the rule would entitle any prospective purchaser to claim against the solicitor is very much more doubtful.

1   As amended with effect from 1 March 1995.
2   See *The Guide* at pp 397–9 for the full text of the rule and the notes which are to be read with it.

(b)   Commercial advice

8.83   As with purchasers a solicitor owes no general duty to give commercial advice to a client who is selling property. In the context of sales of land this issue usually arises where the client has agreed to sell at an undervalue. In *Bowdage v Harold Michelmore & Co*[1] it was held that it was not the solicitor's duty to advise his client that the price at which she had granted an option over her land was unreasonable and to advise her to consult a valuer. In *Johnson v Bingley, Dyson & Furey*[2] the judge also agreed that this was the general rule. However, he found the defendants negligent for failing to advise the client to take fresh valuation advice because (a) the solicitor had a concern about the capacity of the client and the fact that she was taking instructions through her son (who was a wages clerk) and (b) the son had agreed a price reduction which appeared to make no commercial sense.[3] In *Simmons v Pennington*,[4] the Court of Appeal found that a solicitor owed no duty to advise his client to resell the subject property pending proceedings to determine whether the purchaser had lawfully rescinded.

1   (1962) 106 Sol Jo 512 (Melford Stevenson J).
2   [1997] PNLR 392 (Benet Hytner QC).
3   See [1997] PNLR 392 at 408A–G.
4   [1955] 1 WLR 183, CA, considered in greater detail at para 8.84.

(c)   Searches and inquiries

8.84   A solicitor owes a duty to his own client to answer inquiries and requisitions carefully and accurately. It seems that a careless failure to disclose the existence of adverse rights or encumbrances to the purchaser which exposes the client to an action by the purchaser for rescission of the contract or for damages for misrepresentation will also subject the solicitor to a liability in negligence.[1] Of greater difficulty is the case in which the solicitor has obtained information which suggests the existence of an adverse right but is far from conclusive. One example of this sort of information is evidence of the use of a track across the land by neighbours and the occasional member of the public which the client may tolerate without taking action. The definitive map is unlikely to be up to date and show a public right of way and local authority searches are unlikely to be of real assistance. Should the solicitor disclose this information? If it is disclosed the contract may not proceed because the client cannot make a clear or satisfactory title to the land or the purchaser may seek a price reduction. If the evidence is not disclosed and a contract is made the purchaser may later have a claim for rescission for non-disclosure of a latent defect in title. But if the solicitor elects to disclose the information provided and the contract does go off, the client may seek to argue that the disclosure was negligent. *Simmons v Pennington*[2] offers support for the argument that a solicitor should not be held liable to his client in those circumstances. In that case a solicitor was not liable to his vendor client for disclosing to a purchaser that there had been breaches of a restrictive covenant as to user although no attempt had been made to enforce them.[3] It appears that the solicitor had not contemplated that his answer would entitle the purchaser to withdraw and it was held that he could not have been expected to anticipate the purchaser's withdrawal because he gave a standard answer to a standard requisition. If this is the true basis for the decision it is difficult to defend.[4] But we suggest nevertheless that the decision is right. The law encourages the vendor of land to make full disclosure of his title and a solicitor must give adequate disclosure to protect his client. If the consequence is that a purchaser withdraws the solicitor should not be held liable. In *Simmons v Pennington* the solicitor introduced a clause into the contract making the sale subject to any restrictions and he could not have answered the requisition truthfully in any other way. If he could have answered the question fully and truthfully without exposing his client to a liability the decision might have been different.[5]

1   See *Emmet* Vol 1 at 1.022A and *Cemp Properties (UK) Ltd v Dentsply Research and Development Corpn* [1989] 2 EGLR 205 (Morritt J) where the solicitors admitted liability for failure to disclose to the purchaser deeds which contained rights of light and air.
2   [1995] 1 WLR 183, CA.
3   The case is odd because the inquiry about breaches of covenant was made at the requisition stage rather than before contract. The vendor was asked whether there were any restrictive covenants and whether they had been observed; the defendant's clerk answered them truthfully; and this entitled the purchaser to withdraw for repudiatory breach.
4   See chapter 2, paras 2.25ff.
5   See Parker LJ [1995] 1 WLR 183 at 191 rejecting the claim that the solicitor might have used 'some more negative words'. But if this would have had the effect of keeping the contract alive, it is suggested that the solicitor was negligent in failing to do so.

(d)   Leases

8.85   In the same way that the solicitor must advise a potential tenant about the terms of the proposed lease, so must he or she advise a potential landlord. In *Inter-Leisure Ltd v Lamberts*[1] the defendants inserted an 'upwards downwards' rent review clause in the draft lease by mistake and failed to negotiate for an 'upwards only' clause or advise the client that the lease had been executed in this form. In *Theodore Goddard v Fletcher King Services Ltd*[2] the solicitors failed to notice that the part of a rent review clause which ensured that any rent review was upwards only had been removed by mistake. Interestingly they recovered a contribution against the client's agents and surveyors for failing to notice the mistake as well. If the client is proposing to grant a lease to a limited company the solicitor would not usually be required to advise the taking of a guarantee (unless the client had no commercial experience)[3] but in the event that a guarantee is required, the solicitor will be required to ensure that a binding guarantee in proper form is taken.[4] Where the client is an original tenant who has negotiated a sale of the lease the solicitor would be obliged to advise him or her of the continuing liabilities.[5]

1   [1997] NPC 49 (Michael Harvey QC). The cases digested in para 8.55 are equally applicable to landlords.
2   [1997] 32 EG 90 (HHJ Previte QC).
3   See *Allied Maples Group Ltd v Simmons & Simmons* [1995] 1 WLR 1602 at 1616G, CA where Stuart-Smith LJ stated that solicitors for an assignor would probably be negligent if they did not ask for a guarantee by a parent company of a subsidiary which was 'only marginally solvent'.
4   See *McElroy Milne v Commercial Electronics Ltd* [1993] NZLR 39. It is also submitted that it is not enough simply to take a guarantee. The solicitor ought also to consider fully and provide for the tenant company's insolvency.
5   See *Allied Maples* [1995] 1 WLR 1602 at 1608A–B, CA. The finding of negligence was not challenged on appeal. In fact the plaintiff in this case was a purchaser, but a purchaser of shares in a number of companies which had sold on a number of leases. The defendants were found liable for failure to advise the plaintiff of the subject companies' potential first tenant liabilities.

(e)   Making title

8.86   Prior to the introduction of registered land the principal task of the vendor's solicitor was to make title to the subject property. This rarely presents a problem in the modern era and this is borne out by a comparison between the relatively large number of cases in which disappointed purchasers claim against their solicitors as against the number of cases concerned with claims by disappointed vendors.[1]

1   For a case concerned with a vendor's licensed conveyancer failing to make title to an unregistered development site, see *Hitchens v Higgens & Bacchus* [1997] NPC 115, CA.

2   Damages

8.87   The valuation method was applied in *Johnson v Bingley Dyson & Furey*[1] where C would not have sold a freehold property ripe for development if she had been properly advised. She was awarded the difference between the market value at the date of breach (the date of sale) and the sale price. Deducted from the sale price was the amount which was required to pay compensation to a business tenant to obtain vacant possession. The valuation method is likely to provide the appropriate measure of damage where the property is freehold and where the claimant would not have sold it on the terms agreed.

1   [1997] PNLR 392 (Benet Hytner QC).

8.88   Where C is a landlord and the property in question a lease the position is more complicated. The property with which C is left—the reversion—may turn out to be an asset worth far less than anticipated, or even a liability. Where C would not have let and there was an available market for the premises the valuation method applied at the date of the transaction seems most appropriate. Where the defect affects the marketability of the reversion and either C is locked into it or the defect does not come to light until an attempt is made at sale, the valuation method may undercompensate him. In those circumstances the appropriate measure of damages would appear to be the open market value of the premises at the date of transaction less the actual price which C achieved on the sale of the reversion together with any consequential losses such as any lost income. This seems consistent with the extrication and wasted expenditure cases considered above. There is, however, no authority in which this factual situation has been considered. This absence of authority indicates that in most cases the court is unlikely to be faced with a situation in which C would not have let the premises altogether.

8.89   Where the complaint is that D failed to obtain the terms which C instructed him to or would have wished for if properly consulted, the valuation method does not seem appropriate either. In *Inter-Leisure Ltd v Lamberts*[1] the judge found that there was a 75% chance that the tenants would have taken a lease with an upwards only rent review. He also found that there was a 50% chance that the tenants would have exercised a break clause which was available to them until the first review date if they had been faced with an upwards only rent review. Finally, he found that the problem did not come to light until the negotiations for the rent review took place. In those circumstances he assessed damages as the difference between the value of a lease with an upwards only rent review and the lease as granted at the date of the first review. He then discounted this figure by 50% to reflect the chances indicated above. He also added 25% of the difference between the value of the freehold with vacant possession at the same date and the value of the reversion subject to the lease.[2] He rejected assessment at the date of breach because it required the court to undertake an unacceptably artificial valuation exercise. The valuation of the freehold involved the expert valuers picking investment yields appropriate for the property some five years before trial. Given that these yields would involve assumptions or predictions about the behaviour of the market when this behaviour was now known, an assessment of the actual losses suffered since the date of the transaction was more appropriate.[3] He also considered that damages should be quantified at the first review date for a number of reasons: first, an upwards only rent review clause is designed to protect the landlord against subsequent falls in the market; secondly, C did not learn of the defect until the first review; and, thirdly, Ds had continued to act for C in the meantime.

1   [1997] NPC 49 (Michael Harvey QC): see chapter 3, paras 3.17–3.20.
2   On the facts the rent review clause as drafted depressed the value of the freehold below its vacant possession value.
3   For helpful observations about the way in which the court should approach valuation evidence concerned with investment property, see *BBL* at first instance [1995] 2 All ER 769 at 789 et seq (Phillips J).

8.90   *Roker House Investments Ltd v Saunders*[1] also involved a lease of investment property. Ds failed to advise C that a guarantee signed by the French parent of the tenant company was neither valid nor enforceable when C had purchased the freehold and leased it back to the tenant. After three years of receiving substantial rents at above market values, C sought to sell the property subject to the lease in a falling market for £120,000 less than it had originally paid. When a sale had been agreed, the defective guarantee came to light. C then took a surrender of the lease for a reverse premium of £450,000 and sold the freehold with vacant possession. The net sum amounted to only £50,000 less than the price which C had been offered. C sought to argue that the valuation method should be applied *at the date of purchase*, three years earlier. Alliott J directed himself that he 'must ensure that the plaintiff is in the same position as if it had received the £1,015,000 on 11 August 1994, the contractual completion date in the purported Schleider sale' (the sale which went off). This is, therefore, an example of the court assessing damages as the loss on resale. Three points are, however, worthy of mention: first, it was Ds not C who submitted that this was the appropriate measure of damage. Not surprisingly it was not argued that such a loss was too remote. Secondly, this was an investment property and not a residential property. Thirdly, and most importantly, the judge found that if the invalidity of the guarantee had come to light at the time of the original transaction the parent would have rectified the situation and the transaction would have gone ahead.

1   Alliott J, 22 October 1997. The case is briefly reported in [1997] EGCS 137.

8.91   In *McElroy Milne v Commercial Electronics Ltd*[1] where developer C had granted a lease with the intention of taking the property to the market but was unable to do so because the covenant of the tenant for whom the premises had been developed was worthless without a guarantee, C recovered the difference between the price which it would have obtained if it had sold the property with the benefit of the guarantee and the price which it actually realised for the property some years later after a market collapse. The judge found at first instance that the proposed guarantor would have executed the guarantee if it had been asked.

1   [1993] NZLR 39, esp at 41, 48–9.

8.92   Finally the valuation method rule seems particularly inappropriate where C sells a property for more than it was truly worth because D was negligent. In *Cemp Properties (UK) Ltd v Dentsply Research and Development Corpn Ltd*[1] the judge held that the defendant vendor was not entitled to recover from the third party solicitors that part of the sum which the vendor had paid the purchaser which 'represented the difference between the price Cemp paid and the true market value'. But since the purchaser recovered from the vendor the wasted expenditure it had incurred to extricate itself from the lease rather than any loss of value the solicitors were ordered to indemnify their clients against these damages.

1   [1989] 2 EGLR 205 at 207A (Morritt J).

D   PARTICULAR KINDS OF PROPERTY

1   Lease Renewals

8.93   A fertile source of negligence claims against solicitors is the procedural requirements of the Landlord and Tenant Act 1954, Pt II. In a number of cases solicitors have been held liable for failure to comply with its provisions thereby depriving their clients of the protection of the legislation.

(a)   Acting for tenants

8.94   Solicitors have been held liable when acting for tenants for failure to serve a counter-notice under s 25 of the Act and to make an application to court;[1] failure to advise a client or potential client to take these steps;[2] failure to make an application to court;[3] and delay in the conduct of the application with the result that the rent ordered by the court was substantially higher than it should have been.[4] Of greater complexity is the assessment of damages.

1   *Ricci v Masons* [1993] 2 EGLR 159 (Lionel Swift QC).
2   *Whelton Sinclair v Hyland* [1992] 2 EGLR 158, CA.
3   *R P Howard Ltd v Woodman Matthews & Co* [1983] BCLC 117 (Staughton J) and *Hodge v Clifford Cowling & Co* [1990] 2 EGLR 89, CA.
4   *Teasdale v Williams & Co* (1983) 269 Estates Gazette 1040, CA.

8.95   The rent payable under most business tenancies protected by the Act is a market or rack rent but this does not mean that a new lease, when ordered by the court, has no capital value. In most such cases the capital value will be due to the goodwill of the business or the trading location of the premises and the security offered by the Act will enable a tenant who wishes to sell to maximise that value. Where the new lease would have had a premium value but the tenant has lost security of tenure by taking a contracted out tenancy or had to negotiate new and unattractive terms because he has lost the protection of the Act, the lease which he is obliged to accept is likely to have no premium value or to have a value which is substantially lower than could have been expected. In these cases the difference between the value of the lease which would have been ordered and the actual lease negotiated is the most obvious loss. In *Clark v Kirby-Smith*[1] the tenant was unable to prove that the new lease would have had any capital value and recovered nominal damages only. But in *Ricci v Masons*[2] the tenant had a restaurant with a rising turnover and substantial goodwill. Once the protection of the Act was lost he was only able to negotiate a five year contracted out lease with his landlord. The judge found that if his application for a new hearing had been heard, the court would have ordered a ten year lease subject to a redevelopment break clause at a lower rent which could be sold for £100,000 on the open market. In a number of other cases a difference in premium value has also been proved despite the fact that the rent payable under the new lease would have been a market or rack rent.[3]

1   [1964] Ch 506 (Plowman J). The tenant gave up possession and also claimed damages for the terminal repairs liability. This was dismissed on the ground that it was caused by the tenant's own breach of covenant. There was no claim for loss of goodwill or disruption of business. The tenant had allowed options to renew to lapse and had not sought to negotiate.

2   [1993] 2 EGLR 159 (Lionel Swift QC).

3   In *Whelton Sinclair v Hyland* [1992] 2 EGLR 158 (above) the plaintiff vacated and was awarded £5,000 loss of premium value. In *Jolliffe v Charles Coleman & Co* (1971) 219 Estates Gazette 1608 (Browne J) the plaintiff was awarded £250 to reflect the difference in capital values.

8.96   In both *Hodge v Clifford Cowling & Co*[1] and *Ricci v Masons*[2] it was held that the appropriate date for assessment of the tenant's capital loss was the date of breach. In the former there was no suggestion that the tenant intended to sell the lease. In the latter it was found that the tenant did intend to realise both the tenancy and his business at a later date but because the tenant would have had a saleable asset at the date of breach, his present or future intentions were not considered relevant to the date of assessment.

1   [1990] 2 EGLR 89, CA.

2   [1993] 2 EGLR 159 (Lionel Smith QC).

8.97   A direct comparison between the lease obtained and the one which could have been expected is not appropriate, however, where the tenant cannot secure new terms (however disadvantageous) and is obliged to give up possession of the premises. In *Matlock Green Garages Ltd v Potter Brooke-Taylor & Wildgoose*[1] where the tenant company was deprived of the opportunity to obtain a new 10-year lease of a petrol filling station, the tenant was only able to negotiate a short three year lease terminable on three months' notice. The lease was terminated and the company not only closed down the petrol filling station business but also sold off a number of related businesses and assets which were carried out on different sites. The judge awarded damages by calculating the annual net maintainable profits of the company as a whole, making certain adjustments to the profit figures, splitting out the profits attributable to the other businesses and multiplying the figure by the period of occupation which the plaintiff had lost. Two additional points are worthy of note: first, the judge rejected an assessment based on the diminution in value of the business at the date of breach as unreal; secondly, he refused to award damages for the sale of the other businesses on the basis that these losses were too remote.

1   (13 November 1996, unreported) (Wright J).

8.98   Even where the claimant can prove no loss of capital value, the consequence of the solicitor's negligence may be that the tenant is required to pay a higher rent than would have been ordered under the Act. The court may simply assess what the claimant would have paid over the length of the term if his or her rights had been preserved and compare that with the passing rent: see *Teasdale v Williams & Co*,[1] in which the plaintiff took a seven year lease at a higher rent instead of the five-year lease at a lower rent which would have been ordered under the Act. He paid less than he would in years 1 and 2, more than he would in years 3 to 5 and would have applied to court for a new tenancy at the end of year 5. He was awarded the increase in years 3 to 5 less the gain in years 1 and 2. No damages were awarded for years 6 and 7 because the need to apply to court for a new tenancy two years earlier would have cancelled out any increased rent.

1   (1983) 269 Estates Gazette 1040, CA.

8.99   Until or unless the landlord applies for an interim rent the tenant is entitled to pay rent at the old rate until the determination of his or her application for a new tenancy. If, however, his or her solicitor fails to serve a counter-notice or apply to court for a new tenancy in time, the tenancy will come to an end at the expiry of the s 25 notice. In many cases, therefore, the tenant will begin to pay rent at a higher rate much earlier. In *Jolliffe v Charles Coleman & Co*,[1] the judge awarded the plaintiff the increased rent payable during the course of the proceedings as well as his capital loss.

1   (1971) 219 Estates Gazette 1608 (Browne J).

(b)   Acting for landlords

8.100   In *Nadreph Ltd v Willmett & Co*[1] the defendant solicitors served a s 25 notice opposing the grant of a new tenancy on a ground under which the tenant could claim statutory compensation when the plaintiff landlord wished only to recover a part of the premises and would not have served a notice opposing the grant of a new tenancy. The tenant vacated and claimed compensation and the plaintiff claimed against the defendants for the additional amount payable. Damages were agreed as the amount of compensation subject to one point, namely, whether the plaintiff had to give credit for its own use of the premises not only against the loss of rent but also against the compensation.[2]

1   [1978] 1 All ER 746 (Whitford J). The decision appears to be the only reported case in which a landlord has claimed against his solicitor in relation to 1954 Act proceedings.
2   Although the report is not explicit it appears that the plaintiff obtained a benefit from the tenant vacating which exceeded the amount of the rent which the tenant would have paid.

2   Options

8.101   Option agreements themselves, whether for the sale or purchase of land or for the grant or termination of a lease, require no separate treatment.[1] It goes without saying that it is the solicitor's duty to make sure that the client fully understands the terms of, and time for, the exercise of the option when the agreement is made.

1   It is now settled that the requirement for signed writing prescribed by Law of Property (Miscellaneous Provisions) Act 1989, s 2 is satisfied in the case of options by the original contract: see *Spiro v Glencrown Properties Ltd* [1991] Ch 537 (Hoffmann J). Formalities, therefore, present no special difficulties and no reported negligence claims have arisen out of its transitional provisions.

(a)   Reminders

8.102   Ordinarily a solicitor owes no duty to repeat advice once given. But this issue often arises where the advice was about the timing of the exercise of an option. In *Yager v Fishman & Co*[1] the defendants were held not liable for failing to remind their client to exercise a break option in a lease or for failing to exercise it themselves. The case has often been taken as authority for the proposition that a solicitor is under no duty to remind. It is clear, however, that the Court of Appeal were not laying down any particular rule in relation to the exercise of options or the issuing of reminders. This was not a case in which the client had forgotten the date. His complaint was that the solicitors should have advised him to take a different course: the client had guaranteed the tenant company's liabilities, the tenant had gone into liquidation, the liquidator had sublet the premises for a time, and the client was negotiating to take an assignment. He could not decide whether to break the lease or to continue to exploit the premises. He claimed that, in response to a letter which he had written, the defendants ought to have advised him to break the lease. This was held to be a matter of commercial judgment. In *Donmez v Barnes & Partners*[2] by contrast a solicitor who acted for the grantee of a lease which contained an option to purchase the freehold within two years of the commencement of the term was held liable in negligence for failing to ask the plaintiff to come and see him as the time drew near for the exercise of the option.[3] It cannot be said, therefore, that as a general rule a solicitor owes no duty to remind his client about the need to consider exercising an option. Whether the solicitor will owe a duty is likely to depend on (a) the terms of the option and, in particular, how soon and how often the right to exercise it arises, (b) the nature of the original advice and whether it was given in writing, (c) the existence of a continuing retainer and (d) the knowledge and experience of the client.

1   [1944] 1 All ER 552, esp at 558D, CA.
2   [1996] EGCS 129 (HHJ Prosser QC).
3   See also *West London Observer v Parsons* (1955) 166 Estates Gazette 749 (Gorman J): advice given in 1950 (in writing) and 1951 (orally); opportunity to break lost in 1953.

(b)   Exercise of the option

8.103   In juridical terms an option is a privilege not a right. It is well established that the conditions for the exercise of an option both as to time and manner must be satisfied strictly.[1] If the task of exercising the option is entrusted to a solicitor it is almost inevitable that he or she will be negligent if the exercise of the option is invalid because the conditions are not satisfied. In *Tonitto v Bassal*[2] the defendant was held liable for a failure to deliver a signed contract for sale with the notice of exercise and a payment, all of which were required by the option agreement. It was contended that the agreement was uncertain and that the solicitor should not be liable for misconstruing it and this was roundly rejected. In *Roberts v J W Ward & Son*[3] the defendants failed to specify the price in the notice and also to serve one of the parties. It was likewise held that despite the uncertainty in the conditions required by the option agreement, the defendants were liable not only for failing to serve a party but also for serving an invalid notice. In *Titanic Investments Ltd v MacFarlanes*[4] the vendor's solicitors this time were held liable for agreeing to a formula for the determination of the price without advising their clients fully of the terms proposed and obtaining their agreement to them.

1   See *Emmet* Vol I at 2.118.
2   (1992) 28 NSWLR 564.
3   (1981) 126 Sol Jo 120, CA.
4   [1997] NPC 105 (Robert Walker J) and (3 December 1998, unreported), CA.

(c)   Damages (1): grant of the option

8.104   Where the solicitor's breach of duty leads to his client either granting or taking an option on terms which he would not have accepted if properly advised, the appropriate measure of damage is likely to depend on what the outcome would have been if the client had received the proper advice. In *Titanic Investments v MacFarlanes* the court found that agreement would have been reached on some terms and approached the assessment of damages by considering the potential outcomes and evaluating the chances of each occurring. It is considered in more detail in chapter 3.[1]

1   See paras 3.17–3.20.

8.105   In *Amerena v Barling*[1] the defendants granted an option over shares in a company without the authority of the plaintiff. The judge at first instance found that the plaintiff would not have authorised the grant of the option and the Court of Appeal considered the question of damages on the basis that no option would have been granted at all. They applied the valuation method at the date of breach and assessed damages as the difference between the value of the shares subject to the option and their unfettered value at the date of the option agreement. It was argued that the appropriate date for assessment was the date for the exercise of the option by which time the plaintiff had spent £1.75m to buy in the rights under the option agreement and to free the shares. Although the judgment of Peter Gibson LJ is couched in negative terms so that he could see no reason to depart from the usual rule, there were a number of reasons why the date of breach was the appropriate date: first, the subject matter of the option was shares; secondly, it was clear that the plaintiff had made a good bargain and the value of the shares subject to the option at the date of its grant were no less than their unfettered value; thirdly—and perhaps most importantly—there was little or no explanation for the plaintiff's decision to buy back the rights at what appeared to be an inflated price. On this last point the Court of Appeal held that the re-purchase of the shares was not reasonable mitigation given that the plaintiff only opened negotiations some 18 months after the option had been granted.

1   (1993) 69 P & CR 252.

8.106   *Amerena v Barling* may be distinguishable where the subject matter of the option is land and the existence of the option locks the claimant in to a sale at a price which he cannot avoid. If the value of the land changes to the claimant's detriment during the option period, it does not seem just that the claimant should be held to the value at the date of breach. Nevertheless because an option is an inchoate right much may turn on the efforts of the claimant to negotiate a release from the option or to mitigate his loss in other ways. If the claimant becomes aware at an early stage of the defendant's mistake but takes no steps to mitigate his loss the court may adopt the same approach whether shares or land are in issue.

(d)   Damages (2): exercise of the option

8.107   There is little authority on the measure of damage for breach of an option agreement by one of the parties let alone a solicitor's negligence action arising out of such a claim. In *Homsy v Murphy*[1] the court awarded damages based on the difference between the purchase price and the value of the land at the date of exercise of the option. The calculation of the loss was complicated by the fact that the plaintiff had a purchaser for both the option land and his own land at a price which reflected the marriage value of the two interests and it was held that the valuation ought to take into account the marriage value. The general principle also holds good for assessing or quantifying damages where the claimant's complaint is that he has lost the opportunity to exercise an option as a consequence of his solicitor's failure to exercise the option.

1   (1996) 73 P & CR 26, CA.

CHAPTER 9

Wills, estates and trusts

A THE PREPARATION AND EXECUTION OF WILLS

1 The duty to disappointed beneficiaries

(a) The basis of the duty

9.1 A solicitor who accepts instructions to prepare a will owes contractual and tortious duties to his client. These duties survive death and if the client's estate can prove loss as a consequence of such a breach of duty, the estate is entitled to recover compensation for that loss. Losses suffered by an estate are, however, rare. The principal logical difficulty created by claims against solicitors in relation to the preparation of wills is that in most cases the solicitor's negligence has not caused the maker of the will (and, therefore, his estate) to suffer any pecuniary loss but rather has frustrated his or her testamentary wishes.[1] The person who suffers the loss is the disappointed beneficiary.

1   See chapter 1, paras 1.29 and 1.29.

9.2 In *White v Jones*[1] the House of Lords by a majority of three to two held that a solicitor can be liable to a disappointed beneficiary for negligently carrying out the testator's instructions and depriving him or her of an intended legacy. Although all members of the committee delivered speeches, both Lord Browne-Wilkinson and Lord Nolan agreed with Lord Goff.[2] In *Carr-Glynn v Frearsons*[3] Chadwick LJ analysed Lord Goff's speech as follows:

> 'He recognised the need "to fashion a remedy to fill a lacuna in the law so as to prevent the injustice which would otherwise occur on the facts of cases such as the present" (at 268B); but to achieve that end he found it unnecessary on the facts in *White v Jones* to go beyond holding (at 268D):
>
>> "... that the assumption of responsibility by the solicitor towards his client should be held in law to extend to the intended beneficiary who (as the solicitor can reasonably foresee) may, as a result of the solicitor's negligence, be deprived of his intended legacy in circumstances in which neither the testator nor his estate will have a remedy against the solicitor."
>
> Lord Goff went on to say this (at 269C-D):
>
>> "Let me emphasise that I can see no injustice in imposing liability on a negligent solicitor in a case such as the present where, in the absence of a remedy in this form, neither the testator's estate nor the disappointed beneficiary will have a claim for loss caused by his negligence. This is the injustice which, in my opinion, the judges of this country should address by recognising that cases such as these call for an appropriate remedy, and the common law is not so sterile as to be incapable of supplying the remedy when it is required."
>
> Both Lord Browne-Wilkinson and Lord Nolan expressed their agreement with the reasons given by Lord Goff. It must, I think, follow that it is the reasoning in

Lord Goff's speech—and only that reasoning—that can be said to have received the support of the majority in the House of Lords.'

It appears, therefore, that the dicta of Lord Goff quoted by Chadwick LJ will be treated as the ratio decidendi of *White v Jones* and the duty of care owed by a solicitor to a disappointed beneficiary treated as a limited exception to the general principle that a solicitor owes duties only to his client. The extent of the exception is now considered.

1   [1995] 2 AC 207.
2   [1995] 2 AC 207 at 276F and 295D.
3   [1999] 2 WLR 1046 at 1054C–F, CA.

(b)   The extent of the duty

9.3   From the cases which have followed *White v Jones* four limitations on the extent of the duty can be identified.[1] First, the terms of the duty owed to the disappointed beneficiary are determined by the nature and scope of the original instructions given by the testator. It follows from the nature of the exception as explained by Lord Goff that the content of the solicitor's duty to the disappointed beneficiary cannot be wider than that of the duty which he owed to his original client. If, therefore, the solicitor was not in breach of his duties to the testator, the disappointed beneficiary will have no claim even though he may have suffered loss. In *Carr-Glynn v Frearsons*[2] Chadwick LJ stated:

'The duty owed by the solicitors to the specific legatee is not a duty to take care to ensure that the specific legatee receives his legacy. It is a duty to take care to ensure that effect is given to the testator's testamentary intentions. The loss from which the specific legatee is to be saved harmless is the loss which he will suffer if effect is not given to the testator's testamentary intentions. That is the loss of the interest which he would have had as a beneficiary in an estate comprising the relevant property.'[3]

1   These are not dissimilar from those identified by Balcombe LJ in *Clark v Bruce Lance & Co* [1988] 1 WLR 881 at 888–9, CA. In *White v Jones* [1995] 2 AC 207 at 292F–295D Lord Nolan was expressly influenced by the proximity created by the family relationship between testator and beneficiaries. This limitation does not appear to have been picked up in any later cases.
2   [1999] 2 WLR 1046 at 1056F–G, CA.
3   In *Punford v Gilberts Accountants* [1998] PNLR 763, CA, Sir Christopher Slade stated: 'On no conceivable footing can the duty owed by the draftsman to the intended beneficiary be greater than that owed by him to the testator himself.'

9.4   Secondly, the solicitor only owes the disappointed beneficiary a duty of care in relation to the will-making process. He does not owe the beneficiary a duty in relation to any advice which he gave the testator even if it is that advice which causes the beneficiary loss. In *Carr-Glynn v Frearsons*[1] the will-making process was held to extend beyond the preparation and execution of the will to closely associated acts or advice. In that case, the defendants were found liable for failing to advise a testatrix, who owned a property jointly with her nephew but wished to leave her share to her niece, to serve a notice on the nephew immediately severing their joint tenancy. The testatrix who was 81 years old came to the defendants wishing to change her will for the purpose of leaving her half share to the niece; if she failed to sever the joint tenancy it was obvious that the gift would fail; and the defendants themselves recognised the potential need to sever the joint tenancy. It was found that the 'need to take care to ensure that the asset fell into the estate was integral to the carrying into effect of the testatrix's intention

...'.[2] In *Clarke v Bruce Lance & Co*[3] by contrast it was held that solicitors owed no duty of care to a disappointed beneficiary for failing to advise their client not to grant an option for a fixed price over a petrol filling station simply because they had earlier prepared his will in which the station had been left to the plaintiff. The testator was free at any time to deal with his assets as he chose. Although the grant of the option on the advice of the defendants had the effect of reducing the value of the asset which he left to the plaintiff, the advice which the defendants gave about the option was not part of the will-making process. Whether or not the defendants were negligent in advising him about the option, they could owe no duty of care to the plaintiff simply because the testator had chosen to dispose of or fetter one of his assets.[4]

1 [1999] 2 WLR 1046, CA.
2 [1999] 2 WLR 1046 at 1055B–F. The solicitor advised the testatrix to obtain the title deeds from her nephew before serving the notice of severance. There was no reason why a notice could not have been served without waiting for the deeds.
3 [1988] 1 WLR 881, CA. The case is an extreme one and was an application by the defendants to strike out. One oddity is that the claim was not brought by the estate.
4 See also *Punford v Gilberts Accountants* [1998] PNLR 763, CA in which the defendants were a firm of accountants. A more difficult case is *Cancer Research Campaign v Ernest Brown & Co* [1998] PNLR 592 (Harman J), in which it was held that solicitors who acted for a testatrix, who died shortly after her brother, owed no duty to the charitable beneficiaries *under her will* to advise her to execute a deed of variation *of her brother's will* renouncing her interest in favour of them.

9.5 Thirdly, the claimant must satisfy the court that the testator or testatrix intended to confer on the disappointed beneficiary a particular testamentary benefit of which he or she has been deprived. Where there is a formal defect in the will or a delay in its execution, this will usually cause no difficulty. Where, however, the failure consists in failing to advise the testator to adopt a specific testamentary disposition the difficulty is more acute. In cases where the testator did execute a valid will, the court will require convincing evidence both that the will did not represent the testator's wishes and that the testator's instructions to the defendant were not carried into effect. This is a heavy burden and the recent case of *Walker v Medlicott & Son*[1] provides a good example of the difficulties involved.[2] In that case, the testatrix visited the defendant's office without an appointment to make a will. She brought with her a handwritten note in which she had written: 'House and contents to Bobbie Walker [the plaintiff]'. The defendant kept this note. He also kept an attendance note of the meeting, which lasted 18 minutes and which demonstrated that she had changed or modified her wishes in certain respects. In particular, the defendant recorded that she wanted the plaintiff to have a residuary gift of 'all personal chattels' whilst no mention was made of the house. The will was drawn up on the basis of the instructions recorded in the attendance note and the testatrix visited the defendant briefly on a second occasion to sign the will. The plaintiff gave evidence that the testatrix told him after the meeting: 'Well, Bob, I've signed it. The house is now yours ...'; and called nine other witnesses to give evidence that this was her intention. The defendant gave evidence of his usual practice in preparing a will and, although he could not recall the events in question, was convinced that, when the testatrix was in his office, she must have had second thoughts. Although the judge accepted the plaintiff's evidence about his conversation with the testatrix, he dismissed the claim on the basis of the defendant's evidence. This decision was upheld by the Court of Appeal. Sir Christopher Slade said this:[3]

> 'Once the judge accepted, as he plainly did, Mr Medlicott as an honest witness on whose evidence as to facts, such as his usual practice, he could rely, he was

in my judgment fully entitled to attach weight to the inferences drawn by Mr Medlicott as to the probable course of the interview, based on the available documentary evidence and his usual practice, even though he could not actually remember it. Furthermore, having seen Mr Medlicott in the witness box, he was also entitled to take into account his impressions of his professional competence, intelligence and responsibility; and I have no doubt that he did so.

As I have already pointed out, the onus falls on the plaintiff in the present case to prove by convincing evidence that the testatrix instructed Mr Medlicott to include in her will a gift of the house to the plaintiff and that he failed to carry out those instructions in circumstances which constituted negligence. The judge, in the penultimate sentence of his judgment, found that this had not been proved, and I see no sufficient grounds upon which the court would be entitled to interfere with that finding.'

1   [1999] 1 WLR 727, CA.
2   In *Trusted v Clifford Chance* (17 May 1996, unreported) (Jonathan Parker J) (the plaintiff failed to satisfy the court that the testator intended him to have the benefit claimed. In *Horsfall v Haywards* [1999] Lloyd's Rep PN 332, CA, (considered below) it was common ground that the will had been misdrafted.
3   [1999] 1 WLR 727 at 737H–737B. It was accepted that the civil standard of proof was appropriate but following Chadwick J in *Re Segelman decd* [1996] Ch 171 at 184 that 'the probability that a will which a testator has executed in circumstances of some formality reflects his intentions is usually of such weight that convincing evidence to the contrary is necessary.': see 731H–732A.

9.6   In *Walker v Medlicott* the simple question was whether the testatrix intended the plaintiff to have her house. In other cases, however, both the form of will adopted by the testator or testatrix and the form advanced by the disappointed beneficiary may be consistent with the broad intentions expressed to the solicitor by his client and unless the plaintiff can satisfy the court that the testator intended him or her to have the precise testamentary benefit for which he seeks compensation and instructed the defendant to this effect, the claim will fail.[1]

1   See *White v Jones* above at 225E–G, per Sir Donald Nicholls V-C and *Sutherland v Public Trustee* [1980] 2 NZLR 536 at 547–548. In *Cancer Research Campaign v Ernest Brown & Co* [1998] PNLR 592 (see para 9.4), Harman J found that there was no reason to suppose that the testatrix actually wished to vary the provisions of her brother's will however beneficial this might have been to the beneficiaries under her will: see 604G–605A.

9.7   Fourthly, the claim will fail if the beneficiary would not have received the legacy or bequest in any event. This will be the case where the defendant is able to show that the testator would have chosen to dispose of it in his lifetime or would have revoked the will or that the assets in the estate would have been distributed in such a way that the claimant would have received no additional benefit. In practice this latter situation is unlikely to arise in relation to claims based on failure to prepare or procure execution of the will except where the estate is insolvent or the asset in question is required to meet the debts and expenses of the estate. The remedy 'fashioned' by the House of Lords in *White v Jones* was designed to deal with the situation where the only person who had suffered a loss had no title to sue. If the asset in question would have been applied exclusively for the benefit of the estate's creditors, the disappointed beneficiary would have no claim.

9.8   That is not to say that the disappointed beneficiary will be barred from claiming against the solicitors simply because the estate itself is also able to claim.

In *Carr-Glynn v Frearsons*[1] Chadwick LJ recognised that there might be cases in which the disappointed beneficiary and the estate have 'complementary' claims. A change in the disposition of the will might affect both the estate and the disappointed beneficiary, eg by varying the amount of tax payable by the estate. If the result were beneficial to both, there seems to be no reason why both should not recover. Again if an asset would have been sold and part applied for the benefit of the creditors and the balance paid out to the beneficiary, both estate and beneficiary will have complementary claims.[2]

1   [1999] 2 WLR 1046 at 1056G–H, CA. He also stated that although both could claim, it would not be necessary for both to be parties if one or other chose not to claim.
2   There seems to be no reason why *classes* of beneficiaries should not have a claim or individual beneficiaries within a particular class (some of whom might have been better off with the will which was admitted to probate): see *White v Jones* [1995] 2 AC 207 at 226A–B, per Sir Donald Nicholls V-C.

2   Breach of duty

(a)   Preparation and execution

9.9   In the reported cases, solicitors have been found liable to disappointed beneficiaries for failure to carry out a testator's instructions to draw up a new will within a reasonable time.[1] They have also been found liable for failure to ensure that a will has been witnessed properly: in *Ross v Caunters*[2] Sir Robert Megarry V-C. found the defendants liable for failure to warn a testator that a will should not be witnessed by a spouse of a beneficiary and to check that it had been attested properly. As a consequence of this failure, the gift to the beneficiary was void under Wills Act 1837, s 15.[3] In *Seale v Perry*[4] the Supreme Court of Victoria refused to follow *Ross v Caunters* and held that a solicitor owed no duty of care to ensure that a will was properly attested.[5] This decision is not likely to be followed in this country and, in any event, appears inconsistent with the recent decision of *Esterhuizen v Allied Dunbar*.[6] In that case, it was held to be negligent to leave the will with the testator to get it executed and witnessed by himself. The judge stated that 'in ordinary circumstances just to leave written instructions and to do no more would not only be contrary with good practice but also in my view negligent'. He also approved the practice whereby the solicitor must either ensure that the testator comes into the office to execute the will or visits the testator at home with a member of staff to attest the will.

1   See the facts of *White v Jones* [1995] 2 AC 207. See also *Smith v Claremont Haynes & Co* (1991) Times, 3 September (HHJ Barnett QC), *Whittingham v Crease* [1978] 88 DLR (3d) 353 and *Gartside v Sheffield, Young and Ellis* [1983] NZLR 37.
2   [1980] Ch 297. The decision itself was, and remained for a long time, of substantial importance. The reasoning can no longer be relied on, however.
3   See also, to the same effect, *Watts v Public Trustee* [1980] WAR 97.
4   [1982] VR 193.
5   Under s 7 of the Victorian Wills Act 1958, which, as under s 9(d) of the Wills Act 1837 (as amended), provides that an attesting witness must attest and sign or acknowledge the signature in the presence of the testator. The defendant witnessed his client's signature but failed to sign the will himself in the presence of the testator and the other attesting witness and to ensure that the other witness did the same.
6   [1998] 2 FLR 668 (Longmore J). See also Oats in Sol Jo 11 December 1998 at 1132, 1135.

9.10   In *Hall v Meyrick*,[1] where the defendants were engaged to advise two clients who subsequently married thereby invalidating their wills, Hodson LJ stated:

'A question of great importance and interest to solicitors is whether the judge was right in holding, as he did, that there was any duty at all on a solicitor, in the circumstances to draw the attention of the client to s 18 of the Wills Act 1837.[2] I have said that I do not propose to give any concluded finding on this point but I think it right to say this. I would not for one moment suppose that it was the duty of a solicitor in all cases to draw the attention of persons who come into his office to make wills to the effect of marriage on a will. In such a case I must use the words which are so well known that "each case depends on its own particular facts". This is a very special and unusual case. The parties came into the defendant's office, a man and a woman each known to the defendant to be single, each desiring to benefit the other substantially to the extent of their whole possessions before death by their wills. They were known to have been living together for fifteen years as housekeeper and boarder ... On those facts the learned judge's decision at any rate is supported by evidence. I leave that matter, having made it clear, I hope, that I am not going to impose an extravagant duty on solicitors who are making wills for their clients.'

1   [1957] 2 All ER 722 at 724F–I. See also Ormerod LJ at 730B–F. Despite the reluctant conclusion quoted in the body of the text, the action was dismissed for failure to plead the retainer properly, the judge having allowed an amendment after the expiry of the limitation period. The decision predates *Hedley Byrne* and would be decided differently for that reason alone. It is submitted that the court would also be more robust on the issue of substance today.
2   Wills Act 1837, s 18(4)(b) (as amended by the Administration of Justice Act 1982) now contains a saving for the case where the testator was 'expecting to be married' at the date of execution.

(b)   Taking instructions

9.11   There are no reported English cases in which a solicitor has been found liable to a disappointed beneficiary for failing to take adequate instructions or to ensure that the testator fully understands the legal effect of the dispositions which he proposes to make. There are a number of dicta in cases concerned with a testator's want of knowledge and approval which suggest that it would be negligent for a solicitor to take instructions through a beneficiary[1] or to give inadequate advice or information about the effect of the will before execution.[2] In cases where a claim is brought against the solicitor for failing to give adequate advice, the difficulty for the claimant will be in showing whether the advice would have made a difference to the testator's intentions and, in particular, whether the disappointed beneficiary would have received a benefit as a consequence. This difficulty is well illustrated by *Sutherland v Public Trustee*[3] in which a claim was brought against a solicitor employed by the New Zealand Public Trustee for failing to ensure that the testator, who proposed to leave his whole estate to his wife, should include a gift over in favour of his step-children in the event that his wife predeceased him. Although the judge found that the will was 'unwise and inappropriate in its terms' he found that the solicitor had advised the testator of the possibility of an intestacy. He concluded:[4]

'Admittedly what indicators there are suggest that, even pointedly, the testator wished to benefit the Passmore children but *that is not what his will said*, notwithstanding he was given an opportunity to say so. To hold that there was a duty of care to persons the testator deliberately refused to nominate himself would take the law very far beyond its present limits. It would involve specula-tion, albeit with some degree of probability, involvement in the consequences of the act rather than the act itself and, worst of all, what testators ought to do. Although unusual, I do not think it so far fetched as to exclude its likelihood, that the testator meant to have his estate distributed according to the rules of intestacy should his wife predecease him. There could not be a duty of care which might prevent that possibility.'

The claim therefore failed because it could not be said with certainty what dispositions the testator genuinely intended in the event that his wife predeceased him.

1   *Aylwin v Aylwin* [1902] P 203 at 204 (Jeune P). For the general duty to take instructions, see chapter 2, paras 2.32–2.38. Compare, also, the cases considered in chapter 8, paras 8.7 and 8.8.
2   *Wintle v Nye* [1959] 1 All ER 552, HL; *Russell v Fraser* (1980) 118 DLR (3d) 733 at 745–6; and *Morrell v Morrell* (1882) 7 PD 68 at 72–3.
3   [1980] 2 NZLR 536, Supreme Court of New Zealand (Jeffries J).
4   At 548 (the judge's emphasis).

(c)   Notification of personal representatives

9.12   In *Hawkins v Clayton*[1] a majority of the High Court of Australia held that it was the duty of a solicitor, who had prepared a will for the deceased and with whom the will had been left for safekeeping, to take reasonable steps to locate and notify the executor of her estate. Because the defendants failed to do so they were found liable to the estate for the losses it suffered both as a consequence of the estate property falling into disrepair and also of a fine levied for late payment of estate duty. Deane J[2] considered that there might also be circumstances in which the failure by a firm of solicitors to communicate the existence or contents of a will in its custody to a person named as executor and principal beneficiary might constitute an actionable breach of duty of care owed to that person in his capacity as a beneficiary. He gave as an example the failure of a firm of solicitors to disclose the existence of a will causing the assets of the estate to be irretrievably distributed to the next of kin on an intestacy or persons claiming under an earlier will. In *Cancer Research Campaign v Ernest Brown & Co*[3] by contrast Harman J held that a solicitor (who was also the sole remaining executor) was under no duty to notify the residuary beneficiaries of the death of the testatrix, the terms of the will and the material facts about the estate so that they could apply to court for a tax efficient variation of the will.

1   (1988) 78 ALR 69.
2   (1988) 78 ALR 69 at 99, lines 27–44.
3   [1998] PNLR 592. There were a number of residuary beneficiaries which were charitable organisations. We consider that there must be some duty to notify those interested in the will and that the case is confined to its special facts although the extent of the duty may turn on the number and identity of the principal beneficiaries.

(d)   Acting for the estate

9.13   There are no special duties which arise out of the fact that a solicitor has been engaged to act by personal representatives on behalf of an estate and the duties arising will be governed by the terms of the retainer. If the solicitor is instructed (as he or she ordinarily will be) to advise on and deal with inheritance tax, it will be incumbent on the solicitor to consider whether the beneficiaries should agree to a deed of variation or a disclaimer under Inheritance Tax Act 1984, s 142 in order to reduce the liability of the estate.[1] Even if the solicitor is not expressly instructed to consider the need for a variation or disclaimer we consider that it is incumbent upon a solicitor retained by an executor to do so.[2]

1   See *Williams on Wills* (7th edn, 1995) Vol 2 at 1832–43. Insofar as the decision in the *Cancer Research Campaign* case casts doubt on this proposition it is suggested that it goes too far. Further, in that case the principal difficulty appears to have been that the solicitor was also the executor and could not, therefore, claim against himself (or the firm which employed him) for a failure to advise a variation within the statutory period.

2   See *Hurlingham Estates Ltd v Wilde* [1997] STC 627 at 634f. The test used by Lightman J in relation to a commercial tax matter was whether 'Mr Rowe should reasonably have appreciated that Hurlingham needed his guidance in respect of the tax liabilities to which entry into the transaction would expose it.'

3   Claims brought by estates

9.14   In a number of miscellaneous cases claims have been brought by estates against firms of solicitors. What distinguishes these cases is that the solicitor's negligence in acting for the deceased deprives the estate of an asset which would only have accrued on death and for this reason they are considered here. In *Otter v Church, Adams, Tatham & Co*[1] the tenant in tail of settled land who would have become absolutely entitled to it by executing a disentailing deed, received negligent advice from his solicitor that he was absolutely entitled to the property without the need to do so. He died and the property passed to his uncle. His administratrix sued the solicitors. It was argued that damages should be nominal because, had the mistake been discovered in the lifetime of the deceased, it would have been his duty to mitigate his loss by executing the relevant deed. This argument was rejected. The estate was awarded damages for the deceased's loss of opportunity to execute the deed.

1   [1953] Ch 280.

9.15   In *McLellan v Fletcher*[1] Anthony Lincoln J also found a solicitor liable to the deceased's estate for failing to ensure that a life policy securing a mortgage loan was in force on completion of the deceased's purchase of the property. Unlike *Otter* the deceased could never have received the proceeds of the policy during his lifetime and they would only have formed part of his estate if the policy had been in force at his death. Phillips J declined to follow *McLellan* in *Lynne v Gordon Doctors and Walton*[2] on the grounds that the deceased himself had suffered no loss for which the estate could claim. The latter decision is likely to be followed where the proceeds of a life or endowment policy form part of the deceased's estate. Where, as is common, two people purchase a property with the intention of taking out a joint policy which would provide sufficient to discharge the mortgage debt on the death of *either* of them, the same objection does not seem available. Again where the beneficiary of the policy is not the deceased or his estate but some identified third party beneficiary, there seems no reason of policy to deprive the beneficiary of a *White v Jones* type claim.[3]

1   [1987] NLJ Rep 593 and (1987) 3 PN 202. The finding of negligence was itself surprising since the defendants wrote letters to the deceased advising him to put the policy on risk but may be explained by the fact that both experts agreed that a solicitor should ensure, if only as part of his duty to the building society, that the policy is on risk before completion. The deceased was found 75% contributorily negligent.

2   (1991) 135 Sol Jo LB 29. The decision was a preliminary issue on the question whether the plaintiffs could demonstrate any loss. The judge followed the dicta of Kennedy LJ in *Griffiths v Fleming* [1909] 1 KB 805 at 820–1 which was not cited to Anthony Lincoln J.

3   See also *Dunn v Fairs, Blissard, Barnes and Stowe* (1961) 105 Sol Jo 932 (Barry J) in which executors sued the deceased's former solicitors for accepting instructions from her to purchase an annuity at the age of 77 written and sent from the Marie Curie Hospital. The claim was dismissed on the ground that the solicitor had not been negligent.

4 Damages

9.16 Where the disappointed beneficiary is deprived of a benefit through a formal defect in the will, he will recover the benefit under the will to which he would have been entitled if the testator's instructions had been carried out.[1] He will obviously have to give credit for any other benefits which he received from the estate but would not have received if he had received the intended testamentary benefit. He will also have to give credit for any ex gratia payment made by the beneficiaries who received unintended benefits as a consequence of the solicitor's negligence.

1   In *White v Jones* [1995] 2 AC 207 the Court of Appeal awarded the plaintiffs the full amount of their legacies without deduction for any prospect of a last minute change of heart although there had been some evidence of this: see 228A–E. In *Ross v Caunters* [1980] Ch 297 at 323F–324G Megarry V-C rejected a claim for out of pocket legal expenses.

9.17 In other cases the solution may not be so simple. In *Gartside v Sheffield, Young and Ellis*[1] Cooke J stated:

> 'There will, no doubt, be difficulties in assessing the damages but such difficulties do not make assessment impossible—*Chaplin v Hicks* [1911] 2 KB 786. The question must be whether the plaintiff has lost some right of value, something which has reality and substance. Although it may be that this value is not easy to determine it is the duty of the court to do the best it can—*Kitchen v Royal Air Forces Association* [1958] 2 All ER 241. In a given case a court may view the actual loss suffered through the negligence of a solicitor failing to prepare a will as much less than the testamentary provision to be made for him. The possibility of other claims being brought to the detriment of the disappointed beneficiary, had the will been executed, must be taken into account; any amount which the disappointed beneficiary may receive in a claim under the Family Protection Act or the Law Reform (Testamentary Promises) Act will be relevant. In the end a value must be placed upon the benefit that has been lost. Although, therefore, there will be undoubted difficulties in the assessment of any damages I do not think that the courts should shrink from allowing a claim because of them.'

In *Whittingham v Crease & Co*[2] the successful plaintiff succeeded in obtaining the difference between the one third share of residue which he would have obtained had the defendants not been dilatory in taking instructions and the one fifth share to which he became entitled by intestate succession. The damages were then reduced to take account of the potential claim which the testator's other children could have brought under the family provision legislation in Canada.

1   [1983] NZLR 37 at 56 lines 28–42.
2   (1978) 88 DLR (3d) 353 at 374.

9.18 In some cases where the court is satisfied that the beneficiary has proved negligence, the court will have to assess the chance that the testator or testatrix would have executed the will in time; in others the court will have to assess whether the gift would have vested in the disappointed beneficiaries; and in others the court will have to assess the probability that other potential beneficiaries would have brought claims under the Inheritance (Provision for Family and Dependants) Act 1975 and place a value on those claims.

(a)   Rectification

9.19   Solicitors' claims in relation to the preparation of wills also give rise to one specific issue which is not encountered elsewhere. Where a testator's will does not express his true intentions, it is open to his personal representatives to apply to court for rectification of the will pursuant to Administration of Justice Act 1982, s 20. That section provides:

'(1)   If a court is satisfied that a will is so expressed that it fails to carry out the testator's intentions, in consequence—

(a)   of a clerical error; or

(b)   of a failure to understand his instructions,

it may order that the will shall be rectified so as to carry out his intentions.

(2)   An application for an order under this section shall not, except with the permission of the court, be made after the end of the period of six months from the date on which representation with respect to the estate of the deceased is first taken out.'

9.20   Where a claimant seeks damages from a solicitor for failing to record the testator's instructions faithfully in his will, he must establish all the necessary ingredients of a successful claim for rectification under this section before he can succeed against the solicitor. Indeed, the claimant might well succeed in obtaining rectification of the will where he would not succeed in negligence against the solicitor. This is precisely what happened in *Walker v Medlicott*,[1] where the plaintiff brought forward cogent evidence of the testatrix's intention but the court found that the defendant had not acted negligently. Sir Christopher Slade said this:[2]

'If it be asked how that finding is reconcilable with the evidence as to the testatrix's intention and understanding, I think there is one possible simple answer. On the available evidence, I, for my part, on the balance of probabilities would be disposed to draw the inference that there was a genuine misunderstanding between the testatrix and Mr Medlicott ...

There is no evidence as to what either party actually said at the interview. It may well be that, in the context of ascertaining the testatrix's final wishes and intentions, there was some discussion as to the respective values of the house and the testatrix's other assets. It may well be that the testatrix unwittingly gave Mr Medlicott the reasonable impression of intending one thing, while in truth intending another. In view of the paucity of the evidence as to the course of that crucial meeting and the judge's assessment of Mr Medlicott's evidence and his calibre as a witness, there is not in my judgment available evidence of a sufficiently convincing nature to establish that any misunderstanding or failure to carry out the instructions on the part of Mr Medlicott constituted negligence ...

If, as the plaintiff asserts, the will failed to carry out the testatrix's intentions, this must, I think, have been in consequence of a clerical error by Mr Medlicott in recording her instructions in his attendance note, leading to a corresponding error in the will as drafted or of a failure on his part to understand her instructions. At least, at first sight, it is difficult to understand why the plaintiff chose to begin by instituting proceedings for negligence rather than rectification.'

It was accepted that the burden of proof in a claim for rectification and a claim for damages against the solicitor were the same and, as an alternative ground of their decision, the court held that the plaintiff had failed to mitigate his loss by commencing proceedings for an order for rectification. The court distinguished the general principle established by *Pilkington v Wood*,[3] that a claimant is not obliged to mitigate his loss by embarking on uncertain and expensive litigation, on the ground that the evidence in both actions would be precisely the same.[4] Sir Christopher Slade concluded:[5]

'This is a situation in which, as a general rule, the courts can reasonably expect the plaintiff to mitigate his damage by bringing proceedings for rectification of the will, if available, and to exhaust that remedy before considering bringing proceedings for negligence against the solicitor, for example, in relation to costs incurred in the rectification proceedings.'

1   [1999] 1 WLR 727.
2   [1999] 2 WLR 727 at 738B–D.
3   [1953] Ch 770 (Harman J).
4   [1999] 2 WLR 727 at 731G–H and 738G–739H (per Sir Christopher Slade), 742E–G (per Mummery LJ) and 742H–744G (per Simon Brown LJ). See also para 9.5, note 3.
5   [1999] 2 WLR 727 at 739F–G.

9.21   In *Horsfall v Haywards*[1] the general application of this proposition was tested for the first time. In that case, the defendants admitted that they had failed to draft the testator's will in accordance with his instructions. The court did not, however, find that the plaintiff ought to have commenced rectification proceedings for three principal reasons: first, on the facts, the judge doubted whether a claim for rectification would succeed; secondly, the principal asset of the estate was the testator's house and the principal beneficiary, whose share was increased as a consequence of the defendants' negligence, moved to Canada and the proceeds of sale were remitted to her there. Rectification proceedings would have been costly and time-consuming and 'would not have resulted in any material recovery of the funds to compensate the plaintiffs for the loss of their interest under the will'; and, thirdly, and perhaps most importantly, the defendants had acted for the plaintiffs in relation to the grant of probate and had not advised them to take rectification proceedings either before the principal beneficiary moved to Canada or before the time limit for bringing the proceedings had expired. *Horsfall v Haywards* should, therefore, be regarded as an exception to the general rule and where a disappointed beneficiary becomes aware that the solicitor has failed to record the testator's instructions before the expiry of the time limit, he ought, in the first place, to bring proceedings for rectification. Indeed, even where the beneficiary becomes aware of the error after the six month period has expired, it would be sensible to make an application for permission under s 20(1)(b) to bring rectification proceedings out of time before contemplating an action against the negligent solicitor.

1   [1999] Lloyd's Rep PN 332, CA. The leading judgment was delivered by Mummery LJ who was a member of the court in *Walker v Medlicott*.

B   INTER VIVOS TRUSTS AND DISPOSITIONS

5   The duty to trustees

9.22   Where a solicitor acts both as a solicitor and as a trustee it is important to distinguish clearly between his duties to the trust as a professional solicitor and his obligations in equity as a trustee. The content of a solicitor's duties both as a trustee and as a fiduciary are considered in detail elsewhere in this work, particularly in the context of handling client funds.[1]

1   See chapter 4.

Duty to give commercial advice

9.23   Where a solicitor has been instructed by trustees to act on behalf of a trust he or she owes duties in contract and tort to his clients, the trustees. Even though the solicitor may be a trustee himself or have acted for the trust for years, there is no such thing as a general retainer[1] and the nature and scope of the retainer should be determined by the terms of the instructions given by the trustees to the solicitor from time to time. In the nineteenth century it was common for solicitor trustees to have the day to day conduct of all trust matters and to take business decisions on behalf of the trust. *Re Partington*[2] provides an example of this traditional role. In that case a solicitor, who was also a trustee, was held liable for negligently investing trust property on inadequate security. Stirling J stated:

'Mr. Allen, by his own bills of costs, appears to have acted as solicitor on behalf of the mortgagees, namely himself and his co-trustee Mrs. Partington and he has charged, as I understand it, in those bills of costs the full scale fees allowed both for negotiating the loan, for deducing title, and for preparing and completing the mortgage. Therefore he appears to me to have taken upon himself to act, in the words of one of the rules, as solicitor engaged in the whole business relating to the mortgage. By undertaking to negotiate the loan he undertook to procure a borrower from the trustees who was able to give a satisfactory security—that is, a security which would not only be sufficient as regards the legal title, but also ample in point of value to secure the fund which was to be advanced by the trustees, and therefore which would be such a security as the trustees could properly accept.'

1   See chapter 1, para 1.9.
2   (1887) 57 LT 654 at 661–2.

9.24   In the more recent case of *Bayer v Balkin*,[1] however, it was held that the duty of a solicitor trustee to his trust is no more onerous than that of any other solicitor. But that is not to say that *Re Partington* would not be followed where a solicitor (whether trustee or not) acts in the traditional nineteenth century role of a 'man of affairs' and is 'engaged in the whole business' of the trust.

1   (1995) 31 ATR 295 at 305–6 (Cohen J, Supreme Court of New South Wales).

6   The duty to disappointed beneficiaries

9.25   In the normal course the trustees would bring any claims against a solicitor for negligence in acting as solicitor to the trust (after obtaining the leave of the court) whilst the beneficiaries would bring any claims against him for breaches of his duties as trustee. There may, however, be cases analogous to *White v Jones* in which the failure by a solicitor to draw up an inter vivos deed of trust or the failure to do so adequately causes the intended beneficiaries a real loss. In *Hemmens v Wilson Browne*[1] HHJ Moseley QC stated:

'I can well understand that if a settlor, acting on the advice of his solicitor, executes an irrevocable deed of settlement, conferring benefits on X instead of, as intended, Y the solicitor may owe a duty of care not only to the settlor but also to Y. In such circumstances, leaving aside the possibility of recti- fication, it will be beyond the power of the settlor, though still alive, to put matters right, and Y will be able to prove an identifiable loss. I can also well understand that a duty of care may be owed by a solicitor to an employee for whose benefit that solicitor is retained by the employer to draft an effective tax avoidance scheme. If the scheme is ineffective, the tax will be payable and it will be beyond the ability of the employer, even if still alive, to put matters right. I accept therefore that there may be circumstances in which a solicitor may owe a duty of care in carrying out an inter vivos transaction. That, however, does not lead to the conclusion that a duty of care is owed in the context of all inter vivos transactions.'

In that case it was held that no duty of care was owed by the defendant to the beneficiary because the settlor who had promised to settle a sum of money on her but reneged on that promise after the solicitor had failed to carry out his instructions, could still put matters right and had a remedy against the defendant himself for breach of contract.[2]

1   [1995] Ch 223 at 236C–F. The case was decided after *White v Jones* in the Court of Appeal but before the House of Lords. The passage quoted in the text was also, necessarily, obiter dictum.
2   [1995] Ch. 223 at 237B–E.

9.26   In *Hemmens v Wilson Browne*, the defendant drew up a document which was ineffective to create a trust and was not under seal. As a consequence, the plaintiff had no enforceable claim against the settlor. He took advantage of this and reneged on his promise. The court was influenced by the circumstances in which the promise was made and the defendant instructed and the judge found that the plaintiff should have no greater rights against the defendant than she had against the settlor himself. Where, however, the settlor does not change his mind, the position is more difficult. Before a claim will succeed the court must be satisfied that the beneficiary falls within the principle explained by Lord Goff in *White v Jones*. The court must also be satisfied that the settlor, if he is still alive, cannot put things right (either voluntarily or by seeking rectification of the instrument from the court) and has no competing claim against a defendant. If the settlor is dead, the court must also be satisfied that the claimant has no enforceable claim for breach of contract, breach of trust or construc- tive trust against his estate. If, therefore, the settlor in *Wilson Browne* had been killed in an accident rather than changed his mind about making the gift, there appears to be no reason why the plaintiff's claim should not have succeeded even though she had not relied on the defendant's conduct.

CHAPTER 10

Litigation

10.1 In this chapter we consider first the standard of care which solicitors owe their clients in conducting litigation. But even if there is a prima facie case of breach of duty on the pleadings, defendants may apply to strike the claim out as an abuse of process on the basis that it challenges an earlier decision of the court, or as falling within the area of a solicitor's immunity from suit while acting as an advocate. These are the second and third topics examined. Fourthly, as to the causation and assessment of damages it is necessary to consider the question of damages for the loss of a chance. After mitigation, remoteness and the type of damage recoverable, at the end of the chapter we look at claims by existing or former clients, on the basis of breach of fiduciary duty or breach of confidence, to restrain solicitors from acting for others in litigation.

A LIABILITY

1 The standard of care

10.2 As in other areas of practice, a solicitor is liable for the conduct of litigation which falls below the standard to be expected of a solicitor of ordinary or reasonable competence. In 1992, the then Sir Leonard Hoffmann suggested that, in reality, it was wrong to suppose that there was a single standard which applied with equal rigour to all areas of a solicitor's work.[1] In particular, he considered that the courts tended to apply lower standards in judging solicitors' conduct in relation to the handling of litigation than they did in relation to conveyancing. In conveyancing cases, almost any error which prevented the client from obtaining good title would be held negligent, whereas in relation to litigation

> 'I think that the inherently risky and unpredictable nature of litigation is the reason why judges are more generous to solicitors in fixing the standard of care than they are in conveyancing.'

He added that, in the nineteenth century, the courts had applied lower standards to all aspects of solicitors' conduct. The standard which the law expected of solicitors in conveyancing cases had risen in recent times. Although judges did not express the reason for this, it was because solicitors were compulsorily insured, so that a finding of liability would have less disastrous consequences for the individual solicitor.

1 The talk was published: (1994) 10 PN 6.

10.3 It is striking that, in the twentieth century, there have been relatively few reported cases about the standard of a solicitor's duty in dealing with litigation, especially when compared with the number of conveyancing and lenders' cases. A considerable number of nineteenth century cases are helpfully discussed in *Jackson & Powell*[1] and *Cordery on Solicitors*.[2] But in the last thirty years, the two principal sources of reported cases in relation to lawyers' handling of litigation have been advocates' immunity and the collateral attack principle, which we discuss below,[3] and wasted costs orders, which we discuss in chapter 11. One suspects that, in relation to the former, the reason why immunity or abuse featured so largely in the defendant's case was that there was no defence on liability. As to the wasted costs jurisdiction, in most cases the court has to consider whether the conduct of the lawyer in question has been 'negligent'. This is in substance the same question as whether the solicitor has acted in breach of the duty at common law.[4] Thus, the cases discussed in chapter 11 are of considerable help in determining the standard of care which now applies in an action for professional negligence. We do not repeat our discussion of those cases here.[5] It is important to emphasise, however, that the trend of the law in relation to wasted costs orders is that such orders should be made only where the entitlement to a wasted costs order is very clear; in less clear-cut cases, a dissatisfied litigant will still have to bring an action for professional negligence. Further, a wasted costs order will of course compensate only lost costs. A client whose case is that, due to a solicitor's negligence, he has wrongly been convicted of an offence or settled a case on bad terms will still have to sue for professional negligence.

1 *Jackson and Powell on Professional Negligence* (4th edn, 1997), paras 4–141ff.
2 *Cordery on Solicitors* (9th edn, looseleaf), paras J-371ff.
3 Paras 10.13ff.
4 See chapter 11, para 11.34.
5 See chapter 11, paras 11.34–11.49.

(a) Relevance of the nineteenth century authorities

10.4 Should one regard the law as to the standard of solicitors' duties in the conduct of litigation as being stated principally in nineteenth century authorities? In other words, is it possible that the courts will hold that the standard which applies now is higher than set out in those cases? We suggest that it is. The standards which the law applies to all professionals, and in particular solicitors, have generally increased since then. Secondly, insurance is now compulsory for solicitors. Part of Hoffmann's[1] point was that judges should articulate clearly the reasons why they have increased the standards expected of solicitors in conveyancing, that is, because of compulsory insurance. But, at least in 1999, the existence of compulsory insurance does not necessarily mean that the standards expected of solicitors should be increased. As Lord Woolf MR pointed out in *Midland Bank plc v Cox McQueen*,[2] small firms of solicitors are now burdened by high insurance premiums, and finding it difficult to remain viable. Thirdly, there should be little difficulty in assessing whether there has been unreasonable delay in the conduct of litigation. The courts have long experience in determining whether there has been inexcusable and inordinate delay so as to justify striking out for want of prosecution. More recently they have had to deal with many cases where, following automatic striking out pursuant to the former CCR Ord 17 r 11, the plaintiff's solicitors have claimed that they have conducted the litigation with reasonable diligence so as to justify reinstatement.[3]

1 Para 10.2, note 1.
2 [1999] Lloyd's Rep PN 223, CA. See quotation from the case in chapter 1, para 1.2 and see also chapter 7, para 7.35.
3 See *Rastin v British Steel plc* [1994] 1 WLR 732, CA and *Bannister v SGB plc* [1998] 1 WLR 1123, esp at 1159C–D, CA.

(b) The Woolf reforms

10.5 A fourth factor is that many of the procedural issues with which the nineteenth century cases dealt either no longer arise or may well be viewed differently, because of changes in the rules of procedure. On 26 April 1999, the revolutionary new Civil Procedure Rules came into force in relation to civil litigation. These will not generally affect the standards expected of solicitors in relation to the conduct of litigation prior to that date, but they will thereafter. It remains to be seen how this will affect professional negligence actions. Delay in the conduct of litigation will probably be tolerated less than before, and it appears that the courts will be more willing to strike cases out as an abuse of process on grounds of delay.[1] Further, a heavier burden than before will lie on those seeking to engage in last minute amendments which fundamentally alter the nature of the case: such applications will often be refused,[2] so that, if the lawyers should have made the application earlier, they may be liable in negligence. The reforms are intended to produce a culture in which lawyers must act much more quickly than was previously the case. It seems likely that, if this culture is to be reflected in the practice of lawyers, there will also be a corresponding increase in the standard expected of reasonably competent litigators. In relation to cases where the sum at stake is not large, solicitors may point to the requirement of the overriding objective that they deal with cases in a way which is proportionate to, inter alia, the amount of money at stake. This cuts both ways: solicitors will not be obliged to spend large sums preparing small cases, in fact, they may be obliged to refrain from such excesses.

1   *Arbuthnot Latham Bank Ltd v Trafalgar Holding Ltd* [1998] 1 WLR 1426 at 1436E–G, CA.
2   *Worldwide Corpn Ltd v GPT Ltd* (2 December 1998, unreported), CA.

10.6   This discussion suggests that, in at least some cases, the standards which the courts expect of solicitors conducting litigation may now be higher than they were in the nineteenth century. Given the lack of recent cases on this topic, it is hard to form a clear view, but we refer below to two decisions of the Court of Appeal which may point in this direction.

2   Application of the standard

10.7   In the absence of exceptional circumstances, solicitors who failed to issue claims within the relevant limitation period,[1] allowed their clients' cases to be struck out for want of prosecution[2] or pursuant to the former CCR Ord 17 r 11, or allowed their clients to be prevented from defending the claim for procedural reasons,[3] will be liable in negligence. Exceptional circumstances might include failure of the client to provide funds or instructions, or being instructed by the client to delay even though the client is fully informed of the risks of so doing. Further, where the limitation period in a personal injury action has expired, and the defendant's insurer indicates an intention to rely upon limitation, failing to advise the client of the possibility of an application under Limitation Act 1980, s 33 is likely to be held negligent.[4] Moreover, failing to attend counsel at court when necessary,[5] failing to appear at court for a hearing when instructed to do so,[6] or failing to ensure that witnesses are warned to attend court when required,[7] are likely to amount to negligence. Where solicitors appear in court as advocates, they cannot be sued for negligence in relation to work done in court or intimately connected thereto. This is not because they cannot act negligently in court, but because such work is immune from suit.[8]

1   Cf *Saif Ali v Sydney Mitchell & Co* [1980] AC 198, HL, discussed at para 10.40. Failing to advise as to the correct limitation period under European Community law may also be negligent: *JJ Dent v National Farmers' Union* NLD, 17 June 1999 (Evans-Lombe J).
2   *Allen v Sir Alfred McAlpine & Sons Ltd* [1968] 2 QB 229, CA, per Diplock LJ at 256D–E.
3   *Godefroy v Jay* (1831) 7 Bing 413.
4   *Carlton v Fulchers* [1997] PNLR 337, CA.
5   *Hawkins v Harwood* (1849) 4 Exch 503.

6   *Holden v Holden and Pearson* (1910) 102 LT 398. The solicitor's conduct of the case was
    hampered by his work as an agent at the general election.
7   *Dunn v Hallen* (1861) 2 F & F 642, an action by attorneys for their fees. In fact, they won,
    after Bramwell B had directed the jury that they should have the fees unless their services were
    'wholly useless and valueless'. Compare the wasted costs cases in chapter 11.
8   See paras 10.36ff.

10.8   Although solicitors will be liable for errors in pleading if they undertake that
task, deciding which causes of action to plead is a matter of judgment, and it is
certainly not the case that failing to plead a cause of action which is properly arguable
necessarily amounts to negligence.[1] Failing to follow clear advice from counsel to
appeal on a point of law[2] or to obtain specific varieties of evidence before trial[3] are
likely to be regarded as negligent, whereas acting in reliance upon counsel's advice
will generally not be so regarded.[4] Failing to obtain evidence from a witness whom
it is reasonable to suppose would not wish to give evidence is not negligent.[5]
Settlement of an action without the client's authority and for a sum which is
significantly less than she would receive at trial is likely to be held negligent.[6]
Similarly, in matrimonial proceedings, solicitors acting for a wife who failed to
undertake proper investigation of the husband's means, and consequently advised
acceptance of a settlement offer which was too low, were conceded to have been
negligent.[7] Failing to apply for an ouster injunction when necessary,[8] or to seek committal
for contempt of court when an injunction against harassment has been breached,[9] may be
negligent, as may releasing a father's passport which allows him to abduct the children
of the family.[10] Failing to advise a client whose legal aid has been revoked as to the
consequences of the revocation and the options open to him is also likely to be negligent.[11]

1   *McFarlane v Wilkinson* [1997] 2 Lloyd's Rep 259, CA, per Brooke LJ at 277. The case
     concerned pleading by barristers, but the principle must be the same.
2   Cf *Walpole v Partridge & Wilson* [1994] QB 106, CA, discussed at para 10.21.
3   *Acton v Graham Pearce & Co* [1997] 3 All ER 909, Chadwick J.
4   See the discussion of acting in reliance upon counsel's advice in chapter 11, paras 11.47–
     11.49.
5   *Roe v MacGregor* [1968] 2 All ER 636, CA.
6   *Amonoo v Grant, Seifert & Grower* [1999] 01 LS Gaz R 25 (HHJ Overend sitting as a deputy
     High Court judge).
7   *Dickinson v Jones Alexander & Co* [1993] 2 FLR 521, Douglas Brown J.
8   *Dickinson* [1993] 2 FLR 521 at 525.
9   Found at first instance and not appealed in *Heywood v Wellers* [1976] 1 All ER 300, CA.
10   See the discussion of *Al-Kandari v JR Brown & Co* [1988] QB 665, CA, at chapter 1, para 1.22.
11   *Casey v Hugh James Jones & Jenkins* [1999] Lloyd's Rep PN 115, Thomas J.

(a)   Criminal law

10.9   Although most of the cases cited above concerned the loss of civil litigation,
it does not appear that the standard to be applied is any different in criminal law.[1]

1   See Chadwick J's approach in *Acton v Graham Pearce & Co* [1997] 3 All ER 909. Except
     in very limited circumstances, the Crown Prosecution Service is immune from suit in respect
     of the work of solicitors it employs: *Elguzouli-Daf v Metropolitan Police Comr* [1995] QB
     335, CA. But this may change after implementation of the Human Rights Act 1998. See *Osman
     v United Kingdom* (1998) Times, 5 November, ECtHR and *Barrett v Enfield London Borough
     Council* [1999] 3 WLR 79, HL.

(b)   Is the standard rising?

10.10   Two recent decisions in the Court of Appeal suggest that the standard applied
to the conduct of litigation may be rising, so as to bring it somewhat closer to the

standard which Hoffmann identified in relation to conveyancing.[1] In *Martin Boston & Co v Roberts*,[2] the plaintiff solicitors acted for the first defendant in an action brought against him by a company, F Ltd. They applied for security for costs against F Ltd. They compromised the application by accepting an unsecured guarantee from A, a director of F Ltd, at a time when they had only her own assertion as to her financial worth. The majority in the Court of Appeal considered that the solicitors acted negligently in taking the risk that, as ultimately came to pass, the guarantee would be worthless, without at least receiving the client's instructions to take this risk.

1   See para 10.2, note 1. See also *Baxter v Smith* NLD, 19 May 1999 (Rougier J): duty to advise client seeking a liquor licence of all options.
2   [1996] PNLR 45, CA. See chapter 2, para 2.27.

10.11   *Balamoan v Holden & Co*[1] concerned the defendant solicitors' conduct of an action by the plaintiff seeking compensation for personal injuries he had suffered when a supermarket was built near his home. Brooke LJ, with whom Evans LJ agreed, said that the case concerned

> '... the standard of care reasonably to be required of a solicitor in a small country town who is instructed by a legally aided client to pursue what appears to be a comparatively small claim. It is of critical importance for the courts not to apply a too rigorous standard in these circumstances, because when pursuing such a claim a solicitor must always be anxious not to incur costs which he cannot, if successful, recover from the other side, because otherwise the Legal Aid Board's charge will reduce his client's compensation.'

But he added that a one-man firm could not expect a lower standard of care to be applied to it simply because it delegated the work to an unqualified member of staff. Further, the defendants had acted in breach of duty. It is worth quoting further from the judgment because it shows the court engaging in a degree of scrutiny of the defendant solicitors' conduct which, it is thought, is not unlike the approach adopted in the context of, for example, solicitors' conduct of conveyancing transactions.[2] Brooke LJ said that, at the start of their engagement by the plaintiff, the defendants

> '... failed in the duty of care they owed Mr Balamoan to take such steps as were reasonable to ensure either that they took him to see counsel promptly (so that counsel could advise on what evidence should be gathered before the trail went cold) or that they gathered such evidence competently of their own initiative, and that he suffered as a consequence of this breach of duty.
>
> Since the defendants ... did not take Mr Balamoan to see counsel promptly, it was incumbent on them to take the initiative in gathering evidence themselves. Instead, they adopted a reactive stance until it was far too late to remedy the damage. In his witness statement prepared for the present trial Mr Anstee accepted that one of his initial tasks was to obtain a detailed statement from Mr Balamoan. This task, in my judgment, he never performed. A little later he points out, as if he was justifying his conduct, that Dr Hughes's November 1989 report only went as far as saying that it might well be that Mr Balamoan's asthmatic symptoms were exacerbated by dust and fumes. He did not appear to appreciate that his duty to his client and to the Legal Aid Board required him to satisfy himself that Dr Hughes would be willing, if asked, to say that on the balance of probabilities the dust did exacerbate his client's condition. He then complains that Mr Balamoan gave him different information at different times about his trips abroad in 1988, and that no evidence was ever produced showing that they had been taken on medical advice. He did not apparently realise that a reasonably competent litigation solicitor would have obtained clear instructions from his

client at an early date at an appointment in his office and discussed with him the evidence he would need on each aspect of his claim, thereby addressing any weaknesses or inconsistencies in the evidence. He also complains that he did not know Mr Balamoan had seen Dr Dyson between 1985 and January 1987. If he had asked Mr Balamoan and/or Dr Hughes the right questions in, say, January 1989, he would have found out.'

1   (28 May 1999, unreported), CA.
2   Compare the discussion of *Nationwide Building Society v Balmer Radmore* [1999] Lloyd's Rep PN 241, in chapter 7.

10.12   This statement followed a detailed and careful analysis of the steps taken to prepare the plaintiff's action for trial. We have suggested that the approach of the courts to claims of liability for the negligent conduct of litigation may need to be reconsidered in the light of developments since the nineteenth century. Two cases in the Court of Appeal do not prove the point. But that court's approach in those cases does suggest that the standard to be expected of solicitors in conducting litigation is to be assessed by careful scrutiny of each of the steps taken in the litigation and the reasons for them. The court in *Balamoan* did not shrink from findings of negligence in the basic steps taken to prepare for trial.[1] This was not a particularly complicated or technical claim, nor did it appear to the solicitors to involve large sums of money. In relation to litigation started, or steps taken, after 26 April 1999, solicitors who engage in long delay are likely to be reprimanded by pro-active judges. In relation to work done, or not done, before that date, an approach along the lines taken in *Balamoan* would subject the conduct of litigation to a standard not wholly dissimilar to that applied to conveyancing cases. It remains to be seen whether the courts will embrace such a standard.

1   It is possible that Brooke LJ's approach in *Balamoan* was influenced by his experience as one of the three Court of Appeal judges who had to consider the many appeals in relation to CCR Ord 17, r 11, and thus the question, in those cases, of whether solicitors had acted with reasonable diligence in the conduct of litigation: see *Bannister v SGB plc* [1998] 1 WLR 1123, CA.

B   THE DOCTRINE OF ABUSIVE COLLATERAL ATTACK[1]

10.13   The topics which, in the recent past, have provided more reported cases than any other in relation to the negligent handling of litigation are the doctrines of abusive collateral attack and forensic immunity. These are defences which are often dealt with at an early stage of the professional negligence action. The defendant claims that the pleaded case should be struck out as an abuse of process on the basis either that it constitutes an impermissible collateral attack on the decision of another court, or that the acts complained of fall within the advocate's immunity from suit in relation to work done in court or intimately related to such work ('forensic immunity'). These two separate concepts were considered in depth in the recent Court of Appeal decision of *Arthur JS Hall & Co v Simons* ('*Arthur Hall*').[2] The Court of Appeal had noticed that a number of appeals were pending in relation to these questions and, of its own motion, selected four appeals, all concerning the conduct of solicitors, to be tried together.[3] The court's judgment, delivered by Lord Bingham of Cornhill CJ, contains a thorough analysis of the previous cases and a clear and helpful discussion of the principles which apply. In setting out the law, we concentrate in particular on this decision. It is understood that the House of Lords has granted leave to appeal, and that the appeal may be heard around Easter of 2000. It is possible that the House will take the opportunity either to depart from or seriously to modify its earlier decisions, for example to reduce the scope of forensic immunity, and thus to change the law. But until that happens, it is likely that the Court of Appeal's decision in *Arthur Hall* will remain good law.

1   Chapter 5 of Hugh Evans's *Lawyers' Liabilities* (1996) contains a particularly lucid discussion of these subjects, though it should now be read subject to the decision in *Arthur Hall* [1999] Lloyd's Rep PN 47: see para 10.17.
2   [1999] Lloyd's Rep PN 47, [1999] PNLR 374.
3   Williams and Cooke 'Solicitors' Immunity' (1999) 143 SJ 274.

10.14   The analysis in *Arthur Hall* proceeded on the basis that the two doctrines of abusive collateral attack and forensic immunity were separate, though related, and should be considered independently. Further, it was clear that, in every case, the question of whether the claim constituted an abusive collateral attack on an earlier judgment of the court should be dealt with before considering forensic immunity. For this reason, we consider collateral attack first.

10.15   Unlike forensic immunity, the doctrine of abusive collateral attack applies to claims against solicitors whether or not they are acting as advocates.[1] The modern origin of the doctrine is Lord Diplock's speech in *Hunter v Chief Constable of West Midlands Police*.[2] This was foreshadowed by what he had said in *Saif Ali v Sydney Mitchell & Co*:[3]

'My Lords, it seems to me that to require a court of co-ordinate jurisdiction to try the question whether another court reached a wrong decision and, if so, to inquire into the causes of its doing so, is calculated to bring the administration of justice into disrepute.'

Hunter did not concern any allegation of negligence on the part of the lawyers who had handled the original hearing. The plaintiff was one of the 'Birmingham Six' who had been convicted of the Birmingham pub bombings. The case was brought well before the criminal division of the Court of Appeal overturned those convictions. So at the time of the hearing, the plaintiff was regarded, and referred to by Lord Diplock, as a convicted murderer. The House was concerned with a civil action which the plaintiff had brought against the police seeking damages for assault causing him physical injury which he alleged had been caused while he was in police custody after his arrest. This was an issue which the judge at the criminal trial had had to consider, in deciding whether the confessions of the alleged bombers were admissible evidence in that trial. The trial judge had decided that

'he accepted the evidence of the police as establishing beyond all reasonable doubt that there had been no physical violence or threats by them to the defendants and that in his opinion the evidence taken as a whole showed that there had been what he described as "gross perjury" on the part of each of the defendants.'[4]

The confessions were admitted and the accused convicted. There was an appeal to the criminal division of the Court of Appeal, but not on the basis of admission of the confessions. The appeal failed. Lord Diplock said that, when the trial ended, the trial judge's ruling on admissibility of the confessions became a final judgment. The plaintiff's claim in the civil action was essentially that he had been assaulted by the police officers and should be paid damages for this. But the same contention had already been considered in a final decision of a criminal court and rejected, and the plaintiff had not appealed that decision.

1   See *Arthur Hall* [1999] Lloyd's Rep PN 47 at 64.
2   [1982] AC 529, HL.
3   [1980] AC 198 at 222C–D, HL.
4   See [1982] AC 529 at 538F–G.

10.16 Lord Diplock continued:[1]

'The abuse of process which the instant case exemplifies is the initiation of proceedings in a court of justice for the purpose of mounting a collateral attack upon a final decision against the intending plaintiff which has been made by another court of competent jurisdiction in previous proceedings in which the intending plaintiff had a full opportunity of contesting the decision in the court by which it was made ...

My Lords, collateral attack upon a final decision of a court of competent jurisdiction may take a variety of forms. It is not surprising that no reported case is to be found in which the facts present a precise parallel with those of the instant case. But the principle applicable is, in my view, simply and clearly stated in those passages from the judgment of AL Smith LJ in *Stephenson v Garnett* [1898] 1 QB 677, 680–681 and the speech of Lord Halsbury LC in *Reichel v Magrath* (1889) 14 App Cas 665, 668 which are repeated by Goff LJ in his judgment in the instant case. I need only repeat an extract from the passage which he cites from the judgment of AL Smith LJ:

"... the court ought to be slow to strike out a statement of claim or defence, and to dismiss an action as frivolous and vexatious, yet it ought to do so when, as here, it has been shown that the identical question sought to be raised has been already decided by a competent court ..."

The passage from Lord Halsbury's speech deserves repetition here in full:

"... I think it would be a scandal to the administration of justice if, the same question having been disposed of by one case, the litigant were to be permitted by changing the form of the proceedings to set up the same case again."

He added that the proper way in which to challenge the previous decision would have been by appeal to the criminal division of the Court of Appeal, which had not been done. Further, although the subsequent civil proceedings would not amount to an abuse of process if they were based upon fresh evidence, this would have to be evidence which (i) was not available at the time of the trial, and could not with reasonable diligence have been obtained by then, and (ii) was such as "entirely changes the aspect of the case".'[2]

1   [1982] AC 529 at 541B, and 541H–542D.
2   [1982] AC 529 at 545B–D. The phrase 'entirely changes the aspect of the case' comes from *Phosphate Sewage Co Ltd v Molleson* (1879) 4 App Cas 801, 814. It is a stronger test than the test used in the civil division of the Court of Appeal, namely that the evidence 'would probably have an important influence on the result of the case, though it need not be decisive'.

10.17 Although Lord Diplock was not concerned with allegations that the lawyers engaged at the time of the criminal proceedings in *Hunter* had been negligent, it is now established that, in every case where it is alleged that the result of a lawyer's negligence was that a court hearing had a different result from that which it would have had if there had been no negligence, the court considering the professional negligence case must first consider whether the claim is an abusive collateral attack on the earlier decision of the court, which should be struck out. In *Arthur Hall*, the Court of Appeal summarised[1]

'the main features of the law as we now understand it to be in cases where (1) a plaintiff in a later action seeks relief against legal advisers who acted for the plaintiff in an earlier action which ended in a considered decision of the court or an approved settlement, and (2) the plaintiff's claim in the later action is based on negligence allegedly leading to an outcome less favourable than, but for the negligence, the plaintiff would and should have achieved, and (3) the legal advisers sued in the later action apply to restrain further prosecution of the proceedings:

(1) The first question to be asked is whether the plaintiff's claim represents an abusive collateral challenge to the earlier judgment of the court. If it does the claim will ordinarily be dismissed or struck out unless there are grounds for not following that course.

(2) In deciding whether, in any given case, the later proceedings constitute an abusive collateral challenge to the earlier judgment of the court it is always necessary to consider (a) the nature and effect of the earlier judgment, (b) the nature and basis of the claim made in the later proceedings, and (c) any grounds relied on to justify the collateral challenge (if it is found to be such).

(3) In considering the nature and effect of the earlier judgment, even greater weight will be accorded to a criminal conviction than to the final judgment in a contested civil trial, and greater weight will be accorded to the judgment in a contested civil trial than to an interlocutory judgment or order or a consent order approved by the court. It can never, however, be appropriate to explore the extent to which an individual judge considered and appraised the merits of a proposed settlement in any particular case.'

It is thus necessary to consider separately the position in relation to fully contested trials, consent orders, and interlocutory hearings.

1   [1999] Lloyd's Rep PN at 66. The rest of the summary related to consent orders and forensic immunity, which we consider below.

1   Fully contested trials

(a)   When has the now claimaint had a full opportunity of contesting the earlier decision?

10.18   In *Smith v Linskills*,[1] the plaintiff's counsel referred to Lord Diplock's dictum quoted above to the effect that the collateral attack doctrine applied in cases where the now plaintiff had, at the previous hearing, 'had a full opportunity of contesting the decision in the court by which it was made'. He argued that the now plaintiff had not had such an opportunity, because the negligence of his former legal advisers, the now defendants, had prevented him from deploying the full case which he would wish to have deployed. The Court of Appeal rejected this argument. Lord Diplock had been speaking of civil as well as criminal cases, and had meant that the collateral attack doctrine would not apply in cases where, for example, a party's civil law claim was struck out for procedural default or after summary judgment. Those were examples of cases where the now plaintiff might not have had a 'full opportunity' to contest the result. It could not be said that the now plaintiff had lacked a full opportunity to contest the case when[2]

'he had had the benefit of a solicitor and counsel throughout the proceedings, had pleaded not guilty, had attended every day of the trial, had been able to give instructions to counsel on the cross-examination of prosecution witnesses, had given evidence himself, had called witnesses, had sought to establish an alibi, had had the benefit of submissions made to the jury on his behalf, had pursued an application for leave to appeal against his conviction, had settled grounds of appeal drawing attention to some at least of his complaints about the manner in which his case had been conducted by his solicitor, and had renewed his application for leave to appeal to the full court on the initial refusal of leave.'

1   [1996] 1 WLR 763, CA.
2   [1996] 1 WLR 763 at 770B–C.

(b) Claimant's purpose in bringing professional negligence action irrelevant

10.19   The court in *Smith* also rejected the suggestion that, in considering whether a claim amounted to an abusive collateral attack, it was relevant to consider the now plaintiff's purpose in bringing the claim. It was true that, in *Hunter*, Lord Diplock had attached importance to what he took to be the plaintiff's true purpose, which was not to claim damages at civil law but to show that the confession on the basis of which he had been convicted had been induced by police violence, so as to persuade the Home Secretary to reopen the case.[1] By contrast, Mr Smith had served his sentence, and said that his true purpose in bringing the professional negligence action was simply to recover damages. The Court of Appeal held that he could not be exempted from the collateral attack doctrine on this basis. The basis of the collateral attack doctrine was the undesirable effect of relitigating such cases; this was not reduced if the claimant's purpose was simply to recover damages rather than to establish that the earlier decision had been wrong.[2]

1   See [1982] AC 529 at 541F–G. Ultimately, of course, this purpose was achieved, but by other means.
2   See [1996] 1 WLR 763 at 771D–E.

(c)   Application of Arthur Hall *principle (2)*

10.20   It will be recalled that the Court of Appeal's second principle in *Arthur Hall* was that, in considering whether the later proceedings constituted an abusive collateral attack, it was always necessary to consider both the nature and effect of the earlier judgment and the nature and basis of the claim made in the later proceedings. An example of this approach is the Court of Appeal's decision in *LR v Witherspoon*,[1] decided after *Arthur Hall*. The plaintiff sued her former solicitors. The local authority had obtained a care order in respect of her son, and decided that it would be in the best interests of the child if he was removed from his mother's care. LR instructed the solicitors who eventually applied for residence and contact. The county court judge rejected these applications, but he made clear that he might well have made a different decision if it had not been for the 12 month delay on the part of LR's solicitors in making the application. Brooke LJ, delivering the only reasoned judgment, said:[2]

> '... in [the judge]'s view the situation which a judge would have had to assess in January 1992 (absent a 14-month placement with prospective adopters and the birth of a new child) was significantly different from the situation he was being required to assess in January 1993. He would hardly have used words like "tragedy" or stigmatised the solicitors' delay as "incomprehensible" if he had not felt that things might well have turned out differently if LR's solicitors had honoured the duty of care they owed to the mother of this very young child and applied to a court promptly. It is therefore quite wrong, in my judgment, to treat the institution of these proceedings as a collateral attack on [the judge]'s judgment, since he was obliged to weigh, in the exercise of his discretion, significant new factors which would not have been present 12 months earlier.'

Thus there was no collateral attack on the judge's decision, because there was no attack on that decision. The plaintiff was not asserting that the judge had made the wrong decision, but rather that he might have made a different decision if there had been no negligence, because the materials on which he would have had to make the decision would have been different. Similarly, there is no objection to a party suing in relation to his conviction in a criminal court when the Court of Appeal has overturned the conviction: the decision which is impugned has already been overturned.[3]

1   [1999] Lloyd's Rep PN 401, CA.
2   [1999] Lloyd's Rep PN 401 at 407.
3   *Acton v Graham Pearce & Co* [1997] 3 All ER 909, Chadwick J.

(d)   Errors of law

10.21   In *Walpole v Partridge & Wilson*[1] the Court of Appeal considered the application of Lord Diplock's principle in cases where it was alleged not that there was fresh evidence which the subsequent court should take into account, but that the earlier court had made an error of law. The plaintiff was convicted by the magistrates' court of obstructing a veterinary officer in the execution of his duty, and his appeal to the Crown Court was dismissed. He then instructed new solicitors, the defendants, to advise him on the prospect of a further appeal from the Crown Court. He later sued the defendants for negligence, and in particular for having failed to lodge an appeal despite counsel's advice, which was that there were valid grounds for appeal by way of case stated on the basis that the Crown Court had erred in law. The defendants sought an order that the claim be struck out as it was an abusive collateral attack on the Crown Court's decision. Ralph Gibson LJ, delivering the only reasoned judgment, pointed out that the plaintiff relied upon an error of law rather than seeking to introduce fresh evidence, and that the defendants conceded that it was arguable that the Crown Court had indeed erred in law. He said that where the challenge was on the basis of an error of law by the earlier court, there might be no abuse of process in bringing further proceedings, and drew an analogy with the case where a collateral attack was permitted because the fresh evidence entirely changed the aspect of the case:[2]

> 'The collateral attack based upon sufficient fresh evidence, if it succeeds, demonstrates nothing more than that two different courts, acting according to law, may properly reach different conclusions upon the same or a similar issue when the evidence before the two courts is markedly different. A collateral attack based upon a failure to advance a point of law on appeal, if it succeeds, demonstrates no more than the unsurprising fact that a court may go wrong in law. It is because of that risk that rights of appeal are given by Parliament and, if a litigant is deprived of the ability to exercise his right of appeal by the breach of duty of his advisers, then, in the absence of any other defence such as immunity, or estoppel, upon which no reliance is placed in these proceedings, I see no reason why he should not be free to pursue a claim for such damages as he may prove that he suffered thereby.'

He went on to say that to allow the plaintiff's claim would not bring the administration of justice into disrepute and[3]

> 'Upon the assumption that the facts alleged are true, and upon the concession that the point of law put forward is arguable, it would be manifestly unfair to the plaintiff to deny him the right of having his case tried on the merits and it would, I think, bring the administration of justice into disrepute if the court denied him that right.'

1   [1994] QB 106, CA.
2   [1994] QB 106 at 117D–F.
3   [1994] QB 106 at 119F.

10.22   This reasoning introduces the point, which was not present in *Hunter*, that the claimant contends that the reason why the point raised in the professional negligence action was not determinative in the earlier court is that it was not raised before the earlier court due to the very negligence of his lawyers for which he now sues. Ralph Gibson LJ clearly considered that it would be contrary to public policy if the plaintiff, who had lost an arguable point of appeal, were shut out from claiming damages for that loss, *even though* it would involve holding that the earlier court had made the wrong decision. On this approach, *Hunter* could be distinguished on the basis that, in that case, it was not claimed that the reason why the earlier court had made the wrong decision was due to the negligence of the party which was now the defendant. Thus, one could say that the earlier court's decision was not being impugned: if there had been no negligence, it would have had the benefit of materials which in fact it did not have, and would have reached a different conclusion. This is similar to the Court of Appeal's approach in *Witherspoon*.[1] The effect of *Walpole* appears to be that, in relation to errors of law, the collateral attack will not be an abuse as long as it is merely *arguable* that the earlier court erred in law.

1   [1999] Lloyd's Rep PN 401, CA.

(e)   Fresh evidence

10.23   If the analysis set out in the last paragraph is right, it makes a stark contrast with cases where the basis on which the earlier decision is impugned is fresh evidence. Where the collateral attack is based upon an error of law, it will be permissible as long as it is arguable that the earlier court made such an error. But if the collateral attack is based upon matters of fact, that is, fresh evidence, the claimant has to show that it would 'entirely change the aspect of the case,' at least if he seeks to challenge the result of a contested criminal trial. It makes no difference that the claimant alleges that the reason why the court did not previously have the fresh evidence was the negligence of his lawyers which is the subject of his later claim.[1]

1   *Smith v Linskills* [1996] 1 WLR 763, CA: see para 10.18. Further, the Court of Appeal in *Arthur Hall* expressly said that there would be circumstances where it was relevant that the reason why the court reached the decision it did was due to the defendant's negligence: but these were where the court's role was only to give approval to a consent order which the parties had already agreed, and, it appears, not where there had been a contested trial. See *Arthur Hall* [1999] Lloyd's Rep PN 47 at 66.

10.24   Further, as mentioned above,[1] the now claimant must show that the fresh evidence is evidence which, even if he and his lawyers had acted with reasonable diligence in preparing for the earlier trial, they could not have obtained. This will generally mean that it is impossible for the now claimant in a professional negligence action to escape the collateral attack doctrine on the basis of such evidence, for the following reason.[2] In the professional negligence action, it will normally be the now claimant's case that his lawyers' negligence prevented the evidence being available for the earlier trial. So the now claimant will be alleging in the professional negligence action that if his former solicitors had acted with reasonable diligence then the evidence *would* have been available at the earlier trial. If the now claimant is right that, had his previous solicitors acted with reasonable diligence, they *would* have obtained the fresh evidence in time for the earlier trial, then it will be impossible for him to show that, had they acted with reasonable diligence, they would *not* have been able to obtain the fresh evidence in time for the earlier trial. But to escape the collateral attack doctrine, the now claimant would have to show that, had his previous solicitors acted with reasonable diligence, they would *not* have been able to obtain the fresh evidence in time for the earlier trial. Thus it will impossible for the now claimant to escape the collateral attack doctrine.

1   Para 10.16.
2   This point is made by Evans *Lawyers' Liabilities* (1996) pp 98–9.

10.25   Is it possible to reconcile the high threshold which a claimant has to pass to prevent his claim being an abusive collateral attack in cases where he seeks to adduce fresh evidence, and the much lower test applied where he contends that the earlier court erred in law? To do so, one would have to hold as follows. If, in a later professional negligence action, the court holds that an earlier criminal court erred in law, it will not bring the administration of justice into disrepute. But if, in the same professional negligence action, the court holds that the earlier criminal court's conviction should not have been reached because there is fresh evidence which, although it does not wholly transform the case, would have caused enough doubt to prevent a conviction, then the administration of justice *will* be brought into disrepute. Evans suggests that this can be maintained, because it is well known that courts often do come to different conclusions on points of law.[1] Certainly, after the saga involving General Pinochet, the public must be well aware of this. But the passage quoted above from *Walpole* suggested that the same applied to errors of fact. It is doubtful whether, in relation to criminal cases, the law should adopt almost wholly different approaches to the collateral attack doctrine depending on whether the new material is a point of law or a point of fact.

1   *Lawyers' Liabilities* (1996) at 99.

2   Rationale of the collateral attack doctrine

10.26   Delivering the judgment of the court in *Smith v Linskills*, which was decided after *Walpole*, Sir Thomas Bingham MR explained the policy reasons for the collateral attack doctrine and said:[1]

> 'We cannot of course shut our eyes to the possibility that a criminal defendant may be wrongly convicted, perhaps because his defence was ineptly prepared or conducted. When that occurs, it represents an obvious and serious injustice. There are two possible solutions. One is to relax the present restraint on seeking to establish that injustice by civil action. The other is to ensure that, in appropriate cases, the conviction itself can be reviewed. It seems to us clear that it is this second solution which has, over the past century, been favoured: by giving a criminal defendant a right of appeal; by providing a relatively low standard for the admission of fresh evidence on appeal; by empowering the appellate court to order a new trial; by giving the Home Secretary power to refer a case back to the Court of Appeal; and by proposals to establish a new review body.'

This approach may well apply to errors of both law and fact. In either case, it might be said that the principal remedy for injustices in the criminal law system should lie in fair and effective appeal and review procedures in that system, rather than in subsequent professional negligence actions. This would provide a strong justification for the collateral attack doctrine in relation to criminal cases.

1   [1996] 1 WLR 763 at 773D–E.

10.27   In fact, it is possible to appeal against a criminal conviction on the ground that the negligence of one's lawyers caused the conviction. The leading case is *R v Clinton*.[1] The Court of Appeal held that such appeals would succeed only in exceptional circumstances, and mere allegations that counsel had made tactical errors in the course of the trial would not be sufficient. But where, as in *Clinton* itself, it was shown that a decision as to the way in which the case should be handled 'was taken either in defiance of or without proper instructions, or when all the promptings of reason and good sense pointed the other way', then the conviction might be overturned if the court considered that the effect of the errors rendered the conviction unsafe and unsatisfactory. The errors in question could be those of counsel and also of solicitors.[2]

1   [1993] 1 WLR 1181, CA, cited at para 7-82 of *Archbold 1999*.
2   There is a debate as to whether, in order to appeal, it is necessary to allege 'flagrant incompetence' on the part of the former lawyers. The editors of *Archbold 1999* consider that the better view is that it is not.

10.28   This gives some force to the collateral attack doctrine in criminal cases. If negligence of lawyers is said to have caused the original conviction, then there should be a criminal appeal, and, in theory, if the evidence supports such a contention then the conviction should be overturned. That having happened, the collateral attack doctrine will not apply to any subsequent suit against former legal advisers. On the other hand, if the evidence is not sufficiently strong to persuade the criminal division of the Court of Appeal to overturn the conviction, why should the defendant be able to have a second bite of the cherry by suing for damages for professional negligence? It is more doubtful whether the doctrine can be justified in relation to previous decisions of civil courts, because it is harder to appeal in civil cases.[1] One factor supporting it, to which the Court of Appeal adverted in *Arthur Hall*, might be the need to prevent large numbers of hopeless claims, or 'satellite litigation'. But the answer to those may be more rigorous scrutiny and striking out of hopeless cases at an early stage.

1   See Evans *Lawyers' Liabilities* (1996) at 99–101, who argues persuasively that the doctrine is not justified in relation to past decisions of civil courts.

3   Interlocutory hearings

10.29   Lord Diplock's principle expressly referred to collateral attacks on 'a final decision' against the now claimant. This suggests that it would not apply to interlocutory decisions. In *Saif Ali*, after referring to the danger against which the collateral attack doctrine is aimed, Lord Diplock said:[1]

'A similar objection, it may be mentioned, would not apply in cases where an action has been dismissed or judgment entered without a contested hearing, and there is no possibility of restoring the action and proceeding to a trial. If the dismissal or entry of judgment was a consequence of the negligence of the legal advisers or a party to the action, a claim in negligence against the legal advisers at fault does not involve any allegation that the order of the court which dismissed the action or entered judgment was wrong.'

As mentioned above,[2] in *Smith v Linskills*[3] the Court of Appeal accepted that the doctrine would not apply in civil cases where a party's claim was struck out due to procedural default or after a summary judgment hearing, because the party whose claim was lost would not have 'fully contested' the matter.

1   See [1980] AC 198 at 223D–E.
2   See paras 10.18ff.
3   [1996] 1 WLR 763, CA: see para 10.18.

10.30   One might argue that this approach ought to apply to the results of all interlocutory hearings: the collateral attack doctrine does not apply because they are not 'final' hearings. But in *Arthur Hall* Lord Bingham said:[1]

'When, without a fully contested hearing, the court has given an interlocutory judgment ... such judgment ... is of lesser weight, and the conditions which must be met to justify a collateral challenge to such a judgment ... will be less stringent. The giving of such judgments ... are not, however, to be ignored because the full *Hunter* test is not satisfied. They involve an exercise of judicial authority, embodied in an enforceable order of the court. They are not to be lightly disregarded. At the very least, it will be incumbent on a party seeking to mount a collateral challenge to such an order to explain why steps were not taken to set aside or challenge the judgment or order complained of in the original proceedings.'

On the face of it this appears to be an extension of the *Hunter* principle, which is inconsistent with the passages from *Saif Ali* and *Smith v Linskills* to which we have referred: a collateral attack on an interlocutory judgment striking a claim out for procedural default or giving summary judgment would, according to this passage, amount to an abuse unless the condition set out in the quotation was satisfied. But that condition does not appear to be particularly onerous. The now claimant has to explain why steps were not taken to set aside or challenge the interlocutory order in the original proceedings. This is likely to be due to the negligence of the now defendant, so it is something which the now claimant would probably have had to deal with even if he or she did not need to overcome the doctrine of collateral attack. Further, it would be surprising if Lord Bingham had intended to say that the approach which he himself had set out in *Smith* was wrong. For these reasons, it may well be the case that the doctrine of collateral attack will rarely prevent challenges, in later professional negligence actions, to interlocutory decisions, especially in relation to decisions giving summary judgment or striking out a claim.

1   [1999] Lloyd's Rep PN 47 at 64.

4   Compromise in civil cases: consent orders

10.31   In *Arthur Hall*, the court recognised that the extent to which consent orders required the exercise of judicial consideration might vary considerably.[1] For example, the approval of a settlement in say a personal injury case on behalf of a person under a disability requires a considerable degree of scrutiny on the part of the court. On the other hand, where adult parties of sound mind settle a case and decide to embody the agreement in a consent order, the court in approving the order ordinarily engages in no exercise of judgment as to whether the settlement is reasonable. In ancillary relief cases, before approving a settlement the court receives a brief form which summarises key facts such as the age of the parties, the duration of the marriage, and the approximate amount or value of the capital resources and net income of each party. In this type of case, 'it is only if a broad appraisal of the parties' financial circumstances as disclosed to it in summary form puts the court on inquiry that the court should probe more deeply'.[2] Thus these cases fall into an intermediate category: there is some judicial scrutiny of the reasonableness of the settlement, but not much.

1   See [1999] Lloyd's Rep PN 47 at 56 for a discussion of various examples.
2   *Arthur Hall* [1999] Lloyd's Rep PN 47 at 58.

(a)   Consent orders which do not require the approval of the court

10.32   The court in *Arthur Hall* did not need to decide what, if any, weight attaches for collateral attack purposes to a consent judgment which did not require or receive the approval of the court, such as a consent order embodying an agreement between adults of sound mind.[1] But, for the reasons given above in relation to interlocutory judgments, it is hard to see why the administration of justice should be brought into disrepute by alleging that one's solicitor's negligence brought about a consent order, if the order was one in relation to which the court exercised no discretion at all. It is submitted that the collateral attack doctrine should not apply to such cases.

1   See [1999] Lloyd's Rep PN 47 at 64, para 40.

(b)   Consent orders which do require the approval of the court

10.33   The Court of Appeal summarised the position in relation to consent orders which do require the approval of the court in its fourth and fifth principles:[1]

'(4) Where the later proceedings do constitute a collateral attack upon a consent judgment approved by the court in previous proceedings they may, and ordinarily will, be an abuse of the process unless the plaintiff can properly allege a breach of duty which either (a) deprived the plaintiff of a reasonable opportunity of appreciating that better terms were available whether on settlement or at a contested hearing than the plaintiff obtained, or (b) placed the plaintiff in the position of having to accept a settlement significantly less advantageous or more disadvantageous than he should have had.

(5) A plaintiff seeking to mount a collateral challenge to an earlier judgment or order will be required to explain why steps were not taken to set aside or challenge the judgment or order complained of in the original proceedings. The court will be reluctant to sanction the initiation of satellite proceedings against legal advisers, and will never do so without substantial grounds. It will never be enough that the plaintiff is suffering from post-settlement remorse.'

1   See [1999] Lloyd's Rep PN 47 at 66.

10.34   It is doubtful whether, in practice, claimants whose actions relate to consent orders approved by the court, and who have arguable cases, will be much inconvenienced by the requirements set out in this quotation. This appears from the Court of Appeal's decisions in the four cases which it had to consider as part of the *Arthur Hall* judgment. In none of them did the court consider that the claim was prevented by the doctrine of collateral attack, even though, in each, it applied the principles set out in the passage quoted. If claimants cannot satisfy either requirement (4)(a) or (4)(b) in that passage, then it is doubtful whether they will be able to prove causation in the professional negligence action even ignoring the doctrine of collateral attack. Similarly, it can be argued that requirement (5) is another way of expressing the principle that a claimant has a duty to mitigate his or her loss if this can be done by means of alternative legal proceedings which are not complex or difficult to mount.[1] That principle applies whether or not the claim is a collateral attack upon an earlier decision of the court.

1   See para 10.63.

5   Compromise in criminal cases: the guilty plea

10.35   It follows from the discussion above that the rationale of the court's approach should be that, the less judicial consideration there is of any particular decision, the less it is the case that a collateral attack on that decision in a later professional negligence action should amount to an abuse of process. One might think that this should mean that proceedings which amounted to a collateral attack on a guilty plea in criminal law would not be an abuse of process, because it was the accused who decided to plead guilty and not the court which decided that he or she was guilty, so that a subsequent professional negligence claim would not suggest that the court had been wrong. In fact, however, a guilty plea attracts the same degree of protection under the doctrine as a conviction after a fully contested trial.[1] It is thought that, in light of the court's decision in *Arthur Hall* as to consent judgments at civil law, the rule in relation to guilty pleas can be justified only the basis that the position at criminal law is different to that in civil law.

1　See *Somasundaram v M Julius Melchior & Co* [1988] 1 WLR 1394, CA. Contrary to what the headnote says, the court's decision on abuse of process was probably obiter, because it first concluded that the action should be struck out as it was bound to fail even in the absence of collateral attack arguments: see 1397G–H. In any case, in *Arthur Hall* the Court of Appeal said (at 64): '... a collateral challenge in civil proceedings to a subsisting criminal conviction, particularly a conviction upheld or not challenged on appeal, *and whether the defendant was convicted on his own admission or on the verdict of a court or jury,* must be the hardest to justify.' (Emphasis added.)

C　FORENSIC IMMUNITY

10.36　A particularly helpful feature of the Court of Appeal's decision in *Arthur Hall*[1] was the clear distinction which it drew between the doctrine of collateral attack and forensic immunity. The latter is the advocate's immunity for work done in court, or which is intimately related to such work. We develop the definition below. It is clear that forensic immunity now applies to barristers, solicitors, and anyone else lawfully doing the work of an advocate, in relation to such work.[2]

1　[1999] Lloyd's Rep PN 47.
2　Court and Legal Services Act 1990, s 62 and see further below.

10.37　The rationale of the doctrine of abusive collateral attack is to prevent the administration of justice being brought into disrepute by impugning the court's earlier decisions. As the Court of Appeal pointed out in *Arthur Hall*,[1] once collateral attack is seen as being a separate doctrine, 'where later proceedings are objectionable as an abusive collateral challenge to an earlier judgment of the court that fact cannot, on its own, afford a public policy ground for granting forensic immunity'. There must be a separate justification for forensic immunity.

1　See [1999] Lloyd's Rep PN 47 at 66, principle (6).

1　Origins of forensic immunity

10.38　The scope of forensic immunity is determined by its rationale, so it is helpful to consider what the rationale is. We do not claim to be legal historians, but a few comments as to what appear to be the origins of forensic immunity may suggest that the rationales currently being considered for it were largely invented in the 1960s.[1] It appears that, in 1435, the orthodox view in England was that a client could sue an advocate for errors in relation to court work in the same way as he could sue a carpenter or a farrier.[2] The cases were silent about the question during the next two or three centuries, a period in which the profession of barrister began to flourish.[3] The matter was not reconsidered until 1791.[4] In the meantime, however, barristers as a profession were seeking to present themselves as being socially and intellectually superior to solicitors and attorneys, whose profession had also come into existence.[5] To this end, barristers began[6] 'to aspire to the neo-classical ideal of a profession of gentlemen, detached from the pursuit of lucre and united in their devotion to a superior vocation.'

This led to adoption of the notion that, unlike solicitors and attorneys, barristers could not sue for their fees. The fees were an honorarium, a present, from the client, as had nominally been the case in ancient Rome.[7] The reason was that the profession of law was 'such a holy thing that it was not to be debased or evaluated in monetary terms'.[8] This did not in fact cause barristers much inconvenience, as they were usually paid in advance, and the rule avoided champerty if a barrister accepted part of an estate as his honorarium. But it did lead conveniently to the notion that, as there was no contract between barrister and client, the client could not sue the barrister in contract for failure to act with reasonable skill or care. Before 1969, the textbook writers gave this as the principal justification for the rule, which had been established in the nineteenth century, that barristers were immune from suit by their clients.[9] As Hoffmann has observed, one does not have to be a Marxist to see a strong element of class protection in this rule.[10]

1   The sources of our information, but not our conclusion, are Prof JH Baker's article 'Counsellors and Barristers' which was prompted by the decision of the House of Lords in *Rondel v Worsley* [1969] 1 AC 191, and republished in his *The Legal Profession and the Common Law* (1986), and the analysis of Lawton J, who had consulted four versions of the Year Books from the reign of Henry VI, in *Rondel* at first instance: [1967] 1 QB 443 at 455–466.
2   Per Lawton J, [1967] 1 QB 443 at 458–9. A farrier shoes horses.
3   See Prest *The Rise of the Barristers* (1986). Before this, advocates had been almost exclusively serjeants-at-law, a different profession.
4   *Fell v Brown* (1791) 1 Peake 131, cited by Lawton J in *Rondel* [1967] 1 QB 443.
5   But not without the expression of judicial displeasure. Lord Chancellor Egerton unkindly described them as 'caterpillars of the commonwealth': Harding *A Social History of English Law* (1966).
6   Prof Baker (see note 1) at 118.
7   The defining feature of the common law is of course supposed to be that it is not based on Roman law. The *lex Cincia de donis et muneribus* (204 BC) was a *lex imperfecta* which prevented advocates from suing for fees or gifts which clients had agreed to pay or give in return for their services. By Cicero's time the law was not taken seriously, and, if an advocate conducted a client's defence, the client would incur an obligation which he would be expected to discharge at a later date, by means of political support, an interest-free loan, a legacy or a gift: see D H Berry *Cicero—Pro P Sulla Oratio* (1996) p 40. The original rationale for the rule was probably as follows. From the earliest times at Rome, there had been a strong moral duty to appear in court and plead cases for one's dependants and relatives. This moral code was perceived to be breaking down, as some advocates were being paid, hence the law: Watson *Roman Private Law around 200 BC* (1971) pp 73–74. There is, however, no evidence of any such moral code in nineteenth century England. A less uplifting motive for the passing of the law may have been envy of those who had begun to charge fees for advocacy (Dr Berry, in correspondence).
8   Professor Baker (see note 1) at 118, quoting Ulpian.
9   See the argument of Louis Blom-Cooper for the appellant in *Rondel*: [1969] 1 AC 191 at 200B–C.
10 (1994) 10 PN 6: see para 10.2.

2   Modern rationales for the immunity

10.39   If this rationale were correct, it would provide a complete immunity from suit for all barristers, whether working in court or out, and no immunity for solicitors, whether working as advocates or not. In modern times, the notion that barristers are so grand that they cannot be sued for negligence need only be stated to be rejected out of hand. In any case, the rationale based on the absence of a contract was destroyed by the House of Lords' decision in *Hedley Byrne & Co Ltd v Heller & Partners Ltd*.[1] Following that decision, the House of Lords was asked to consider the status of forensic immunity in *Rondel v Worsley*.[2] It held that a barrister was immune from suit for negligence in relation to work done in court during the course of a criminal trial. It was accepted that the immunity applied not only to barristers but also to solicitors doing work as advocates.[3] The basis for the immunity was public policy. The different judges had different notions of precisely what the relevant public policy was, and of the extent to which it would provide immunity for work done outside the confines of a trial.

1   [1964] AC 465, HL.
2   [1967] 1 QB 443.
3   [1969] 1 AC 191 at 232, 267, 284 and 294. As mentioned above, Courts and Legal Services Act 1990, s 62 now gives solicitors this immunity, when acting lawfully as advocates.

10.40   Eleven years later, the issue of forensic immunity returned to the House of Lords in *Saif Ali v Sydney Mitchell & Co*.[1] By a 3–2 majority, the House held that a barrister was not immune from suit in relation to negligent advice, given out of court and before expiry of the limitation period, as to who should be party to a running down action, or for settling proceedings on the basis of that advice. Lord Diplock, one of the majority, pointed out that the immunity of advocates could no longer be justified on the basis that barristers did not enter contracts with their clients. Further, the immunity was an exception to the general principle that professional people were liable to their clients for failing to act with reasonable skill and care. The extension of liability for professional negligence had proceeded apace since *Rondel*. This rendered the immunity harder to justify. If public policy justified an advocate's immunity from suit, it had to be for reasons which did not apply in relation to any other type of professional. Further, in order to decide how far the immunity extended, it was necessary to determine what the rationale for the immunity was.

1   [1980] AC 198, HL.

10.41   Lord Diplock considered various rationales which had been proposed in *Rondel*. His reasoning in rejecting the first three candidates is compelling.[1] The first was that barristers owed a duty to the court. But all this meant was that they must obey professional rules, as must other professionals. So this could not provide a justification which did not apply to other professions. Secondly, barristers had to make finely balanced and difficult decisions at speed and under pressure; but so did other professionals such as surgeons and salvors. Further, the standard of care took account of this, as there would be a breach of duty only if the defendant had acted in way in which no reasonable barrister would have done. Thirdly, barristers were subject to the cab rank rule, and might have to act for[2]

> 'an obstinate and cantankerous client who is more likely than more rational beings to bring proceedings for negligence against his counsel if disappointed in the result of his litigation; but the existence of this risk does not, in my view, justify depriving all clients of any possibility of a remedy for negligence of counsel, however elementary and obvious the mistake he had made may be. There are other and more specific means of disposing summarily of vexatious actions.'

1   See *Saif Ali* [1980] AC 198 at 219E–221B.
2   [1980] AC 198 at 221E–F.

10.42   Lord Diplock did, however, consider that there were two rationales which justified forensic immunity. The second rationale was essentially that which underlies the doctrine of abusive collateral attack, which we considered above. But, once that doctrine is treated as being free-standing, and a prior question, as required by the Court of Appeal's decision in *Arthur Hall*, this rationale cannot of itself justify forensic immunity.[1] Lord Diplock's first rationale for the immunity was:[2]

> 'that the barrister's immunity from liability for what he says and does in court is part of the general immunity from civil liability which attaches to all persons in respect of their participation in proceedings before a court of justice, judges, court officials, witnesses, parties, counsel and solicitors alike. The immunity is based on public policy, designed, as was said by Lord Morris of Borth-y-Gest ([1969] 1 AC 191 at 251), to ensure that trials are conducted without avoidable stress and tensions of alarm and fear in those who have a part to play in them. As was pointed out by Starke J in *Cabassi v Vila* ((1940) 64 CLR 130 at 141), a case in the High Court of Australia: "The law protects witnesses and others, not for their benefit, but for a higher interest, namely, the advancement of public justice." The courts have been vigilant to prevent this immunity from indirect as well as direct attack, for instance by suing witnesses for damages for giving perjured evidence or for conspiracy to give false evidence: see *Marrinan v Vibart* [1963] 1 QB 528.
>
> In *Watson v M'Ewan* [1905] AC 480, this House held that in the case of witnesses the protection extended not only to the evidence that they give in court but to statements made by the witness to the client and to the solicitor in preparing the witness's proof for the trial, since, unless these statements were protected, the protection to which the witness would be entitled at the trial could be circumvented.'

1   See *Arthur Hall* [1999] Lloyd's Rep PN 47 at 66.
2   *Saif Ali* [1980] AC 198 at 222A–D.

10.43   It remains to be seen whether, in the further appeal in *Arthur Hall*, the House of Lords considers that even this rationale is sufficient basis for the immunity. To Lord Diplock's regret, in *Saif Ali* the House of Lords had not had the benefit of argument from counsel to the effect that the immunity should be abandoned altogether.[1] It may well be necessary to protect *witnesses* from 'avoidable stress and tensions of alarm and fear', even in some cases professional expert witnesses,[2] but is there really a compelling public interest, sufficient to deny compensation to those who have suffered loss due to incompetence, in protecting advocates from such fears? Is it not part of the very essence of being an advocate that one should be able to cope with the stress and alarm of conducting a trial in court? Is there really a strong public interest in protecting nervous advocates and their insurers from having to pay for their negligent mistakes in court?[3]

1   See [1980] AC 198 at 223F–G.
2   Compare *Stanton v Callaghan* [1998] 4 All ER 961, CA.
3   See Evans *Lawyers' Liabilities* (1996) p 91.

10.44   It is also possible that the immunity may constitute a disproportionate restriction on the right of access to a court, in breach of Art 6.1 of the European Convention on Human Rights,[1] which will be directly enforceable in English law when the Human Rights Act 1998 comes into effect.[2]

1   Compare *Osman v United Kingdom* (1998) Times, 5 November, ECtHR.
2   At the time of writing, it is not clear when this will be.

3   Scope of the immunity

10.45   The extent of conduct which falls within the immunity depends on the rationale for it. But as there is no clear agreement as to the rationale, the extent of the conduct covered is unclear. In *Saif Ali*,[1] each member of the majority accepted the test for the scope of the immunity formulated by McCarthy P in the New Zealand Court of Appeal in *Rees v Sinclair*:[2]

> 'I cannot narrow the protection to what is done in court: it must be wider than that and include some pre-trial work. Each piece of before-trial work should, however, be tested against the one rule; that the protection exists only where the particular work is so intimately connected with the conduct of the cause in court that it can fairly be said to be a preliminary decision affecting the way that cause is to be conducted when it comes to a hearing. The protection should not be given any wider application than is absolutely necessary in the interests of the administration of justice, and that is why I would not be prepared to include anything which does not come within the test I have stated.'

Commenting on this passage, Lord Wilberforce said:[3]

> 'I do not understand this formulation as suggesting an entirely new test, ie a double test requiring (i) intimate connection with the conduct of the cause in court and (ii) necessity in the interests of the administration of justice. The latter words state the justification for the test but the test lies in the former words.'

Each member of the majority in *Saif Ali* considered that the work of advising who should be joined to proceedings in a running down action, before expiry of the limitation period, fell outside the test and thus outside the immunity.

1   [1980] AC 198, HL: see paras 10.40ff.
2   [1974] 1 NZLR 180 at 187.
3   See [1980] AC 198 at 215D–E.

10.46   In *Arthur Hall*, the Court of Appeal held that the immunity would apply to a solicitor only insofar as he or she was doing the work of an advocate. Thus, in cases where a solicitor instructs counsel, he or she will normally be unable to rely upon the immunity. Further, the court indicated that:[1]

> 'Save where a claim relates to the acts or omissions of an advocate conducting a contested case in open court, forensic immunity is not to be recognised on the application of any blanket rule. It is always necessary to look with care at the specific complaint of negligence made against the lawyer in the context of the particular case.
>
> *Saif Ali* indicates that there are certain forms of advice (such as decisions made on strategic or professional grounds on whether witnesses should or should not be called, or whether claims or defences should or should not be pleaded) which would be covered by forensic immunity if made in court in the course of a trial and are likely to be similarly protected if made out of court before a trial. We cannot, however, accept that a similar immunity should attach to allegedly negligent decisions made out of court on, for example, the legal strength or weakness of a claim, or the legal admissibility of evidence, or the approximate value of a claim. It may very well be, of course, that the lawyer will succeed in rebutting any accusation of negligence; but the question whether the lawyer is negligent is quite distinct from the question whether he is immune.
>
> If our foregoing analysis is correct, it must follow that there can be no general rule that counsel is, or is not, immune from liability in settling a case or, as it

should more properly be put, in advising his client that the case should be settled. Nor, in our view, can it safely be said that such advice given at the door of the court on the day of the hearing, or even during the hearing, is necessarily immune, and advice given at any earlier stage is not: all must depend on the advice given, the reason for it and the complaint made about it. Advice based on the advocate's assessment of the strength of the evidence, or the likelihood of a finding of contributory negligence may be one thing; advice based on a palpable error of law or deficient research may be quite another. Whatever the advice in question, and whenever and wherever the same is given, the basic question must always be whether public policy requires the recognition of immunity in the case in question. Any doubt must be resolved against the grant of forensic immunity, since such immunity derogates from what we have described as a fundamental principle and the law should be slow to grant its own practitioners a protection denied to members of other professions.'

1   [1999] Lloyd's Rep PN 47 at 64–65.

10.47   This passage, together with the court's application of it to the four cases it had to decide in *Arthur Hall*, suggests that, apart from work done in court in the conduct of a contested trial, forensic immunity should now be very closely circumscribed. Of previous decisions in which it had been said that forensic immunity applied, the Court of Appeal disapproved three at first instance,[1] declined to comment on a further two at first instance as they were the subject of appeals,[2] and declined to follow a previous decision of the Court of Appeal itself.[3] As the court indicated, where the case concerns a 'palpable error of law', there is unlikely to be immunity for out of court preparation. Circumscribed in this way, it is doubtful whether the immunity serves any purpose. The examples given of cases which fall within it tend to relate to decisions of advocates not to follow a particular course for tactical reasons, or in order to comply with a duty to the court. But decisions of these types would generally be unlikely to be regarded as negligent even if there were no immunity. They would probably be negligent only if utterly misguided; if they were utterly misguided, why should they be the subject of immunity from suit? The immunity of advocates in court in relation to defamation must clearly remain, but it is doubtful whether immunity in court can be justified in relation to negligence. It is possible that, when the House of Lords reconsiders the matter, the law will move forward to the position which it adopted in 1435,[4] so that advocates may be sued for negligence in court in the same way as the builders who build the courtroom.

1   *Landall v Dennis Faulkner & Alsop* [1994] 5 Med LR 268 (Holland J), *McFarlane v Wilkinson* [1996] 1 Lloyd's Rep 406 (Rix J), and *Griffin v Kingsmill* [1998] PNLR 157 (Timothy Lloyd J).
2   *Atwell v Michael Perry & Co* [1998] 4 All ER 65 (Sir Richard Scott VC) and *Griffin v Kingsmill (No 2)* (20 February 1998, unreported) (Buckley J).
3   *Kelley v Corston* [1998] QB 686, CA.
4   See para 10.38.

D   CAUSATION AND ASSESSMENT OF DAMAGES

1   General principles relating to loss of civil claims

10.48   The type of loss most commonly claimed in actions for the negligent conduct of civil litigation are loss of the following types of opportunity: (i) to proceed with a claim to trial, (ii) to defend a claim, (iii) to obtain a settlement of a claim, or (iv) to obtain a better outcome than was in fact achieved, whether at trial or by settlement. The types of negligence most likely to give rise to items (i) to (iii) are striking out of the claim or the defence or allowing the limitation period to expire without issuing a valid claim. Similarly, in relation to negligent handling of criminal litigation, there may be claims for loss of the opportunity either to have the prosecution dropped or to have won an acquittal, or to have received a more lenient sentence. All these varieties of claim require the court trying the professional negligence action to assess what might have happened in the previous litigation. Although this may often be a complicated exercise, it is in fact similar to what lawyers do every day in advising their clients as to the likely outcome of litigation, which they have to do in order to advise whether claims should be settled. Thus the features which the court trying the professional negligence action has to consider are likely to be factors which practitioners in the relevant area of law are considering on a daily basis. The judge trying the action may not be an expert in the particular field of law in question, but that is a different problem, and in principle surmountable by reference to the specialist textbooks.[1]

1   Compare *Bown v Gould & Swayne* [1996] PNLR 130, CA: see chapter 2, para 2.15.

10.49   The precise nature of the claim will of course depend on what the parties contend would have happened if there had been no negligence, and, as in other areas of the law of damages, the principal task in every case is a careful analysis of the facts and assessment of what would probably have happened in the absence of breach of duty. Thus the role of authority in indicating how the court should approach any particular case is likely to be relatively limited. But there are some broad general principles which apply. The starting point in assessing damages in this area of the law is a passage from the judgment of Lord Evershed MR in *Kitchen v Royal Air Forces Association*.[1] The plaintiff's husband had been electrocuted and killed in his kitchen. She alleged that his death had been caused by faulty wiring in the cooker, which was the responsibility of an electricity company. The defendant solicitors acted for her in relation to her potential claim against the electricity company, but they failed to issue a writ before expiry of the limitation period. This was negligent. Counsel for the defendants contended that, in relation to damages, the plaintiff had to show, on the balance of probabilities, that, had there been no negligence, she would have won the action, and that, if there was a lower than 51% chance that she would have won the action, she had failed to satisfy that burden, and should recover nothing. The Court of Appeal rejected this, as being the wrong approach to assessing damages in this type of case. Lord Evershed MR said:[2]

'If, in this kind of case, it is plain that an action could have been brought, and, that if it had been brought, it must have succeeded, the answer is easy. The damaged plaintiff then would recover the full amount of the damages lost by the failure to bring the action originally. On the other hand, if it be made clear that the plaintiff never had a cause of action, that there was no case which the plaintiff could reasonably ever have formulated, then it is equally plain that she can get nothing save nominal damages for the solicitors' negligence. I would add, as was conceded by counsel for the plaintiff, that in such a case it is not enough for the plaintiff to say: "though I had no claim in law, still, I had a nuisance value which I could have so utilised as to extract something from the other side, and they would have had to pay something to me in order to persuade me to go away."

The present case, however, falls into neither one nor the other of the categories which I have mentioned. There may be cases where it would be quite impossible to try "the action within the action", as counsel for the second defendants asks.

It may be that for one reason or another the action for negligence is not brought until, say, twenty years after the event, and in the process of time the material witnesses, or many of them, may have died or become quite out of reach for the purpose of being called to give evidence. In my judgment, assuming that the plaintiff has established negligence, what the court has to do in such a case as the present is to determine what the plaintiff has lost by that negligence. The question is: Has the plaintiff lost some right of value, some chose in action of reality and substance? In such a case it may be that its value is not easy to determine, but it is the duty of the court to determine that value as best it can.'

The trial judge had held that the most the plaintiff could have recovered at trial would have been £3,000, and reduced it to £2,000 because of difficulties in the action. The Court of Appeal agreed with his approach to assessing damages, though it would have awarded less than £2,000 if there had been an appeal as to quantum.

1   [1958] 1 WLR 563, CA.
2   [1958] 1 WLR 563 at 574–575.

10.50 The Court of Appeal considered *Kitchen* in the context of a solicitor's negligence more widely in *Allied Maples Group Ltd v Simmons & Simmons*,[1] which is discussed fully in chapter 3.[2] It held that, where the court had to assess the claimant's loss by considering what a third party would have done if there had been no negligence, the correct approach was as follows. First, the court had to consider whether the claimant had shown that there was a real or substantial chance that, absent negligence, the third party would have acted in the way that the claimant asserted. If the claimant failed to prove this, he recovered only nominal damages; if he proved it, the court then assessed the value of the chance which the claimant had proved, and discounted his damages in accordance with that chance. The discount might give a figure of less than 50%. The court rejected an argument that, if the chance was less than 50%, the claimant had failed to prove loss on the balance of probabilities and should recover nothing. In the context of litigation, in *Mount v Barker Austin*,[3] two separate firms of solicitors who were acting for the plaintiff had allowed two successive sets of proceedings to be struck out for want of prosecution. Simon Brown LJ, with whom Ward LJ agreed, set out the following principles in relation to assessing loss in cases were negligence had caused an action to be struck out:[4]

'(1) The legal burden lies on the plaintiff to prove that in losing the opportunity to pursue his claim (or defence to counter-claim) he has lost something of value ie that his claim (or defence) had a real and substantial rather than merely a negligible prospect of success. (I say "negligible" rather than "speculative"— the word used in a somewhat different context in *Allied Maples Group Ltd v Simmons & Simmons* [1995] 1 WLR 1602—lest "speculative" may be thought to include considerations of uncertainty of outcome, considerations which in my judgment ought not to weigh against the plaintiff in the present context, that of struck-out litigation.)

(2) The evidential burden lies on the defendants to show that despite their having acted for the plaintiff in the litigation and charged for their services, that litigation was of no value to their client, so that he lost nothing by their negligence in causing it to be struck out. Plainly the burden is heavier in a case where the solicitors have failed to advise their client of the hopelessness of his position and heavier still where, as here, two firms of solicitors successively have failed to do so. If, of course, the solicitors have advised their client with regard to the merits of his claim (or defence) such advice is likely to be highly relevant.

(3) If and insofar as the court may now have greater difficulty in discerning the strength of the plaintiff's original claim (or defence) than it would have had at the time of the original action, such difficulty should not count against him, but rather against his negligent solicitors. It is quite likely that the delay will have caused such difficulty and quite possible, indeed, that that is why the original action was struck out in the first place. That, however, is not inevitable: it will not be the case in particular (a) where the original claim (or defence) turned on questions of law or the interpretation of documents, or (b) where the only possible prejudice from the delay can have been to the other side's case.

(4) If and when the court decides that the plaintiff's chances in the original action were more than merely negligible it will then have to evaluate them. That requires the court to make a realistic assessment of what would have been the plaintiff's prospects of success had the original litigation been fought out. Generally speaking one would expect the court to tend towards a generous assessment given that it was the defendants' negligence which lost the plaintiff the opportunity of succeeding in full or fuller measure.'

These principles apply when a claim or counterclaim has been struck out for want of prosecution. By analogy, they would probably also apply to cases where the claim was struck out for failure to comply with the former CCR Ord 17, r 11. Principle (1) applies to all cases in which there is a claim for loss of litigation, due to the authority of *Kitchen*[5] which we have already discussed. It seems likely that principles (2) to (4) will also apply where the litigation is lost as a consequence of failure to issue the claim within the limitation period: in those cases too, it seems unlikely that the court will wish to be over-generous to the negligent solicitors.

1   [1995] 1 WLR 1602, CA.
2   See chapter 3, paras 3.15ff and 3.54.
3   [1998] PNLR 493, CA. See chapter 3, para 3.16, note 1.
4   [1998] PNLR 493 at 510D–511C.
5   [1958] 1 WLR 563, CA.

10.51   There is no doubt that the correct approach is as set out in *Kitchen*, though the test requires further elaboration. The court must consider the evidence as to what would have happened if there had been no negligence. As mentioned above, in relation to loss of civil litigation, broadly two possibilities are likely to arise: either the case would have been fought to trial, or it would have settled. We consider these two possibilities, and then the position in relation to criminal litigation.

(a)   Trial or settlement?

10.52   Strictly speaking, the court should first consider whether it is likely that, in the absence of negligence, the case would have settled, or gone to trial. If the court assesses damages purely by reference to the likely outcome at trial, it implies that there would have been no settlement. Alternatively, in *Amonoo v Grant*[1] there had in fact been a settlement, but, if there had been no negligence, the case would not have settled and would have gone on to trial. Thus the court had to compare the settlement made with the sum which would have been awarded at trial. If, on the other hand, the court considers that, absent negligence, the case would have settled, then what it should assess is the figure at which it is likely that the claim would have settled, and compare that to the figure which was in fact received, if any. There is, perhaps, a danger of over-elaboration in asking whether the court should assess the question of whether the case would have been tried or settled by reference to a balance of probabilities test, or the percentage chance of each happening. The better approach is probably to assess this by reference to the balance of probabilities and then ask what would have happened in the hypothetical trial or settlement.

1   [1999] 01 LS Gaz R 25 (HHJ Overend sitting as a deputy High Court judge).

10.53   Although settlements tend be calculated by reference to what the parties think the court would award at trial, there may be subjective factors, specific to the parties, which would have determined their attitudes to a settlement. There may, for instance, be reasons why one party would have been keen to get rid of the litigation quickly but at a higher price. It all depends on the evidence in the particular case. For example, in *Dickinson v Jones Alexander & Co*,[1] a claim relating to ancillary relief proceedings, Douglas Brown J considered that it was very unlikely that the husband would have compromised the wife's claim, so he ignored the possibility of settlement and looked simply to what the court would have awarded at a hearing. On the other hand, in *McNamara v Martin Mears & Co*,[2] another claim relating to ancillary relief proceedings, Peter Pain J considered that the most likely outcome would have been that the husband *would* have settled, though at a figure which represented accurately the value of the claim. Thus he concentrated on what would have happened if the case had settled.

1   [1993] 2 FLR 521, Douglas Brown J. See also *Cook v Swinfen* [1967] 1 WLR 457 (Lawton J).
2   (1982) 127 Sol Jo 69 (Peter Pain J), and see the Lexis transcript, pp 16–17.

(b)   Means and willingness to pay of the other party to the lost litigation

10.54   Where the claim is that, absent negligence, the claimant would have had either a judgment or an agreement to pay from the other party to the lost litigation, it is necessary to consider (i) whether that party would in fact have been able to afford to pay, at the time when he or she would have been asked for the money, and (ii) whether it would have been necessary and possible to enforce the judgment, if the other party would have been unwilling to pay.[1]

1   See pp 16–17 of the Lexis transcript of *McNamara* (1982) 127 Sol Jo 69, para 10.53.

2   Civil cases: loss of a trial

(a)   Time at which the assessment is made

10.55   The first questions are when, if there had been no negligence, the trial would have taken place, what evidence would have been available at the trial, and what the claimant could have expected to recover at most at trial. The latter figure is then discounted for the loss of a chance.[1] This could lead to surprising results. Imagine that the claim is for the loss of a personal injury action. If there had been no negligence, trial would have taken place in 1995, when it would have appeared that the claimant, aged 25, would never work again due to the negligence of the then defendant. What he has lost is an award of damages, assessed in 1995, for loss of earnings for his full working life. Then suppose that trial of the professional negligence action takes place in 1998. By this time there is evidence available that the claimant has made a wonderful recovery and is able to play football for Manchester United, with an enormous salary, so that by 1998 it appears that he will suffer no loss of earnings for the period after 1996. In theory, evidence of his condition in 1998 is irrelevant, because what the court is assessing is the amount of damages which would have been awarded at trial in 1995. It might be relevant to show what, had there been a trial, would have been said at that trial in 1995 as to the future prognosis. But, if the evidence is that in 1995 no one would have realised that he might recover, then he ought to receive compensation for lost earnings for life, even though he will not actually suffer such a loss. This is because he is being compensated in 1998 not for the lost earnings, which he will now not lose, but for loss of a trial in 1995, at which he would have been awarded loss of earnings for life. In theory, if the evidence is that, at trial in 1995, no one would have realised that he might recover, so that he would have been awarded all his lost earnings for life, then it is irrelevant that by 1998 when the professional negligence action is tried he has recovered in full.[2] Of course, on different facts, the variation between 1995 and 1998 might be greatly to the detriment of the claimant and to the benefit of the defendant: in the intervening period the claimant's condition may have worsened fundamentally, but in a way which would not have been foreseeable in 1995. This too would be irrelevant to trial of the professional negligence action. It is thought that, if a case were ever to arise in which the facts were as extreme as those quoted in our example, the court might feel that, while in strict logic it should follow the approach of ignoring developments after 1996, in practice it might be prepared to take them into account in order to give effect to the overriding principle of achieving fair compensation, and avoiding an over-mechanistic application of the principles of compensation.[3]

1   See *Yardley v Coombes* (1963) 107 Sol Jo 575, Edmund-Davies J.
2   See *Johnson v Perez* (1988) 82 ALR 587, High Court of Australia, and *Nikolaou v Papsavas, Phillips & Co* (1988) 82 ALR 617, High Court of Australia, cited by *Jackson & Powell* at para 4-230.
3   Compare *County Personnel (Employment Agency) Ltd v Alan R Pulver & Co* [1987] 1 WLR 916, CA.

(b)   Nominal damages

10.56   In assessing the likely outcome at trial, one begins with Lord Evershed's three categories of case.[1] The Court of Appeal will generally not be prepared to interfere with the assessment of the first instance judge who tried the professional negligence action.[2] If the claim would have been hopeless, or, in Simon Brown LJ's words, if it would have had a negligible prospect of success, then only nominal damages will be awarded[3] and, as mentioned in the passage quoted from Lord Evershed above, the claimant should not be awarded damages for the nuisance value of the claim. Similarly, if a case in fact settled but the claimant alleges that it should not have been settled and that, if it had fought, more would have been awarded at trial, there will be nominal damages if more would not have been awarded at trial.[4] Again, if solicitors negligently fail to advise a claimant as to his rights in the event of legal aid being withdrawn, the claimant will recover only nominal damages if, had there been no negligence, legal aid would not have been reinstated and, had it been reinstated, he would have had no real prospect of success at trial.[5]

1   See para 10.49.
2   See *Paffett v Trier* (2 December 1994, unreported), CA.
3   See, for example, *Buckley v National Union of General and Municipal Workers* [1967] 3 All ER 767 (Nield J).
4   *Green v Cunningham John & Co* (1995) 46 Con LR 62, CA.
5   *Casey v Hugh James Jones & Jenkins* [1999] Lloyd's Rep PN 115 (Thomas J).

(c)   Strong cases

10.57   Even the strongest case is not free from risk,[1] and so one would imagine that it would be a rare case in which the court would award the claimant the full sum which it considers he or she could have hoped to achieve, at best, at trial. But in *Dickinson v Jones Alexander & Co*,[2] Douglas Brown J rejected the notion of any discount, on the basis that the husband would not have settled, and that there was no, or only a negligible, risk of the wife obtaining anything less than the proper award. It is thought that this will be the right approach only where there can be very little doubt as to the correct amount of damages.

1   *Jackson & Powell* para 4-227.
2   [1993] 2 FLR 521.

(d) Intermediate cases

10.58   It is doubtful whether, once the principles on which loss is to be assessed have been established, the citation of authority can help much, especially in relation to intermediate cases. Each case turns on its facts, so the assessment of the probabilities in any given case will depend on the facts of that case and not of others.[1]

1   Some examples are: *Yardley v Coombes* (1963) 107 Sol Jo 575 (Edmund-Davies J)—employers' liability claim, chance assessed at one third; *Gregory v Tarlo* (1964) 108 Sol Jo 219 (McNair J)—employers' liability claim, chance assessed at 75%; *Malyon v Lawrance, Messer & Co* [1968] 2 Lloyd's Rep 539 (Brabin J)—road accident in West Germany, assessment of likely damages in German court, 50% reduction for likely contributory negligence finding; *Gascoine v Ian Sheridan & Co* [1994] 5 Med LR 437 (Mitchell J)—medical negligence claim, chance assessed at 60%.

(e) Appeals

10.59   In some cases the court has to make an assessment of the outcome of not one but two hypothetical further hearings. Thus in *Corfield v DS Bosher & Co*,[1] the plaintiff's case was that the defendant's negligence had caused him to lose the opportunity to appeal from the award of an arbitrator to the Commercial Court; further, if the appeal had taken place, the Commercial Court would have remitted the matter back for hearing before a fresh arbitrator. Thus the court had to assess the likely outcome of both the appeal hearing and the hearing before the fresh arbitrator, and discount the plaintiff's claim for the risk of failure at both stages. While this may be complicated, it is of course similar to the exercise which lawyers have to undertake in advising clients of the likely outcome of an appeal which, if allowed, would lead to the case being remitted for a further hearing. This is difficult but not impossible.

1   [1992] 1 EGLR 163 (Judge Crawford QC sitting as a deputy High Court judge).

(f) Costs

10.60   The courts seem generally to have ignored the incidence of costs in assessing damages for loss of a trial.[1] The court should approach the matter in the same way as an advocate advising a client on the prospects of settling the case. If the claim was for a maximum award of £100,000, and there was a 90% chance of success, then there was a 10% chance that the claimant would have lost and had to pay the defendant's costs. Ignoring for the moment the element of untaxed costs, if the claimant had won the £100,000 then he or she would have had his or her own costs paid by the defendant. If costs on both sides would have been £10,000 each, then what the claimant has lost is a 90% chance of winning £100,000 and having to pay no costs, but he or she has also escaped a 10% risk of winning nothing and having to pay both sides' costs (£20,000). The value of what the claimant has lost can be expressed as (90% x

£100,000 = £90,000) – (10% x £20,000 = £2,000), giving a total of £88,000 rather than £90,000. Of course, if the prospect of winning £100,000 is only 50%, then the calculation is (50% x £100,000 = £50,000) – (50% x £20,000 = £10,000) = £40,000 rather than £50,000. But even this analysis may be too simple, if the likelihood is that the claimant would have recovered damages in a range between say £60,000 and £80,000, or if there might have been a payment into court which would have been rejected. In principle, risks in relation to costs should be dealt with expressly in judgments, and are capable of a reasonable degree of arithmetical elucidation.

1   See Evans *Lawyers' Liabilities* (1996) ch 7, pp 131–135, where the point is developed. There is some reference to costs in *Corfield v DS Bosher & Co* [1992] 1 EGLR 163 (see para 10.59), *McNamara* (1982) 127 Sol Jo 69 (see para 10.53), and *Port of Sheerness Ltd v Brachers* [1997] IRLR 214, Buckley J, discussed at para 10.61.

3   Civil cases: losing a settlement, or obtaining a worse settlement than deserved

10.61   In *McNamara v Martin Mears & Co*,[1] Peter Pain J considered it most unlikely that, in the absence of negligence, the husband would have wished to go to court for a hearing in relation to ancillary relief. Instead, he would have made a shrewdly judged settlement offer. Thus the questions were when, and in what amount, it was likely that he would have made it. In the events that had happened, the husband had in fact made a much lower settlement offer. Damages thus comprised the difference between the amount of the settlement which was in fact offered, and that which would have been agreed absent negligence, making deductions for the hazards of litigation and costs. Further, there was a deduction in that, in the events that happened, the plaintiff had been paid earlier than she would have been if there had been no negligence. In *Port of Sheerness Ltd v Brachers*,[2] the defendants negligently advised that, if the plaintiff dismissed its dockers on the ground of redundancy, the only payments it would have to make would be redundancy payments. The negligence was in failing to mention the risk of unfair dismissal proceedings, which were then brought and settled for a further £10,000 per docker. Buckley J found that, if there had been no negligence, (i) the likelihood was that the plaintiff would have settled with the dockers for a lower sum; he assessed the value of the chance at £2,000 per docker; (ii) there was a 90% chance that proceedings would have been avoided, so the plaintiffs were awarded 90% of the costs of those proceedings.

1   (1982) 127 Sol Jo 69 (Peter Pain J), and see the Lexis transcript; discussed at para 10.53.
2   [1997] IRLR 214 (Buckley J).

4   Criminal cases

10.62   In *Acton v Graham Pearce & Co*,[1] the plaintiff was himself a solicitor, who was charged with obtaining money from the Law Society by deception, on the basis that he had submitted green forms to the society for payment when he knew that they contained false information. The defendants represented him in the criminal proceedings. He instructed them that responsibility for operation of the scheme in his office had been delegated to an employee, S, and that S had been forced to leave her previous firm. He further suggested that memoranda written by S, on which the prosecution relied, were not authentic. The defendants negligently failed to submit the memoranda to an expert to check their authenticity, or to take statements from the partners of S's previous firm. The plaintiff was convicted. On appeal, the Court of Appeal admitted fresh evidence from both those sources, and quashed the conviction. Having held the defendants negligent and rejected a claim to immunity, Chadwick J assessed the claim as one for damages for loss of the chances that, if the plaintiff had been properly represented, either the prosecution would have withdrawn the case, or he would have been acquitted at trial. He considered the various events which would have happened, and said:[2]

> 'The quantification of the value of a chance lost cannot be an exact science. The task is made more difficult when, as in the present case, the value of the chance lost depends on the evaluation of a sequence of chances; each of which contributes to the loss of a favourable outcome overall. I do not think that the task is assisted by over-refinement. The court must make the best estimate it can.'

He assessed the chances that, absent negligence, the plaintiff would have escaped conviction at 50%. He was not asked to consider the amount of compensation to which this 50% figure should be applied, and directed an inquiry as to that.

1   [1997] 3 All ER 909, Chadwick J.
2   [1997] 3 All ER 909 at 935.

E   MITIGATION OF LOSS AND TYPES OF DAMAGE RECOVERABLE

10.63   If the effect of a solicitor's negligence is that the claimant loses the opportunity to bring or defend the claim at all, then it will not be possible for the negligent solicitor to contend that the claimant should have mitigated his or her loss by bringing alternative proceedings. There may, however, be cases where such a contention is arguable. We dealt with mitigation in the sense of bringing alternative proceedings in chapter 3.[1]

1   See paras 3.40ff.

10.64   Damages for mental distress arising out of solicitors' breaches of duty are in general not recoverable, because, in general, the object of the contract made with solicitors is not to provide comfort or pleasure, or the relief from discomfort.[1] But if solicitors negligently fail to enforce an injunction to prevent harassment, and the client is harassed further, they may be liable for this further mental distress,[2] or if their negligence causes the client wrongly to be convicted of a criminal offence, they may be liable for mental distress caused to the client who perceives himself, wrongly, to be seen as a criminal by his friends, family and acquaintances.[3] They may also be liable for mental distress if their negligence causes a client to be made bankrupt.[4] Further, if solicitors are aware that the client is suffering from an anxiety syndrome related to the litigation, and that the syndrome will probably terminate as soon as the litigation does, if their negligence causes the litigation to go on longer than necessary they may be liable for the increased period for which the anxiety syndrome is suffered.[5]

1   *Hayes v Dodd* [1990] 2 All ER 815, CA.
2   *Heywood v Wellers* [1976] QB 446, CA.
3   *McLeish v Amoo-Gottfried & Co* (1993) 10 PN 102 (Scott Baker J).
4   *R v Graham and Oldham* (29 June 1999, unreported) (McKinnon J).
5   *Malyon v Lawrance, Messer & Co* [1968] 2 Lloyd's Rep 539 (Brabin J).

F   RESTRAINT OF SOLICITORS ACTING IN LITIGATION

10.65   In *Prince Jefri Bolkiah v KPMG*,[1] the House of Lords recently reviewed the circumstances in which the court will grant an injunction, at the behest of a solicitor's existing or former clients, to prevent the solicitor acting as a solicitor for third parties in litigation. In other words, if A perceives his interests to be contrary to those of B, in what circumstances may A seek an injunction to prevent S, his solicitor or former solicitor, from acting as a solicitor in litigation for B? Although the case concerned the conduct of accountants, they had been doing the work of solicitors in preparing litigation, and conceded that the principles which applied were the same as those which applied to solicitors. Lord Millett, with whose speech the other judges agreed, said that it was necessary to distinguish between two situations. First, if the application is made by an existing client whose interests conflict with those of the third party, then the basis for the application is breach of fiduciary duty. Secondly, if the application is made by a former client, then its basis is the risk of misuse of confidential information. We consider these two situations in turn. In either case, the court has power to grant an injunction restraining the solicitors in question from acting for the third party in the litigation.

1   [1999] 2 WLR 215, HL.

1   Claim brought by an existing client: breach of fiduciary duty

10.66   Lord Millett said that, where an application for restraint was made by an existing client of the solicitor,[1]

> '... a fiduciary cannot act at the same time both for and against the same client, and his firm is in no better position. A man cannot without the consent of both clients act for one client while his partner is acting for another in the opposite interest. His disqualification has nothing to do with the confidentiality of client information. It is based on the inescapable conflict of interest which is inherent in the situation.
>
> This is not to say that such consent is not sometimes forthcoming, or that in some situations it may not be inferred. There is a clear distinction between the position of a solicitor and an auditor. The large accountancy firms commonly carry out the audit of clients who are in competition with one another. The identity of their audit clients is publicly acknowledged. Their clients are taken to consent to their auditors acting for competing clients, though they must of course keep confidential the information obtained from their respective clients. This was the basis on which the Privy Council decided *Kelly v Cooper* [1993] AC 205 in relation to estate agents.'

Thus, a solicitor cannot without consent act for two existing clients whose interests conflict. If consent is expressly given there is no difficulty. If it is not expressly given it may be inferred, but Lord Millett implies that it will not often be inferred in the case of solicitors. Where a lender and a borrower both instruct the same solicitor, the borrower is taken to consent to the solicitor passing information relating to title to the lender,[2] but it is thought that such consent will rarely be inferred in relation to the conduct of litigation.

1   [1999] 2 WLR 215 at 222H–223C. This passage was obiter, but of considerable weight.
2   See chapter 7.

10.67 Where a practising solicitor acts as a deputy judge, he owes no fiduciary duties to any client of his firm's, and thus does not act in breach of fiduciary duty if he tries an action which may have an effect upon the interests of one of his firm's clients.[1]

1   *Locabail (UK) Ltd v Bayfield Properties Ltd* [1999] 20 LS Gaz R 39 (Lawrence Collins QC sitting as a deputy High Court judge).

2   Claims brought by a former client: breach of confidence

(a)   The test which the court applies

10.68 Lord Millett went on to deal with the position where a former clients seeks to restrain a solicitor from acting in litigation:[1]

'Where the court's intervention is sought by a former client, however, the position is entirely different. The court's jurisdiction cannot be based on any conflict of interest, real or perceived, for there is none. The fiduciary relationship which subsists between solicitor and client comes to an end with the termination of the retainer. Thereafter the solicitor has no obligation to defend and advance the interests of his former client. The only duty to the former client which survives the termination of the client relationship is a continuing duty to preserve the confidentiality of information imparted during its subsistence.

Accordingly, it is incumbent on a plaintiff who seeks to restrain his former solicitor from acting in a matter for another client to establish (i) that the solicitor is in possession of information which is confidential to him and to the disclosure of which he has not consented and (ii) that the information is or may be relevant to the new matter in which the interest of the other client is or may be adverse to his own. Although the burden of proof is on the plaintiff, it is not a heavy one. The former may readily be inferred; the latter will often be obvious. I do not think that it is necessary to introduce any presumptions, rebuttable or otherwise, in relation to these two matters. But given the basis on which the jurisdiction is exercised, there is no cause to impute or attribute the knowledge of one partner to his fellow partners. Whether a particular individual is in possession of confidential information is a question of fact which must be proved or inferred from the circumstances of the case.'

Thus the rationale for restraint in relation to former clients is quite different: it is the danger of misuse of confidential information rather than breach of fiduciary duty. The applicant must satisfy the two criteria numbered (i) and (ii), but this will not be hard. Once the applicant has done this, Lord Millett said that[2]

'... the court should intervene unless it is satisfied that there is no risk of disclosure. It goes without saying that the risk must be a real one, and not merely fanciful or theoretical. But it need not be substantial.'

1   [1999] 2 WLR 215 at 223C–G.
2   [1999] 2 WLR 215 at 226H.

(b)   Application of the test of 'real but not fanciful' risk of disclosure: Chinese walls

10.69 Briefly, the way in which this test applied to the facts of *Prince Jefri* was as follows. KPMG, the very large international firm of accountants, had acted for the plaintiff, Prince Jefri Bolkiah, in relation to major litigation in which he was personally involved. They had acted for 18 months ending in May 1998. The work was done by KPMG's forensic accounting department and included a large amount of work normally done by solicitors. But KPMG did it on its own without the intervention of external solicitors. One hundred and sixty-eight members of KPMG's staff were involved, including 12 partners and 81 people of assistant manager status or above. KPMG were paid around £4.6m for the work. Prince Jefri was the youngest brother of the Sultan of Brunei, and the chairman of the Brunei Investment Agency ('BIA') until 1998. He was then removed from the BIA and the government of Brunei commenced a major investigation into its activities. In early July 1998 the government of Brunei engaged KPMG's forensic accounting department to undertake investigations into the activities of the BIA. Lord Millett said that this might well lead to civil or criminal action against Prince Jefri, and that it was common ground that it was clear by this stage that (i) some of the confidential information which KPMG had obtained while acting for Prince Jefri would be relevant to this further investigation, and (ii) the interests of Prince Jefri were adverse to those of the BIA. KPMG decided that it could properly act for the BIA, which it commenced to do, without seeking Prince Jefri's consent or notifying him of its action. 50 of its staff worked on the new project, of whom 11 had previously done work for Prince Jefri, though KPMG contended that none of them was in possession of any confidential information.

10.70   KPMG's case was that the information barrier, or Chinese wall, which it erected was sufficient to prevent any risk of misuse of confidential information, and it offered an undertaking not to misuse any information confidential to Prince Jefri. It had used different personnel, different computer servers, and had ensured that the work was done in a secure office in a different building from where Prince Jefri's work had been done. The findings of the judge at first instance, that KPMG and its staff were honest and would do their best to fulfil their obligations, were accepted. Nevertheless, the House of Lords considered that these measures were inadequate:[1]

> 'The Chinese walls which feature in the present case, however, were established ad hoc and were erected within a single department. When the number of personnel involved is taken into account, together with the fact that the teams engaged on [Prince Jefri's work] and [the BIA's work] each had a rotating membership, involving far more personnel than were working on the project at any one time, so that individuals may have joined from and returned to other projects, the difficulty of enforcing confidentiality or preventing the unwitting disclosure of information is very great. It is one thing, for example, to separate the insolvency, audit, taxation and forensic departments from one another and erect Chinese walls between them. Such departments often work from different offices and there may be relatively little movement of personnel between them. But it is quite another to attempt to place an information barrier between members all of whom are drawn from the same department and have been accustomed to work with each other. I would expect this to be particularly difficult where the department concerned is engaged in the provision of litigation support services, and there is evidence to confirm this. Forensic accountancy is said to be an area in which new and unusual problems frequently arise and partners and managers are accustomed to share information and expertise. Furthermore, there is evidence that physical segregation is not necessarily adequate, especially where it is erected within a single department.'

1   [1999] 2 WLR 215 per Lord Millett at 228G–229B.

10.71 We have quoted from the facts of *Prince Jefri* in some detail, because subsequent cases are likely to turn on a careful analysis of the facts to see whether they demonstrate more than a fanciful risk, bearing in mind the House of Lords' approach. It would appear that it will be difficult to contend that Chinese walls maintained between different parts of the same department of large firms of solicitors will be effective, at least if they occupy the same building. On the other hand, Laddie J distinguished *Prince Jefri* in *Young v Robson Rhodes*.[1] The plaintiffs were suing Pannell Kerr Forster ('PKF'), a large accountants' firm, for negligence. They employed the defendants, who worked in the forensic account- ancy department of Robson Rhodes ('RR'), as expert witnesses to support their case. Suddenly the plaintiffs were informed that RR and PKF were proposing to merge, so that their expert witnesses would be part of the firm they were suing. There was no doubt that the experts had confidential information about the plaintiffs which was relevant to the litigation. But Laddie J declined to grant an injunction delaying the merger until after the trial. He considered that effective measures could be taken to prevent the risk of disclosure of confidential informa- tion. The information was confined to only four fee earners and two secretaries. Undertakings were given to ensure, inter alia, that those who had worked on the plaintiffs' case would not have any professional contact with those working on defending the case, and would be housed in separate buildings.

1   (1999) Times, 11 May.

10.72 In *Davies v Davies*,[1] the Court of Appeal held that there was more than a fanciful risk of conflict where a wife had consulted a solicitor who specialised in matrimonial matters in 1991 and discussed matters relating to her marriage with him, and her husband engaged the same solicitor to act for him in divorce proceedings against the wife in 1997. The House of Lords in *Prince Jefri* overruled the Court of Appeal's statement of the law in *Rakusen v Ellis, Munday & Clarke*,[2] but it is clear from Lord Millett's speech that he considered that the result reached in that case had been correct. He summarised the facts as follows:

> 'It concerned a small firm of solicitors with only two partners who carried on what amounted to separate practices, each with his own clients, without any knowl- edge of the other's clients and with the exclusive services of some of the clerks. The plaintiff consulted one of the partners in relation to a contentious matter. After he had terminated his retainer, the other partner, who had never met the plaintiff and was not aware that he had consulted his partner, was retained by the party opposite in the same matter. The judge granted an injunction to restrain the solicitor from acting. The Court of Appeal found that there was no risk of disclosure of confidential information and discharged the injunction.'

This, and the *Robson Rhodes* case, suggest that, even where the claimant shows that Lord Millett's first two requirements for the grant of an injunction are made out, there will still be some cases where the solicitors are able to show that the risk of misuse of confidential information is no more than fanciful so that an injunction should not be granted. In addition to the requirements of the case law which we have discussed, solicitors acting in these circumstances will also wish to consider their professional duties set out in *The Guide to the Professional Conduct of Solicitors*.[3]

1   (4 March 1999, unreported), CA.
2   [1912] 1 Ch 831. See [1999] 2 WLR 215 at 222A and 228G.
3   (7th edn, 1996), discussed by Lush and Satyadeva (1999) 143 SJ 610.

3   Conflict of interest when acting as an advocate

10.73   Rule 4.1(e) of the Law Society's Code for Advocacy provides:

'Advocates must not accept any brief if to do so would cause them to be professionally embarrassed, and for this purpose advocates will be professionally embarrassed ... (e) if they have been responsible for deciding on a course of action and the legality of that action is in dispute in the proceedings ...'

The Court of Appeal considered the effect of this provision in *Christie v Wilson*.[1] David Price, a solicitor with expertise in defamation law, had advised the editor of a magazine called *Spiked* in relation to the publication of an article about the athlete Linford Christie. After conversations with journalists of *Spiked*, he had advised the editor that there was no significant risk that the editor would be sued for libel as a result of publishing the article. The editor published the article and Linford Christie sued for libel. The defendants to the libel action engaged Mr Price to conduct their defence. The plaintiff alleged that, in doing so, Mr Price was acting in breach of rule 4.1(e) because he had advised in relation to the article which was the subject of the action; thus he had been responsible for deciding on the course of action of publishing the article, and the legality of that action was in dispute in the proceedings. The Court of Appeal disagreed. It was necessary to distinguish between deciding on a course of action, which would have triggered operation of the rule, and merely advising on the merits of a course of action, which would not. Mr Price had done only the latter, so he was not covered by the rule. It may be observed that this is a fairly fine distinction, which may prevent rule 4.1(e) from operating in many cases. If Mr Price had considered that his action in advising publication might have been seen as negligent, then it is submitted that he would have had to have ceased acting. But it looks from the report as if no one had suggested this. He had had conversations with journalists from *Spiked*, but was unable to divulge their contents, probably because he was bound by privilege and obligations of confidentiality from doing so. It seems likely that, had the contents of those conversations been known, they would have shown that it could not be suggested that Mr Price had acted negligently.

1   [1998] 1 WLR 1694, CA.

PART 3

Procedure

CHAPTER 11

Orders that solicitors pay the costs of litigation personally

A CIRCUMSTANCES IN WHICH THE COURT MAY ORDER THAT SOLICTORS PAY COSTS PERSONALLY

11.1   In addition to the risk of being sued for negligence or breach of contract by their own clients, solicitors face the possibility of orders that they pay the costs of proceedings personally. The principal jurisdiction under which the courts may make such orders in civil proceedings, is the wasted costs jurisdiction, which was introduced with effect from 1 October 1991 by Supreme Court Act 1981, s 51(6).[1] Most of the discussion in this chapter relates to civil proceedings, but provisions relating to criminal proceedings are considered at the end of the relevant sections.

1   This provision does not have retrospective effect: *Fozal v Gofur* (1993) Times, 9 July, CA.

11.2   Before examining the rules as to wasted costs in detail, it is helpful to consider the court's other powers to make costs orders against solicitors. In *Tolstoy-Miloslavsky v Aldington*,[1] Rose LJ said that there were only three categories of case which could give rise to an order for costs against a solicitor. The first was pursuant to the wasted costs jurisdiction. The others were:

> '... (ii) if it is otherwise a breach of duty to the court such as, even before the Judicature Acts, could found an order, eg if he acts, even unwittingly, without authority or in breach of an undertaking; (iii) if he acts outside the role of a solicitor, eg in a private capacity or as a true third party funder for someone else.'

This was approved by Lord Woolf MR in *Hodgson v Imperial Tobacco Ltd*, where he also made clear that the court should consider making an order under the second head only after it had considered whether to make a wasted costs order.[2] Following Lord Woolf's approach, in this chapter we first consider wasted costs orders, and only then look at Rose LJ's second and third categories of order.

1   [1996] 1 WLR 736 at 745H–746A, CA.
2   [1998] 1 WLR 1056 at 1066H, CA.

B WASTED COSTS ORDERS

11.3   Wasted costs orders provide a means whereby solicitors and barristers may be ordered to compensate either their own client, or a party to litigation other than the client for whom they act, for costs incurred by that party as a result of acts done or omitted by the solicitors or barristers in their conduct of the litigation.[1] The definition to be used in conjunction with the Civil Procedure Rules 1998 ('CPR') is:[2]

> 'A wasted costs order is an order that the legal representative pay a specified sum in respect of costs to a party or that costs relating to a specified sum or items of work be disallowed.'

Making an application for a wasted costs order is not straightforward. The cardinal point is that the court will grant such an order only in plain cases, which are capable of being dealt with quickly and in summary fashion.[3] There are further pitfalls which we also discuss below.

1   See *Ridehalgh v Horsefield* [1994] Ch 205 at 225F, CA. That case was not concerned with orders against solicitors' or barristers' own clients.
2   See para 2.8 of the *Practice Direction about Costs Supplementing Parts 43 to 48 of the Civil Procedure Rules—Directions Relating to Part 48—Costs—Special Cases*, Section II (hereafter 'the *Part 48 Practice Direction*').
3   See paras 11.6ff.

11.4   The Civil Procedure Rules have altered the text of the procedural rules to be followed in seeking a wasted costs order, but not the statutory provision granting jurisdiction to make the order, which remains Supreme Court Act 1981, s 51 of which the relevant parts state:

'51(1)   Subject to the provisions of this or any other enactment and to rules of court, the costs of and incidental to all proceedings in—

(a)   the civil division of the Court of Appeal;

(b)   the High Court; and

(c)   any county court,

shall be in the discretion of the court ...

(6)   In any proceedings mentioned in subsection (1), the court may disallow or (as the case may be) order the legal or other representative concerned to meet, the whole of any wasted costs or such part of them as may be determined in accordance with the rules of court.

(7)   In subsection (6), "wasted costs" means any costs incurred by a party—

(a)   as a result of any improper, unreasonable or negligent act or omission on the part of any legal representative or any employee of such a representative; or

(b)   which, in the light of any such act or omission occurring after they were incurred, the court considers it unreasonable to expect that party to pay ...

(13)   In this section "legal or other representative", in relation to a party to proceedings, means any person exercising a right of audience or right to conduct litigation on his behalf.'

11.5   We begin this section by considering the procedural rules which apply when making a wasted costs order, and then the substantive rules as to the circumstances in which the court will make such an order. In considering both the procedure and substance of the law, the leading case is the Court of Appeal's unanimous decision in *Ridehalgh v Horsefield*[1] ('*Ridehalgh*'), though some of the points made there would now be decided differently as a result of changes made by the CPR.

1   [1994] Ch 205, CA.

1   Procedure

11.6   The key point is that the wasted costs jurisdiction is intended to be a reasonably simple and summary form of procedure, to be used only in clear cases, where the issue can be dealt with relatively quickly and without the need for lengthy pleadings or hearings lasting weeks. The general principles of the procedure were set out by Sir Thomas Bingham MR in *Ridehalgh*, in a passage which merits quoting in full:[1]

'The procedure to be followed in determining applications for wasted costs must be laid down by courts so as to meet the requirements of the individual case before them. The overriding requirements are that any procedure must be fair and that it must be as simple and summary as fairness permits. Fairness requires that any respondent lawyer should be very clearly told what he is said to have done wrong and what is claimed. But the requirement of simplicity and summariness means that elaborate pleadings should in general be avoided. No formal process of discovery will be appropriate. We cannot imagine circumstances in which the applicant should be permitted to interrogate the respondent lawyer, or vice versa. Hearings should be measured in hours, not in days or weeks. Judges must not reject a weapon which Parliament has intended to be used for the protection of those injured by the unjustifiable conduct of the other side's lawyers, but they must be astute to control what threatens to become a new and costly form of satellite litigation.'

In *Warren v Warren*,[2] Lord Woolf MR, with whom the other judges agreed, quoted this passage, emphasised the concluding words, and added that, in *Warren*, it would have been better if the application had never been made. Similarly, in *Wall v Lefever*, the other judges agreed with Lord Woolf, who said:[3]

'... in relation to a decision of a judge of first instance who has heard the evidence and seen the witnesses, and who had come to the conclusion that a wasted costs order should be refused, great caution should be exercised before launching on an appeal. The wasted costs jurisdiction is salutary as long as it is not allowed to be a vehicle which generates substantial additional costs to the parties. It should not be used to create subordinate or satellite litigation, which is as expensive and as complex as the original litigation. It must be used as a remedy in cases where the need for a wasted costs order is reasonably obvious. It is a summary remedy which is to be used in circumstances where there is a clear picture which indicates that a professional adviser has been negligent etc. If a judge has come to the conclusion that the case is not one which falls within that category, then an appeal will only be justified if there is some point of principle involved which indicates that the judge's approach was wholly wrong.'[4]

This approach is now reflected in para 2.5 of the *Part 48 Practice Direction*[5] which provides that

'the court will give directions about the procedure that will be followed in each case in order to ensure that the issues are dealt with in a way that is fair and as simple and summary as the circumstances permit.'

Now that the CPR are in force, applicants must bear in mind the principle of proportionality.[6] Further, Lord Woolf MR has stated that the wasted costs jurisdiction is unlikely to be appropriate in cases which call for detailed investigations of fact, or in which allegations of dishonesty on the part of lawyers are made.[7]

1   [1994] Ch 205 at 238G–239A, CA.
2   [1997] QB 488 at 494–5, CA.
3   [1998] 1 FCR 605 at 614a–d, CA.
4   Parts of this passage were cited with approval by Simon Brown LJ in *Fletamentos Maritimos SA v Effjohn International BV* (10 December 1997, unreported), CA (the Court of Appeal's decision on aspects other than wasted costs in this case appears at [1997] 2 Lloyd's Rep 302). Further, in *Tolstoy-Miloslavsky v Aldington* [1996] 1 WLR 736, CA Roch LJ said at 747H that the jurisdiction should be exercised only in a clear case. See also *Turner Page Music Ltd v Torres Design Associates Ltd* (1998) Times, 3 August, CA.
5   See para 11.3, note 2.
6   *Re Merc Property Ltd* (1999) Times, 19 May (Lindsay J).
7   *Manzanilla Ltd v Corton Property and Investments Ltd* [1997] 3 FCR 389, CA.

(a)   Appeals to the Court of Appeal in relation to refusals to make wasted costs orders

11.7   The effect of the passage quoted in the last paragraph is that the Court of Appeal is keen to discourage appeals against judges' refusals to make wasted costs orders. This was underlined by the order which the Court of Appeal made in *Wall*: the appellant had to pay the costs of the appeal taxed on the indemnity basis. Lord Woolf MR said that[1]

> '... this is an area where this court is very unlikely to interfere with a decision, made in the exercise of the discretion of the judge below, unless a very strong case indeed is made out.'

Following those indications, parties who fail to obtain wasted costs orders from the judge will wish to appeal to the Court of Appeal only in the strongest cases. Appeals will be slightly less risky in cases where it is said that the judge wrongly *made* a wasted costs order: in those cases, the appellant will be able to rely on Lord Woolf's indication that such orders should be made only in clear cases and after summary proceedings. But they may still be subject to the court's desire to prevent the growth of expensive satellite litigation, and will probably wish to appeal only where the merits of the appeal seem particularly strong, that is, where the judge has plainly erred in principle.

1   [1998] 1 FCR 605 at 617f, CA.

11.8   A clear example of allegations not suitable for the summary procedure of the wasted costs jurisdiction is *Re Freudiana Holdings Ltd*.[1] The applicant's points of claim seeking the wasted costs order were 40 pages long; there were 35 pages of points of defence on behalf of counsel and 40 on behalf of the solicitors, followed by 20 pages of points of reply. The respondents' costs of defending the wasted costs application were of the order of £400,000. Skeleton arguments to the Court of Appeal amounted to 100 pages. The Court of Appeal upheld the trial judge's decision to discharge his earlier order, which had required the respondents to show cause why they should not pay wasted costs. It was quite clear that the case was wholly inappropriate for a summary procedure, and would essentially involving re-trying the original action, as well as considering the knowledge of the lawyers who had acted in it. The crux of the case for those seeking to apply for wasted costs orders was as follows. The court considered that the application had been made unsuitable for a wasted costs order by the conduct of the lawyers applying for it: if they had kept their allegations brief, and alleged simply negligence rather than 'knowing participation in an attempt deliberately to mislead the court and to pervert the course of justice' then it might well have been possible to deal with the matter under the wasted costs jurisdiction.[2] But once such serious allegations had been made against solicitors and counsel, it was inevitable that they would seek rigorously to defend them, thus increasing the length of the pleadings and issues. Thus the message of *Freudiana* for those seeking wasted costs orders is to keep the allegations short, and avoid extravagant allegations of bad faith on the part of the lawyers.

1   (1995) Times, 4 December, CA.
2   See Millett LJ's judgment.

11.9   On the other hand, it will be in the interest of those defending such applications to emphasise the extent to which a hearing will be long and cumbersome, dealing with many issues, and ultimately unlikely to produce a clear conclusion. For example, in *Re Hallewell Bunyard*,[1] Neill LJ's prima facie view was that there had been a serious piece of negligence by the solicitor, but he considered that a wasted costs order should not be made, because it was a matter which required further examination, and, in particular, interrogation of the solicitor. As this was not possible on a wasted costs application, it was not possible to conclude that the case was sufficiently clear to make a wasted costs order.

1   (5 June 1996, unreported), CA.

(b)   Interrelationship with other remedies, and advocates' immunity

11.10   It might be said that the courts' emphasis on the summary nature of the wasted costs jurisdiction gives an unfair advantage to solicitors and counsel responding to such allegations, since they essentially obtain the benefit of any doubt or unclarity as to the merits. But where the application is made by a client against his own lawyers, it is still open to the aggrieved client to bring an action for negligence, so that the client is not unduly prejudiced by the court's declining to make the wasted costs order. Note, however, that this is unlikely to assist parties making applications against other parties' lawyers. Further, where a party sues his own lawyers in relation to litigation, he may be met with the defence of advocates' immunity from suit.[1] In relation to applications for wasted costs orders, there is no immunity from judicial scrutiny for the conduct of the advocate in court. In this respect, the wasted costs jurisdiction favours the apparently aggrieved party, though note that the policy reasons supporting the immunity still apply, so that the court will make an order in relation to conduct in court only in a clear case:[2]

> 'Any judge who is invited to make or contemplates making an order arising out of an advocate's conduct of court proceedings must make full allowance for the fact that an advocate in court, like a commander in battle, often has to make decisions quickly and under pressure, in the fog of war and ignorant of developments on the other side of the hill. Mistakes will inevitably be made, things done which the outcome shows to have been unwise. But advocacy is more an art than a science. It cannot be conducted according to formulae. Individuals differ in their style and approach. It is only when, with all allowances made, an advocate's conduct of court proceedings is quite plainly unjustifiable that it can be appropriate to make a wasted costs order against him.'

1   For the complexities of this doctrine, see chapter 10.
2   *Ridehalgh* [1994] Ch 205 at 236F–H.

(c)   Procedural rules

11.11   An application for a wasted costs order must be made pursuant to CPR Part 48.7, which provides:

> '48.7(1)   This rule applies where the court is considering whether to make an order under section 51(6) of the Supreme Court Act 1981 (court's power to disallow or (as the case may be) order a legal representative to meet, "wasted costs").
>
> (2)   The court must give the legal representative a reasonable opportunity to attend a hearing to give reasons why it should not make such an order.
>
> (3)   For the purposes of this rule, the court may direct that privileged documents are to be disclosed to the court and, if the court so directs, to the other party to the application for an order.
>
> (4)   When the court makes a wasted costs order, it must specify the amount to be disallowed or paid.

(5)   The court may direct that notice must be given to the legal representative's client, in such manner as the court may direct—

(a)   of any proceedings under this rule; or

(b)   of any order made under it against his legal representative.

(6)   Before making a wasted costs order, the court may direct a costs judge or a district judge to inquire into the matter and report to the court.

(7)   The court may refer the question of wasted costs to a costs judge or a district judge, instead of making a wasted costs order.'

11.12   The following comments may be made. First, the requirement of a fair hearing is expanded upon in the *Part 48 Practice Direction*.[1] Secondly, the need for any order made to specify the amount of money to be paid or disallowed (Part 48.7(4)) was introduced by the CPR, and reflects the general approach of those rules in favour of the immediate assessment of the amount of costs, though the court may instead refer the whole matter to a costs judge or a district judge (Part 48.7(7)). Thirdly, there is a new power to order that notice be given to the lawyer's client (Part 48.7(5)).[2]

1   See para 11.15.
2   See also part 44.2.

(d)   Privilege

11.13   Fourthly, the power to direct that privileged documents be disclosed, in Part 48.7(3), is also new. 'Privilege' is defined in the glossary as 'the right of a party to refuse to disclose a document or produce a document or to refuse to answer questions on the ground of some special interest recognised by law'. Before this provision was introduced, there was a particular difficulty where a party sought a wasted costs order against another party's lawyers. If the other party did not agree to privilege being waived, they might be unable to reveal matters which would provide a good defence.[1] The court had to give the lawyers the benefit of the doubt, if it had not seen the privileged material.[2] Now that the court has power to direct that privileged documents be disclosed either to itself, or to the other party to the application for a wasted costs order, it has the power to circumvent this problem, so that it may see precisely what happened and why. It remains to be seen how this power will be exercised, and whether suggestions that the rule is ultra vires or contrary to the European Convention on Human Rights will prove correct.[3]

1   There was less difficulty in cases where a party sought an order against his own lawyers: if he did not agree to waive privilege, then the court could make adverse inferences against him.
2   *Ridehalgh* [1994] Ch 205 at 237.
3   See Lewis and Bowden 'Wasted Costs under the Woolf Regime' (1999) 143 SJ 237.

(e)   Part 48 Practice Direction

11.14   More rules on the procedure to be followed appear in the *Part 48 Practice Direction*,[1] the relevant parts of which provide:

'2.1   Rule 48.7 deals with wasted costs orders against legal representatives. Such orders can be made at any stage in the proceedings up to and including the proceedings relating to the detailed assessment of costs. In general, applications for wasted costs orders are best left until after the end of the trial.

2.2   The court may make a wasted costs order against a legal representative on an application under Part 23 or of its own initiative.

2.3   A party who wishes to apply for a wasted costs order must first give to the legal representative against whom the order is sought notice in writing—

(a)   of what the legal representative is alleged to have done or failed to do, and

(b)   of the costs that he may be ordered to pay or which are sought against him.

The notice must be given at least 3 days before the hearing.

2.4   It is appropriate for the court to make a wasted costs order against a legal representative only if—

(a)   he has acted improperly, unreasonably or negligently,

(b)   his conduct has caused a party to incur unnecessary costs, and

(c)   it is just in all the circumstances to order him to compensate that party for the whole or part of those costs.

2.5   The court will give directions about the procedure that will be followed in each case in order to ensure that the issues are dealt with in a way that is fair and as simple and summary as the circumstances permit.

2.6   As a general rule the court will consider whether to make a wasted costs order in two stages:

(a)   in the first stage, the court must be satisfied—

(i)   that it has before it evidence or other material which, if unanswered, would be likely to lead to a wasted costs order being made, and

(ii)   the wasted costs proceedings are justified notwithstanding the likely costs involved.

(b)   At the second stage (even if the court is satisfied under (a) above) the court will consider, after giving the legal representative an opportunity to put forward his case, whether it is appropriate to make a wasted costs order in accordance with paragraph 2.4 above.'

1   See para 11.3, note 2.

(f)   Stages of the application

11.15   The effect of these directions is that an application may require the applicant to take as many as four steps: first, the applicant notifies the legal representative in accordance with para 2.3;[1] secondly, the court makes directions for the summary disposal of the application (para 2.5); thirdly, there will generally be the first stage of the court's consideration of the application, as provided for by para 2.6(a). At this third level, the court considers essentially whether there is a case to answer, *and* whether the application is justified bearing in mind the costs involved.[2] It is possible that the second and third of these steps will take place at the same time. Fourthly, if the applicant wins the third level, there is the second stage of the court's procedure, as provided for in para 2.6(b). At what we have called the third level, which is the first stage of the court's consideration of the application, the making of an order that the application proceed to the final stage

'... is not something to be done automatically or without careful appraisal of the relevant circumstances. The costs of the inquiry as compared with the costs claimed will always be one relevant consideration. This is a discretion, like any other, to be exercised judicially, but judges may not infrequently decide that further proceedings are not likely to be justified.'[3]

As to the final stage, the court is not bound to make an order even if improper, unreasonable or negligent conduct, and causation, are made out (see para 2.4(c)),

'but in that situation it would of course have to give sustainable reasons for exercising its discretion against making the order.'[4]

1   Compare *S v M* (1998) Times, 26 March (Pumfrey J) decided under the old regime: the notification should be in clear terms.
2   The court will have the part of the CPR's overriding objective relating to proportionality well in mind at this stage.
3   *Ridehalgh* [1994] Ch 205 at 239B–C.
4   *Ridehalgh* [1994] Ch 205 at 239E–F.

(g)   Court initiating the application

11.16   The court has power to initiate an application (para 2.2), but should be slow to do so except in very clear cases, such as failure to appear, lateness, gross repetition or extreme slowness. The reason is that, if the application is lost, the court will not compensate the parties for the wasted costs of the application itself.[1]

1   *Ridehalgh* [1994] Ch 205 at 238D–F.

(h)   Timing and judge of the application

11.17   Generally speaking applications for wasted costs orders are best made at the end of the trial.[1] An example of an exceptional case in which it was appropriate, before the end of the trial, to make a similar order, against the Legal Aid Board rather than lawyers, for the costs of an adjournment, was *Kelly v South Manchester Health Authority*.[2] The court was apprised of all relevant material at the interlocutory stage and so it was appropriate to make the order then. Wherever practicable, the application should be dealt with by the judge who dealt with the matter which gives rise to the wasted costs application.[3]

1   Para 2.1, and compare *Ridehalgh* [1994] Ch 205 at 238B–D, approving *Filmlab Systems International Ltd v Pennington* [1995] 1 WLR 673 (Aldous J).
2   [1998] 1 WLR 244.
3   *Re Merc Property Ltd* (1999) Times, 19 May (Lindsay J).

(i)   Settlement of an application

11.18   Where the court has decided that there is material which, if unanswered, would lead to a wasted costs order, but the application is subsequently settled, the lawyers involved risk being deprived of the opportunity to clear any blot from their reputations by the settlement of the application. *Manzanilla Ltd v Corton Property and Investments Ltd* was such a case. Lord Woolf MR said:[1]

'In such a case as this, the court should be prepared to allow a written statement to be placed before the court, so that it can be transmitted to the judiciary who were previously involved, without counsel or other lawyers having to attend, as long as it is first produced to the other parties and they raise no objection to it being submitted. The statement should be short and succinct and not one which goes into unnecessary detail. It would also be desirable that, wherever possible, the statement is agreed by the other parties. However, where no agreement is possible, the position of the other parties can be protected by their also being allowed to submit an equally short statement in response to that of the initiator of the procedure. There it must end because otherwise the costs which I would seek to avoid being incurred would be incurred in producing a multiplicity of lengthy written statements which are not going to assist the court.'

1   [1997] 3 FCR 389 at 391E–G, CA.

(j)   Applications by those who are not parties to the litigation

11.19   Wasted costs orders may be made only in favour of those who are parties to the litigation.[1] This led Sedley J to hold, in *R v Camden London Borough Council, ex p Martin*,[2] that there was no jurisdiction to make a wasted costs order in favour of the respondent to an ex parte application for leave to move for judicial review: until leave was granted, the application was expressed to be 'ex parte', and so the respondent was not properly a party. But in the later case of *R v Immigration Appeal Tribunal, ex p Gulsen*,[3] Buxton J held that the court did have power to make such an order pursuant to its inherent jurisdiction. Further, in *Lubrizol Ltd v Tyndalls*,[4] Carnwath J held that *Ex p Martin* did not apply in a case where the application for leave to move for judicial review included an application for an interlocutory injunction. In that case, it was established that it was appropriate for the respondent to appear at the oral hearing seeking the injunction, so that the respondent was a party, and there was jurisdiction to make a wasted costs order in its favour.

1   See the definition of wasted costs in Supreme Court Act 1981, s 51(7).
2   [1997] 1 WLR 359.
3   [1997] COD 430. See para 11.66.
4   (8 April 1998, unreported).

(k)   Interrelationship between wasted costs orders and orders for costs against the Legal Aid Board

11.20   If the case is one in which a wasted costs order should be made, this will normally be a reason for not making an order that the Legal Aid Board pay the costs. But, except in the clearest of cases, a party which applies for costs from the Legal Aid Board is not obliged also to seek an order that other lawyers pay wasted costs. At most, a party seeking costs from the Legal Aid Board need only mention to the court that it is possible that a wasted costs order should be made; if this is done, the court may then choose to inform the Legal Aid Board that it may wish to object to being ordered to pay costs, on the basis that a wasted costs order should be made instead. If the Board does this, then the court will have to consider the issue of a notice to show cause to the lawyers in question.[1]

1   *Re O (wasted costs order)* [1997] 1 FLR 465, CA. See Lord Woolf MR's judgment at 472A–D.

2   Basic requirements for the making of a wasted costs order

11.21   The basic requirements for the making of an order are that it be shown that the lawyer has acted improperly, unreasonably or negligently, that this has caused costs to be wasted, and that it is just in all the circumstances that an order be made.[1] The first three requirements will be considered individually; then there is consideration of various subsidiary issues which arise in relation to those three issues; next, the issue of causation is dealt with, and finally the overall justice of making an order.

1   *Part 48 Practice Direction*, para 2.4.

11.22   Although it is of some assistance to consider the concepts of improper, unreasonable and negligent conduct separately, nevertheless[1]

> 'conduct which is unreasonable may also be improper, and conduct which is negligent will very frequently be (if it is not by definition) unreasonable. We do not think any sharp differentiation between these expressions is useful or necessary or intended.'

1   *Ridehalgh* [1994] Ch 205 at 233E.

3   Improper acts and omissions

11.23   Improper conduct was defined in *Ridehalgh*[1] as follows:

> 'The adjective covers, but is not confined to, conduct which would ordinarily be held to justify disbarment, striking off, suspension from practice or other serious professional penalty. It covers any significant breach of a substantial duty imposed by a relevant code of professional conduct. But it is not in our judgment limited to that. Conduct which would be regarded as improper according to the consensus of professional (including judicial) opinion can be fairly stigmatised as such whether or not it violates the letter of a professional code.'

1   [1994] Ch 205 at 232D–E.

11.24   Three points may be made. First, it is likely that conduct which is improper will also be unreasonable, so that it is unlikely to be necessary to rely upon this category alone. Secondly, although the passage quoted in para 11.22 suggests an overlap between the three concepts of improper, unreasonable and negligent conduct, note that, in that passage, the overlaps suggested are

(i)   improper conduct may overlap with unreasonable conduct, and

(ii)   negligent conduct may overlap with unreasonable conduct.

While it is undesirable to adopt an over-technical approach, it is submitted that it is helpful to consider the cases as falling into two broad categories. The first category, improper/unreasonable conduct, is conduct which tends not to be careless, but rather to be deliberate or intentional use of legal procedures in a way which is considered unethical or bordering on the unethical. The second category, negligent/unreasonable conduct, is conduct which is careless or based on ignorance, as in the familiar tort of negligence. This division mirrors the familiar distinction between intentional wrongdoing and negligence. We do not suggest that the cases expressly set out this distinction in terms, but we do suggest that it provides a helpful way in which to think about them.

11.25   Thirdly, the fate of the wasted costs application in *Re Freudiana Holdings Ltd*,[1] shows that it is generally undesirable for those applying for wasted costs orders to make extravagant allegations of impropriety against lawyers, except in the clearest circumstances. The more morally culpable the allegation, the more the lawyer is likely to wish to defend the matter vigorously, and the harder it may be for the court to reach the conclusion that the lawyer has plainly acted improperly.

1   (1995) Times, 4 December, CA, see para 11.8.

4   Unreasonable acts and omissions

11.26   Again, the key definition was given in *Ridehalgh*:[1]

'"Unreasonable" ... aptly describes conduct which is vexatious, designed to harass the other side rather than advance the resolution of the case, and it makes no difference that the conduct is the product of excessive zeal and not improper motive. But conduct cannot be described as unreasonable simply because it leads in the event to an unsuccessful result or because other more cautious legal representatives would have acted differently. The acid test is whether the conduct permits of a reasonable explanation. If so, the course adopted may be regarded as optimistic and as reflecting on a practitioner's judgment, but it is not unreasonable.'

1   [1994] Ch 205 at 232E–G.

(a)   Agreeing expert evidence

11.27   This definition has been considered in a number of subsequent cases. *Greenhoff v J Lyons & Co*[1] is a relatively simple one. In a personal injury action concerning relatively low levels of damages, the medical experts were in agreement on all points except one. The plaintiff's solicitors refused to agree the evidence. Agreement would have avoided the need for the experts to come to court. The recorder held that the plaintiff's solicitors ought to have agreed the reports, subject to agreement that their client could raise in evidence the one point on which she disagreed with the defendants' expert. Their failure to do so did not admit of a reasonable explanation, so it was unreasonable. He ordered the plaintiff's solicitors to pay the costs of the doctors' attendance at court. The Court of Appeal accepted that this conclusion was open to the recorder, and declined to overturn his decision.

1   (30 June 1998, unreported), CA.

(b)   Vexatious conduct: the distinction between hopeless cases and abuse of the process of the court

11.28   In two remarkable cases, *Tolstoy-Miloslavsky v Aldington*[1] and *Fletamentos Maritimos SA v Effjohn International BV*,[2] the Court of Appeal found that lawyers' conduct was vexatious and amounted to abuse of the process of the court. Before considering the facts of those cases, it is necessary to consider the distinction between advancing hopeless cases, which is not improper or unreasonable, and abusing the process of the court, which is:[3]

'A legal representative is not to be held to have acted improperly, unreasonably or negligently simply because he acts for a party who pursues a claim or a defence which is plainly doomed to fail ... Barristers in independent practice are not permitted to pick and choose their clients ... solicitors are not subject to an equivalent cab-rank rule, but many solicitors would and do respect the public policy underlying it by affording representation to the unpopular and unmeritorious. Legal representatives will, of course, whether barristers or solicitors, advise clients of the perceived weakness of their case and of the risk of failure. But clients are free to reject advice and insist that cases be litigated. It is rarely if ever safe for a court to assume that a hopeless case is being litigated on the advice of the lawyers involved ...

It is, however, one thing for a legal representative to present, on instructions, a case which he regards as bound to fail; it is quite another to lend his assistance to proceedings which are an abuse of the process of the court. Whether instructed or not, a legal representative is not entitled to use litigious procedures for purposes for which they were not intended, as by issuing or pursuing proceedings for reasons unconnected with success in the litigation or pursuing a case known to be dishonest, nor is he entitled to evade rules intended to safeguard the interests of justice, as by knowingly failing to make full disclosure on ex parte application or knowingly conniving at incomplete disclosure of documents. It is not entirely easy to distinguish between the hopeless case and the case which amounts to an abuse of process, but in practice it is not hard to say which is which and if there is doubt the legal representative is entitled to the benefit of it.'

A qualification to this passage may be required, in light of the provision in the CPR allowing the court to override privilege.[4] In cases where this power is exercised, it will enable the court to see whether a hopeless case has been brought in spite of advice from the lawyers that it is hopeless, or in the absence of such advice. In hopeless cases where no such advice has been given, this will make it easier for the court to conclude that the lawyers have acted either improperly or negligently in allowing the action to proceed.

1   [1996] 1 WLR 736, CA.
2   (10 December 1997, unreported), CA (the Court of Appeal's decision on aspects other than wasted costs in this case appears at [1997] 2 Lloyd's Rep 302).
3   *Ridehalgh* [1994] Ch 205 at 233–4.
4   See para 11.13.

11.29   A relatively simple example of abuse of process of this kind appears in *In re a Company (No 006798 of 1995).*[1] The question was whether the court should make a wasted costs order against a solicitor who had sworn an affidavit in support of the winding up of a company, at a time when he believed, contrary to what he swore in the affidavit, that the company was able to pay its debts. Chadwick J said:

'... a solicitor who, in swearing an affidavit in the short statutory form to support a winding up petition, asserts on oath a belief that a debt is owing and that the company is insolvent acts improperly if he does not have that belief; and acts unreasonably if there are no grounds upon which a competent solicitor could reach that view on the material available to him.'

The background of the case was that it appeared that the winding up petition was bound to fail, and that the application was launched not in order to wind up the company, but rather for the collateral purpose of putting illegitimate commercial pressure on the company.[2]

1   [1996] 1 WLR 491 (Chadwick J). See esp 506E.
2   For a case relating to the compromise of an application to wind up a company, which the Court of Appeal considered fell on the other side of the line and did not involve unreasonable or improper behaviour, see *Philex plc v Golban* decided at the same time as *Ridehalgh*: [1994] Ch 205.

11.30   We have already considered the Court of Appeal's emphasis that wasted costs orders should be made only in plain cases. The facts of the *Tolstoy* and *Fletamentos* cases demonstrate the sort of circumstances which will be sufficiently exceptional to justify a wasted costs order on the basis of improper or unreasonable behaviour. In both cases, the court concluded that the solicitors' conduct had crossed the line from merely taking hopeless points into abuse of the process of the court. So remarkable are the facts of these cases that it is hard to convey their full import by way of summary, and ideally they should be read in full. In the first, Rose LJ summarised the circumstances which led him to conclude that there had been abuse of process by the solicitors acting for the plaintiff, Count Tolstoy.[1] In particular: this was the second and possibly the third occasion on which Count Tolstoy had sought to defeat Lord Aldington by litigation in relation to the same matters; Lord Aldington had been harassed by the various proceedings; the proceedings were prima facie an abuse as they were a collateral attack on the final decision of a court of competent jurisdiction; the new evidence on which Count Tolstoy relied was extremely weak; Count Tolstoy had not paid Lord Aldington the enormous costs of the first action, was bankrupt, and there was no prospect of him paying the costs of this action. In Ward LJ's view the key factors were that:

(i) 'as hopeless cases go, this really was plumbing the depths':

ii) given the background of the previous litigation and insolvency of Count Tolstoy, the litigation was vexatious as it 'heaped fraud and perjury upon the vicious calumny of the allegation of being a war criminal';

(iii) the action was instituted to harass Lord Aldington, and no reasonable solicitor could have considered otherwise.[2]

1   At [1996] 1 WLR 747.
2   See [1996] 1 WLR 736 at 752C–E.

11.31 Similarly astonishing are the facts of *Fletamentos*.[1] In this case it was significant that the allegedly wasted costs were the costs of an appeal to the Court of Appeal. Thus, the appellants had already had the opportunity to make their arguments in court, before Morison J. The question was whether the decision to bring the appeal amounted to an abuse, and unreasonable behaviour. Simon Brown LJ analysed each proposed ground of appeal, and showed that each one was extraordinarily weak; some of them were 'absurd'. In relation to the solicitors, Zaiwallas, he concluded:

'I have the clearest impression that Zaiwallas saw their role essentially as one of assisting their clients at all costs to stave off the evil day of judgment, meanwhile taking all possible points in an attempt to disrupt the arbitral process and achieve, if possible, a more compliant Tribunal ... These, in short, were wrecking tactics, designed rather to obstruct than to further the fair disposal of this arbitration. This litigation permitted of no reasonable explanation. It failed the "acid test". It amounted to an abuse of process.'

Other relevant points were that it was likely that there would be difficulties for the other party in enforcing costs orders against Zaiwallas' client, and that this was an appeal from an interlocutory rather than a final decision, so that there was less need to appeal.

1   See para 11.28.

11.32 Morritt LJ too analysed each ground of appeal, and considered them all hopeless. He also inferred that the appeal had been instigated by the solicitor Mr Zaiwalla rather than his clients Marflet. Mr Zaiwalla was motivated in part by his personal feelings in relation to one of the arbitrators involved in the case. This was unreasonable conduct. Mr Zaiwalla had failed to disclose material matters on an ex parte application for leave to appeal; this was improper. Morritt LJ added, obiter, that it was possible that it might amount to vexatious conduct to advance a point which, though not utterly hopeless, had some small chance of success, if the conduct in question was intended to harass the other party rather than advance the resolution of the case. Waller LJ agreed; a summary of his reasons appear on the last page of the Lexis transcript. They are similar to those already set out.

11.33   We can summarise as follows. The Court of Appeal had emphasised that wasted costs orders will be made only in plain cases. So far as improper and unreasonable conduct is concerned, the *Tolstoy* and *Fletamentos* cases provide examples of the sort of circumstances in which orders will be made. But the facts of those cases were extreme. With the exception of the specific examples in relation to experts' reports and affidavits given above, practitioners will wish to be cautious in deciding to apply for wasted costs orders on these bases.

5   Negligent acts or omissions

11.34   In defining negligent conduct for these purposes, as before, the starting point is *Ridehalgh*:[1]

> '... we are clear that "negligent" should be understood in an untechnical way to denote failure to act with the competence reasonably to be expected of ordinary members of the profession.
>
> In adopting an untechnical approach to the meaning of negligence in this context, we would however wish firmly to discountenance any suggestion that an applicant for a wasted costs order under this head need prove anything less than he would have to prove in an action for negligence: "advice, acts or omissions in the course of their professional work which no member of the profession who was reasonably well-informed and competent would have given or done or omitted to do"; an error "such as no reasonably well-informed and competent member of that profession could have made": see *Saif Ali v Sydney Mitchell & Co* [1980] AC 198, 218 per Lord Diplock.'

Thus, although technicalities are to eschewed, the test of negligence is broadly the familiar common law test, as it applies to professionals.

1   [1994] Ch 205 at 233.

(a)   Conduct held not to be negligent

11.35   It is instructive to consider the Court of Appeal's application of the test on the facts of the individual cases dealt with as part of the consolidated appeals in *Ridehalgh*. On the facts of *Ridehalgh v Horsefield* itself, the court found that the solicitors, acting for a tenant in a possession action, had made a concession to the landlord which should not have been made because it was based upon a misunderstanding of the law. The concession made it easier for the landlord to obtain an order for possession. The court nevertheless held that the solicitors had not been negligent in failing to understand the law correctly. The law was complex. The solicitors consulted textbooks which did not give a clear answer. The county court judge did not intervene to correct the error. The solicitors were not to be treated by the standard to be applied to specialist counsel, nor could they reasonably expect to be paid for prolonged research.[1] At first sight it might seem a surprising conclusion that lawyers who failed to understand the law correctly might not have been negligent, but it is submitted that this approach, in relation to a complex area of law being interpreted by high street solicitors, is realistic rather than utopian.[2]

1   *Ridehalgh* [1994] Ch 205 at 242. See also chapter 2, paras 2.10 and 2.12.
2   See also *Warren v Warren* [1997] QB 488, CA. The Court of Appeal held that a solicitor had not acted unreasonably in issuing a witness summons against a district judge, even though the judge was not a compellable witness. It is clear from Lord Woolf MR's judgment that the law as to the compellability of the district judge was, before that judgment, unclear and disorganised.

11.36 The next individual case which the Court of Appeal considered in *Ridehalgh* was *Allen v Unigate Dairies Ltd*.[1] The plaintiff had claimed damages for noise-induced hearing loss which he alleged was caused by exposure to a decrater machine at his place of work. On the first day of trial, the plaintiff abandoned the claim as it was accepted that the workplace had not been dangerously noisy. The judge ordered the plaintiff's solicitors to pay the wasted costs, on the basis that they should have found this out earlier and had negligently failed to so. But the Court of Appeal held that the solicitors had not acted negligently. They had taken the plaintiff's instructions and relied upon advice from an expert and counsel, none of whom had adverted to the reason which ultimately led to the case being abandoned. The reason was that there was a solid wall between the plaintiff and the decrater. But there was nothing in the defence, the defendants' expert's report, or the defendants' solicitors' correspondence, to suggest the existence or relevance of this wall. Thus it was not negligent of the plaintiff's solicitors to have failed to find out about it.[2]

1   [1994] Ch 205.
2   See *Ridehalgh* [1994] Ch 205 at 245–6.

11.37 A similar case is *Wall v Lefever*.[1] In the course of cross-examination the plaintiff's expert made a concession which led to the plaintiff, on the advice of his solicitors and counsel, abandoning the claim. The defendants sought a wasted costs order against the plaintiff's lawyers, presumably on the basis that they ought to have detected this weakness in their case at an earlier stage. The trial judge rejected the application, on the basis that there was evidence that counsel and solicitors had prepared the case very carefully. Lord Woolf MR said that his reasons could not be faulted.[2]

1   [1998] 1 FCR 605, CA.
2   Ironically, in considering the effect of the expert's concession on the trial, Lord Woolf considered that it had not meant that the plaintiff's case was bound to fail. But if the concession did not mean that the plaintiff's case was bound to fail, why was it that, as a result of it being made, the plaintiff did abandon his case, following the advice of his solicitors and counsel? This would suggest an alternative error on the part of solicitors and counsel, namely, abandoning the case when it was unnecessary to do so. The consequences of such alternative negligence were not explored in the judgment.

11.38 The court's approach in *Sampson v John Boddy Timber Ltd*[1] was perhaps more surprisingly lenient on the lawyer. Sir Thomas Bingham MR originally thought the conduct in question was negligent, but, as the other two judges disagreed, accepted that it was not a sufficiently plain case for the making of a wasted costs order. In a personal injury action, the defendant's insurers wrote that they were 'prepared to negotiate a settlement of the plaintiff's claim on a compromise basis'. The letter was not marked 'without prejudice'. No settlement was agreed. The defendants listed the letter in their list of documents. Shortly before trial, the plaintiff's barrister told the defendant's barrister that he proposed to read the letter to the judge. The defendant's barrister objected strongly, on the grounds that the letter was an offer to compromise which was inadmissible, and warned that, if the letter was read to the judge, he would ask that the trial be adjourned to be heard before a new judge. The plaintiff's barrister contended that the letter was admissible because it did not bear the words 'without prejudice'; the defendant's barrister made clear that he rejected that view. At trial, the plaintiff's barrister nevertheless read the letter to the judge. The defendant's barrister objected. After argument, the judge adjourned the trial on the ground that he should not have been read the letter; he rejected the argument that it was not privileged because it did not bear the words 'without prejudice'. The question was whether the plaintiff's barrister should pay the costs wasted by the adjournment. The Court of Appeal held that he should not. Although the letter was privileged, the contrary was fairly arguable, so that it was not negligent of the barrister to have argued it. This case shows how the rule that wasted costs orders should be made only in plain cases works in favour of legal representatives, even when the lawyer's conduct is said only to be negligent rather than improper. The same principles would presumably apply to a solicitor advocate appearing in court.

1   [1995] NLJR 851, (1995) Independent, 17 May, CA.

11.39   In *Turner Page Music v Torres Design Associates Ltd*,[1] the Court of Appeal held that solicitors who declined to reveal to the opposing party in litigation that their client's insurance cover was limited, or to advise their client to settle, were not negligent. Further, solicitors who are under great pressure to act fast to seek accommodation for a client who has had to sleep outside the previous night may not be negligent in launching an application which, with careful consideration and hindsight, turns out to have been doomed to fail.[2]

1   (1998) Times, 3 August, CA, and see the transcript.
2   *R v Westminster London Borough, ex p Geehan & Butler* [1995] COD 204 (Dyson J).

(b)   Negligent conduct

11.40   In *R v Horsham District Council, ex p Wenman*,[1] Brooke J was unable to make a wasted costs order because the principal errors had occurred before the wasted costs jurisdiction came into effect. He nevertheless indicated that, in judicial review proceedings, lawyers should not regard it as unnecessary to write a letter before action merely because they believed it inevitable that the proposed respondent would deny their clients' claim. Further, judicial review proceedings were wholly inappropriate for cases which bristled with factual disputes. Thirdly, it was wrong to fail to draw the attention of the judge, on the ex parte application for leave, to alternative remedies and evidence which told against the applicant's case.[2] Though this case was decided before *Ridehalgh*, and these comments were obiter, it nevertheless supplies helpful guidance.

1   [1995] 1 WLR 680 (Brooke J).
2   On the facts of *Wenman*, the solicitors had not acted negligently as they had relied on specialist junior counsel. See below for reliance on counsel.

11.41   Next, in *D Walter & Co Ltd v Neville Eckley & Co*,[1] a firm of solicitors was advising the plaintiff, who was the managing director of a company in compulsory liquidation, in an action against the company's liquidator. They instructed junior counsel who specialised in company law. The liquidator's solicitors pointed out to the plaintiff's solicitors that the action against the liquidator lay in the company, not the plaintiff, and sent them a copy of a case called *Re Embassy Art Products Ltd*,[2] which they said was relevant. The plaintiff's solicitors decided not to refer this to counsel, as they trusted their own judgment that the case was irrelevant. Sir Richard Scott V-C decided that the case was highly relevant, and that the solicitors had been negligent in failing to consider the case properly. Further, in counsel's written opinion he had said that there were grounds for proceeding but that this must be re-considered if further evidence showed that the company's financial position was worse than thought. The solicitors subsequently received a letter showing that the financial position was much worse, but they failed to consider the effect of this on the application, with or without counsel. This too was negligent. A wasted costs order was made.

1   [1997] BCC 331 (Sir Richard Scott V-C).
2   [1988] 3 BCC 292.

11.42   One relevant factor in the *Fletamentos* case[1] was that the costs in question were the costs of an appeal. The appellant had already had one opportunity to argue his points, and for the most part they had been rejected in clear but careful terms by the judge at first instance. In *Re J (A Minor)*,[2] a barrister was held to have been negligent in advising an appeal where all the supposed grounds of appeal were matters of fact in relation to which the Court of Appeal would not interfere with the judge's findings. The solicitors narrowly escaped a wasted costs order, on the basis of their reliance on counsel's advice (see below).

1   (10 December 1997, unreported), CA. See para 11.31.
2   (25 March 1997, unreported), CA.

11.43   In principle it is irrelevant to the exercise of the wasted costs jurisdiction that a party's lawyers' fees are being paid by legal aid, because of the terms of Legal Aid Act 1988, s 31(1). Further, those acting for legally aided clients should be no more at risk of wasted costs orders than those whose clients are privately funded.[1] But there are some regulations which apply only to those acting for legally aided clients, breach of which may be relevant to the exercise of the jurisdiction. In *Re Stathams*,[2] the Court of Appeal held that a solicitor acted negligently when, in breach of his duty under the civil legal aid regulations, he failed to serve notice of discharge of the legal aid certificate of the plaintiff, for whom he acted, on the defendants. The defendants were given the false impression that the plaintiff was legally aided with a full certificate and that, on the appeal in question, if they won they would have the right to claim costs from the Legal Aid Board. In fact he did not have legal aid, there was no prospect of the Board paying the costs, and the plaintiff himself was impecunious. If the defendants had known this, they could have applied for security for costs, which they did not in fact do.

1   *Ridehalgh* [1994] Ch 205 at 234–5.
2   [1997] PIQR P 464, CA.

11.44   In *Veasey v Millfeed & Co Ltd*,[1] the solicitors in question issued and served a writ in which they named the plaintiff as a partnership of father and son, when in fact the partnership had already been dissolved, and only the son had instructed the solicitors. The defendants knew that the son was legally aided so that costs would not be recoverable from him, but were given to believe that the father was a party, not in receipt of legal aid, so that he might be able to satisfy a costs order. In truth, the father was not a party at all and the only plaintiff was the legally aided one. Had the defendants known the truth they would have settled the case in the sum at which they ultimately settled it when they discovered the truth. The Court of Appeal held that the solicitors had acted negligently in serving proceedings which named the father as well as the son as the plaintiff, when the father was not in truth a party. They were liable for the costs caused by the delay in settlement.

1   [1997] PNLR 100, CA.

11.45   The relevance of legal aid arose again in *Shah v Singh*.[1] The plaintiff's solicitors applied for an adjournment of the trial, a few days before it was due to begin. The partner dealing with the matter sent a litigation clerk to make the application, but failed to ensure that the clerk emphasised to the court that legal aid for the trial had only recently been granted. The application was rejected and the plaintiff lost the trial, but, on appeal, a re-hearing was ordered. The Court of Appeal held that it had been negligent of the partner to fail to ensure that the court was told of the recent grant of legal aid; if it had been told, an adjournment would probably have been granted, and the costs of the appeal avoided. Thus the plaintiff's solicitors were ordered to pay the costs of the appeal.

1   [1996] 1 PNLR 83.

11.46   Delay in the conduct of litigation may be so great as to amount to negligent conduct, though it may be hard to show that the delay has caused any loss of costs.[1] Negligence of solicitors for the purposes of a wasted costs order may also depend upon their use of counsel, which we consider next.

1   *Kilroy v Kilroy* [1997] PNLR 66, CA.

6   Solicitors' reliance upon counsel

11.47   In *Locke v Camberwell Health Authority*,[1] Taylor LJ stated principles relevant to solicitors' reliance upon counsel:

'(1)   In general, a solicitor is entitled to rely upon the advice of counsel properly instructed.

(2)   For a solicitor without specialist experience in a particular field to rely on counsel's advice is to make normal and proper use of the Bar.

(3)   However, he must not do so blindly but must exercise his own independent judgment. If he reasonably thinks counsel's advice is obviously or glaringly wrong, it is his duty to reject it.'

This was endorsed by the Court of Appeal in *Ridehalgh*, which added:[2]

'A solicitor does not abdicate his professional responsibility when he seeks the advice of counsel. He must apply his mind to the advice received. But the more specialist the nature of the advice, the more reasonable it is likely to be for a solicitor to accept it and act on it.'

In *R v Luton Family Proceedings Court, ex p R*,[3] the Court of Appeal overturned a decision that a solicitor had not been entitled to rely upon the advice of specialist junior counsel in relation to judicial review. There was no evidence as to the extent of the solicitor's own expertise in judicial review, nor was counsel's advice obviously wrong.[4] It is thought, however, that it might have been different if there *had* been evidence that the solicitor was himself an expert in judicial review: that would have made it easier to show that he ought to have taken a different view or pointed out errors in counsel's approach.

1   [1991] 2 Med LR 249, CA. See also *Davy-Chiesman v Davy-Chiesman* [1984] Fam 48, CA, and in chapter 2, para 2.11.
2   [1994] Ch 205 at 237G.
3   [1998] CLY 496, CA.
4   See also *Reaveley v Safeway Stores plc* [1998] PNLR 526, CA: reasonable reliance on counsel not negligent.

11.48   The solicitors in the slightly earlier case of *Re J (a minor)*[1] escaped by a much narrower margin. Ward LJ held that two barristers who advised appeal from a county court judge's decision as to a care order were both negligent. There was no evidence from the appellants' solicitors that they had applied their minds to counsel's advice on appeal at all. But they escaped a wasted costs order because counsel's advice was not glaringly wrong. Ward LJ said:

'It seems [the solicitor] relied blindly on counsel and abdicated his professional responsibility to give independent consideration to whether or not this was a proper appeal. Such a lamentable failure to exercise any judgment at all seems to me to be a negation of professional responsibility. Solicitors and counsel work as a team, and as a team, each has an equally valuable contribution to make. They are lawyers, each of them, and they should be judged as lawyers, not as outdoor clerks. It is, therefore, with considerable reluctance that I find myself grudgingly accepting the submission advanced on behalf of the solicitors that the advice of counsel, also adopted as it was by those advising the local authority, was not so glaringly without some superficial attraction that the solicitors should have rejected or questioned it. I say begrudge that conclusion because, implicit within it, is an acceptance that the level of competence by which the standard is fixed must be pretty low and such conclusion is, in fact, the antithesis of the regard I have for the solicitors' profession.'

There is in this passage the germ of an argument that the standard to be applied to solicitors who rely upon counsel should be raised.[2] Presumably those trained as solicitor advocates are already subject to a higher standard, as they hold themselves out has having skills similar to barristers. It remains to be seen whether this point will be developed in later cases.

1 (25 March 1997, unreported), CA.
2 Compare our discussion of solicitors' liability for the conduct of litigation in chapter 10, and see also *Dace v Redland Aggregates Ltd* [1997] EGCS 123 (Blackburne J). Counsel's advice that there had been a reasonable prospect of success in asserting the existence of an agricultural tenancy was unreasonable and negligent, and the solicitor had not been entitled to rely on it blindly.

11.49 In the *Fletamentos* case,[1] however, it was no excuse for the solicitor that, on the eve of the doomed appeal, leading counsel had advised by telephone that the application had a fair chance of success. As observed above, the circumstances of that case were exceptional. The solicitor had already received advice from two different leading counsel specialising in commercial law to the effect that the appeal was hopeless. He did not formally brief the third leading counsel to advise on the prospects of success. Further, there was a catalogue of other bizarre features.

1 (10 December 1997, unreported), CA. See paras 11.28ff.

7 Contribution and indemnity in wasted costs orders

11.50 *Fletamentos* also contains some obiter discussion of what should be done if more than one party was to blame for the wasted costs, for instance, both solicitors and counsel. Simon Brown LJ considered that, if the court made an order against solicitors, it probably did not have power to go on and make a contribution order in their favour against counsel, if the aggrieved party to the proceedings had not sought an order from counsel.[1] Morritt LJ, on the other hand, thought that it might be possible to order one legal representative to indemnify another in respect of payments to the applicant. In his view, however, normally the court would assess the percentage of the wasted costs which each lawyer should pay to the applicant.[2] Authority is needed on this point.

1 Lexis Lexform transcript, p 14.
2 Lexis Lexform transcript, p 27.

8   Relevance of legal aid and conditional fee agreements

11.51 As long as legal representatives comply with legal aid regulations, funding by legal aid makes no difference to the likelihood of a wasted costs order being granted, and such legal representatives should not allow their conduct to be tempered by fear that it might.[1] In particular, it is inappropriate for privately funded clients to apply for wasted costs orders against those who act for legally aided clients, simply on the basis that costs cannot be obtained from the legally aided clients.[2]

1   *Ridehalgh* [1994] Ch 205 at 234–5.
2   See Otton LJ's observations in *Wall v Lefever* [1998] 1 FCR 605, CA at 615–6.

11.52 The same applies in relation to lawyers who act pursuant to conditional fee agreements, as long as the agreements comply with both the Solicitors' Practice Rules[1] and Courts and Legal Services Act 1990, s 58. Such lawyers are in no different position from lawyers who act for claimants who have legal aid certificates requiring no contribution from the client.[2]

1   See *Hughes v Kingston upon Hull City Council* [1999] 2 WLR 1229, DC.
2   *Hodgson v Imperial Tobacco Ltd* [1998] 1 WLR 1056 esp at 1066A–C, CA.

9   Causation

11.53 The Court of Appeal stated in *Ridehalgh*:[1]

> '... the court has jurisdiction to make a wasted costs order only where the improper, unreasonable or negligent conduct complained of has caused a waste of costs and only to the extent of such wasted costs. Demonstration of a causal link is essential. Where the conduct is proved but no waste of costs is shown to have resulted, the case may be one to be referred to the appropriate disciplinary body or the legal aid authorities, but it is not one for the exercise of the wasted costs jurisdiction.'

This makes the position quite plain.

1   [1994] Ch 205 at 237E–F.

11.54 As to application of the test of causation, in *Sawrij v Lynx (Helping Abused Animals) Ltd*[1] the defendant had consistently been in default of its obligations with regard to discovery. The plaintiff applied at trial for the defence to be struck out on that basis, and two days were spent dealing with the application, at the end of which it was rejected. The Court of Appeal nevertheless accepted that the trial judge had been entitled to find that the making of the application had been caused by the defendants' defaults in discovery, so that a wasted costs order against the defendants' solicitors was justified in relation to those two days. It was not necessary for the plaintiffs to show that they were prejudiced by the failure to give discovery; all they had to show was that it was reasonable to have made the application.[2] On this approach, the test of causation may be relatively favourable to applicants. On the other hand, in *Kilroy v Kilroy*[3] the applicant was unable to show that lengthy delay by solicitors in the conduct of litigation had caused any specific costs to be wasted.

1   (21 February 1997, unreported), CA.
2   See Pill LJ's judgment at p 34 of the Lexis Lexform transcript.
3   [1997] PNLR 66, CA.

11.55   It will be recalled that Supreme Court Act 1981, s 56(7) provides:

'(7)   In subsection (6), "wasted costs" means any costs incurred by a party—

(a)   as a result of any improper, unreasonable or negligent act or omission on the part of any legal representative or any employee of such a representative; or

(b)   which, in the light of any such act or omission occurring after they were incurred, the court considers it unreasonable to expect that party to pay ...'

What is the ambit of subsection (b)? Imagine that I carefully spend a day preparing a trial and arrive at court the next day to present the trial. You, the barrister or solicitor instructed to appear for the opposite party, sleep in, miss the train, and the hearing has to be adjourned. You acted unreasonably or negligently, and this caused costs to be wasted, but your negligence occurred after I had done the work of preparing. It is submitted that it is this type of case at which subsection (b) is aimed.

10   Justice in all the circumstances

11.56   As mentioned above, in *Ridehalgh*[1] Sir Thomas Bingham MR made clear that, if the applicant shows that improper, unreasonable or negligent conduct has caused costs to be wasted, though the court is not bound to make a wasted costs order, it will need to provide sustainable reasons if it decides not to do so. *R v Secretary of State for the Home Office, ex p Wong*[2] was such a case. The solicitor of an applicant for judicial review should have come off the record when legal aid was withdrawn, and should have notified the respondent of the withdrawal. But Schiemann J decided not to make an order because, if the solicitor had come off the record, then the point which ultimately caused the applicant to win might never have come to light, so that an injustice would have been done because he would have lost a case which he deserved to win. Similarly, in *Pelling v Bruce-Williams*,[3] solicitors had negligently failed to serve an affidavit in support of an application to commit the appellant to prison. But the committal application related only to the appellant's failure to serve an affidavit of means, and only £200 was at stake. The making of a wasted costs order was not proportionate to the scale of the matter, so no order was made.

1   *Ridehalgh v Horsefield* [1994] Ch 205.
2   [1995] COD 331 (Schiemann J).
3   (16 December 1998, unreported), CA.

11   Criminal law

11.57   So far we have dealt only with provisions relating to civil proceedings. Supreme Court Act 1981, s 56 does not relate to criminal proceedings. But those are governed by almost identical provisions, which were introduced at the same time, and appear in Prosecution of Offences Act 1985, s 19A and Costs in Criminal Cases (General) Regulations 1986, regs 3A–3D.[1] The wording of these provisions is very similar to the equivalent provisions in civil law, and the Court of Appeal in *Ridehalgh* expressed the hope that its decision there would be of guidance in criminal cases, while realising that it could not be authoritative. It seems likely that the criminal division of the Court of Appeal would wish to follow the guidance given in *Ridehalgh* unless there is good reason not to do so. For example, in *Re a Solicitor (wasted costs order)*,[2] the criminal division of the Court of Appeal had to consider the meaning of the words 'improper, unreasonable or negligent' which appeared in the criminal statute. Giving the judgment of the court, Beldam LJ referred to the definitions suggested in *Ridehalgh*, and effectively adopted them. The court held that no reasonably competent solicitor would have issued a witness summons for the recovery of documents unless there was more than a speculative basis for believing that they might be relevant to the case; as there was no such basis, a wasted costs order was made. Similarly, in *R v Basra (wasted costs order)*,[3] a solicitor had applied for a witness summons when there was no proper basis to do so. The criminal division of the Court of Appeal upheld the making of a wasted costs order against the solicitor. But in *Neill v Crown Prosecution Service*,[4] no order was granted because the solicitor had not acted improperly when he requested an old-style committal in circumstances where there was good reason to believe that the prosecution case might collapse at that stage.

1   SI 1986/1335. Regulation 3 also gives the court power to order that one party pay costs to another party, if the costs have been caused by the 'unnecessary or improper act or omission'. of the first party.
2   [1996] 1 FLR 40, CA.
3   [1998] PNLR 535, CA.
4   [1997] COD 171, DC.

11.58   As in civil proceedings, proving causation is a necessary element of applying for a wasted costs order.[1]

1   *Re Lakha & Booth* (6 November 1998, unreported), CA. Cf *R v Wood Green Crown Court, ex p DPP* [1993] 1 WLR 723, DC, a case relating to an order that another party pay the costs, rather than a wasted costs order.

11.59   In a case decided before *Ridehalgh*, the criminal division of the Court of Appeal set out six guidelines relating to the jurisdiction in criminal cases.[1] It is possible that these may need some reconsideration in light of *Ridehalgh*, not in the sense that they are inconsistent with it, but simply on the basis that the court might wish to expand upon them to a degree, taking into account what was said in *Ridehalgh*.[2] A further degree of guidance, which also pre-dates *Ridehalgh*, appears in Lord Taylor of Gosforth LCJ's *Practice Direction (Costs in Criminal Proceedings)*.[3]

1   *Re a Barrister (wasted costs order) (No 1 of 1991)* [1993] QB 293, CA.
2   Although the Court of Appeal suggested that settlement of wasted costs applications was inappropriate, it is submitted that what the court had in mind was what had happened in that case: the judge had called the barrister to his chambers and discussed the matter with him for two hours, in part trying to persuade him to accept responsibility for what had happened. In other circumstances settlement may be appropriate: see para 11.18.
3   93 Cr App R 89.

C   ORDERS MADE PURSUANT TO THE COURT'S INHERENT JURISDICTION OVER SOLICITORS

11.60   Before the introduction of wasted costs orders, the court had an inherent jurisdiction to make costs orders against solicitors. Lord Woolf MR considered the exercise of this jurisdiction, in civil cases, after the introduction of the power to make wasted costs orders, in *Hodgson v Imperial Tobacco Ltd*.[1] He said that 'this limited jurisdiction is only going to be relevant in a very small minority of cases'. He added:

'Mr Brennan makes three submissions about this jurisdiction which are not controversial except in one respect. The first is that it is limited to orders against solicitors and does not extend to orders against counsel. The second is that it must be regarded as having been supplanted in circumstances falling within the statutory wasted costs jurisdiction; and the third is that it should not be exercised until after a consideration whether an order should be made under the wasted costs jurisdiction. The point which might be controversial is whether today the courts would take the view that the inherent jurisdiction is limited to orders against solicitors. This is not a point which we have considered and as it does not arise we express no opinion on it.'

1   See [1998] 1 WLR 1056 at 1066E–H, CA.

11.61   Thus it appears that the court will rarely make orders under this jurisdiction. In particular, if the facts justify a wasted costs order, then the court will not move on to consider an order under this jurisdiction. In most cases, if the court is not prepared to make a wasted costs order, it will not be appropriate to make an order under this jurisdiction. What are the exceptions? Two examples given by Rose LJ in the *Tolstoy* case[1] were acting without authority, or in breach of an undertaking.

1   *Tolstoy-Miloslavsky v Aldington* [1996] 1 WLR 736, CA.

1   Acting without authority

11.62   It is likely that a solicitor who purports to act for a client, but does not in fact have that client's authority to act, will be found to have acted negligently and thus be liable to a wasted costs order. For instance, a solicitor who purports to act for a corporation, but fails to obtain its authority, is likely to be held negligent, as is a solicitor who acts for a bankrupt in relation to a cause of action which is vested in the bankrupt's trustee.[1] A solicitor who ignores a clear need to consider whether a client is under a mental disability will probably be held negligent.[2] If the solicitor is found to have been negligent, then, given that the court must first consider the wasted costs jurisdiction, it will not be necessary to go further and consider orders for costs under the present heading. On the other hand, in cases where the solicitor had no authority but nevertheless did not act improperly, unreasonably or negligently, the court will have no power to make a wasted costs order. It may, however, have jurisdiction to make an order for costs against the solicitor on a basis akin to breach of warranty of authority.

1   See *Nelson v Nelson* [1997] 1 WLR 233 at 240C–E per Waller LJ, CA.
2   *Re O (A Minor)* [1994] 2 FLR 842 at 847E per Connell J.

11.63   A distinction must be drawn between:

(i)   a solicitor who believes himself to have been retained by someone who has no authority to retain solicitors at all; and

(ii)   a solicitor who believes himself to have been retained by someone who has limited authority to retain solicitors, such as a bankrupt.

In both classes of case, by purporting to act for a party in litigation, the solicitor impliedly warrants that he has a client, that the client bears the name of the party to the proceedings, and that the client has authorised him to act for the client in the proceedings.[1] In the first class of case, the representation that the client has authorised him to act in the proceedings is incorrect, because the client has no authority to do so. Cases in the first class include a solicitor who purports to act for a defunct corporation, or for a minor or person of unsound mind who does not act by means of a next friend. In these cases, the effect of the misrepresentation is to give rise to the inherent jurisdiction of the court to order the solicitor to pay the other party's costs. This jurisdiction may be exercised even if the solicitor acted with reasonable skill and care, and was not negligent in failing to discover the want of authority.[2]

1   *Nelson v Nelson* [1997] 1 WLR 233.
2   As to persons of unsound mind, see *Yonge v Toynbee* [1910] 1 KB 215, CA. See also Waller LJ's analysis in *Nelson* at 240.

11.64   The second class of case was the subject of *Nelson v Nelson*.[1] The solicitors in question had, without negligence, purported to commence proceedings to protect the interest of their client in property. Unknown to them, the client was a bankrupt, so the right to take proceedings to protect his property was vested in his trustee in bankruptcy,[2] not in him. The trustee had not authorised the proceedings. McCowan and Peter Gibson LJJ held that the bankrupt did have the authority to retain the solicitors to commence the proceedings, so that the solicitors had not acted in breach of warranty of authority, and there was no breach of duty giving rise to the court's inherent jurisdiction. It was true that the bankrupt did not have a good cause of action, so that the action could have been stayed at any time on the basis of the bankruptcy and lack of authority from the trustee; but the solicitors gave no warranty as to the strength of the cause of action, so they were not in breach of warranty.[3]

1   [1997] 1 WLR 233.
2   By Insolvency Act 1986, s 306.
3   Waller LJ's judgment raises some questions. In his view, solicitors in the first category of case which we have set out were in breach of warranty because the warranty was that a client had authorised the solicitors, and this was false because the minor or person of unsound mind was unable to give that authority. But he then went on to say that a bankrupt was incapable of bringing proceedings in relation to property without the agreement of his trustee. If that is correct then it would seem that the bankrupt is in the same category as the child or person of unsound mind: he cannot give authority to his solicitors at all, so there is a breach of warranty by solicitors who act for him and warrant that he has authorised them to act. Nevertheless, Waller LJ held that the solicitors warranted only that the bankrupt existed and had authorised the proceedings, and that this warranty had not been breached. What is unclear is how, in Waller LJ's view, it was possible for the bankrupt to give the solicitors authority to act in the proceedings when he had an 'incapacity' to bring proceedings.

2   Breach of solicitors' undertakings

11.65   The court has power to enforce solicitors' undertakings by summary procedure, and, if it does so, to order the solicitor to pay the costs of such proceedings.[1] This jurisdiction is part of the power to enforce solicitors' undertakings.[2]

1   *Udall v Capri Lighting Ltd* [1988] QB 907, CA.
2   See *Cordery on Solicitors* (9th edn, looseleaf) at F [964]ff.

3   Orders in favour of non-parties

11.66   The court's jurisdiction to order costs in favour of non-parties in judicial review proceedings has already been discussed at para 11.19. As to the standard required of solicitors pursuant to this jurisdiction, before Supreme Court Act 1981, s 51(6) came into effect, the Court of Appeal had held that, in civil cases, the court could make an order against a solicitor pursuant to its inherent jurisdiction if the solicitor had acted unreasonably or improperly, or if costs had been thrown away by his incompetence; it was not necessary to show a serious dereliction of duty on the part of the solicitor.[1]

1   *Gupta v Comer* [1991] 1 QB 629, CA.

4 Criminal law

11.67 In criminal cases, the court also has an inherent jurisdiction to order solicitors to pay the costs of proceedings, but the jurisdiction is exercisable only if there has been a serious dereliction of duty on the part of the solicitor; mere mistake, error of judgment or negligence will not suffice.[1] For this reason, it is likely that, in criminal cases as well as civil, the wasted costs jurisdiction will be used more frequently than the court's inherent jurisdiction.

1   *Holden & Co v Crown Prosecution Service* [1990] 2 QB 261, CA.

D ORDERS PURSUANT TO THE GENERAL JURISDICTION OF THE COURT OVER COSTS

11.68   In *Aiden Shipping Co Ltd v Interbulk Ltd*,[1] the House of Lords established that the court has jurisdiction, pursuant to Supreme Court Act 1981, s 51(1) and (3), to make orders that non-parties pay the costs of proceedings. In a subsequent decision, the Court of Appeal indicated that it was likely that such an order would be made in circumstances where a non-party had maintained the action, in the sense of:[2]

> 'wanton and officious intermeddling with the disputes of others in [which] the meddler has no interest whatever, and where the assistance he renders to one or the other party is without justification or excuse.'

This raised the question of whether solicitors who acted for no fee might be liable for the other party's costs, pursuant to s 51(1) and (3). The ratio of the Court of Appeal's decision in *Tolstoy-Miloslavsky v Aldington*[3] is that there is no jurisdiction to award costs against solicitors, pursuant to s 51(1) and (3), merely because they act for no fee. The jurisdiction under s 51(1) and (3) could be exercised against a solicitor only 'if he acts outside the role of solicitor, eg in a private capacity or as a true third party funder for someone else'.[4]

1   [1986] AC 965.
2   *Murphy v Young & Co's Brewery plc* [1997] 1 WLR 1591, CA per Phillips LJ at 1601, referring to the test which Lord Mustill set out in *Giles v Thompson* [1994] 1 AC 142 at 164, HL. See also Balcombe LJ's guidelines in *Symphony Group plc v Hodgson* [1994] QB 179, CA.
3   [1996] 1 WLR 736.
4   *Tolstoy* [1996] 1 WLR 736 per Rose LJ at 746A. Ward LJ agreed: 751B. See also Roch LJ at 750D–F. The House of Lords dismissed a petition for leave to appeal: 752G. Further, Lord Woolf MR referred to the decision with approval in *Hodgson v Imperial Tobacco* [1998] 1 WLR 1056 at 1066H, CA.

11.69   The court in *Tolstoy* was not suggesting that a solicitor could never be the subject of an order pursuant to Supreme Court Act 1981, s 51(1) and (3). A solicitor could presumably be made the subject of such an order if he truly maintained another's action, in the sense of intermeddling set out above. For instance, he might be liable in this way if he funded a third party's action in which he was not himself instructed as a solicitor, and in relation to which he had no connection and no reason for such support.[1] It will be recalled from the discussion above that, in *Tolstoy*, the court considered that the solicitors had engaged in considerable meddling and interference in the litigation, for their own personal reasons. Yet, even on those facts, the court did not consider that there was jurisdiction to make a costs order under s 51(1) and (3): instead, the appropriate course was to make a wasted costs order under s 51(6). That being the case, it seems unlikely that, in a case where the solicitor is acting as a solicitor, the court will consider that it has jurisdiction to make an order under s 51(1) or (3).

1   Further, see *Nordstern Allgemeine Versicherungs AG v Internav Ltd* [1999] 23 LS Gaz R 33, CA: an order was made against a solicitor, but he had not been instructed to act as a solicitor in the proceedings in question. In *Globe Equities Ltd v Globe Legal Services Ltd* [1999] BLR 232, CA the defendant company had been formed by solicitors to hold the lease of their offices; the solicitors were the guarantors under the lease; it was appropriate to order them to pay costs as they were 'the real defendants'.

11.70   In the earlier case of *Mainwaring v Goldtech*,[1] the Court of Appeal had been prepared to assume, for the sake of argument in that case, that a solicitor might be liable for the other party's costs

> '... if he conducts the litigation in the knowledge that there is no real likelihood of his ever having his costs and expenses reimbursed by or on behalf of the client, save in the event of the litigation being successful.'

But this was not part of the ratio, because the court did not hear argument on it, and counsel for the solicitors was prepared to accept it for the purposes of the appeal. It must now be considered in light of the decision in *Tolstoy*. In particular, Rose LJ's judgment in that case emphasised that it was in the public interest, and perfectly proper, for solicitors and counsel to act without fee.[2] It is submitted that the passage quoted from *Mainwaring* was originally obiter and should now be treated as effectively having been overruled by the decision in *Tolstoy*, especially as *Mainwaring* was cited in argument in *Tolstoy*.[3]

1   (1991) Times, 19 February, CA.
2   [1996] 1 WLR 736 at 746B–D.
3   See [1996] 1 WLR 736 at 738C. Note also that Lord Woolf MR observed in *Hodgson v Imperial Tobacco Ltd* [1998] 1 WLR 1056 that the court's jurisdiction to make an order against solicitors under Supreme Court Act 1981, s 51(1) and (3) would be exercised only in 'a very small minority of cases': [1998] 1 WLR 1056 at 1066F.

11.71   Applications against the Solicitors' Indemnity Fund Ltd for costs pursuant to this jurisdiction, on the ground of delay in deciding to withdraw a solicitor's insurance cover because the claim arose out of a dishonest act, will generally fail.[1]

1   See *Bristol and West plc v Bhadresa* and *Bristol and West plc v Mascarenhas* [1999] Lloyd's Rep IR 138 (Lightman J).

CHAPTER 12

Disclosure and privilege

A   PRE-ACTION REMEDIES

1   Introduction

12.1   It is reasonably common for clients, particularly institutional ones, to ask their solicitors to send the file to them or to send it to a new firm of solicitors either for safekeeping or to enable copies to be taken. Sometimes the request is made immediately a transaction is completed and sometimes it is made years after the retainer has been terminated. Sometimes the request is made as part of a storage or an auditing process and sometimes it is made as a prelude to commencing litigation. Some confusion surrounds the obligations of the solicitor in these circumstances, particularly where he or she is, or has been, retained by more than one client and this confusion is at least in part due to the competing principles of ownership, the client's contractual rights, the client's statutory right to the delivery of a bill (and to have it taxed) and the court's inherent jurisdiction to police solicitors as officers of the court.

2   Delivery up or production of documents

12.2   A defendant to an action is under no obligation to list or produce documents to the claimant in advance of the commencement of proceedings unless the documents fall within one of the categories of pre-action disclosure. The Civil Procedure Rules have extended the availability of pre-action disclosure to all claims for breach of contract or tort. It remains to be seen how widely the relevant provisions will be interpreted but the remedy is unlikely to be widely available in standard negligence actions.[1] A client is only entitled, therefore, to see documents in advance of proceedings if he can establish some other right to the documents: a property right, a contractual right under the terms of any retainer or pursuant to statute or the inherent jurisdiction of the court.

1   See CPR 31.16 and *Burrells Wharf Freeholds Ltd v Galliard Homes Ltd* (1 July 1999, unreported) (Dyson J). An application for *Norwich Pharmacal* relief, ie a free-standing action for disclosure against a non-party, remains available where the solicitor has been mixed up in the wrongdoing of a third party.

12.3   Subject to any lien, the court may order a solicitor to return all documents which belong to him to the client or his personal representatives pursuant to the inherent jurisdiction of the court to regulate the conduct of solicitors.[1] RSC Ord 106, r 3 also provides a specific remedy whereby the court may order a solicitor to deliver a cash account, money or securities or a list of securities to his client or the client's personal representatives.[2] Finally, the court has a specific jurisdiction under Solicitors' Act 1974, s 68 to require a solicitor to deliver a bill of costs and at the same time to deliver up any documents in his possession, custody and power in non-contentious business. Where costs remain outstanding, the usual practice before the CPR was to apply for an order for taxation and delivery up of all documents upon payment by the client.[3] The jurisdiction was a summary one and would be exercised unless there was a genuine dispute as to the client's entitlement to the documents.[4] There is no reason to suppose that interim relief will not be granted on the same basis under the new rules of court.

1   See *Cordery on Solicitors* 9th edn (1998 issue) Vol 1 at F[486].
2   See CPR 50.1(2) and Schedule 1.
3   See the *Supreme Court Practice* (1998 edn) Vol 2 at 15G-8.
4   See *Ex p Cobeldick* (1883) 12 QBD 149, CA. Part 8 of the CPR (Alternative Procedure for Claims) applies to such applications.

12.4   In the past it has been common practice for solicitors to hand over the entire file at the termination of the retainer for the sake of convenience but this does not mean that every document on the file belongs to the client or that he is entitled to possession of it. It is obvious that the client is the owner of cash or documents which he has given to the solicitor for safekeeping and the specific remedy afforded by RSC Ord 106 exists in this instance to enable him to recover his money or valuable documents of title or securities quickly. The client will also be the owner of documents which the solicitor receives or creates in his capacity as agent for the client, eg correspondence with a third party or his or her solicitors. The client is entitled to have and see these documents as well because he owns them.

12.5   Although the principle is easy to state, it is more difficult both in litigation and transactional work to identify which parts of the solicitor's working papers or work product belong to him and which to the client. Both *The Guide to the Professional Conduct of Solicitors*[1] and *Cordery*[2] contain detailed analysis of the ownership of the documents on a file and that analysis is not repeated here. In any event, in most cases where proceedings are contemplated the client is not interested in physical possession of the file as much as seeing and then taking a copy of the relevant documents. Little judicial time has been focused on the difference between the right to possession of documents and the right to production of them for the purpose of copying but there is authority that the court may order production of a file for inspection and copying by a client under its inherent jurisdiction.[3] If this is right a client is entitled to a summary order before action giving him access to the file.

1   (6th edn, 1999) '*The Guide*': see Annex 12A.
2   9th edn (1998) Vol 1 at E[676] and Vol 2 at 4[21] et seq. For more detailed consideration and citation of all the relevant authorites see *Cordery* 8th edn (1988) at 88–91.
3   *Re Crocker* [1936] Ch 696 (Clauson J). It may be that the true analysis of this is that it is an example of the wider duty to disclose all relevant information to the client: see *The Guide* at para 16.06. The case has barely been cited and in *Nationwide v Various Solicitors (No 3)* [1999] PNLR 52 at 71G–72F (Blackburne J), quoted in para 12.8, the judge drew a distinction between documents which a client was entitled to see and information which the solicitor was bound to disclose.

3   Joint and multiple retainers

12.6   The right of a client to obtain a remedy which entitles him to take copies of documents which he does not own becomes more important where the solicitor is acting either under a joint retainer or a multiple retainer,[1] eg, where he acts for vendor and purchaser or lender and borrower. If the view expressed in the last paragraph is right, the client ought to be entitled on a summary application to delivery up of all documents which belong exclusively to him and to take copies of all documents which belong to the solicitor or the other client in which he has an interest and is entitled to see.

1   This term is used here to describe the situation in which the solicitor is instructed *separately* by two or more clients but the retainer involves the solicitor in carrying out the *same* task for all of them.

12.7   Which documents belonging to the second client is the first client entitled to see and copy? If documents are brought into existence whilst the solicitor is working for both clients, each is entitled to a copy although neither can take physical possession of the original without the consent of the other.[1] Where the solicitor acts for both vendor and purchaser or borrower and lender, these documents will be relatively few in number. If documents are brought into existence whilst the solicitor is acting exclusively for the second client the first client is only entitled to see them with the express consent of the second. In certain circumstances, however, it may be possible for consent to be implied. In *Mortgage Express Ltd v Bowerman*[2] Millett LJ stated:

> 'A solicitor who acts both for a purchaser and a mortgage lender faces a potential conflict of duty. A solicitor who acts for more than one party to a transaction owes a duty of confidentiality to each client, but the existence of this duty does not affect his duty to act in the best interests of the other client. All information supplied by a client to his solicitor is confidential and may be disclosed only with the consent, express or implied, of his client. There is, therefore, an obvious potentiality for conflict between the solicitor's duty of confidentiality to the buyer and his duty to act in the best interests of the mortgage lender.
>
> No such conflict, however, arose in the present case. It is the duty of a solicitor acting for a purchaser to investigate the vendor's title on his behalf and to deduce it to the mortgagee's solicitor. He has the implied authority to communicate all documents of title to the mortgagee's solicitors.'

It is suggested that 'documents of title' is being used here in the extended sense of all documents copies of which the solicitor could have been expected to receive if he had been deducing title for the mortgagee. In the case of a standard conveyancing transaction this will include all preliminary inquiries, documents of title, searches and correspondence with third parties, eg the vendor's or landlord's solicitors, where that correspondence is material to the mortgagee's retainer.

1   See *The Guide* Annex 12A, para 2.
2   [1996] 2 All ER 836 at 844j–845b. See also *Bristol and West Building Society v Mothew* [1998] Ch 1 at 20D–G and *The Guide* above at para 3.

12.8   This implied consent is limited, however. The first client is not entitled to see or take copies of confidential communications passing between the solicitor and the second client. In *Nationwide Building Society v Various Solicitors (No 3)*[1] the judge held that a borrower was entitled to maintain privilege in all confidential communications to or from his solicitor even though he had authorised the solicitor to reveal certain information to the lender for the purpose of carrying out his duty to the lender to report on title. He said this:[2]

> 'He [counsel for the defendants] submitted that the question is essentially one of what authority the borrower is impliedly giving to his solicitor in respect of the information in question. The authority, he submitted, is merely to pass on to the Nationwide the information. It does not extend to divulging the confidential communication—for example, a letter—in which the information is passed to the solicitor.
>
> In my judgment, Mr Davidson is correct. The fact that the borrower authorises his solicitor to divulge to the Nationwide, or its solicitor, information which he has passed to his solicitor in the course of confidential communications does not mean that the communication in question ceases to be privileged. The fact that the solicitor also happens, with the borrower's consent, to be acting for the Nationwide can make no difference. As the quoted passages from the judgments of Millett LJ in the *Bowerman* and *Mothew* cases make clear, a solicitor who acts for both borrower and lender in a transaction owes separate duties of confidence

to each client. The question in each case is whether the communication in question is confidential; and, if it is, what information contained in the communication the borrower has authorised the solicitor to disclose to the lender?

The reason why, in the *Bowerman* case, the solicitor has the borrower's implied consent to communicate the documents of title to the lender and to hold them, as solicitors for the lender, and not just as solicitors for the borrower, was because deducing title involves showing the person to whom title is to be deduced the very documents of title themselves. The position is different where the implied consent concerns only the provision of information.'

Accordingly, the appropriate test in each case is to consider which documents (as opposed to information) the solicitor would have received if both clients had been separately represented and he had been acting exclusively for one rather than the other.

1   [1999] PNLR 52 (Blackburne J).
2   [1999] PNLR 52 at 71G–72D.

12.9 If the solicitor mistakenly hands over the entire file to the first client at the expense of the second or permits a copy to be made, the solicitor cannot recover the documents without the authority of the second client whatever liability he may incur for breach of confidence.[1] This is not because there has been a waiver of privilege or confidentiality but because only the client and not the solicitor has a right of action to recover them.

1   *Nationwide v Various Solicitors (No 2)* (1998) Times, 1 May (Blackburne J).

B DISCLOSURE

1 Introduction

12.10 It usually presents no difficulty to identify the material documents in a claim of negligence or breach of duty against a solicitor. In many cases the solicitor's file will provide the only relevant documents. In other cases where the claimant is an institution, each party will have a file and the forensic inquiry will be limited to an analysis of the two files. The most difficult disclosure issues in solicitors' cases usually arise where the defendant has acted for the claimant on other transactions or for a third party whose conduct is central to the claim. The issues which most commonly arise are, first, whether the conduct of other transactions is relevant to the issue between the parties; secondly, the extent to which the documents relevant to the transaction in question or other transactions are privileged; thirdly, whether the claimant may rely on the iniquity exception to obtain an order for production of privileged documents; and, fourthly, whether the claimant may be taken to have waived privilege in relation to other transactions in which the defendant or other solicitors acted on his behalf. The Civil Procedure Rules now limit the duty of a party to make disclosure to those documents located by a reasonable search.[1] But even before the new rules came into force, the court was reluctant to permit a roving search of a defendant solicitor's files.[2]

1   It will be clear from the disclosure statement in the defendant's list whether he considers other transactions relevant: see CPR 31.10(6). If the number of files in question is small and can be easily located, the proportionality test will be satisfied and it will be reasonable for the defendant to conduct a search for them: see CPR 31.7.
2   See *Portman Building Society v Royal Insurance plc* [1998] PNLR 672 at 675C–D, CA referring to the 'potentially poisonous effect of an over-literal application of the *Peruvian Guano*'.

2 Relevance of other transactions

12.11   In civil cases the court will not order disclosure of documents which go solely to credit and more often than not evidence of what occurred on other occasions goes purely to the credibility of the evidence of one or other of the parties about the facts in issue. If one party's behaviour on another occasion was wholly inconsistent with the account he now gives, this earlier behaviour will cast doubt on his credibility. The policy of the law is to limit the forensic inquiry to evidence which is logically probative of the facts in issue and, unless the evidence is compelling, exclude more prejudicial material. In *Thorpe v Chief Constable of Greater Manchester Police*[1] the court refused to order disclosure of documents relating to earlier convictions or disciplinary findings against two police officers who were the subject of a claim for damages for assault and false imprisonment. It was held that evidence of this kind would be likely to be directed solely to cross-examination as to credit and the application was refused.

1   [1989] 1 WLR 665, CA.

12.12   In civil cases, as in criminal cases, evidence of other transactions will be admitted if that evidence does not go solely to credit but is so strikingly similar to them as to be logically probative of the facts in issue.[1] In *Bradford & Bingley Building Society v Boyce Evans Shepherd*[2] where a lender claimed to be the victim of a number of mortgage frauds the judge permitted it to amend its pleadings to allege fraud in reliance on a second, copycat, transaction. He distinguished *Thorpe* on the ground that evidence of the second transaction was sufficiently similar to be evidence of system. He said this:[3]

> 'It seems to me the various similarities between the two transactions on which the plaintiff wishes to rely are such that there is a case based on dishonesty which can properly be pleaded against the defendants in relation to their involvement with the instant transaction. As in many different sorts of matters in which the court has to make a judgment, the demarcation between cases where the evidence to be relied on is "to give a dog a bad name" and where it is being relied on for justified similar fact purposes is often hard to identify. I bear in mind the fact that the plaintiff does not seek to rely upon Mr Jeremy's involvement in the no 15 transaction purely for the purpose of providing similar fact evidence: it also contends that the subject transaction (ie that relating to the flat) was part of a scheme of mortgage frauds, involving the same personnel, the same type of system. Accordingly, I have reached the conclusion that the plaintiff ought to succeed on this issue.'

1   *Mood Music Publishing Co Ltd v De Wolfe Publishing Ltd* [1976] Ch 119.
2   [1998] PNLR 250 (Neuberger J), upheld on this point by the Court of Appeal (6 July 1998, unreported), CA.
3   [1998] PNLR 250 at 255F-256A.

12.13   The evidence of other transactions may also relate to other claims brought by the claimant against the defendant. In *Maes Finance Ltd v Leftleys*[1] the judge gave leave for a number of actions against the defendants involving allegations of negligence and breach of fiduciary duty in relation to a number of transactions to be tried together on the grounds that the evidence in each action would be relevant evidence in the other claims.

1   [1998] PNLR 193 (Jacob J). Upheld on appeal: (1998) Times, 13 November, CA.

12.14   Evidence of other transactions may also be directly relevant to questions of causation and reliance even if there is no striking similarity. In *Lillicrap v Nalder & Son*[1] the defendant admitted negligence for failing to advise his clients of the existence of a right of way over land which they later purchased but argued that they would have proceeded with the transaction if properly advised anyway. The court held that evidence of their conduct in six other transactions in which the defendants had acted for them was directly relevant to the defendants' defence. Dillon LJ stated:[2]

> 'I do not regard this as a strict case of similar fact evidence. It is merely a question of trying the issue in civil proceedings of whether, on the balance of probabilities, the plaintiffs would or would not have resiled from the transaction, or taken some other course other than they did, if they had been properly advised about the rights of way, the presence of one and the absence of another.'

The court did, however, reserve the right of the trial judge to exclude the evidence on grounds of prejudice in the exercise of his discretion. At the interim stage, however, the defendants were entitled to plead the transactions and obtain disclosure of the relevant documents. The critical point here is that evidence of other transactions may not only be relevant to the hypothetical question whether the client would have withdrawn from the transaction if properly advised but the most cogent evidence by which the court can assess his answer.

1   [1993] 1 WLR 94, CA. Dillon LJ delivered the lead judgment in both this case and *Thorpe*.
2   [1993] 1 WLR 94 at 100F–H.

12.15   Even so, the court will not admit evidence of all other transactions. In *Lillicrap v Nalder & Son* the six transactions had all taken place prior to the transaction which was the subject matter of the claim. In *Nyckeln Finance Ltd v Edward Symmons & Partners*[1] by contrast the court ordered disclosure of one transaction which had taken place prior to the transaction in question on the ground that it was relevant to reliance and contributory negligence but refused to order disclosure of a number of transactions which post-dated the transaction which was in issue in the action. They threw no light on the state of mind of the client's officers at the relevant time.

1   [1996] PNLR 245, CA.

3   Documents which are privileged

12.16   The leading modern authority on the scope of legal advice privilege is *Balabel v Air-India*[1] in which disclosure was sought of all communications between the defendant and its solicitors (apart from those seeking or giving legal advice), drafts and working papers, attendance notes and memoranda of the defendant's solicitors and internal communications of the defendant. The Court of Appeal refused to order discovery of any of these categories. Taylor LJ gave the following guidance about the scope of the privilege:[2]

> '[T]he test is whether the communication or other document was made confidentially for the purpose of legal advice. Those purposes have to be construed broadly. Privilege obviously attaches to a document conveying legal advice from solicitor to client and to a specific request from the client for such advice. But it does not follow that all other communications between them lack privilege. In most solicitor and client relationships, especially where a transaction involves protracted dealings, advice may be required or appropriate on matters great or small at various stages. There will be a continuum of communication and meetings between the solicitor and client. The negotiations for a lease

such as occurred in the present case are only one example. Where information is passed by the solicitor or client to the other as part of the continuum aimed at keeping both informed so that advice may be sought and given as required, privilege will attach. A letter from the client may end with such words as "please advise me what I should do." But, even if it does not, there will usually be implied in the relationship an overall expectation that the solicitor will at each stage, whether asked specifically or not, tender appropriate advice. Moreover, legal advice is not confined to telling the client the law; it must include advice as to what should prudently and sensibly be done in the relevant legal context.

It may be that applying this test to any series of communications might isolate occasional letters or notes which could not be said to enjoy privilege. But to be disclosable such documents must be not only privilege-free but also material and relevant. Usually a letter which does no more than acknowledge receipt of a document or suggest a date for a meeting will be irrelevant or non-disclosable. In effect, therefore, the "purpose of legal advice test" will result in most communications between solicitor and client in, for example, a conveyancing transaction being exempt from disclosure, either because they are privileged or because they are immaterial or irrelevant.'

The dicta of Taylor LJ were directly applied in the recent case of *Nationwide v Various Solicitors (No 3)*[3] in which the judge stated:

'I take the decision of the Court of Appeal in that case to mean that in an ordinary conveyancing transaction communications passing between the solicitor instructed in the matter and the client, being confidential communications made in connection with the matter, will be privileged if, although advice is not specifically sought or given in relation to any particular communication, the communication is made with the view, albeit unspoken, to legal advice being given if appropriate; or, as Peter Gibson J tersely put it in *In Re Konigsberg (a bankrupt)* [1989] 1 WLR 1257, 1263:

"Privilege attaches where information is passed by the solicitor or client to the other in the course of keeping each other informed so that advice may be sought and given as required."'

Applying this test the judge found that the following classes of document were privileged as part of the 'continuum' of communications:[4] (a) letters passing between solicitor and client (although the letters from the client contained no express request for advice and all but one of the letters from the solicitor contained no formal advice); (b) letters passing between the client's agent and the client sent to the solicitor by the client for his information; and (c) completion statements and their earlier drafts. He found, however, that client account ledger entries were not privileged.[5]

1   [1988] Ch 317.
2   [1988] Ch 317 at 330D–331A.
3   [1999] PNLR 52 (Blackburne J).
4   [1999] PNLR 52. It was accepted that all documents of title and communications with third parties rather than the borrower were not privileged.
5   In *R v Manchester Crown Court, ex p R* (1999) Times, 15 February, CA it was also held that a solicitor's appointments diary and time sheets were not privileged. Bills rendered by the solicitor to the client would, of course, be privileged.

12.17   Both *Balabel* and *Nationwide* involved conveyancing files. *NRG Holding NV v Bacon & Woodrow*[1] provides a good example of the scope of legal advice privilege outside the conveyancing context. The claim concerned due diligence work done by the defendant actuaries and accountants for NRG in relation to a number of insurance companies. In the course of the action a bill was disclosed containing a description of the work undertaken by NRG's solicitors. It was conceded that there was no privilege in documents written or copied by the solicitors to NRG's other advisers (including the defendants), notes of meetings with the non-legal team (save to the extent that those notes contained advice in addition to what was said at the meeting) or notes of meetings with the vendors (save to the extent that they contained the views of the solicitors on what had passed).[2] But the accountants also sought production of the legal advice given by the solicitors and NRG's foreign lawyers on two grounds: first, that the advice was commercial and not legal and, secondly, because it was not confidential or privileged. The judge rejected both submissions. He said this:[3]

> 'As Taylor LJ observed, a solicitor's professional duty or function is frequently not exclusively related to the giving of advice on matters of law or, in the context of this kind of case, on drafting or construction of documents. It not infrequently relates to the commercial wisdom of entering into a given transaction in relation to which legal advice is also sought.'

He also rejected[4] the second submission on the ground that it was implicit in the retainer of the solicitors that they had the authority to disclose the legal advice which they had given to their client to the other advisers in the team to the extent that they thought necessary. But this did not mean that they owed no duty of confidentiality to their client. Far less did it mean that there was no duty of confidentiality in relation to the advice which the solicitors had given to the client and which had not been disclosed to the rest of the team.

1   [1995] 1 All ER 976 (Colman J).
2   [1995] 1 All ER 976 at 981h–j.
3   [1995] 1 All ER 976 at 983j.
4   [1995] 1 All ER 976 at 984b–f.

7   Joint and multiple retainers

12.18   Where the solicitor represents more than one client, it may become necessary to consider whether documents which are brought into existence for the purpose of seeking or obtaining legal advice are confidential to one client and privileged from production to the other. It is now well settled that clients who retain a solicitor jointly to act for them cannot maintain privilege against each other or against their successors in title. Where, however, the solicitor is instructed under a separate retainer by two clients at the same time, each will be able to maintain privilege against the other.[1]

1   See *Re Konigsberg (a bankrupt)* [1989] 1 WLR 1257 (Peter Gibson J); and *The Sagheera* [1997] 1 Lloyd's Rep 160 (Rix J).

12.19   It is a question of fact whether a solicitor is engaged under a joint retainer or separate retainer. In cases where the solicitor writes an engagement letter and submits bills to both clients, the question is easily answered. In *Re Konigsberg*, however, which involved the sale of one property and the transfer and remortgage of another by a husband and wife the judge held that at various times the solicitor was acting under a single separate retainer from the husband and a joint retainer from both husband and wife. He rejected the 'broad view of this question' and refused to hold that 'throughout the bankrupt and Mrs Konigsberg were the joint clients of the solicitors'.[1] He also held[2] that the wife could not assert privilege against the trustee in bankruptcy of her husband as his successor. The critical question is not whether the parties are acting in the same interest but whether they instruct the solicitor jointly.[3]

1 [1989] 1 WLR 1257 at 1262D–G. Peter Gibson J also stated: 'But the fact that Mrs Konigsberg provided the money used to pay the solicitors ... does not mean that throughout she was the client, either alone or jointly, of the solicitors. Advice can be given to A by a solicitor but subsequently paid for by B without B becoming at the time of the advice or thereafter the client of the solicitor in relation to that advice.' See also chapter 1, para 1.8.
2 [1989] 1 WLR 1257 at 1266D–1267G.
3 See eg *The Sagheera* [1997] 1 Lloyd's Rep 160 (Rix J) in which the parties were a ship owner and war risk insurer or *Shore v Bedford* (1843) 5 Man & G 271. For an extended discussion of when a joint retainer arises see *Phipson on Evidence* (14th edn, 1990) para 20–17.

8 The iniquity exception

12.20 It is also well established that the client may not continue to assert privilege in relation to documents which were brought into existence for the purpose of furthering a criminal or fraudulent purpose.[1] No exhaustive definition of the conduct to which the exception applies has yet been attempted. In *Ventouris v Mountain*[2] Sir Thomas Bingham MR used the term 'iniquity' and this term was adopted in *Barclays Bank plc v Eustice*[3] where the court ordered the defendant to produce privileged documents relating to a transaction in fraud of creditors within Insolvency Act 1986, s 423.

1 The leading authority in this context is *O'Rourke v Darbishire* [1920] AC 581.
2 [1991] 1 WLR 607 at 611E.
3 [1995] 1 WLR 1238 at 1248H–1250D.

(a)   The facts of the case

12.21 The claimant may seek production of the privileged material on the grounds that the original transaction of which he complains was fraudulent or tainted by iniquity. In *Birmingham Midshires Mortgage Services Ltd v Ansell*[1] the judge held that the exception did not apply where a borrower misled a lender about the purpose for which he required a remortgage. Blackburne J refused to follow *Ansell* in *Nationwide v Various Solicitors (No 3)*[2] and held that:

> 'Deceiving a person into lending money in circumstances where, if no deception had been practised, no loan might well have been forthcoming is, in my respectful view, at least as iniquitous as entering into a transaction for the purpose of putting one's assets beyond the reach of one's creditors or otherwise prejudicing the interests of those creditors. The fact that the motive was to relieve financial pressure does not seem to me to matter.'

Furthermore the judge also held that in order to invoke the exception it is not necessary for the applicant to satisfy the court that the solicitor was a party to the crime or iniquity in the sense that he was engaged to assist his client to further that purpose or knew that his involvement would be of such assistance.[3] Indeed in *Barclays Bank plc v Eustice*[4] the Court of Appeal accepted that the exception might be invoked even if the client and solicitor shared the view that the scheme designed to put assets out of the reach of creditors was lawful.

1 (6 November 1997, unreported) (Jonathan Parker J).
2 [1999] PNLR 52 at 73G.
3 [1999] PNLR 52 at 74A.
4 [1995] 1 WLR 1238 at 1252C–D.

12.22 In *Eustice*[1] the Court of Appeal left open the question whether it was necessary for the applicant to establish a prima facie case of iniquity or a strong prima facie case.

In *Nationwide Building Society v Various Solicitors* the judge, whilst recognising that there may be little difference between them, adopted[2] the view expressed by Viscount Finlay in *O'Rourke v Darbishire*[3] where he said this:

> 'It is not enough to allege fraud. If the communications to the solicitor were for the purpose of obtaining professional advice there must be, in order to get rid of the privilege, not merely an allegation that they were made for the purpose of getting advice for the commission of a fraud but there must be something to give colour to the charge. The statement must be made in clear and definitive terms and there must further be some prima facie evidence it has some foundation in fact.'

1   [1995] 1 WLR 1238 at 1241H.
2   [1999] PNLR 52 at 74D–E.
3   [1920] AC 581 at 606.

(b)   Evidence gathering

12.23   The parties may also allege that the way in which evidence has been gathered involves fraud or iniquity. In *Dubai Aluminium Co Ltd v Al Alawi*[1] there was a strong prima facie case that Dubal, the plaintiff, had obtained details of the defendant's bank, credit card and telephone accounts from inquiry agents who had made 'pretext calls' impersonating the defendant. These calls involved both fraudulent misrepresentations and criminal offences under the Data Protection Act 1984 and Swiss banking legislation. The defendant sought disclosure of the reports and other documents relating to the investigation. The judge held that criminal or fraudulent conduct undertaken for the purposes of litigation is no different from advising on, or setting up, a fraudulent or criminal transaction and ordered disclosure.[2]

1   [1999] 1 All ER 703 (Rix J).
2   [1999] 1 All ER 703 at 709b–d. He did not, however, consider that searching dustbins and copying material found in them amounted to criminal or fraudulent conduct for the purposes of the rule: see 707h.

9   Implied waiver of privilege

(a)   The principle

12.24   In order to pursue his claim against the defendant, it is always necessary for the client to waive privilege in relation to the defendant's file for the transaction which is the subject matter of the claim. Otherwise it would be impossible for him to establish that the defendant gave the wrong advice or failed to advise him with skill and care. When, however, the defendant seeks to obtain disclosure of documents which demonstrate how the client behaved on other occasions, for example, when he received legal advice from the defendant in relation to similar transactions or when he received independent advice from another solicitor in relation to litigation with third parties, the client may assert privilege in those documents despite their relevance to the proceedings.

(b)   The defendant's files

12.25   In principle a client who commences proceedings against his former solicitor will be found to have waived privilege in the defendant's own files to the extent that it is necessary to enable the court to adjudicate on the claim fully and fairly. In *Lillicrap v Nalder & Son*[1] the Court of Appeal held that there had been an implied waiver of privilege in relation to six other transactions. Dillon LJ stated:

'Thus, the client has the right to insist on his professional legal privilege and it is for him to choose whether or not to waive it. But it is accepted that the waiver may be implied and that there is an implied waiver when the client brings proceedings against the solicitor. Mr. Bennett suggests that the waiver is only in respect of documents and information concerned with the particular retainer. This may, in general, prima facie, be so but it is not difficult to envisage scenarios where it is apparent that the waiver must have a wider scope ...

For my part, I accept May J's formulation of the scope of waiver. He said in his judgment:

> "I return to what I regard as the heart of the matter—waiver. A client who sues his solicitor invites the court to adjudicate the dispute and thereby in my judgment waives privilege and confidence to the extent that it is necessary to enable the court to do so fully and fairly and in accordance with the law of evidence. I suspect that at the fringes each case will depend on its own facts. Normally the waiver will extend to facts and documents material to the cause of action upon which the plaintiff sues and to the defendant's proper defence to that cause of action. The bringing of a claim for negligence in relation to a particular retainer will normally be a waiver of privilege and confidence for facts and documents relating to that retainer, but not without more for those relating to other discrete retainers."

I agree with that. The waiver can only extend to matters which are relevant to an issue in the proceedings and, privilege apart, admissible in evidence. There is no waiver for a roving search into anything else in which the solicitor or any other solicitor may have happened to have acted for the clients. But the waiver must go far enough, not merely to entitle the plaintiff to establish his cause of action, but to enable the defendant to establish a defence to the cause of action if he has one. Thus, it would extend to matters under earlier retainers, as in the hypothetical example I had given[2] which established that the experience of the client was, to the knowledge of the solicitor, such that the solicitor was not in breach of the duty as alleged.'

1   [1993] 1 WLR 94 at 98B and 99A–E, CA.
2   [1993] 1 WLR 94 at 98C–H.

12.26   In *NRG Holding NV v Bacon & Woodrow*[1] the defendants sought to argue that the plaintiff had waived privilege over advice given by their legal advisers in relation to a share purchase by proceeding against its other advisers, who were accountants and actuaries. Colman J, after citing *Lillicrap v Nalder*, said this:

'The true analysis of what the courts are doing in such cases of so-called waiver of privilege is, in my judgment, to prevent the unfairness which would arise if the plaintiff were entitled to exclude from the court's consideration evidence relevant to a defence by relying upon the privilege arising from the solicitor's duty of confidence. The client is thus precluded from *both* asserting that the solicitor has acted in breach of duty and thereby caused the client loss and, to make good the claim, opening up the confidential relationship between them and at the same time seeking to enforce against that same solicitor a duty of confidence arising from their professional relationship in circumstances where such enforcement would deprive the solicitor of the means of defending the claim. It is fundamental to this principle that the confidence which privilege would otherwise protect arises by reason of the same professional relationship between the parties to the litigation. The underlying unfairness which the principle seeks to avoid arises because the claim is asserted and the professional relationship opened for investigation against the very party whose duty of confidence is the basis of the privilege. It is against the unfairness of both opening the relationship by asserting the claim and seeking to enforce the duty of confidence owed by the defendant that the principle is directed.'

He held that by commencing proceedings against the non-legal advisers the plaintiff had not waived privilege in relation to confidential legal advice.

1   [1995] 1 All ER 976 at 986c–f.

(c)   The files of other solicitors

12.27   Although the views expressed by Colman J suggested that the principle was confined to dealings between the claimant and the defendant, both *Lillicrap v Nalder* and *NRG v Bacon & Woodrow* left open for decision the question whether a client who sues one solicitor will be taken to have waived privilege in relation to advice which he received from another firm of solicitors. A number of conflicting first instance decisions then followed. In *Kershaw v Whelan*[1] the judge ordered discovery of privileged documents relating to advice given by other solicitors. She found that Colman J's dictum was 'not directly in point'.[2] She also said this:[3]

'The solicitors' files of the plaintiff's former solicitors are in the hands of his present solicitor. In my judgment, they are subject to the same rules of discovery as the files of his present solicitors, which means that letters and other communications between solicitor and client will be privileged as will advices, opinions, and file notes. I can see no logical basis for distinguishing between those files and those of the plaintiff's present solicitors where the various solicitors were dealing with essentially the same subject matter.'

In *Banque Bruxelles Lambert SA v Simmons & Simmons*[4] on the other hand the judge held that the implied waiver extended only to 'communications between the client and the solicitor whom he is suing' and that the plaintiff, which had commenced proceedings against its external solicitors, had not waived privilege in relation to advice provided by its in-house lawyers. In *Hayes v Dowding*[5] the judge declined to follow *NRG* and ordered the plaintiff to make disclosure of privileged communications relating to a compromise agreement. Finally, in *Burdge & Burdge v John Hodge & Co*[6] the judge held that the implied waiver did not usually extend to require disclosure of documents privileged in the hands of another solicitor instructed after the act of negligence complained of.

1   [1996] 1 WLR 358 (Ebsworth J)
2   [1996] 1 WLR 358 at 369E.
3   [1996] 1 WLR 358 at 370D.
4   (24 November 1995, unreported) (Blackburne J), transcript, p 40.
5   [1996] PNLR 578 at 589C–F (Jonathan Parker J). The claim was not a claim against a solicitor but against parties to a compromise agreement.
6   (11 March 1996, unreported) (Longmore J).

12.28   This conflict of authority has now been resolved by the decision of the Court of Appeal in *Paragon Finance plc v Freshfields*.[1] In that case the plaintiffs, a group of mortgage lenders, syndicated their mortgage books by selling the loans to special purpose vehicles and issuing a series of loan notes to investors. Sun Alliance and Eagle Star guaranteed the loans on terms that the lenders met certain lending criteria which were then specified in the mortgage guarantee policies. When the insurers refused to indemnify the lenders against heavy losses sustained by the plaintiffs for failure to comply with these criteria, the plaintiffs sued the insurance companies. This litigation was compromised and the lenders then commenced proceedings against the defendants who had advised them on the terms of the policies. The defendants sought production of the communications between the lenders and their new solicitors and counsel in the actions against the insurers. It was common ground that these documents were relevant to the proceedings but the Court of Appeal refused to order disclosure. Lord Bingham MR who delivered the judgment of the court made this important statement of principle:[2]

> 'When a client sues a solicitor who has formerly acted for him, complaining that the solicitor has acted negligently, he invites the court to adjudicate on questions directly arising from the confidential relationship which formerly subsisted between them. Since court proceedings are public, the client brings that formerly confidential relationship into the public domain. He thereby waives any right to claim the protection of legal professional privilege in relation to any communications between them so far as necessary for the just determination of his claim; or, putting the same proposition in different terms, he releases the solicitor to that extent from the obligation of confidence by which he was formerly bound. This is an implication of law, the rationale of which is plain. A party cannot deliberately subject a relationship to public scrutiny and at the same time seek to preserve its confidentiality. He cannot pick and choose, disclosing such incidents of the relationship as strengthen his claim for damages and concealing from forensic scrutiny such incidents as weaken it. He cannot attack his former solicitor and deny the solicitor use of materials relevant to his defence. But, since the implied waiver applies to communications between client and solicitor, it will cover no communications to which the solicitor is not privy and so will disclose nothing of which he is not already aware.
>
> Thus, on the present facts, by bringing these proceedings the plaintiffs impliedly waived any claim to legal professional privilege in relation to confidential communications between them and Freshfields concerning the transaction briefly described above, up to the moment when Freshfields ceased to act. That is not in issue. The question is whether the plaintiffs have also impliedly waived any claim to legal professional privilege in relation to confidential communications between them and Slaughter and May relating to the pursuit and settlement of claims arising from those transactions. Approaching this question as one of pure principle, we conclude that they have not. The plaintiffs have not sued Slaughter and May. They have not invited the court to adjudicate on any question arising from their confidential relationship with Slaughter and May, and so have not brought that confidential relationship into the public domain. They have done nothing to release Slaughter and May from the obligation of confidence by which they are bound. They have chosen to subject their relationship with Freshfields to public scrutiny, but not their relationship with Slaughter and May. They are not seeking to pick and choose among the confidential communications passing between themselves and Slaughter and May: none of them is (so far) in the forensic arena. It is open to Freshfields, by way of defence, to rely on any communication passing between themselves and the plaintiffs; to hold that the plaintiffs have impliedly waived privilege in relation to confidential communications between themselves and Slaughter and May would be, not to enable Freshfields to rely on communications of which they are already aware, but to disclose to them communications of which they have no knowledge.'

The court restricted the application of *Lillicrap v Nalder* to former transactions handled by the defendant, approved both *NRG v Bacon & Woodrow* and *BBL v Simmons & Simmons*, disapproved Ebsworth J's reasoning in *Kershaw v Whelan* and overruled *Hayes v Dowding*.

It remains unclear, however, following *Paragon*, whether the doctrine of implied waiver can ever extend beyond a case where the solicitor in question is also the defendant. In *Paragon* itself the files in question were relevant to the defendant's case of contributory negligence and failure to mitigate, and it was unnecessary for the court to consider a case where the claimant has put in issue the legal advice which he has received but the adviser is not the defendant. It is clear that the principle of implied waiver extends only to cases in which the claimant has brought the legal relationship into the public domain. The difficulty is to identify the limits of that principle.[3] If it is limited to cases in which the relationship is the subject of the action and the claimant releases the defendant from his obligation of confidentiality so that he can defend himself, the doctrine is very narrow indeed. But if it extends to all cases where the claimant has put in issue the advice which he received either expressly or by implication the doctrine will be of wider application.

1   [1999] 1 WLR 1183.
2   [1999] 1 WLR 1183 at 1188D–1189C.
3   See Style and Hollander *Documentary Evidence* (6th edn, 1997) pp 238–242, which suggests that the principle is of narrow application.

(d) Reliance on legal advice

12.29   Where the issue is whether the claimant received and acted upon the legal advice of the defendant, he or she will normally be taken to have waived privilege. Closely related to the question whether the claimant did in fact rely on the legal advice which he received is the question whether he would have relied on the advice which he now alleges he should have been given. As stated above, in *Lillicrap v Nalder & Son*[1] the Court of Appeal held that privilege had been waived in relation to six earlier transactions because they were directly relevant to the question whether the plaintiffs would have avoided the loss if advised in the way which they should have been.

1   [1993] 1 WLR 94, CA.

(e) Limitation defences

12.30   Where the claimant's claim is barred by a primary limitation period, he may need to rely on Limitation Act 1980, ss 14A or 32. As we discuss earlier in this book,[1] it is not easy to decide whether ignorance of the legal position enables a claimant to take advantage of the longer limitation periods. Here, we consider whether a claimant is obliged to disclose the legal advice which he or she has later received. In *Kershaw v Whelan*[2] the defendant pleaded that the plaintiff's claim was statute-barred both in contract and tort. In reply the plaintiff relied on Limitation Act 1980, s 32 and alleged that he did not and could not with due diligence have discovered the facts upon which his claim was based before April 1985 because they had been deliberately concealed from him by the defendant. It was held that this plea involved an implied waiver of the privilege in legal advice relating to the concealment and discovery of his claim.[3] In *Paragon* the Court of Appeal left open the question whether the case had been wrongly decided although they disapproved the dictum of the judge quoted in para 12.27.[4] If *Paragon* is applied with full rigour, we consider that the decision cannot stand and no order should have been made. By commencing proceedings the plaintiff was not bringing his relationship with his subsequent solicitors into the public domain and reference in general terms to the advice which he has received in a party's pleadings does not usually amount to an express waiver of privilege.[5] If, however, the wider interpretation of *Paragon* is adopted, the decision was the right one. By asserting in his reply that he could not have discovered the facts on which his claim was based, the plainitff put in issue the knowledge of his former solicitors and the advice which he received.

1   Chapter 5, paras 5.38–5.59.
2   [1996] 1 WLR 358 (Ebsworth J).
3   It appears that Ebsworth J ordered disclosure not only of the litigation files of the plaintiff's former solicitors but also of his current solicitors: see the headnote at 359B–D. It is not entirely clear, however, from the terms of the judgment but see the form of the summons and order at 360D–F and 370H–371A.
4   [1999] 1 WLR 1183 at 1192–1193B.
5   See Style and Hollander *Documentary Evidence* (6th edn, 1997) pp 228–232.

12.31   That said, in order to prove his case at trial a claimant who seeks to rely on either s 14A or s 32 will have to establish when he first received advice about the claim and, depending on the facts, he may also have to reveal the terms of that advice. This will normally require him to make a conscious decision to waive privilege. He may have to meet a request for further information and he will have to deal with the advice which he received both in his witness statement and in cross-examination. The extent to which any of these actions involves a waiver of privilege in individual documents or a course of correspondence will depend on normal principles[1] and a decision whether to waive privilege is best taken as soon as the defendant raises a valid limitation defence.

1   The fact that a party is now required to make a statement of truth in relation to his case and that he is able to adduce the opposing party's witness statements in evidence may lead to the conclusion that waiver of privilege takes place at an earlier stage.

(f)   Damages

12.32   A similar problem arises for a party who claims damages for the costs of abortive litigation. In *Burdge & Burdge v John Hodge & Co*[1] the plaintiffs claimed as damages the costs of litigation on which they had embarked to extricate themselves from the consequences of the defendant's negligence. These proceedings ultimately proved fruitless. Consistently with *Paragon*, the judge held that the files of the solicitors who handled the proceedings were relevant but privileged. He added, however, that although there was no implied waiver, it was likely that the plaintiffs would be obliged to *consent* to waive privilege if they wished to prove a causal connection between the negligence and the costs.

1   (11 March 1996, unreported) (Longmore J).

(g)   Settlements and compromises

12.33   In *Biggin & Co Ltd v Permanite Ltd*[1] it was held that a plaintiff who sought to recover as damages the amount which he had paid to compromise a claim had to satisfy the court that the settlement was a reasonable one. In a number of cases[2] disclosure of legal advice has also been sought on the grounds that by relying on a compromise with a third party and asserting that it is reasonable a party has waived privilege in relation to the legal advice which he received. We consider that

Paragon has resolved this issue too. Even if the legal advice is relevant to the reasonableness of the claimant's conduct, he cannot be ordered to disclose it. He is free to choose whether to waive privilege and introduce evidence of the legal advice which he received or to rely on the terms of the settlement and open correspondence by themselves.[3]

1   [1951] 2 KB 314, CA, a sale of goods case.
2   *Oceanic Finance Co Ltd v Norton Rose* (26 March 1997, unreported) (Moore-Bick J), *The Society of Lloyds v Kitson Environmental Services Ltd* (1994) 67 BLR 102 (HHJ Havery QC, ORB) and *DSL Group Ltd v Unisys International Services Ltd* (1994) 67 BLR 117 (HHJ Hicks QC, ORB).
3   In both *Oceanic Finance* and *DSL* (see note 2), it was held that the advice was not relevant because the test of reasonableness was an objective one. In *Oceanic Finance* Moore-Bick J distinguished the decision in *Muller v Linsley & Mortimer* [1996] 1 PNLR 74, CA, in which Hoffmann LJ adopted a subjective test in ordering disclosure of without prejudice communications. In *Paragon* [1999] 1 WLR 1183 at 1191F Lord Bingham indicated that no real principle could be derived from the case.

Index

Abuse of process
application to strike out as, 10.1
decision to bring appeal amounting to,
11.31, 11.32
unreasonable act, as, 11.28–11.33
wasted costs order on, 11.28–11.33
Abusive collateral attack, doctrine of
application of, 10.15
consent orders, variation of–
approval of court, not requiring, 10.32
approval of court, requiring, 10.33,
10.34
judicial discretion, exercise of, 10.31
criminal cases–
force in, 10.28
guilty plea in, 10.35
defence, 10.13
forensic immunity, separate consideration
of, 10.14
forms of, 10.16
fully contested trials–
application of principle, 10.20
errors of law, 10.21, 10.22
fresh evidence as basis of impugning
decision, 10.23–10.25
opportunity of contesting earlier
decision, 10.18
purpose of bringing professional
negligence action, irrelevance
of, 10.19
interlocutory hearings, application to,
10.29, 10.30
negligence, consideration of, 10.17
origin of, 10.15
policy reasons for, 10.26
rationale, 10.26–10.28
Action for money had and received
lenders' cases, 7.113

Breach of duty
duty to advise, extent of–
advice, nature of–
commercial matters, on, 2.36–2.38
generally, 2.34, 2.35
legal document, as to, 2.35
client, nature of, 2.32, 2.33
commercial significance, of, 2.38

Breach of duty—*contd*
duty to advise, extent of—*contd*
general approach, 2.37
generally, 2.30, 2.31
third party, instructions by, 2.33
wisdom of transaction, as to, 2.36
fiduciary. *See* FIDUCIARY DUTY, BREACH OF
vendor and purchaser, acting for, 8.04,
8.05
Breach of trust
action amounting to, 4.07
actual fraud as, 4.11
breach of contract amounting to, 4.07
client account, unauthorised payment
from, 4.05, 4.06, 4.08, 4.09
common law and equitable claims, overlap
of, 4.02
constructive trust–
basket of remedies, 4.17
fraud, defendant implicated in, 4.18,
4.19
meaning, 4.17
solicitor's liability to client, 4.18
criminal conspiracy, 4.13
deliberate, 4.13–4.16
deliberate or inadvertent, 4.03
dishonest, 4.10–4.12
equitable compensation, claims for, 4.01
express trusts, 4.03, 4.04
fraudulent, 4.10–4.12
implied trusts, 4.05–4.09
innocent, 4.14
lenders' cases, 7.114
limitation–
constructive trusts, 5.72–5.74
exceptions, 5.71
statutory provision, 5.70
loss or destruction of asset, leading to, 4.56
remedies–
account of profits, 4.37, 4.66
assessment of compensation, 4.56, 4.57
causation, proof of, 4.40
compensation, 4.37
purpose of, 4.41
elastic nature of, 4.03
mitigation, 4.52, 4.53
nature of, 4.37

341

Breach of trust—*contd*
  remedies—*contd*
    plaintiff, conduct of, 4.42–4.46
    presumptions, 4.58
    restitutionary, 4.39, 4.54
    third parties, conduct of, 4.47
    traditional, 4.03
  resulting trusts, 4.05–4.09

Client
  nature of, 2.32, 2.33
Conditional fee agreements
  wasted costs order, relevance to, 11.52
Consent orders
  abusive collateral attack, doctrine of–
    approval of court, order not requiring,
      10.32
    approval of court, order requiring,
      10.33, 10.34
    judicial discretion, exercise of, 10.31
Contract
  contributory negligence. *See* CONTRIBUTORY
    NEGLIGENCE
  limitation. *See* LIMITATION
  retainer. *See* RETAINER
  solicitor's duties in–
    collateral contract, implication of, 1.08
    express terms, 1.01
    obligation, breach of, 1.02
    particular result, achieving, 1.03
    reasonable care, taking, 1.02
    restriction of liability for breach, 1.05,
      1.06
Contribution
  amount of, 6.22
  application, 6.22, 6.23
  contributory negligence, interrelation with,
    6.24, 6.25
  differing extent, liability in, 6.18
  dishonest defendant, claim by, 6.23
  issues, 6.1
  lenders' cases, in, 7.92
  nature of damage, formulating, 6.17
  protection from claim, 6.21
  same damage, liability for, 6.17
  scope, 6.16–6.21
  settlement of claim with one party, 6.19,
    6.20
  statutory provisions, 6.16
  wasted costs order, in, 11.50
Contributory negligence
  ambit of–
    breach of fiduciary duty, in case of, 6.6
    contract, claims in, 6.3, 6.4
    fraudulent and negligent
      misrepresentation, in, 6.5
    lenders' cases, in, 6.7, 6.8
    statutory provisions, 6.2
  application–
    claimant's employees, negligence of,
      6.13
    fault, determining, 6.14
    lenders' cases, in, 6.9–6.12

Contributory negligence—*contd*
  application—*contd*
    reduction, basis of, 6.15
  breach of fiduciary duty, in case of, 6.6
  claimant's employees, negligence of, 6.13
  contract, claims in, 6.3, 6.4
  contribution, interrelation with, 6.24, 6.25
  defence of, 4.51
  fault, determining, 6.14
  fraudulent and negligent
    misrepresentation, in, 6.5
  issues, 6.1
  lenders' cases, in–
    allegations, nature of, 7.82
    ambit, 6.7, 6.8
    application, 6.9–6.12
    basic or attributable loss, reduction
      from, 6.9
    benchmark for awards, 7.3
    deduction, levels of, 7.84
    excessive LTVs, 7.85–7.87
    mortgage indemnity guarantee, taking,
      7.87
    non-status lending, 7.88
    overvaluation, direct contribution to,
      6.10
    staff, inadequate training of, 7.83
    warranty of authority, breach of,
      7.112
  reduction, basis of, 6.15
  reductions on account of, statutory basis
    for, 6.2
  statutory provision, 6.2
Conveyancing
  certificates of title, provision of, 8.39–8.40
  damages–
    defective purchase, for–
      care, cost of, 8.79, 8.80
      extrication cases, 8.74–8.76
      planning restrictions, discovery of,
        8.75
      resale, loss on, 8.77, 8.78
      rights of access, defective, 8.76
      valuation method, application of,
        8.73
    delayed purchase, for, 8.72
    inconvenience, for, 8.81
    loss of opportunity to purchase, for,
      8.71
  exchange of contracts, 8.56, 8.57
  lease renewals–
    landlords, acting for, 8.100
    reminders, 8.102
    statutory provisions, failure to comply
      with, 8.93
    tenants, acting for–
      capital loss, date for assessment,
        8.96
      counter-notice, failure to serve,
        8.94
      higher rent, requirement to pay due
        to negligence, 8.98, 8.99
      new lease, capital value of, 8.95

Conveyancing—*contd*
lease renewals—*contd*
tenants, acting for—*contd*
possession of premises, obligation
to give up, 8.97
more than one party, acting for–
binding, whether words or actions
being, 8.09
client or clients, obtaining authority of,
8.07–8.10
co-owners, acting for, 8.09
contract of retainer, nature of, 8.08
different forms of ownership,
explaining, 8.10
joint names, conveyance of property
to, 8.10
mortgagors, mortgagees and sureties,
8.11–8.33
third parties, duties to, 8.34–8.44
vendor and purchaser, 8.01–8.06
mortgagors, mortgagees and sureties,
acting for–
both mortgagors, for, 8.24, 8.25
claims arising, 8.11, 8.12
duty when acting for lender and
guarantor, 8.28–8.31
guarantor, for, whether instructed by
guarantor or lender, 8.21–8.23
guarantors' or mortgagors; claims to set
aside mortgages, 8.13–8.20
lender alone, for, 8.26
lender and mortgagors, for, 8.32, 8.33
lender and principal mortgagor, for,
8.27
options–
breach of agreement, 8.107
client understanding, 8.101
conditions, not satisfying, 8.103
exercise of, 8.103
damages for negligence in, 8.107
grant, damages for negligence in,
8.104–8.106
reminders, 8.102
pre-contract inquiries–
disclaimer, 8.37, 8.38
liability in respect of, 8.35–8.38
purchaser, acting for–
completion, duties on–
fraud or defalcation, risk of, 8.66
procedure, 8.64–8.66
stamping of transfer, 8.70
undertaking to discharge mortgage,
8.67–8.69
damages–
defective purchase, for, 8.73–8.80
delayed purchase, for, 8.72
inconvenience, for, 8.81
loss of opportunity to purchase, for,
8.71
duties before contract–
commercial advice, giving, 8.45
deposits, mortgages and surveys, as
to, 8.46–8.51

Conveyancing—*contd*
purchaser, acting for—*contd*
duties before contract—*contd*
entering into binding contract,
explanation of effect, 8.49,
8.51
leasehold purchasers, to, 8.55
searches and inquiries, 8.52, 8.53
special property, purchase of, 8.50
terms, advice on, 8.54
duties post-contract–
advice, giving, 8.63
conditions, satisfaction of, 8.60
encumbrances, discharge of, 8.59
occupiers, as to, 8.61, 8.62
searches and investigation of title,
8.58
exchange, duties on, 8.56, 8.57
searches and inquiries–
boundaries and dimensions, 8.53
easement and restrictive covenants,
8.53
local authority, 8.53
rates and tenancies, 8.53
requirements for, 8.52, 8.53
third parties, duties to–
certificates of title, provision of, 8.39–
8.40
circumstances for, 8.34
damages, recovery of, 8.44
father of client, instructions by, 8.43
financial information, reference in
relation to, 8.42
pre-contract inquiries, 8.35–8.38
vendor and purchaser, acting for–
breach causative of loss, proof of,
8.03
conflict, danger of, 8.01
double employment rule, 8.02
duty of care, breach of, 8.04, 8.05
Solicitors' Practice Rules, 8.01
vendor, acting for–
commercial advice, giving, 8.83
contract races, 8.82
damages–
invalid guarantee, in case of, 8.90,
8.91
rent review, defect in, 8.89
resale, loss on, 8.90
reversion, in case of, 8.88
valuation method, 8.87, 8.88
wasted expenditure, recovery of,
8.92
leases, advice on, 8.85
searches and inquiries, answering, 8.84
title, making, 8.86
Costs
damages for loss of a trial, consideration
on, 10.60
Legal Aid Board, order against, 11.20
non-parties, order against, 11.68
Solicitors' Indemnity Fund, applications
against, 11.71

Costs—*contd*
solicitors, orders against–
  acting without authority, on, 11.62–
    11.64
  breach of undertakings, on, 11.65
  categories of case, 11.2
  criminal proceedings, in 11.67
  general jurisdiction, under, 11.68–11.71
  inherent jurisdiction, 11.60–11.67
  jurisdiction, 11.1, 11.2. *See also* WASTED
    COSTS ORDER
  non-parties, in favour of, 11.66
wasted costs order. *See* WASTED COSTS ORDER
Counsel
advice–
  failure to obtain, 2.12
  reliance on, 2.11
forensic immunity. *See* FORENSIC IMMUNITY
solicitor's reliance on, relevance of,
  11.47–11.49

Damages
assessment–
  criminal cases, negligence in, 10.62
  date of–
    breach, date of, 3.48
    breach date rule, 3.48–3.51
    diminution in value rule, 3.52–3.59
    flexible approach, 3.51
    postponement of, 3.59
    transaction, date of, 3.49, 3.50
    valuation method, 3.52–3.59
  loss of civil claims, for–
    approach to, 10.49
    general principles, 10.48–10.54
    means and willingness of other
      party to pay, 10.54
    nature of claim, 10.49
    negligence causing action to be
      struck out, where, 10.50
    no negligence, consideration of
      situation on, 10.49, 10.51
    starting point, 10.49
    trial or settlement, likelihood of,
      10.52, 10.53
    types of loss claimed, 10.48
    want of prosecution, striking out
      for, 10.50
  loss of trial, for–
    appeals, 10.59
    categories of case, 10.56
    costs, incidence of, 10.60
    intermediate cases, 10.58
    nominal damages, 10.56
    strong cases, 10.57
    time of, 10.55
    settlement, losing, 10.61
    worse settlement than deserved,
      obtaining, 10.61
attributable loss, 3.7–3.10
causation–
  burden of proof, 3.14
  chance, loss of–
    commercial negotiations, 3.17–3.20

Damages—*contd*
causation—*contd*
  chance, loss of—*contd*
    evaluation of, 3.17–3.21
    generally, 3.15
    rent review, in case of, 3.18, 3.19
    sale of property, in, 3.21
    substantial, 3.16
  claimant acting on advice, 3.11–3.14
  connection between act or omission
    and loss, 3.22
  negligence as effective cause of loss,
    3.22–3.24
  principle of, 3.1–3.3
  relevant considerations, 3.23
  reliance on advice, relevance of, 3.13
  third parties acting on advice, 3.15–
    3.21
  trading losses, 3.25–3.27
common law, purpose of, 4.54
conveyancing transactions, in. *See*
  CONVEYANCING
diminution in value rule, 3.52–3.59
general principles–
  application, questioning, 3.2
  attributable loss, 3.7–3.10
  causation, remoteness and mitigation,
    3.1
  contract and tort, in, 3.1–3.3
  explanation of, 3.1
  misrepresentation, for, 3.4–3.6
  separate consideration of, 3.3
interest as, 3.60, 3.61
loss of particular asset, limited to, 4.55
mental distress arising from solicitor's
  breach of duty, for, 10.64
misrepresentation, for, 3.4–3.6
mitigation. *See* MITIGATION OF DAMAGE
presumptions, 4.58
remoteness. *See* REMOTENESS OF DAMAGE
responsibility for losses, extent to which
  assumed, 3.9
scope of solicitor's duty, action within,
  3.9
valuation method–
  acquisition of property cases, in, 3.57
  claimant would have acted differently,
    where, 3.54
  date of breach, application at, 3.55,
    3.56
  diminution in value rule, 3.52
  flexible approach, 3.55, 3.56
  lenders' cases, in, 3.58
  suitability of, 3.53
Deceit
common law action for, 4.11, 4.12, 4.16
damages for, 3.4
fiduciary duty, breach of, 4.22, 4.23
Disclosure
causation and reliance, relevance to, 12.14
credit, documents going to, 12.11
issues arising, 12.10
joint and multiple retainers, where existing,
  12.18, 12.19

Disclosure—*contd*
material documents, identification of,
12.10
other transactions, relevance of, 12.11–
12.15
pre-action, categories of, 12.02
privileged documents. *See* LEGAL ADVICE
PRIVILEGE
Documents
delivery up or production, 12.02–12.05
disclosure. *See* DISCLOSURE
joint and multiple retainers, where existing,
12.06–12.09
request for delivery of, 12.01
return to client, court ordering, 12.03
solicitor or client, belonging to, 12.05
storage by solicitors, 12.01
termination of retainer, return at, 12.04
Duty of care
assumption of, 1.08
breach. *See* BREACH OF DUTY
client, to–
contractual obligation, independent of,
1.10
retainer, determination by terms of,
1.10, 1.11
nature of, 1.10
standard of care. *See* STANDARD OF CARE
third parties, to–
accuracy of statements, for, 1.23
advice, giving, 1.14
assumption of responsibility, 1.14–
1.18
basis of liability, 1.16
claims against solicitors, 1.17–1.21
direct contract, where, 1.24
direct responsibility, assumption of,
1.22
disclaimer of liability, 1.25–1.27
exclusion of liability, 1.25–1.27
foreseeability, proximity and
reasonableness, test of, 1.13
Lloyd's Names, duty of managing
agent to, 1.20
nature and scope of, 1.12
potential beneficiary, to, 1.28, 1.29
pre-contract inquiries, duty to potential
tenant concerning, 1.19–1.21
principle underlying, 1.14–1.16
proximity, 1.17
reliance on advice, indication of, 1.17,
1.18
services, provision of, 1.14–1.16
solicitor's role, stepping outside, 1.22–
1.24
special relationship test, 1.14, 1.15
will, in preparation and execution of. *See*
WILL

Engagement letter
express terms set out in, 1.01
lack of, 1.07
Equity
breach of trust. *See* BREACH OF TRUST

Equity—*contd*
compensation in–
account of profits, 4.66
causation–
fact, in, 4.48, 4.49
full disclosure, absence of, 4.45
need for proof of, 4.40
plaintiff, conduct of, 4.42–4.46
third parties, conduct of, 4.47
contributory negligence, 4.51
difficulty in assessing, 4.56, 4.57
interest on–
account of profits, 4.66
compound, 4.63, 4.64
enhanced rate of, 4.62
equitable fraud, in case of, 4.64
history of jurisdiction, 4.59–4.63
inherent jurisdiction, 4.59
rate of, 4.60, 4.61, 4.65
loss of particular asset, limited to, 4.55
measure of, 4.54–4.58
mitigation, 4.52, 4.53
opportunity to exploit land, loss of,
4.47
presumptions, 4.58
purpose of, 4.41, 4.54
remoteness of damage, 4.50
restitutionary remedy, as, 4.39, 4.54
specific restitution, as substitute for,
4.50
types of remedies, 4.37
fiduciary duty, breach of. *See* FIDUCIARY
DUTY, BREACH OF
lenders' cases, 7.114, 7.115
limitation. *See* LIMITATION
relevance of, 4.01, 4.02
Estate
acting for, duties arising, 9.13
claims brought by, 9.14, 9.15
life policy forming part of, 9.15
Expert evidence
agreeing, 11.27
jurisdiction to admit, 2.21
solicitor, of, 2.23, 2.24
standard of care, as to. *See* STANDARD OF CARE
ultimate question, as to, 2.22

Fiduciary duty, breach of
breach of duty of care, and, 4.20
contributory negligence, 4.51, 6.6
deputy judge, solicitor acting as, 10.67
double employment rule, 4.28–4.31, 4.38
good faith, duty of, 4.32–4.36
intervention of equity, purpose of, 4.38
lenders' cases, 7.115
limitation, 5.75
more than one client, conflict of duties to–
actual conflict rule, 4.33, 4.35
disclosure, 4.29
double employment rule, 4.28–4.31,
4.38, 8.02
estate agent, by, 4.30
good faith, duty of, 4.32–4.35
impossibility of acting, 4.31

Fiduciary duty, breach of—*contd*
  more than one client, conflict of duties
      to—*contd*
    lender and borrower, 4.27, 4.34
    one client, acting against interests of,
        4.35
  personal interest, conflict with–
    actual fraud, cases of, 4.23
    deceit, action in, 4.22, 4.23
    equitable relief, jurisdiction, 4.23, 4.24
    fraudulent intention, 4.23
    full disclosure, duty of, 4.25, 4.36
    plaintiff, conduct of, 4.43, 4.44
    restatement of law, 4.25
    strict standard, 4.26
    vulnerability of client, protection of,
        4.21
  pleading, 4.36
  remedies–
    account of profits, 4.66
    circumstances of case, meeting, 4.38
    conflict on interest and duty, in case of,
        4.43, 4.44
    failure of claim, 4.46
    mitigation, 4.52, 4.53
    nature of, 4.37
    plaintiff, conduct of, 4.42–4.46
    presumptions, 4.58
    restitutionary, 4.39, 4.54
    third parties, conduct of, 4.47
  restraint of solicitors acting in litigation,
      application for, 10.66, 10.67
  trust and confidence, relationship of, 4.21
Forensic immunity
  abusive collateral attack, separate
      consideration of, 10.14
  circumscription of, 10.47
  conduct falling within, 10.45
  defence, 10.13
  disproportionate restriction on right of
      access to court, as, 10.44
  fees, inability to sue for, 10.38
  justification of, 10.42
  meaning, 10.36
  modern rationale, 10.39–10.44
  origins, 10.38
  professional negligence, extension of
      liability for, 10.40
  protection of advocates, whether
      necessary, 10.43
  rationale, 10.37
  scope of, 10.13, 10.36, 10.45–10.47
  solicitors, application to, 10.39, 10.46
  standard of care, 10.41
  sufficient basis for, 10.43
Fraud
  breach of trust as, 4.10–4.12
    defendant implicated in, 4.18, 4.19
  conveyancing, risk in, 8.66
  equitable, 4.64
  fiduciary duty, breach of, 4.23
  lenders' cases, in, 7.99, 7.100
  limitation period, extension of, 5.4, 5.62,
      5.69

Fraud—*contd*
  limitation period, extension of—*contd*
    constructive knowledge, 5.68, 5.69
    effect of, 5.61
    statutory provision, 5.60
  meaning, 7.99
  mortgage transactions, 7.12–7.14

Guilty plea
  abusive collateral attack, doctrine of, 10.35

Husband and wife
  same solicitor engaged by in matrimonial
      proceedings, 10.72
  wife's signature forged on documents,
      7.102–7.109

Injunction
  restraint of solicitors acting in litigation–
    circumstances for, 10.65
    existing client, claim brought by,
        10.66, 10.67
    fiduciary duty, breach of, 10.66, 10.67
    former client, breach of confidence
        claim brought by–
      Chinese Walls, use of, 10.70, 10.71
      husband and wife, same solicitor
          engaged by in matrimonial
          proceedings, 10.72
      real but not fanciful risk of
          disclosure, test of, 10.69–
          10.72
    test applied, 10.68
Interest
  claimant locked into investment, where,
      3.65
  damages, as, 3.60, 3.61
  date on which cause of action arose and
      date of payment, between, 3.62
  equitable compensation, on–
    account of profits, 4.66
    compound, 4.63, 4.64
    enhanced rate of, 4.62
    equitable fraud, in case of, 4.64
    history of jurisdiction, 4.59–4.63
    inherent jurisdiction, 4.59
    rate of, 4.60, 4.61, 4.65
  lenders' claims, in, 3.65
  rate of, 3.63, 3.64
  rule for, 3.60
  statutory, 3.62–3.65

Legal advice privilege
  documents subject to, 12.16, 12.17
  implied waiver–
    damages for costs of abortive litigation,
        claim of, 12.32
    defendant's files, 12.25
    legal advice, reliance on, 12.29
    limitation defence, 12.30, 12.31
    other advisers, proceedings against,
        12.26
    other solicitors, files of, 12.27, 12.28
    principle of, 12.24

Legal advice privilege—*contd*
  implied waiver—*contd*
    scope of, 12.25
    settlements and compromise, claim as
        to, 12.33
    statement of principle, 12.28
  iniquity exception–
    conduct to which applying, 12.20
    evidence gathering, 12.23
    facts of case, 12.21, 12.22
    strength of case, 12.22
  joint and multiple retainers, where existing,
      12.18, 12.19
Legal aid
  wasted costs order, relevance to, 11.43–
      11.45, 11.51
Lenders' claims
  action for money had and received, 7.113
  breach of trust, 7.114
  causation–
    report, duty to, 7.57–7.61
    test of, 7.57
  contract and negligence–
    attributable loss, 7.70–7.80
    back to back sales, 7.12–7.14
    basic loss, 7.62–7.69
    causation, 7.57–7.61
    contribution, 7.92
    direct payments, 7.12–7.14
    express and implied terms in mortgage
        transaction. *See* MORTGAGE
        TRANSACTIONS
    generally, 7.1, 7.2
    lender and solicitor, roles of, 7.7–7.11
    mitigation, 7.89–7.91
    multiple lenders, loans by, 7.93–7.98
    sub-sales, 7.12–7.14
  contribution, 7.92
  contributory negligence. *See* CONTRIBUTORY
      NEGLIGENCE
  damages, valuation, 3.58
  equity, relevance of, 7.114, 7.115
  fiduciary duty, breach of, 7.115
  fraud, 7.99, 7.100
  interest in, 3.65
  key issues, 7.3–7.6
  limitation. *See* LIMITATION
  losses–
    attempt to recover, 7.1
    attributable–
      basic loss, reduction of, 7.70
      contributory negligence, effect of,
          6.9, 7.81
      interest, 7.74
      meaning, 7.62, 7.70
      solicitors, claims against, 7.75–7.80
      valuers, overvaluation by, 7.71–
          7.73
    basic–
      amount claimed, 7.64
      contributory negligence, effect of,
          6.9, 7.81
      interest on, 7.65–7.69
      meaning, 7.62

Lenders' claims—*contd*
  losses—*contd*
    basic—*contd*
      negligent valuation, high rate on
          interest on, 7.63
    types of, 7.62
    warranty of authority, breach of, 7.111
  managed lists of actions, 7.2
  mortgage transactions. *See* MORTGAGE
      TRANSACTIONS
  multiple lenders, loans by–
    contract claims, 7.94–7.96
    sets of facts, 7.93
    tort claims, 7.97, 7.98
  solicitors, against–
    losses–
      attributable, 7.75–7.80
      breach of duty, not attributable to,
          7.76, 7,77
      lender not wishing to make advance
          to borrower on proper
          reporting, 7.80
      valuation, breach of duty relevant
          to, 7.78, 7.79
  warranty of authority, breach of–
    causation, 7.110
    contributory negligence, 7.112
    liability–
      purchasers/borrowers of lender,
          solicitor acting for, 7.106–
          7.109
      vendors, solicitor purporting to act
          for, 7.102–7.105
      wife's signature forged, where,
          7.102–7.109
    measure of loss, 7.111
    mitigation, 7.112
Life policy
  proceeds forming part of deceased's estate,
      9.15
Limitation
  benefits under will, loss of, 5.37
  common law claims–
    benefits under will, loss of, 5.37
    cause of action, accrual of, 5.2
    contract and tort, in, 5.2
    contract, in, 5.9–5.14
    court, approach of, 5.2
    depression, claim of damages for, 5.7,
        5.8
    fraud or deliberate concealment,
        extension in case of, 5.4
    ignorance of accrual of action, 5.2, 5.3
    issues, 5.5
    lenders' cases, 5.26–5.34
    litigation, loss of, 5.35, 5.36
    negligence, in, 5.15–5.25
    personal injuries, 5.6–5.8
    statutory provisions, 5.2, 5.3
  contract, claims in–
    cause of action, accrual of, 5.2, 5.9
    continuing duty, 5.10–5.14
    matrimonial home, failure to protect
        continuing interest in, 5.12, 5.13

Limitation—*contd*
contract, claims in—*contd*
option, failure to register, 5.11
equity, claims in–
breach of trust, 5.70–5.74. *See also*
BREACH OF TRUST
fiduciary duty, breach of, 5.75
issues arising, 5.1
legal advice, disclosure of, 12.30
lenders' cases–
cause of action, accrual of–
basic comparison, 5.27–5.31
before default of borrower, 5.32,
5.33
borrower defaulting to some
degree, 5.33
comparison of cases, 5.34
evidence, obtaining, 5.29
measure of loss, 5.28
sale of property, on, 5.30
security worth less that advance,
where, 5.31
security, property acquired as, 5.27
interest payable, 5.26
litigation, loss of, 5.35, 5.36
negligence, claims in–
cause of action, accrual of–
agreement as to payment of capital
gains tax, 5.19
date when loss suffered, 5.15, 5.16
legally recoverable loss, at tie of
accrual, 5.2
matrimonial home, failure to protect
continuing interest in, 5.23
mortgage deed, date of entry into,
5.18
purchasers' cases, in, 5.24, 5.25
relevant facts, ignorance of, 5.3,
5.41
restrictive covenant, date of taking
effect, 5.20–5.22
risk to be guarded against, date of
accrual, 5.17
contingency, loss dependent on, 5.25
ignorance of relevant facts, 5.41
litigation, loss of, 5.35, 5.36
valuation, in case of, 5.24
new causes of action, addition after
expiry–
different duty, pleading, 5.80
different facts, addition of, 5.81
limitation defence, depriving defendant
of, 5.83
meaning, 5.79–5.83
new regime, 5.77
rule for, 5.78
same or substantially same facts, arising
from, 5.84
treatment of, 5.82
personal injuries, three year period for,
5.6–5.8
privilege, implied waiver of, 12.30, 12.31
protective writ, issue of, 5.76

Limitation—*contd*
statutory extensions to period of–
fraud, deliberate concealment or
mistake, in case of–
constructive knowledge, 5.68, 5.69
deliberate concealment, 5.63–5.66
effect of, 5.61
fraud, 5.62, 5.69
mistake, 5.67
statutory provision, 5.60
ignorance of relevant facts–
actual knowledge, construction of,
5.44
burden of proof, 5.43
constructive knowledge, 5.56–5.58
effect of provision, 5.40
employment contract, negligent
advice as to, 5.54
error of law, negligence alleged
being, 5.50–5.58
knowledge that damage attributable
to act or omission alleged to
constitute negligence, 5.45–
5.49
lender's claim, 5.58
occupational pension scheme,
transfer of surplus under,
5.52, 5.53
scope, 5.41
separate causes of action, knowledge
in relation to, 5.59
starting date, 5.42
statutory provisions, 5.3, 5.39
Litigation
abuse of process, application to strike out
as, 10.1
abusive collateral attack, doctrine of. *See*
ABUSIVE COLLATERAL ATTACK, DOCTRINE OF
advocate, conflict of interest when acting
as, 10.73
costs. *See* COSTS
damages. *See* DAMAGES
forensic immunity. *See* FORENSIC IMMUNITY
negligence, liability in, 10.7, 10.8
pleading, errors in, 10.8
restraint of solicitors acting in–
circumstances for, 10.65
existing client, claim brought by,
10.66, 10.67
fiduciary duty, breach of, 10.66, 10.67
former client, breach of confidence
claim brought by–
Chinese Walls, use of, 10.70, 10.71
husband and wife, same solicitor
engaged by in matrimonial
proceedings, 10.72
real but not fanciful risk of
disclosure, test of, 10.69–
10.72
test applied, 10.68
settlement without authority, 10.8
standard of care–
application of, 10.7–10.12

Litigation—*contd*
  standard of care—*contd*
    criminal law, in, 10.9
    level of, 10.2, 10.6
    nineteenth century authorities,
      relevance of, 10.4
    one-man firm, of, 10.11
    reported cases, lack of, 10.3
    rising, possibility of, 10.10–10.12
    small claim, in, 10.11
    steps in litigation, scrutiny of, 10.12
    Woolf reforms, 10.5

Misrepresentation
  damages for, 3.4–3.6
  fraudulent or negligent, contributory
    negligence, 6.5
Mitigation of damage
  collateral benefits, receipt of, 3.44–3.47
  equity, in, 4.52, 4.53
  further litigation, 3.40–3.43
  general compensatory principle, as
    reflection of, 3.40
  general principle, 3.1–3.3
  implied covenant of title, suing on, 3.42
  lenders' cases, in, 7.89–7.91, 7.112
  possession action, in, 3.43
  principles on which court acting, 3.41
  solicitor's breach of duty, arising from,
    10.63
Mortgage transactions
  back to back sales, 7.12–7.14
  borrower's covenant, value of, 7.9–7.11
  change in purchase price, allowances,
    7.22
  charge, forged signatures on, 7.34–7.36
  conveyancing. *See* CONVEYANCING
  direct payments–
    badge of fraud, as, 7.24
    fraud, 7.12–7.14
    reporting, 7.23–7.26
    true purchase price not price stated in
      offer, failure to report
      circumstances, 7.21
  existing mortgages, redemption before
    completion, 7.28
  express contractual terms, liability for
    breach of–
    allowances, 7.22
    categories of allegation, 7.19
    construction of terms, 7.37
    direct payments, reporting, 7.23–7.26
    existing mortgages, redemption before
      completion, 7.28
    forged signatures on charges, 7.34–
      7.36
    incorporation into contract, 7.16–7.18
    material changes in circumstances,
      obligation to report, 7.29
    proper security, failing to obtain on
      completion, 7.30, 7.31
    resident borrower, 7.27
    solicitors, by, 7.15

Mortgage transactions—*contd*
  express contractual terms, liability for
    breach of—*contd*
    true purchase price not price stated in
      offer, failure to report
      circumstances, 7.20, 7.21
    undertakings agreed between banks
      and Law Society, forms of,
      7.32, 7.33
  fraud, 7.99, 7.100
  guarantors' or mortgagors' claims to set
    aside mortgages–
    non est factum, 8.13
    undue influence–
      categories of, 8.15
      constructive notice, 8.19
      issues arising, 8.14
      notice of, 8.16–8.18
      substantial disadvantage, terms to,
        8.20
  implied contractual terms, liability for
    breach of–
    confidentiality of borrower, implied
      waiver of, 7.54, 7.55
    creditworthiness of borrower, as to,
      7.47–7.51
    information learnt from other
      transactions, reporting, 7.56
    matters relevant to value of security,
      implied duty to report, 7.39–
      7.46, 7.52, 7.53
    reasonable skill and care, solicitor
      acting with, 7.38
    remortgage, duty as to, 7.46
    terms of retainer, 7.42
  key issues, 7.3–7.6
  lender and solicitor, roles of–
    borrower's covenant, value of, 7.9–
      7.11
    security, value of, 7.8
    typical transaction, in, 7.7
  losses–
    attributable–
      basic loss, reduction of, 7.70
      contributory negligence, effect of,
        6.9, 7.81
      interest, 7.74
      meaning, 7.62, 7.70
      solicitors, claims against, 7.75–7.80
      valuers, overvaluation by, 7.71–7.73
    basic–
      amount claimed, 7.64
      contributory negligence, effect of,
        6.9, 7.81
      interest on, 7.65–7.69
      meaning, 7.62
      negligent valuation, high rate on
        interest on, 7.63
    types of, 7.62
    warranty of authority, breach of,
      7.111
  material changes in circumstances,
    obligation to report, 7.29

Mortgage transactions—*contd*
    matters relevant to value of security,
        implied duty to report, 7.39–7.46,
        7.52, 7.53
    more than one party, acting for. *See*
        CONVEYANCING
    multiple lenders, loans by–
        contract claims, 7.94–7.96
        sets of facts, 7.93
        tort claims, 7.97, 7.98
    negligence, liability in–
        creditworthiness of borrower, as to,
            7.47–7.51
        matters relevant to value of security,
            implied duty to report, 7.39–
            7.46, 7.52, 7.53
        reasonable skill and care, solicitor
            acting with, 7.38
    offer of advance, 7.11
    proper security, failing to obtain on
        completion, 7.30, 7.31
    security, value of, 7.8
    sub-sales–
        fraud, 7.12–7.14
        true purchase price not price stated in
            offer, failure to report
            circumstances, 7.20
    true purchase price not price stated in
        offer, failure to report
        circumstances, 7.20, 7.21
    typical, 7.7
    undertakings agreed between banks and
        Law Society, forms of, 7.32, 7.33

Negligence
    breach of duty. *See* BREACH OF DUTY
    lenders' claims. *See* LENDERS' CLAIMS
    limitation. *See* LIMITATION
    mortgage transactions. *See* MORTGAGE
        TRANSACTIONS
    routine mistakes, and, claims involving,
        2.28
    standard of care. *See* STANDARD OF CARE
    test applied, 2.30
Negligent misstatement
    damages for, 3.5

Personal representatives
    notification, duty of, 9.12
Privilege. *See* LEGAL ADVICE PRIVILEGE
Professional standards and practice
    difference of opinion as to, 2.19
    medical cases, in, 2.13
    novel defence, where, 2.18
    routine practice, negligent, 2.16, 2.17
    rules of conduct, 2.14–2.19

Remoteness of damage
    equity, in, 4.50
    foreseeability–
        contract and tort contrasted, 3.28
        fall in market, effect of, 3.35
        increased building costs, 3.33

Remoteness of damage—*contd*
    foreseeability—*contd*
        inflation, effect of, 3.34
        market changes, treatment of, 3.32–
            3.35
        reasonableness, 3.28, 3.29
        resale of property, loss of profit on,
            3.36, 3.37
        special contracts, 3.36, 3.37
        type and extent of loss, 3.29–3.31
    general principle, 3.1–3.3
    intervening acts, 3.38, 3.39
Retainer
    bringing into existence, 1.07
    continuing, 1.09
    conveyancing, acting for more than one
        party in. *See* CONVEYANCING
    duty of care, determining nature and scope
        of, 1.10, 1.11
    formation, 1.07–1.09
    informal creation of, 1.07
    joint and multiple–
        disclosure of documents, 12.18, 12.19
        documents, relevance to, 12.06–12.09
    legal services, taking reasonable care in
        providing, 1.04
    standard of reasonable conduct under, 2.1
    termination on reasonable notice, 1.09
    terms of contract, governed by, 1.01
Rules of conduct
    failure to comply with, 2.14
    standard of care, relevance to. 2.14–2.19

Solicitor
    client, relationship with, 1.01
    contract, duties in. *See* CONTRACT
    duty of care. *See* DUTY OF CARE
    expert evidence by, 2.23, 2.24
    instructions, declining, 1.09
    qualification, statutory requirement, 2.3
    tort, duty of care in. *See* DUTY OF CARE
Standard of care
    contract and tort, in, 2.1
    counsel's advice–
        failure to obtain, 2.12
        reliance on, 2.11
    difficulty in identifying, 2.5
    errors of judgment–
        court not punishing, 2.25
        hindsight, without benefit of, 2.26
        matters characterised as, 2.27
        moral fault, no attribution of, 2.29
        routine mistakes, and, 2.28
    expert evidence, relevance and
        admissibility of–
        generally, 2.20
        jurisdiction, 2.21
        professional negligence cases, in, 2.22
        solicitor, of, 2.23, 2.24
    expert, of, 2.7
    expertise, level of, 2.3–2.7
    failure to achieve, liability in negligence,
        2.2

Standard of care—*contd*
  fees, level of, 2.8
  law, knowledge of, 2.9, 2.10
  litigation, in conduct of. *See* LITIGATION
  professional standards and practice,
      relevance of—
    difference of opinion as to, 2.19
    medical cases, in, 2.13
    novel defence, where, 2.18
    routine practice, negligent, 2.16, 2.17
    rules of conduct, 2.14–2.19
  reasonable competence—
    counsel's advice—
      failure to obtain, 2.12
      reliance on, 2.11
    experience and knowledge, level of,
        2.7
    expertise, level of, 2.3–2.7
    failure to achieve, liability in
        negligence, 2.2
    fees, level of, 2.8
    insufficient expertise, having, 2.6
    law, knowledge of, 2.9, 2.10
    unqualified surveyor, of, 2.4
  retainer, under, 2.1
  rules of conduct, relevance of, 2.14–2.19
Surveyor
  unqualified, standard of reasonable
      competence, 2.4

Trading losses
  causation, 3.25–3.27
Trust
  breach of. *See* BREACH OF TRUST
  constructive—
    fraud, defendant implicated in, 4.18,
        4.19
    limitation period, 5.72–5.74
    meaning, 4.17
    operation of law, arising by, 4.18
    solicitor's liability to client, 4.18
    types of, 4.18
  inter vivos—
    disappointed beneficiaries, duty to,
        9.25, 9.26
    ineffective creation of, 9.26
    solicitor and trustee, solicitor acting as,
        9.22, 9.24
    trustees, duty to—
      commercial advice, giving, 9.23,
          9.24
      nature of, 9.22

Wasted costs order
  application for—
    amount of money paid or disallowed,
        specification of, 11.12
    client, notice to, 11.12
    court, initiation by, 11.16
    fair hearing, requirement of, 11.12
    judge dealing with, 11.17
    persons not party to litigation, by,
        11.19

Wasted costs order—*contd*
  application for—*contd*
    plain cases, in, 11.3
    privileged documents, disclosure of,
        11.13
    procedure—
      approach of court, 11.6
      general principles, 11.6
      Practice Direction, 11.14
      rules, 11.4, 11.5, 11.11
      summary, allegations not suitable
          for, 11.8
    proportionality, 11.6
    settlement, 11.18
    stages of, 11.15
    timing, 11.17
  causation—
    criminal proceedings, in 11.58
    requirement of, 11.53
    statutory provision, 11.55
    test, application of, 11.54
  conditional fee agreements, relevance of,
      11.52
  contribution and indemnity, 11.50
  criminal proceedings, in 11.57–11.59
  definition, 11.3
  delay in conduct of litigation, on, 11.46
  improper acts and omissions, on, 11.23–
      11.25
  jurisdiction—
    criminal proceedings, in 11.59
    generally, 10.3, 11.1
    statutory provisions, 11.4
    use of, 11.6
  justice in all the circumstances, provision
      for, 11.56
  legal aid, fees paid by, 11.43–11.45, 11.51
  making, basic requirements for—
    generally, 11.21, 11.22
    improper acts and omissions, 11.23–
        11.25
    negligent acts or omissions, on—
      delay in conduct of litigation, 11.46
      legal aid, fees paid by, 11.43–11.45
      appeal, in, 11.42
      concession leading to abandonment
          of claim, 11.37
      conduct held not to be negligent,
          11.35–11.39
      conduct held to be negligent,
          11.40–11.46
      definition, 11.34
      failure to find out facts, 11.36
      failure to settle action, 11.38
      inappropriate actions, 11.40
      relevant case, failure to consider,
          11.41
    unreasonable acts and omissions—
      abuse of process, 11.28–11.33
      appeal amounting to abuse, 11.31,
          11.32
      definition, 11.26
      expert evidence, agreeing, 11.27

Wasted costs order—*contd*
    making, basic requirements for—*contd*
        unreasonable acts and omissions—
            contd
            hopeless cases, advancing, 11.28–
                11.33
            vexatious conduct, 11.28
    negligent acts or omissions, on–
        appeal, in, 11.42
        concession leading to abandonment of
            claim, 11.37
        conduct held not to be negligent,
            11.35–11.39
        conduct held to be negligent, 11.40–
            11.46
        definition, 11.34
        delay in conduct of litigation, 11.46
        failure to find out facts, 11.36
        failure to settle action, 11.38
        inappropriate actions, 11.40
        legal aid, fees paid by, 11.43–11.45
        relevant case, failure to consider, 11.41
    order for costs against Legal Aid Board,
        interrelationship with, 11.20
    other remedies, interrelationship with,
        11.10
    plain cases, in, 11.3
    proportionality, 11.56
    refusal, appeals from, 11.7–11.9
    solicitor's reliance on counsel, relevance
        of, 11.47–11.49
    unreasonable acts and omissions, on–
        abuse of process, 11.28–11.33
        definition, 11.26
        expert evidence, agreeing, 11.27
        hopeless cases, advancing, 11.28–
            11.33
        vexatious conduct, 11.28
Will
    breach of duty as to–
        damages–
            claim for rectification, establishment
                of ingredients of, 9.20, 9.21

Will—*contd*
    breach of duty as to—*contd*
        difficulties in assessing, 9.17
        estate, acting for, 9.13
        instructions, taking, 9.11
        marriage, invalidation by, 9.10
        personal representatives, notification
            of, 9.12
        preparation and execution, in, 9.09,
            9.10
        proper attestation, 9.09
        retainer, duties governed by terms of,
            9.13
    disappointed beneficiaries, duty to–
        basis of, 9.01, 9.02
        beneficiary not receiving legacy or
            bequest in any event, 9.07, 9.08
        damages–
            benefit, recovery of, 9.16
            chance of executing will in time,
                assessing, 9.18
            claim for rectification, establishment
                of ingredients of, 9.20, 9.21
            credit for benefits received, 9.16
            difficulties in assessing, 9.17
        death, surviving, 9.01
        extent of, 9.03–9.08
        instructions, taking, 9.11
        intended legacy, depriving beneficiary
            of, 9.01
        intention of testator, proving, 9.05,
            9.06
        new will, failure to draw up in
            reasonable time, 9.09
        specific testamentary disposition,
            failure to advise on, 9.05, 9.06
        terms of, determining, 9.03
        will-making process, in relation to,
            9.04
    loss of benefits under, limitation, 5.37
    rectification, application for, 9.19–9.21
Writ
    expiry of limitation period, issue to escape,
        5.76